PELICAN BOOKS

A576

A SHORT HISTORY OF
RELIGIONS

E. E. KELLETT

E. E. KELLETT

A Short History of Religions

PENGUIN BOOKS

Penguin Books Ltd, Harmondsworth, Middlesex
AUSTRALIA: Penguin Books Pty Ltd, 762 Whitehorse Road,
Mitcham, Victoria

—

First published by Gollancz 1933
Published in Pelican Books 1962

—

Made and printed in Great Britain
by Richard Clay & Company, Ltd,
Bungay, Suffolk

Set in Monotype Baskerville

CONTENTS

PREFATORY NOTE

THE design of this book is not to satisfy, but to stimulate, the interest of serious-minded people in its theme. There are many signs that the world is awakening to a renewed sense of the paramount importance of religion: men are thinking about it; and one of the best aids to right thinking is to know something of what has been thought in the past. Religion is an affair of growth – or rather it is a life; and life cannot be understood unless it is followed through all its stages.

Much, of course, has necessarily been omitted; and it may well seem to many that some points that have been omitted are of more importance than some that have been mentioned. But it is hoped that the reader will at any rate not find much that he will have to unlearn.

In certain cases the chapters overlap, and the continuation of a subject touched on in one may have to be sought in another. Thus, for example, it is impossible to give the history of the Church of England without speaking of Calvinism, the full development of which is shown in the Church of Scotland. In such cases a reference to the Index will usually provide assistance. In the Index, also, the explanations of certain difficult phrases will be found.

Absolute impartiality is not possible: but I have, to the best of my powers, tried to live up to the motto of one of the greatest of religious leaders, and to be 'the friend of all, the enemy of none'.

CHAPTER I

RELIGION: ITS NATURE AND ORIGIN

A PRECISE definition of religion is probably impossible.
Matthew Arnold's attempt is well known:[1] religion, in his
view, was 'morality touched with emotion'. Unfortunately,
in almost all nations, till comparatively recent times, that
which all are agreed to call religion had little or nothing to
do with morality: and often the first step in the construction
of ethical systems was to denounce the current religion as
at best non-moral. The great teachers, for example, alike
in Palestine and in Greece, those men whose doctrines form
the basis of modern 'religion', are conspicuous for the vigour
with which they combated the religion of their times.
Isaiah would have nothing to do with incense or vain oblations; Micah asserted that Yahweh cared nothing for gifts or
thousands of rams: yet incense, gifts, and rams were the
very essence of religion as understood by the men of that
time. Xenophanes, Socrates, Plato are full of censures of the
immoral tales told of the gods and heroes whose altars
crowded every town in Greece; and Homer, in whose poems
these tales were told, was politely but ruthlessly banished
from Plato's moral commonwealth. The Iliad was the Bible
of the people, and the basis of religion, but the ethical
teacher must get rid of it. If we go back earlier, the divorce
between religion and morality becomes, if possible, still
clearer. 'Divorce', however, is the wrong word; for the two

1. *Literature and Dogma*, chap. i, § 2. Of other definitions I might mention
Max Müller's, 'Anything that lifts man above the realities of this material
life is religion'; Newman's, 'the essence of religion is authority and obedience'; Schleiermacher's, 'it is a feeling of absolute dependence'. Contrast
with these the assertion of a well-known German writer that it is an
infectious disease, the rapid spread of which is due to the social instincts
of mankind! We shall see many proofs that it is infectious: whether it is a
disease or not is a question which has been debated through the centuries.

had never been united. Religion was a series of external actions, or of abstentions from action, intended to propitiate supernatural powers: it said nothing as to what we today call 'good conduct', and if purity of heart existed, it existed almost in spite of religious taboos. Let the reader consider the Ten Commandments as given in the thirty-fourth chapter of the Book of Exodus – a code which seems to have directed the religious life of the Hebrews till it was superseded, somewhat late, by the Ten Words of the twentieth chapter. In the earlier commands there is not one but had to do with childish superstitions, not one which is concerned with the moral law, as we understand it. There is no prohibition of murder or theft, but we are straitly forbidden to seethe a kid in its mother's milk. Nothing is said about covetousness or undutifulness; but we must not keep the fat of God's sacrifice until the morning.

Even 'holiness', which we now regard as the very sublimation of morality, consisted then in ceremonial purity merely: it meant nothing but the avoidance of any uncleanness which might annoy the gods. To kill a man was nothing; but to touch a corpse was a horror, and necessitated a tedious process of getting rid of the taint. This sort of thing persisted, even in Judaism, down to a very late time. We are accustomed to think of the Founder of Christianity as holy. This is exactly what, in the view of the formalists, he was not. Nothing irritated these 'religious' more than his disregard of technical holiness, or than his contempt for the outside washings of cup and platter.

The more deeply we probe into early religion, the more clearly we perceive how little it has to do with the morality of which Arnold speaks,[1] however strongly it might be

1. 'It is often asserted,' says Monier-Williams (*Brahmanism and Hinduism*, preface, vii), 'that the Hindus are the most religious people in the world. Those who make this assertion ought of course to define what they mean by the word *religious*. What is really meant, I think, is that among all the races of the world the Hindus are the greatest slaves to the bondage of immemorial tradition – not so much in its bearing on religious beliefs, or even on moral conduct, as on social usages, caste practices, and domestic ceremonial observances': and Monier-Williams refers

touched with emotion, and that, though sometimes the emotion of hope, far more often the emotion of fear. And, looking again, we discover that the second element entering into it was, strange as it may seem, an infantile and elementary, but none the less genuine, physical science. Surrounded with unknown influences, tormented with terrors of ghosts, demons, spirits of all kinds, men searched, timidly and hesitatingly, into the causes of these plagues, and leapt eagerly at the first possibilities that presented themselves for avoiding or mitigating them. Like our own people during Black Deaths and other catastrophes, they ran after everyone who could promise them immunity, and seized greedily on any talisman which happened to have been worn by someone who had himself escaped. And, as whole ages were ages of perpetual plague, and the whole world a nest of contagion, everybody was then as superstitious as our own grandfathers were during the cholera. Any man who professed to know was like an advertiser with his panacea today: that is, he was a man of 'science'. The science might be mistaken, but it was none the less dominating, and had all the force of an oecumenical council.[1] The antagonism

---

in illustration to the marriage-customs, which are certainly what is usually called 'religion', but equally certainly have nothing moral about them whatever.

1. Many thinkers, e.g. Singer (*From Magic to Science*), refuse to give to these crude guesses the name of 'science'. Though, of course, this is largely a matter of definition, it seems to me that no clear line can be drawn between these inductions, based as they were on the simplest enumerations, and the careful experiments of a Faraday. We should, I think, call Anaxagoras a man of science, though his attempts to measure the moon were largely guess-work. From thence we pass forward without perceptible break, to Eratosthenes' measurement of the latitude of Alexandria, and so on to modern more exact measurements. If we pass *backward* from Anaxagoras, I can see no point at which we can say 'here *science* begins'.

'Science,' says Jevons, 'arises from the discovery of Identity amidst Diversity.' In early days, men 'discovered' Identity where it did not exist; but I think the mental process was not so dissimilar to that of a Newton or an Archimedes that we need hesitate to use the same name for both.

between physics and religion, which filled so great a space in modern history, did not exist in early times: on the contrary, religion was the natural development of physics, and without physics could scarcely have arisen. The priest was in fact the professor, and the minister was the medicine-man. People went to him for explanations of natural phenomena, and for relief from the fears those phenomena aroused. Out of his esoteric knowledge, such as it was, he prescribed for their diseases and dispelled their anxieties. 'Do this or that,' he said to them, 'and these terrors will vanish.'

Thus, while not every philosophy is a religion, every religion is a philosophy. Religion, to be worth anything, must cast out fears, allay bewilderment, solve perplexities: and this cannot be done without the formation of theories, that is, without philosophizing. No one can conceive an object of worship, however crude or loathsome, unless he has first reflected on the 'cause of things': and without such reflection he will be the victim of 'terror and insane distress', of which we can hardly imagine the least advanced of human beings not to desire to rid himself.

A much more satisfactory definition of religion than Arnold's is that proposed by Sir James Frazer: 'a propitiation or conciliation of powers superior to man which are believed to control the course of nature or of human life':[1] but this considers certain actions of men rather than the state of mind leading to such actions. If we *do* consider that state of mind, we may prefer the account given by the American, Howerth, and endorsed with the weighty approval of Warde Fowler:[2] 'Religion is the effective desire to be in right relation to the Power manifesting itself in the universe.' We might perhaps prefer to call this a definition of *religiousness* rather than of religion, and to adopt Frazer's words for the acts such religiousness induces: and if so, we shall have a fairly satisfactory working definition both of the rituals and of the kind of mental attitude from which ritual springs. But it will, I think, be seen that religion and re-

1. *Golden Bough*, I, 62.
2. *Religious Experience of the Roman People*, p. 8.

ligiousness, thus understood, alike imply a philosophy. For it needs a philosophy to conceive of such a Power or Powers as are here postulated: and it needs still more philosophy to believe that they can be conciliated. As was said by a profound student of religion in a later stage, 'He that cometh unto God must believe that he is, and that he is a rewarder of them that seek after him':[1] and such belief cannot arise unless the believer has first *thought* about the universe. That he first *wondered* about it is of course true; wonder is the necessary preliminary to examination. So far we may admit that emotion enters into religion. But there is not the slightest sign that the early thinkers regarded the Power they conceived to exist as in any sense moral.

If we may plausibly guess about these philosophers, we are almost constrained to imagine that, at some stage or other in the history of men, the higher minds among them began studiously to ponder on the strange phenomena presented to their senses: the stars, the winds, the floods, or even perhaps the mysteries of birth and death. To the common herd these were but a congeries of unintelligibilities; but the precursors of Newton and Maxwell were not content simply to be tossed hither and thither 'each way and move': they had to ask questions and find answers. So soon as they guessed at[2] an explanation, they were philosophers, and straightway began to exert the influence which those who know can always exert over the ignorant. Knowledge enabled them to invent schemes for averting from themselves and others the harm which natural agencies were all too capable of doing. Out of this knowledge sprang religion, which the men of science taught, and the common people believed. These terrible and arbitrary powers, the storm, the flood, the thunder, must be by some means placated: the men of science had, it was thought, discovered the means; and these means, when adopted, absurd and futile as they might be, were a cult.

1. Hebrews xi, 6.
2. Or 'arrived at'; they must have done *some* analysing: *guessing* is perhaps too severe a term.

We cannot, of course, speak with any certainty as to 'primitive' man; and indeed it is as well to shun the word 'primitive' altogether. Even what we call 'early' man is early only in relation to our own times; he may well be late if reckoned from the enormously distant period of the actual beginning. A hundred thousand years ago may be but yesterday. Precision is out of the question. It is practically impossible to distinguish between the first man and the last of his anthropoid ancestors: we can never say, 'At this point man appeared on the earth.' Still less can we say how or when he began to think, or when his indistinct cerebrations began to be tinged with reason. We can but argue from more or less dubious analogies and more or less vague probabilities. We can go back, with some confidence, a trifle of ten or twenty thousand years; for the millenniums before that we must be content, for the most part, with plausible conjectures.

This is not, however, to say that we are compelled to give up our search, at the very outset, as altogether hopeless, and, through fear of dogmatism, to run into the extremes of Pyrrhonism or utter scepticism. In the first place, we may be reasonably sure that human nature is tolerably uniform – that, in the common phrase, it is 'the same all the world over'. If you prick Jew, Christian, or heathen, he will bleed; if you tickle him, he will laugh; if you wrong him, he will revenge: and that, within limits, has always been the case. We are not unjustified, therefore, in arguing to the unknown past from the known present, and, making due allowance for changes of environment, we have some right to believe that men of old reacted to certain conditions as the men of today react to them. Human emotions may not be, as Spinoza thought, no less definable than the properties of lines and circles; but they are not lawless and chaotic. Again, to speak paradoxically, the *variations* of human nature are also tolerably uniform. We find everywhere, and at all times, whenever we have an opportunity of judging, the same contrasting types as now; the credulous, the sceptical, the servile, the rebellious, the courageous and the timid, the strong-minded and the weak. Time makes no radical difference to such characters as these: prehistoric man had his Hampdens and his Straffords, his Luthers and his Tetzels, his Hal of the Wynds and his Conachars. The artists who have left, in their drawings of the stag and the cave-bear, specimens of their pictorial genius, obeyed the same impulses as Leonardo and Rembrandt; and the fathers that begat us harboured our suspicions, and believed our beliefs as we do, though their memorial is perished with them. Those who prefer to follow priestly guidance, and those who trust a priest as Hamlet trusted adders fanged, had their prehistoric precursors; the saint and the sinner dwelt side by side in lake-dwellings as they dwell in London today; the miser hoarded his cowrie-shells and the prodigal scattered them, in the reign of Assaracus as, in the reign of Elizabeth II, he hoards his bits of paper. There is nothing absolutely new under the sun; and man is no exception to the rule.

We are not surprised, therefore, when we find in the present world much that has the obvious mark of a *survival*, and that can be explained only as a relic of a past which admits of fairly plausible reconstruction. As, in looking at the monuments of Easter Island, or at the pyramids of Yucatan, we can form some conception of the civilizations out of which they sprang, so, in contemplating certain beliefs still existing, we can envisage, within limits, the previous beliefs from which they have developed. And these existing beliefs have now, by the labours of innumerable devoted investigators, been collected, compared, and analysed for our use. We know, fairly well, what men now think; and we are therefore not entirely without indications as to what their fathers thought. Nay, if we but turn our minds inwards, and consider what we ourselves think, we may often guess what our own ancestors thought thousands of years ago: for there is no living religion which has not in it much of ancient heathenism, and no living philosophy which is not the result of the simple logic and the blind gropings of the distant past.

Studying ancient beliefs, then, in the light of such records as have come down to us, and comparing them with beliefs still held by backward tribes, we are driven to the conclusion that one of the primary factors in early religion was fear of the unknown. Nature was horrible and incalculable. The wind blew where it listed, and none could tell whence it came or whither it went: all, however, could be sure that it was at times savagely ruthless and destructive. The 'red eyes of the lightning' were ferocious and terrifying; and the thunderbolt smote not only with irresistible force, but with the capricious irresponsibility of an Oriental sultan. The stars moved in a perplexing and frightening fashion: and, to people who had not yet learnt to count, even the sun's diurnal course must have appeared mysterious, as beyond doubt his alternating tyranny and tenderness must have been past finding out, and his motives for hiding his face during an eclipse must have been sinister. He was assuredly now angry and now pleased: but *why* was he either the one or the other?

The explanations given were bound to be anthropomorphic. No one can step out of his own shadow; and early man had nothing to reason from save his own feelings. The stone that hurt his foot must be, literally, animated with malignity; the storm that baffled him must *mean* to baffle him. He knew that when *he* struck he meant to hurt; when Nature struck *him*, she must have a like intention. 'Reasoning' from analogy, he ascribed to everything in the world human motives. He himself moved; winds and rivers moved also; therefore winds and rivers were like him in other respects. When he observed that they also 'spoke', he inevitably gifted them with a human voice, and the evidence that they were entirely human gained double force. Conrad's Captain MacWhirr could not help feeling that the typhoon he was facing had an opposing *will*: Achilles did not doubt that Xanthus *meant* to overwhelm him. Even more sure, if possible, would a MacWhirr or an Achilles of the immemorial past have been, when caught in a flood or a tempest. As to animals, the thing was so obvious that proof was needless:

they were instantaneously perceived to be men, differing only in the insignificant detail of physical shape. Adam would have needed no divine instruction to tell him that beasts and birds were his equals and his companions.

> *Is not the earth*
> *With various living creatures, and the air,*
> *Replenished? ... Know'st thou not*
> *Their language and their ways? They also know,*
> *And reason not contemptibly.*

Everything in the world, being thus animated, was, as I said, conceived as in the main hostile to man, and had to be flattered, cajoled, or in some way or other rendered harmless. A few easy observations or experiments, like those stigmatized by Bacon as *merae palpationes*, scratches on the surface of phenomena, or at best *inductiones per enumerationem simplicem*, would be sufficient for these early men of science to establish a general law. 'Chaos umpire sat; next him, high arbiter, chance governed all': and two or three accidental coincidences would satisfy minds that had not learnt to doubt and to discriminate; as, in fact, they satisfy similar minds today. The same childish logic which assumes that because one misfortune has happened on a Friday therefore all Fridays are unlucky, of that because one man has been killed by a falling ladder therefore we must never walk under ladders – this logic must have operated in full vigour thousands of years ago. We cannot believe that *post hoc non propter hoc* was a maxim any better remembered and applied by early man than it is in certain circles today. Unless, like John Howe, we hold that Kepler and Descartes were 'but the rubbish of an Adam', we must hold that early man, through no fault of his own, reasoned on slight premisses, and leapt precipitately to conclusions. The psychological law of the Association of Ideas – useful when checked and corrected, but terribly deceptive when allowed to run wild – worked havoc in the minds of our ancestors. Nor was it likely to be kept in control when along with it was working the distorting influence of fear.

The man of 'science', whether medicine-man, magician, or priest, having once obtained power by establishing a superstition, was not likely easily to abdicate. The love of ruling is one of the strongest of all human passions, and one of those which most subtly disguise themselves as virtuous and altruistic. The great man does not find it hard to persuade himself that he remains in his position not for his own sake but to benefit the community. How often today do we hear the statesman complain of the burdens of office, which only a high sense of duty prevents him from laying down! If any human sentiment is innate, this is innate: and assuredly it arose in man very early. No sooner then had a man of science obtained power over the minds of others by the successful use of a spell, than he would endeavour by all means to retain it. He had, once or twice, relieved others from fear of certain influences: it was now his business to inculcate fear of himself. That force which had driven away the storm or saved men from a wild beast could be equally well exerted in bringing the storm or inciting the beast: it might also, by simply refraining from exercising itself, remove the protection, and allow untold calamities to rush in. Offend him, and the defences would fall, and the offender would be crushed.

When once such a dominion was established over the minds of men, its strength was tremendous. There are many cases of men dying, from sheer imagination, when a spell was laid upon them, or when they simply beheld that the countenance of the ruler was changed. The witch who killed by means of the evil eye is a faint reflection of the spell-binder of earlier times or of uncivilized regions: as also the witch who cured diseases by a few muttered words is a faint reflection of the medicine-man who cured by the potency of his barbaric incantations.

The powers whom it was the business of the magician to control were everywhere. Every beast, bird, insect, pebble was the seat of an influence that might be malignant: and less palpable forces might be still more dangerous. Diseases – fever, a sudden stitch in the side, a toothache – all were the work of gods or demons – two words for the same thing. Against all these the magician offered protection; and to him the trembling victim inevitably had recourse.

It is unnecessary to inquire how it was that he kept up his power despite the scores of failures he must have made. It would be easy for him to throw the blame upon others, to camouflage failure as success, to play upon the fact that a single lucky coincidence is remembered when a thousand discrepancies are forgotten – a fact which Bacon has noted, but which it does not need the intellect of Bacon to discover. Above all, it was easy for him to start against the doubter the charge of blasphemy, and to suppress the heresy by killing the heretic – the favourite method of despots in all times. Thus it was that beliefs which could not have stood a week's impartial examination retained an unchallenged position for century after century, and added to their other advantages the prestige of immemorial antiquity. 'With us,' the priests could say as the Friends said to Job, 'are the grey-headed and the very aged men, much older than thy father.' It is one of the miracles of history that this immensely powerful prescription should ever have found a single sceptic to utter a whisper against it. Possibly, but for the impact of tribes with one set of superstitions upon tribes with others, the world might never have escaped from this crushing thraldom – that is, if it ever does fully escape. It may be that the sole means of ridding ourselves of one superstition is to adopt another.

Not the least widely spread of these superstitions is the belief in imitative magic: a belief due to the inability of uneducated man to distinguish between similarity and identity.[1] Thus, in the simple philosophy of early man, any

1. This inability appears in very curious ways. It is hardly too strong a statement, for example, that certain languages scarcely possess any word for 'is like', 'resembles', 'represents', 'consists of', and use 'is' instead. Thus Hebrew and Arabic say: 'All thy garments are myrrh', 'The vale of Siddim was slime-pits', 'I am prayer', 'the season was showers', 'The whole earth was one speech'. These expressions, which are disguised in our translation, are plainly retentions from a time when the loosest relations were actually confused with identity.

Again, in a different sphere of thought, the familiar fact that twins, phenomenon might be compelled to occur by imitating it. In hot seasons a breeze may be desired. This is gained by the exercise of swinging, which is indulged in not for present pleasure, but in order to constrain the wind-gods to give a similar breeze in the near future. To get rainy weather, or dry, as circumstances demand, ball-games are played, the ball, being dark, representing the dark clouds: and the coming storm or drought follows the result of the game. Elijah, we cannot doubt, brought famine upon the land by means of such an imitative spell, as he certainly brought the rain by a sevenfold enchantment which mimicked the storm. Every child knows the stories of disease and death called upon an enemy by making an image of the victim and pricking it with pins, or, after the fashion of Rossetti's Sister Helen, melting it before a fire. To burn a man in effigy was, in old days, not a mere harmless way of showing enmity: it was an infallible method of ensuring his death within a very short time. The Lord Bute of 20000 B.C. would have actually died when the jackboot was thrown into the flames; nor would it have been long before the Princess of Wales followed the cremated petticoat into the next world.

It is this imitative magic that lies at the root of many of the games which still survive as children's amusements. All games, in fact, that have naturally arisen, and have not been deliberately invented, were once religious ceremonies. Dolls are deposed idols – though the two words have no ety-

---

because they were alike, were supposed to be the same human being miraculously doubled is a further illustration of the tendency to confound the similar with the identical. Examples gross as earth instruct us; I will give but two. In the Saga of Hervor we are told that Arngrim had twelve sons, the two youngest of whom, both called Hadding, were twins, and did the work of one man between them; this was because they *were* but one. In the Eastern legend, St Thomas is the twin of Christ, and is constantly mistaken for him. The widespread custom of calling twins by the same name, as in the case of these Haddings, Bede's two Ewalds, Shakespeare's two Dromios, is but another example of the confusion. The name *was* the man; it was beyond the power of early thought to distinguish between the noun and the thing. Hence, as the twins were one person, their names must be one.

mological connexion. The tug of war – formerly a sex-conflict, women holding one end of the rope and men the other – was a spell to promote fertility. Knucklebones controlled the caprices of chance. Still more portentous was the game of skittles, the rumbling sounds of which, being like thunder, had the power of bringing on the beneficent thunder-shower of early summer; or, if necessary, of being so manipulated as to prevent a maleficent one. A similar game was played by King Salmoneus of Elis, who, in order to constrain Zeus to discharge his bolt, drove his chariot along the ways, with torches to imitate the lightning and with the rattle of drums for the thunder. Doubtless he thought, and his admiring people thought also, that by this process he had actually turned himself at least for the time being into Zeus and had annexed Olympian prerogatives. His pious purpose was, however, sadly misunderstood by later generations, whose ideas of divinity had changed. He was represented as blasphemously defying the Almighty, and as having been deservedly smitten with a real thunderbolt. As Virgil tells us, he was found expiating his crime in Tartarus:

> *Vidi et crudeles dantem Salmonea poenas*
> *Dum flammas Jovis et sonitus imitatur Olympi:*
> *Quattuor hic invectus equis et lampada quassans*
> *Per Graium populos, mediaeque per Elidis urbem*
> *Ibat ovans, divomque sibi poscebat honorem*
> *At pater omnipotens densa inter nubila telum*
> *Contorsit, non ille faces nec fumea taedis*
> *Lumina, praecipitemque immani turbine adegit.*[1]

1. Thus 'translated' by Dryden:

> *Salmoneus, suffering cruel pains, I found,*
> *For emulating Jove: the rattling sound*
> *Of mimic thunder, and the glittering blaze*
> *Of painted lightnings, and their forky rays.*
> *Through Elis, and the Grecian towns, he flew:*
> *Th' audacious wretch four fiery coursers drew;*
> *He wav'd a torch aloft, and, madly vain,*
> *Sought godlike worship from a servile train.*
> *Ambitious fool! with horny hoofs to pass*
> *O'er hollow arches of resounding brass*

Very similar ideas lay behind the universally diffused belief in the lot. The lot, representing the man, *was* the man; and as it fell, so would the man's fate befall. 'The lot is cast into the lap, but the whole disposing thereof is of Yahweh.' It was thus that, by a succession of casts, Yahweh picked out tribe, family, household, and finally Achan; and all Israel stoned him with stones and burned him with fire. It was thus that the god decided between Saul and Jonathan, one being Urim and the other Thummim (two sacred and fateful stones), as to which had been guilty of transgressing a taboo; and it was thus that the eleven Apostles decided between the two candidates for the place left vacant by the treason of Judas. Unluckily, it is not always that the lot gives so unexceptionable a verdict.

All these proceedings, and a thousand others of the kind, were emphatically religious services, with, be it noted, no touch of morality about them, but involving a good deal of elementary science in the form of magic: all designed either to ascertain the will of a set of capricious or malignant deities, to gain their favour, or finally to compel them to act in a certain way. The same may be said of a vast number of ceremonies designed to *avert* the evils which the gods were suspected of planning against men. Such were the eclipse-ceremonies, which the Romans continued to practise in their most civilized days: the 'vapulation' of the moon with a 'rhombus', of which Martial speaks, the spells alluded to by Propertius for dragging her down to earth, the beating of drums and the blowing of trumpets vainly tried by the mutinous soldiers of Drusus, as so vividly described by Tacitus. In India today the *dosadh* or pork-butcher, though (or because) he is an untouchable, is set to perform the task of frightening away the demon Rahu who is trying to de-

---

To rival thunder in its rapid course,
And imitate inimitable force!
But he, the king of heaven, obscure on high,
Bar'd his red arm, and, launching from the sky
His writhen bolt, not shaking empty smoke,
Down to the deep abyss the flaming felon struck!

vour the luminary during an eclipse. We are assured by those who have attended this service that the noise is tremendous, and that if Rahu had human ears he *must* be driven away by it. The Jews, we are told, needed a *dosadh* only for an eclipse of the sun; for, having taken the precaution of adopting a lunar calendar, they were unaffected by what happened to the moon. 'Learn not the ways of the Gentiles,' says Jeremiah to his countrymen; 'and be not dismayed at the signs of heaven, for the Gentiles are dismayed at them.' None the less, the Jews continued to be dismayed, and took care to make sun-images and bow down to them; for they felt the sun, at least, to be a powerful enemy. When Job cursed the day of his birth, he could think of no worse imprecation than that it should be left out of the lunar calendar, and that the dragon should swallow the sun on that day every year.

For the averting of these catastrophes, and of others of every kind, the priests alone knew the secrets, or could interpret the mysterious signs by which the gods revealed what they were about to do. No Roman or Greek general ever went to battle without consulting the diviners, any more than Nebuchadnezzar would have advanced against Jerusalem without looking at the liver or watching where the arrows,[1] ceremonially shot, happened to point. If, in spite of favourable omens, disaster supervened, the augurs knew how to shirk the responsibility. We cannot doubt that Flaminius took all proper precautions; but when Trasimene had ruined his army, and he was dead and unable to defend himself, it was no hard matter to circulate the rumour that he had disregarded a multitude of supernatural warnings. When Claudius had lost a naval battle, it was easy to say that he had flung the sacred chickens into the sea, remarking that if they would not eat they should at any rate drink. Cicero, himself an augur, had no belief in augury: yet he found it expedient to declare Caesar's laws invalid because he had ignored the omens which his political opponents endeavoured to use in order to hinder their passing.

1. See Ezekiel xxi, 21.

There is no more interesting work in the world than Cicero's little book on Divination, in which crowds of instances are collected showing the survival, into a highly cultured age, of a belief in dreams, in the flight of birds, in premonitions, and in all the other methods by which the purposes of the gods were supposed to be detected – if only those means had been less ambiguous. That Cicero, though he did not believe in them, yet thought they must not be treated with disrespect, is shown by the fact that he puts their defence in the mouth of his brother Quintus, and allows that they have the support of great philosophers, and the prestige of immemorial antiquity. That, indeed, all these ideas, and others of the same kind, were held from the very earliest ages, it is certain as such things can be; and there is no nation, however it may boast its freedom from ancient fancies, which is yet emancipated from them. We can easily guess the power gained by those who claimed the ability to interpret the obscure signs vouchsafed by the gods; nor are we left to guess-work. A Joseph became the vizier of Egypt, second only to Pharaoh, because the spirit of the gods was in him, and he could explain a prophetic dream: a Daniel was the third ruler in the kingdom of Darius for a similar reason. There must have been hundreds of Daniels and Josephs whose names have not come down to us. Agamemnon was the nominal commander-in-chief of the Greeks at Troy, and Achilles their greatest warrior, but the real imperator was Calchas; and 'vixere augures ante Calchanta multi'.

It is the view of some scholars that the wise men did more than this: that, in addition to bringing or averting calamities, and swaying the destinies of tribes, they were also the conscious authors of the myths on which the rituals were a practical commentary. They were deliberate inventors, on this theory, of the stories of gods and heroes which answered the questions put by the uninitiated. For example, if a 'man of science' were asked by a bewildered pupil to account for the strange behaviour of the sun, he explained the phenomenon, possibly to his own satisfaction, and usually to that of his hearer, by *inventing* a myth, and the tale of Phaethon, the story of the cattle of Helios, or the account of the way in which Odin became one-eyed and acquired his azure cloak, would be the result. His myths were probably less artistic than those of Plato, but they had a like origin and design. That very able scholar, Mr Ray Knight, goes even further. He regards some of these early myth-makers as philosophers of a very advanced order – so highly advanced, indeed, that we have not even yet overtaken them – and he thinks that in their myths they set forth in mystical garb, some of the profoundest metaphysical truths. The myth of Perseus, for instance, he regards as intelligible only if it is viewed as the symbolical expression of the philosophical conceptions of some prehistoric Mahatma or Patmian visionary. I am not sure that I agree unreservedly with this theory. At any rate, I believe that the *majority* of myths are of popular origin: like our old ballads, they had no author, or, what is the same thing, many authors: they grew insensibly from invisible beginnings. Only thus can I explain the rise of similar myths in countries that can scarcely have had intercourse with one another. The widely diffused myth, for example, which is found in places so far apart as Greece and Samoa, describing how the heaven was forcibly sundered from the earth,[1] and thenceforth held in its place by trees, mountains, or pillars, seems to me to be a folk-story, and hardly likely to be an esoteric allegory. But whether this is the true account or not, the priests would know how to adapt the stories to their own ends, and would be as capable as a Philo Judaeus of making a given tale mean what they wished it to mean. If popular fancy pictured an eclipse as the swallowing of the sun by Leviathan, the priest would easily advance to the rhetorical question, 'And who but me knows how to frighten Leviathan away?' If the common people looked upon Orion as a giant who in his folly[2] had lifted his hand against Yahweh, and had been hurled in chains into the sky,

1. The Japanese say that their empire began at the very moment when this separation took place.
2. The Hebrew Orion is Kesil, the Fool.

the priest might well utter the warning, 'Take heed, ye ignorant, for it is in my power to bind the influences of the Pleiades, and to loose, for your destruction, the bands of Orion.' There are, however, in my opinion, some myths, and even some of very great antiquity, which seem to bear the marks of purposed priestly authorship; they show a distinctly philosophic character, and are apparently beyond the scope of ordinary minds. Some few, indeed, have so profound a meaning that we must, with Mr Knight, assume their originators to have been men of very exceptional intellect. That the priests alone held, or claimed to hold, the key to their significance, would add indefinitely to the prestige of the priestly class, much as the ability to read added to the prestige of clerks in the Middle Ages. Again, some men of philosophic bent might attach to a popular myth a sequel, or give to it a turn, which would lend it a meaning never dreamt of by its first begetter. We have instances of such refashionings in historical times. Thus, when Protagoras subjoins an appendix to the myth of Prometheus, in order to explain the way in which man became a social and political animal, or when Pindar gives to Epimetheus a daughter Prophasis, or 'Excuse', we see that they are deliberately enlarging and expounding an ancient story for a certain end; and it is probable that much earlier teachers did the same thing. As we shall notice later, this is exactly what Zarathushtra did with the Iranian mythology, translating its crudities into some of the most difficult and abstract doctrines ever propounded to the world.

Among the myths which would lend themselves to this treatment were what I may loosely call Myths of Mind: those which deal with mental processes, with birth and death, with a future life, or with the creation of the universe. Savage conceptions of death, in particular, as far as we can discern, were excessively naïve: there are still tribes which cannot understand that the dead man is anything but asleep, or playing a conjuring trick upon his neighbours with nefarious intent. Other tribes have advanced far enough to perceive that heat has gone out of him, that the 'thin flame' of life is extinct; others that the breath, that is, air, has departed from him. That breath is the man's spirit – something physical and material, but for the most part invisible. Whither it has gone, and what are its feelings, the learned man alone can tell; and according to the stories he relates, so will the customs he bids the people observe and the rites he bids them perform. Not least important is this, that he alone can interpret the dying man's inarticulate mumblings, and reveal who has murdered him. For a *natural* death was all but inconceivable to our ancestors; when a man died, an enemy must have caught him, either by shooting an invisible arrow, or by sending him a Nessus gift,[1] or by some fatal spell. It is necessary for the tribe to know who this slayer is: and the priest or medicine-man undertakes the investigation. He asks the question of the dying victim, and out of the sibylline mutterings concocts a name; or he lies down, sleeps, and dreams, and sees the murderer in the dream. From fancies like this spring whole cults and rituals. Should the spirit be hovering near the corpse, it must be removed to a distance, cajoled, tricked, or forcibly kept back: for it may well be planning vengeance. The priest knows the ways of making him harmless, ways differing at sundry times and in divers places, but all inspired by practically the same motives. 'Mourning'-garb may have to be assumed, in order that the angry ghost may fail to recognize its relatives; this dress is no sign of sorrow, but a disguise due to fear. Again, if the man has died in the house, you must carry him out, not by the door he has been accustomed to use, but by some other passage which he does not know. You break down the wall, and push him through, or you lift the corner of the tent. Or, just as he is dying, you raise the window and let the soul fly out, taking care, however, to shut it at once, lest he return. If you carry him out to bury or burn him, you must come back by another way, having first brushed the grave with a branch in order to sweep away the spirit. You hold a secret conclave, speaking in whispers lest he should hear, and you decide, with the help of the medicine-man,

1. As the Centaur Nessus sent a poisoned shirt to Heracles.

on the means you shall use to make him hie to his confine. All these are *religious* rites; and it is hardly too much to say that half the religious services of the early world were due to fear of the dead. From Brittany to Samoa, as Frazer says, it is not affection for the lost but fear of his spirit that stirs men to these ceremonies. But it must be observed also that the fear is controlled by a philosophy, a science, or, if we prefer the word, a creed, dictated by men who, in comparison with the rest of their tribe, may be called learned. This is specially indicated by the fact that dread of pollution from a corpse is an almost universal feeling. In the view of some, this may have been due to rudimentary medical knowledge; and the methods of purification, though often ludicrously puerile, are sometimes such as a modern doctor would recommend. There are worse prophylactics than 'to bathe one's flesh in water and to be unclean until the evening' – an injunction certainly not first found in the Mosaic Law. But it is not an injunction likely to have occurred to the ordinary savage; it seems to show observation and reflection.

The immense influence of the person whom we have called indifferently the priest, the medicine-man, and the philosopher, could not, of course, have been gained unless there had been a community of interest, and a common basis of knowledge, between him and the ordinary people. He was but the highest specimen of their class, and his ideas were but the highest expression of theirs. If they were willing to follow him, that was because he was never too far in front of them. If they accepted his explanations of natural phenomena, it was because they felt themselves to have been dimly groping after similar explanations. Often, doubtless, he led them because he really followed them: he had the ruler's talent for catching up popular notions, and giving them back to the people as if they were his own: and they won acceptance because they were already the people's. He rode on the wave of vulgar opinion: and he rarely made the mistake of going directly and obviously against it. How great is the strength of an opinion thus skilfully swayed, no examples are necessary to show: and the rigid conservatism with which a people will cleave to views once formed can be observed today by anyone with eyes in his head. Even folk-stories must be cautiously altered, and never utterly transformed. Children will not lightly permit their parents to change their nursery-rhymes or fairy-tales; and in the childhood of the world a mythological story, once started, remained essentially unaltered. The tribal Pantheon, with all its intricacies and genealogical relationships, is the same from generation to generation: the discrepancies we sometimes notice are due not to time but to place, or to the intrusion of foreign elements. Nay, should an alien cult impose itself on the tribe, the old mythology has a trick of persisting, even though the conquerors may substitute new names for the old. '*Graecia capta ferum victorem cepit*'. In Britain, many a heathen spell, and many a Northern rite, survived with the mere change of Thor and Odin into Matthew and Mark: the ancient creed, like Shelley's Cloud, may change, but it cannot die. The rites, in fact, are still more rigid than the spells or stories. Their efficacy, having been 'demonstrated' by an immemorial experience, cannot be discredited by any number of exceptions, any more than the efficacy of a patent pill can be discredited, in the minds of the faithful, by a thousand failures. Short work is made of a sceptic who even hints his doubts. Nor, for century after century, can the struggling ethical sense, probably latent though it be in all men, produce the due impression. 'If it had might as it has right,' said Bishop Butler, 'conscience would govern the world': but its might is small, and its march excessively slow. Against moral ideas, uneasily felt to be revolutionary and destructive, a stubborn inertia opposes an apparently invincible resistance.

Whether early man ever hit on the idea of a Supreme Being, in anything approaching our sense of the word – whether he conceived of God, as distinct from a multitude of Gods – this is one of the questions, so easy to put, which may never be solved. It is the theory of some, especially of those who take a strict view of the revelations of Scripture, or of those who regard the great religions of the Far East to have been originally monotheistic, that mankind also was originally monotheistic, and that polytheism is a corruption of a purer religion. To them, the evidence seems to point to the fact that men, so far from having, more or less steadily, struggled upwards from savagery, have declined from a state of moral and mental enlightenment. The story of the Fall of Adam is to them a representation of the truth. Alike in men's behaviour and in men's conception of the Deity, the first ages were the best; and we have by no means recovered the Paradise we have lost.

This is a theory worthy of all respect; it was held by the great ancients who believed in a Golden Age; it was held by the Hebrews and the Early Christians; and it is still a basic conception of Catholicism; nor is the number of archaeologists who hold it contemptible. To me, however, it appears untenable. It is to my mind more likely that man, in the manner hinted at above, has evolved all his ideas from savage beginnings, and that even in the cases in which he has declined from a comparatively high stage, that stage was originally attained by ascent from a lower. History is full of such advances and retrogressions, and progress is scarcely ever continuous. In any case it is fairly certain that early man had no idea of God in any way approaching the abstract and refined conceptions of modern philosophers. The definition of him as 'an Infinite and Eternal Spirit', set forth in so many catechisms, would have been far beyond the profoundest Palaeolithic thinker. Nor do I think it yet firmly established that *all* nations have reached an idea which even the Moabites or Ammonites would have regarded as worthy of being set beside their Chemosh or Moloch. Demons of the stone, the wood, or the stream I think it not improbable that they had; though some explorers claim to have discovered tribes to which even these were unknown, and which lived in a state of utter materialism, accepting things as they came, and making no attempt to explain them.[1] It is hard to think either that men whose

1. In both aspects the difficulties of mutual understanding between explorers and savages are great. It is hard for the questioner to avoid

ancestors were enlightened should have fallen so low, or
that after evolving from *Pithecanthropus* they should not have
evolved a little further. But be this so or not, it seems to me
all but certain that the idea of *God* is of slow growth, and
that only by very gradual steps are his cruder anthropomorphic characters stripped from him. It was very timidly
and imperfectly, as we shall see, that even the Jews advanced
to monolatry, or the conception of one God to one country:
more gradually and more tentatively still was it that their
great thinkers – religious geniuses of the highest order – went
forward to proclaim the doctrine of a God ruling the whole
earth, the heaven, and Sheol under the earth. In Greece a
similar process took place – and took time. In many countries philosophic minds may have contrived to reconcile
monotheism with the prevalent polytheism by picking out,
more or less arbitrarily, one god, out of the vast number of
possible candidates, to be the chief of the hierarchy. But the
reconciliation was nominal. The Zeus of Cleanthes was not
the Zeus of the populace: and when Paul hinted at his
identity with the Father whom he preached, he was speaking
not to the populace but to an audience of philosophers. He
knew the difference quite well when, in Lycaonia, the crowd
tried to worship Barnabas as Zeus and himself as Hermes.

But in any case, whether early men ever reached the idea
of a Supreme Being or not, it is certain that they, like the
majority of their descendants to the present hour, paid comparatively little attention to him. He was 'too far from every
one of us', and had to be approached, if at all, through inter-
mediaries. To 'feel after him and find him' was a task too
difficult for most. The services offered to Zeus in Greece – far
removed as Zeus was, in the ordinary mind, from the One
God of the philosopher – were few compared with those
offered to nymphs, heroes, demigods, and the spirits inhabiting trees, fountains, and stones. It has been well remarked that the supreme divinity of the Romans was not

---

putting ideas into the minds of the questioned. On the other hand, it is
hard, if the savage *has* ideas of a metaphysical kind, to find language,
intelligible to his interlocutor, in which to express them.

Jupiter Optimus Maximus, but the Eternal City herself – a sort of anticipation of the Hegelian goddess, the State, who played so great a part in German history during the last century. But even Rome, at no time, we may be sure, received anything like as regular and continuous worship as the Lares and Penates, Terminus, Pales, or Vertumnus and Priapus. In India, for one prayer to Brahma there are probably millions paid to the fertility-images that are so visible in every street. In less enlightened parts of the Catholic world, even today, it is the saints who receive the adoration; God the Father is a vague Personage in the background; precisely as, if we may believe the Prophets, the people of Israel neglected Yahweh and worshipped their local Baals and Astartes under every green tree and on every high hill. There is no reason to think that 'primitive' man acted otherwise.

The worship was a ritual consisting rather in a series of symbolic acts, and the crooning of incantations, than in prayer: though prayer was not entirely absent – at least if we count flattery and cajolery as forms of supplication. But the ritual almost always included some offering which would titillate the senses, or satisfy the appetite, of the god. 'The Lord smelled a sweet savour', and came down to take a goodly share of the feast. The best must be given to him – one must not, like Prometheus, give the god the least tasty or digestible portions of the victim. In many cases the god was known to prefer blood to any other drink, and plenty was given him. In the early days, even of Judaism, he claimed every first-born, whether of man or of beast, and human sacrifices were freely offered. It was not till later that he graciously permitted the first-born of human parents to be redeemed by means of an *Ersatz* or substitute. Even when this costly present had been long discontinued, it might be resumed in times of disaster, as the Romans sacrificed men during the Hannibalian terror, or as Mesha rescued his country when it was in the last stage of despair during foreign invasion. What so horrified the Spaniards in the ritual of the Mexicans was, if they had but known it, exactly what their own ancestors had done some centuries before. The Hebrews loathed those who made their children pass through the fire to Moloch; but David himself, to turn away the wrath of Yahweh, ceremonially sacrificed to him the ill-fated descendants of Saul.

The god loved music, or at least noise; and an almost invariable part of the ritual was the beating of drums and tom-toms, the playing of timbrels, and violent dancing or corroborees. There can be little doubt that, in the excitement thus caused, the worshippers felt the actual presence of the deity, and actually, in some cases, *saw* him. What Miss Jane Harrison called the 'congregational god' is a reality; the devotees of Dionysus saw him in their midst, and I have been assured by travellers that American Indians, when duly worked up, see their tribal god among them. The method of bringing him down is fully understood by the priests, regularly practised, and almost invariably with success.

There is an astonishing likeness, amid trifling differences, in the rituals of all nations, in all parts of the world, at certain stages of their religious development. As I have said, the ritual, once established, displays an obstinate tenacity, and is often not driven out save by foreign conquest and the forcible imposition of a new cult. Even then, like the spells of which I spoke above, it may continue an underground existence, as the worship of the Horned God went on in Europe for centuries despite clerical denunciations of Satanism, and despite all the terrors of the Inquisition. The *Malleus Maleficarum* itself did not entirely break to pieces that ancient ritual: nor did Islam entirely suppress Parseeism in Iran. Sometimes the vanquished religion is strong enough to compel the victor to make a treaty, and steals into the very ritual which imagines itself to have utterly eradicated its rival: as we can trace elements of Mithraism, or of the cults of Iris and Attis, in some still living Christian services. In our own country many signs of such fusion are visible to the instructed eye: Freyja and Odin are assuredly not yet quite dead. Our beliefs are composite, and our religion may be compared to that of the East Anglian king of whom Bede speaks, who built a church at one end of which was the Sacramental Table, and at the other an altar to Thor.

But – and here we enter upon a theme which will occupy us, more or less constantly, through our whole discussion – even without external violence the established religion cannot escape the silent corroding influence of time. Not even a Venetian or Spartan oligarchy remains unchanged: and not even a religion rooted in antiquity and buttressed by superstition can stand foursquare for ever against the wind and weather. 'Knowledge' cannot be confined to priests, *all* heresies cannot be extirpated, *some* heretics will whisper, and their whispers will have their effect on the thoughts of others. At last, a favourable concurrence of circumstances having arisen, the heretics speak out loud and bold, and the ancient religion discovers that it is weaker than it fancied, and that it needs to employ new weapons of defence.

There are two main lines on which this revolution usually proceeds. The one is that of philosophy, in which we may include natural science. I said at the beginning that natural science is one of the chief elements of early religion. But it is the characteristic of science to be progressive, whereas, in comparison, religion is almost stationary. The friendship between the two, therefore, can hardly be lasting. The physicist asks questions which go to the root of the religious organism, and the answers he gets are often such as seriously to shake it. When some early Anaxagoras reaches the conclusion that the sun is a red-hot mass of stone, larger than the Peloponnese, he is inevitably accused of impiety by those who have taught that the sun is a maiden pursued by a wolf, or a charioteer driving flaming horses across the sky, and who have based on this mythology a lucrative ritual of sun-worship. The quarrel of Galileo with the Inquisition, or of Huxley with Bishop Wilberforce, is only a replica of what must have happened many times over in prehistoric days. We know how Macaulay hoped to destroy Hinduism by simply teaching a scientific geography: for the religious system of Hinduism is bound up with a geography so absurd that a second-standard child in a council school must laugh at it. When early philosophers discovered that *their* religion was similarly bound up with false science, they probably did not laugh – the case was too serious – but they felt contempt, none the less keen because they had to conceal it.

Sometimes allied with this form of philosophy, and sometimes antagonistic to it, but equally hostile to the dominant religion, was, as we have already seen, the science of ethics. A prehistoric Socrates might deny that he had anything to do with Anaxagoras, and might loudly declare that the physics of Anaxagoras were at once impious and ridiculous – that the books in which the doctrines were proclaimed were dear at a drachma each – but it was useless for him to say that his own theories were not, in their tendency, as subversive as astronomy or geology. The instinct of Anytus and Meletus was not at fault: the Socratic morality meant the end of mythology, and with the mythology the gods must ultimately disappear also. From their point of view the conservatives were right in banishing Anaxagoras and in condemning Socrates. We find similar movements, with characteristic differences due to time and race, almost everywhere. Men arise to whom ritual is not only useless and based on scientific error, but positively repugnant; who cannot abide vain oblations, and who detest the priest; who demand right conduct rather than sacrifices, and purity of heart rather than corroborees or ceremonial cleanliness. Such men were the Jewish prophets, who were in perpetual hostilities with the priests of Bethel and Dan; and such are those today who dislike institutional and sacramental religion, and tend to regard true worship as a matter between the individual and the Deity. Some of these men have become solitaries or mystics: some, like Milton, absent themselves from public worship altogether; others, like Micah, openly announce that God cares nothing for ceremonies, and desires merely the doing of justice, the love of mercy, and a humble walk.

It would of course be a great mistake to imagine that these ideas had rigid and impassable boundaries, or that they did not often melt insensibly into one another. Many institutional religions have found it possible to make room for the solitary, the prophet, and the mystic: others have contrived a compromise with physical science; and no great religion of today divorces itself from morality. On the contrary, the claim of most is that true morality is inseparable from religion; many theologians indeed will assert that the truest morality is only to be found in *their* religion, that any goodness to be detected outside is either derived from that religion or a poor mimicry of it. Perhaps the most important revolution in history is this annexation of morality by a system which once had nothing to do with it. Nevertheless, we must bear in mind that the two things are historically two and not one; and it is as well to keep apart in thought what, in actual fact, we may find inextricably interwoven.

We shall be able to trace these elements, almost without exception, ritual, prophetism, priesthood, philosophy, mysticism, practicality, ethics, in each of the religions we are about to study. They will be present in differing degrees, and in very varying proportions, but they will be there. We shall often, also, trace a kind of circular movement in the process; sacerdotalism yielding to mysticism and reasserting itself after a total or partial eclipse; institutionalism giving way to personal religion, and then returning; morality asserting itself against ritual, and then retiring into the background. Jupiter may depose his father, but '*redeunt Saturnia regna*'; Paul may outshine Peter, but Peter recovers his prestige; a Reformation comes, but a counter-Reformation follows, to be succeeded in its turn by another counter-Reformation. The tide advances, and seems irresistible; but it declines, and the sands reappear, to be covered again when the appointed time arrives.

CHAPTER 2

JUDAISM

No religion is more interesting than the Hebrew, and scarcely any is better known to us. Through the labours of many scholars we are now able to follow its development almost from its beginnings, as the cult of a mere Bedouin tribe, down to the present time: and as a commentary on the general outline which I gave at the beginning it cannot easily be surpassed. We can also see, with tolerable clearness, how and why one section of it grew into Christianity, and how and why Christianity nevertheless found in Judaism its most relentless antagonist. Had it no other claim on our attention, its amazing vitality would be enough to attract the student of religion: and, had it died when Titus took Jerusalem, it would yet have demanded and gained the eager investigation of the historian. In it we see the contending forces of priestcraft and prophetism, of institutionalism and mysticism, at perhaps their keenest; and we see the most remarkable, and most nearly successful, attempt to establish a pure theocracy which the world has ever witnessed. We no longer believe that it was in the possession of a unique revelation: that Israel alone harboured the truth, while other nations lived under the dominion of a falsehood. Few nowadays would maintain that Judaism was a spiritual land of Goshen, enjoying perpetual light, while the rest of the world was groping in an eternal darkness that could be felt. But this only deepens the instruction which we can gain from Hebrew history, and from the analogies which can be drawn between Jewish experiences and those of other peoples. We find in the Scriptural records accounts of struggles between the kingship and the priesthood like those between Henry II and Becket; and of arguments between Amos and Amaziah like those between Christian and Formalist. There are times when the throne patches up for a moment its quarrel with the altar, and when we can almost overhear a Jeroboam saying, like James I, 'No bishop, no king.' Still more interesting – we can watch the long and doubtful conflict between the polytheism of the common people, aided as it was by the paganism of the conquered Canaanite, and the henotheism based on the Temple services: a conflict in which, as usual, the vanquished were far from being entirely overcome. Augustine, we know, did not drive out heathenism from England, nor did Boniface exterminate it in Germany: and the worship of the local deities went on in Palestine long after Yahweh had chosen one place to set his name there.

We can hardly begin our study before the time of Moses. We have, it is true, traditions of an earlier time; of tribal wanderings represented by the stories of Abraham, Isaac, and Jacob, of relations established with the kingdom of Gerar and with the princes of the Hittites. Sacred stones, altars, and wells, at which the Hebrews worshipped in later times, are associated in the tradition with these names. We have also, in Egyptian records, indications that Hebrew septs had settled in Palestine long before the invasion of Joshua: and there is no reason to doubt the firmly held belief of the Jews that they came originally from the banks of the Euphrates – that 'their fathers dwelt on the other side of the river in old time'. That they carried thence many Babylonish beliefs is a matter of likely inference, and is indeed not merely admitted, but emphasized, in later Jewish legends. A very close kinship was claimed with the Aramaeans of Damascus and its neighbourhood, and one hardly less close with Edom, Moab, and Ammon. All these might be called tribes of Israel, though they were never assimilated, and often fought as ferociously with the twelve acknowledged tribes as did the seven nations whom Israel ultimately conquered and endeavoured to exterminate.

A tradition preserved in the Book of Genesis records a sojourn of 'Abraham' in Egypt, and it is probable enough that the Pharaohs gladly permitted the immigration of a small but hardy tribe. A later immigration, on a much

larger scale – perhaps of three or four tribes – is symbolized
for us in the immortal story of Joseph. At first it was certainly welcomed by the Pharaohs; and the settlement lasted
a long time – the tradition says two hundred or four hundred
years. But later, 'a king arose who knew not Joseph'; and
the foreigners were sorely oppressed: the land of Goshen was
turned into the house of bondage. So far, it seems impossible
to identify this king: he may have been Ramses the Second,
about 1300 B.C., or, as is now generally believed, a Pharaoh
of two centuries earlier. Whoever he was, his tyranny led to
revolt, and the oppressed tribes were not without a leader,
who is known to all the world as Moses. Amid the mass of
myth and legend that has accumulated round that name, we
can clearly discern that Moses was one of the truly great
and dominant men of history, ranking with Mohammed,
with Charles Martel, and with the few others who have
made the world what it is. Under his guidance, the people –
like the Kalmuck Tartars in 1772 – determined to depart.
Like the Kalmucks, they were pursued, and, like them,
made good their escape. Pharaoh, or one of his generals,
followed them, and they were saved only by what the whole
nation ever afterwards regarded as a miracle. The fugitives
had reached the 'Sea of Reeds', Yam-Suph – probably a
lake close to the Mediterranean shore, which is known to be
subject to such accidents. A strong wind arose, and made
the lake passable: the Israelites went over 'dry-shod'. The
Egyptian army, following on their heels, were just in the
midst of the hollow when the waters returned, and Pharaoh's chariots and horsemen were drowned in Yam-Suph.
The marvellous deliverance was never forgotten: a song,
ascribed to Moses himself, describes it in detail; but there
is scarcely a writer or speaker in the whole of Hebrew history who does not refer to it. The Christian author of the
Epistle to the Hebrews, a millennium and a half later, finds
no better example of the power of faith than the story of
this miracle: 'By faith the children of Israel passed through
the Red Sea as on dry land; which the Egyptians assaying to
do were swallowed up.'

After this escape – one of the decisive episodes in world history – the tribes wandered about from oasis to oasis in the wilderness; the tradition says for the conventional period of forty years, or a whole generation. What religious rites they practised we cannot easily discover; the records are overlaid with accretions, and much that cannot have arisen till later times has been thrown back into the nomad life. Many accounts, as is well known, have been combined to make the Pentateuch as we know it, some dating from the ninth century, some from the eighth, and some from the fourth: and the tendency was always to gain prestige for a new regulation by ascribing it to the great original lawgiver. Just as trial by jury was supposed to be due to Alfred, so the complicated legislation of Exodus and Leviticus, much of which is applicable only to a settled agricultural community, was put into the mouth of Moses, the leader of a desert sept, changing its abode every few months. Nay, with a charming *naïveté*, a whole book, known to us as Deuteronomy or the Second Law, which cannot be earlier than the days of Manasseh, revises and modifies the old code, giving it a far more humane character, and yet deliberately casting it into the form of Mosaic discourses. It is as if the whole of Sir Robert Peel's transformation of our criminal system, his creation of the police force, and his suppression of the death penalty for a hundred offences, had been asserted to be the work of Queen Elizabeth, lost for three or four centuries and discovered in a muniment-chest by the Archbishop of Canterbury.

When we remove these additions, and reconcile these contradictions, we are led to perceive that the religion of Mosaic times differed but in detail from the religion common to the Bedouin tribes, and had a marked Semitic character. The Hebrews, like their kinsfolk, had their own tribal god, differing scarcely more than in name from the gods of Moab and Ammon; they had all the superstitions, the rituals, and the modes of worship which we find in the peoples around them: they worshipped stocks and stones, set up sacred pillars, adored magic wells, believed in dreams,

and raised the dead, in order, from the twitterings of the
ghosts, to learn the future. The wisest man could not have
foreseen that in this mass of credulity there lay hidden the
germ of moral enlightenment, or that this barbaric cult,
rather than the Assyrian, the Aramaean, or the Phoenician,
was to give birth to a religion which would sweep over the
whole Western world, and harbour reasonable hopes of universal dominion.

Nor was there in the character of the Hebrew deity anything that presaged such a metamorphosis. Yahweh, Yah,
or Yahu – the exact pronunciation of the name is uncertain
– was, as we have already said, much the sort of deity we
should expect an Arab tribe to adopt. All gods are, inevitably, the creation of men, and tribal gods are the creation
of the tribe. They express their peoples as clearly as a book
reveals its author, and can never rise above the mental and
moral capacity of their makers. What the Hebrews were at
any time, such was Yahweh: precisely as the German God
is a German and the British God a Briton.

We do not know when Israel first made his acquaintance.
The early traditions tell us unsuspiciously that Abram built
an altar to Yahweh, that Yahweh appeared unto him in
Egypt, and 'made room' for Isaac in Rehoboth; nay, that
he set a mark upon Cain, the second man, and – inconsistently enough – that in the third generation of mankind
'men *began* to call upon the name of Yahweh . . .' A later tradition, however, states positively that to Abraham, Isaac,
and Jacob the god was known as El Shaddai, and that by
'the name Yahweh he was not known to them'. It would
seem as if, in the view of some, he was first revealed to Moses
in the Arabian desert; and certain obscure allusions make it
possible that he was the god of a tribe of which Jethro or
Hobab, 'the priest of Midian', was the sheikh. We are told
that Jethro was the father-in-law of Moses, and that there
was close friendship between the 'children of the Kenite'
and Israel. It may well be, therefore, that the one tribe
adopted the god of the other, or at any rate gave his name
to their own chief divinity. Be this as it may, Israel always

recognized that Yahweh was a southerner. 'God came from Teman, and the Holy One from Mount Paran,' says Habakkuk; 'Yahweh, thou wentest forth out of Seir, thou marchedst out of the field of Edom,' says the song of Deborah; and that great ode, the sixty-eighth Psalm, borrowing the phrases of Deborah, merely substitutes Sinai for the mountains of Seir. We cannot, then, carry the history of the god, with any safety, much further back than the period of the wanderings. A strong and persistent tradition, magnificently rendered, tells of a portentous theophany, accompanied by thunder and lightning, on some southern mountain, called in one record Sinai, in another Horeb. Here Yahweh is said to have manifested his presence, if not for the first time, yet unmistakably and unforgettably, to his people, and to have delivered to them a code of 'Ten Words' written with his own hand on two tables of stone. Ever after he was the god of mountains, and, as the nation wandered northward, he annexed one by one the 'high hills' of Bashan, Ebal and Gerizim, Tabor, and finally Zion and Moriah. Inevitably also he was the Zeus or Thor of Israel, armed with the lightning-flash and the thunderbolt – the natural weapons of a mountain deity. 'The voice of Yahweh,' says the poet of the twenty-ninth Psalm, 'is powerful; it is full of majesty; the voice of Yahweh breaketh the cedars of Lebanon; he maketh them also to skip like a calf, Lebanon and Sirion like a young aurochs.' The Syrians were right, then, when they said that the Israelite god was a god of the hills, and when they preferred to fight him in the plains. Nothing showed his anger with Saul more clearly than his permitting him to fall down slain on Mount Gilboa. Rarely indeed did he give his people victory in the valleys: it was only with the help of Kishon and the stars in their courses that they triumphed over Sisera in the plain of Esdraelon. Israel drove out the inhabitants of the mountain, but could not drive out the inhabitants of the valley; the chariots of iron were too formidable for Yahweh.

His power, in fact, was strictly limited, exactly like that of Anath, Ram, or Gad, the 'abominations' of neighbouring tribes. He gave certain territories to Israel, because they were his own to give; but Jephthah, in arguing with the Ammonites,[1] does not deny that Chemosh has equal right to give other districts to *his* people. 'From thy face shall I be hid,' said Cain to him when banished from his native soil. Still more noteworthy are David's words to Saul: 'If it be Yahweh that hath stirred thee up against me, let him smell an offering; but if it be children of men, cursed be they before Yahweh; for they have driven me out this day that I should not share in the inheritance of Yahweh, saying, *Go, serve other gods.*' At the court of Achish, David would worship Dagon; in Moab, Chemosh, exactly as Ruth, when leaving Moab, says to Naomi, 'Thy people shall be my people, and thy god my god.' The only way in which Naaman could contrive to show his gratitude to Yahweh while avoiding offence to his Syrian deity was to carry with him to Damascus two mules' burden of Israelite earth, in order to worship the foreign god on foreign territory. But when he stepped off that Hebrew plot, he bowed down in the house of Rimmon. Elisha was quite content, and bade him go in peace.

Nor was Yahweh the god of the dead, but of the living. In Sheol, the land of darkness and shade, where even the light was as darkness, whither the gibbering ghosts of men fled after death, there was no remembrance of him, and none to give him thanks. Much later, when Job is seeking an escape from the arrows of Yahweh, he knows that death is a sure refuge: 'For now shall I lie down in the dust, and thou shalt seek me diligently, but I shall not be there.' Hezekiah, when doomed, as he thought, to death, said, 'I shall not see Yahweh, for Yahweh is in the land of the living; Sheol cannot praise thee, death cannot celebrate thee; they that go down into the pit cannot see thy truth.' It was not till a new revelation had been given that Joyan could cry to God out of the belly of Sheol and be heard.

If we may believe the prophet Amos, Yahweh demanded

---

1. Or rather, with the Moabites, for (by some confusion) all the arguments apply to Moab, and none to Ammon (Judges xi, 18 ff.).

no sacrifices in the forty years' wandering in the wilderness. He may have contented himself with sharing in the feasts, and 'smelling sweet savours'; but other authorities, as early as Amos, speak of him as accepting the burnt offerings of Noah and Abraham; and the received account of the wanderings allows him no lack of victims. In any case, after his arrival in the Promised Land, he makes up fully for any abstinence of the kind. There are many signs that even human sacrifices were not, on occasion, abhorrent to him. He showed no objection to the fulfilment of Jephthah's fatal vow: nor did he refuse the offering of seven of Saul's kinsmen to appease the Gibeonites and to turn away a famine from Israel. When Samuel hewed Agag in pieces before Yahweh in Gilgal, the deed was in the nature of a sacrificial act. At one time the god required all the first-born, both of man and of beast: and it was not till later that the human victims could be redeemed by the substitution of an animal. We may well believe that in the earliest story Abraham actually offered up Isaac; when the progress of morality had made the deed detestable, the ram caught in a thicket took the place of the lad, as, in later forms of Greek story, Iphigenia was snatched away from the altar at Aulis, and a stag, or an old woman, slain in her stead. The universal Semitic custom, familiar to us from the history of Carthage, Phoenicia, and Moab, found no exception in Israel. Micah, it is true, speaks of thousands of rams as common victims, but he also plainly hints that the first-born was given for transgression, and the fruit of a man's body for the sin of his soul.

But, of course, as a patriotic god, with all that concentrated patriotism which we find only in small countries surrounded by dangerous enemies, he preferred victims from hostile nations to those of his own chosen people. War was his chief province, and his special designation is 'Yahweh Sabaoth', Yahweh of the Armies. He 'goes forth with his hosts', and if he is favourably disposed to them they are victorious. 'Yahweh is a man of war,' says Moses: 'he teacheth my hands to war,' says David, 'so that mine arms do bend a bow of brass.' He breaks his enemies, and dashes them in pieces like a potter's vessel. He teaches his generals stratagems, by which they capture cities, or lures the embattled foe to destruction. But in return for all this he asks payment; often nothing less than every captured man, woman, child, and precious thing. When the King of Arad, the Canaanite, came and fought against Israel, and took some of them captive, Israel vowed a vow unto Yahweh, and said, 'If thou wilt deliver this people into my hand, I will put their cities to the *herem*' – that is, 'I will sacrifice them utterly, and without exception.' And Yahweh hearkened to the voice of Israel, and delivered the Canaanites into their hand, and they put the cities to the *herem*; and the name of the place was called Hormah, or 'Utter Destruction'. The same was the fate of Amalek, of Jericho, of Ai: and 'Joshua did to the king of Makkedah as he had done to the king of Jericho.' The blackened walls of these cities can still be seen, a lasting witness of the terrible savagery which a savage nation can ascribe to a god they fashion in their own likeness. This is exactly parallel to Shalmaneser's account of the battle of Karkar: 'With the might which Asshur the Lord has given me, and with the weapons which Nergal, going before me, has bestowed upon me, I fought with the enemy, and made an end of them. Fourteen thousand of their warriors I caused to be slain with the sword.' Or we may compare the inscription of Mesha of Moab – who had, it is true, many wrongs to avenge – 'And Chemosh said to me, Go up against the city and take it. And I fought against the city of Kiriathaim and took it, and I strangled every man that was therein as a sacrifice to Chemosh, god of Moab.' There is but little difference, save in name, between Yahweh and Asshur or Chemosh, or between the Chosen People, at this stage of their history, and those which were not chosen.

We think of God as pre-eminently unchanging: but to the Hebrews, who had as yet no idea of the uniformity of Nature, he was as capricious as Rehoboam; his ways were most emphatically past finding out. A god who could depose Saul for sparing one man out of his host of Amalekite prisoners, who could slay Uzzah for touching the Ark, who could blaze out into fury against his own chosen people for slight provocation or none, was certainly not easy to understand; and we hear that his worshippers, like Samuel and David, were angry with him at times – not without cause. His conduct when he allowed all Israel to be defeated by the small tribe of Benjamin, for no assignable reason whatever, was assuredly remarkable: and – though here the lot gave some sort of explanation – that thirty-six men should be killed at Ai because one man had stolen a goodly Babylonish garment from the *herem*, is not the conduct one would expect from a magnanimous deity. Perhaps most astonishing of all is his treatment of Balaam. First refusing to let him go to Balak, he then permits him, but his anger is kindled because he goes; he stands in a narrow path to kill the prophet, but, because the ass on which Balaam is riding turns aside three times, he spares the seer's life, and lets him go on his way. No wonder that Balaam thought he might still be circumvented by a few enchantments and a few changes of place.

We can, however, follow, more or less imperfectly, the steps by which he gradually developed into a deity worthy of respect and finally of true worship. To David, as we have seen, he was a god of whims and caprices. His image, or teraph, was a rude representation of a man, which might in fact be used to delude Saul's emissaries. His will might be discovered by the priest, who would consult, with proper incantations, another image known as the ephod. The god would, as a rule, if duly propitiated, assist David in his wars, and would be pleased when the captured Moabites were measured with the line – two lines to put to death, and one to keep alive. As a tree-god, he might make 'the sound of a going' in the top of the mulberry-trees, in sign that the king should go out in confidence to smite the Philistines. Like Odin in his Wild Hunt, he might rush through the woods, or ride upon a cherub and fly, yea, fly on the wings of the wind.

Perhaps a hundred years after David, we have a picture of Yahweh as painted by the school of Judaean writers known by the symbol J. These writers, in a series of stories of incomparable charm, present a portrait of Yahweh as a sort of super-David or Haroun-al-Raschid. He is a man all over, as human as Homer's Zeus, differing from man only in excess of strength. He makes Adam out of clay, and breathes into his nostrils the breath of life – he is a man, but with magic power. Like an Oriental sultan he walks in a garden in the cool of the evening having doubtless had his siesta in his upper chamber like Eglon of Moab. He allows Enoch and Noah to go about with him, and talks to Moses as a man speaks to his friend. He smells the sweet savour of Noah's burnt offerings and enjoys a meal of cakes, butter, and milk at Abraham's tent. He repeatedly appears in human form – which seems indeed to be conceived as his natural shape – and, as the so-called 'Messenger of Yahweh', visits the homes of men as Zeus and Hermes visited Philemon and Baucis: but he can disguise himself as a pillar of cloud by day or a pillar of fire by night, revealing himself, however, by his voice, for we are told that 'the pillar of cloud descended and talked with Moses'. He can be affable; but also dangerous: those who have seen him, like Manoah, expect to die, and even Moses is allowed only to see his back for a moment: his real glory is invisible, and his face must not be seen. Centuries later, when Isaiah beholds him enthroned in the Temple, he cries, 'Woe is me, for I am undone, mine eyes have seen the King, Yahweh of the Armies.' In earlier times, he must have been still more terrible.

Yet, with the inconsistency almost invariably to be found in mythologies, his terrors might be faced and overcome; as Diomede could overcome the mighty Ares, and as, in Norse story, Gunnarr Helming wrestled with Frey, put him to flight, and actually went about the country in the guise of the god. There are similar tales in Hebrew legend. Jacob, returning from Paddan-Aram, meets Yahweh, and wrestles with him till the breaking of the day; nor, though he suffers in the sinew of the hip, does he come off defeated.[1] An obscure passage in another place speaks of Levi as similarly contending with the god, whom he 'proved at Massah, and with whom he did strive at the waters of Meribah': obscure as the passage is, it seems clearly to imply that Levi had the victory.[2] A yet more mysterious tale, which has obviously been doctored by the editors, presents Yahweh in the character (so familiar in Christian legend) of the Divine Bridegroom. Like Asmodaeus, he is angry that Moses has stolen his marital privileges, and seeks to kill him, as Asmodaeus killed the successive husbands of Sarah. Zipporah his wife, however, by a symbolic act, makes Moses a 'blood-husband', and saves his life. Yet another truncated narrative, which, though it does not occur in J, seems to come from very early times, speaks of Jacob as being 'met', that is, 'attacked', by the angels of Yahweh, whom he recognizes as the hosts of the god: so far as we can see, he escapes without defeat. In a less material contest, Abraham, by a long argumentative petition, prevails upon Yahweh to promise to spare Sodom and Gomorrah if he can discover ten righteous men in them; but such 'repentance' or change of mind on the part of this deity, is too common to need illustration.

Though the Hebrews, unlike the Egyptians and the Greeks – unlike also their Assyrian and Babylonian kinsmen – were never distinguished for their skill in the pictorial or graving arts, and were later actually forbidden to practise them, there was, in the times with which we are now dealing, no prejudice against fashioning some rude representa-

1. I have no doubt that this is the Hebrew metamorphosis of a story of a contest between some other hero and a river-god, who, like rivers in all countries – the Hellespont, the Gyndes, the Achelous – objected to being crossed. A well-known Icelandic saga tells a similar story of a streamtroll fighting with Gretti till the breaking of the day. See Frazer, *Folk-lore in the Old Testament*.

2. Though this passage is late, it points back to some much earlier tradition, in which the incidents at Meribah and the origin of the name, Strife, were narrated differently from the way in which they now appear. Exodus xvii, 1–7.

tion of Yahweh, or of things in heaven above, in the earth beneath, or in the waters under the earth. Every village, every township, had its 'Baal' or local Yahweh, and worshipped the obelisks, teraphim, stones, and 'Asherim'[1] in which he was supposed to dwell: as the Virgin of Lourdes, La Salette, or Embrun is adored by those to whom she is at the same time one and many; or as a Greek hero might be worshipped in a score of places where his bones were supposed to lie. No distinction was drawn between the image and the god it symbolized. David carried an ephod with him in his wanderings and consulted it regularly in times of emergency: Rachel took teraphim (which Laban unhesitatingly calls his 'gods') with her on her flight from Aram; and Michal, as we have seen, found them ready in the house when she wished to deceive her father's emissaries. In one of the very oldest narratives we hear of a man named Micah, who makes a molten image of Yahweh, an ephod, and teraphim, and consecrates the grandson of Moses as the priest. A remarkable conflation of two stories here reveals a later change: for one form of the tale tells us that Micah made a *graven* image (*pesel*): this is doubtless due to the emergence of the code which forbade *molten* images (*massekahs*): a still later code forbade graven images as well. This cult was shortly transferred to the northern sanctuary of Dan, where a molten calf of gold was long worshipped, in blissful ignorance that Moses, the grandfather of the first priest, would later be credited with terrific denunciations of this very form of worship. In Dan, and in the more famous sanctuary of Bethel, Yahweh was adored as a golden calf for centuries, perhaps as a reminiscence of the Egyptian worship of Apis. That this had been a legitimate ritual was so completely contrary to subsequent belief that the whole history was modified: Jeroboam, who set up the calves, was spoken of as the man 'who made Israel to sin'; and an episode was introduced into the narrative of the desert-wanderings

1. Wooden pillars, or trees roughly shaped to human form: strangely translated 'groves' in our old version. We may compare the stone Hermae of Athens.

showing how the calf-worship had been practised by Aaron,
and sternly suppressed by Moses himself.

The character of Yahweh during these centuries shows
little change and less improvement. The 'jealousy' or exclusiveness which afterwards so clearly distinguishes him is
still absent: though he is the national god, he does not appear to have resented the presence of other gods: Solomon
set up shrines to Moabite and Ammonite divinities on the
Mount of Olives near Jerusalem; and there is no sign that it
was as yet known as the 'opprobrious hill'. As the Canaanites were gradually absorbed, they inevitably brought with
them their own 'abominations'; inter-marriages took place,
and the Baal of Tyre, Ram, Anath, Ashtoreth, Saccuth,
Chiun, came in as the dowry of the wives. But more important than these – lower in rank yet nearer to the daily life
of the people – were the Daemons of home and field, the
spirits of the dead, the powers informing the animals. These,
indeed, did not vanish for centuries – if they have yet vanished. So far as they have disappeared at all – in our own
country as in Israel – they have faded not before religion,
but before science. The Talmud, fifteen centuries after J, is
full of daemons. 'There is not,' says one writer, 'the space
of a quarter of a *kab* in the universe in which there are not
nine *kabs* of daemons'; and Rabbi Johanan says there are
three hundred species of male daemons in the small Galilean
town of Sichmin; as for the females, their number is beyond
his arithmetic. They dwell thus everywhere, but they prefer
ruined buildings, cesspools, and dormitories. By means of
spells and incantations their footprints can be traced; they
may be put to flight, as Samson destroyed the Philistines,
with the jawbone of an ass, or by beating the ripples on a
pool with spades and shovels. The story of Tobit is mainly of
Gentile origin; but, as we have seen already, Asmodaeus the
demon-bridegroom, who could be expelled only by a 'fishy
fume', would have been recognized by the Hebrew as but
one more of the phantasms familiar to his own experience.

If this continued to be the belief so late, we may be sure
that it prevailed in, if possible, exaggerated form long before

Tobit or the Talmudic sages: and our authorities, despite all expurgations, have left us ample proof that this was so. The Old Testament provides us with daemons in good measure, pressed down and running over, and the story of the Gadarene swine would have seemed a poor and single business to the Hebrew of the early kingship.

Their name is Legion, for they are many; and it must content us to pick out from the vast multitude a mere handful as typical of the rest. There is Lilith, whom later legend regarded as Adam's first wife, and as particularly malignant to the daughters of her successor in childbirth, or to the man who sleeps alone in a house. To Isaiah she was the haunter of ruined cities: she, along with the owl and the pelican, would lurk in the waste places of Edom, and scare away the traveller. If we can trust a plausible emendation of a passage in the Book of Job,[1] she would dwell in the tent of the wicked, and add to the terrors which chased him at the heels. Along with her went the Sha'ir, a goat-monster who, like the horned devil of our own ancestors, or the satyr of the Greeks, dwelt also in lonely places, shrieking to his neighbour, and filling the air with horror. To the same class, apparently, belonged Azazel, the daemon of the desert, to whom, on the Day of Atonement, the sins of the congregation were handed over. Two goats were chosen, and, by the decision of the lot, one was selected for Yahweh, the other for Azazel. The chosen of Yahweh was duly sacrificed; the other, the 'scapegoat', loaded with the transgressions of the people, was ceremonially led to the edge of the wilderness, and let loose to carry the impurity to its rightful owner.[2]

There is the 'Aluqah, not improbably a vampire-daemon, a bloodsucker to whom the Book of Proverbs assigns two insatiable daughters, perhaps twins, for their names are 'Give' and 'Give'. There is the night-terror, the daemon

---

1. Job xviii, 15: 'There shall dwell in his tent that which is none of his': for 'none of his' (*lilo*) read Lilith.

2. In similar fashion Zechariah (v, 9) beheld the woman, typifying the wickedness of Judah, carried away in an ephah from Jerusalem and settled safely in the land of Shinar.

that hurls his dart in the day, the pestilence-daemon that walketh in darkness, and the *Qoteb* that deals sunstroke at mid-day. There are the fire-daemons[1] to whom Eliphaz is probably alluding when he says that man is born unto trouble, as the 'sons of Resheph' tend to fly upward. To these, according to the Psalmist, Yahweh gave up the flocks of his people when they provoked him to anger; and Habakkuk tells us that, when Yahweh came forth to war, before him went Pestilence, and Resheph at his heels; while his hand, like that of Zeus, grasped the lightning.

Not all these spirits were malignant. Some were as kindly as Raphael was to Tobit; and those that dwelt in plants and animals might be helpful. A rod, like Aaron's, could dispel a plague, and a stick, like Elisha's, might restore life and health. By a common form of imitative magic, the venom of serpents might be nullified by making a serpent of brass, at which men might gaze and be healed. An undrinkable Marah could be made sweet if a benevolent tree were cast into the waters, and Elisha removed death from a pot by throwing in meal. The love-apples which Reuben found in the field had the power to restore Jacob's affection for Leah, as well as to remove from Rachel the curse of barrenness. Other things like the fruit of the tree of knowledge, had higher virtues, and could make one wise. Honey, as we learn from the story of Jonathan, had the same effect as the commandments of Yahweh: it 'enlightened the eyes': though the author of the nineteenth Psalm is careful to tell us that the commandments are the sweeter. 'My son,' says the sage in the Book of Proverbs, 'eat thou honey, for it is good, and the honeycomb which is sweet to thy taste; so shalt thou know wisdom to be unto thy soul: if thou hast found it, somewhat will surely follow.' It was a shrewd idea of Samson's to eat the honey from the body of the lion: had he done likewise before meeting Delilah, he might have escaped her snare.[2]

1. Reshaphim. In Psalm lxxvi, 3 we learn that arrows might be informed with Resheph, but that Yahweh could break their power.

2. The reader will recall the tale that a swarm of bees rested on the lips of the boy Pindar when he was asleep, and thus gave him the gift of

With invisible forces all around, with the ghosts of the
dead ready to take vengeance, and the daemons of the air
hovering on every breeze, it was obviously desirable to
know the means of discovering their purposes, and of averting the harm they might do. Such means were to be found
in plenty. The third chapter of Isaiah, in the midst of a
Quaker-like denunciation of over-adornment in apparel –
of mufflers, pendants, sashes, and shawls – reveals that the
daughters of Jerusalem went about with amulets and soul-
boxes, in which the souls of their lovers or of their enemies
were kept in security: and Ezekiel is equally severe on the
women who sew fillets upon their elbows, and make ker-
chiefs to capture souls. In a very remarkable passage Abigail
tells David that his soul will be bound up in 'the bundle of
life' with Yahweh, while the souls of his enemies he will hurl
out as from a sling: his soul, in fact, is to be hidden in a stick
or twig, and carefully stored away under Yahweh's protection. If, however, all these mascots and charms proved in-
effective, there were experts to give advice, and a store of
occult knowledge on which the anxious person might draw
to any extent. In that village was a wise woman; in the
other a soothsayer: there a hydromancer, here a man with
second sight.[1] Saul has not wandered very long in search of
his father's lost asses when his servant tells him there is a
Roeh or seer who can infallibly tell him all about them.

---

poetry (which is much the same as the gift of prophecy). Pindar himself
calls the prophetess of Delphi a bee; and in another place he tells us that
the serpents fed the prophet Iamus with the 'drug of bees' – that is with
inspiring honey. So, in the Homeric Hymn to Hermes, the Fates derive
the power of prophecy from honey:

> They, having eaten the fresh honey, grow
> Drunk with divine enthusiasm, and utter
> With earnest willingness the truth they know:
> But if deprived of that sweet food, they mutter
> All plausible delusions.

(Shelley's translation, line 748; original, line 556.)

1. The innumerable enactments against witchcraft ('Thou shalt not
suffer a witch to live') prove, by their very frequency, that they totally
failed to effect their purpose.

Joseph used a special wine-cup, not merely for drinking, but for divining – the word here used being derived from that for a serpent: he had the wisdom of that subtle animal.[1] This startles us when we read in the eulogy of the Chosen People put in the mouth of Balaam: 'Surely there is no enchantment with Jacob, neither is there divination with Israel.' More common, apparently, than the hydromancer was the dealer in Qasam, who seems to have been an augur, or reader of omens and caster of lots. Where this man failed, there was the Wise or Knowing Man, the *yidde'oni* – a word rendered 'wizard' in our versions – a sorcerer who knew the ways of familiar spirits, and was an adept in black magic. Like him, though not called by the same name, was the 'wise woman' (*hachamah*). One of these dwelt at Tekoa, and persuaded David to bring back Absalom from exile: another lived in Abel-beth-maacah, a city to which men resorted for counsel, and, when they had obtained it, regarded the matter as settled. The power of this woman was such that when she declared her will, the guards of Sheba the son of Bichri refused to defend him, and killed him without hesitation. There must have been many such women in Abel to account for its great reputation.

Still more terrible was the 'Mistress of Ob', the woman who could raise the dead. Saul, we are told in a doubtful parenthesis, had put away the *yidde'onis* and the oboth out of the land. If in truth he had tried to do so, he had failed; for when he himself had need of them, his servants had no difficulty in finding a Mistress of Ob not far off at Endor: and, as we learn from a narrative of matchless impressiveness, she did her work. 'Divine for me [*qasomi*] by Ob,' said Saul, 'and bring up him of whom I tell thee'; and she raised from Sheol the godlike shade of Samuel, who declared to the king, all too accurately, his coming doom: 'Tomorrow shalt thou and thy sons be with me.' The voice of Samuel,

---

1. Later interpreters took the passage (Genesis xliv, 15) to mean, 'Know ye not that such a man as I could certainly find it all out?' – as we today use 'divine' simply for 'detect'. This interpretation shows that men were shocked to think that Joseph was a mere magician.

like that of the ghosts seen by Odysseus on the shores of
Ocean, though distinct, was a bat-like twittering: Isaiah, in
foretelling the fate of 'Ariel', can find no more forceful figure
than that her speech shall be low out of the dust, and her
voice as of Ob out of the ground.

Sometimes men dispensed with the services of these
'mistresses', and consulted the shades for themselves; they
lay all night in the tombs, and took, as infallible oracles, the
words they heard in the nightmares that followed. This
lasted long. Among the sinners denounced by the great
prophet of the Exile [1] – among those who prepare a table for
Gad, the ancient god of Luck, and fill up mingled wine for
Meni, the god of Destiny, who sacrifice in gardens and burn
incense on bricks – we find those who sit upon graves and
lie all night in the vaults of the dead.

But more powerful than all these, and more trusted as
having direct access to Yahweh himself, were the Nebiim or
prophets; a strange class of men who exercised a vast influence on the fortunes of the nation. These enthusiasts resembled the dervishes familiar today in the East, and would
not arouse surprise in any who know the force of religious
excitement in uncivilized countries. They had the habit of
casting themselves into trances, in which they ascertained
the will of Yahweh and foretold the future. A rational man
would look on them with interest mingled with disgust: and
there are signs that some of the more enlightened Israelites
had the same feelings – along with a not unnatural fear.
The infection of their frenzy was very strong; it occasionally
seized on an unwary spectator and stretched him on the
ground 'prophesying' – that is, foaming at the mouth, wal-
lowing hither and thither for hours, and uttering strange
sentences of gibberish which a skilful interpreter might
translate as '*Neum Yahweh*', the oracle of God. Their actions
at other times were less wild, but equally characteristic: they
would wander in symbolic nakedness through the streets, or
wear horns of iron as a proof that the Syrians would be
pushed back as by an ox till they were consumed. Rightly

1. Isaiah lxv.

were these prophets called Nebiim, or the Foamers; and in their calmest moments they were extraordinary enough never to be mistaken for anything but what they were. Their single garment might be a leathern girdle, and their meat, when they condescended to take any, might be locusts, and the wild honey which gave them not only bodily sustenance but supernatural wisdom. During the whole period between the Exodus and the destruction of the kingdoms they exerted a power, both for good and for evil, that cannot be easily exaggerated. They destroyed the dynasty of Omri, shrinking from no crime in pursuance of their end; and, by their excess of political folly, they contributed not a little to the ruin of the dynasty of David and the destruction of Jerusalem. For there was no means of discovering whether they spoke truth or falsehood save the event. Micaiah and Zedekiah both opened their prophecies with 'Thus saith Yahweh', and both, there is no reason to doubt, believed themselves inspired by him: Ahab obeyed the wrong one, and went to his doom at Ramoth-gilead. The same was the case two centuries later: Jeremiah ingeminated peace with Nebuchadnezzar, Hananiah confidence in Egypt. The miserable king, tossed hither and thither between prophets with apparently equal credentials, knew not what to do, and finally, after the manner of weaklings, made the irrevocable and fatal choice.

With the growth of morality and knowledge, the prophetic power declined. We find Amos, for example, even before the fall of Samaria, rigidly refusing the title of Nabi; and a writer whose verses are bound up with the visions of Zechariah, but whose floreat is probably before the Exile, speaks of the order with undisguised contempt. It was not for many hundred years that it revived: its place was taken during a long period by a series of authors who set forth their ideas in symbolic visions called apocalypses.

Over against the prophets, and to a great degree opposed to them, were the priests, who, during the regal period, were gradually establishing themselves as a distinct and exclusive caste. In the early days every chief of a clan, every head-man of a village, was a priest, performing the sacrifices to the local Lord or Baal, and acting as the human representative of the community in its relations to its divine ruler. At the various feasts – the ingathering of the grapes, the harvest, the atonements, he, or a man chosen by him, did the honours. When Micah had fashioned his *pesel* and his *ephod* he 'filled the hand' of one of his sons, who became his priest – a proceeding which to the later historian seems astonishing, and to be accounted for only by the fact that, as there was then no king in Israel, 'every man did that which was right in his own eyes'. Even Micah, however, if we may believe another version of the story, was glad to welcome a Levite, a descendant of Moses, into the office; and, when Jonathan appeared, accepted him with joy, saying, 'Now know I that Yahweh will be good to me, seeing that I have a Levite to my priest.' With the growth of the conception that the local Baals were but inferior manifestations of Yahweh, and with the establishment of great altars at Shiloh, Dan, Bethel, and Jerusalem, we note the intensification of the feeling that the priests are a class apart; and among the twelve tribes one, which had failed to secure a local habitation, assumed the name of priestly *par excellence*. This was the tribe of Levi, which, along with that of Simeon, had been practically annihilated in a feud with a Canaanite city: it had been 'divided in Jacob, and scattered in Israel'. By slow degrees this clan succeeded in monopolizing the great services: and one family, that of Aaron, claimed the sole right to the high priesthood. Of Aaron, whom tradition called the brother of Moses, we hear very little in the earliest narratives; his glory was the natural result of the triumph of a particular household. The family of Eli, which held the priesthood in Shiloh till it was destroyed, and took charge of the sacred chest under David, was finally deposed by Solomon, and that of Zadok substituted. That the Aaronites did not gain their position without a contest is indicated by a story told in the Book of Numbers, where we hear that another Levite clan, the sons of Korah, made a determined effort to break the monopoly, and were ruthlessly suppressed. But the kings for a long time retained the priestly power, which, indeed, seems to have been from ancient times regarded as an essential part of kingship. Saul sacrificed, and Solomon not only dedicated the Temple, but offered the burnt offering, the meal offering, and the fat of the peace offerings: while Jeroboam, after setting up the golden calf at Bethel, himself stood by the altar to burn incense – the very sin for which, according to the author of the Book of Chronicles, King Uzziah was thrust out of the Temple by Azariah the priest, and smitten with leprosy by Yahweh. 'It pertaineth not to thee, Uzziah, to burn incense before Yahweh, but to the priests the sons of Aaron, that are consecrated to burn incense.' This was a doctrine which would have seemed strange to the real Uzziah, who would probably have made short work of a priest who propounded it. The Chronicler's story shows how complete the victory of the priestly caste had become by the time of the Exile.

The religion everywhere was a religion of sacrifices. Yahweh, as the tutelary god of the nation, and as in a sense the nation itself, demanded and received a share of all its possessions: the first-born of men and cattle, and above all the savour of blood.[1] The people must not offer to him that which costs them nothing; for the protection which he offers them from disease, the scab, pestilence, famine, the locust, or the enemy, is worth paying for. Thus, right down to the destruction of Jerusalem in the first century after Christ, the altar drips with the blood of the victims.

During the latter part of the period represented by the authors called comprehensively J, a formidable and decisive movement, led by the prophetic order, arises for the accomplishment of one main purpose – the assertion of the principle that the land is *exclusively* Yahweh's, and that he will tolerate no foreign rival. Under Solomon, who had endeav-

1. To the blood, which was the life, Yahweh laid an exclusive claim: it was his alone, as much as the breath which he had breathed into the nostrils of animals to make them 'living souls'. When Cain killed Abel, the voice of the blood – still living – cried unto Yahweh from the ground. No wonder then that the covenant between Yahweh and his people was sealed with the sprinkling of blood.

oured to strengthen himself by foreign alliances, and make
himself, like the Hapsburgs, 'happy' by marriages, 'other
gods' had been seen and worshipped close by Jerusalem;
the absorption of the Canaanites had – to judge by the frequent denunciation of the prophets – introduced many
others; and under the house of Omri, which had, after
Solomon's fashion, allied itself with Tyre and Sidon, the
Phoenician Baal (to be distinguished from the local Baals
which were but Yahweh in another form) had entered
Samaria and dangerously threatened the sovereignty of the
native deity. No fewer than four hundred 'prophets' are
said to have ministered to him in Samaria alone: and he
advanced so rapidly that – probably in too 'heightened and
telling' a style – those who had not bent the knee to him
were counted as but seven thousand. There is no reason to
think that Ahab and his sons themselves deserted Yahweh,
but they *tolerated* the alien cult, and Jezebel, the Tyrian
Queen, was so forceful a character that the Yahwites feared
the total extirpation of their religion. This was anathema to
the sons of the prophets. Under Elijah the Tishbite, the very
type and image of the prophetic order, a terrible massacre
of the priests of Baal was consummated on Mount Carmel:
and after Elijah's disappearance a revolt against the dynasty
was engineered by his successor Elisha. With a frightful ferocity the house of Ahab was wiped out by one of the generals
of the king, Jehu the son of Nimshi, who 'rode furiously' to
the slaughter, and slew not only every member of the royal
house, but every devotee of Baal on whom he could lay
hands. Yahweh proved himself indeed a 'jealous god'.

Lest we censure the reformers too hastily, however, we
must remember that in one respect they represented a moral
advance. The rites of Baal were savage, cruel, and filthy;
they were closely bound up with religious prostitution and
with the deification of the reproductive powers. *Kedeshim*
and *kedeshoth*, chartered libertines of the altars, thronged
the temples of Baal, and human sacrifices were not unknown. Though the worship of Yahweh himself had at one
time involved these rites, the slow growth of ethical feeling

was banishing them; and in driving out Baal Elijah and Elisha were thus on the side of moral progress. A man of keen foresight, accordingly, when challenged to 'choose this day whom he would serve', might hesitate when he thought what a hideous murder was to follow, but would yet choose Yahweh as the god of the future. A patriot, again, would assuredly have felt that he did well to drive Baal over the border into his native land, and thus to assert that Yahweh was the sole god of Israel. Only through monolatry was it possible for monotheism to arise.

We do indeed perceive just at this time the infant stirrings of a genuine ethical feeling in the religion of Israel; the first attempts, even in the midst of Elisha's treasons and Jehu's murders, to transform the jealous and fierce deity of the country into a god of mercy. A new race of prophets arose, represented to us mainly by the two great names of Amos and Hosea, but probably strong and widespread. To these the savage intolerance of Elisha and his school was wholly repugnant. They utterly rejected the foreign Baal, but they detested the means by which he had been expelled; and they went further: they denounced the sacrifices of the priests, declared that Bethel and Dan were no better than any other place, and proclaimed that without justice and charity sacrifice and offering were futile. 'Woe unto them that sell the righteous for silver and the needy for a pair of shoes.' 'Come ye not to Gilgal, nor go up to Beth-aven' (Hosea's name, House of Evil, for Beth-el, House of God), 'nor swear, As Yahweh liveth.' No victims, no incense, will avail, in the absence of a pure heart and clean hands. Along with this went the totally new conception – slow indeed in translating itself into actuality – that Yahweh's dominion was not confined to Israel, nor even to the habitable earth. His wrath would pursue the unjust and cruel man even to the stars; if he fled into the sea, it would command the great dragon and he would devour him; if he went down into Sheol itself, it would find him out there. And, on the other hand, as Yahweh was the God of all the earth, Israel must not expect his special favour, unless earning it by special obedience. Yahweh had brought him out of Egypt – but equally he had brought the Philistines out of Caphtor and the Aramaeans out of Kir. 'Are ye any more to me, O children of Israel, than the children of the Ethiopians?' – a lesson which the children of Israel were not to learn for centuries yet.

It is not unnatural that all this, so new, should appear as a return to the old, a reformation rather than an innovation; this is the mark of reformers generally, and not of Hebrews only. We are not then surprised to find that about this time the history of Israel is rewritten, and that a new emphasis is laid upon certain episodes, while the picture of Yahweh now drawn showed a great advance upon that hitherto given. This history, which in some degree reflects the spirit of Amos and Hosea, is known by the symbol E: it is Ephraimite in origin, and for the most part uses the name Elohim instead of Yahweh. The writer has not the full narrative-power of J: but he is theologically ahead of him. The anthropomorphism is less crude, and the spirituality of God is more clearly brought out. By one of the happiest chances in the history of the world, the work was not destroyed when, in 722, Samaria was sacked by the Assyrians. It escaped like Lot from the midst of the overthrow, and found a refuge in the Southern Kingdom, where, later, it was incorporated with J, to form a document known as J E. We can still, however, in many cases disentangle it from its surroundings: and the reader who takes the pains to do so will be richly rewarded. Merely by running through the fragments of E embedded in Genesis he will obtain a good idea of its character. There still, of course, remains a good deal to which modern feeling might take exception. The 'covenant' between Israel and Yahweh, for example, is represented as too much in the nature of a business-bargain. 'If,' says Jacob, 'God will be with me and will keep me in this way that I go, and will give me bread to eat and raiment to put on, then shall Yahweh be my God.'[1] But there is

1. This idea, of course, leads to the converse: 'If Yahweh does *not* give us bread and raiment, he shall *not* be our God': and it was inevitable that

much of a loftier tone, and much that seems to mark a *deliberate* attempt to raise the morals of the people. The exquisite chapter (xxii), for example, describing the so-called sacrifice of Isaac, though falling short of the full spirit of Amos and Hosea, yet marks, as we have seen, a notable advance on earlier thought. The older narrative, we can hardly doubt, represented the slaughter as actually consummated, and as proleptically justifying human sacrifices in certain instances; but to E the story was shocking. The first-born must no longer, in any circumstances, be considered an acceptable gift to Yahweh; and in their stead the lower animals must invariably be chosen. This does not attain to the full stature of Micah, who rejected all sacrifices, and would have nothing of thousands of rams or rivers of oil; but it answers his indignant question, 'Shall I give my first-born for my transgression, the fruit of my body for the sin of my soul?' Such sacrifices should be left for Mesha to pay to Chemosh; they were, henceforward, an abomination to Yahweh.

Equally noteworthy, on another side, is E's substitution of the 'Ten Words' of the twentieth chapter of Exodus for the older code now found in the thirty-fourth. Retaining the regulation as to the Sabbath, the new school cut out the merely ritual commands, and put in their places a moral law which is still thought worthy of being recited in our churches every seventh day, and is in fact the foundation of modern ethical systems. Doubtless this code was at first very concise; it has certainly been enlarged more than once; but in its shortest form it marks a long step in human progress.

The same Micah, of whom we have just spoken, and his illustrious contemporary Isaiah, carried the work of the northern prophetic order still further, and gave it an immortal and incomparable expression. With unsurpassed

---

those who held this idea should argue as John the son of Kareah and his friends did to Jeremiah (Jeremiah xliv, 17): 'when we worshipped the Queen of Heaven we had plenty of victuals; when we worshipped Yahweh we had none: therefore we will go back to the Queen of Heaven.'

poetic genius, Isaiah, in particular, laid down the great moral principles on which religion, if it is to be worth anything in the long run, must rest: and his words remain as necessary and as forceful today as two millenniums and a half ago. To them Jesus returned, and it is out of them that Christianity sprang. 'To what purpose is the multitude of your oblations unto me? saith Yahweh. I am full of the burnt offerings of rams, and the fat of fed beasts. Bring no more vain oblations; incense is an abomination unto me: new moon and sabbath, the calling of assemblies, I cannot away with. Wash you, make you clean; put away the evil of your doings from before mine eyes; cease to do evil, learn to do well; seek judgement, relieve the oppressed, judge the fatherless, plead for the widow.' Nothing higher than this was to be heard for hundreds of years; but the swing of the pendulum, which is as regular in religion as in politics, was to take place, and a reaction – fortunately not complete – was speedily to be seen.

The worship of the local Baals, that which the prophets speak of as adoration on every high hill and under every green tree, still went on, although the destruction, first of Shiloh and then of Dan and Bethel, had inevitably increased the prestige of the great sanctuary at Jerusalem. Isaiah himself speaks without repugnance of the asherim and the massekahs. It was, however, naturally to the interest of the priests of the capital that the 'high places', the Bamoth, should be removed, and the services concentrated in one spot over which they had control. We hear that for centuries the kings refused to destroy the Bamoth, and the priestly historians, even when admitting the piety of such kings as Asa and Jehoshaphat, add the posthumous censure, 'Howbeit the high places were not taken away' – a censure which no one in the times of those kings would have understood. But, a hundred years after Isaiah, the work of removal was vigorously taken in hand – at the cost of how much silent rebellion we are able only to guess. There had been, during the long reign of Manasseh, a return to the old rites, a renewal of human sacrifices, and even the admission of foreign gods. Under Manasseh's grandson all this was swept away, and at the same time a determined effort was made to abolish every form of sacrifice except that of the chief Temple. The 'discovery' of a book ascribed to Moses himself, in which all other worship was forbidden, aided the movement – this book, which was unquestionably the gist of what we call Deuteronomy, maintained that from the very first, Moses had foreseen how, after the conquest of Canaan, Yahweh would choose 'one place to set his name there', and would reject worship paid to him in any other. Not a single Israelite of earlier times, not David or Solomon, and still less Jeroboam or Jehu, with all their devotion to Yahweh, would have understood this prohibition: but the young Josiah obeyed it in an access of religious enthusiasm, and made a clean sweep of all the Bamoth within the reach of his armies. In particular, he destroyed what was left of the ruined altar of Bethel which Jeroboam had set up, burned the Bamah and the Asherah, and reduced the whole to powder. The 'Chemarim' – the priests of the Bamoth whom earlier kings had ordained to burn incense in these places – he ruthlessly put down; and indeed carried out a reformation as thorough and as merciless as that of Thomas Cromwell when he abolished the monasteries. It was Elijah and Elisha over again.

That it was premature is obvious enough. Before the work could be finished, Josiah was killed in battle with Pharaoh Necho at Megiddo – a terrible blow to the Jerusalem party. Not only was his personality lost to the cause, but his death at thirty-nine appeared to shatter the whole Deuteronomic theory, which had boldly proclaimed that worldly prosperity and length of days were the certain reward of obedience to Yahweh. 'If thou shalt hearken diligently to his voice,' the Deuteronomic 'Moses' had declared, 'Yahweh thy god will set thee high above all the nations of the earth: and shall cause thine enemies that rise up against thee to be smitten before thee: they shalt come against thee one way and shall flee before thee seven ways.' Unfortunately, it was the army of Josiah that had fled the seven ways; and the shock to belief was tremendous. The followers of Josiah mourned – with a mourning that became a proverb of grief; Jeremiah wrote the dirge; but the king's successors, and a very large proportion of the nation, fell back instantly into the old ways, worshipping the Baals on every high hill and under every green tree, reintroducing the cult of sun and moon, and offering sacrifices to the 'Queen of Heaven'. The fatal doctrine that we must judge by the result was found to cut both ways. The argument with which the remnant of Judah met the indignant remonstrances of Jeremiah must have been hard to meet: 'Since we left off to burn incense to the Queen of Heaven, and to pour out drink-offerings unto her, we have wanted all things, and have been consumed by the sword and by the famine.'

Nevertheless, the theory persisted, and fate came to its aid. Despite all the incense and the drink-offerings, the Queen of Heaven failed her worshippers. The party of the Baals made the ruinous error of relying on the broken reed of Egypt, and fell before the energy and rapidity of Nebuchadnezzar. 'Pharaoh king of Egypt was but a noise,[1] he let the appointed time pass by.' After the decisive battle of Carchemish it ought to have been plain that Egypt would give no effective help, but a large proportion of the nation still, in besotted folly, trusted in the 'noise' and had the assistance of an army of prophets foretelling success. The king, a well-meaning but weak youth, tossed to and fro between opposing factions, was a paper-boat upon the waves. Now he hearkened to one side, now to the other: at one moment he permitted Jeremiah to be flung into a dungeon, and at another he visited him in prison and sought for the advice which he did not dare to take. Finally, in an evil hour, he declared for Egypt, and broke his oath of allegiance to Nebuchadnezzar. The result was the capture of Jerusalem, and the deportation to Babylon of all the chief families of the people. Deuteronomy had vindicated itself:

1. There seems to be an obscure pun in this phrase: some translate it 'Pharaoh's name is Crash or Downfall' (Jeremiah xlvi, 17).

'And the generation to come, and the foreigner that shall come from a far land shall say, when they see the plagues of Judah, and the sicknesses wherewith Yahweh hath made it sick, wherefore hath Yahweh done this unto this land? What meaneth the heat of his great anger? Then men shall say, Because they forsook the covenant of Yahweh, the god of their fathers, which he made with them when he brought them out of the land of Egypt, and went and served other gods, and worshipped them, gods whom they knew not, and whom he had not given unto them; therefore the anger of Yahweh was kindled against this land; and Yahweh rooted them out of their land in anger, and in wrath, and in great indignation, and cast them into another land.'

The captivity, which lasted half a century – which indeed, for the vast majority, was a permanent exile – was bound to have an enormous effect both upon the character of the people and upon their religion. One band settled in Egypt, and established there a temple and a worship similar to that of Jerusalem. Other bands were planted in Babylonia, and thence scattered all over the nearer East. In Babylon they came into contact with a nation more civilized than themselves; one which had, in particular, through its pursuit of astrology, penetrated deeply into mathematical knowledge and into the science of the stars. By intercourse with these people the exiles inevitably gained a vast enlargement of mind, and lost much of the insularity which had previously characterized the nation. Many thousands must have conformed to their surroundings, and must have been absorbed by the populations among which they found themselves. Even those who held fast by their religion and nationality show signs of having felt the foreign influence. Even Ezekiel, a priest, and one of the earliest of the exiles, fashions the remarkable imagery in which he clothes his visions on the model of the sculptures and other wonders which he saw all around him by the canal of Chebar; and even those who sat down and wept by the rivers of Babylon, remembering Zion, could not altogether help breathing the atmosphere around them.

When, in 538, Cyrus became master of Babylon, the Jews found themselves in contact with a nation more sympathetic than their former conquerors. One of the first acts of Cyrus was to allow the return to Judaea of such as so desired; and some thousands availed themselves of the permission. Under a prince of the royal house, Zerubbabel, accompanied by Joshua the High Priest, the exiles came back, and after some delay rebuilt the Temple and re-established the services. Many, of course, remained behind: some indeed, as we learn from the story of Nehemiah, had high positions under the new empire. Others were too widely scattered, and too firmly settled in their new homes, to be able or willing to make the venture: there were among them 'Parthians, Medes, Elamites, and dwellers in Cappadocia, in Pontus, in Phrygia and Pamphylia, in Egypt and the parts of Libya about Cyrene, Cretans and Arabians'. There seems to have been so far little prejudice against them; and they mingled freely with their neighbours. In the dominant Persian religion there was much to attract them, and they borrowed much from it. There is every reason to think that it was from Persian theology they took the conception of Satan, the great Adversary of Yahweh. They had already the name. In the Book of Job,[1] the Satan is one of Yahweh's servants: he goes up and down in the earth, and wanders to and fro in it, to see if God's commands are obeyed, and if his worshippers are genuine; and he appears regularly before him with the other 'sons of God' to make his report. So late as the reign of Darius, the prophet Zechariah sees him performing the same function – watching the High Priest Joshua, perhaps too cynically, to note if his heart is pure before Yahweh. But, under the influence of Zoroastrianism, he speedily takes on the character of Ahriman, the spirit of Evil who is always contending with Ahura-Mazda, the spirit of good, whom the Jews naturally identified with Yahweh. He has armies of spirits in attendance on him, and his rule is over 'the powers of the air'.

1. Though, in my view, the *poem* of Job comes from a late period in the Exile, the prose narrative may well be based on a much earlier tradition.

Along with him came in what we may now call the 'angels' – no longer mere messengers of Yahweh, but princes of the universe to whom are assigned special provinces of the world, and special spiritual functions. Many of these angels receive names: thus Raphael watches over Tobit, and the Book of Daniel, written in the second century, speaks of Michael the Prince of the Jewish nation, and of Gabriel (to say nothing of the unnamed Princes of Persia and Greece) as if these angels had long been familiar to his hearers. They are, though apparently faithful servants of Yahweh, represented as contending among themselves for superiority, as the lesser gods of Homer, though yielding a loose allegiance to Zeus, yet took different sides in the war of Troy, and sometimes, more or less furtively, followed a course of which Zeus disapproved.[1] From these beginnings grew the later portentous hierarchy of 'Thrones, dominations, princedoms, virtues, powers', over against the similar hierarchy of evil spirits; the two armies between them occupying every hole and corner of space: a growth which would have astonished the Persian myth-makers from whom the system was derived.

Below these mighty 'Princes' were the angels who guarded individual men, in something like the manner in which the 'genius' presided over the fortunes of the Roman, '*Natale comes qui temperat astrum, naturae deus humanae*':[2] *albus* or *ater* according to circumstances. This 'angel', of whom we hear nothing in early Hebrew history, seems to have been borrowed from the Persian *fravashi* (which may itself have been of Buddhist origin), though the conception underwent important developments in Jewish mythology. The *fravashi* was not exactly a guardian angel, but apparently rather the external soul of the man, sharing in the elevation or determination of the rest of his personality. If the man were righteous, his fravashi was righteous, and was

1. As the reader will remember, it was these 'angels of kingdoms' that Dryden proposed to use as the celestial 'machinery' of his projected epic poem.

2. Horace, Ep. ii, 2, 187.

worshipped after his death. With the Jews, it became the Michael or Gabriel of the man's 'little kingdom', and was regarded as separate from him but always in close attendance; while yet it retained enough of its old character to be in a sense his 'double'. By the time of Christ the idea had attained full vigour: Jesus tells his disciples that the angels of children do always behold the face of the Father, and that every 'offence' done to the children is therefore likely to be fully avenged. To the author of the Epistle to the Hebrews, the angels, including the *fravashis*, were all ministering spirits, sent forth to minister to them that should be heirs of salvation. By the time we reach the Talmudic age, angelology has become almost a systematized science: the lore of the subject is quaint, minute, and astonishingly voluminous. What we would specially note about the whole doctrine is this, that there are many traces of angel-worship. Monotheism is, apparently, a creed which men find it hard to put consistently into practice; it requires to be diluted before the common people can fully accept it. Jewish monotheism is no exception. Like other professedly monotheistic religions, it suffered modifications and alleviations.

While thus the Jews of the Dispersion were inevitably being moulded into something less Jewish, those who had returned and founded their little settlement in and about Jerusalem equally inevitably were passing through very different experiences. Their leaders were so fearful lest their followers might be absorbed into the surrounding tribes, and lose the identity which they had preserved even in Babylon, that they formulated perhaps the most rigid set of rules ever devised for keeping a community pure. Within a few miles were the Samaritans – the remnants of the Northern Israelites left by Sargon – who had mingled with the colonists planted in the land by the Assyrians; 'men from Babylon, and Cuthah, and Hamath, and Sepharvaim'. These, though they worshipped Yahweh, were looked upon by Zerubbabel and his company as a mongrel race, contaminated with heathenism, and unfit for the Society of the only true Chosen People. The Samaritans made efforts to fraternize, but were ruthlessly repulsed : those Jews who made 'strange marriages' were cast out. Finally, under the leadership of a prince named Manasseh, the Samaritans abandoned the attempt at friendship, withdrew from the Church, and set up their own worship on 'this mountain' of Gerizim. Thenceforward 'the Jews had no dealings with the Samaritans'. But the little Samaritan Church still survives, still recognizing, out of the whole Old Testament canon, the 'Books of Moses' only; and even now worshipping, to the number of two or three hundred, at the ancient city of Nablous or Shechem.

At the same time, the priesthood was organized on a similarly exclusive system. The 'sons of Aaron' claimed the highest posts, and kept the 'Levites' down in a subordinate position: the services were strictly regulated, and the officials were duly graded.

All this would probably have meant the total ruin of the colonists, who might well have perished like the first Virginian settlers, if, in the year 458, a new accession had not come from Babylon, under Ezra the Scribe, a sort of Calvin, who came with the fixed resolve to carry out the exclusive policy to the full, to keep out rigidly from the Church the 'Sons of the Land', to confine the religious privilege to the 'Sons of the Exile' (Benê Haggôlah), and to introduce and enforce the observance of a new Priestly Code which had been growing into shape in Babylonia. For this purpose he was armed with a rescript from Artaxerxes the Great King.

There were in Ezra all the force, the perseverance, and the caution which mark the man of one compelling idea, '*Ohne Hast, ohne Rast*', he went steadily on his way. At first he kept his new code in the background, and seemed to be acting solely on Deuteronomic principles. For fourteen years he laboured quietly, preparing the soil for the work; nor, even then, did he venture to act openly till assured of the support of the Governor, Nehemiah the son of Hacchelejah,[1] a Jew high in favour with Artaxerxes, who had at his

1. In my opinion, Nehemiah *preceded* Ezra, but I retain the traditional chronology.

back the whole force of the Persian Empire. Then, probably
in 444, on the 'first of Tisri', the new Law was read to the
people, and a little later the nation, purged of incompatible
elements, was bound by a Solemn League and Covenant to
keep it. This is the 'Priestly Code' which, known by the
symbol P, is easily recognizable in the Books of Moses; with
its set legal phrases, its chronological data, its rigid monotheism it runs like a steel thread through the whole of the
Pentateuch, and is indeed traceable in Joshua and other
books also. The old history was rewritten with a definite
aim: awkward facts were omitted, and suitable additions
made. The first chapter of Genesis, for instance, represented
the Sabbath as an institution dating from the beginning of
the world; the story of the Flood was told so as to agree with
the Priestly theory of 'clean and unclean' beasts – which, by
that theory were unknown in the time of Moses – and, in
the seventeenth chapter, the practice of circumcision was
declared to have been imposed by God on Abraham himself, and thus to have the prestige of immemorial antiquity.
The rest shows the same tendency, and is informed throughout by the intent to exalt the priesthood and to insist on the
sole sanctity of the Temple of Jerusalem, the very measurements of which had been prescribed by Moses in the wilderness. At a somewhat later time – if not under the direction
of Ezra himself yet under the influence of his system – the
Books of Chronicles were composed, in which the history
of the kingship was similarly rewritten, and a twist given
to it in accordance with the views of the Temple mini-
strants. The author may well have been a devout chorister
or acolyte: a series of 'Midrashim' or moral stories appears
in his work, in which long speeches are ascribed to prophets,
victories are won against frightful odds by priests and Levites
who merely blow trumpets, and 'kings of armies flee'; the
Northern Kingdom is practically ignored, and dubious incidents in the life of David or Solomon are studiously
omitted. The Deuteronomic theory is still maintained;
Asa, as a punishment for some sin, is diseased in his feet;
Uzziah is stricken with leprosy for invading the rights of the

priests; the pious Jehoiada lives a hundred and thirty years. The death of Josiah is explained by the strange assertion that Necho came up by the will of God; and the long life of Manasseh, the renegade and idolater, by a narrative of a repentance unmentioned by early authorities. That God should have urged David to the sin of numbering the people is intolerable to the chronicler; it was Satan who stood up against Israel and drove the king on.

In this substitution we see, unquestionably, a higher view of the deity than has appeared before; and, similarly, in P's account of the Creation, borrowed as it is from Babylonian sources, God assumes a loftier and less anthropomorphic character, not merely than that of J (which in our Bibles follows immediately after it), but than that of E or, in some respects, than that of the Deuteronomist; and the Psalms of the Exile and of the Return show, on the whole a similar advance. In fairness to the Priestly party, we must remember that, with all their bigotry and officialdom, they stood for progress in this respect. Their policy drove out not only Manasseh and the Samaritans, but other sects as well; and it imposed a yoke upon the people which, as Peter declared centuries later, 'neither their fathers nor they were able to bear'. We can see the signs of many feuds between priest and populace, and many signs that the Temple was turned, if not into a den of thieves, yet into a nest of extortioners. The system was a theocracy of the strictest kind, and, being conducted by human beings, aroused, like all theocracies, bitter resentment, and sank from a theocracy into a bureaucracy. But it had one great virtue. History shows that such a policy is the toughest and most enduring of all organizations. However small the community which maintains the system, it keeps its vitality amid almost all vicissitudes. It sheds members, and casts out heretical sects, but it persists. It is to the legislation of Ezra that we owe the existence of the Jewish people at the present day; it was the force breathed into the nation by him that enabled the Jews, alone among a hundred tribes, to resist the might of Rome, and to offer an insoluble problem to the Emperors, who

could slaughter but not overcome. The power which could
conquer and reconcile the Gaul or the Spaniard broke itself
on the obstinacy of the Jew. We must remember, also, that
the oppressive yoke did not burden too heavily the Jews
outside the Holy Land, who were far more numerous than
the 'Benê Haggôlah'; and, while these were retained in
allegiance, the Church believed it could afford the schisms,
more especially as, in those days, Judaism was a proselytiz-
ing religion, and indeed increased its numbers so rapidly as
to perplex the imperial rulers. The heretics were therefore
ruthlessly cast out. It was not till long afterwards that a Jew
arose who proclaimed the doctrine of a wider unity; to
whom even Samaritans were as Jews; and who was in consequence greeted by the more rigid of his countrymen as
himself a Samaritan and a demoniac, the friend of outcasts
and sinners.

What materially aided the process we have been describing was the fact that the Persian kings naturally preferred the rule of priests to a secular satrapy, and that thus
the sacerdotal caste could build up its power, quietly but
determinedly, under imperial protection. How great that
power was, and how stubborn the fanaticism engendered by
the religion, was shown long after Persia had fallen, when it
was subjected to a strain more subtle and more dangerous
than almost any it has endured in its long history. When
Alexander died, Palestine came at first into the hands of the
Greek kings of Egypt, whose rule was for the most part
tolerant and mild. Later, however, the Seleucids of Syria
obtained the suzerainty, and under one of these kings a
tyranny at once crafty and violent, attractive and repellent,
came in. Antiochus IV added the lure of Hellenism to the
force of persecution. Antiochus was a very remarkable man.
Having driven Egypt entirely out of Syria, he invaded the
land of the Nile, and would have subjected it but for the
intervention of Rome, whose envoy, in a famous scene, drew
a line round him on the ground, and bade him not cross it
till he had decided either to leave Egypt or to face a Roman
war. Having been fourteen years a hostage in Rome, he

knew what her legions were like: and he decided to leave
Egypt. Thus foiled in one ambition, he turned to another,
which was to Hellenize the 'Beauteous Land'. His character was very peculiar. He was unquestionably able, kingly
in his magnificence and generosity, a royal builder in his
capital city of Antioch, and extraordinarily skilful in forming and concealing his designs. But he had a touch of eccen-
tricity so marked that his contemporaries, punning on his
title Epiphanes, called him Epimanes or the Madman. He
was at times entirely undignified; he loved like Philip II
of Spain or Haroun-al-Raschid, to put off his robes of state
and wander alone through the streets in search of low adventure; but unlike them he took no pains to conceal his
vagaries; and he was capable of playing very unregal practical jokes. All these characteristics are noted by the Jewish
writer who has given us the Book of Daniel, and who in that
book describes Antiochus's 'unyielding countenance' and
talent for 'dark sentences' or dissimulation. He was Greek
by descent, half Roman by education, and had an Occidental turn of mind which led him to seek the complete
Hellenization of his widely spread dominions, Judaea
among them. He doubtless felt himself an enlightened despot, civilizing barbarians, as Peter the Great civilized Russia.
He was not, of course, without allies among the Jews themselves. A large party favoured what appeared to very many
the side of culture and progress; they already spoke Greek,
and often called themselves by Greek names; some of
them, indeed, occupied high positions in the priesthood.
The King knew some of these, and may well have thought
them more numerous and influential than they were. By the
orthodox Jews they were inevitably regarded as traitors,
'transgressors of the law, who made a covenant with the
Gentiles, and sold themselves to do evil': while to Antiochus they must have seemed like those distinguished
Romans whom he had known in Italy, students of Greek
literature and pioneers of the Greek culture which was so
speedily to make a conquest of its conquerors. He was blind
to the dangers of his policy, and made haste to carry out his

design of unifying the religion of his whole vast empire. He
was perhaps not the first, and he was certainly not the last,
to break himself to pieces on the rock-like obstinacy of Jewish monotheism. He fancied that a few bribes and decora-
tions, a few executions and imprisonments, would finish the
work; he died before he had found out the real magnitude of
his error. Like so many persecutors, he merely enlarged the
numbers, and intensified the enthusiasm, of those he hoped
to suppress.

The result is well known to all who have read the Book of
Daniel and the First Book of Maccabees. The 'evil root' –
such is the title given to Antiochus – began by threatening
death to all worshippers of the Name; the Temple was to
be made a shrine of the Olympian Zeus; and altars to other
heathen deities were to be erected, not only in Jerusalem,
but all over the land. To these deities all were to be compelled to sacrifice; and unclean meats were to be forced
down the throats of the true believers. On the 15th of
Chisleu, 168 B.C., an idol known to all the world as the
'Abomination of Desolation'[1] was set up on the very altar
of burnt offering; the Books of the Law were sought out and
destroyed; and the recalcitrant were put to death. Many
conformed, but there were many martyrdoms, and the
horror aroused by the persecution was never forgotten.

At length the feeling broke out into open rebellion. Led
by Mattathias, a priest of Modin (a small village twenty
miles from Jerusalem), the faithful banded themselves together, and under Mattathias and his sons, the 'Maccabees', they won an astonishing series of victories. Three
years after the desecration, the sanctuary was purified and
restored. Antiochus died in the Far East, and his general,
Lysias, granted toleration to the Jews.

It was during this troubled period that the extraordinary
Book of Daniel made its appearance – a work of amazing influence, not only in its own time, but for a score of

1. A characteristic play on words. The idol was Zeus Hash-Shamayim,
Zeus of Heaven: the Jews altered *shamayim* to *shomem*, thus turning
'heaven' into 'causing horror'.

centuries afterwards. Written to encourage and console the suffering saints, it begins with a series of didactic fables, in which the triumphs of earlier Jewish confessors, symbols of the persecuted faith, were narrated. The 'Three Children', cast into the burning fiery furnace by Nebuchadnezzar, and coming out unhurt, betokened the nation under the oppression of Antiochus, and prophesied deliverance. Daniel, saved from the den of lions, repeats the lesson. From these stories the writer turns to a series of apocalyptic visions, in which, though the history is often false, the prophecy is marvellously correct. The Maccabees did indeed prevail as he foretold. But his chief importance lies elsewhere. His book is the chief and triumphant expression of that belief in a resurrection which was beginning to emerge as the old Deuteronomic conception of a reward in this life was proving a failure. That conception had already received a staggering blow from one of the greatest poets in the whole history of the world – the author of the Book of Job, who had taken the legend of an ancient sage, overwhelmed with misfortune though perfect before God, and had turned it into a matchless denunciation of the old and simple theory.[1] The Book of Daniel, taking the name of a legendary saint who might be fairly balanced against Job himself, met the problem by stating clearly the doctrine of a resurrection of the just to eternal life, and by setting forth (for the first time as far as we know) the parallel doctrine of the future punishment of the wicked. These views, thus proclaimed in a work of enormous power and authority, became the badges of the 'Hasidim' or Holy Men who supported the Maccabees, and of the 'Pharisees' who grew out of the Hasidim party; and it was, as is now fully acknowledged, from the Pharisees that Christianity drew much of its inspiration. No Old Testament writing, indeed, has borne a greater part in the formation of Christian doctrine than this ultra-Jewish pamphlet – and that though it does not contain a single unmistakable

1. Job, indeed, attacked the doctrine with such ruthless force that the book could not be admitted into the canon without some drastic editing, involving large orthodox additions.

reference to the Messianic hope.[1] The words of Jesus swarm with references to the book; and when Paul was brought before a Jewish tribunal he proclaimed himself a Pharisee and the son of Pharisees: 'touching the hope and resurrection of the dead am I called in question.'

The Book of Daniel is one of the latest-written books of the Old Testament canon; but we should make a great mistake if we imagined that it marks a cessation in the growth of the Jewish religion. During all the confused political changes which filled the post-Exile period, steady and continuous changes had been taking place in the character of Jewish literature. To the primary and authoritative 'Torah', the Law of 'Moses', which had been formed by welding together J, E, the Deuteronomist, P, and various smaller fragments, were added the historical books, the three Major Prophets, and at least some of the Twelve Minor Prophets. The struggle against Antiochus produced a stream of poetry of which our Book of Psalms preserves some vigorous specimens; the victories of the Maccabees inspired a writer under John Hyrcanus, about 130 B.C., to write their story. But we now find, for the first time apparently, the impulse towards the writing of romances 'with a purpose'. Of such are the Book of Judith, written to encourage the Jews in their warfare with Syria; Tobit, to inculcate the full observance of the Law; Esther, to help the recognition of the Feast of Purim (a book in which we have the great advantage of marking with clearness the tendency to interpret and to add: for its latest form is twice the length of its earliest). To this class belong the first chapters of Daniel. At the same time, the Pharisaic party was not behindhand in the production of psalms and other poems glorifying the Law and the Temple services: these, as is natural, are more meritorious in their intent than in their accomplishment; the

1. The famous passage, ix, 26, declares distinctly that the 'Anointed One shall be cut off' – this of course has no reference to a Messiah of the later Jewish belief, who is to reign for at least many years. The corrupt phrase, translated 'but not for himself', probably means, 'and shall have no successor'.

longest and most characteristic of them is the huge acrostic numbered 119 in our collection of Psalms. Alongside of these are the moral and gnomic works of Ben Sira (Ecclesiasticus), and a whole series of pseudonymous philosophical writings, in which the problems of life are handled with remarkable force and freedom. Some of them seem to show traces of the impact of Greek thought, and are certainly very different in tone from the earlier Biblical books. Of these, the most famous are the sceptical *Koheleth* or Ecclesiastes, and the indignant orthodox reply to it, the Book of Wisdom. Both of these assumed the name of Solomon, and gained a hearing by the device. But it is one of the ironies of literary history that while the heretical work, with the assistance of some interpolations and annotations, obtained admission to the canon of the Church, the orthodox reply failed to escape from the Apocrypha. It is perhaps a sign of the reaction against Deuteronomism that the Book of Chronicles, despite its legalism and its eulogies of priest and Levite, only just, and at the eleventh hour, secured admission into the sacred volume. Nor did any of the later books attain a position equal to that of the Law: the belief was that prophecy would fail, and the historic books cease to be; but the Law would live for ever.

None the less, there was one class of literature which, at least for a time, exerted an influence hardly second to that of the Law itself; and which marks a distinct advance both in religion and in ethics. This is Apocalyptic – a class of works till recently somewhat neglected by Biblical scholars, but one which powerfully stirred the early Christian writers, gave birth to the so-called 'Revelation of St John the Divine', inspired the *Divine Comedy* of Dante, and moved the imagination of Swedenborg and Blake. With the decay of prophecy proper, Apocalyptic came inevitably into prominence, and in some respects carried on its work. We do indeed see a few survivals of the old prophets: nay, Josephus calls John Hyrcanus himself a prophet; and the revival of the order among the early Christians shows that it must have had some vital principle. But the best writers no longer chose the prophetic method of teaching. They preferred the style adopted, in most of his work, by Ezekiel, and made popular by the vast prestige of the book ascribed to Daniel. And yet, as Professor Charles has well shown, there are many points in which the two schools are essentially as one. Thus the prophet's knowledge of the will of God, like that of the apo-calyptist, came through visions, trances, and spiritual illu-mination. But it is to Apocalyptic that we owe an enormous development, especially in the conception of the future life and its rewards and punishments – a conception which, it is needless to say, has great influence upon ordinary morals. Hitherto, for instance, Sheol, the shadowy abode of the dead, is entirely devoid of any ethical significance; good and bad alike are there, and no distinction is made between them. Yahweh has no dominion there; the master and the servant, the tyrant and the slave, Hezekiah and the Baby-lonian king, are alike covered with an eternal shade. But, as we have seen, the Book of Daniel marks a distinction between the fates of the just and the unjust; and this doc-trine was carried further by the apocalyptic writers, until it could be taken over almost unchanged by Christianity. It was accepted by the whole body of the Jews, save only the Sadducees.

Again, the idea of a 'new heaven and a new earth' had hitherto been materialistic. A Messiah was to come and re-store all things, but his kingdom was to be of this world, and he was to be but a second David, with greater power and a longer reign. A gradual transformation of this view took place in the last century before Christ, and prepared the way for his ideas. This world was not fit for the saints: they looked to another and a spiritual world. 'Here they had no continuing city, but anticipated one whose builder and maker was God.' And this city was not for the Jewish nation, but for those only who were worthy of it – a vast change from the time when Israel regarded itself as, *in the mass*, a Chosen People. We are at the dawn of the idea that the blessings of God may be bestowed on the saints of all nations, and refused to the unsaintly of the Jews.

Apocalyptic, again, asserted a catastrophic end of the world, when the earth and all things in it should be dissolved, and the heavenly bodies should melt with fervent heat. Nothing less tremendous would suffice to root out evil, and prepare an abode for the good. It is needless to prove that this conception, also, was taken over by early Christianity – and, indeed, is still a belief of many Christians. It was part of the apocalyptic philosophy, which surveyed past, present, and future, and endeavoured to see a divine purpose in the whole of history. We can see here the germ of some of St Paul's ideas – his conception of the Gentiles who, having done right without revelation, might share in the pardoning grace of God, and, after the catastrophe, be found among the saints. For, after the catastrophe, just judgements would be dealt out. Ezekiel had proclaimed the abolition of the old law that the fathers had eaten sour grapes and the children's teeth were set on edge. Men who sinned, said he, would themselves die. But Apocalpytic thrust this aside and declared that whether the righteous and the wicked 'died' in this world or not, they would receive their deserts in the great consummation. This was a conception which Job[1] would have welcomed, and which was actually welcomed by Christ and his apostles.

These apocalypses were all pseudonymous, and doubtless gained authority from being ascribed to commanding names like Enoch, Noah, or Daniel. But, in thus seeming to base themselves on antiquity, they allowed, and even demanded, a reinterpretation of ancient ideas, in order to accommodate themselves to modern views while yet yielding due reverence to a past that was supposed to have been inspired – a process with which we are quite familiar today, and which is indeed the very mark of a living Church. It is hardly too much to say that Judaism survived through this power of reinterpreting old conceptions. The soul, spirit, Sheol, Para-

---

[1]. Whatever be the true interpretation of the famous passage (Job xix, 25), 'I know that my *Goel* liveth' (and I think it has no reference to a future life), I believe there are signs that dimly and uncertainly Job did hope for some justification after death.

dise, the Messianic kingdom, the Resurrection, all these, as
Charles truly says, were transformed not once, but often,
not suddenly but continuously. Even the legalists, with all
their stubborn formalism, could not escape the influence of
Apocalyptic, and interpreted the cruder Old Testament
ideas into a higher dialect. Strangely enough, some of the
most rigid devotees of the Law were at the same time mystics worthy to be compared with Böhme or Tauler.

It is now, perhaps, that we find an attempt so to re-inter-
pret the ancient oracles as to make them consistent with the
ethics of a better age. Those old oracles were a mass of self-
contradiction, in which, however, the higher ethics usually
had the worst of it. David, the man after God's own heart,
was represented, in certain places, as the most savage of
conquerors and the most revengeful of despots: how to reconcile this with the 'vengeance is mine' of the Deuteronomist, or with the words ascribed to David himself, 'With
the merciful thou wilt show thyself merciful'? In Leviticus
the Hebrew is commanded not to hate his brother in his
heart, and not to take vengeance or bear grudge against the
children of his people: 'thou shalt love thy neighbour as
thyself.' This, it is true, limits the love of a Hebrew to the
Hebrews, and allows him to hate the foreigner as much as
he pleases: but it is, even so, inconsistent with those Psalms
which tell how the poet hated some of his 'neighbours' with
perfect hatred, and counted them his enemies. The ferocious
'imprecating Psalms', which pious and mild Christians still
chant on Sundays in blissful ignorance of their meaning –
'The righteous shall rejoice when he seeth the vengeance; he
shall wash his feet in the blood of the ungodly' – are hard to
harmonize with the injunction in Proverbs, 'say not thou, I
will recompense evil; wait on Yahweh and he will save
thee'; and it runs directly counter to the noble boast of Job,
that he rejoiced not at the destruction of him that hated
him, nor lifted himself up when evil found him. 'Curse ye
Meroz,' says the Song of Deborah; 'curse ye bitterly the
inhabitants thereof': but Job, though a curse would have
rid himself of his enemy, refused to utter it. 'Happy shall he

be,' says the Psalmist 'who taketh the children of Babylon and dasheth them against the stones.' 'If thine enemy hunger, feed him; if he thirst, give him drink,' is the exhortation of a sage; 'for in so doing thou shalt heap coals of fire on his head.'

But, though there is much true morality in the Old Testament, its general tone is unquestionably savage and revengeful. Yet it was inspired: the Torah at least, was inspired in every jot and tittle. How then was it to be reconciled with the growing feeling that God was a moral God, merciful and gracious, a hater of evil, transgression, and sin? The new thinkers did not shrink from the task, and accomplished it, in the long run, with a considerable measure of success. The sacred text, it is true, suffered from torture in the process. All sorts of devices were adopted – allegory, symbolism, even anagram and arithmogram. Long before Ignatius Donnelly used the cryptogram to make Shakespeare announce that he was Bacon, a crowd of Jewish commentators had applied similar methods to make their Scripture mean something altogether different from what it said. At the same time, they were, in their own names, propounding a moral system on which it is hard to improve. Many of their maxims, indeed, are so lofty that Jesus himself had little to do but to select from them, to give them a slightly different emphasis, or to make positive what had often been negatively expressed: to turn, for example, 'Do nothing to a man which you would not wish him to do to you' into 'Whatsoever you would that men should do to you, do ye even so to them.' It is but the merest justice to say that by the first century before Christ Judaism had become a moral religion. That there was more of precept than of practice in it is true; but it is true of Christianity today. That there were many who compounded for sins they were inclined to by the performance of ceremonial acts, is true also: but such people are not unknown among ourselves. It is true also that though Hillel might bid his disciples love their enemies, few Jews loved the Romans; a similar phenomenon might have been observed among Christian nations in 1914.

'Scribes and Pharisees' have been judged unjustly. Some of them, doubtless, were too prone to washing the outside of the cup and the platter; but many of them, like Paul, lived in a good conscience towards God and man. When all is said, it remains true that Pharisaism was a '*Praeparatio Evangelica*', and that the system, with all its human failings, was not unworthy to be the germ from which Christianity took its rise. It is the rock from which the Church was hewn, and the hole of the pit from whence it was digged; and the Christian ought to look back on it with regard and piety.

Like all vital religions, Judaism could find room within itself for many very different minds, and for many very different schemes of life. During the centuries at which we have arrived, it could embrace Pharisaism in all its forms, the worldly and political creed of the Sadducees, whose first object was so to direct their course as to leave the Romans without an excuse for 'taking away their place and nation', the fiery Zealots, who were ultimately the ruin of the people, and the mystic and monastic Essenes, of whom Josephus has left so remarkable an account. 'They neglect wedlock, but they adopt other people's children, and form them according to their own manners. They despise riches, and are so charitable that we must admire them. It is their law that everyone who comes among them must share his goods among all. They have no fixed city, but many of them dwell in every city; and when they leave one place they take nothing with them, for they will be welcomed by their brethren in another. As for their piety, it is amazing, for before sunrise they speak not a word about profane matters, but offer prayers they have received from their forefathers: after which they are dismissed to exercise those arts in which they are individually skilled. Thereafter they reassemble, and bathe their bodies in cold water. Their food is plain, but good; and none tastes of it till grace has been said. The silence they observe is such that to strangers it seems like a portentous mystery. All things are done according to a rule, save only to help those in need and to show mercy – which things are left to their own discretion. He that wishes to join them has years of probation, and before admission has to take tremendous oaths, that he will show piety to God and justice toward men; that he will love truth and detest falsehood; that he will never seek to outshine others; that he will be obedient to the Government, for governors are ordained of God; that, even at the hazard of life, he will never reveal the doctrines of the sect.' Their philosophic ideas, in which Josephus sees a likeness to those of the Greeks, were that bodies are corruptible, but souls immortal, being emanations from the most subtle air; that the souls are drawn to the bodies by a natural attraction, and there, for a time, imprisoned, but when set free from the bondage rejoice and mount upward.[1]

The Essenes were few, but experience shows that the influence of such sects and communities is totally out of proportion to their numbers: and, in appraising the character of Judaism we must no more neglect to count Essenism than we must neglect St Anthony or St Benedict in appraising early Christianity, or the Society of Friends in measuring the force of religion in England today. Like the Friends, also, they had all the influence which comes from the brave endurance of martyrdom: for, according to Josephus, they suffered even more terribly from the Romans than any other sect, and bore their tortures with the sublimest patience.

Which of these three sects should survive was decided by the great catastrophe of A.D. 70. Sadduceeism, which was bound up with a rigid observance of the ritual Law, and with the strict performance of the Temple services, was certain to disappear when the Temple was destroyed. The Essenes, scattered as they already were, faded out of existence, or were gradually absorbed by other religions. But the Pharisees had, it is said, foreseen the disaster and prepared for it. The great teacher Hillel, perhaps through his early

1. Readers may recall De Quincey's strange theory that Josephus was here describing not a Jewish sect, but the Christians whom, with characteristic prejudice, he refused to name. This is a paradox; there is this, however, to be said, that some of the Essene doctrines and practices were probably annexed by Christianity, especially in the East.

life in Babylon, had preached a less rigid observance of the Law, using for his purpose every allegorical device of re-interpretation: it was possible for a Jew to keep Hillel's precepts even when there was no central sanctuary, while it was impossible for a man to obey the commands of a Sadducee High Priest when priest and altar had alike disappeared. A pupil of Hillel's, Johanan ben Zakkai, having failed in his endeavours to prevent his countrymen from provoking the might of Rome, secured the favour of Vespasian, and induced the conqueror to spare 'a remnant' of sages in the little Philistine coast-town of Jamnia. Vespasian held to his bond; Jamnia was spared, and became the new seat of the Sanhedrin and the new spiritual capital of the people. In a sense it may be called the cradle of the Talmud – that vast collection of Jewish learning, ethical teaching, and Biblical exegesis. There is much in the Talmud that seems to us childish, trivial, and superstitious; but there is much also of high spiritual significance. The destruction of Jerusalem was not an unmixed misfortune – it made inevitable the moralization of the Jewish religion and put an end to the rigid formalism which, if unchecked, might have been its spiritual death.

There were millions of Jews already in the Roman Empire, and thousands beyond its Eastern boundaries. To these, as we have already seen, the rigour of the Law was, by force of circumstances, far looser than at the centre. Space, of itself, would have worked to relax the strain; but contact with other nations hastened the process. The very zeal of the colonists helped in time to diminish zealotry. The Jews at that period, as we know, compassed sea and land to make proselytes, and made them in thousands; but everyone they made brought with him something of the idea in which he had been educated. A converted Mede Medised Judaism; a converted Greek introduced into it a touch, or more than a touch, of Hellenism. We can guess, to some extent, the strength of this foreign element from the fact that Paul found in it the most fruitful field for evangelization. Hellenistic Christianity had for its harbinger Hellenistic

Judaism; and it was this that aroused the hostility of the Jews against the Apostle. He was poaching on their preserves.

Of the degree to which Greek philosophic thought penetrated the higher Jewish minds, it is possible to form some judgement from the case of Philo of Alexandria. We need, however, to be on our guard against judging too hastily from this single case. For, first, Alexandria was a centre – perhaps the chief centre – of Greek culture; and secondly, Philo was one of the choicest spirits and most receptive minds of antiquity. What affected a man of his intellectual power might well fail to influence the ordinary man. Nevertheless, with due caution, we may take him as a type, though a very lofty type, of the man of strict Jewish principles who yet felt, and welcomed, the full impact of Greek philosophy.[1] A short sketch of Philonism – the first great and comprehensive attempt to philosophize Judaism – may therefore not be out of place at this stage.

Born about 20 B.C., and living till about A.D. 50, Philo saw the tremendous change which we associate with the name of Augustus: Egypt had just become a Roman province, and was gradually learning to accept the new conditions. He was far from being a mere recluse, and we learn that, at least for a time, he was carried away in the whirlpool of politics. But, like Cicero, he found his real interest in philosophy, and, like Cicero, he is distinguished rather by his omnivorous reading, and by his capacity for absorbing something from all systems, than by original philosophic power. He utterly fails, if indeed he ever tried, to formulate a consistent set of doctrines. But his love of truth was a consuming passion, and, unlike the Roman, he was sure he had the

1. The susceptibility of ordinary Jews to external influences is I think shown by the prevalence of Eastern heresies in the Colossian Church. If, as I think likely, the converts were largely Jews, their acceptance of these heresies, and their retention of them even after they had embraced Christianity, proves the eagerness with which they had assimilated them in the first instance, and the tenacity with which they clung to them when once received. A similar conclusion may perhaps be drawn from the history of Gnosticism in the early Church.

means of finding it. Truth was in the books of Moses, if only he could interpret them aright: nay, it was, verbatim and literatim, in the Septuagint version, which he was firmly convinced had been made under the direct inspiration of God. The seventy translators he held, had sat in seventy separate rooms, turning the Hebrew into Greek – and, after working seventy days, had compared their results, which did not differ in a single iota. But the 'most holy Plato' was also inspired, if not quite to the same degree as the 'divine Moses', yet equally by God; and God cannot contradict himself. Plato and Moses, he concluded with a mingling of *naïveté* and daring, must be reconciled; and not only these two highest of men, but the other God-aided sages, Pythagoras, Zeno, Panaetius, Posidonius, and the authors – probably Alexandrian – of the Book of Wisdom. In the works of all these writers Philo was steeped, and he read them all in the light of a profound religious feeling. God to him was an ever-present influence; prayer was his hourly resource; what he studied came to him always as a revelation of the Unseen. He was, as Novalis called Spinoza, a *Gottbetrunkener Mann*, a man intoxicated with the Divine. 'If a yearning come upon thee, O soul,'[1] cries he, 'to possess the good, which is divine, forsake not only thy country (the body), and thy kindred (the sense-life), and thy father's house (the reason),[2] but flee from thyself and depart out of thyself, in a divine madness of prophetic inspiration as those possessed with Corybantic frenzy. For that high lot becomes thine, when the understanding is rapt in ecstasy, feverishly agitated with a heavenly passion, beside itself, driven by the power of Him who is True Being, drawn upwards towards him.' 'The soul anticipates its expectation of God,' he says again, 'with an early joy. We may liken it to that which happens with plants. For these, when they are to bear fruit, first bud and blossom and put forth shoots. The day, too, laughs in the early dawn as it waits for the sunrising; a dimmer

1. I quote from H. A. A. Kennedy's translation, *Philo's Contribution to Religion*, to which these sections owe much (p. 16 ff.).

2. Cp. Christ's words, Luke xiv, 25, which are also, I think, allegorical.

radiance proclaims the fuller blaze.' In other places, perhaps without full consistency he adopts a Pantheistic vocabulary. 'To speak of God as coming down to view a city and a tower is manifest impiety. He that comes down must leave one part of space and occupy another. But the whole universe is filled by God.' Yet again, 'we must strive after the vision of the Existent, and if we cannot attain this, at least of his Image, the most sacred Logos, and next, of this universe of ours, the most perfect of his works.'

How to reconcile any of these views – whichever was Philo's most permanent and most certain, with the Mosaic representation of a deity who walked in a garden, who made man of clay and conversed with him, who accepted burnt sacrifices and smelled sweet savours? To us the task may well appear insoluble; but Philo, though he seems at times to realize its difficulty, had the means to hand, provided by a long succession of interpreters; and he had but to apply it more vigorously and more consistently than those predecessors. The method consisted simply in an unsparing use of that allegorical system of interpretation which already prevailed – and which was to prevail for many centuries, in Judaism, in Catholicism; which was to be employed by Paul, by Clement, by Origen, by Gregory the Great, by Dante, by Swedenborg, by Blake, and to which even Erasmus did not deal the death-blow. It was already reduced to rule, and – though it unquestionably allows the reader to transform anything into anything else, is less arbitrary than at first sight it appears. That Philo was perfectly sincere and innocent in its use is certain; and that, by its aid, he touched the Mosaic spirit to finer issues is indubitable. We have already seen an example of his application of the principle. A few more it may be desirable to give, in order to show how the rigid legalism of the Torah could be made elastic, and thus be compelled to yield doctrines of which its authors had no conception. We should do the method injustice if we did not recognize that it had a *vitalizing* power; that it could breathe life into the most arid of dead bones, and that, till the discovery of the historical and comparative method of studying religion, it was the only way by which progress was possible. Nothing can have a future which is not rooted in the past: and any other system, in Philo's time, would have involved a ruinous breach of continuity. It may be held that Philonism is the death of Judaism; if so, he made her die that she might live. In truth, however, he was a revolutionary who worked by breathing new life into the forms of the *ancien régime*.

Thus, in commenting on the creation of Eve, he says, 'The literal narrative is a myth, for how could anybody believe that woman was made out of the rib of a man?' Similarly, he rejects the story of Moses's fiery serpents – the incident never happened, but the hidden meaning is eternally true. When the Law demands that the sacrificial victims be without blemish, the inner, that is the real, significance is this, that those who offer the sacrifice must themselves be raised above the power of passion. The story of Hagar is for him practically worthless as history, but as symbolism is full of suggestion. Abraham is the soul, which has left Ur of the Chaldees – the love of this world – and is on a pilgrimage towards the knowledge of God. He unites himself first with Sarah, divine wisdom, and then with Hagar, intermediate or preparatory training; the Egyptian slave, as contrasted with the Hebrew princess. Abraham's alliance with Sarah at first is fruitless, for he is not yet ripe for spiritual gnosis. She therefore bids him wed the handmaid – devote himself to secular knowledge; and this alliance produces fruit at once. When the secular instruction has done its work, he again unites himself to Sarah, and now – the preparation being complete – the union is blest with a son – nay more, with an offspring as the sands of the sea for multitude. 'The barren woman hath borne many.'

But Philo does not stop here. The two sons are contrasted like the two mothers; Isaac is spiritual wisdom – here perhaps Philo is thinking of the Stoic Wise Man – while Ishmael is worldly wisdom, which ever tends to sophistry, and must be banished. Therefore, 'cast out the bondwoman and her son'.

The reader will here inevitably be reminded of Paul's treatment of the same story in his letter to the Galatians, so like and yet so different; and many pages have been written on the two famous allegories. But also – again amid difference – a parallel is worth drawing between the Abraham of Philo's Pilgrim's Progress and Humanity in Dante's Vision. Dante, like Abraham, is 'wedded' to Beatrice, Divine Wisdom; but he too is not yet ripe for it; he must be handed over to the guidance of Virgil, the highest type of human knowledge, until, as he approaches the promised Land, human knowledge becomes exhausted, and fades away. Paradise cannot be realized by Reason – the eye of Beatrice alone can gaze upon the sun.

But not only does Philo draw out of a story, certainly once meant as literal fact, a spiritual significance; by doing so he rids the sacred books of a piece of immorality which must have staggered many a pious Jewish soul, as it has staggered many a Christian since. Abraham's conduct to Hagar is certainly unworthy of the Friend of God; and Sarah's is still worse. Precisely so, replies Philo: and it is this very fact that ought to show you the incident never happened. God cannot sanction iniquity; if a story seems to say that he does sanction it, we ought on that very account to search into its real intention, which can only be holy, just, and good. To the buttressing of this system every allegorical device is pressed into service; not least the proper names, which – as Hebrew names almost always have a meaning – can usually be twisted in any direction. Isaac – laughter – is the joy which comes to those who have cognisance of God; Sarai is special divine knowledge. Sarah divine knowledge in general.

A score of other passages could easily be adduced to show this moralizing and spiritualizing tendency in Philo. But almost more important is his attempt to give a metaphysical colour to the Old Testament writings. Here his difficulties were still greater; for there is no metaphysic in the Hebrew Scriptures, and no language is less philosophical than that in which they are written.[1] The Jews were concrete, direct, personal. It would be a hard task to detect in the Old Testament so much as a single *oratio obliqua*; and even adjectives are rare. In the so-called 'Wisdom Literature' we do indeed find a faint shadow of philosophical thought; there is the conception that God made the world by 'Khochmah' or 'Sophia'; but we are a long way from the metaphysics of the *Timaeus* of Plato; and it was the *Timaeus* that Philo desired somehow to find concealed in the still less philosophical Pentateuch. He achieved the task by a *tour de force*. 'Moses,' he tells us, 'who had reached the summit of philosophy and had received instruction by divine revelation concerning the most important aspects of Nature, recognized that among existing things there must be on the one hand an active Cause, on the other a passive, and that the active is the Mind (*nous*) of the universe, perfectly pure and unmixed, better than knowledge, better than the good-*per-se* and the beautiful-*per-se*, while the passive is lifeless and motionless, but when moved and shaped and quickened by Mind becomes transformed into the most perfect product, this universe of ours.' God, realizing that a perfect copy could not come into being apart from a beautiful pattern,[2] and that none of the things perceived by sense could be flawless which was not made after the image of an Archetype and a spiritual Idea, formed first the ideal world, so that he might produce

1. The Talmudic writers had practically to invent a vocabulary to express the philosophical ideas they desired to propound. They had to face a still harder task than that which Cicero and Lucretius had to meet when trying to force Greek conceptions into Latin; '*Graiorum obscura reperta difficile inlustrare Latinis versibus.*'

2. The reader will recall Spenser ('Hymn in Honour of Beautie', stanza 5): who is following the same passage in the *Timaeus* which Philo has in mind:

> *What time this Worlds great Work maister did cast*
> *To make all things such as we now behold*
> *It seemes that he before his eyes had plast*
> *A goodly Paterne, to whose perfect mould*
> *He fashioned them as comely as he could,*
> *That now so faire and seemely they appeare,*
> *As nought may be amended any wheare.*

the bodily by the use of an incorporeal and most godlike pattern, the later modelled on the earlier, and intended to contain as many classes of sensible things as there were ideas in the archetypal world.[1] 'If anyone would know why the universe was created, he might say (as Plato said) that the Maker of all things is gracious, and did not grudge to lend his perfection to Matter, though in itself Matter is disordered and abounding in difference. Thus it became ordered, vital, harmonious.'

This is indeed a transformation of the simple words of Genesis, 'The earth was Tohu-wa-Bohu, formless and void', and would have bewildered the Priestly author of that chapter. Similarly, when we are told that 'God saw all things that he had made, and behold they were very good', Philo's comment is that God did not praise Matter, which in itself is a *rudis indigestaque moles*, but he praised Matter as reduced to order and finished by his own single regulating power, according to a perfect design.[2]

In much the same fashion Philo deals with the making of man, who, in the Septuagint version, is said to have been 'moulded' of clay by God's plastic power. 'There is,' says he, 'an immense difference between the man now moulded and him who had earlier *become* according to the image of God. The man now moulded was perceptible to sense, while he who was made after the divine image was an Idea or Soul, apprehensible only by thought, incorporeal, neither male nor female, immortal by nature. And when God breathed upon him, there entered into him a breath from

1. I again avail myself of Kennedy's translation, op. cit., p. 64.
2. In a famous stanza of the 'Adonais' Shelley adapts the same Platonic theory to poetical expression:

> *The One Spirit's plastic stress*
> *Sweeps through the dull dense world, compelling there*
> *All new successions to the forms they wear,*
> *Torturing the unwilling dross, which checks its flight,*
> *To it own likeness.*

But Shelley assuredly was not concerned to reconcile this with the Mosaic cosmogony.

that blessed and happy nature. If its visible part is mortal, its invisible part possesses immortality.'

Like many later thinkers, Philo was perplexed to explain by what process God reveals himself to man. All philosophies have to face this problem; but Jewish and Christian perhaps more compulsorily than most. The Gnostic systems, as is well known, tried to bridge the chasm between the Infinite and the finite by conceiving a hierarchy of 'aeons': Spinoza, centuries later, by a series of infinite 'modes'. Philo, though he is certainly not distinguished here by consistency of thought, imagines a number of mediating essences, among which the 'Logos' holds the most important place. There are Powers and Angels that come to aid the soul in its pilgrimage, but the supreme Guide is this Divine Reason, which is not God himself, but dwells nearest to him, and is sometimes, if not always, described in language that suggests personality. 'The Logos,' he says, 'is a suppliant for transitory mortals'; it is 'the first-born of God', a 'divine Man', a 'protagonist', a 'counsellor and champion'. How far this is merely figurative is hard to tell; there are passages in which the Logos appears as a tendency, a stream of influence, or an ideal at which man should aim. At times Philo identifies it with the 'Wisdom' of the Book of Proverbs; at others he seems to mean no more than philosophy in the Greek sense of the term. But, despite all this wavering, there can, I think, be little doubt that the concrete Jewish mind, studying the works of Philo, conceived the Logos as a person; and (though this has been the subject of the acutest controversy) that it was, mediately or at first hand, from Philo that the Johannine conception of Jesus as the incarnate Logos was derived. Though, as Kennedy says, it would have appeared to Philo an 'inversion of all values' that the Evangelist should have dared to say 'The Logos became flesh and dwelt among us', yet it seems to me incredible that, whatever developments the doctrine suffered after it was annexed by Christianity, the first seed should have been sown independently of Philo.

Whence Philo himself derived it, is difficult to decide. He

may, as Kennedy hints, have found it in Heraclitus's idea of
Logos as the principle of order and unity in the world; or it
may have been floating about in the loosely harmonized
philosophies which were current in Alexandria in his time.
By identifying it with the Proverbial Wisdom he may once
again have been reconciling Hebraism with Hellenism. But
his attempt remains an attempt; it was left for Christian
thinkers, of whom he was the chief Jewish forerunner, to
carry the reconciliation to something approaching real
fusion.

He is more successful, in my opinion, when, availing himself of his allegorical method and relying upon some of the
more 'religious' passages in Plato or the Stoics, he deals with
the higher ethics – with man's yearning for God, with the
sense of sin, with conscience, with repentance. Here, as I
think will be generally admitted, the Hebrew mind is deeper
than the Greek; and Philo would find more to inspire him
in the Psalms, in Jeremiah, or in Isaiah than in the Academy
or the Porch. To him, Sin was not a mere error, nor was
Right a mere mean between two extremes. The fountain of
sin is passion; the love of pleasure is the cause of transgression; and sin is not merely wrongdoing, it is *ungodly*; that
is, it is a wandering from God. Men, not loving God as they
ought, but through love of self, fall into all kinds of vice,
and end in the utter scorn of things divine. But God has
placed in our hearts a test of action, which, if we follow its
guidance, will enable us to build up our character in accordance with his will. This *elenchus* or testing-power is Conscience, which warns us against evil and directs us to the
good: it is the True Man in every man, the Rational Man
as opposed to our irrational self; now acting in us as ruler
or umpire, and now taking the place of the accuser; innate
in every one of us, and to be disregarded at our peril. It is,
in fact, a fragment of God within us. When we have done
wrong, Conscience stands at the bar against us, and reveals
to us that we have been deserting God. Then follows Repentance: 'We are in pain because of our former mode of life,
and in grief at its wretchedness we weep, groan, and sigh.

Wretched men that we are, who have been stricken by the disease of senselessness and folly.' But Repentance, though painful, is given to us by the mercy of God, and is the first sign of moral convalescence, the first indication that the disease of sin has passed its worst. The cure is inevitably toilsome, for sin recedes but slowly from the human mind, as the waters of the Flood took many days to dry. The dove of grace finds first the olive-branch and then the twig; only after a long time will it cease to need to return to Noah at all. Never, of course, do we attain perfection; none is truly good but God. We can, however, like Abraham, cast ourselves wholly on God, and that will be counted to us for righteousness. Faith is our firm conviction that the One Cause exists and that his providence rules the world. As Abraham's faith secured him a country, though he possessed no foot of land, so our faith gives us an inheritance, and secures to us that goodness which we cannot gain by ourselves. Through it, despite our imperfections, we share in the limitless perfections of God. It is a 'true and stable good, a consolation of life, a fulfilment of hope, a famine of evils, a full harvest of blessings'. Men cannot of themselves possess pure and unadulterated good, but the fixing of our anchor firmly in the Solely Existent issues in a glad *parrhesia* or fearlessness, and gains for us that which alone is worth having. Abraham's faith earned for him the cheering divine words, 'Fear not, I am thy shield and thy exceeding great reward.'

This reward cannot in its fullness be gained on earth. But the soul is immortal, and will receive its guerdon after death. When the faithful man dies, he is, like Abraham, 'gathered to his own people'; that is, to the company of the angels and the saints. Till then, he must wait in patience. Nevertheless, every now and then God grants him a foretaste of the future blessedness, a Beatific Vision of Himself. Even the effort after goodness brings a preliminary satisfaction; but the attainment, even if not absolute, is a revelation of the Highest which raises man above himself. It is possible that the revelation may but reveal the incomprehensibility of God, as the vision granted to Moses did not show him God's face;

but even the skirts of the Infinite are worth beholding. When the soul, driven by an irresistible impulse to search for God, is wrestling in prayer with groanings that cannot be uttered, a bright bodiless ray darts forth, purer than the ether, and bids the struggling spirit look and see the ideal world, guided by God in the way it should go. 'The soul, though dazzled by the intense radiance, endures the pangs, through her longing for the sight of God. Then the Father and Saviour, pitying her pains, and seeing how she longs and yearns, withholds not the Vision of himself, so far as it is possible for a created and mortal nature to bear it.'

It is in this state, which Philo exhausts his vocabulary to describe – enthusiasm or possession by God, Epitheiasm, divine rapture, Bacchism, Corybantism, Theophorism, madness, frenzy, holy eroticism, ecstasy – that the prophets received their messages. God, loving Adam, threw him into an ecstasy, and created Eve for him. 'About the setting of the sun, ecstasy fell upon Abraham.' Such trances 'fall upon' the prophets, who then see things invisible to the senses; the Divine Spirit becomes one with theirs, and they utter words not their own, but 'Neum Yahweh', the Oracle of the Lord.[1]

Those who have followed even this meagre sketch will have been constantly struck with the likeness to early Christianity. Intellectually, the author of the Epistle to the Hebrews is another Philo, often employing phrases which Philo might have used, and always adapting Philonian thoughts to Christian ends.[2] Whether the Johannine

1. As false prophets pass into trances like the true, Philo has some difficulty in distinguishing their visions and utterances from those of the servants of God. He falls back upon the view that the false prophet proclaims *his own* ideas; the true yields himself entirely to God, and disregards self. Thus true 'possession' will visit only those whose lives are true, and whose wills are deliberately subjected to God's. All fine and noble natures may become prophetic: no bad man is ever divinely possessed. In modern language, judge the message by the man: what the good man says is worth listening to; what the bad man says is worthless.

2. If this author was Apollos, a Jew of Alexandria, 'mighty in the Scriptures' – that is, skilled in the allegoric system of exegesis – his likeness to Philo is easily accounted for.

'Logos' is *derived* from him or not, the author of the Fourth
Gospel belongs to some sect or other of the Philonian school,
and his symbolic history – his treatment of symbolism as
fact – is but the converse of Philo's treatment of fact as symbolism. The mysticism of Paul, his view of sin, his conception of the body as a clog on the soul, to be beaten black and
blue and compelled into subjection, his ecstasies and
trances, his visionary translation into the heaven of heavens,
his transcendental view of Christ alongside of his almost
total disregard of the historic Jesus, to say nothing of his
allegorizing interpretation of Old Testament narratives –
all this can be understood only by realizing it in relation to
the spiritual and intellectual atmosphere breathed by the
Higher Judaism of the time; and that atmosphere is, for us
at least, best represented by the great Alexandrian Jew. In
mere trifles the similarity is equally manifest. Both Paul and
Philo contrived to combine a belief in the literal inspiration
of the Scriptures with a reliance upon a verbal memory not
always exact. The original Hebrew was inspired, and so was
the Greek version even when it differed from it; and so was
an inaccurate recollection of either. Paul could build an
argument upon the use of the singular *seed* instead of the
plural *seeds*; there are many parallels in his contemporary.
Both, in fact, were Jews and both Greeks; and both were
full of Jewish and Greek ideas which they did not always
know how to reconcile.

Small wonder, then, that Christianity, beginning as a
branch of Judaism – a development of Pharisaism not impossible of fusion with the Jewish system – and gradually
adopting Gentile ideas which were perceived to be incompatible with it, should come to be regarded by orthodox
Judaism first as a somewhat troublesome sect, and then as a
heresy to be exterminated. But it is still less surprising that
Judaism should continue to regard it *as* a Jewish heresy,[1]

1. Similarly, Christianity regards Mohammedanism as but the most
powerful and dominant of the innumerable army of Christian sects.
Mohammed is an heresiarch – of the same class as Pelagius or Valen-
tinian, though more dangerous.

as a child that had disowned its parent, and should pursue it with something of the animosity with which Churches always pursue heresies. It is easier to tolerate a member of a totally different religion than one who has broken off from your communion.

CHAPTER 3

RELIGION IN THE ROMAN EMPIRE

IT is a commonplace of history that Christianity found the way prepared for her by the existence of the Roman Empire, vast, peaceful, and well organized. It was providential that Jesus was born in the days of Caesar Augustus, by whose single decree 'all the world was enrolled'. Had the Nativity come a hundred years earlier, the seas would have been infested by pirates, and the land overrun by war-lords constantly fighting with one another, and all preying on the unhappy common people. The conditions which Paul found so favourable to this work – the presence of Roman governors and 'Asiarchs' keeping order, the good roads, the seas in which storms alone were to be feared, all these were due to the pioneer-work of Augustus, the even-handed justice of Tiberius, and the tradition they had established.

But in other ways also the Empire was a *Praeparatio Evangelica*. Before the advent of Rome, it is hardly too much to say that every nation had its own religion, and almost every village its little cult. There had been attempts, like those of Antiochus Epiphanes in Syria, to impose uniformity of religion upon large empires; but these had failed, and so far as they went seem to have been inspired by Roman influence. The very idea of a world-religion had occurred to nobody save a few Jews, who were, however, at once so broad and so narrow as to be neither. The Kingdom of Yahweh was to be universal; the Jewish God was willing to be the God of anyone who would consent to become a Jew – but the terms were too high. Many religions had persecuted other religions, and many gods had overcome and carried captive other gods, as Asshur carried away the gods of Hamath, Arpad, and Sepharvaim; but there is no sign that the Assyrians thought of making Asshur the one god of the whole world.

Now, however, the single imperial power of Rome, compelling a unity in secular affairs, and, by its easy system of roads and sea-ways, familiarizing one people with another, aided the growth of the idea of unity in religion also. Narrow patriotism died out. A man was far more proud of being a Roman citizen than of being a Cappadocian or a Numidian. When Julius Caesar enfranchised the Gauls, he made them, in a sense, cease to be Gauls altogether. And with local patriotism the local gods died also; or, if we prefer so to put it, the enlargement of the Cappadocian into the Roman meant that the Cappadocian god put on the character of Jupiter Optimus Maximus. The tiny deities of Lycaonia became manifestations of Zeus and Hermes; the single Imperial Power was accustoming men to think of a single religion; and peoples which had been worshipping the most diverse gods began to discover that they had really been worshipping the same divinities after all. It is, then, not unnatural that in Imperial times, and not before, we mark the appearance of religions deliberately making universal claims. Of these the most important, but far from the only one, was Christianity.

A short sketch, therefore, of the state of religion in the Roman world at the time when Christianity was about to invade it, may be desirable. Such a sketch must be tentative and inadequate; for, in the first place, we do not know as much as we should wish even about the outward frame of the religion; and, in the second place, we know still less about the vitality of the beliefs on which those forms rested, and which in turn were modified by the forms. We cannot tell how far they were sincerely held, or how far they really influenced men's life and thought. But we are in the same case today with our own religions – no one knows how sincere his neighbour is, and perhaps no one knows how sincere he himself is. We must be content with more or less plausible guesses.

The Roman religion, when we catch our first sight of it, was an affair of the *pagus* or collection of homesteads,[1] and

1. The *pagus* is hard to define: it was an area, distinctly marked off from other areas, and loosely ruled as *one*: it contained an indefinite

had little to do with the individual. It was, as Warde Fowler puts it, a *religio* in the sense of a 'nervous anxiety as to taboo': a fear of infection from this thing, that, or the other: the individual was concerned in it so far as his infection might change the luck of the *pagus*. If, for instance, a vestal was supposed to have so behaved as to disturb the relations between the hearth-goddess Vesta and the community, short work was made of her.[1] Should infection seize the *pagus*, there must be a 'lustration' or purification of some kind. Touching a corpse, or even speaking unguardedly to a *hostis* or stranger, might be sufficient to bring disaster upon the whole community: the religious services were in a sense medical precautions against the spread of a disease. Much the same is seen when we descend from the *gens* to the family, from the hamlet to the home. Here again the 'anxiety' was about the family itself and the house itself: the inmates must act so as not to offend the friendly spirits, and to keep out or placate the hostile. There was a spirit of the door, another of the threshold, another of the hinges: all these must be kept in good humour. Vesta, the goddess of the hearth, the Penates or gods of the *penus* (the store-room), the Genius or spirit that kept up the life of the family, all must be propitiated. Silvanus, on the other hand, the spirit of the forest, must be prevented from intruding. In the field, the *di agrestes* must be worshipped, and the festivals of seed-time and harvest duly kept.

Of the greater Roman gods we know but little, and that little has had to be unearthed by the diligent research of specialist scholars. It has been noticed that many of their names are adjectival – Saturnus, Neptunus, Vertumnus – as if the Romans thought more of the things with which the

---

number of *familiae* or households. Probably it began as the amount of land allotted to a *gens* or clan. It is not exactly what we mean by a village community, which corresponds rather to the *familia* and its land.

1. We may compare the case of Achan in the Book of Joshua. By taking to himself the 'goodly Babylonish garment' which was taboo, he had infected the whole of Israel, which had to be purified by his death and that of all his family.

gods were associated than of the gods themselves: and many
again appear in bands, like the Lares, the Penates, and the
Lemures. They are, in fact, so impersonal that some have
thought the Romans had hardly any gods, in the strict
sense, at all. What they really worshipped was the *numen* or
will of the deity, though they had not yet arrived at a distinction between the will and the willer. But the necessity
of addressing the deity rightly compelled the gradual
discovery of the proper names – even though this might give
information to an enemy, and enable him, by possessing
himself of the name, to steal away the god.[1] Even Jupiter
was addressed by the priest with the words, 'Jupiter best
and greatest, or by whatever name thou choosest to be
called.'[2]

As the households coalesced into the city, the deities enlarged also. Janus, originally the spirit of the hut door, became the god of the city gate; Vesta now had a hearth on
which the sacred fire of the city was kept perpetually burning. And, as the verge of Rome extended, as she obtained
the primacy first among the Latin cities and then in Italy
itself, foreign gods, more personal and more clearly visualized than the native deities, were introduced. Hercules, for
example, came in as a trade-god, probably through intercourse with some Greek colony; and the 'Great Twin
Brethren', Castor and Pollux, perhaps entered in the same
way, though the famous tradition ascribes their coming to
gratitude for their aid in battle. Minerva, a craft-goddess,
was borrowed from the Tuscans, who had themselves
annexed her from some Italian tribe. Diana, the wood-spirit
of Aricia, became a Roman goddess when Rome became
head of the Latin League, of which Aricia had been the
religious centre. In a sense even Jupiter Optimus Maximus
is a new god – his titles imply that, among all the Jupiters

1. The name (as we have seen), in practically all early nations, *is* the
person. When the son of Shelomith blasphemed the name, he insulted the
god (Leviticus xxiv, 11). When a man's nature was changed, his name
was changed, and *vice versa*.
2. '*Matutine pater, seu Jane libentius audis*' (Horace, *Sat.* ii, 6, 20).

worshipped by the Latins, he, as the Roman deity, is now the best and greatest.

And so the endless annexations went on. Never was a nation more receptive, on this side, than the Roman. One special addition to their Pantheon is particularly famous. During the terrible war with Hannibal, as was to be expected, the people were '*moti in religionem*'; portents were everywhere related: wolves appeared in unexpected places, and a bull actually climbed upstairs in a house, and threw itself from an upper storey. The augurs were kept busy interpreting the omens, and the State 'attended to' them by means of a 'procuratio'. The city was purified; Juventas, the deity of young recruits, was entreated, and a supplication was decreed to Hercules. Even after the decisive battle of the Metaurus, the 'religio' or anxiety was felt. Hannibal was still in Italy, and while he was there the terror still remained. Strong steps were necessary. It happened that there was a rain of pebbles; the Sibylline Books were consulted, and some ingenious augur declared that the sibyl bade the people bring the 'Magna Mater', Agdistis or Cybele, from Asia Minor. Attalus, King of Pergamum (a city ever honoured by Rome), gave his consent; the oracle of Delphi approved; the goddess came in the form of a black stone; and no less a man than Scipio, soon to be Africanus, welcomed her. The story tells that the ship ran aground on a shallow at Ostia. Only a chaste maid, said the oracle, could move it; whereupon Claudia, whose reputation had been traduced, took hold of the cable and easily drew it in to harbour. The goddess did what was expected. Next year Hannibal and his veterans left Italy for ever.[1]

1. As we shall see in the next chapter, 'Magna Mater' was primarily a corn-goddess. There was, not unnaturally, a famine in the land: the introduction of the Great Mother was followed by an abundant harvest. This, by itself, would be enough to establish her cult firmly.

What, I think, helped the growth of the cult was the fact that the Romans could easily identify Cybele with their own goddess of the Wealth of Earth, Ops or Plenty, who was regarded as the wife of Saturn (the Sower).

The 'Bona Dea', another foreign goddess introduced later, seems to

The Magna Mater was the first Oriental deity to be introduced into Rome, but far from the last. The cult of Isis,
despite the opposition of the authorities, found many adherents. The Jews, who very early were everywhere, and
who – it must be remembered – were at this time zealous
propagandists, must have been in Italy long before the end
of the Republic; and Syrian worship would come in with
Syrian traders. But the chief foreign influence was the
Greek. Centuries before the Romans had gained a name,
the Greeks had entered Southern Italy, and founded a number of colonies, which were so powerful, wealthy, and widespread that the country was known as Magna Graecia or
Great Greece; indeed, if these cities had but been united,
they would have offered an insurmountable barrier to
Roman advance. As it was, they submitted one by one, but
every city added to the Roman dominion meant a deeper
penetration of Greek ideas. The Greeks, though politically
and militarily vastly inferior to the Latins, had the superiority in civilization, the speculative gift, and the arts of peace
generally. They entered the Roman Empire nominally as
conquered, really as conquerors: and the outward and
visible sign of their conquest was the introduction of their
gods and their god-myths. The process was curious. The
Roman gods retained their names, but put on Greek characters: and the tales attached to them were often singularly
incongruous. Zeus became Jupiter, Artemis Diana, Herē
Juno, Poseidon Neptune, on the ground of some superficial
likeness; but the result was often a complete metamorphosis.
Some of the freaks of Zeus hardly suit the sober Jupiter
Optimus Maximus, and, apart from the fact that Ares and
Mars have both to do with war, there is little in common be-
tween the father of the Roman people and the barbarous
Thracian deity who cuts so poor a figure in the Homeric
poems. Yet the Romans yielded to the spell; and the poets

have been, like the 'Magna Mater', a deity of fertility. To her mysteries
only women were admitted. It was the intrusion of the reprobate Clodius
into these rites that led to some very decisive events in the life of his
enemy Cicero.

vied with each other in ransacking Greek story for legends of the gods which they could tack on to Roman names. Ovid, in particular, confounds the persons and divides the myths, in a delightful but bewildering fashion. It is often, indeed, very difficult to distinguish the genuine Italian substratum from the Greek accretion, except perhaps by noting the greater frivolity of the Hellenic element. The confusion, however, is but another sign of the receptivity of the Roman religious mind.

At the same time, as all religion involves a philosophy, which in its turn modifies the religion, the Romans admitted, more or less feebly and unconsciously, the philosophy which very early was brought to bear on the Greek myths, and on the questions which myth endeavours to solve. Among the philosophic religions of Magna Graecia the most remarkable was Pythagoreanism, a strange blend of mathematics, ritual, and Oriental mysticism, which, to uneducated minds, might be hardly distinguishable from atheism. This unquestionably began to insinuate itself, very early, into Roman society; and, as the Roman was neither mystical nor metaphysical, the effect it produced was rather atheistic than philosophic, rather destructive than constructive. By the end of the Hannibalian War this scepticism had made considerable headway, the authorities, busied with other things, having neither time nor inclination to check it. It will be no surprise to anyone familiar with human nature that this process should have gone on simultaneously with the growth of such superstitions as the belief in prodigies, and with ideas like those which led to the introduction of a new cult from Phrygia. Such phenomena were common during our own great war of 1914 to 1918 – a vast increase in superstition and a willingness to believe in any religion that could mitigate the horrors, along with a growing disbelief in everything. Men would worship any god, and men would deny that any god existed. So it was in Rome, in the still greater terrors of a war at the very gates, and devastation visible from the walls. Doubtless also, as in our time, there were some who reflected that while they were relying on their

gods, the enemy were relying on *theirs*; that if they prayed
to Jupiter for their victory, Hannibal also had prayed to
Melcarth at Gades for *his*. Which was the true God? Or was
there no god at all? No wonder that about this time there
were many who could not believe that, if gods there were,
they took any interest in human things. There was at least
one man who said this openly. The poet Ennius fought in
the Second Punic War, and is said to have distinguished
himself in it. He may have looked on as Magna Mater was
drawn up the Tiber. But in one of his plays – and plays are
not read in secret – he declares that gods may exist, but
cannot possibly care what happens to us. He was one of
those men born on the borders of many nations, and three
languages, Oscan, Latin, and Greek were native to him.
From Greek he translated into Latin the famous treatise of
Euhemerus, which says that the gods are only dead men,
thought too highly of after their death. Still more significant
is the case of Plautus, the most popular dramatist of the day,
who brings gods on the stage in the most absurd and degrading situations – here also borrowing from the Greeks –
and there is no reason to think that the *Amphitruo* was not
received with laughter and applause. About the same time
the sacred name of Numa, the most pious of the early
Roman kings, and the Moses of the Roman religious dispensation, was deliberately used to subvert religion. A
book appeared, full of crude Pythagoreanism, which professed to be the work of Numa, and – like Ecclesiastes
stealing the name of Solomon – preached exactly the
opposite of what Numa was supposed to have taught: it
meant the destruction of religion, and thus of the State
authority with which religion was bound up. The Senate
suppressed the book, but could not destroy its effect – for
the poison was working secretly, and the spirit of the time
was in favour of it: nay, some Senators themselves felt the
influence.

The process was not likely to slacken during the astonishing century in which, from being scarcely the mistress of
Italy, Rome became the virtual ruler of the whole Medi-

terranean world. These conquests might increase the prestige of Urbs Roma – the real deity of the conquering people
– but hardly of gods as a whole. They were not made by
piety or faith, but by a combination of force, fraud, and
good luck. They helped the worship of Fortuna, but not
that of Jupiter: and they were followed by a time of frightful desolation, in which Rome turned her arms against herself, and all but tore herself to pieces. The Civil Wars convinced many besides Lucretius that the gods sat apart in
Olympian calm, where no sound of human sorrow mounted
to disturb them. On one side was the ruffian Marius, on the
other the more sinister and terrible, because more deliberate
and politic, Sulla. Those that escaped the battle were massacred in proscriptions, and those that escaped the proscriptions were harassed by a brutal soldiery, turned loose to do
its will. Men took refuge either in a sad scepticism or in a
despairing half-trust in the lowest magic and in the most
contemptible of superstitious rites, borrowed from anywhere
and practised anyhow. Nay, we find this confusion repeatedly in one and the same man; the greatest as well as
the least show the wildest inconsistencies both of belief and
of conduct. Shakespeare's picture of Caesar 'superstitious
grown of late', of the Epicurean Cassius 'partly crediting
things that do presage', of the godless Antony worshipping
Hercules, is accurate and typical. Amid all the consultations
of augurs, the magical rites, the peerings into the future, ran
a disbelief in them. The augurs were ridiculed; Cato said he
wondered that two of the guild could meet without laughing, and Cicero, himself an augur, says openly that he has
no belief in omens. Caesar, the Pontifex Maximus, or Chief
Priest, avowed in the Senate that he did not believe in a
future life, and the speech made a great impression, largely
on account of that very avowal. And yet much of the poem
of Lucretius, written at that very time, is devoted to combat-
ing the fear of punishments in the future life – a fear which
he obviously regards as general,[1] and general among

1. The poem is addressed, and could be addressed, only to the class
from which Senators were drawn – the very class that heard Caesar's

Senators. There was always a *possibility* that the old tales were true: and it was a comfort to hear a man like Caesar saying confidently they were childish inventions. Or, when Lucretius told them that Acheron and Tartarus were mere symbols of the torture of conscience in this life, they rejoiced; for conscience they could easily educate, but the 'apparition, the veiled sign', the doubt as to the coming penalty, they could not quite get rid of. Their attitude was not that of unqualified and unhesitating denial; it was, in the strict sense of the word, scepticism, leading to an ennui and weariness of life; what the great poet calls a 'weight in the soul, tiring itself with its own burden'.[1] Much of this scepticism, doubtless, was due to the terrible decline of morality and the disappearance of the old Roman virtues. For when once a union between morality and religion has been established – we have seen that the two had little enough to do with each other originally – the decline of one leads to the decline of the other: and no nation has ever seen a more sudden moral declension than the Roman in the last century or two before Christ. The war with Hannibal, the too easy conquest of the East, the rapid influx of wealth not earned by labour, the irresponsibility of the proconsuls, and the examples of tyranny and rapacity set by them, all these causes, and many others, had produced their natural effects. Men believed in Mammon, and it is impossible either to serve or to believe in God and Mammon at the same time. The corruption was rank. A shrewd barbarian declared that Rome was a city for sale, if but there were anyone rich enough to buy it; and he was only just not rich enough himself. Inevitably, therefore, belief in the divine government of the world suffered decay. Even the good men began to doubt it:

words with approval. These men approved Caesar's words because they *hoped* they were true, but *feared* they were false. They were like Clough's with *them*.

1. That most pathetic picture which Cicero draws of himself after the death of his beloved daughter, can never be forgotten by those who have once seen it. He wavers to and fro between the hope of seeing her again and the fear that she is lost for ever.

they cried, like Job, 'Why do the wicked live, grow old, and wax mighty in power?' There could be no gods if men like Verres and Gabinius went unpunished: or, if gods there were, they were a feeble folk. '*Aut Deus non vult tollere mala, aut non potest. Si non vult, non est bonus; Si non potest, non est omnipotens.*' As for the bad men, it was obviously to their interest that there should be no gods: and it was no long step to conclude that what was to their interest was the truth. Thus we have on the one hand the high-souled Lucretius proclaiming that the gods, at best, were indifferent, and on the other hand his friend Memmius tyrannizing over his province in the happy confidence that the gods took no notice.

The times being thus out of joint, it fell to Augustus to put them right. It is not impossible that he was a believer; it is certain that he thought it desirable for the common people to believe. Hence, along with his political reforms, he set to work to bring about a religious restoration. Temples were to be repaired or built. The victory of Actium was ascribed to the direct favour of Apollo, and a temple to the god was built on the height overlooking the scene of the battle, in which, as the flattering poet says, Apollo's quiver was first emptied upon the foe, and the spear of Augustus followed next.[1] As the famous inscription of Angora records, he built or rebuilt[2] temples to Apollo on the Palatine, to Jupiter Tonans, to Quirinus, to the Lares and Penates, and to many others – Virgil tells us three hundred. This work was only the external sign of his wish to restore religion. He desired also to restore inward reverence and true morality – a harder task. As Pontifex Maximus he could reform ritual; as *censor morum* he tried to reform manners and character. Several attempts were made to encourage marriage and

1. Propertius, v, 6:

> *Dixerat, et pharetrae pondus consumit in arcus;*
> *Proxima post arcus Caesaris hasta fuit:*
> Vincit Roma fide Phoebi.

2. Ovid, *Fasti*, ii, 63:

> *Templorum positor, templorum sancte repostor.*
> (Holy founder, holy refounder, of temples.)

diminish licentiousness; several others, in the good old Roman fashion, to diminish external shows of wealth and luxury, by 'sumptuary laws' – which always fail. For this purpose he, and his minister Maecenas, enlisted the services of the poets. Horace, who was a kind of Laureate, in more than one of his Odes, endeavoured to help on the good work. The Romans, he said, would pay the penalty for the sins of their forefathers unless they rebuilt the temples and cleansed the images from the dust of neglect. But still more energetically must they cleanse their morals, and return to the simple Sabine virtues which had repulsed Hannibal and tilled the Latin fields. There had been a sad degeneracy. Their fathers were worse than their grandfathers, and unless they reformed, their sons would be worse than *they*. That neither Augustus nor Horace lived up to his precepts need not surprise us: they may well have seen that the vices they practised would be ruinous if practised by the people at large. Nor did they wholly fail: there is no question that the world was not only vastly happier but much more moral in the days of Augustus than at any time during the previous hundred years. If the Emperor had done nothing else than suppress the tyranny and venality of the provincial governors, he would have deserved well of the world; and he did much more. Here, as has been comparatively recently shown, his work was carried on and greatly extended and deepened by the much-maligned Tiberius. Men, having gained peace after war, port after stormy seas, began once more to believe in the protecting power of the gods, and specially in a deity that watched over the fortunes of Rome. The favour of the gods, and nothing else, could have brought the empire safely through such disasters and perils. This feeling is seen clearly in the poems – and we cannot doubt would be seen, if we had the records, in the life – of Virgil, whose writings bear everywhere the impress of a sincere religious sense. Specially, perhaps, in the Georgics do we recognize this *pietas*, this submissiveness to the divine power, which bids the soil teem and the corn grow, informing even the herds and the flocks. In the *Aeneid* this feeling

widens to embrace the State, which is mighty, not in its own
strength, but in its dependence on the higher will. Happy is
he who recognizes the *di agrestes*: happy is he also who owns
the supreme God who has made Rome what she is, and will
keep her so long as she obeys him. Go back to your ancient
faith, says Virgil, perform the ancient rites, practise the
ancient virtues, and Rome will never cease to rule, for she
will deserve to rule. It is this which made so many of the
Fathers see in Virgil an *anima naturaliter Christiana*: and it was
this which led Constantine to read the Fourth Eclogue to
the assembled Bishops at the Council of Nicaea – this, and
the dim consciousness that Virgil, being so saintly, might
well be dowered by God with the gift of prophecy. A French
writer,[1] in his heightened and telling Gallic style, goes so far
as to say that to those who have read Virgil there is nothing
surprising in Christianity. At least, they will see that there
was in the Roman world a soil prepared for the reception of
the new religion.

But in the list of temples inscribed on the Angora monument there is one which we must certainly not omit to mention – for it marks what was at once a hindrance and a help
to Christianity in the later time. Along with Apollo, Jupiter,
and the rest, occurs the name of Divus Julius: Augustus has
set his uncle among the gods; and he sees to it that the worship of Julius shall be no less ceremonious and solemn than
theirs. This was the formal inauguration of what we may
almost call the real religion[2] of the Roman Empire – the
worship of its head. Julius was no longer living; but even
when living he had received practically divine honours: the
chariot of the gods had been drawn before him in procession, a month had been named after him as if he were the
peer of Janus and Mars, his image had been placed among
those of the gods, and a priest had been consecrated to perform the due ritual to him; nay, the East, which had made
a god of Alexander, and could still see coins of Antiochus IV

1. Sainte-Beuve, quoted by Warde Fowler, *Religious Experience of
Romans*, p. 404.
2. The Emperor was *Urbs Roma* personified.

as 'Zeus manifest', went further, and proclaimed Julius openly as divine. Much the same happened to Augustus himself. Very early men discovered that his birth was miraculous; and the poets were not slow to hail him as a god on earth. When he restored to Virgil the ancestral farm, Virgil said, '*Deus haec otia fecit*'; and Horace pictured him as already sitting in heaven between Pollux and Hercules, quaffing the nectar of Olympus. Nor was this mere metaphor: it is certain that the common people, and the Easterns particularly, took these phrases with a good deal of literality. No sooner was he dead, than the full measure was given him by a solemn apotheosis. The calm and somewhat morose good sense of his successor Tiberius rejected this flattery for himself; he would have no temples, no priests, and forbade his statue to be placed among those of the gods: even his birthday he would scarcely allow to be celebrated, and the proposal to call September 'Tiberius' he laughed to scorn. That after his death he was not called *Divus* would have seemed to him exactly appropriate. But even his sardonic contempt could not prevent the fashion from growing: he had his worshippers, much as he despised them. His successor, the madman Caligula, had in his lifetime plenty of these honours, though he too was denied them in the grave. Claudius, on the other hand, though almost openly mocked at in life, received a solemn apotheosis when dead: and if Seneca made somewhat lugubrious fun of the ceremony in the *Apocolocyntosis* or *Pumpkinification of Claudius*, yet the poor pedant still remains on the list of *Divi* where Nero placed him. Nero himself, the Beast of the Apocalypse, died and remained a mere artist; but from Lucan he received an immortality which even deification could not give him. 'Let him be what god he will: let him be Jupiter, or let him guide the chariot of Phoebus; only let him be careful not to set his throne too near the Pole, lest the weight should disturb the balance of the world.' Even Vespasian, the rough commonsense soldier, had to perform miracles against his will, and when dying muttered, '*Ut puto, Deus fio*'[1] – a

1. 'As I fancy, I am becoming a god.'

prophecy which was shortly fulfilled: he too became a *Divus*.

At length, emperor-worship became so thoroughly established that the recognition of it was a test of loyalty – the
experimentum crucis which infallibly distinguished the Christian from other Romans. You might refuse to worship
Jupiter; but to refuse the simple sign of adoration of Caesar
was fatal. This was the 'mark of the Beast' of which the
author of the Book of Revelation speaks so often: that mark
in the foreheads of renegade followers of Jesus which
stamped them as of the tribe of Cain. 'Victory' over this,
and over the image of Caesar, was what ensured eternal
glory to the faithful saints: whereas those who gave way,
and had the mark of the Beast, and worshipped his image –
for them the mystic bowl was poured out that became a
great and grievous sore:[1] these were the men who were deceived by the Beast and the False Prophet; they were cast
down into the pit, while those who refused to worship the
image nor received the mark lived and reigned with Christ
a thousand years. It was the attribution of godship to the
Emperors, perhaps more than anything else, that destroyed
the empire: for it was inevitable that a religion which owned
but one God should deny allegiance, and should, if it itself
survived, be the death of the organism within which it
worked. It was useless for the Christians to say that they
prayed for the Emperor so long as they would not pray to
him; and the State saw that this sect was a deadlier enemy
even than the Jews: for it had no earthly country to be
ravaged, and no earthly Jerusalem to be destroyed.

It is true, of course, that no sensible man, in talking of
Divus Caesar, really confused him with the Zeus of Aratus
or Cleanthes – with him who alone rules the world, in whom
we live and move and have our being. It is ridiculous to
suppose that a Plotinus who enjoyed the Beatific Vision of
the divine, and yet was the close friend of Gallienus,
imagined Gallienus to be the human manifestation of God:
nor, with all Pliny's regard for Trajan, can we believe that
he looked on Trajan as more than a most excellent and

1. Revelation xv, 2; xvi, 2; xx, 4.

noble man, willing as he was to call him conventionally by
the supreme name, and consenting as he did, though reluc-
tantly, to punish those who would not follow the convention.
He was honestly perplexed by their obstinacy, as well as
irritated – much as a Tory is irritated today when a Communist refuses to stand up during the singing of the National
Anthem. Even the Jews, he knew, after the destruction of
Jerusalem, contributed the Temple-dues to the upkeep of
the shrines in Rome: what possessed these stubborn sec-
tarians to boggle at a mere trifle, and that though in so
many other ways they were citizens of a useful and decent
kind? We can hardly wonder that some of the very best of
the Emperors were the most strenuous persecutors of the
religion: they felt, and felt rightly, that there was something
in it incompatible with the safety of the State. They knew
themselves to be tolerant; if Christianity would only be
satisfied with the admission of another god into the Pantheon, they would not object:[1] but here was a sect that
would be content with nothing less than the destruction of
all the gods, and the State-god with them. Christianity,
though it did not know it, was starting a civil war; and the
State, in self-defence, had to take sharp measures.

Nevertheless, Christianity was right. The claim that
Caesar was in any sense divine ran counter to the first principle of true religion – 'Hear, O Israel, the Lord thy God is
one Lord.' We may regret the fanaticism with which so
many, seeking the crown of martyrdom, went out of their
way to insult the ruler and maltreat the idols; but if God
and man were to be kept apart, if the doctrine were to be
established that One alone is worthy of adoration, then the
Christian had no choice. When put to it, he must be faithful,
and serve God rather than man. That he afterwards compromised, and, as we shall see, admitted Godlings into his
own Pantheon, says nothing against those who, in earlier
generations, resisted even unto blood: and most of the com-

1. The tale that Tiberius wished to have Christ worshipped as a god is
of course a fiction; but it expresses the attitude of Rome with tolerable
exactness.

promises came when the Emperor had himself renounced the claim to be worshipped.

There was, in fact, an advantage for the Christian in the existence of this single test. It marked out a precise and easy boundary between him and the world, and served as a watchword serves a soldier. A soldier indeed he was – a unit in a garrison in the midst of a hostile territory; and it was as well he should have a comprehensive sign by which he could distinguish friend from foe, as well as – what was equally important – the comrade who would face the worst from the weakling who would flee when the battle became fierce.

Despite all the work of Augustus and his successors, there can be little doubt that after a time world-weariness and disillusion returned upon the Empire. Apart from the outlying provinces, the larger portion of mankind seems to have relapsed into a state of mind in which hopelessness was the chief feature. Gibbon, it is true, gravely doubts whether any period in history was better worth living in than the age of the Antonines – the eighty or ninety years from the death of Domitian to the death of Marcus Aurelius. But – even if we refrain from asking for *which* class this happiness was provided, and trouble ourselves not at all about the artisans, the poor, or the slaves – the happiness, to judge by what we read, was of the passive kind: it was rather a somewhat sullen submissiveness, degenerating often into fatalism, than anything approaching cheerfulness. Men were in the world, and had to make the best of it: the sooner they were out of it the better. Families were small – why should so poor a thing as life be passed on to others? Hence, in part, the decline in population which made the Empire, a century or two later, the ready prey of the barbarian, and turned once crowded regions into deserts, to be sometimes voluntarily handed over by the Emperors to Goths or Dacians. In this state of mind people naturally fell victims to the quack-philosopher, the wonder-worker, or the prophet. Anything was worth trying, and nothing was worth trying for long. The world swarmed with charlatans, such as those described by Lucian, who were eager to sell contentment – for a price: and learned and ignorant alike thronged to hear the latest physician, till a later one appeared, with the same message dressed in slightly different language. The old gods were dead, and any new one that seemed to be alive was gladly welcomed.

We find this in the first century, and traces of it are to be seen in the Acts of the Apostles. The proconsul of Cyprus, whom Luke describes as a sagacious man, had Elymas the sorcerer with him,[1] and was clearly in a state of mind that was ready to welcome a better adviser. The people of Samaria had their Simon Magus, whom they regarded as a manifestation of the deity, and who was himself willing to learn from one whom he regarded as a greater magician than himself. At the very time when Paul was growing up in Tarsus there was in that city a great miracle-worker known as Apollonius of Tyana, the founder of a religion which professed to be directly revealed from heaven. The life of Apollonius, written by his admirer Philostratus, is another Gospel: it tells of a semi-divine man who went about healing the sick, raising the dead, casting out devils, and prophesying things that shortly came to pass. In the next century arose Alexander of Aboniteichos, whose life was written by no admirer, but by the unbelieving Lucian: and who appears as an impostor of astonishing ingenuity and craft. Had the life been written by a disciple, it would have been that of yet another Messiah; for Alexander was believed in by thousands from the highest to the lowest, and died in the odour of sanctity and in the full blaze of glory.

Miracles, indeed, today perhaps a hindrance rather than a help to faith, were then so common that the difficulty of the Christians was not to induce people to believe in them, but to show that there was anything specially remarkable in the Christian brand of Thaumaturgy. How was Paul's healing of the sick superior to the cures of Apollonius, or how was Peter a higher sort of Magus than the other Simon? The

1. A hundred years before, the great general Marius had carried about a Jewish prophetess called Martha, whom he habitually consulted.

Christians themselves never denied that the heathen performed miracles. They owned that the Pythian Apollo prophesied correctly and told what Croesus was doing though
hundreds of miles away: that Castor and Pollux appeared at
Regillus, and that Tuccia carried water in a sieve.[1] Their
only resource was to declare that these wonders were done
by the agency of demons, in which they, like the Jews and
the heathens, undoubtingly believed. 'If magicians,' says
Tertullian in his famous *Apology* written at the end of the
second century, 'do set before your eyes a pageant of
spectres, and by their black arts, or direful forms in necromancy call up the souls of the dead:[2] if they throw children into convulsions, and after a while make them vent the
madness in oracles, if by their juggling wiles they delude the
senses with the abundance of mock miracles, and inject
dreams in the dead of sleep,[3] by first invoking the assistance
of their angels and demons, by whose sophistry even goats
and tables are wont to divine; if then these evil spirits will
do so much by the impulse of men, what will they not do by
their own impulse and for their own interest? But let a
demoniac be brought into court, and let the spirit which
possesses him be commanded by any Christian to declare
what he is, he shall confess himself as truly to be a demon as
he did falsely before claim to be a god. Let the celestial Virgin, the great procurer of rain, or Aesculapius, the great
improver of medicine, who recovered those that otherwise
would not have lived a day – if these, I say, do not declare
themselves to be devils, not daring to lie in the presence of
a Christian, that Christian is ready to answer for the cheat
with his own blood. You may say this is done by magic, but
what can be objected against that which is made plain as
naked truth?'

1. All these absurdities are spoken of by Tertullian as true: *Apology*,
cap. 22.

2. '*Defunctorum animas infamant, aliter inclamant*' – two different forms of
necromancy.

3. Contrast the contempt of Horace and Juvenal for these charlatans,
called variously *grammatici* and *magi*. But even the powerful mind of
Tiberius was moved by them.

Thus when, as we are told, the Christians cast out demons, healed the sick by imposition of hands, or even raised the dead by pronouncing the name of Christ, they were giving the heathen no very striking arguments for the truth of the new religion: these things were being done daily by wonder-workers all over the known world, and had been done from time immemorial. It might have been to their advantage, at least in their efforts to convert the wise according to this world, if they had refrained from performing these feats. But there can be no doubt that the ignorant, the poor, and the miserable would expect their performance, and, if the Christians had refused them, would have gone somewhere else. In an atmosphere impregnated with miracle, it was necessary that the missionaries should breathe the same air, and be infected with the same germs, as their neighbours, if they were to have any influence. And, coming as they did with a full belief in these constant interferences with the course of nature, it was as well that they found a world not only unlikely to be repelled by their miracles, but ready to accept them and even demanding them. Had everybody been like Celsus and Lucian, convinced that nature is uniform and works by law, there can be little doubt that the miraculous claims of the evangelists would have blinded the world to the moral excellences of the religion, and we should have lost the enormous benefits it has conferred upon us. We can discern how some men of science were in actual fact thus repelled: they saw the Christians behaving, externally, just like the charlatans with whom they were familiar, and concluding, wrongly but naturally, that this religion was but one more of the innumerable and 'detestable'[1] superstitions that deluded the vulgar. It was, after all, a good thing that the Christian missionaries were at once *intellectually* no better than their contemporaries, and morally superior.

1. Tacitus, *Annals*, xv, 44: 'Those men whom, through hatred of their crimes, the vulgar called Christians. ... This detestable superstition spread not only through Judaea, the home of the pest, but through Rome, to which all horrible and shameful things tend to flow.'

CHAPTER 4

THE GREEK RELIGION

THE religion of the Greeks, like many other religions, sprang from the feelings of wonder and fear, and was just as savage and crude as the religion of any African or Polynesian tribe. That we are inclined to think otherwise is due to the fact that the literature in which it has been enshrined for us is more artistic than that of other nations, and lends a delusive glamour to stories and rituals which we should easily perceive to be barbarous if we met them unadorned. Some of the earliest records, again, like the Homeric poems, seem to have been doctored by late editors, and, as in the case of the Hebrew Scriptures, we have to look carefully for traces of the more primitive customs and beliefs.

Looking thus, we find plenty of evidence of that fear of the dead which is almost universal. The dead still lived in their tombs, and needed regular offerings of food. In early times it was felt that they would be lonely without their wives and their slaves, who were sacrificed and buried with them. Their weapons or tools were carefully provided, that they might carry on the work that had pleased them when alive. If neglected, their *kēres* or souls would exact terrible vengeance: there were myriads of these *kēres* around, ready to bring disease and death. The soul was not exactly the man; the man's self was his body;[1] but the soul had the man's shape,[2] and was exactly like him except that it was more tenuous substance, and that its voice was thin and bat-like. If you were courageous enough, you could go to the tomb with a bowl of fresh blood, draw out the ghost by incantations, and let it drink. As it drank the blood, which

1. The wrath of Achilles sent the *souls* of heroes down to Hades, but gave their *selves* to dogs and birds.
2. Not that it might not often take the shape of a snake, a bird, or any other animal.

was the life, a temporary vitality returned to it, and you could compel it to answer questions. It was thus that Odysseus induced Teiresias to tell him of the future.

If the dead man had been a king like Agamemnon, or a chief of a tribe like Achilles, he was worshipped at his tomb as a 'Chthonian' or underground deity. He was regarded as still controlling the city or clan over which he had ruled when alive; and we can sometimes trace the wanderings of a tribe by noting the successive places where the chief was thus worshipped. Achilles and Hector had each perhaps a dozen tombs: this means that their clans had migrated from place to place, or that other clans had thought it desirable to secure their favour. The tomb was the social and religious centre of the tribe, and the hero was looked upon as its divine ancestor. It is the opinion of many that Greek tragedy, which was essentially a religious service, owed its origin, at least in part, to this ancestor-worship. Dithyrambs were composed and chanted in memory of the hero, and sacred dances were organized in his honour; from these, at two or three removes, might come the plays of Aeschylus.

In order duly to worship these beings it was necessary to be pure. Touching a corpse, for example, involved at least uncleanness, if not actual danger from the dead; and the man who had had such an accident must be cleansed from defilement in water, and preferably in 'living' or running water from the sea or from a river. This the Greeks called *catharmos* from *cathairo*, to cleanse. Thus in the *Iphigeneia in Tauris* of Euripides the priestess tells the king that the two strangers whom he wishes to sacrifice are tainted with bloodshed, and must first be purified. 'In fountain-waters, or in ocean's wave?' asks the king. 'The salt sea,' she replies, 'cleanses all pollutions': and not only the victim, but the sacrificer, must be cleansed in like manner. If the suppliant desired to receive anything from the god, he approached him in due fashion, prostrating himself to the earth or lifting his hands to heaven; and he used a set form of words: for a prayer, which was hardly distinguishable from a spell, had a magic power over the deity. A vow generally accompanied the spell; for the gods, being, to all intents and purposes, human, could be propitiated by gifts. 'Many burnt offerings of cattle did Hector offer to me on the peaks of many-folded Ida,' says Zeus in the Iliad, 'and many in the lofty city; therefore does my heart pity him': and he ponders whether he shall not, on that account, save him from impending death. Thus men, hoping to win favours in return, offered the gods food and drink, or the sweet savour of a holocaust.

But divine power resided not only in the dead, nor only in the great and plain phenomena of nature: there was a spirit in everything, however small. Before Apollo came to Delos, the islanders worshipped a stone, and long after he came to Delphi, a stone continued to be worshipped by the Delphians. So late as the time of St Paul, we all know, the Ephesians worshipped the 'image that came down from Jupiter'. Such stones were called by the Semites 'Bethels', houses of God, and the Greeks called them by the same name, slightly altered – 'Baïtyls'. Trees, rivers, fountains, birds, beasts, were all divine, and must be propitiated; and there were priests to show how the propitiation should be done. Old phrases still remain in the later language, showing that houses were once regarded as thinking, or other inanimate things as speaking.[1] No wonder then that casual sayings of human beings, which happened to bear a meaning the speaker did not intend, were accepted as omens. Thus Telemachus, in the second book of the *Odyssey*, takes it as a *phēmē* or word of good luck, when a man has accidentally invoked a blessing on him without knowing it. And the will of the gods and daemons might also be revealed in all sorts of ways, especially by natural phenomena the causes of which were not understood, and which were therefore ascribed to deities regarded as even more capricious than human beings. A sudden flash of lightning, an eclipse, the flight of birds, a stumble, or a sneeze, might be charged

1. 'This house thought of being rich,' says Telemachus in the *Odyssey*, meaning *used to be* rich; somewhat as in the Book of Jonah we are told that the ship '*thought* it was being broken'.

with portentous significance. In a very enlightened age, when some men already knew that an eclipse of the moon is possible only when the moon is full, such an eclipse, interpreted by soothsayers, forced an Athenian general to remain inactive in his camp for a whole month, and brought about the total ruin of his army. The soothsayer Calchas, at the beginning of the Iliad, foretells the length of the war from the curious behaviour of a serpent; and every day for a thousand years such predictions were made.

The Greeks did not always live in Greece: they came from the north, and gradually drove earlier tribes into the corners of the peninsula. Some tribes of Greeks came later, and subjected Greek tribes that had arrived earlier: thus in the Peloponnese, the Dorians made the Achaeans their subjects. New customs and new gods thus came in, not often destroying the old, but mingling with them. Hence a great confusion as to the powers of the deities. The supreme god of one tribe had to settle questions of precedence with the supreme god of another; and the questions were not settled without compromises and a good deal of overlapping. As in Norse mythology we cannot always tell where the domain of Thor stops and that of Odin begins, so, and for the same reasons, we cannot mark out exactly the boundaries between the kingdom of Apollo and that of Helios, or between that of Hecate and that of Artemis. And similarly, when men began to burn the dead instead of burying them, the ideas of the soul became confused. Though they conceived the soul as a kind of fire or breath, they continued to picture it as a sort of body: and, though the soul still remained near the tomb or pyre, it nevertheless wandered in the regions below the earth; while it could also be sometimes seen fluttering in the air. Such inconsistencies, of course, are not peculiar to Greece; they are found everywhere, and exist in our own country today.

The underworld was conceived, like the Sheol of the Hebrews, as a place of darkness visible and of unsubstantial life. According to Homer, there was but one among all the ghosts, the prophet Teiresias, who still retained full intelli-

gence – the rest flitted about as shadows: and the ghost of
Achilles tells Odysseus,

> *Rather would I, in the sun's rays divine,*
> *Serve with a churl who spends his days in grief,*
> *Than the whole lordship of the dead were mine.*

Four rivers bounded the place; Styx, of hate; Acheron, of
sorrow; Phlegethon, of fire; Cocytus, of wailing: and far off
from them was Lethe, the stream of forgetfulness. When the
soul arrived on the banks of Styx, the ferryman Charon took
him over the river. Hence it was the custom to put an obol
or penny-piece in the mouth of the corpse, that Charon
might receive his fare. From this realm, which was known as
the House of Hades (the Invisible), there was no return;
though there were later legends of demigods like Heracles
and Theseus who had made the journey and come back in
safety. Certain ravines, such as Taenarus in Laconia or that
near Avernus in South Italy, were supposed to be the entrance to this abode.

It does not appear that at first there was any ethical idea
about the conception of Hades. Later, we find the moral
view of Retribution or Reward expressing itself in pictures
of an Elysium, where the favourites of the gods enjoy eternal
bliss, or of a Tartarus, to which great rebels are condemned
by the three judges, Minos, Rhadamanthus, and Aeacus.
There are (probably interpolated) passages in Homer which
speak of the punishment of such criminals as Tantalus and
Sisyphus: in later poets these fancies become common. To
Homer, the avengers of crime are the Erinyes, which appear
as winged dogs, chasing the sinner over land and sea. These
are not exactly conceived as the personified pangs of conscience, but rather as the souls of the injured pursuing the
injurer in bodily form. They dwell in Hades, and an in-
cantation draws them up to work their will on earth. In the
typical case of Orestes, who had slain his mother, they seem
to represent the next of kin, whose duty it was to avenge the
death: as Orestes, the slayer was himself the next of kin, the
Erinyes undertook the duty at once for him and against him.

There are many others of these daemonic beings – the Harpies, who may be the swift winds, and who are represented as winged women carrying away the souls of children; the Sirens whom Odysseus met, and who charmed sailors to destruction by their singing; the three Fates, who span the destinies of men; the Gorgon Medusa, the sight of whom was fatal; and scores besides.

When we come to the great gods, we find, in spite of the attempts of poets and philosophers to reduce them to something like order, plain traces of similar confusion, and of their origin in primitive natural science and primitive hopes and terrors. Zeus, for instance, has by the time of Homer become recognized as in a sense supreme, and when he chooses to assert his will the other gods may grumble but they give way. That he did not attain this position without difficulty is shown by the stories of his contests with other deities. There are tales of frightful battles with the Titans, but he is helped by Titans and sometimes appears as a Titan himself. His father Cronos, who had deposed his own father Uranus, he drives out and hurls to Tartarus – but the very fact that he is represented as the son of Cronos indicates that he, in some measure, stands for the same natural phenomena. He was, almost certainly, a sky-god: and even when, like Yahweh, he takes on the character of a tree-divinity, the celestial power remains. In Dodona he manifests his will by the sound of a gong in the leaves of the oak-trees; but this is because the lightning often strikes the tallest trees, and thus a blasted oak becomes a clear sign of his power. He is shown as grasping a thunderbolt in his hand, and with an eagle perching close by. Men found in him the explanation of volcanoes like Etna or of the upheavals in Cilicia – these are the Titans whom Zeus has conquered, but who are still struggling vainly beneath the earth. He is Zeus Hyetos, Zeus of the Rain; Zeus Nephelegereta, the cloud-compeller; Coryphaeus, the mountain-god; Olympius, because he has specially chosen Olympus, the mountain, of all mountains known to the Greeks, nearest to heaven. All the phenomena of air and sky are his doings, performed either personally or through his agents. He may almost be called the child of man's sense of helplessness in the presence of external nature.

He has as many wives as Solomon, though the vast majority are of the ephemeral kind. 'All places that the eye of heaven visits' are to him like ports to a sailor, and afford him a temporary consort. He visits Danae in a shower of gold – this is the rays of the sun. Elsewhere he meets Semele, to whom his embrace is fatal – this is perhaps the murderous thunder cloud. He weds Leto, and becomes the father of Apollo and Artemis, who – at least in later times – figure the sun and the moon. He weds Demeter, Mother-earth, and the result is Korē or Persephone, who is carried down to Hades and kept there three months every year. This is that union of sun and earth which brings forth the corn in its season; and Korē, the Maiden, represents at once the youth of mankind and the fruitfulness of spring. But such is the confusion that, while Demeter is Zeus's wife, Ge or Mother-earth is the mother of Cronos, and thus Zeus's grandmother. Like Demeter, and naturally enough, Ge is associated not merely with birth but with death; we came from earth and to earth we return.

Were we to follow the other great gods of the Greek Pantheon in similar fashion, we should find the same confusion and the same underlying awe of nature. We have dozens of sea-gods, and only gradually does Poseidon assert his superiority over them; the sea is feared and worshipped, and so are the individual billows and the white foam of the waves, which sometimes deceive and sometimes, like Leucothea in the *Odyssey*, spread their scarf under you and bring you safe to land. As for the gods and goddesses of birth, their name is legion. The chief, and finally the only, wife of Zeus is Herē; she, little by little, assumes to herself the guardianship of women, aids them in childbirth, avenges their wrongs; but we can see that in each of her offices she is taking the place of some goddess, perhaps that of a vanquished tribe; and again and again Artemis does the work which Herē is supposed to do. Thus, as Eileithyia, Herē helps *laborantes utero puellas*; but who does not know that this is the function of Artemis also? Again, we have just seen that Korē or Persephone is the goddess of the lower world, and the wife of Pluto;[1] but we often find Pluto confounded with Zeus, and his wife with Herē. This does not prevent the mythographers from telling us that Artemis, under the name Hecate, also rules in Hades.

We must be careful to distinguish the personifying power of myth from the allegorizing tendency which, so far as we can see, works later, and indicates the growth of reflection and elaboration. Many names of gods and goddesses we are tempted to regard as allegories, and they were certainly allegorized in later times: but originally, when everything, even an idea, was a person, the allegory was probably not perceived. Thus in Homer Hēbē, youth, is the daughter of Zeus and Herē; she is certainly not conceived, in the manner of Spenser's Una or Error, *first* as an abstraction and afterwards as a person. Later, of course, as thought became more philosophical, the process was reversed, and the person was allegorized. Thus, in the old myths, Metis or Wisdom is spoken of as the wife of Zeus and the mother of Athenē; in more sophisticated ages she is resolved into a phantom. Themis, Law or Order, is another wife of Zeus; in Aeschylus we find her not only now identified with Ge and now treated as Ge's daughter, but made the mother of Prometheus the Fore-sighted: a clear, if unelaborated, allegory. As thought advanced, the allegorization was carried further: Themis, in works of art, is pictured as holding the scales of justice. Similar is the case of the Horae or Seasons. Themis is their mother because they come according to law or rule; but we must not imagine that this idea was formally or philosophically worked out. They are figured as dancing in time, and regularly returning to the same place; they are maidens. 'To them,' says Homer, 'hath been entrusted great heaven

1. This may be because *Plutus* ('earth's increase and foison plenty'), the wealth which comes from fertile soil, is represented as the son of Demeter, and Persephone is her daughter: Pluto and Plutus being probably but forms of the same word.

with Olympus, for the opening and shutting of the gates thereof'; these are not abstractions, but, so to speak, divine human beings, with arms and hands. In another portion of the Iliad, Sleep and Death carry the body of Sarpedon from the plains of Troy to Lycia; though (in the opinion of many) this passage is late, yet the poet does not seem to have reached the stage in which allegory is practised. But in a still later passage, in which we are told of 'Prayers, daughters of great Zeus, lame, wrinkled, and side-glancing, who follow after Até or Mischief though she has gone far before them, and heal the harm she does', it appears to me that the writer is allegorically philosophizing in the simple manner of a Greek Bunyan, and *deliberately* making abstractions into persons. He might almost be a Pindar, who, as we have seen, gives Epimetheus or After-thought a daughter, Prophasis or Excuse.

In the same way we must beware of thinking Moira a *mere* personification of Destiny; she is a real goddess, with the usual human attributes of a deity. Nor is Até, of whom we have just spoken, mere mischief: she is a goddess who delights in mischief, a very different thing; Plutus is not wealth, but a god of wealth; Charis is not grace or beauty, but a gracious creature, and the actual wife of Hephaestus the Fire-god. When Achilles is thinking of killing Agamemnon, and Athenē (unseen by others) comes to deter him, she is not a personified conscience, but the daughter of Zeus herself: a deterring impulse *was* a goddess, as to Socrates a warning thought *was* a deity or daemon.

But of course, as time went on, the elaborating process developed more and more speedily, until there was hardly an abstraction that had not been more or less purposely personified: until Aidōs or Respect for Right, and Nemesis (something like the censure passed on 'bad form' by public opinion) actually had their altars; until, as readers of the Acts know, the Athenians imagined that Paul was bringing them a new goddess, Anastasis or Resurrection. But this process is not the simple anthropomorphism of earlier times. To Homer the Muses are song-goddesses, not Song: Iris is not the rainbow, but a messenger of Zeus: Poseidon is not the sea, but the ruler of it and driver over it: and even the Kēres, the souls of the dead, are black women in a bloody dress.

In the sense thus illustrated we may speak of many of the deities as personifications of the heavenly bodies. Helios is the sun, Selene the moon; and both were worshipped daily at their rising and setting. At Rhodes, as everyone knows, was the Colossus representing Helios – one of the Seven Wonders of the World. Odysseus in his wanderings lighted on the island where the cattle of Helios grazed; and the mad folly of his men in eating of the sacred herds led to their ruin:

> They perished every one, by their own mad deeds did they fall,
> For they slaughtered the kine of the Sun and devoured them – fools
> were they all.

As in so many mythologies, Helios drives through the sky in a four-horse chariot: the story of Phaethon (the Bright), who perished while driving in place of his father, may be the myth of an eclipse. Similarly the winds are represented as swift horses. Helios, and the winds, are *real*.

But far more important, perhaps, than all these cults is the worship of Reproduction, whether that of the fruits of the earth or that of human beings. These powers were, like other natural energies, personified and made into deities; and some of the most remarkable and significant of all religious services had to do with these gods. It is impossible here to describe, however briefly, all these services. I will take one or two, which, alike by attraction and by repulsion, had some influence, in all probability, upon Christianity.

The first is the cult of Aphrodite, the goddess of love. She appears not to have been originally of Greek origin: there is every reason to believe that she is the Syrian goddess Ashtoreth or Astarte, whose worship probably reached the Greeks when they advanced as far as Cyprus. Some elements, doubtless, were borrowed from the worship of the

Phrygian Cybele and the Hittite, Derkĕto, both of whom show, in some regard, considerable likeness to Astarte. No cult, in fact, is more widely spread than this. Under other names, Aphrodite is worshipped almost everywhere: we shall see the reproductive principle adored, with very similar rites, in India: and the numberless prohibitions of it in the Mosaic Law show that the Hebrews not only found it prevalent among the Canaanites, but were under a constant temptation to practise it themselves.

Those who wish a full account of the worship, may find it in the essay of Lucian, the second-century Greek writer, entitled *The Syrian Goddess*: a most curious and interesting work. I must content myself with a short account of the festival known as 'Aphrodisia', which was celebrated all over Greece, but specially in the city of Paphos in Cyprus – one of the first Gentile places, incidentally, where St Paul preached the gospel. No bloody sacrifices were permitted: the only offerings were pure – fire, incense, and flowers. If, as is sometimes said, goats were sacrificed, it must have been solely for the purpose of obtaining omens, and it must have been outside the temple: though the sacrificial feast was probably held within. 'At Paphos,' says Virgil with poetic exaggeration, 'Venus has her temple, and there a hundred altars glow with Sabaean incense and breathe with fresh-plucked flowers.'

There were two cities called Paphos, the Old and the New: at the appointed time men and women assembled at New Paphos, formed in ranks and marched in solemn procession seven miles to the old city, headed by Agetor ('Leader'), the priest of Aphrodite. Arrived there, they performed the solemn acts of worship, and in the following 'mysteries' those who desired initiation, boys and girls alike, were admitted into the fellowship of the goddess: this, as in so many religions, involved religious prostitution. No disgrace, but rather high honour, attached to this ceremony: indeed the Jews, and afterwards the Christians, were the only nation that found anything objectionable in it. In return for a piece of money, the devotee received a measure of salt – the type of purity, and the phallus, the symbol of natural reproductive power.[1]

The close connexion between this and the reproductive power of the fruits of the earth is well illustrated by the festivals of a number of gods in different parts of Greece and the Near East, such as those of Hyacinthus, Hylas, Adonis, Attis, and Dionysus the wine-god. These, and the myths associated with them, are remarkably similar to those of Indian gods, to that of Osiris the Egyptian deity, to that of Mondamin the Red Indian maize-god, and to that of our own John Barleycorn. Had we fuller information, we should probably find that they bore also some resemblance to some of the early Hebrew feasts, such as that of the Treading of the Grapes, referred to in the history of Abimelech,[2] or possibly to the four days' mourning which was kept up annually for the daughter of Jephthah.[3] The full ceremony of the worship of Adonis or Tammuz was, as we know, practised by Jewish women, to the horror of the prophet Ezekiel. 'Thou shalt yet see other great abominations which they do. Then he brought me to the door of the Lord's house, and behold, there sat the women weeping for Tammuz.'[4] I shall here give a short account of the myth and ritual of Attis, because this not only profoundly influenced Christianity, but was spread over almost the whole Roman Empire, and was familiar in Rome itself; while the very similar cult of Adonis, though practised throughout the Greek world, did not penetrate into the West. The resurrection of Attis took place on the twenty-fifth of March, the beginning of spring –

1. This symbol was everywhere in Greece, as in India today. It was particularly prominent in the festivals of Dionysus, which were essentially what we regard today as indecent. Hence the unabashed indecency of the old comedy of Greece, which was really part of a religious service in honour of Dionysus. Our own ancestors had something like it: we learn that St Olaf, in his endeavours to convert Norway to Christianity, had some difficulty in suppressing the 'volsi-game', which, from the description given of it, must have been a ceremony in honour of the reproductive principle.

2. Judges ix, 27.   3. Judges xi, 40.
4. Ezekiel viii, 14: alluded to by Milton, *Paradise Lost*, i, 455.

the very day on which, according to many Christians,
Christ rose from the dead, and the very day on which,
according to Jewish tradition, God finished the work of
creation.[1]

Attis was a Phrygian youth, the son (or the herdsman) of
the Great Mother Cybele. He was born of a virgin who conceived by putting a ripe almond to her breast. According to
one story, he mutilated himself under a pine-tree and bled
to death; according to another he was, like Adonis, killed
by a boar. His priests, or Galli, were eunuchs, dedicated to
the service of Cybele. Every year, at springtide, the twenty-
second of March, a pine-tree was cut down, brought to the
Temple of Cybele, decked like a corpse, and treated like a
god. A band of tree-bearers (Dendrophori) attended it,
wreathed it with violets, and tied to it the image of a young
man. On the next day, there was a great blowing of trumpets. On the third, the Day of Blood, began a wild and
tumultuous dance, led by the chief Gallus, in which the
devotees, in their frenzy, 'cut themselves after their manner
with knives and lancets', and many of the novices, like the
youth in the poem of Catullus, 'assumed the god', became,
so to speak, each an Attis, and mutilated themselves. The
symbols of fertility were afterwards gathered up and buried
in the earth, where they apparently aided in restoring Attis
to life. All these horrors might be more or less exactly
paralleled in the rites of Artemis of the Ephesians, the
'Syrian goddess', or the Ishtar of Babylon: and the ceremony was a wailing-rite for the dead god, like the well-
known mourning for Tammuz.

Then followed the sudden resurrection, a carnival of joy
and licence, not unlike our own Christmas festival of the
Lord of Misrule. 'The god had risen.' On the next day the
exhausted revellers rested; and on the twenty-seventh of
March, the priests, in solemn procession, went down to the

1. According to others, Christ was *crucified* on the twenty-fifth of March
(A.D. 29), and his resurrection accordingly was fixed on the twenty-
seventh. This is the more curious, as it seems impossible to harmonize
this date with that implied in the Gospels.

river, and washed the image of the god and 'all the pur-
tenance thereof', and returned to their place. The effigy of
the god was kept for one year and then burned.

Alongside of all these ceremonies went a Mystery or
Sacrament. The applicant for admission to the inner circle
of worshippers first fasted and wept with the mourners; he
then ate from a drum and drank from a cymbal, the two
instruments used in the sacred rites. He was then 'baptized'.
He descended into a pit over which there was a grating. On
to this grating a bull was driven, and slain with a consecrated spear. In the blood the neophyte bathed himself and
his garments, and emerged, with all his sins eternally
washed away in the blood of the bull. This blood-bath was
called the 'Taurobolium' – many traces of this rite have
been found in Rome, in Gaul, and in Germany.[1]

That Attis was a vegetation-god – he may of course have
been much besides – seems certain. He was called the 'Very
Fruitful', and is again and again identified with the corn,
which 'falls into the ground and dies', and rises again from
the dead to bear fruit. A statue of him represents him with
ears of corn in his hand, and a cap on his head from which
ears of corn are sprouting: he wears a wreath of pine-cones,
pomegranates, and other fruits. His mother, whether the
virgin Nana or the great goddess Cybele, is a deity of universal fertility: all forms of reproductiveness, human, animal, and vegetable, being under her care. The sowing of
the seed means that it gone down to Hades – therefore
men mourn. Its first sprouting means its return from Hades,
therefore men rejoice. This death and resurrection of the
corn are, of course, so closely allied with the death and resurrection of the sun that they are often confused. Persephone is in Hades at the same time as the corn is under the
earth, and at the same time as the sun is weak. Thor's
hammer is hidden during the winter; he recovers it just
when the thunder-shower is about to break up the clods and
bring forth the fruits.

1. A fuller account may be seen in Frazer, *Adonis, Attis, and Osiris*,
pp. 167–73.

Attis, like Adonis, was a foreign god, and his cult was borrowed. But the Greeks must have recognized that he was but doing the work which some of their own ancestral gods had done from time immemorial. The festival of Hyacinthus had been celebrated in Laconia for perhaps thousands of years before Attis came: and it was celebrated in much the same fashion as the festival of Attis: mourning for the dead god, followed by rejoicing as he rose from the dead and ascended to heaven.

The still more famous worship of Dionysus was also borrowed, but the Greeks took to it with a rapidity which shows how natural it was to them; as indeed some sort of worship of the kind seems natural to all men. Dionysus came in from Thrace, and the Thracians were akin to the Phrygians of Asia Minor, who had their god Sabazius; Sabazius is like Attis; and Attis is like Adonis. When Dionysus came to Greece, he would be recognized as like what the Greeks had known already, except that his worship was wilder and more fanatical than that to which they were accustomed. Dionysus was adored at night-time by women, who wandered in the mountains with torches (the symbols of life) in their hands, and as the strains of music, the intoxication of wine, and the 'crowd-psychology' wrought in them, they went mad with frenzy. They are thus variously called Bacchae, shouters, Maenads, mad-women, or Thyiades, furious ones. In this state of ecstasy, like the devotees of Attis, they not only *saw* the god, but *became* the god: their souls left their bodies and united with the deity. It was these strange rites that Euripides watched with a curious mixture of scepticism and sympathy: and the result was his immortal play the *Bacchae*. Such a union with the god must be symbolized in act: when the frenzy was on them, the women tore to pieces snakes or other animals which were supposed to be the god in visible form; they devoured the flesh and drank the blood, 'which was the life thereof', wrapped themselves in the skins, and pursued the dance until their natural powers could endure no more and they sank down in utter exhaustion to the ground. Euripides noticed the reaction

which followed in the morning, when they realized what
they had been doing. All sorts of myths arose, attempting to
illustrate both the cult itself and the antagonism which it
had aroused in many quarters. Thus one tale tells how
Lycurgus, King of Thrace, had opposed the god, and had
chased him and his 'nurses', that is the Maenads, out of the
country; and how the god took a terrible revenge. The story
of Agāvë, who tore her own son Pentheus to pieces in the
corroboree – the story which Euripides tells in the *Bacchae* –
may be based on a similar opposition and vengeance: but it
is more probably of different origin. Pentheus was the god
himself, torn and eaten by his worshippers: a mistaken reading of the rite led later to his being regarded not as the god
but as the god's enemy, deservedly destroyed. A similar
story tells how Orpheus was in like manner torn to pieces.

As people began to reflect upon such myths and such rites,
a *new* symbolic meaning was attached to them. The gods
had been personifications of natural processes, which, by the
laws of the human mind, could not but be treated as persons. It is probable that, in very early times, philosophical
thought had dwelt on these deities, and had developed a
highly symbolic form of worship, especially for the benefit
of the initiated. This form was known as a Mystery – its
essential doctrines were secret. To the outer world the
myths and the rites remained crude and vulgar; the gods
were worshipped in total ignorance of their origin. But the
Mysteries still went on, and with the growth of general civilization, the Mystery-worship began to be preferred to all
other kinds: it represented so obviously a profounder emotion and a truer religious sense, and answered so clearly to
men's higher desires that for a very long time it was probably by far the highest expression of the Greek attitude towards the divine. We may, I think, detect a *return* to the
mysteries about the fifth century before Christ: and, despite
Christian opposition, they lasted till the fourth century of
our era. The Fathers, to whom we owe much of our knowledge of them, speak of them with horror – partly, doubtless,
because they saw such skilful Satanic imitation of their own

rites: but it is the belief of some that as a matter of fact the borrowing had been on the other side, and that Christianity had been imitating heathenism.[1]

Of the great number of Greek Mysteries the most famous were the Eleusinian, celebrated (at first exclusively) at Eleusis in Attica. So famous were they, indeed, that when we hear in Greek or Latin authors of *The* Mysteries, the Eleusinian are meant. That they had to do with fertility is clear, for they were in honour of Demeter and Persephone, and all the myths which explain their origin speak of them in connexion with a supply of corn to the country.[2] Demeter, wandering over the world in search of her lost daughter, sat exhausted on the stone of Grief at Eleusis (a sort of Baityl), gave the inhabitants corn, and instituted the Mysteries. This gave Eleusis a special sanctity, and, even when Athens became the political head of the country, the little city remained the religious capital. The chief priestesses claimed to be descendants of Eumolpus, an ancient Eleusinian hero; others were 'daughters' of a King Celeus; the third class, the 'Heralds', were also perhaps of Eumolpid descent.

There were the Greater and the Lesser Mysteries: the Lesser, according to the myth, were instituted to allow Heracles, though a stranger, to be initiated as a reward for his services to Athens. At the Lesser, held in 'Flowermonth' or March, the primary initiations took place, and the candidates became 'Mystae'. The Greater were held in September, and lasted nine days. In that month the Mystae

1. In my opinion, this view is erroneous. The Christian Mysteries were retentions of *Eastern* esoteric ceremonies, which Christianity modified in its own sense. But these, being products of natural human instincts, were inevitably *similar* to the Greek, even though the Greek may have arisen independently. The Greeks themselves were struck with the likeness to foreign customs, and some of them held that their Mysteries were derived from Egypt. In similar circumstances, and in parallel stages of thought, different nations develop almost identical systems. There is something, even in Mexican religion, not unlike the Greek Mysteries.

2. Similarly, as we have seen, the introduction of Magna Mater to Rome in time of famine secured an abundant harvest in the following summer.

assembled in Athens: the first day they waited. On the second they went for purification to the sea: on the third they fasted till evening, when they were given a meal of honey-cakes. On the fourth, a second procession took place, in which, as Virgil tells us, there was a wattled crate, of symbolical no-value, containing pomegranates and poppy-seeds (symbols of fertility), which was carried in the 'slow rolling wain of the Eleusinian Mother' (it was drawn by oxen), women following on foot with mystic caskets in their hands. Not till the fifth evening, the 'Day of Torches' (symbols of life), did the Mystae set out for the Temple of Demeter at Eleusis: the following night they spent in prayers and meditations. On the sixth day the statue of Iacchus[1] was carried, bearing a torch in his hand, amid shouts of joy from vast multitudes of followers, said sometimes to exceed thirty thousand. That night, the heralds bade all the 'profane' depart, and the Mystae were initiated into the vision or 'Epopty', the final secret, which they had to take a solemn oath never to disclose: they were then led into the inner shrine, where they were allowed an 'Autopsy' or personal sight, of what none but the Mystae ever saw. No ancient writer tells us what the vision was.[2]

The seventh day was given up to the wildest rejoicings. Everybody abused everybody else, especially at the bridge over the Cephissus on the way back – so much so that 'to bridge' became a common word for 'to insult'. The eighth and ninth days were supplementary – perhaps not originally included. The final ceremony was to fill two small vessels

---

1. Said to be the son of Demeter.

2. Near Lindus, in the island of Rhodes, is an inscription of the age of Hadrian, which shows the conditions on which men might enter the temple which formerly stood there. 'First, they must be pure in hands and heart, and free from consciousness of wrong-doing.' This will remind the reader of Psalm xxiv: 'Who shall ascend the hill of Yahweh? he that hath clean hands and a pure heart.' Then the stone deals with other things, and names the days required before certain pollutions can be wiped out. 'After eating cheese, one day; after abortion, forty days; after family bereavement, forty days.' Here the reader may think of Acts xv.

I owe this note to Moulton's *Religions and Religion*, p. 62.

with water or wine, and dash the liquid, from one vessel to the east, from the other to the west, while the priest uttered words of mystical meaning.

There can be little doubt that all this was a sacred drama, showing forth the story of Demeter; and that the Mystae received some explanations of the symbols seems equally likely. The Fathers dwell upon this dramatic character, and hint at the instructions given to the neophytes. That the Christian Sacrament was also originally a drama of like kind, setting forth the death and resurrection of Christ in vivid and palpable form, and that it too possessed its exoteric and esoteric doctrines, precisely like the Greek religion, is the view of many scholars: but it is not, in my opinion, necessary to assume that the one was directly borrowed from the other. Sacramental religion seems to satisfy the deepest wants of certain minds, in all times and in all places, and probably arose independently, to answer these wants, all over the world. So strongly was this feeling rooted in Greece that the Mysteries survived when the gods in whose honour they were celebrated had, to all intents and purposes, ceased to exist. When the Church obtained power, and began to retaliate on heathenism the persecution she had suffered under it, attempts were made to suppress the Mysteries; but it was not till the sword of Theodosius was called in that they were successful. That great but most fanatical Emperor destroyed them with almost as much vigour as he showed against the heretics.[1]

We have thus seen three kinds, or stages, of Greek religion, which, it is true overlapped each other: a simple nature-worship and hero-worship, based on fear of the dead and of

1. Clement of Alexandria, who in his heathen days had probably been initiated, thus exclaims: 'What patent shamelessness! Of old, night, which drew a veil over the pleasures of the temperate, was a time of silence: but now, when night is for those who are being initiated a temptation to licentiousness, talk abounds, and the torch-fires convict unbridled passions. Quench the fire, thou priest. Shrink from the flaming brands,. torchbearer. The light convicts your Iacchus. Suffer night to hide the Mysteries. Let the orgies be honoured by darkness.' (I quote from F. A. Wright, *History of Later Greek Literature*, p. 315.)

elemental powers; the development of this into a more or less regular and systematic cult of gods recognized as persons of human character and form; a reversion to a mystical interpretation of the lives and deaths of these gods and heroes. But there remains a fourth stage, which in some respects is more like what we know as religion than any of these, and which formed assuredly a preparation for the reception of Christianity by higher minds. This was moral philosophy, which unquestionably took the place of religion with many men for whom the old cults had ceased to have any attraction. Long before Christianity, some of the best men had denounced the stories of the gods as immoral. It was impossible for them, in the absence of any science of comparative religion, to detect the origin of these stories, and to perceive that the myths of the amours of Zeus or the hateful ceremonies of Aphrodite-worship, had sprung from natural causes, and they expressed their loathing pretty plainly. When Euthyphro defended his unfilial conduct by telling Socrates that Cronos had mutilated his father Uranus, Socrates left him in no doubt, despite his ambiguous and ironical language, as to what he thought of the tale. Xenophanes also, rejected all such stories: Euripides put some of them on the stage, and made his heroes utter their opinions of the dubious actions of Apollo and Herē: Plato turned Homer out of his Republic. The defence which Plato puts into the mouth of his master denies that Socrates disbelieved in gods, but to the intelligent his disbelief was vocal enough: Socrates did not believe in the gods of Athenian legend. In spite of the condemnation of the 'atheist', the slow penetration of men's minds went on, and it was the growth of morals that did the work. By the time of Cicero, a hundred years before Christ, hardly a single intellectual man believed in the gods of Greece and Rome, whose official worship, for political purposes, the rulers none the less maintained.

In place of this dead religion the better minds welcomed philosophy, and found in it some consolation. They had plenty of philosophies to choose from; there were almost as many systems in the Roman Empire as there are religions today in the United States. But there were two which stood out above all the rest; the two which Paul found flourishing in Athens while the altars of gods in whom none of them believed crowded every street and met him at every corner. The strength of both lay far less in their theories of the Universe than in their moral appeal.[1]

EPICUREANISM, as represented to us by the great poem of Lucretius, starts with an uncompromising rejection of the common religion, and with a denunciation of the crimes it has urged men to commit. Its object is to *arraign* the ways of gods to men, and to deliver us from our fear of them. It does not in so many words deny their actual existence, but it relegates them to a region where, in total indifference to our joys and sorrows, they enjoy eternal repose. 'If anyone thinks proper to call the sea Neptune and corn Ceres, and chooses rather to misuse the name of Bacchus than to utter the term that belongs to that liquor, let us allow him to declare that the earth is mother of the gods, if only he forbear in earnest to stain his mind with foul religion.'[2]

Nevertheless, Epicureanism was a religion itself. Like other religions, it gave an account of the origin of the world, though it reduced the universe to Atoms and Void, and did not derive it from the fiat of a deity. It has been called a secular Church, with Epicurus as its saviour. Study the nature of things, said he, that you may gain *ataraxia*, serenity of mind; for what we need is not vain opinion, but to pass our lives without alarm. And the worst of alarms is the dread of death. In some of the finest lines ever written, Lucretius girds himself to attack the monstrous fables which have made men think the next world a place of torment, and to reconcile men to a perpetual sleep in which even the

1. When Virgil announced that, so soon as the Aeneid was finished, he would renounce poetry and give himself to philosophy, this was his way of saying that he would devote his last years to religion. He was a Prospero, drowning his book of magic, and retiring to a monastery.

2. 'My dear friend, clear your *mind* of cant. You may *talk* as other people do; but don't *think* foolishly.' Boswell's *Johnson*, 15 May 1783.

world-shaking clash of Rome and Carthage will not disturb them. The river of Acheron is *here*; the rock of Tantalus is nothing but the terrors of the guilty; the vulture of Tityos is the gnawing of conscience. When immortal death has taken away our mortal life, he that no longer *is* can have nothing to fear, nor can it make any difference whether he was ever born or not. As, a hundred years ago, we were not troubled by the convulsions of the world, so a hundred years hence no convulsions will fret us. This being so, it remains to make the best of this life; and that is done by avoiding unnecessary pain. Among unnecessary pains are avarice, ambition, gluttony, and sensual 'pleasure'. 'O purblind race of men,' cries Lucretius, 'who fail to see that there are but two things needful, a body kept free from pain and a mind at ease.' And, said Epicurus, what we need is attainable and what is unattainable we do not need. Pleasure, in this sense of wise passiveness and acquiescence, is the supreme good. Wisdom and self-control will enable us to secure in life a balance of pleasure: courage will enable us to endure with patience the pains that cannot be avoided; and justice will gain for us the goodwill of others.

This was the creed which its enemies, and even its friends in jest, called Porcine. But Epicurus, as has been well said, was no swineherd. His pleasures were noble, and no Stoic ever asked less from life than the founder of this Hedonistic system. Although Epicurus recommended his followers to live hidden from the world – though he insisted on the *personal* character of his gospel – yet, in the inculcation of the pleasures of true friendship, and in the practice of domestic virtues, he showed that he was not blind to social evils and that he knew the way to mitigate them. From Epicureanism the early Christians, though they would not have confessed it, might have learnt much, and did learn something.

Epicurus was an Athenian. His great rival, Zeno, was of Eastern origin, and there is much that is Oriental in his thought. This is why so many of the more liberal Fathers recognized in his system something akin to Christianity, and why some even fancied that the Stoic Seneca might have met St Paul and have borrowed something from him. That STOICISM prepared many minds for Christianity is certain. It came precisely at the right time, when the world had returned to chaos, when men were more than usually doubtful about the morrow, and when the wheel of fortune turned with more than ordinary caprice. Epicurus told men to make the best of it in these bad times: Zeno told them that, rightly understood, pain was no evil; the only evil was to do wrong. Nothing else mattered. Even the slave was free if he did right and served God. And Zeno had seen many thousands of freemen made slaves.

Whereas Epicurus derived the world from Atoms and Void, which, in infinite time, had accidentally made the world we see, the Stoics asserted that the world was contrived by Reason or Logos, the Eternal Fire which 'lives through all life, extends through all extent, spreads undivided, operates unspent', and which is ultimately the same as that which rules the human mind. Thus the same law which regulates the paths of the stars must regulate our lives: the Duty which keeps the ancient heavens fresh and strong must direct the humble actions of man. This Logos had many names – the common people call it Zeus. 'Of thee we are the offspring, and the universe as it rolls willingly obeys thee,' says Cleanthes in the poem which St Paul may have had in mind when speaking at Athens; and in another poem he says, 'Lead me, O Zeus, and Thou, Eternal Fate; thee will I follow unshuddering, and if through weakness I be unwilling to follow, follow will I nevertheless.'

Along with this belief in an ordered government of the world, in a Pronoia or Foresight in the Creator which knew whither the world was going because it *meant* it to move thither, went a kind of cosmopolitanism. The whole universe, as Manilius says, is a republic, ruled over not by chance, but by the order of a God most high:

Sic etiam in magno quaedam respublica mundo est,
Quam natura facit, quae caelo condidit Urbem.

Of that Republic we are citizens, and all men partake its privileges. Everyone of us has two fatherlands, the country in which he happens to be born, and the Empire on which the sun never sets. In that Empire all men join in fellowship, sharing in Reason, which is the law of Nature. It is a passage in which this universal brotherhood is proclaimed, that is specially chosen by a Father of the Church to show that Stoicism was a preparation for Christ.

Pain being no evil, and riches or poverty, kingship or slavery, being things that do not concern the real '*I*', Stoicism had to contend with common feeling, which cannot but regard these 'things indifferent' as matters of very considerable importance: and there can be little doubt that it met the difficulty with a certain amount of sophistry, and some degree of inconsistency. If pain became intolerable (though how what is no evil can ever become such neither Zeno nor his followers explained) you had the right to change your intolerable earthly country for your heavenly, to 'swoon into the infinite', in other words to kill yourself. Scores of Stoics, including Zeno himself, thus swooned away, in 'the high Roman fashion'; when Cato saw that if he lived at all he must live under the unendurable domination of Caesar, he assisted his own passage into the other world; and Brutus did the same when defeated by a second Caesar. Aristotle, the philosopher of common sense, asserted that bodily health was good, prosperity and a competence were good, and a sufficiency of friends was good: Zeno declared that virtue was the only good, and virtue consisted in a good will. In themselves, no *actions* are either good or bad; it is the intention that makes them so. No one who has not attained true virtue *can* have this good will; and hence all have sinned, and come short of the glory of God. One sin is as bad as another: a man one inch below the surface drowns as certainly as at fifty fathoms. This was a conception which the common man found it hard to stomach, and it was justly ridiculed by Horace, the poet of the common man. Zeno himself found it necessary to modify it. There are, he said, *actions* which are 'expedient', things of worth which the practical Stoic finds useful in daily life. This looks at first sight like an anticipation of the Catholic doctrine of two standards – one for the saint and one for the ordinary man; but, in a way which is not fully made clear, Zeno contrived to reconcile it with the theory that good is but one. He held to it that there is but a single absolute canon of right, which is exemplified solely by the *spoudaios* or perfect man; and that there is thus an impassable boundary between the true Stoic and the world.

No religion, in its earlier stages, has ever lost by setting forth a rigid law of excellence; in fact the success of a religion seems to be measured by the sternness with which it forbids things that to the ordinary mind seem innocent or even praiseworthy. Early Christianity, early Calvinism, early Methodism, rejected ornaments in dress, would have nothing to do with dancing, scorned the theatre. Compromise, in all cases, came later. Stoicism showed the same audacity. Believing in another life, it defied the terrors and allurements of the present: and no martyrs have shown greater courage than its adherents in standing up alike against the tyranny of rulers and the more subtle pressure of popular convention. But it made its compromises, which were real and great. Unlike Epicureanism, it accepted the ordinary superstitions, defended the belief in omens, auguries, dreams, and witchcraft; and professed belief in the gods, while for the members of its own Church it had its esoteric and allegorical interpretations of the myths on which the common herd fed so greedily. Something like this is not unknown among ourselves: it means, as a rule, an arithmetical gain but a spiritual loss.

It is impossible to study either the lives or the works of some of these old philosophers without a feeling of intense admiration, mingled, it is true, with occasional surprise or even repugnance. The *Meditations* of Marcus Aurelius, and still more the *Manual* of Epictetus, reveal characters comparable with those of the highest Christian saints – except in one point. There is a certain pride in their virtue, a certain lack of sympathy. The Perfect Man is too perfect; he stands aloof in haughty superiority from the untaught masses. He saves his own soul; other souls he thinks hardly worth saving. There is no touch of that charity which led Paul to cry that he could wish himself accursed if he could thus redeem his people. A Stoic, it has been well said, would tell you in words that all men were brothers; but in act he was the elder brother, and the rest were hopeless prodigals. As we shall see, the charge he brought against Christianity was precisely this, that it killed the fatted calf for the wanderer. He himself drove back his brother to the husks that the swine did eat. The good Emperor says, 'as far as particular individuals interfere with my proper functions, man is to me indifferent, less than sun or wind or beast of the field'; and the noble slave compares wife and child to a shell or a flower picked up by a sailor when he reaches port. Let the captain call you aboard, and you throw the shell aside, run to the ship, and leave the 'things indifferent' behind. There have been Christians like Aurelius and Epictetus; but they have not been true imitators of Christ, who sent his messengers to the highways and hedges and welcomed to the feast the outcasts found there.

None the less, as that great and liberal Christian Father, Clement of Alexandria, was bold enough to say, 'all sects of philosophy contain a germ of truth: Greek philosophy purges the soul and prepares it beforehand for the reception of faith, on which Truth builds up the edifice of Knowledge.'

CHAPTER 5

GERMANIC RELIGION

ALL religions, in their early stages, are confused and self-contradictory; the powers of one god are constantly annexed by another, and a deity is now omnipotent and now almost contemptibly feeble; now he rules all others and now is ruled by them. Few religions, however, have come down to us in a more confused state than that, or those, of our own Germanic ancestors; and the reason is that no great teacher came to compel the creeds and cults into something like unity, and to lend them a philosophic character.

We owe our knowledge, such as it is, to Roman and Greek historians, like Caesar, Tacitus, Procopius, Jordanes, but above all to the great Icelandic writer Snorri Sturluson, who, living in the twelfth century, came just soon enough to collect, in the so-called *Edda*, the popular myths before they were modified out of recognition by Christianity, and to Bishop Saemund, who gathered the early epics and other poems into what is known as the *Elder Edda*. Scattered fragments of myth, unearthed from all parts of the Germanic world, and amounting in the total to an enormous mass, have been patiently sifted and analysed by a whole army of scholars; and many of the stories are now so easily accessible that they are told to our children in the schools.

The general characteristics of this religion are those common to all mythologies that have arisen by popular reflection on natural phenomena; but the fear which lies at the root of all such reflection has been strangely crossed by the courage which is so marked a feature of the race. There is also, as might be expected, a conspicuous lack of the sort of metaphysics which we find, for example, in Hinduism; all, or nearly all, is concrete material, and crudely anthropomorphic. The gods are often actually called men, and there are few signs of the worship of abstractions like

Concord, Fortune, or Wealth. The ghosts are walking corpses, solid and tangible; and Fate or Weird herself, the goddess whose presence was everywhere felt, is less a principle than a stubborn and unconquerable virago. War, which the tribes understood thoroughly, is personified as a band of furiously riding maidens, 'Choosers of the Slain'.

The cosmogony is obviously based on the physical nature of the home of the race. Towards the north, the universal abode of demons in our hemisphere, lay Niflheim, the home of cloud; to the south Muspelheim, the Bright Home. Out of Niflheim rose Hwergelmir, the Boiling Cauldron, and the icy streams called Elivagar. By some means, vaguely hinted, there arose the Aesir, or gods: these separated day from night, and harnessed the horse Ar-vakr (Early-waker) to his chariot; the maiden Sol, or the Sun, was the driver; behind her, ever pursuing, was the boy Mani, or the Moon.

Gradually grew up the Ash of Yggdrasill, the World-Tree. Its highest point overshadowed Valhalla, the Hall of the Slain; its roots reached, through Midgard, where men dwelt, to Jotunheim, the realm of the Giants, to the kingdom of Hel, the goddess of the Lower World. The Aesir lived in Asgard, a place not definitely fixed but apparently not in the highest branches of the Ash of Yggdrasill: there are myths which seem to indicate that it could be reached without leaving Midgard. Somewhere in Midgard dwelt also the Vanes, another band of gods, who at one time were at war with the Aesir. A peace, however, was made, and the Vane god Njord was given to the Aesir, the Aesir-god Hoenir to the Vanes. It is not impossible that we have here an adumbration of some compromise between Scandinavians and Finns: but no certainty is attainable.

In Asgard, according to Snorri, dwelt twelve gods and eight Asynjur or goddesses: but here we seem to have an attempt at precision where precision was impossible. We hear of other gods beside these, and some of the twelve are very dimly conceived. We shall give here a sketch of the functions of the more important gods only.

In Tacitus we are told that the chief deity was Mercury,

who must be Woden or Odin, whom we still commemorate on Wednesday (Mercredi): but the likeness to the Roman god is not very close. Odin, whatever the derivation of the name,[1] seems to have been adopted from another race, and to be primarily an air-god; but he has of course a multitude of other characters, which have to some extent eclipsed his original features. He is a bard and the god of bards; he gives oracles, and is the inspirer of learning: he is thus, so far, rather Apollo than Mercury. As All-Father, he is a Jupiter, the maker of mankind; as Gautr he is the maker of the world: he has scores of other names, each of which emphasizes some act or function in which he is concerned. He is usually pictured as an old man, tall, one-eyed,[2] and mighty, clothed in a blue mantle, with his hat drawn far over his eyes. He carries the spear Gungnir, and rides furiously in his 'Wild Hunt' (as he still does in some places today) on his eight-footed steed Sleipnir, the Slipper or Runner. From his seat on Hlidskialf he gazes all over the world: two ravens, Huginn and Muninn, Thought and Memory, fly hither and thither to bring him news. Through them he can learn all things; yet he often sets out to explore for himself. As Guest or as Grimnir the Hooded, or as Vegtamur the Way-worn, he visits men and discovers their ways. In the form of a snake he penetrates the stronghold of Suttung, the giant who guards the cauldron Odrerir in which is the draught of wisdom.[3] He seeks the well of Mimir, to gain knowledge of the future, and purchases it by giving up one of his eyes. This knowledge he locks up in runes or sacred letters; and these runes enable him to teach men science, or magic spells; it is through them that he even remembers the long list of his own names. It is by the knowledge won from Mimir that he foretells Ragnarök, the Twilight of the Gods, in which the Fire-demon Surt will rush upon the world, and

1. Some compare *vates*, a seer: others, more probably, connect the word with the root *wa*, to blow, whence our *wind*.

2. He is thus like Polyphemus, the Sun.

3. So Indra, in the Vedas, disguises himself as a hawk, and brings to the gods the soma-juice of knowledge.

the elements will melt with fervent heat. Hence his care for warriors. Whom he loves he kills, that they may be ready to help him in the great battle with the demons on Vigrid's Plain; he sends forth his Valkyries to 'choose' them, and when they have fallen they feast with him in Valhalla, the Hall of the Slain, till the great day. Sometimes he fights himself, with the same end. He breaks the sword of Sigmund, and slays him, for he needs him in the battle; he slays Harald Hilditonn, because he loves him; and when Eric Blood-axe falls, he rises from his throne to welcome him as a recruit for his army of Einherjar, or chosen warriors. More strange still, he 'gives himself to himself'; he hangs nine nights on the gallows, wounded by the spear. Though he dies in the last battle, he still lives; men have seen him on his horse rushing through the woods, with the Choosers of the Slain following him, and the Einherjar at his side.

Second to Odin, if second, is Thor, the strongest of the Aesir, whom we still remember on Thursdays. He was identified with Jupiter, as his name, Thunder, clearly suggested. He is the special deity of the Norsemen, more so than Odin himself: and the number of personal names beginning with Thor is nothing less than bewildering. He is a mighty warrior: but his special function is to watch over the household and the crops; hence the care, by naming children after him, to secure his friendship. He was gentle to those who worshipped him. Even his terrible hammer, Mjollnir the Miller or Crusher, betokens less the destroying bolt than the beneficent thunder-shower. At marriages the hammer consecrates the bond: boundaries are still seen marked by the hammer which Christianity, when she displaced the old religion, skilfully transformed into the cross.[1] His sons are, it is true, Magni and Modi, Strength and Courage; but his regular attendants are Thjalfi and Roskva, Delver and Ripener. He is the chief god of the husbandman, and the favourer of the common people. If we could go back beyond our records, we should probably find that he was the chief

1. Compare the swastika of Hinduism, which, at least in later days, represents the bolt with which Vishnu slew the demons.

god of the Norseman, accommodated into Asgard by the simple device of making him Odin's son when that god arrived in the land.

'None,' says Snorri, 'is so wise as to tell all Thor's mighty works.' We need not repeat here the story of his adventure with Utgarda-Loki, told once for all by Carlyle, nor the tale of Thrym's theft of the hammer and its recovery. The eight leagues below the earth where Thrym has hidden it obviously mean the eight months' winter of the Far North; and the slaying of the giants betokens the breaking of the ice in summer; but Thor has many other characters. He rows out with Hymir the giant to capture the Midgard's serpent which holds the world together; this *may* signify that he is sometimes the cause of mighty cataclysms. He brings back Orwandill from Jotunheim in a basket, but Orwandill's toe freezes; he breaks it off and throws it into the sky, where it still is, our Morning Star.[1] His wife is Sif, whose hair Loki cut off: whereupon Thor compelled him to get new golden hair for her from the dwarfs; this is plainly the golden corn of harvest. Like Odin, he lived long after the 'White Christ' came to the North. When Olaf Tryggvason was exercising his rowers in his great ship the Long Serpent, he saw a solitary sailor in a boat. He bade his oarsmen pursue him. After a long chase they overtook the boat, and saw that the rower was Thor. 'Had my brother been with me,' said Thor, 'you would never have caught me'; dashed his foot through the bottom of the boat, and sank from sight. When the Icelander Thorgisl forsook him for Christ, the god plagued him and bruised him, even pursuing him all the way to Greenland in the form of an auk. Nothing, in fact, is more needful to remember than that, to our ancestors, even after they embraced Christianity, the old gods were real. All that had happened was that Christ was a stronger warrior. Slowly the gods faded into demons, fairies, or pixies: but many

1. Orwandill is mysterious. In other legends he appears as the father of Hamlet, who seems to have been originally a sea-god. The connexion is not obvious. In our early Christian poetry 'Earendel' or the Morning Star is used as a symbol of Christ.

of the tales attached to them were annexed by saints or angels.

A god who has apparently come down in the world is Tiw. If it be true that his name is the equivalent of Zeus or Jupiter, he will have been a sky-god, and may once have been supreme. The myths largely ignore him, and his past glory has to be gathered from the *kennings* or periphrases so common in Germanic poetry. *Tir*, renown, is constantly used for warlike fame: the Apostles, in our early Christian epics, are called *Tir-eadige haeleth*, Tiw-glorious heroes. In some tribes the very name appears to have been forgotten, and the descriptive title Dings (god of the Thing or Assembly) has taken its place; hence the German Dienstag for our Tuesday. We can however detect that he was not only a sky-god, but a god of war. A statue discovered in 1883 represents him as a warrior, with helm, spear, and shield. His rune was engraved on the sword, and brought certain success; thus, when the sword fell into the hands of Attila, that 'scourge of God' became invincible.

In contest with the horrible Fenris-Wolf, Tiw lost his right hand, thus postponing, but not averting, the Last Battle. The wolf is bound with the chain Gleipnir, made of the footfall of cats, the beards of women, the roots of mountains, and the breath of fish; but the chain will break and the wolf will escape: then Tiw will fight with the dog Garm, and both will perish.

All the gods are enigmatical, but Loki is an insoluble riddle. He is the Satan of Northern mythology – indeed some think he has borrowed some features from that Christian devil. He is the cause of evil, the murderer of Balder, the father of the Fenris-Wolf and other monsters, the master of treasons and lies. It is he that brings about the Twilight of the Gods. Yet he is also at times the companion and friend of Thor and Odin. In his proper form he is of transcendent beauty; but he loves to take all sorts of bestial shapes: he is now a god, now a giant, and is equally at home in Asgard and in Jotunheim. Hel is his daughter, and the World-Serpent his son. He penetrates unbidden into the feasting-hall of the gods, and mocks them one and all in his 'senna' or jeering. In revenge they capture him, and bind him with chains, under the dripping of poison. His wife Sigyn catches the poison in a bowl, but every time the bowl is full and she has to empty it, he groans with agony and strives to turn: thence arise terrible earthquakes. Yet it is he who saves the gods from the machinations of a giant who, for the promise of the sun, the moon and the goddess Freyja, offers to build the walls of Asgard by the first day of summer. All but the gate is finished, but just in time the craft of Loki prevents the accomplishment of the fatal task. He obtains the spear Gungnir from the dwarfs for Odin, and the wonder-ship *Skidbladnir* for Frey. Yet he slays the herald of the sea-god Aegir, and the list of his crimes is interminable. He remains a riddle; and that our ancestors also were at a loss to understand him is shown by the fact that, like Belial, he had no altars and no worship.

Frey is the special god of the Swedes: under the name Ing he appears as the ancestor of a royal line. There is, however, some obscurity about him. The word Frey is descriptive; it means 'Lord', and may have taken the place of another name. Some think he is Tiw; others, with more probability, identify him with Njord. But here again there is difficulty. Tacitus tells us of a *goddess* called Nerthus or Earth, who is worshipped by seven tribes descended from Ing. But Njord is a god, and a sea-god, dwelling in Noa-tun, the place of ships. His wife is the Finnish maiden Skadi, who was allowed to choose any god she pleased, on condition she saw their feet only. She was thus deceived into choosing Njord instead of Balder. As we have seen, Njord is one of the Vanir, and seems to have been a god imported from some non-Germanic tribe. As we know him later, he is a God of fruitfulness.

The story of Balder is one of the most familiar in the world. He appears in Snorri as a full god, son of Odin, and beloved of all. He is fair as the flower called Balder's brow. All his judgements are just, everything about him beautiful. But Fate hangs over him; he dreams of approaching death.

His mother, Frigg, goes round to all created things, and exacts a vow that none will harm him. Thenceforward it is the sport of the gods to aim darts at his invulnerable breast. But Loki is displeased. He goes to Frigg and asks her if *all* things have sworn to spare Balder. 'All but the mistletoe,' says she; 'her I deemed too weak.' Then Loki went, and put the mistletoe in the hand of the blind god Hodr, who shot, and Balder fell dead: 'and that was the greatest grief that ever happened to gods or men'. But for the 'grith' or peace of the time, the gods would have taken vengeance on Loki. One thing alone is possible: if all things will weep for him, Hel will give him back. All things weep, men, animals, stones, and plants, 'even as it is seen when things come out of cold to heat'. But the giantess Thokk, who is Loki in disguise, says she will 'weep with dry eyes'; and thus Balder, and Nanna his wife, who refused to survive him, remain in Hel's abode.

As this exquisite tale stands in Snorri, the element of nature-myth is plain to see, and the admixture of Christian traits have been discerned by some. As told by Saxo Grammaticus, the Danish historian from whom, at second or third hand, Shakespeare derived the legendary basis of *Hamlet*, it is an ordinary story of a strife between two heroes, rivals for the hand of Nanna, with the usual apparatus of magic foods and supernatural aids. Which is the earlier form would be hard to decide.

Other gods are scarcely more than names to us. Hoenir, who may be Tiw, is fleet of foot, but so dull of mind that when the Aesir make their composition with the Vanes, he is reckoned as no fair exchange for Njord, and the giant Mimir is thrown in with him. Ullr, a genuine Swedish god, hardly appears in the myths; he is best known to us from the monuments, in which he is represented as standing on skates or snow-shoes. He dwells in the Dale of Bows, and presides over war and the chase. Vidar and Vali are two sons of Odin: Vidar avenges his father after the great battle by slaying the Fenris-Wolf. Vali, as we learn from an early poem, is born immediately after the death of Balder, and, before he is a day old, accomplishes the vengeance: 'hands he washed not, head he combed not, till Balder's foe to the pyre he bore' – a hint, apparently, that in one form of the myth Hodr was a willing slayer. Bragi is the god of poetry, but there is some reason to believe that he was originally a human bard, transformed into a deity, and borrowing some of the functions of Odin. Hermod we know almost exclusively as the god sent down the nine-days' journey to the abode of Hel in order to plead for the return of Balder. Many of the gods seem to be mere personifications – the nearest approaches to abstraction our ancestors made. Thus Modi and Magni are the sons of the mighty Thor – the Kratos and Bia (Strength and Force) of our mythology. Vili and Ve, Odin's brothers, seem to be similar allegories; and Forseti, the son of Balder, though reckoned by Snorri among the foremost twelve, may be nothing but Law or Justice, a sort of male Themis – one perhaps, of Odin's aspects.

The goddesses are not sharply discriminated in the records that remain to us: their names are many, but their natures are few. To put it somewhat loosely, they are the visitors of houses, and the teachers of household arts, such as spinning or weaving or tending the hearth: though of course, as in all religions, they are the deities of beauty and of love. We hear, in the *Germania* of Tacitus, of several not known from other sources; he speaks of Nerthus (Mother Earth), who may, as we have seen, be allied to Njord, of a Swabian 'Isis', of Tamfana, and of Baduhenna. Others are known to us from inscriptions; such are Sunna and Sandraudiga, as well as the Netherland Nehalennia. In folklore we learn of Bertha, the goddess of spinning, with her train of children who have died young, and of the little girl who follows her with a pitcher of tears. Still more famous is Holda, the 'Frau Holle' of Grimms' *Fairy Tales*. In the Twelve Nights she rides through the air like Odin; when it snows, she is making her bed and the feathers are flying; when it rains, she is washing her veil. Some of her functions have been transferred to witches, others to the Virgin Mary.

The chief goddess is Frigg, the wife of Odin: but she

seems later to have been confused with Freyja, the sister of
Frey. Frigg knows the future, and Odin consults her as to
coming events: she weeps beforehand for the death of
Balder. Perhaps she was once the heroine of the great neck-
lace-myth, which was afterwards assigned to Freyja. Four
dwarfs had made the Brising necklace, and Freyja, to gain
possession of it, surrendered herself to each in turn. Scarcely
had she received it when Loki stole it, and when Odin recovered it and gave it back to her, it was to be kept only as
long as the two kings on Ha-ey should continue fighting.[1]
Freyja has other treasures – the magic dress of eagles'
feathers, which gives the speed of winds, the chariot drawn
by cats, and tears of gold. In many respects she is the
Aphrodite of the North; she presides over love, and is the
fairest of all the denizens of Asgard. But she also rules over
war, and Odin gives her a half-share in the heroes that fall in
battle.

Of other goddesses we know many names but little besides.
Poets compare their lovers to Eir, Gefu, and Lofn: we hear
of Gifjon, who may be the same as Geofon, the Old English
ocean-goddess; and of Idun, the wife of Bragi, Snorri tells a
story, mingled of grotesquesness and beauty, the interpretation of which will probably occupy scholars till Ragnarök. Hel, the pale queen of the lower world, receives the
souls of all who do not die in battle. In the story of Balder
we are told of Hermod's ride to rescue him from Hel's
dominion: 'nine nights he rode till he came to the river
Gjoll, and rode over Gjoll-bridge; that bridge is covered
with bright gold. Modgud is the maiden named that guards
the bridge.' Not even a god could look on the face of Hel.
Her hall is Misery, her dish Hunger, her knife Greed; Idle-
ness was the name of her man, Sloth of her maid, Ruin of
her threshold, Sorrow of her bed, and Fire of her curtains.

---

1. They fight all day till all are slain, and are raised to life every morning by Hilda's enchantments: the everlasting battle goes on till Ragnarök. This is clearly a myth of day and night: the Brising necklace is the
sun. In *this* instance Loki seems to represent eclipse. The Brising necklace
is referred to in *Beowulf*, 1195, as 'carried off to the bright burg'.

In Hwergelmir, the roaring cauldron, the dragon Nidhogg devours the corpses of evildoers. In front of her dwelling stands the hound Garm, from whose jaws the blood drips as he snarls at the pilgrims from the upper world.

But it would be a mistake to assume that the sole, or even the chief, objects of fear and worship were the great deities. As in all nations, the witches, the demons, the dwarfs, were omnipresent, and demanded to be appeased. Tacitus tells us of the wise woman Veleda, who stirred up Civilis to revolt against Rome, and was regarded as a goddess. To Thorgerd Holgabrud, the terrible Earl Hacon built a temple, and prayed with tears; yet she was hardly more than a sorceress. The Valkyries, who chose the slain for Odin, are often almost human, though invisible and mighty. The elves cause side-ache or stitch, and are ever-present: and the dwarfs, though they can be made to work for men, may, if offended, lay a curse upon the instrument they have made that will work through generations. The giants, though Thor has slain them, still live and stride from fell to fell. Luckily, they are usually stupid, and can be circumvented with a little cunning.

Of the sea-gods, Aegir seems to be the most powerful: he may, on the whole, represent the sea in its kindly aspect. His wife Ran, however, is the sea as the handmaid of death. In her net, spread round a sinking ship, she drags the sailors to doom. Their nine daughters, Bylgja, Kolga, and the rest, are the billows.

Our ancestors were fatalists. A man's destiny was settled long before his birth by the three Norns – Urd, the Past; Verdandi, the Becoming or Present; and Skuld, the Future. Weird, or Fate, cannot be altered. Many a time a warrior escapes from almost certain death because it is not the will of Weird that he shall die: on the other hand, when his time comes, he must submit. A curse laid on a sword by the dwarfs that made it brings ill luck to the owner, and even compels him to do 'nithing's work', scoundrelly deeds, with it. Yet Weird could be controlled by spells. In Egil's Saga, Egil erects a nid-stang or spite-stake against his enemy Eric

Blood-axe, and it does not fail of its effect. To set up a horse's head so as to point in the direction of an enemy's army would ensure evil to it, as to throw a spear over it was to give it to Odin. Runes, properly spoken or carved, could bring good or harm as desired. The art of the physician was still the art of the sorcerer; nor is the draught of forgetfulness which made Tristram forget Isolt and Sigurd desert Brunhild to be distinguished from the healing medicines which occur so often in the sagas. When false runes, graven on the gills of fish, failed to cure a sick girl, Egil came along, and, by changing the false runes to true, saved her life.

The form of witchcraft called *seidr* has attracted special attention, for it seems to be peculiar to Norseland. It is usually employed for bad ends, but sometimes for good: it is ascribed to Odin, and Gullveig the thrice-born and thrice-burnt virgin. The seidrman or woman sat on a high seat, accompanied by singers who chanted 'warlock-songs' to draw down the prophetic power.[1] We hear of a seidr-woman named Heid who had thirty such attendants. In the Saga of Eric the Red (so well known as the saga which tells the story of the Norse discovery of America) there is a full description of the ceremony. Thorbjorg was a 'spa-woman' or prophetess, the last survivor of ten sisters: she was called the Little Volva or Sibyl. As there was a famine in the land, the chief bade her to his house. Every man gave her greetings, 'but she took every man's greetings according as he was agreeable to her'. In the evening, after the meal, she said she must yet sleep a night in the place: and afterwards, when the time had come for her to perform the seidr, Gudrid sang the warlock-song, which drew the spirits down to hear it, so that the spa-woman could see many things that before were hidden. Thus inspired, she foretold that the famine would not last, and that the harvest would be good, 'and the sickness which hath lain upon you shall mend rather sooner than later'.

To detect a murderer, lots were drawn, as Joshua drew

[1] Compare the story of Elisha, who called for a minstrel with the same purpose (2 Kings iii, 15).

them for Achan; bird-omens were understood, and the future was learnt (as by the Persian lords in Herodotus) by the neighings of milk-white horses. But perhaps the chief omen was the dream. Scarcely a saga is without its apparatus of prophetic dreams; indeed, such an apparatus came to be regarded as a necessary element in a story, and the saga-man, if the tale came to him without it, inserted it to lend his work the due literary flavour.

The Germanic ideas as to the spirit-world follow the usual lines. The soul is a thin material body, sometimes air, sometimes flame. The dead still live, in a fashion. The old Celtic legend tells how, when they were ferried over from Brittany to Cornwall, the boat sank to the gunwale with the weight; when it returned empty, it stood high from the waves. The dead reside, more or less conscious, in the howes and barrows: when Odd of Tongue was dying, he bade his kin 'Flit him up to Skaney-fell after he was dead, for he wished still to look down upon the whole Tongue; and it was done even as he commanded.' Gunnar of Lithend, the hero of Njal's Saga, was heard singing a song in his house. Thorolf had such regard for a certain fell that he made it holy, and trusted that he and his house should 'die into it'; and so it was; for when his son Thorstein was drowned, a shepherd saw him marching towards the fell, which opened to receive him, and a voice was heard saying that Thorstein must sit on the high seat over against his father.

The soul might appear in another manner as a man's *fylgja* or fetch. As a rule the soul dwells in the body, but it may be descried apart from it. If thus descried, it portended calamity, especially if a man saw his own. It might even take another form, and appear as an animal. In this form it would be called a *hamingja* or disguise: it might be regarded as a sort of astral body disguising the physical one. There are many instances of the transformation (usually of this kind) of men into animals: werwolves, vampires, and aftergangers are common features in half the old stories. Storolf and Dufthak were transformed into a bear and a bull, and fought fiercely at night in those shapes: next day, in human form, they were found maimed and exhausted. The well-known Glam, in Gretti's Saga, was a demon that had possessed itself of the body of a dead man.

Of actual transmigration there are few traces; but in the early legends there are accounts of rebirths. Helgi Hundingsbane is born again at least twice: St Olaf was said to be an ancient king reborn: and it is just possible that Beowulf was a reincarnation of the old hero Beowa.[1]

Of spirits presiding over families and households (something like the genii of the Romans) we find many traces. There was a stone at Gillwater which the whole family held in reverence, for an *armann* or genius dwelt therein, until the spirit was overcome by the spell of the Cross, and fled to his confine. The family, like the individual member, had its fetch, which watched over it, and was jealous when the White Christ or a saint came to take its place.

Of the cosmogony of our ancestors (which is closely bound up with their eschatology) the best account is that found in the great poem called the Voluspa or Prophecy of the Sibyl. Unluckily, the poem is very difficult: scholars dispute as to the order in which its stanzas are to be read, as to which lines are corrupt, and as to the correct emendations of the corruptions. More important, they differ as to how far the poem, especially in its account of the Last Things, has been touched by Christian influences. There are striking parallels to the Babylonian cosmogony – are these accidental, or was there some obscure path by which the Babylonian myth was carried to Scandinavia? Such as the poem is, I give here a hasty abridgement of it.

Sitting in the midst of the Assembly of the Gods, the Volva tells of the origin of things. In the beginning there was naught, neither sea nor earth nor heaven; only Gin-

1. The separability of the soul is well illustrated by a story in Vatnsdaela Saga. When Ingimund was about to change his home, he shut up three Finns in a room (the Finns, to the Scandinavians, were the chief of sorcerers). The Finns sent their souls on a journey, and when they returned described the place they had seen. Ingimund went in search of it, found the exact spot in Vatnsdale, and settled there.

nunggap, the Yawning Void, and the giant Ymir. Then the sons of Bor drew Midgard out of the chaos, and the Sun appeared out of the south, but the sun knew not her home, nor the Moon his dominion, nor the Stars their place. Then the gods established Morn, Noon, and Evening, and called them by their names, that the seasons might be duly counted. After that they met in the plain of Ida, built themselves palaces, and lived in bliss, playing at tables nor lacking gold. But then came three Thurs-maidens (giantesses), loathsome of aspect, and the happy age was over; evil entered and war began.

Ymir was slain by Odin, Vili, and Ve: out of his blood they made the sea, out of his flesh the earth, out of his bones the rocks, and out of his skull the cavity of heaven. Then they took counsel, and fashioned many dwarfs that dwell beneath the earth; these in their turn made images of men. Two of these images the gods chose, and made the first man and woman, Ask and Embla, ash and alder. Breath had they not, nor speech, nor feelings: Odin gave breath, Hoenir feeling, and Lodur (is this Loki?) speech and fair hues.

To this poet, then, the universe is eternal; the gods are its shapers, not its makers; it has been before them and will survive them. As has been said, they stand, not at the beginning of creation, but at the beginning of history.

It is to them we owe the division of the world into Asgard, Midgard, and Outgard, the home of giants and monsters. Around Midgard, as in Homer, runs the Ocean-stream, wherein lies Jormundgandr, the great dragon (the Rahab of Hebrew myth), whom Thor once or twice nearly lifted from his lair. Had he done so, the earth would have flown asunder. Far in the north-east, on the edge of ocean, lies Jotunheim, the abode of the giants. Over all extend the branches of the evergreen ash, on which Odin once hung as a sacrifice, 'himself to himself'; hence it is called the Ash of Yggdrasill, the Ash of the Gallows of Odin. At the foot lies a fountain by which the Norns have their abode, and from the waters of which (by the usual hydromancy) they forecast the fates of men. Close by is the Place of Judgement, where the gods assemble to decide cases of justice and order. The three roots reach to the realms of gods, men, and giants, nay, to the dwelling of Hel. A squirrel runs ever up and down the tree, striving to create enmity between the eagle that sits on the top and the dragon lurking at the foot. Every day the Norns water the tree from their fountain, whence came dews and rivers over the earth.

In the realm of Hel lives the dragon Nidhogg, and the Fenris-Wolf, who at the last day shall slay even Odin. It is that last day, ever impending, drawing ever nearer, that is the one drop of misery in the cup of the gods. Ragnarök is always before their eyes. Vain is it to chain Loki beneath the dropping venom, vain to choose the valiant from the battle: the kingdom of darkness is at hand: it is the last hour.

Fearful is that winter: Odin, who knows all things, trembles on his high seat; the cock Gold-comb crows loud; the Einherjar rise from sleep; the hell-hound Garm begins to howl. Strange times come; brother betrays brother, families are divided. Heimdall blows his horn, and the whole universe rocks on its axis. The World-Tree shivers, dwarfs groan in their caves, the powers of evil break their chains. A wolf devours the sun, another the moon, and the stars fall from heaven. Earth shakes, for the great serpent is stirring; the Fenris-Wolf has broken loose. The dread ship *Naglfarr* sails the sea, built of the nails of corpses. Loki leads from the north the ice-giants and the hosts of Hel; Surt, the fire-demon, brandishes his flaming sword; Odin falls before the Fenris-Wolf; Thor before Jormungandr; Frey before Surt. The Vigrid plain is covered with the corpses of gods, the race of men vanishes, and earth herself sinks beneath the sea. To all this rings the refrain, 'Fiercely bays Garm before the cave of the Rock; the chain is broken and the Wolf ranges free.'

But from all this rises a new heaven and a new earth. 'Lo, I see,' cries the Sibyl, 'another vision; earth upstarts from the sea, green and fresh; the eagle, fisher of the waterfalls, flies overhead. Again the gods meet on Ida-plain; they remember the great decrees, and the runes of Fimbul-Tyr (the mysterious god). Golden tables will be found in the grass, such as they had of yore. Unsown the fields yield their increase; bale shall turn to bliss. Balder shall return, and he with Hodr, reconciled at last, shall dwell in the glorious home of Odin. Know ye yet or what?'

When the flames of Surt have ceased to burn, and the waters of Aegir to toss, Resurrection comes, calm and fair. A new race of men appears, born of Lif and Lifthrasir, who, hidden in the world-tree, have escaped the ruin, and have nourished themselves on morning-dew. Another sun, not less fair than her mother, is seen in heaven. 'Then shall Hoenir choose the rods of divination, and the sons of the Two Brethren shall dwell in Windhelm. Know ye yet or what?'

The Sibyl then turns to describe the doom of the righteous and of the wicked, in verses which, whether themselves borrowed from Christianity or not, supplied figures and *kennings* to later Christian poets when elaborating their pictures of heaven and hell. 'I know a hall that stands fairer than the sun, roofed with gold, on the Lea of Gems; there shall the righteous dwell and for ever enjoy their bliss. Northward on the Hill of Darkness stands a hall of gold for the race of Sindri (the Dwarfs) and another on Un-cold, the drinking-hall of the Jotun, and its name is Brimir. Far from the sun, on the Strand of Corpses, I see a hall whose doors face northward.[1] Poison-drops fall through its roof, and the roof is thatched with adders. A river flows from the east through Venom-Dale, and its waves are knives and swords: Slid is the name of the river. There shall perjurers and murderers wade through stubborn streams, along with those who have betrayed another's wife: the serpent Nidhogg sucks the corpses, and a wolf devours them. Know ye yet or

---

1. From the north, in all mythologies of our hemisphere came all evils, and in the north dwell the demons. We may compare the passage in Isaiah xiv, so admirably used by Milton, where the 'Son of the Morning' sets up his throne upon the Mount of the Congregation in the uttermost parts of the north.

what? The fiery Nidhogg comes flying from the Hill of Darkness, bearing corpses on his wings.'

With these words the Sibyl sinks into silence, leaving us with many questions to ask. Did she speak of herself, or did she borrow something from the seer of Patmos? Is the hall of the Jotun the origin of the tradition that Satan's seat is on the northern hill, or did that tradition give rise to the Sibyl's words? These and many like problems call aloud for solution, but will probably remain unsolved. Such difficulties confront us everywhere. *Beowulf*, for example, has most certainly been interpolated by Christian scribes, and when once such an influence has been recognized, one can rarely be sure that any part of the work is entirely untouched by it.

To draw a rough comparison, the period to which our thousand years of Teutonic growth are most similar is that which we conveniently call the 'heroic age' of Greece. We do not know how far our one authority, Homer, has been overlaid by later accretions; nor do we know how far Homer himself is describing any one age: we do not know whether he was idealizing his own, or whether he was mingling together a confused medley of traditions of former times. But, roughly, the parallel holds. Odin is not unlike Zeus, as Gunnar is not unlike Achilles; Thor is a nobler Ares, Njal a nobler Nestor.

The parallel holds in other respects also. It has often been noticed that to the Greeks there was little connexion between religion and morality. So in the Germanic world. Tacitus draws a most engaging picture (perhaps inspired by the wish to satirize the Rome of his time) of the simple morality of the tribes of Germania. To be faithful to their chief, to vie with one another in valour, to tell the truth, and to be chaste, these were the virtues of the Germans. But none of them has a religious sanction (unless we assume that Voluspa was original and very ancient). The gods, in fact, were not distinguished for truth-telling or for chastity, and even in bravery they were surpassed by their worshippers. Criminals, it is true, were sacrificed to the gods; but this was not because the gods hated crime as such; it was because punishment was a tribal act, and its tribal character could be symbolized only by performing it to the tribal god. War, drinking, singing, and revelry were all in this sense religious – they were the doings of the tribe as a whole, and the god welcomed war and drunkenness on that account. The god *was* the tribe; he defended the tribe in the Thing or assembly, and led it when it became a Heer or army. He avenged all offences against the *frith* or peace of the Thing-tide, and all breaches of camp-discipline. So far he is a moral being, but so far only.

Vastly superior to the gods are the heroes. As Achilles, with his detestation of falsehood, is higher than Zeus or Ares, so a Sigurd or a Beowulf is higher than Odin or Frey. In such men, with all their faults, we can discern the germs of that chivalry which softened the horrors of the Middle Ages, and deserved something of the glowing eulogy of Burke. The sense of an irresistible fate, so far from crushing their spirits, raised them to a dauntless nobility. To die laughing, like Ragnar Lodbrok, to welcome the sword, like the Vikings of Jomsborg – this is the 'high calling' of men. To tell the truth marks them as it did the Ancient Persians. It has been noticed that in the old Saga of Amleth (Hamlet), the hunted prince, with all his craft, never tells an actual lie. His very equivocations – a trait wonderfully caught by Shakespeare – are verbally true.

Much of the homely morals of the Norsemen may be gathered from that remarkable collection of proverbs called the Hava-mal, or Speech of the High One (Odin) – a collection not unworthy to be compared with the Proverbs of Solomon. I give here a few, to which the reader will at once supply the Hebrew parallels.

'The flocks know their folding-time, but a fool never knows the measure of his appetite.'

'Better burden beareth no man abroad than wisdom; better is it than wealth in a strange place.'

'Better is one's own home, though it be but a cottage; strong is every man in his own home.'

'Too soon came I to one man's house, too late to another's: the ale was drunk at the one, and not yet brewed at
the other. He that is unwelcome is never exact to time.'

'Long is the path to an ill friend, though he live close by;
to a good friend the ways are short though he live far off.'

'As brand kindles brand, so through speech man draws
near to man.'

'A fool lieth awake all night thinking of all things: weary
is he when morning cometh, and his troubles are none the
better.'

'No one can tell a fool till the fool opens his mouth.'

'Middling wise should each man be, never wise in excess;
for the heart of a truly wise man is seldom glad.'

'Stay not in the same house long, but go; for love turns
to loathing if a man stays long on another's floor.'

'Bandy not words with fools, for ill is thy reward from an
ill man's mouth.'

'Laugh not at the hoary head: oft is that good which old
men say.'

When Christianity touched the Germanic tribes, it made
at first but little difference. The conversion of Iceland, for
example, was one of the most calm and commonsense
political transactions known to history. As the new religion
seemed likely to split the State, a shrewd 'Deemster' suggested a compromise. The heathen should give up eating
horse-flesh and other objectionable habits: the Christian
should look the other way when a sacrifice to Thor was performed quietly and unostentatiously. On these terms the
heathen agreed to be baptized – when they found a geyser
not too hot to make the ceremony uncomfortable. Slowly
and gradually the old gods faded out – nor is the process yet
complete.

Of the retention of heathen ideas in a Christian atmosphere, indeed, the most curious examples may be found in
almost any Anglo-Saxon poem. The old charms survived
with the simple substitution of Christian saints for Thor and
Odin: the Apostles appear as warriors of the Beowulf or
Sigurd kind: God is *Metod*, the measurer, a title probably of

Odin as the Terminus or god of boundaries: Earth is still Midgard: Constantine wears the sign of the boar on his helmet, though the poet does not tell us that the boar is the emblem of Frey: when armies meet, the terror of Hilda stands over them, and the wolf 'conceals not the war-rune': when day dawns, Night takes off her helmet; and when a warrior dies, the poet says that Weird has taken him, precisely as Beowulf says, before his fight with Grendel, that 'Weird goeth ever as she must.' And, as we have seen, when the Christian poet Cynewulf wishes to give Christ the highest possible title, he calls him Orwandill, the name of a giant whom heathenism had made a star.

THE EARLY CHRISTIAN CHURCH

HE who writes on Christianity is like the Roman historian, spoken of by Horace:

> *Tractat et incedit per ignes*
> *Suppositos cineri doloso:*

everywhere his steps are on the smouldering fires of controversy. He will be accused of credulity by the adherents of Strauss, Drews, or Robertson, to whom the Christ-story is but one among a thousand myths: and of scepticism or even atheism by the Fundamentalist, to whom the words of the Parables (perhaps even those in the Authorized Version) are exactly, verbatim and literatim, those uttered by Jesus on the Mountain or the Plain. He will be charged with insularity if he claims that Christianity is in some points superior to other religions, and with slavish superstition if he treats other religions with what may seem to him decent respect.

Again, what *is* Christianity? Which of its Protean forms is the real one? 'As the number of thy cities are thy gods, O Judah,' said the prophet; and as the number of the cities of Christendom are her sects and denominations, some of which have denied the very name of Christian to the others, and the most liberal of which imagine that they possess an important something that is absent in the rest. These divisions, like those of Reuben, must cause the conscientious historian great searchings of heart: to find a formula elastic enough to embrace them all will strain his powers to the utmost. As for the sects that have perished, they are, like the dead of the human race, more numerous than the living. They began almost as soon as Christianity was born, and so early as the end of the second century they had increased and multiplied. Hippolytus 'refutes' thirty or forty, and alludes to others which he does not think deserving of a re-futation. Even in his time there were some that claimed to hold the one gate to heaven. Not only did the 'Catholic' Church make this claim, but some of the tiniest sects con-soled themselves for their smallness by arrogating to their 'little flock' the sole right to the Kingdom. Acesius, Bishop of an insignificant Roman Church, was one of these zealots. He was eager to make his community consist solely of pure saints, and to exclude all others from future blessedness. Constantine, whose sanctity was not of the strictest kind, laughed at him. 'Take your ladder, Acesius, and climb up alone to heaven.' But the impartial historian of Christianity as a whole must be broader than Acesius, and even more catholic than the Catholic Church. He must be willing to treat as Christians all who profess and call themselves such.

It is not unlikely, indeed, that many of these so-called heresies (I might mention in particular the Pelagian,[1] the Montanist, some of the Gnostic, and in later times the Cal-vinist) represent each an important aspect of Christian be-lief, to which, it may be with undue emphasis, they call special attention, and which the other forms of Christianity tend to neglect. Truth has many facets, and no one man, or set of men, can view all with an impartial and duly-proportioned gaze. Even when the heresy is entirely mis-taken, it has often had its use in compelling the orthodox to restate their view with greater precision. But this only makes the task of the historian more difficult: for, to give a just appreciation of Christianity as a whole, he must endeavour to understand and sympathize with those teachers who have either carried a certain 'true' theory too far, or, by pro-pounding a 'false' one, have exercised – if only by reaction – a powerful influence upon the Church. This task is, to speak frankly, impossible, and is rarely even attempted. Even to-day one knows candidates for Holy Orders who have never made the slightest attempt to investigate the distinguishing

1. John Wesley and many others have held that Pelagius has been mis-takenly classed among heretics. The errors of Origen, also, are separated from orthodoxy by the narrowest of lines.

doctrines of the Nonconforming Churches all around them, although these are comparatively few, and though the works in which they are presented are easily accessible. Much more difficult is it to appreciate rightly views like those of Novatian, Marcion, Basileides, or Arius, which are often expressed in language hard to comprehend, and are the product of forms of thought long since dead.

The brief account of Christianity here set forth, then, must be taken as only tentative. An attempt will be made to describe the religion, not from the point of view of a believer, but as it might be described by an intelligent Hindu or Chinaman, looking on it objectively as merely one of the many interesting endeavours of the human race to solve the great mysteries of life and death. That the objectivity will be complete is more than can be expected: the writer's own ideas will necessarily colour the narrative. Every reader will have his own ideas also, and will often dissent, sometimes perhaps with violent revulsion. But this may have its advantages. In speaking of a religion that is but little known, there might be a risk of unintentionally deceiving the reader; here, where the reader already knows something, and has a body of ideas ready-made, he will not be likely to accept any dubious assertion without examination.

The first opinion the intelligent Hindu would be likely to form is that Christianity, as a whole and in its parts, in its doctrines and in its institutions, is constantly changing, whether for better or for worse: that it *moves*, and is no more capable of continuing in one state than any other creation of the human mind.[1] From the very first it was altering. The mere increase of numbers involved an organization which was unnecessary when those who were gathered together were but a hundred and twenty. The admission of Hellenists into the Church led to the appointment of Gentile deacons to serve tables. The original communistic system had to give

1. I am not denying that Christianity has a divine element; but its institutions are, and must be, worked by men, and its creeds are, and must be, expressed in human language and accommodated to the human intellect.

way before the spectre of starvation. With the advance to Antioch a relaxation of legalism became imperative: the Torah was reduced to three or four commands, and, when the Church crossed the Aegean, there is small sign that even these three or four were obeyed. The Apostle of the Gentiles, to judge by the letters he has left, was a man of most receptive mind, whose practical ideas were always expanding, and whose theology was always growing. The ruling conception of the whole body, that Christ would reappear before that generation was exhausted, had to be abandoned when the generation died out and there was no *Parousia*: nay, if the Second Epistle to the Thessalonians be Pauline, the idea had to be profoundly modified within a very few years. With the dawn of the second century change became if possible still more rapid: we see, for example, the emergence of an episcopacy – something very different from the presbyterate of the earlier years: and before long the Bishop is becoming something of a despot, controlled not by his brother-presbyters but by the other Bishops. Since then, the history is one of continuous change, sometimes perhaps of advance and improvement, sometimes of retrogression and degeneration. The process can be variously regarded. A sarcastic unbeliever once proposed to 'prove the divinity of Christianity by the permanence of its name despite its total change of character': a Newman looks on these variations as proofs of vitality. The plant that does not change is dead.

The earliest hints as to the life of Jesus that we possess, as given in Paul's Epistles, are very few and very scanty. We learn that he was betrayed into the hands of his enemies, and that on the night of his betrayal he performed a mystic ceremony which became a memorial-service in the churches. This is nearly all. After his death he appeared, at intervals, to many of his disciples, and also to his brother James, who does not seem to have been one of his followers till this apparition convinced him, but who became thereafter the chief pillar of the Church at Jerusalem. Later, Jesus appeared in a vision to Paul himself, 'as to one born out of due time'.

For many years, so far as we know, there were no written records. None of those who had conversed with Jesus wrote any account of what they had seen and heard. But, as the first generation began to die away, collections of his 'Logia' or 'Sayings', which were mostly brief, pointed, and figurative, were put together. About fifty years after the Crucifixion a short memoir was published, in which some of the facts of the life were set down along with some of the characteristic parables and Logia. This little work, which is rough in style, but particularly vivid and striking in effect, is ascribed with much probability to Mark, an associate of Peter, the most prominent of the early disciples. It has about it many of the signs of an eye-witness, and is noteworthy both for what it omits and for what it says. There is not a word about the birth and early days of Jesus: the story of the Resurrection, so far as we possess it,[1] is plain and sober; and generally, if we compare it with biographies of other religious leaders written so long after their deaths,[2] it is astonishingly free from tales of miracles: in fact it is not too much to say that there is hardly a marvel in it that cannot be rationally explained.

Alongside of Mark, we can dimly discern a more or less ordered collection of parables and sayings. These, of course, had been floating about, carried in the memories of the disciples, and repeated from mouth to mouth: some, perhaps, were 'set in note-books, conned, and learned by rote'. But there is reason to believe that they had been formed into something like a book, which, for convenience, is known by the symbol Q. This book does not appear to have contained narratives of fact, except so far as to explain the Logia. Of Q, Mark, for some reason – perhaps because he wished to confine himself to first-hand information, perhaps because it did not exist in his time – made no use. Still less did he use the mass of floating tradition which was appearing and in-

1. The last few verses of the Gospel are lost. The lack has been variously supplied.
2. In the earliest accounts of the 'Bab' there are no miracles. Within twenty years the biographies swarm with them.

creasing, as it inevitably does where men are eager to learn more and more about a beloved and revered teacher, and where accurate documentary records are not in existence to correct the fancies. Even today, legend is rife about every great man; he is made to say things he never said, and to do things he never did. Much more so in the East and in a comparatively illiterate age. Even in Rome, at that very time, Augustus had been subjected to this treatment; his birth had become miraculous, and his actions had been surrounded with a supernatural atmosphere. So with Jesus: people were no more content then than now not to know, and tales grew up about him without conscious intention, every one more marvellous than its predecessor. As Jesus was the Messiah, it was still more necessary that tales should gather round him; for his life must be made to harmonize with what was supposed to be Messianic prophecy, and incidents attached themselves to him because Isaiah or Micah[1] had said something more or less ambiguous about the coming Deliverer. A Hebrew or Aramaic Gospel seems to have adopted these tales and to have reduced them to order. The Gospel of 'Matthew', perhaps translating from the Hebrew, and certainly using the same sources, made out of them, by combining them with Mark's Gospel and Q, a most extraordinary book, in which the supernaturalism is perhaps the most striking feature. Dreams abound, all sorts of prophecies, many of which have to be sadly distorted for the purpose, are 'fulfilled', and Jesus appears as a fully developed thaumaturge. The omissions of Mark are boldly supplied: to 'fulfil' a prophecy which originally applied to the age of Tiglath-Pileser, and which even so was mistranslated, Jesus is born of a virgin, like so many divine men of all races: an elaborate story is told to explain how the child of Nazarene parents came to be born in Bethlehem, whence another prophet had said a 'Governor' was to

1. As an example, it was the belief, and the boast, of the early Fathers that Jesus was the reverse of handsome. This was because the 'suffering servant' of Isaiah liii was said to have a countenance more marred than the sons of men.

arise; and the infant is even sent down to Egypt in order to fulfil yet another prediction, which, without Matthew's assistance, no human being would have suspected to have any reference to Jesus whatever. Finally, a number of prophecies are ascribed to Jesus himself, referring to the 'end of the world' – prophecies significantly accurate as far as they relate to the destruction of Jerusalem, but becoming vague when they deal with later events. This by itself is sufficient to fix the date of the Gospel as subsequent to A.D. 70. If we suppose it to be ten to fifteen years later than Mark, we shall be struck once more with Mark's sobriety and with the rapidity with which legends grew.

We are told that there were many other Gospels, setting forth the things which had been accomplished among the early believers, as there were, later, many which have survived to show how legends accumulated and degenerated, or how the life of Jesus was touched to doctrinal issues.[1] All the earlier ones, however, have disappeared: they were superseded by an almost perfect masterpiece, which Renan called, not unjustly, the most beautiful book in the world. This is the Gospel of Luke, which is certainly by the same cultured and most sympathetic writer who has given us the Book of Acts. It may have been written, as a very strong tradition asserts, by the companion of Paul, who shared so many of his trials and successes: and there can be no doubt that the author was a Greek, a scholar, and one who knew how to use his materials. He had studied earlier biographies, and had 'perfect understanding of these things from the first'. The book is dedicated to 'His Excellency', a man of high position, to give him full knowledge of the things in which he had already received some instruction. It is worthy both of its author and of the man to whom it is sent. In style and manner it formed a strong contrast to the rough colloquialisms of Mark, whom it uses freely and quotes, 'with advantages', at every turn. The book has an unsurpassed charm, and that indefinable quality which, though the

1. The 'Gospel of Peter', for instance, gives the incidents a 'Docetic' tinge.

author keeps himself in the background, makes us love him.

But, thinks the intelligent Hindu, we must be on our guard. Luke is a Greek writer, and writes like a Greek historian. In some cases, it is to be feared, he makes speeches of his own for his heroes; and a beautiful story seems true to him because it is beautiful. No more exquisite tale was ever told than that contained in his first two chapters, narrating the births of John the Baptist and Jesus. But it is hard to believe that it is history. The psalms sung by Zacharias and by Mary (the latter modelled on that ascribed to Hannah in the Book of Samuel) are obviously the work of poets meditating on the events, and are no more the composition of the supposed authors than Cowper's lines are the composition of Alexander Selkirk. The whole story is a popular legend, taken over and rewritten with deceptive charm by a man of Herodotean gifts. We are not shocked into scepticism as we are by Matthew; but that is simply because Luke is an artist.

The Logia and Parables, incomparable in their simple wording and depth of meaning, were taken by Luke from Q, and are probably fairly exact transcripts of the words of Jesus in very many cases. Words like his – and 'never man spake like this man' – would rivet themselves to the minds of the hearers, and be passed on almost unaltered through many years. Luke may have added an occasional literary touch, but he has generally been very careful to leave their sense unchanged – a temptation to which Matthew sometimes yielded. Thus, for instance, when Jesus said, 'Blessed are ye poor,' Luke adds not a word: but Matthew interprets, most likely inaccurately, into 'Blessed are the poor in spirit.'

Probably much later than Luke, a Gospel appeared of an entirely different kind, and picturing a Jesus of a vastly different character. Around this Gospel controversy has constantly raged, and still rages. Tradition assigned it to the 'disciple whom Jesus loved', the third of the select three with whom he shared his special confidences, John the son of

Zebedee, who was supposed to have migrated from Palestine to Ephesus, to have lived to a very great age, and to have composed this Gospel to supply what he regarded as wanting in the others, and occasionally to correct their errors. It is not yet decided whether this ascription is correct: the tendency of recent scholarship is perhaps in the other direction.[1] The question, though of vast importance – for it is plain that the authority of such a witness must outweigh any other we have – is yet less important than the other question which presses on us as we study every verse of his book: 'What sort of history was he writing?' For we have not gone far in our reading before we suspect that his work is not history in our sense at all, nor even history in the sense of Matthew and Luke: and that it belongs to an altogether different world from the simple and natural narrative of Mark. That he dissents from these 'Synoptics' in certain matters of fact is a trifle. It is a small matter in comparison that he gives Jesus three Passovers (at least) in Jerusalem instead of one, that he changes the Synoptic date of the Crucifixion, that he puts the 'cleansing of the Temple' at the beginning instead of the end of the ministry. It is even a comparatively small matter that the *man* Jesus, as we have learnt to know him from the earlier Gospels, is quite unrecognizable in this new portrait – two observers often see two very different sides of a man with whom they are both on friendly and intimate terms.[2] What is really important is

1. It may be taken as agreed that the author is the same as the author of the Epistles of John, or at least of the First Epistle. It is also widely admitted that, whoever he was, he did not write the Apocalypse, which belongs to an entirely different school of thought, and is not improbably a Jewish work enlarged and adapted to Christian purposes.

There is another tradition, that John the son of Zebedee died early and never went to Asia Minor: the existence of this tradition, though it is not very strongly attested, shows on what thin ice the historian is skating when he is dealing with these early times.

2. Yet 'John's' portrait is perhaps so different as to pass the bounds of probability. Though the Johannine Jesus, in his relations to his disciples, shows a touching tenderness, in his relations to the Jews he is unpleasant and repellent: continually demanding that they should recognize him as 'He', yet refusing to offer evidence; and continually provoking them by

the transcendental and metaphysical character of the whole work – the presentation of Jesus not as a man but as a personified idea. The very first verses identify him with the conception of the Logos, a conception apparently assumed to be already familiar to the reader; and this is followed by the tremendous assertion that the Logos was made flesh and dwelt among us. After this come speeches, exactly in the style of the author, but bearing no resemblance to any recorded by the other Evangelists; all in a mystical strain, and shading off into the author's own narrative so imperceptibly that no one can tell where Jesus ends and 'John' begins. From the very first Jesus seems conscious that he is in some mysterious fashion identical with the Divine – that he is the Only-Begotten[1] Son of the Father, and that this ought to be obvious to everyone at the first glance: if the leaders of the Sanhedrim do not acknowledge it they 'shall die in their sins'. A series of very peculiar miracles 'manifests forth his glory' – they are all symbolic, and differ *toto caelo* from those we have met already. Closely analysed, they scarcely seem to be miracles at all, but parables of the work which, the Incarnate Logos is doing. Thus the turning of the water into wine appears to mean the sublimation of the old religion by the infusion of Christ's spirit: and the healing of the man born blind denotes the Vision of Truth granted to the Jew who should yield himself to the Christ-doctrine. It is hard, indeed, to find a single incident which is viewed simply and objectively *as* an incident; every one, or nearly every one, interests the writer not as fact but as the expression of a metaphysical doctrine. Names, dates, persons, are all pressed into the service in the manner habitual, as we have seen, with Philo: and events, as with the writer of Chronicles,

---

haughty and unintelligible speeches. But for the glamour of the later chapters it is unlikely that the harsh controversialist thus presented would prove attractive to a simple and liberal mind.

1. This word I believe to mean not God's only son, but 'begotten by God alone', without other help. That the word has some transcendental, almost incomprehensible, significance is plain: it seems to be meant to refute some Gnostic errors.

are narrated, not as materials for history, but as the themes for Midrashim: nay, the facts are speedily entirely forgotten, and the Midrash goes on its way untrammelled by any 'solidity or compound mass'.

All these features, and others of the kind, compel us to recognize what we have already hinted – that as Philo and his school treated history as allegorical doctrine, so this author, conversely, works backward from the doctrine to 'fact'. The doctrine is there first, and the so-called history is invented to provide a substratum for it. Already – for instance, in the Epistle to the Colossians – Paul had formed a Christology practically independent of factual history: he had conceived a Christ almost sundered from Jesus, 'the image of the invisible God, the first-born of all creation, in whom were all things created, through whom and unto whom all things were made, who was before all things, and in whom all things consist'. This doctrine the Johannine writer carried still further; a step in advance made the 'first-born' the Logos, and clothed him with all the attributes in which the Alexandrian school had visualized that conception. But to make this idea *carry*, it was necessary to give it an apparently historical background: and a symbolical biography was written in which metaphysics were in a manner brought down to earth: the Logos, in fact, was 'made flesh', and had to be given a human career. It was, in its way, like the *Faerie Queene* of Spenser, in which Holiness dons armour, and goes on an adventure, attended by Truth in the form of a woman, and hampered by Bodily Infirmity in the shape of a lagging dwarf. But no one has taken the Knight's conflicts as the real battles of a real St George.[1]

1. The Eastern critic would also recollect how many other religious teachers have been transformed into deities or metaphysical entities. Zoroaster made no claim to be more than a man; but his followers, in writings purporting to be written or inspired by the prophet himself, represent him as a supernatural being. The earliest lives of Buddha (Gautama) picture him as a human being; the later turn him into a manifestation of the divine, not dissimilar to the Logos. Even Confucius, the most commonsense and prosaic of teachers, hardly escaped a similar fate.

There is great philosophic and theologic value in these Johannine myths: as there is, to a lower degree, in Spenser's poem; but we must not look in them for a concrete chronicle. For that we must seek in the Synoptics; and even there, with their load of legendary accretion, the disentangling of the truth is a task of enormous difficulty. The 'Quest of the Historical Jesus' is a journey on which many have set forth: and scarcely two have agreed in what they have finally discovered. Each is the victim of his own personal sense of the probable: what a Loisy thinks the real Jesus could never have said or done, another traveller, with equal scholarship and equal reverence, thinks *exactly* the thing most characteristic of the Jesus he has discovered. One thing alone is certain, that Jesus was a person of amazing impressiveness, force, and charm; that even after death he yet speaketh, and that today there are millions who, reading his words and contemplating his acts, cannot explain him but as in a sense divine: they feel him working in their hearts, controlling their lives, and inspiring an undying love. As in Galilee, so in England, he 'goes about doing good'.

For what it is worth, I give here one of the many rationalistic views. Jesus, an artisan of Nazareth in Northern Palestine, the son of the carpenter Joseph and his wife Mary, had meditated on divine things from his earliest youth. He had been brought up to the knowledge of the Scriptures, and had read them in the light of his own spiritual feeling. He was profoundly dissatisfied with the formalism and legalism he saw around him: penetrated as he was with the sense of the Fatherhood of God, he recognized also the brotherhood of man, and saw in the Jewish race first, and later in the whole world, one family, which ought to be knit together in paternal love. Constant prayer, and incessant communion with his Father, strengthened these feelings. With a

---

It may be that an Oriental thinker (or even the author of the Johannine Gospel himself) would be surprised to find that Westerners take him literally; as writers of Midrashim certainly do not expect their moral stories to be regarded as plain fact. 'Plain fact', indeed, is something that rarely comes within their intellectual horizon.

confidence totally untinged with vanity, he conceived that it was his duty to communicate these ideas to others, and to form a band of adherents who should be inspired with the same love and burn with the same zeal. As he was thus pondering, he heard of another teacher who was proclaiming a like message; who also seemed to be convinced that a new day was dawning, and that repentance for the past might open the door to a better future. With humble hope Jesus went, like many others, and submitted to baptism at the hands of John: after which, in true prophetic fashion, he went into the wilderness and communed in solitude with his own soul. He returned, strengthened in the conviction that his Father had sent him, that he was to preach the coming Kingdom, and also that God had given to him a fuller revelation than even to John, whom yet he reverenced as one great and good Teacher will always reverence another.

He speedily gathered round him a small community of disciples, for the most part simple men of the working class, and women of the same rank or lower. With an unerring eye for the good and true, he always recognized, even in 'publicans and sinners', the germs of better things, and totally disregarded the ordinary respectable conventions: the only things that drew stern words from his lips were formalism and hypocrisy. Thus, while the common people heard him gladly, officialdom was very early antagonized, and the antagonism soon grew into bitter hatred. His miracles of healing, which assured the multitude that he was a prophet of the Elijah kind, were, in the view of the scribes and Pharisees, done by the aid of Beelzebub.

At what time the belief rose in him that he was the promised Messiah we do not know: it may have been expressed in early days in his home, for we know that his mother and his brothers were irritated by what they thought his wild pretensions – so inconsistent with what they knew of his family life: and he himself recognized that Nazareth, where he had been a plain carpenter, was the last place where honour would be done him. But whenever he formed the idea, it was no vulgar one. He was to be a king, but his king-

dom was to be within the hearts of his subjects; his victories
were to be over vice and sin, and the vanquished were to
submit themselves willingly: force was to be eschewed, and
love was to take its place. This was a conception far too
spiritual even for the closest of his followers. 'Lord,' they
said, even after he had died and risen again, 'wilt thou not
at this time come and restore the kingdom to Israel?' It
was no purpose of his to take the sword and expel the
Romans. To those of his enemies who tried to entrap him
into words that might savour of rebellion, he answered,
'Render unto Caesar the things that are Caesar's and unto
God the things that are God's.' Again and again he explained that the Kingdom of Heaven had nothing to do
with this world: it was like leaven, it was like a grain of
mustard-seed, it was like a treasure hid in a field, it was like
seed sown which springs up man knoweth not how. But all
this fell uselessly on minds obsessed with the idea that the
Messiah was to be a new David, breaking the nations with a
rod of iron, and dashing them in pieces like a potter's vessel.
The priestly rulers, when they heard of his claims, feared
that another frenzied revolutionary had arisen, and that the
Romans would come and take away their place and nation:
it was not long before they determined to seize the first
chance of suppressing him. The Pharisaic order, also,
though they could have found much in his teaching with
which their own sages agreed, were alienated by his disregard of the Sabbath, by sayings which seemed to hint
at the coming abrogation of the whole Law, and by his
obvious indifference to their prestige.

In one point probably, the Johannine Gospel is right –
that Jesus made more than one visit to Jerusalem. Only thus,
apparently, can the intense hatred of the rulers be easily
explained. They had seen more than once the crowds that
followed him and disturbed the peace of the city: they had
more than once met him in argument and been foiled by his
meek superiority. The third or fourth time set the seal upon
their resolve. He must be removed at any cost. After a final
scene of tumultuous triumph, in which the mob acclaimed

him with the fatal title of Son of David – 'Blessed is the *kingdom* that cometh' – the priests delayed no longer. A bribe was offered to one of his disciples to betray him: he was captured in the Garden of Gethsemane, and handed over to the Roman procurator. The mob, with its usual fickleness, deserted him; all his disciples forsook him and fled; and Pilate, apparently much against his will, gave him up to the death of the Cross.[1]

In any other case this would have been the end; but in this it was but the beginning. It was not possible that such a personality should be holden of death. As the disciples recovered from the shock, gracious and prophetic words returned to them, which they had not understood at the time, but which now put on a new meaning: words which seemed to imply that he must leave them but that if he went away from them his spirit would visit them. A series of apparitions followed, in which he did visit them. The first to see him was Mary Magdalene, 'out of whom', as the Evangelist naïvely tells us, 'he had cast seven devils': a loving soul, and one easily susceptible to occult experience. Next, he appeared to Peter and perhaps John, then to the Twelve, and then to above five hundred of the brotherhood at once. Later, as we are authoritatively told, he appeared to his brother James – a decisive event, for, as we have seen, his brothers had at one time not believed in him. Finally, in a manifestation on the Mount of Olives, he was carried away from them into the air: and 'two men in white apparel' told the disciples that as they had seen him ascend so they should see him descend from heaven.

The effect of these revelations was immediate, and has not yet worn away. The timid disciples were changed into bold and eloquent preachers of the Name: the band daily grew of those who were disposed to eternal life: and the rulers, who had killed the Master, were afraid to deal drastically

1. It seems certain that Jesus had anticipated this catastrophe, and had even welcomed it. Many sayings, which there is no reason to suspect, indicate his clear prevision. But it is quite unnecessary to imagine that he purposely rushed on death as the only way out of a hopeless *impasse*.

with the pupils. A few imprisonments, a few stripes, were all that they dared to inflict. It soon appeared, also, that the new sect was but Judaism with two or three added doctrines. The Apostles were observers of the Law; James, in particular, was as strict as the strictest Pharisee, and was known to all as The Just. The converts did indeed hold that Jesus was the Messiah, and that the rulers had unjustly (if in ignorance) condemned him. They held also that he had been – to use the remarkable expression of one of them – 'put to death in the flesh, but raised again in spirit',[1] and that, in accordance with the prophecy of the 'two men in white', he would speedily return in the clouds. But they 'were continually in the Temple', and if they 'broke bread', did so at home. They were, in fact, setting a good example to the people at large. A few thousand men and women, living in common,[2] sharing their goods with each other, and distinguished by the regularity with which they attended the services, could do no harm even if they did hold a set of transcendental opinions and perform some simple miracles. The rulers,

---

1. 1 Peter iii, 18. I see no good reason for denying this Epistle to Peter, more especially if it be taken as written late in his life.

2. The communism did not last, even in Jerusalem, and never extended beyond the city – though, as we shall see, the Church always regarded itself as bound to see that the poorer members were provided for. Apparently, even in the communist society, no one was compelled to give up all his property. Even Barnabas did not do more than sell an estate and hand over the proceeds to the common fund.

Our 'intelligent Hindu' would refuse entirely to believe the story of Ananias and Sapphira – and that quite apart from its miraculous character. These two people simply wished to gain credit for generosity and yet to retain a little nest-egg for themselves in case the communistic experiment should fail. This involved deception and a lie or two; but no one has yet regarded a lie as punishable with death. Again, if Peter did kill them, it was gross negligence on the part of the police not to interfere: more especially as there was no concealment about the business.

But still more decisive against the story is this, that if Peter did so act, he was again, and more unpardonably, denying his Master, who had repeatedly forbidden the use of force. He who had told his disciples not to imitate Elijah, would certainly have told Peter that 'he knew not what spirit he was of': and the cock would assuredly have crowed thrice three times as Ananias and Sapphira died.

therefore, after a time were content to follow the advice of Gamaliel, and let the sect alone. If the movement were not of God, it would of itself come to naught: if it were of God, it was useless to contend against it.

Things, however, became altogether different when bold and ardent Gentiles, or Hellenistic Jews of liberal opinions, were added to the Church. A grievance on the part of these started a movement which speedily assumed great importance. The widows of the Hellenists were neglected in favour of the Hebrews in the distribution of food: and the question came before the Apostles, who appointed seven ministers, or 'deacons', to see to this organizing work, while they themselves devoted their energies to evangelization. Every one of these deacons bears a Greek name: and their appointment, even to a subordinate office, seems to show that the Apostles recognized how the Church was gradually outgrowing its Jewish character. It was soon plain that this was so: these Hellenists were so far from being strict keepers of the Law that they openly proclaimed the coming end of the Temple and of the legal system. Men were found to declare that they 'spoke blasphemous things against Moses and the Holy Place'. Their Leader was Stephen, the chief of the seven, 'a man full of grace and of the Holy Ghost', that is, in modern phraseology, a man of uncompromising piety and of fiery eloquence. It was not long before his words were reported to the Sanhedrim – it is noteworthy that his accusers were mainly Jews of the Dispersion, who would naturally be angry that one of their own number was betraying the very citadel of their position, and pointing the way to their separation from the Jews of Jerusalem. He was roughly seized and dragged before the rulers, who must at once have perceived that there were, in the harmless sect, possibilities of mischief which they had not suspected, and which put the *far niente* policy of Gamaliel out of the question. Stephen's defence, if it is accurately reported, was certainly provocative enough. The audience did not hear it through to the end. A plain assertion that the real Temple was not on earth but in heaven exasperated them beyond measure: and he was stoned to death in a tumultuary rush of his indignant hearers. Among those who watched the scene with approval, and kept the clothes of the witnesses while they did their horrible work, was a young Pharisee, a pupil of Gamaliel, whose name was Saul.

The martyrdom of Stephen was followed by a great persecution of the Church in Jerusalem, in which little discrimination was made between the Judaizing Christians and the Hellenizing party. It would appear that the Apostles, however, were known and spared; for whereas 'all' were scattered through Judaea and Samaria, the Apostles, we are told, remained in the city. The result of the persecution was to carry the Gospel far and wide, and eventually to alter its whole character. It spread very rapidly to Damascus and to the great Gentile capital of Antioch, where it was bound to suffer an enormous transformation. There, converts were admitted who had never been Jews, to whom the Law was nothing, and who had no intention of submitting to its burdens. They soon received a most notable accession of strength.

The ardent and tireless Saul, a Pharisee of the Pharisees, but also a Roman citizen, and a native of the highly cultured city of Tarsus in Cilicia, had 'consented unto the death of Stephen': but one victim was not enough for his zeal. In the terse words of the historian, he made 'havoc of the Church, and entering into every house, and haling men and women, committed them to prison'. Thus noted as an Inquisitor, he obtained letters from the High Priest to the synagogues of Damascus that he might carry out a similar work there. But a revolution, of which he was hardly as yet conscious, was going on in his own mind. He had been, without realizing it, deeply impressed by the sight of Stephen's fearlessness, and by the humble steadfastness of his prisoners. There was something in their courage which irresistibly appealed to his own courageous soul: he was an Alexander who could appreciate a brave enemy. Who knows, also, that his upbringing in Tarsus, and his Roman citizenship, did not impel him to conceive the vague idea that in Stephen's visions there lay the germ of a transformed Judaism which should transcend the limits of Palestine, and become a spiritual empire conterminous with the material dominion of Rome. Jesus might have been right: his kingdom, just because it was not of this world, might be world-wide.

With all his energy and practicability, Saul was also – that rare and irresistible combination – a mystic and a visionary. He was John Wesley and Swedenborg in one. We know that in the midst of his preaching and organizing labours he had trances in which he was caught up into the heaven of heavens, and heard things not lawful for men to utter. On his way to Damascus, he had one of these visions, which altered his whole life, and with it changed the history of the world. Suddenly, as he was riding on his persecuting journey, he was struck to the ground, and Jesus appeared to him in a blaze of supernatural light, which left him blinded for days. We have – brief as the Book of Acts is – three separate accounts of this occurrence.

Immediately after this he was baptized in Damascus, and, in the very same synagogues to which he had received his persecuting commission, 'confounded the Jews, proving that Jesus was the Messiah'. No wonder that they were astonished, and that they even plotted against his life; so that he was forced to leave Damascus. His own brief summary of what happened afterwards[1] – which it is difficult to reconcile with the account of the Acts – runs thus: 'when it pleased him who had separated me from my mother's womb to reveal his son in me, that I might preach him among the Gentiles, straightway, instead of conferring with any human being, or going up to Jerusalem to those who were Apostles before me, I went off into Arabia, and then returned to Damascus. Not till three years later did I go up to Jerusalem to visit Peter, with whom I remained a fortnight: and other of the Apostles saw I none, save James the Lord's brother.'

Much surprise has been felt that a man who had so re-

1. Or, more probably, his Arabian sojourn took place immediately after his conversion, and the debates with the Jews on his return to the city.

cently been converted from one faith to another should make no attempt for three whole years to see the leading exponents of his new belief, and still more that he should make this very omission a ground for the confidence of his own Galatian converts. But Paul insists on the fact – 'What I write unto you, behold before God I lie not': and the case becomes less astonishing when we reflect that to him, as is obvious to anyone studying his letters, the *historical* Jesus was entirely secondary. A great revelation of the Divine Man had been made to him in vision; on that vision it behoved him to meditate, alone, in the desert, until its full meaning should be made clear to him as the *Neum Yahweh* was made clear to the prophets of old: human instruction was no help but a hindrance. 'The Gospel which was preached by me,' says he to the Galatians, 'was not after any human standard; for I did not myself receive it from man, nor was taught it, but it came to me by revelation from Jesus Christ.' A faith thus gained was certain to differ from that of a man like Peter, who had actually walked and talked with his Master in the villages and fields of Galilee, and whose first sermon had spoken of 'Jesus of Nazareth, *a man* approved of God by wonders and signs'. Three years of meditation might well seem desirable to Saul in order so deeply to root in his mind his conception of Christ that it might be strong enough to resist contact with Peter's more human and mundane view.

Though he stayed but a fortnight in Jerusalem, it was long enough for him to be discovered by his old associates, who, like those of Damascus, formed a plot against his life. Learning of this, the brethren took him down to Caesarea, whence he was dispatched to his native city of Tarsus. He was thus totally unknown by sight to the Churches of Judaea. What he did during the next few years we are not told: a slight phrase[1] permits us to guess that he spent some time preaching in the country round Tarsus, and that he made a considerable name as a preacher. Probably also, he did not confine his ministrations to Jews. He must, at any rate, have speedily become known as a leader of the Liberal party. We

1. 'The parts [*climata*] of Syria and Cilicia' (Galatians i, 21).

are told that certain 'men of Cyprus and Cyrene' began to 'speak unto Greeks'.[1] When the news of this daring step reached Jerusalem, the Apostles sent down Barnabas of Cyprus, one of their leading men, to inquire into the circumstances. Barnabas soon became a supporter of the movement, and, in order to secure the best possible help, set out at once for Tarsus, and brought Saul to Antioch. He would hardly have done so if Saul had not already become famous, and famous as a pillar of the wider Christianity. With Barnabas he worked in the great Gentile city for a whole year. It seems to be implied that he made many Gentile converts, who would immensely strengthen his hands. As he thus toiled, the great idea occurred to him of casting his net yet wider, and attempting to evangelize cities beyond the borders of Syria itself – cities of Cyprus, Pamphylia, or even of the half-barbarous Lycaonia. That so social a man kept this idea to himself we cannot believe: he would talk of it here, there, and everywhere, and it would finally become a great popular desire, perhaps inarticulate, but none the less keen. All eyes would be upon Saul and Barnabas as the men for the work. After the two leaders, about the year 44, had been up to Jerusalem to carry a much-needed contribution to the starving Church,[2] and had returned to Antioch, the smouldering fire burst into a flame: the great idea, which had been slowly and silently penetrating the minds of the members of the congregation, suddenly came to open expression during a fast. To use the Oriental phrase of the historian, 'the Holy Ghost said, Separate me Barnabas and Saul for the work whereunto I have called them.' The unanimous wish of the community had found a voice: the two Apostles were ordained for the enterprise, and set forth on the first and most momentous of all Christian missions. They were a small company – Barnabas, Saul, Mark the

1. Acts xi, 20. I have no doubt that the true reading here is 'Hellenas', Gentile Greeks, and not 'Hellenistas', Grecian Jews.

2. Paul was always charitable, and not least to his 'brethren' the Jews: but this step was also likely to placate the still dubious authorities in Jerusalem.

cousin of Barnabas as their attendant, and a few others; but
the expedition of William the Conqueror was less pregnant
with destiny.

The system they invariably adopted was to go to the
Jewish synagogue in each town, to give the Jews the offer of
the Gospel, and – if the offer was rejected – to turn to the
Gentiles: and it was among the Gentiles that they met their
chief successes. In each place they set up a little Church,
loosely organized, which assembled in any convenient
house. When they had reached their proposed limit, they
turned back, visiting each town in succession, and 'confirm-
ing' the members in the faith. If, as seems likely (most
scholars incline, as against Lightfoot, to the view of Ramsay),
these are the 'Galatians' addressed by Saul – who is henceforth known by his Gentile name of Paul – we have first-
hand means of knowing their nature, and the kind of trials
through which they had to pass.

Whatever the Church of Jerusalem had thought of previous isolated cases of Gentile conversion, it had now to face
the larger question, and to determine how the new problem
was to be solved. Aliens were now Christians, and that in
numbers which bade fair to cast the Jewish Church into a
secondary place. The issue was soon joined, and concentrated itself mainly on two or three decisive points. Were
Greek Christians to be circumcised after the manner of
Moses, or not? What about their relations with their neighbours? Were they to eat meat that had been offered to
heathen gods? Were they to abstain from things strangled?[1]
To decide all this, what is sometimes known as the first great
council of the Church was held at Jerusalem.[2] The result, as

1. Despite the presence of this phrase in the two great manuscripts, I
am not quite certain that it is genuine. But the question would certainly
be debated between the two parties.
2. The account of this council in Acts xv is difficult and obscure. The
chief speech, that of James – a Hebrew of the Hebrews – bases its argument on a passage in the prophet Amos as given in the Greek version,
which is very different from the original. It is true that the original would
have afforded him no help, and that we have seen how Philo contrived to
believe at once in the inspiration of the Hebrew and in that of the Greek,

usual in conferences, was a compromise. Through the influence of Peter and James, circumcision was declared unnecessary, but fornication,[1] the eating of meat offered to idols, and perhaps the eating of things strangled, were forbidden.

Like most compromises, this in the long run satisfied few. We learn from Paul's letters that shortly afterwards[2] Peter came down to Antioch, fell into the company of the Judaizing party, 'men who had come from James',[3] and removed himself from fellowship with the Gentilizers. Paul, whose fiery nature could not brook timidity, rebuked him publicly and fiercely. When Barnabas was carried away by the same 'dissimulation', he felt even keener pain; and this weakness of his old companion had perhaps its influence in the contention which shortly followed. Proposing to Barnabas a second missionary journey, he found that Barnabas wished to take Mark with them, though the young man had shown want of courage on the former expedition. On this point the friends quarrelled and parted. Paul, choosing a 'prophet' named Silas, already distinguished in the Church at Antioch, set forth on a mission which was to cover Asia Minor and a large part of Greece, and was to be the beginning of European Christianity.[4]

---

even when they were at variance. But it is hard to believe that, with a jealous opposition ready to mark every word, there should not have been voices to cry out, 'Quote the Hebrew.'

1. By this is perhaps meant religious prostitution, such as was common in Antioch and other Eastern places.

2. So one would gather from the passage, Galatians ii, 11. As Lightfoot says, any other date is hardly possible. Further, it is Peter's *inconsistency* that roused Paul's indignation; and it cannot be denied that such vacillation on the part of Peter is quite in character.

3. Why this expression, if James had really been on the side of the Liberals? It is points like this which led the Tübingen school to believe that there was not only argument, but an actual bitter schism, between 'Paul and the Three', which it was the object of the author of Acts to gloss over. It is, in my opinion, probable that the Tübingen school exaggerated the dissension: but I believe that it was keener than the orthodox theory admits.

4. Possibly, before this, Christianity had been carried by isolated members of the Church to Rome: but that there was a 'Church' there is

The two chief Churches founded on this mission were Corinth and Ephesus, in each of which great cities the Apostle had astonishing success – accompanied, it is true, with many anxieties and disappointments. He made numerous converts, but they were erratic and sometimes even rebellious. The mixed population of Corinth, in particular, gave him much trouble: even when he was there they required tactful management, and in his absence they ran wild: quarrels were incessant, and there were even open factions, one calling itself after Paul himself, another after Apollos, another after Peter, and a fourth – which does not appear to have been any more truly Christian than the rest – after Christ. It is from two or three of the letters which Paul wrote to this Church that we get the most vivid account of what a congregation might be like when formed of turbulent people and meeting in a mixed population. What elsewhere might be quiet and orderly services – a psalm, a lesson from the Scriptures of the Old Testament, the kiss of peace, and the communion – in Corinth degenerated into frenzied orgies. 'Prophesyings' – which, it would appear, many despised – 'speaking with tongues' – that is, insensate gabblings in any language or none – haranguings, discordant songs; these, Paul tells us, went on in such a fashion that the heathen would have thought madmen were raving.[1] It took a leader of great authority to keep these excesses within bounds; and Paul was handicapped by the fact that he himself was liable to be carried away, and that he was quite uncertain as to where the Holy Ghost ended and Satan began. For ecstatic rants were the sign of the descent of the Holy Ghost, and yet it was precisely these ecstatic moments that

doubtful. Such church as there was had no individual founder. Paul, writing to these very Romans, says in one and the same breath that he had been long anxious to come to them, and that he was always careful not to build on another man's foundation. Had Rome been the preserve of anyone else, he would clearly have left it alone.

1. Similar phenomena are not unknown in revival services both here and in America. 'Speaking with tongues', as all know, occurred in Edward Irving's Church in the last century: and observers like Frank Newman were struck with the likeness to the Corinthian scenes.

the devils chose as favourable for attack. Demons, indeed, were present in every church assembly in uncountable numbers – invisible but active: and angels also, because of whom, in an enigmatic sentence, Paul says that women ought to have 'power on their heads' – that is, probably, ought to keep their heads covered in church lest the angels should know them too well.[1] The women, who usually sat apart from the men, might easily forget themselves in these excitable moments: some, we know, even wanted to preach: and the dangers were the greater because of the very over-confidence which conversion engendered. Another enigmatic sentence hints that some Church-members, proud of their self-control, led about with them 'sister-wives'[2] – a practice which caused great scandal to the heathen and was afterwards suppressed. It will thus easily be realized that the Corinthian services bore little likeness to the decorous matins to which we are accustomed in an Anglican Church today. As to the compromise of Jerusalem, Paul, who was 'all things to all men', took no notice of it at all. He told his followers that idols were nothing, and that if meat were set before them they should not ask awkward questions as to whether it had ever been offered to those nonentities. Sabbaths and other holy days were also nothing: some might esteem one day above another, and others esteem all days alike: the great thing was to be fully persuaded in one's own mind. At the same time, there must be charity and forbearance: if meat caused a brother to stumble, Paul was quite willing to give up meat altogether.

The organization was of the simplest. In each city-church a small brotherhood of elders, also called overseers or Bishops, was ordained by the laying-on of hands. These were equal in position, though it was of course inevitable that in many cases the man of most ability, energy, rank, or prestige should gain some sort of more or less permanent authority over the rest. These leaders were assisted by minis-

1. Probably in this phrase there lies hidden a reference to the Divine Bridegroom, who, as we shall see, appears so often in the martyrologies.
2. Well known to psychologists as productive of ecstasies and trances.

ters (deacons) and deaconesses, whose chief business may
have been to attend to the distribution of the charitable
funds and to the needs of widows and orphans: a task which
demanded (as it does today) special experience and discrimination. Already the Church was assuming the character of a relieving-society; already it was finding that some
persons were joining it less for spiritual sustenance than for
material food: and Paul had to lay down the sound rule that
idlers should be rejected: 'If any did not work, neither
should he eat.'[1]

Less precisely defined varieties of ministry were desig-
nated according to the special *charismata* or divinely ordered
talents with which they were endowed. Good readers,
though laymen, might read the lessons or the letters from an
absent Apostle: natural orators – and unfortunately sometimes those who had no claim to that title – might preach:
the speakers with tongues had to have their fling; the
exorcists – a most important class at a time when half the
diseases of humanity were ascribed to devils – had to ply
their functions; and – though of these we hear little – there
must have been precentors, singers, and men skilled in the
writing of hymns[2] and the composition of tunes. But,
though there were these 'diversities of charismata', the
underlying assumption was that all were equal 'in the
Lord'; bond, free, male, female, barbarian, Scythian, all
were one brotherhood: and even the highest officers were
chosen for their posts by the brethren. This equality, marked
by the constant 'kiss of peace' which formed part of every
service, was the real strength of the community – the Church
was the first institution to offer a welcome to the sinner, the
outcast, the degraded, the slave. There is nothing like this in

1. Despite the help of the ministers, the presbyters seem to have been
entangled in this work: and within a very few years, we know, the Bishops
were often almost absorbed in organizing work to the detriment of their
spiritual functions.

2. Fragments of these hymns, doxologies, and Christian psalms are to
be found scattered in the Epistles, sometimes imitating Hebrew rhythms,
sometimes, I believe, in Greek metres. No revivalistic Church has ever
been able to dispense with these aids.

earlier history. Even the kind-hearted Cicero could never have written a letter like that of Paul to Philemon, in which the injured master is urged, with exquisite tact, to receive his runaway slave as a brother beloved: and, whatever we may think of the intellectual strength of Origen's reply to Celsus, there can be no question that the Christian had in this point the better of the philosopher.[1]

This equality, however, must not lead us to imagine that Christianity was a form of Socialism. It began as a religion, and as a *personal* religion: such social feeling as came in was a consequence, and not a cause, of the religious sentiment. This is typified by the fact that deacons were introduced after other ministers, and were always inferior to the overseers. But a society based on love *must* be in a sense Socialistic; and the early Christians not only helped each other, but helped other Churches, as Paul collected alms for the Church of Jerusalem. As the religion started in the East,

1. 'Other religions', says Celsus, 'proclaim, "Let him draw near who is pure from stain, who has lived an upright life". But let us hear the call of these Christians: "Whoever is a sinner, foolish, unlettered, in a word, whoever is wretched, him will the kingdom of God receive".' This, which philosophers made a reproach, Paul rightly claimed as a glory: and Origen, in his reply, adopts the defence of Paul. It is, of course, true that, in admitting the ignorant and foolish, the Church raised up for itself many difficulties: but it was emphatically worth while.

Aristotle's defence of slavery, and his exclusion of slaves from citizenship in his ideal policy, stands in glaring contrast to the Christian view. It is not to be denied, however, that many Greek thinkers held slavery to be immoral; and, as W. L. Newman shows (*Politics of Aristotle*, I, 139 ff.) the tone of Aristotle seems to indicate that he is arguing against a belief held by a good many. The Stoics and Cynics, also, were opponents of the institution – rather, perhaps, because they held all institutions 'indifferent' than because they detested the cruelty and injustice of this particular institution. Epictetus, himself a slave, does not, I think, attack slavery itself: he teaches that a philosopher, even though a slave, may be superior to his surroundings. There is a wide gulf fixed between this and the Christian view.

As to the 'sinner', Greek philosophy as a rule either scorned him or ignored him.

Thus, though Christianity made no direct attempt to abolish social distinctions, it is I think only just to say that it paved the way for their abolition.

where the cleavage between social strata was less clearly marked than in the West, and as also the *Pax Romana* had tended to the revival of a middle class to which an appeal could be made with some hope of success – as, further, 'not many noble' or rich people came in at first – it was possible for Christianity to ignore, to some extent, differences of rank and wealth.[1] After all, as the fashion of the world was soon to pass away, what did such differences matter? Hence we find that Paul, while insisting that all are equal before God, confesses that men are unequal in destiny, and bids them recognize these inequalities. Masters and slaves – both are there: the masters must deal to their slaves that which is just and equal; the slaves must remember the respect due to the masters. Doubtless the opinions of Paul as to such matters were largely influenced by his own position as a Roman citizen, and by the fact that his ministry was mainly carried on in great towns. Jesus, in a simpler civilization, had little need to think of such things; his Apostle came up against them at every turn.[2]

To what extent Christianity was *already* a 'Mystery' religion: how far it had adopted symbolic ceremonies from the Orphic and Eleusinian rites – or, as is perhaps more probable, from Eastern religions – is a difficult question. The astonishing likeness, for example, between the baptismal ceremony and the purificatory rites of Attis and Adonis cannot fail to strike every student: and the Christian religion has at all times shown a remarkable power of taking into itself what suits it from other religions. Much of Paul's language seems hardly to be explained save on the assumption that he had already welcomed hints of this kind; and it is pretty certain that very early the Church practised secret *orgia* and kept an esoteric doctrine for its initiates.

1. Though, if the Epistle of James be really a Christian document, snobbery was at a very early stage found to be a rampant evil.

2. On all this Troeltsch, *Social Teaching of the Christian Church*, has much that is illuminating to say. This book, and, in slightly less degree, Uhlhorn's *Christian Charity in the Early Church*, are of the highest value to the student.

Baptism, the Agapae, and the Eucharist contained the germs of such doctrines and ceremonies, and the admission of converts from heathenism made it almost inevitable that customs which had been found spiritually beneficial in the old creed should be gradually introduced into the new. No growing and aggressive Church but sooner or later becomes thus syncretistic – a cause, and an effect, both of strength and of weakness: and Paul was far from the least receptive of great and aggressive revivalists.

Be this as it may, every step he took, whether to cast off old trammels or to accept new ideas, was certain to arouse the hatred of the Jews and the Judaizing Christians, who pursued him with persistent and relentless hostility. The Jews in every city were his open foes: they accused him to the Romans of turning the world upside down – that is, of treason to the empire: they raised tumults against him, stirred up the mob, and endeavoured to poison the ears of the magistrates. At times they dealt with him themselves: we know that five times he suffered at their hands the frightful infliction of 'forty stripes save one', a torture which would have killed many men of greater muscular strength but less tough constitution. From actual murder he was saved repeatedly by the Roman governors; and he rightly availed himself of his Roman citizenship to avoid unnecessary danger. But it is probable that he found the Judaizing Christians even worse enemies, as more subtle and secret – they were the foes of his own household. Whenever he had established a Church, and assured his converts of 'the liberty wherewith Christ had made them free', these men crept in, and by stealthy insinuations endeavoured to persuade the infant believers that Paul was an impostor, or at best but half a Christian; that 'except they were circumcised after the manner of Moses they could not be saved'. Of their machinations we have a pretty clear account in the letter to the Galatians, where we learn that in a very short time they had practically undone his whole work: and we can see how bitterly his sensitive and affectionate nature felt the blow. He saw clearly, of course, that if these men

prevailed, the conversion of the West was quite impossible:
but their narrow fanaticism was impenetrable, and nothing
but determined opposition was of any use. Particularly in
Asia Minor[1] their tireless activities fretted him. In one of the
most pathetic scenes recorded in the Acts, we are told how,
taking what he knew to be his last chance, he sent for the
elders of his beloved Ephesus, and warned them how, after
his departure, grievous wolves would enter in, not sparing
the flock: reminding them of the trials which had befallen
him by the plots of the Jews, and pleading with them to
abide by 'the whole counsel of God'. They all wept sore,
and sorrowed greatly; but there is every reason to believe
that his words were vain.

The animosity persisted long after his death. Whether the
Pauline doctrine is actually attacked in the Apocalypse or
not,[2] he is certainly the 'Simon Magus' of the *Homilies* and
Recognitions which bear the name of Clement of Rome. In
the *Homilies* Peter is represented as saying, 'Shun any
Apostle who does not first compare his teaching with that
of James my Lord's brother, and has not come to thee with
witnesses – such as Simon, who came sowing error under the
pretence of truth, and preaching in the name of our Lord.'
Again, 'Simon,' says Peter, 'if Jesus was made known to
thee in a vision, it was because he was angry with thee. Can
anyone be made wise unto doctrine by visions? How shall
we ever believe thee that he was seen of thee?[3] If by being
seen of him for a single hour thou wast made an Apostle,
then preach his words, expound his teaching, love his
Apostles, do not fight against me his companion. For thou
hast withstood me,[4] the rock on which the Church is

1. Even in Corinth, perhaps, they worked against him – they may be
those who said, 'We are of Cephas.' Compare also 1 Cor. ix.

2. Many think that it is Paul who is denounced in that half-Jewish
book under the name of Balaam, 'who cast a stumbling-block before the
children of Israel, to eat things sacrificed to idols, and to commit fornication' – exactly the offences which the Judaizers would impute to
Paul.

3. 1 Cor. ix, 1: 'Am I not an Apostle, have I not seen Jesus our Lord?'

4. Gal. ii, 1.: 'I withstood Peter to the face.'

founded. Nay, in saying I stood condemned,[1] thou accusest God who revealed Christ to me.' In the romance called the *Recognitions* there was similar abuse; and in other works he is even stated to have tried to murder James. Nay, he was, so it was averred, really a Gentile by birth, who, wishing to marry the High Priest's daughter, became a proselyte: but, being disappointed in his hope, turned round and furiously attacked the Mosaic Law. Slanders like these continued to be propagated till the middle of the third century, and point clearly to the existence of a hatred far more ferocious than we might suspect even from Paul's own words. That Peter and James held themselves apart from it we may, if we so choose, believe; but they could not prevent their followers from using their names.

The question was settled at last by the inexorable logic of events. After the deaths of Paul and Peter, both of whom were martyred at Rome in the reign of Nero,[2] the great catastrophe occurred; the Jews broke out into rebellion. With the details of that most heroic, most savage, and not far from most important, of all wars, we are not here concerned: they are recorded by a Jew who contrived, after fighting for some time for his countrymen, to make his peace with the enemy. But in the effects which we, at this moment, are feeling, we are inevitably interested. The disaster had been foreseen by the Jewish Christians in Jerusalem: passages in the Gospels indicate their belief that Jesus himself had foretold it. Like the prophets of old, they had denounced the crimes which must lead to it, and like them were regarded as traitors and enemies of their country. Exactly as Jeremiah had been denounced as a pro-Chaldean, so these men were denounced as pro-Roman. All chance of renewing the old friendliness between Jew and Jewish Christian was shattered for ever. A short time before the outbreak of the war, the most prominent leader in the whole Church, James the brother of Jesus, who in devotion to the Law was more

---

1. Gal. ii, 11: 'Because he stood condemned.'
2. There is no certainty as to this: but the tradition seems too strong to be disregarded. The date *may be* 64.

Jewish than the Jews themselves, was stoned to death by order of the High Priest Ananus.[1] As the storm drew nearer, the Christians, remembering or inventing some warnings of Jesus, 'when ye see Jerusalem compassed with armies, then let them that are in the midst of her depart out', left the city *en masse*, and settled in Pella, on the east side of Jordan. From that moment the hatred of the Jews for their traitor-kinsmen was intense and lasting: and curses against them became a regular feature in their daily prayers. The feeling will be intelligible to those who remember what was thought of 'Pro-Boers' among ourselves in 1899, or of 'conscientious objectors' in 1916: it was hardly less strong among those Jews who had at first opposed the war than among the Zealots themselves; for it was held to be the duty of all patriots, when once the war had begun, to support it to the best of their ability. We know what Jews, even today, think of Josephus: and we can imagine what, at the time, they thought of men who, as they would put it, ran away at the first threat of danger. Thenceforward, Jew and Judaizing Christian were sundered. What is equally important, the desertion revealed the distinction to the Romans. Hitherto they had confounded all alike in one – Pauline, Petrine, Judaizing – as mere quarrelling sects of the familiar strange and obstinate religion. Like Gallio, they had left them to see to their idle legal disputes for themselves, or, like Nero,[2] tortured all indiscriminately: but now a decisive and essential severance manifested itself, which I do not think the majority of Romans henceforward failed to observe – except deliberately. Judaism and Christianity were both, to the cultivated Roman, 'detestable superstitions'; but they were

1. As Ananus was a moderate, and had no wish to quarrel with Rome, he may have put James to death because his denunciations disturbed the peace, and merely provoked the Zealots to greater fury against the Romans. The act was disapproved of by many of the Jews, and apparently not least by Agrippa, who understood the Christians, and was the firm friend of the Roman rule.

2. I imagine that Nero's persecution of the 'Christians' in 64 was a persecution of Jews as well: this is the view of Gibbon and many other historians.

different, nor did he ever confuse them unless he desired to turn the hatred felt for the one upon the other also.

At Pella, it was impossible to maintain the strict observance of the Law after the manner of James and his followers: and though, under the guidance of Simeon, another relative of Jesus, the community did its best to keep up a sort of Judaism of the Diaspora, in the style of the Daniels or Tobits of an earlier exile, circumstances were too strong for the best intentions. In the little Peraen city, Gentile Christians were inevitably introduced into the Church: and when, after the capture of Jerusalem by Titus in 70, some of the band returned to the city, more Gentiles would attach themselves to it. We hear, as we should expect, of many dissensions – there was room for every variety of opinion as to the amount of conformity to the Law now imperative or expedient. And worse was to follow. Simeon, who seems to have been a moderating influence, was martyred in 106: and schisms became even more numerous. Thirty years later, under one of the many Messiahs who appeared in these troubled times – Bar-cochba, the Son of the Star, prophesied by Balaam – the indomitable nation rebelled again. Once more the Christians 'fled to the mountains'. The insurrection was crushed by Hadrian with even more severity than the earlier one by Titus; Jerusalem was destroyed, and a new city, Aelia Capitolina, was built on its ruins, from which the Jews were excluded – only a wall being left, by which, in after times, they were permitted to weep. To this city the Church of the Circumcision once more returned, but, inevitably, as Gentiles and not as Jews. Even of these there were many sects, two sufficiently important to be noticed. There were those who still held to the Law (as far as possible) themselves, but did not wish to impose it on others; and there were those who still, with pathetic obstinacy clave to the old doctrine, and denied salvation to 'such as were not circumcised after the manner of Moses'; nay, who held by the belief that Jesus, though the Messiah, was a mere man.

Meanwhile, the Pauline religion was advancing by leaps

and bounds, while the Church of the Circumcision was not only dwindling but splitting into these exiguous fragments. Numbers prevailed: Providence, as usual, was on the side of the big battalions; and, by one of the ironies of history, that which had been the dominant and orthodox branch of the Church sank gradually into a despised and 'heretical' sect. Among the 'heresies' denounced by the Fathers, the Nazarenes, and the Ebionites, holding the views of James the Lord's brother,[1] are constantly mentioned with reprobation, tempered only by a sense of their weakness and insignificance.

1. And, as some think, of Peter and John throughout their lives: certainly through many years of their lives.

GENTILE CHRISTIANITY

WE are thus led to consider Gentile Christianity – the only Christianity familiar to the ordinary man. For, from this time onward, as Harnack and many others have noticed, Christianity proved totally unable to make any impression on the religion out of which it sprang, and of which it was at one time considered, not unjustly, as merely a sect. More and more rapidly it forgot the rock from which it was hewn, and, like Paul, finding the Jews 'unworthy of eternal life', turned to the Gentile world. Its success in this enterprise was prodigious. Investigations in the Catacombs (where the Christians buried their dead) and careful comparisons of the various statements of the Fathers with the admissions of pagan writers, prove, full allowance being made for prejudice and exaggeration, that it grew like a grain of mustard-seed. In those Catacombs are perhaps four million graves – certainly not less than two million – and interment in them ceased with the sack of Rome by Alaric in 410. By the time of Hippolytus this would mean that there were at least 150,000 Christians alive in Rome alone. As early as A.D. 64, according to Tacitus, an *ingens multitudo* were involved in Nero's persecution. Justin Martyr asserts that in his time (about 160) 'there was not a single race of men, barbarian, Greek, or whatever it was called, nomads, vagrants, or tent-dwellers, among whom prayers and giving of thanks were not offered in the name of the Crucified'. The famous letter of Pliny to Trajan (112) says that in his province of Bithynia and Pontus Christianity was professed by many '*omnis aetatis, omnis ordinis, utriusque sexus*', that the temples of the gods were '*prope iam desolata*', that the '*solemnia sunt intermissa*', and that all this had been going on for a long time. 'We are but of yesterday,' says Tertullian about A.D. 198, writing to the Roman authorities; 'yet we overspread your empire; your cities, islands, forts, assemblies, camps, palace, senate, forum, all swarm with Christians. Were we but to abandon you, the loss of so many men of all ranks and degrees would leave a hideous gap; you would stand aghast at your desolation, and be struck dumb at the general silence and horror, as if the whole world had departed.' Nor was this growth confined to one class – the high-born, the educated, lawyers, rhetoricians, philosophers, were all entering the Church. A moderate calculation puts the numbers of the Christians, about Tertullian's time, at one-sixth of the total population of the empire;[1] but what terrified the rulers was less this lateral and numerical extension than the 'vertical' growth – the fact that there were Christians in every stratum. An Emperor's own cousin might be a Christian; a high official in the palace might be an adherent of the 'detestable superstition'; a proconsul or prefect might be converted at any moment.[2]

1. Gibbon's estimate, that in the time of Constantine (330) the Christians were about six million, or a twentieth of the total population, though endorsed by high authorities, is almost certainly ludicrously below the truth.

2. No satisfactory explanation of this marvellous growth has ever been given. The Church herself explains it as miraculous; but even miracles need favouring circumstances. And, if the rise of Christianity was miraculous, why did it fail anywhere or at any time? One miracle is no harder than another; and if Christianity conquered Rome in three centuries, why has she failed to conquer the rest of the world in nineteen? Christianity, nominal or real, is in the main confined to countries affected by Roman influence: the vast populations of the Far East stubbornly reject it, and whole nations in the Near East prefer Mohammedanism. In certain places Mohammedanism still makes scores of converts where Christianity makes one.

It is clear, then, that there was something in the Roman civilization, and in the times at which Christianity arose, specially favourable to it. Rome, in destroying so many nationalities, had to a great extent simplified their religions – instead of one religion for each tribe, there was one compounded and jumbled religion for the whole empire, or, what comes to much the same thing, an indifference that tolerated all. There was but one real cult, one ceremony only that was compulsory, the worship of the Emperor.

A religion that preached hope for the slave, that proclaimed the brotherhood and equality of all men, that emancipated women from the

But this portentous increase was far from being all gain. Among the converts were many whom the Church could well have dispensed with: Christians in name only. Large numbers of these were found out in times of persecution, and 'lapsed' to heathenism under that stern test. Many were not even then detected, for it is to be feared that martyrdom, with its promise of earthly glory and future bliss, had an attraction, not only for the genuine saint, but for the wolf in sheep's clothing. Hundreds of fanatics, far from holy in their daily lives, deliberately provoked the persecutors to put them to death; and it became necessary for the Church to decree that men who thus invited martyrdom should not be counted as martyrs. The fact that the Church was, as we have seen, a great relieving organization, led to the inclusion in its nominal membership of many who sought loaves and fishes rather than the bread of life. Ambition introduced numbers who sought distinction in the assemblies which would have been hard to gain outside. Some Bishops and presbyters, if we are to believe other Bishops and presbyters, were unworthy, and visibly unworthy, of their position. In fact, the Church, in overcoming the world, was in serious danger of becoming worldly.

It is about this time that we perceive the rise of a theory which, overtly or tacitly, has often since been held – the theory of two standards of conduct set before Christians, one for the saint and another for the average man. As the Church made her way, she had to face all sorts of questions which before had not greatly troubled her. Was she to hold social intercourse with pagans? Were her members to trade in anything that might possibly be used in pagan worship?

---

degrading servitude in which they languished, while at the same time there was nothing 'highbrow' about it, had every chance at that time. Its philosophy did not run counter to the prevailing superstitions of the age; miracles, exorcisms, demonology, were everywhere, and Christianity believed in all.

We have seen in our own days religions rise and advance with almost torrential speed: Mahdism in the Soudan, Christian Science in the West. We may perhaps add Gandhi's revival to the list, for the same force which drives a new religion often impels the revival of an old one.

Could a Christian be a soldier? We hear much of these and similar questions in the writings of Tertullian, who, holding that the power of the Church consisted in her obvious moral superiority to heathenism, would permit of no compromise.[1] Christians must of course avoid heathen pleasures, such as the theatres and the gladiatorial shows; but besides this they must hold no public offices, and even give up teaching in schools. But the struggle was in vain, and Tertullian was driven out of Catholicism into MONTANISM – a Phrygian revival of primitive Puritanism which held many strange tenets, but which, in the strictness of its views, satisfied Tertullian's conscience. The Church could not sacrifice the many thousands of members whom a rigid system would have expelled. When Callistus, the enemy of Hippolytus, relaxed the penitential system, and received even adulterers into renewed communion, Tertullian and many others went over into another 'denomination'. Nothing short of the highest sanctity would satisfy him. But the Church won. Montanism is a heresy, and Tertullian was too saintly to become a saint.[2] There is little doubt that, on the point at issue, Paul or James would have agreed with him; but a great and settled community has to admit much which a loose and small one can reject.

Other elements were introduced as the conquest advanced. The simplicity of the primitive organization, and the simplicity of the primitive creed, were alike corrupted, or, as some might think, improved, by the direct or indirect influence of foreign admixture. So early as the end of the first century we find one of the presbyters, in many of the churches, gradually assuming a monarchical authority, and becoming a 'Bishop'. The letters of Ignatius[3] are full of this

1. If a Christian went near a temple, he exposed himself to the attacks of the demons who haunt such places: such is Tertullian's idea.

2. Every religion, after the first or second generation, has to meet these difficulties. The history of Methodism, Quakerism, Scottish Calvinism, supplies many illustrations.

3. I think that Lightfoot has settled, with great probability, the genuineness of *some* of these strange epistles.

despotic sentiment; the most important point for this man, on a journey he expects to end in martyrdom, is the necessity that Church-members should obey their Bishops. More or less simultaneously with this growth of episcopal authority runs an increasing rigidity in the separation of the offices, and an enlargement of their numbers. We have, before the end of the second century, an order of sub-deacons, who assisted the deacons in their secular duties; a distinct order of lectors, whose business it was to read the Scriptures[1] to the congregation, and to take care of the copies used in the church; acolytes, who waited on the Bishop; exorcists, now more firmly established than ever; and *ostiarii* or vergers, who cleansed and arranged the church, and opened and shut it at the due times. Such multiplication of offices was clearly necessary as congregations grew; but it is plain also that it tended to exalt the chief men, and to diminish that equality which had once been so happy a feature in the communities. The Bishops, it is true, were still chosen by the congregation, and not imposed on them either from without or from above: and the election was usually a perfectly genuine voice. We hear also of frequent consultations with the presbyters on the part of the Bishops; more than once even so despotic a man as Cyprian says he does not wish to decide questions without their advice. And there can be no doubt that episcopal authority helped to exclude heresy, or what was supposed to be such, from the flocks which, without such a defence, it might have contaminated. Thus, to take but one out of a thousand examples, Serapion, Bishop of Antioch, hearing that the brethren in the Church of Rhossus, a little Cilician town, were in the habit of using the Gospel of Peter in their services, and, finding on inquiry that the Gospel was 'Docetic', condemned it.[2] But

1. In which (with variations in the different cities) were now included books of the New Testament in addition to those of the Old (which alone were 'Scripture' at the beginning of the first century).

2. Serapion was appointed Bishop of Antioch in or about 191. So early, then, we find Bishops of large sees exercising authority over smaller Churches within their sphere of influence.

there was unquestionably another side to all this. There are few things in all history more terrible than the spiritual tyranny exercised by some of these Bishops – a tyranny all the more dreadful because it *was* spiritual, and depended entirely on the imagination of the victim. Nor could the victim escape it by leaving the town and joining another Church: for more and more were the Churches being formed into federations, and more and more were the Bishops forming unions among themselves, meeting in synods, and combining to exalt their order.

The chief weapon was excommunication, and the chief excuse for excommunication was 'heresy'. One cannot quite lay the invention of this sin to the sole charge of Christianity: it existed among the Jews, and the Persians had something like it;[1] but it is safe to say that Christianity carried the idea to a height utterly unknown before, and that the principle, on which Christianity acted for hundreds of years, that an intellectual error is a crime to be punished by spiritual penalties[2] in this world, and by eternal torture in the next, almost counterbalances the benefits she had brought upon the world. Nothing astonished and disgusted the tolerant Romans more than this. Celsus, for instance, speaks with just indignation of the fury with which a heretic – that is, a man whose opinions differed from those of the majority – was pursued by those who professed a religion of love. 'They slander one another with all sorts of charges mentionable and unmentionable, refusing to yield the smallest point for the sake of concord, and hating one another with a perfect hatred.' The Church, regarding itself as the sole depositary of truth, denied the very name of Christian to any man who thought for himself. The thing began early. No book preached more beautifully on the

1. Herodotus is astonished at the bigotry with which the Persians attacked religions not their own, and destroyed the temples of the conquered nations.

2. Too soon, alas, physical penalties were added: as soon as the Church gained the power, she called in the secular arm, and with a refinement of hypocrisy, while disclaiming their use herself, saw to it that the State applied them.

text 'Love one another' than the Epistle of John. Yet this same John, if we may believe tradition, being at the bath and hearing that the heretic Cerinthus was on the premises, rushed out rather than see him.[1] The noble-minded Marcion meeting his old friend Polycarp after many years, went up to him and said, 'Don't you know me, Polycarp?' 'Yes,' answered the saint, 'I know you, the first-born of Satan.' Since they had last met, Marcion had been promulgating opinions which there is no reason to believe he did not honestly hold, but with which Polycarp did not agree. Why waste politeness on heretics? 'We have expounded their doctrines,' says Hippolytus, 'that they, ashamed lest we should prove them to be infidels, might to some extent abandon their absurd and wicked principles. But since they are not at all put to shame by our moderation, nor reflect that the God they blaspheme is slow to anger, I am compelled to expose their secret mysteries once again.' But there is worse than impoliteness. It is hard to find a single heretic whose private character is not blackened by the orthodox. We are already in the era of the *odium theologicum*. Nemesis, however, sometimes provides the appropriate penalty. Few of the Fathers exceed Tertullian in the ferocity with which heretics are assailed. Before very long, Tertullian becomes a heretic himself.

The heresies, as we have already seen, are countless: but the majority of those of the first two centuries, though differing widely among themselves, are often comprehended under the single name of GNOSTICISM, and have indeed something in common. Gnosticism was a system, or set of systems, based on the attempt to combine with Christianity elements derived from Greek and Oriental philosophies – especially the more mystical and transcendental theories of Pythagoras and Plato. In this endeavour the Gnostics often lose sight of historical fact entirely, and appear to consider Christianity as a mere system of metaphysics. It is probable

---

1. The tradition has high authority: but, even if false, shows that Christians saw no inconsistency in John's thus acting while bidding the disciples love one another.

that the Gospel of John was written in opposition to some early forms of Gnostic speculation: indeed, it has itself been called an exposition of Christian Gnosis. The theory of one of the chief of these Gnostics, Valentinus, is preserved for us by Hippolytus, and – though he tells us that even among the Valentinians there were great diversities – may be sketched here as a fair type of Gnostic views generally. 'Some,' says Hippolytus, 'in Pythagorean fashion, hold that the Father sits solitary, without a female principle or consort. Others, thinking that no existence could spring from a male principle alone, postulate Silence (Sigë) as a consort, in order that he might become a Father.' The Father, who is unfathomable, and whose best name is Buthos or the Abyss, is all Love; but Love must have an object, and, after endless ages spent in contemplation of its own perfections, the Abyss (with or without the aid of Silence) produces Mind and Truth (Nous and Aletheia), and then, in descending scale of pairs, the Logos and Zoë (Life), Man and Ecclesia (the Church), and no less than eleven other pairs. These thirty 'Aeons', among whom the Christ – to be carefully distinguished from the Messiah – is one of the chief – constitute the divine Pleroma or Fullness, and mark the gradual transition from the Infinite God to the visible world – a passage which all philosophies have found it difficult to bridge. The visible world, named Pathos (because passive), is created by God through the agency of Sophia, the actual labour of creation being undertaken by the Demiurgos.[1] When divine Wisdom has thus made Man, he is at first placed in Paradise, one of the many heavens of this cosmogony; but on his fall into sin he is cast down to earth. The chaos and confusion caused by sin demand a healer and a remedy: to accomplish this task the Demiurgos commissions the Messiah, on whom the Aeon Christ descends. The Messiah pursues his reconciling course until the Crucifixion: but here the philosopher is faced with an impossibility. Only the human Messiah can die: the Christ

1. The Demiurgos, or work-master, is obviously borrowed from Plato's creator-god.

is eternal. Before the end, therefore, the Aeon deserts him and ascends to the upper heaven.

This symbolic system, with all its modifications, is enough to show the hardihood with which men brought up on the Timaeus and Pythagorean mysticism attacked the problem of blending transcendentalism with the simple Gospel story. Such attempts must have been made very early. It is clear that among the Colossian converts to whom Paul wrote in the middle of the first century there were philosophers of this kind; and Paul in his letter indicates the limits within which he thought their speculations might safely play. Christ was the first-born of the creation; in him all things were created, visible and invisible, thrones, dominations, princedoms, powers; in him all the Pleroma was pleased to dwell, and by him the great Reconciliation, the Peace-making which harmonized things in heaven and things on earth, was brought to pass. Many years later, the Johannine Gospel further defined the orthodox boundaries of the theory, identifying, as we have seen, the Christ with the Logos-Aeon, and laying down the doctrine that this Aeon was actually made flesh. But it was impossible that the enthusiasm of philosophy should stop with the comparatively general phrases of Paul and John: a more detailed hierarchy was necessary, and with every added detail the door was opened for a new 'heresy'. Strange and fantastic as all this may seem to the concrete mind of today, it was not altogether alien to Christianity; there is much Gnostic mysticism in the orthodox creed. But, lending itself as it did to endless modifications according to the predilections of its successive exponents, it was inevitable that it should develop into forms which shocked the feeling of the Church – though all, or nearly all, of its teachers regarded themselves as no less Christian than the most pedestrian and literal-minded of Bishops. Cerinthus, though a Jew in origin, apparently thought his views as sound as those of John himself. Marcion, whose Gnosticism was a curious blend of practicality and visionariness, did not set up a separate Church till late in his career. Bardesanes, who lived beyond the bounds of the empire, mingled with his ideas a good deal of Chaldaean astrology, but remained, in his own opinion, a Christian. Simon Magus, around whom a vast mass of legend accumulated, was, according to Acts, a 'believer', despite the sorcery and charlatanry with which, if we may trust tradition, his doctrine was tainted. And, as we have seen, 'Docetism' was long innocently absorbed by Churches like Rhossus, which had no idea they were heretical. Docetism, in fact, was a philosophy only too easy to deduce from the Logos-theory of the Gospel of John. It was a natural, if false, corollary of that theory that the Christ, a divine Aeon, could not suffer; hence the Docetics (a name derived from the Greek *doceo*, to seem) held that the Jesus who perished on the cross was no actual man but a phantom.[1] The Gospel of Peter, which the Rhossians so eagerly read, declares that amid all the torments which preceded the Crucifixion, 'he himself was silent, as feeling no pain'.[2] It was left to the Bishops and other doctors to decide at what point Gnosticism ceased to be orthodox; and a very knotty question they found it to be.

Gnosticism, with all its eccentricities, compelled the Church to philosophize, and to attempt to reconcile the creed with reason; and the work was undertaken by many of the Fathers, with results often hardly less fantastic than those reached by the heretics. By the Alexandrian school, represented by two of the greatest names in all literature, Clement of Alexandria and his pupil Origen, the attempt was made with an energy, ingenuity, and learning scarcely ever surpassed. These men, by the aid of allegory in the style of Philo, and of a charity too rarely seen in the Church, tried to show that Greek philosophy was really a feeling after the truth: Socrates, Plato, and the Stoics were Christian

1. Some maintained that Simon of Cyrene was substituted for Christ, and was 'compelled to bear the cross' in the full sense of the words.
2. This phrase has been otherwise translated; but that the Gospel is Docetic is beyond dispute, whatever interpretation we give to this particular verse.

in intention, and by their noble lives and thoughts had prepared the way for Christ; while the Old Testament writers,
if properly interpreted, could be shown to be really Platos
and Zenos with a Hebraic tinge. No more stupendous *tour
de force* was ever undertaken: it is a proof of the powers of
Clement and Origen that it all but succeeded – though it
ran directly contrary to the common doctrine of the Church,
'*Extra ecclesiam nulla salus.*' As one reads these expositions,
one wonders what the Founder of Christianity would have
thought of them, or whether the original disciples would
have recognized their own religion in the system which
these philosophers had made of it. But this is always so.
Within the same Church there are always the learned and
the unlearned, and the creed of the one is never the same as
the creed of the other.

Heresy, then, ever reappearing, forced the Church constantly to redefine its views, and to lend precision to what
had been left vague by its original teachers: and the history
of Christianity in the third century is the history of successive endeavours to give exact expression to philosophic ideas
the very germ of which had, in many cases, never occurred
to the first generation of disciples. Every such expression
meant the shedding of a considerable number of adherents,
the creation of a new set of heretics, and the condemnation
to eternal flames of new multitudes. It was an exciting
game, of which, especially in the Eastern Empire, people
never seemed to tire: and it led, again and again, to open
tumult and to actual bloodshed. Anathemas and counter-
anathemas were bandied to and fro like the notes and pro-
tocols of diplomatists. Bishops are condemned and deposed,
absolved and restored, again condemned and again sent
into banishment. The furious attack of Hippolytus upon
Calistus, Bishop of Rome at the end of the second century, is
typical of what went on almost everywhere. If we are to believe the Bishop of Portus, the Bishop of Rome was a thief,
an embezzler, a cheat, and a convict. Worst of all, he was a
Noetian heretic. Whether the charges were justified or not,
is hardly important: they were made, and both accuser and

accused have been canonized by the Church. Cyprian, Bishop of Carthage, makes hardly less violent assaults on the Pope of his own time, though he is quite willing to avail himself of Papal aid when he needs it against Bishops in his own country. When Rome agrees with you, '*Roma locuta est*,' the question is decided; when Rome differs, her Bishop is a heretic, or at least in gross error.

By the end of the third century, though the number of disputed doctrines was still great, the attention of the Church, or at any rate of the Greek portion of it,[1] was mainly concentrated upon one. It was by this time pretty well agreed that Christ was divine; but it is obvious that there is room for disagreement as to the exact measure of divinity which his nature involves. He was the Son of God: what was the precise meaning of this phrase, which is plainly metaphorical? He was 'begotten' of the Father, before all worlds: *when* was he thus begotten? How far does Sonship imply subordination? The authoritative documents are either silent or ambiguous on these and similar points; but the Greek mind, inquisitive and subtle, was incapable of leaving them alone; and when once mooted they had to be settled – or, if they could not be settled, one out of the many possible theories must be selected and arbitrarily declared correct.

The man who forced these problems to the front was ARIUS, a presbyter of Alexandria. He does not appear to have been a person of profound or clear intellect, nor does he appear to have in the least intended to stir up the trouble which his lucubrations aroused. He meant simply to defend the doctrine of the Trinity against Sabellianism and Gnosticism. A rigid ascetic – 'having the form of godliness' as his enemies declared – he had, in an age of asceticism, far more influence than his mental powers deserved to gain; and his views were listened to with attention by many. The Son, he said, was produced by the Father, before all time, as perfect God, only begotten, immutable, but subordinate

1. The Western, or 'Latin', mind was far less prone to metaphysical abstraction than the Greek.

to the Father, and distinct from him. In a careless phrase, he even spoke of Christ as created by God, to be the Logos or Sophia by whose mediacy God intended to create the world. No sooner was this doctrine promulgated, than Alexander, Bishop of the city, assembled a conference, condemned Arius, and excluded him from communion with the Church. Thus began a storm which convulsed the world for centuries. Sensible men, like the historian Eusebius, deprecated equally the raising of a question beyond human power of solution, and the precipitancy with which Alexander had dealt with the defendant. But passions had been aroused, and the violent had to have their way.

It happened that about this time the Roman Emperor had taken the portentous step, pregnant with so much good and so much evil, of declaring himself a Christian. Years before, in conjunction with his colleague Licinius, he had, by the Edict of Milan, proclaimed toleration to the religion which his predecessors had persecuted; and since then he had gradually advanced until it is hardly an exaggeration to say that Christianity was the established creed of the State. His motives have been, and are, disputed: it may well have been the doctrine, always preached by the sect, of passive obedience to the king, that weighed most strongly in his mind. He was, it is certain, little more than a nominal Christian; his life after his conversion was no better than it had been before; and he took care to delay his baptism for a long while. But circumstances compelled him to pay attention to the disputes in the Church; for they bade fair to destroy the peace which it had taken him so many battles to gain: and the Arian was the chief of these disputes. It was not to be expected that a busy soldier and statesman should be able to find time for a personal investigation of so abstruse a question: Constantine was at the mercy of any theologian who happened to catch his ear at an opportune moment. At first he was persuaded, it would seem by Eusebius of Caesarea, afterwards his eulogistic biographer, that the quarrel was about a distinction without a difference: and he accordingly wrote to Alexander and Arius bidding them recognize each other as Christian brethren. Philosophers, he hinted, could differ on minute points without rancour; why could not theologians do likewise? But Constantine, though he knew barbarous mercenary soldiers, did not know the bitterness of theologians. The quarrel went on despite his exhortations, and soon threatened something like civil war. Strong measures were necessary; and in the year 325, Constantine summoned the so-called First Oecumenical Council of Nicaea in Bithynia. Three hundred and eighteen bishops, it is said, attended; and such was the throng of ecclesiastics and their attendants that the postal service of the empire was seriously disturbed.[1]

Among these Bishops, the party of Arius was very thinly represented; nor was the opposite party[2] much larger. The majority, like most of the Eastern Christians, were semi-Arians, occupying an intermediate position, and for the most part following the lead of Eusebius of Caesarea. These were anxious for peace, and endeavoured to induce the Arians to modify their extreme expressions, trying also to convince the anti-Arians that Arius was not as bad as he was painted. Eusebius therefore presented a creed, composed for the most part in Biblical phraseology, which the Arians might be willing to accept, and which their enemies could not refuse. The Arians did accept it; but the anti-Arians, who now had the ear of the Emperor, would not do so without adding articles condemning the 'blasphemies' of Arius. As usual, the determined minority prevailed over a vacillating majority. After a series of very unedifying

1. That Constantine convoked this council cannot be disputed, and there is no evidence worthy of notice that the Pope (Sylvester) was so much as consulted. That Constantine sought the advice of certain Bishops is, of course, probable enough; and Rufinus (about 370) says that he acted *ex sententia sacerdotum*. The evidence is, as usual, very fairly stated by the Catholic historian of the Councils, Bishop Hefele of Rottenburg.

2. Known as the Homoousian – that is the party which regarded Christ as of one substance with the Father. Another party, the Homœousian, was content to say he was of *like* substance: hence the common but superficial jibe that the controversy was about a diphthong.

scenes, the middle party, after the fashion of the Plain in the French Revolution, yielded to the energetic Homoousians, and subscribed the articles.[1] The Emperor, who, having listened to his anti-Arian advisers, had now been converted to Homoousian views – he was to change repeatedly in the sequel – did not hesitate to employ all the resources at his disposal to coerce doubters: and, like James I at the Hampton Court Conference, but with less excuse, he was vain of his theological knowledge and acumen. If we may believe Eusebius, he delivered a divinity-lecture, and called on all to accept his decisions. Disobedience was to be treated not merely as heresy but as treason.[2] Not many were found willing to contend with the master of thirty legions. Fifteen Arian Bishops yielded, not to conviction but to fear. Two only refused to be cowed, and utterly rejected the creed. Their names should be mentioned with the respect always due to conscientious courage, whether in a mistaken cause or not. Theonas of Libya and Secundus of Ptolemais ought to be as immortal as Virgil's two Trojan heroes:

> *Fortunati ambo si quid mea carmina possunt,*
> *Nulla dies unquam memori vos eximet aevo.*

They were not quite alone. Two Bishops, Eusebius of Nicomedia and Theognis of Nicaea, though not Arians, and though willing to subscribe the creed, declined to agree to the clauses condemning Arius, who did not, they maintained, hold the opinions which were censured. After a long and angry dispute, in which Christianity was all but lost in theology, the Emperor announced his final decision. Arius and his two supporters were condemned and deposed: those who should preserve their writings were actually, in good despotic fashion, threatened with death. Three months

1. With explanations intended to justify their action in the future Eusebius stated that he yielded for the sake of peace.
2. Men were plainly told that unless they conformed they would be acting *contra divina statuta*, as a Christian writer strangely puts it. This does *not* mean 'against the Laws of God', but 'against the imperial decrees'.

later, Eusebius and Theognis also were condemned and banished.

Selden, the great English jurist, once said that he would never believe 'the odd man to be the Holy Ghost'. On this occasion the 'odd man' was unquestionably Constantine, who had carried through by the strong hand what otherwise could not possibly have passed the Council. Nor was it long, as we have hinted, before his theological views, never based on sound knowledge, underwent an almost complete change. Partly through the influence of his sister, who was of the Arian persuasion, and partly through his own reflection, he began to fear he had been hasty. Arius was allowed to present an apology, which satisfied the Emperor; and within four years of the Council, the heresiarch was restored to favour; Theognis and Eusebius returned to their dioceses; and Constantine showed himself again eager to suppress discussion. The point at issue was, he now declared, of but trifling import, and those who desired his favour should never mention the subject. He met, however, a man not to be suppressed, who was determined to mention it. Athanasius, who, though a mere archdeacon, had been the real soul of the Homoousian party, was now Bishop of Alexandria. An uncompromising logician, and far more than a match for Constantine in stubbornness of purpose, he directly disobeyed the commands of the Emperor to restore Arius. The result was bitter dissensions in the city, leading often to open and violent riots. Athanasius was accused of fomenting these disturbances, and actually of treason against the Emperor, who, for the sake of peace, banished him to Trèves, at the other end of the empire. Shortly after this, a notable event happened. Arius was now in Constantinople, high in favour with the court. The Bishop of the capital, a strong Homoousian, was bidden to receive the heretic back into communion. Driven to distraction, he uttered the most un-Christian prayer, that God would remove either *him* or Arius from the world. That very day Arius suddenly died – a coincidence which occasioned Gibbon's famous saying that we are given an option between poison and miracle. The orthodox, of course, saw in it a divine judgement[1] – forgetting the words of Christ about the Tower of Siloam – while the Arians ascribed it to sorcery. Had there been any proof of poison, they would not have been slow to point it out.

For interminable years the feud continued, its fortunes varying not so much with the real opinions of the Church as with the attitude of the Emperor for the time being. One Emperor dies, and his successor restores Athanasius: that successor perishes, and Athanasius is again in trouble. One council declares in favour of Arianism, the next reverses the decision. Nor is it only kings, Bishops, and doctors who engage in these disputes. The populace is as eager in theological discussion as a British crowd in talking of a prize-fight or a football-match. 'Every corner of the city,' says Gregory of Nyssa, 'is thronged with men arguing on incomprehensible subjects. Ask a man how many obols a thing costs, and he dogmatizes on generated and ungenerated essence. Inquire what is the price of bread, and you are answered, The Father is greater than the Son, and the Son is subordinate to the Father. Ask about your bath, and you are told, The Son was created out of nothing.' But these are more dangerous themes than the relative merits of two footballers.

Enough may seem to have been said to show that Christianity was by now all but ceasing to be a moral religion, and was becoming a system of dogmas. The Sermon on the Mount was being forgotten, and theology substituted. It was enough to be 'orthodox', that is to profess the creed which, by any means, could contrive to be dominant for the time. Added to this was the influence of worldly ambition, which of course cannot be altogether excluded from the purest religion, but which rushes in as soon as the religion has court-favour, social prestige, or wealth, on its side.

1. It is due to Athanasius that, at least in his writings, he refuses to rejoice over the death of his enemy.

Those who are interested in the vagaries of the human mind may read Newman's chapter on the death of Arius in the *Essay on Miracles*.

Very early in the history of Christianity, James the Lord's brother had seen many of these evils creeping in, and had denounced them with vigorous emphasis: 'If there come into your synagogue a man with a gold ring, and a poor man in vile clothing, and ye have regard to the rich man, and say, Sit thou here in a good place, and to the poor man, Stand thou there, or sit under my footstool, are ye not making distinctions, and have ye not become judges with evil thoughts?' In the time of Constantine, James would have had more to say.

Within a hundred years things had grown worse. No more painful story exists than that of Nestorius of Constantinople and Cyril of Alexandria. These two great Patriarchs were rivals: the ancient city could not bear inferiority to the mushroom growth of Byzantium. Cyril, a man of unbounded ambition, of great skill in intrigue, totally indifferent to the means he used to gain his ends, in fact as un-Christlike a prelate as it would be easy to find, was determined to assert himself against the Bishop of Constantinople. For this purpose, the one simple device was to accuse him of heresy; and Nestorius, a monk suddenly elevated to a high position in the midst of a crowded and mundane city, soon provided his enemy with the desired opportunity. Vain, perhaps, of his own eloquence, he gave vent to some unguarded expressions. Particularly, he indulged in his sermons in attacks upon the phrase 'Mother of God' (*theotokos*) as applied to Mary. This phrase had often been used before, though its exact meaning had not yet been defined; it was popular; and it was easy for Cyril to arouse feeling against one who denounced its use. With stealthy and unrelenting animosity he worked his will, undermining Nestorius's influence at court, making friends for himself by bribery and flattery, by vulpine adulation securing the aid of Pope Celestine, and finally gaining the Emperor's consent to the summoning of a council, which he packed with his own adherents, and from which he contrived, till the decisive moment was over, to keep out the friends of Nestorius. The result, where such arts are employed against simplicity, is never in doubt. Nestorius was condemned and deposed. But the malignity of his foe was not yet appeased. Banished at first to a monastery near Antioch, Nestorius lived for a while in peace. But this was too close to the centre of affairs to suit Cyril. The Emperor was persuaded to exile him to an oasis in Egypt, where the only people who showed him kindness were a horde of barbarians who had made him prisoner. From Christians he received none. Despite the infirmities of age, he was dragged about from place to place on the borders of Egypt, and the letters he wrote to the governor were disregarded. How he died we do not know; but a charitable Church historian tells us that his tongue, the organ which had uttered his blasphemies, was gnawed away by worms, after which he was taken to the eternal torments of another world. Not all Christians, fortunately, are like this historian. 'Who,' says Milman, 'would not meet the judgement of the Divine Redeemer loaded with the errors of Nestorius rather than with the barbarities of Cyril?'

Nor were fellow-Christians alone the objects of Cyril's hatred. The Church, having been persecuted, had now become a persecutor, and bade fair to outdo Decius or Maximin in the ferocity with which it attacked those who did not accept its teachings. The Bishop, taking advantage of a riot in which Jews and Christians had been engaged, appeared at the head of an armed force, expelled the Jews from the city, and watched calmly while their houses were sacked. Five hundred monks came from outside, sword in hand, to defend him against Orestes, the prefect of the city, who not unnaturally resented his conduct: they surrounded Orestes, called him heathen and idolater, and all but killed him. But the people rescued their governor, seized the man who had wounded him, and put him to death. Cyril retorted by preaching a sermon in this scoundrel's praise, giving him the honours of a martyr, and naming him Thaumasius, the Wonderful. As for an even more atrocious crime, the murder of Hypatia, in which Cyril is not unjustly suspected of being accessory before the fact, the story is too well known to need repetition.

A Church like this, living in apparent negation of every principle laid down by its Founder, might seem ripe for destruction. The better men within it sorrowed over its degradation; the heathen without mocked at the contrast between its professions and its practice. 'The shepherds are driven out,' says Basil; 'in their place grievous wolves come in, not sparing the flock. The houses of prayer are empty; the deserts are full of mourners.' The hideous slaughter by which Damasus gained the Bishopric of Rome from his rival Ursinus – the battle cost a hundred and fifty lives – drew from the honest heathen Ammianus Marcellinus a sarcastic comment: the splendour of a Bishop's position, he says, its wealth, its luxury, are such that any crime may be excused which enables a man to attain it. No wonder that things like these made Julian desire to restore the old religion. Wild beasts, he knew, did not hate men as Christians hated one another.

From a church like this,[1] it is pleasant to learn, thousands turned away in disgust and shame. It is these scandals that in large measure explain the rise and rapid growth of eremitism and MONASTICISM. Since the world had captured the Church, and since there were no signs that Christ was yet coming to regenerate her, it was necessary to flee altogether from a Church that was indistinguishable from the world. For it is of the first importance to recognize that monasticism was in the first instance a determined revolt against ecclesiasticism. Strange as it may seem when we remember how in later times the monks became the Pope's Praetorian Guard, and how he took them under his special protection, we must not fail to see that in origin monasticism was a practical heresy, hateful to the episcopal order, differing from other heresies only in the fact that it was too strong to be suppressed. It was all but entirely a lay movement; clerics were admitted rarely and cautiously. Monks, as such, were not ordained, and only with great difficulty could they be induced to accept ordination and come out, like

1. And also to escape the attention of demons – an end not always attained.

Nestorius, into the world: some even mutilated themselves in order to escape the danger of being made Bishops. Nay more: they avoided Church services, and – especially when they lived alone – made it impossible for themselves to share in them in any form. Anthony, whose life was written by Athanasius, and who is a renowned saint of the Church, never observed any of her rites. By the very fact that monks and hermits separated themselves from men, they rejected Church ordinances with more than Quaker determination; they received no sacraments, made no confessions except to God, heard no sermons, died without the oil. Their whole system implied antagonism to an institution that had proved itself unfaithful to its Founder. Not for long did the clerical enemy, seeing that it could not overcome this spirit, contrive to harness it to its own uses: during the first centuries it detested and feared monasticism; the life of a monk was hardly safe if he appeared in a city; and but for the fact that the system harmonized with the spirit of the age, and that vast multitudes revered the sanctity of the ascetics, the Church would have crushed it as ruthlessly as Cyril crushed Nestorius. Fortunately for her own permanence, she failed in the attempt; for, with all its fanaticism and extravagance, monasticism was, at least in its earlier manifestations, the saving salt of Christianity.[1]

1. In connexion with Monasticism a word may perhaps be desirable about the Culdees, though they were not a sect, nor in any sense heretical. They were originally from the south of Ireland, and were thus attached not to the views of Columba or Aidan, but to the Roman communion. They celebrated Easter according to the Roman rule, and had the Roman tonsure. They seem to have been discontented with monastic life, and to have preferred therefore to revive the system of solitary anchoritism. When the Pictish King Nechtan expelled the North-Irish sectaries from his kingdom, the Culdees came to Scotland in considerable numbers, and some of their cells may still be seen. By the time of Malcolm Canmore they had apparently degenerated, though his pious Queen, Margaret, recognized the merits of many of them, and associated with them for religious reasons. Under David, they degenerated still further, and were somewhat ruthlessly 'reformed' by him. A hundred years later they had almost entirely disappeared.

They sought their homes in the most out-of-the-way places, not least

How far this form of asceticism may have been influenced by Far Eastern example – to what extent is started by imitation of Buddhist practice – we do not know; but its advance in the Roman world can be clearly traced to the desire to free oneself from the contamination of city life, and to the impulse towards personal religion as contrasted with mere membership of an institution. The Church, like the State, had overrated her importance: as has been well said, she had come to imagine that the individual lived for her, and not she for the individual. The rush to the desert, therefore, was like the old Exodus of the Israelites – it was undertaken that the emigrants might find a place, at three or four days' distance, where they might worship God in peace. It was this combined fear of infection and longing for solitary communion which led to those amazing extravagances associated with the names of Simon Stylites and Thalelaeus; how was it possible to talk with angels unless first we renounced talk with mankind? Jerome was a scholar and a man of social instincts; but if we read his letters we shall be inclined to believe that he saw no merit save in bookless and friendless solitude. Nevertheless, vast as was the prestige of the lonely saint on his pillar, or of the anchorite in his cell, the real strength of the movement lay in the monasteries in which numbers of men lived together. It was these that, as we have seen, strengthening one another's fanaticism, made a bodyguard for Cyril; and it was these that gave Athanasius a band of fighters against Arianism.

It was, indeed, the anti-Arianism of the monks that

---

on rocky islets about the coast. Many, it seems, went even further. When the Norsemen came to Iceland, about 870, they found there relics of the 'Papas', who they perceived were Christians, for they had left behind Irish books, bells, and crooks. These were almost certainly Culdee hermits. According to the Icelandic historian Ari, there were 'English' books which told of frequent early intercourse between the British Isles and Iceland. Only one, the Latin work of the Irish geographer Dicuil, is now known which thus speaks.

The word Culdee or Keledei is probably derived from the Latin Deicola, servant of God, which appears in Irish as Ceile Di, taken over into Scottish as Keledei or Culdee.

finally reconciled the institutional Church to them. Though the Bishops disliked the censure of episcopal arrogance implied in the withdrawal of so many laymen from their sphere of influence, though many[1] denounced their exaltation of celibacy over the married life, and though there were some who regarded the monastic system as a cowardly shirking of one's duty to one's neighbour, yet they were too useful allies in the war against heresy not to be, after a time, welcomed by the official Church.

Though there can be no doubt that monasticism and asceticism were a necessary reaction against the growing worldliness and luxury which threatened to undermine true Christianity, there are serious deductions to be made. Apart from the fanaticism inevitably produced when men of one way of thinking withdraw themselves from contact with men of other ideas, there was a self-centredness in the monks not easily to be harmonized with true humanity. The monk was intent, not on saving the world, but on saving himself. 'What he did more than this,' says Newman, 'is the accident of the hour.' 'Historians have supposed,' says Montalembert,[2] 'that Benedict intended to regenerate Europe, to stop the dissolution of society, to reconstruct public order. I firmly believe that he never dreamed of regenerating anything but his own soul.' Had the monks enlarged their ideas, and sought the salvation of others, the history of Christianity might have been different. Again, in their exaltation of celibacy, which was part of their belief in the essential wickedness of the flesh, they strengthened an evil superstition which has been the cause of much misery, while incidentally they promoted that Mariolatry which was soon to take possession of the Church. Paul's preference of celibacy to marriage, moderate as it was, rested on his conception that the fashion of the world passes away. But the monks, seizing on the Eastern idea of the inferiority of

1. e.g. Jovinian, who is best known to us by Jerome's ferocious and unseemly attacks upon him.

2. I take these quotations from Workman, *Evolution of the Monastic Ideal*, p. 12; a most suggestive work.

matter, degraded the very thought of marriage. There can be little doubt that the view put forth by Helvidius is the right one: the 'brothers of the Lord' were his full brothers, sons of Joseph and Mary. But this was a horror to the monk Jerome and his followers; and Jerome built up a theory, based avowedly on his own conjectures, that James, Simon, and the rest were the children of Mary the wife of Alphaeus, and thus not brothers but cousins of Jesus. In this manner, as he boasted, he saved the virginity, not of Mary only, but of Joseph also. To this the step, long afterwards taken, to the assertion that Mary herself was 'immaculately' conceived, was a natural successor.[1]

Such fancies were already in the air, especially in the air of the East. In the *Acts of Thomas*, an Edessan legend, we are told that the Apostle persuaded a young bride and bridegroom to live a celibate life after marriage. In the *Acts of Paul and Thecla*, Paul pronounces a blessing on those who have wives and are as if they had them not. There are very many, and very early, stories of brides who chose a celestial husband rather than the man to whom they had been wedded: one of these is familiar to all students of English literature from Chaucer's *Canterbury Tales*:

> ' *I have an angel which that loveth me,*'

says Cecilia to Valerian,

> ' *And if that he may felen, out of drede,*
> *That ye me touche or love in vileinye,*
> *He right anon wol slee you with the dede,*
> *And in your youthë thus ye shulden dye:*'

and it is with great appropriateness that the poet puts the story in the mouth of a nun. The mischief that these ideas caused can scarcely be exaggerated; and it is to monasticism that we owe, if not their origin, yet their wide and rapid

1. As Lightfoot points out, Jerome claims no traditional sanction for his theory: nor did he himself always hold it. It was invented for a polemical purpose.

diffusion. In our own history kingdoms have been rent to pieces by them.

The chief defect in such conceptions is this – that human nature is often too strong for them in practice: that suppression in the long run produces excesses of revulsion. We need not go far to find proof that monks and nuns did not always keep their vows: the *History* of Bede is full of instances. The same thing is true of their other renunciations. The monks could give up wealth, but could not resist avarice; and all sorts of ingenious devices were invented to combine poverty and riches, to serve God along with Mammon. There is *something* to respect in the man who openly says money is worth having and bends his energies to the gaining of it: but the man who pretends to despise it and yet contrives to get it is deserving of nothing but contempt. Monasticism, in its strictness, is possible only for the few; when, by the influence of fashion or caprice, it is adopted by the many, its ideals are certain to be degraded, and the scandal of professions belied by conduct is all the greater because the professions have been lofty. In the long run, as is well known, it was the inconsistency of monkish life with the monkish ideal that gave the first impulse to the storm which broke the Church to pieces.

Along with this movement, as none will be surprised to learn who know the tendencies of history, went one which ran, at first, directly contrary to it: the movement to institutionalize the Church still more, and make its orders and offices still more distinct and rigid. We have seen this process already beginning within half a century of the foundation of Christianity; the gradual assumption by the Bishops of supremacy over their brother-presbyters, and the substitution of a fixed form of Church government for the loose and free constitution of the earliest communities, and we have seen how, by the end of the second century, the offices were still more exactly graded and subdivided. We have now to see how this process was accelerated and strengthened, until even Bishops were subordinated to Archbishops, and finally the Archbishops themselves owned the suzerainty of one or two great Patriarchs. It was a natural, and perhaps inevitable, process, easily explained by historical circumstances, and fraught, like most changes in human life, with both good and ill.

Even so late as the end of the second century, we find Bishops still called presbyters; and, when writing to the presbyteral body, they often call themselves fellow-presbyters. The right of electing the Bishop was still in the hands of the whole Church, including the laity, though usually the presbyters seem to have selected one from their own order for the congregation to approve or reject. When chosen, he was still only 'primus inter pares'. But, in the case of strong-willed and ambitious men, this was already more a theory than a fact: and we can trace, in many districts, the fatal confusion between the Christian presbyter and the Jewish priest which gradually transformed the old equality into complete subordination. The presbyterate became a sacerdotal caste, and the Bishop a High Priest. As soon as this confusion became rooted, the Old Testament furnished many precedents which would encourage the advance of monarchism: there were the sons of Aaron, the priests, the Levites, for all of whom parallels were imagined in the Church. As the clergy rose, the laity were depressed. At one time a layman, if indeed we can call him such, might teach, preach, and administer the sacraments. Now, he became an inferior being. To the aid of Judaism came in the Roman system: the senatorial ordo, as contrasted with the plebs, provided a model for the constitution whereby the Church had its 'Orders' for the clergy, to which the plebeian laity were expected to acknowledge inferiority. Sometimes, it is true, the plebs rebelled, and remembered the words of Peter that they were all kings and priests: but circumstances were too strong for them. It is only just, moreover, to say that in many cases the Bishops earned their power by their constancy in times of trouble. Theirs was the post of danger, and they did not shrink from facing it. In the Decian persecution of 250, two Bishops of Rome suffered martyrdom. It is not surprising, then, that shortly after the date of this persecution the episcopal order made a great leap forward in prestige and power.[1]

Among these sufferers was Cyprian, Bishop of Carthage, who, though he was not, as yet, to die for the cause, had endured great privations. Perhaps more than anyone else, Cyprian was the man who stabilized the distinction of orders. Through his influence, the clergy were now forbidden to engage in trade or in any secular pursuit. This appeared to him as a renunciation of the world: the holy priesthood must not be entangled with things mundane; it was, in the phrase of the Epistle to Timothy, an army set free from civilian cares.[2] In this Cyprian showed himself a good organizer; but he was less successful in preventing the intrusion of spiritual pride, which is always likely to come in when one class of men is set above another: and the multiplication of orders within the order, which we have already noticed, hastened that degeneracy of the higher ranks which so fretted the minds of the better Christians and provoked the sarcasms of the heathen.

Each town had its one Church, and each Church had its Bishop, who in theory had been the equal of every other Bishop. As was repeatedly asserted, the size of a city had nothing to do with the sanctity or orthodoxy of its inhabitants: the Bishop of Portus did not hold himself in any way inferior to the Bishop of Rome, and rebuked him without fear or favour. And, on the well-known Irish principle that one man is as good as another, yes, and better too, Acesius, in his tiny see, thought himself better than either.

1. It must be remembered that in early days a Bishop might be a slave or handicraftsman, working for his living. Not till well-to-do men like Cyprian pressed into the Church, nor till she had the legal right to hold property, did the Bishops gain anything like full power.

It was not without good reason that, as rich men began to crowd in, and to gain high posts, Tertullian wished to compel all Christians to return to apostolic poverty. After the time of Constantine the Bishops became almost State officers – 'Poor-law Commissioners' – and this further increased their already swollen authority.

2. Thus Paul, who kept himself by tent-making, was represented as desiring the clergy to have no secular occupation.

But there was one ground, difficult to dispute, on which a certain moral superiority might be based. Those Churches which had been unquestionably founded by Apostles were not unnaturally held to be safer depositaries of the tradition than others, and, when doctrinal questions arose, appeals would be made to them: 'What has been handed down to you from St Paul or St John on this point?' Every such appeal inevitably increased the prestige of an *apostolica sedes*. It was thus that, in early days, Polycarp of Smyrna spoke with authority; he had, years before, listened to the living voice of John. It was the belief that Alexandria was evangelized by Mark, the minister of Peter, which lent so much weight to the opinions of Athanasius: and we know how often the Bishop of Antioch, associated with the names of Paul and Barnabas, was consulted by his brethren, and how anxious, conversely, Cyril was to keep him out of a council lest his vast influence might countervail Cyril's own. It was rarely that a country Bishop, *chorepiscopus*, could lay claim to such an apostolic origin; but there are traces that, in early days, when he could make this claim, he was listened to with respect. As, however, the Apostles for the most part confined their ministrations to the cities, the great centres of population had the double advantage of apostolicity and size – the one great exception being of course Constantinople.

And, of course, as Christianity spread from the cities to the small towns around, and – more slowly – into the villages, these smaller Churches felt their dependence on the metropolitan communities, and something like the modern conception of dioceses arose; these dioceses often corresponding in area with the imperial provinces. The Bishop of Antioch was the spiritual proconsul of Syria, the Bishop of Alexandria the prefect of Egypt. To these great personages lesser Bishops could not help looking for advice, or for protection against the terrible charge of heresy. Thus grew up the archbishopric – a conception which would have horrified a Timothy or a Titus. As usual, however, we must beware of generalization: there were, till very late, many

Bishops who still clave to the old idea of equality. As we have seen, as many as three hundred and eighteen were summoned to Nicaea; and each vote counted for *one*. Nor has the theory yet died out; at the Vatican Council of 1870 the vote of a Bishop *in partibus* – that is, of a Bishop without a see – was ranked as equal to that of an Archbishop of Paris. None the less, size always counts in one way or another.

Of all the cities, the greatest was Rome, not only in population but in imperial position, in the splendour of her past history, and even in her future; for all alike, Christian and heathen, assumed she would live for ever.[1] Nor less was Rome renowned for the number of her martyrs: her Church, placed 'where Satan's seat was', was always liable to suffer more intensely than any other. In smaller cities, again, it was possible for the whole Church to meet in one place: in Rome, it is said, there were no fewer than forty-six 'parishes'[2] administered by presbyters. It is clear that, in such a Church, the chief presbyter must be set distinctly apart from the rest in order duly to organize so great a system: and the man who is set apart is often set on high. The Bishop of Rome, then, had more authority over the presbyters than the Bishops of most other cities: and authority rarely disputed at home tends to be respected abroad.

There were few cities indeed that could have hoped to rival Rome in the struggle, which was certain to arise, for the hegemony of Christendom. Jerusalem, where the religion began and which for thirty or forty years held unquestionably the first place, had long since, by circumstances with which Christianity had nothing to do, dropped out of the race. First Titus, and then Hadrian, fancying they were conquering Jerusalem for a heathen Rome, were really winning the victory for a Christian one. The logic of facts, also, had shown that Christianity was to be, in the main, a Graeco-Roman religion; the East, on the whole, was not to adopt it, and the Jews had already decisively rejected it.

1. The author of Revelation himself, when he prophesies the fate of 'Babylon', puts it at the end of the world.

2. To use a convenient but inaccurate word.

Jerusalem, therefore, could no longer be the 'Omphalos' of the world: the geographical centre, and consequently the religious centre, was transferred to Italy.

Thus, among all the Bishops, who were in theory equal, the Bishop of Rome took naturally a high rank, and very early came to hold a leading position: a sort of vague precedence was allowed him, which, though largely a matter of courtesy, might be construed into a practical reality. Not that even this was not on occasion vehemently denied. If, as now and then happened, he lapsed into heresy, or denounced as heretics those whom the general Church accepted, he was treated with no more ceremony than Nestorius of Constantinople or Paul of Antioch. Liberius, when he became a semi-Arian, did not escape censure from the orthodox because he was Pope; now, when he returned to orthodoxy, did the Arians spare him. When Victor excommunicated the Churches of Asia Minor for celebrating Easter on the 'wrong' date, Irenaeus told him plainly what he thought of him. At most, he was among Bishops, *primus inter pares*, occupying about the same ambiguous position as the original overseer of an individual Church among his brother-presbyters: it remained to be seen whether he would make this mild primacy a sovereignty.

He was aided by the other great Bishops themselves, who often, when they wanted his assistance, used polite phrases which might easily be, and have been, interpreted as meaning that they owned his superiority. In reality, as their expressions on other occasions clearly show, they meant nothing of the kind: the compliments were like Ephron the Hittite's offer to Abraham, 'the field I give thee for nothing' – a prelude to a very shrewd bargain for a good price. They were, however, written, and the Popes took care that the *litera scripta* should remain.

But was the Church of Rome, in addition to its physical greatness, also apostolical? Could it rival Corinth, or Ephesus, or even Philippi, in this one most necessary point? Here tradition came to her help. Paul was known to have visited her and to have written to her one of the greatest of his letters. Peter was said to have come to her; after his escape from Herod's prison, he 'went to another place', and what could that place be but Rome? In his catholic letter, too, he speaks as if representing the Church of Babylon, and Babylon is a common synonym for the imperial city. Nay, it was all but certain that, like Paul, he had been martyred there. It was an easy leap to the conclusion that he had founded the Church, that Paul had collaborated with him, and that – though, if there is anything assured in history at all, it is this, that the Apostles were never Bishops – he was the first Bishop of the Roman Church. He was, in fact, the Rock of which Christ had spoken at Caesarea Philippi, on which not only the Roman but the universal Church was to be built; the chief of the Apostles and the first of Bishops.

This claim would have gone for little but for a political event. Already Diocletian had removed the centre of government from Rome, and established his fourfold sultanate elsewhere. A few years later, by the foundation of Constantinople, Constantine completed the work, and permanently transferred the seat of empire to the Bosphorus. Even when the rule was divided, the Italian Emperor was usually a mere *fainéant*: and when, in 476, the Western Empire was destroyed, the Pope was left to rule the city without a rival. While, then, the Patriarch of Constantinople, which was not even an *apostolica sedes*, was kept in his place by the pressure of the court, the See of Rome was free from lay domination, and could enlarge its claims almost without limit. 'The ghost of the Roman Empire' haunted the abode where the body had dwelt: and, as the robes of Western Bishops are the garments of imperial officials, so the Pope is the successor not so much of St Peter as of Augustus. He still bears the title which Augustus assumed among so many others, Pontifex Maximus; and, like Augustus, he has been addressed as Divus.[1] Nothing is easier to explain, on historical

1. One very significant difference between Pope and Patriarch may be found in the coronation-ceremony. No Western Emperor, after the reestablishment of the Western Empire by Charles the Great in 800, was more than Emperor-elect till crowned by the Pope. In the Eastern

and rational principles, than the growth of Papal power. But it *was* a growth: there was very little power to begin with, and what there was was often denied.

At once a cause and an effect of the gradual union of the smaller Churches into large provincial combinations, was the habit of convening provincial synods, in which questions of doctrine and organization were discussed, and which enabled men to meet and know one another. Such were the three synods held at Antioch to deal with the heresies of Paul of Samosata, which ended after some years (in 269) in Paul's condemnation and deposition. Such was the Synod of Elvira in the south of Spain, which was held, apparently, after the great persecution of Diocletian,[1] and decided what should be done with the 'lapsed' – that is those who had given way in time of trial. These synods were a natural preliminary to the great Oecumenical Council of Nicaea in 325, of which some account has already been given. This was followed by many others; in particular by that of Constantinople in 381, by that of Ephesus in 431, and by that of Chalcedon in 451. These four 'Oecumenical' Councils are, on the whole, recognized as authoritative by Protestants as well as by Romanists: but, by the Twenty-first Article of the Church of England it is laid down that general Councils may err, and sometimes have erred. It is, in fact, not so much the Council that is infallible as the common voice of the Church, and its 'oecumenical' authority is decided not beforehand but afterwards. Thus the Council of Ephesus in 449 was certainly meant to be oecumenical, but as its decrees did not harmonize with general opinion, they were reversed, and – though not

---

Empire, when the throne was vacant, the new Emperor was crowned by a representative of the electors, who was usually (but not always) the Patriarch; at least once he was a layman: when the Emperor appointed a colleague to succeed him, without a vacancy, after his death, he crowned him himself.

Had the Emperor remained in Rome, it would have been impossible for a Hildebrand to claim supremacy over kings.

1. The date is uncertain: the guessers differ by as much as seventy years.

more turbulent than many that have been recognized – it is known as the 'Robber Synod'. A thousand years later, the Council of Constance also met as oecumenical, but its decisions did not suit Papal claims, and it was removed from the list. On the other hand, the Council of Trent, in 1545, excluded the Protestants, and yet is perhaps the most highly honoured, in Catholic view, of all the councils. It is clear, then, that 'oecumenical' is a somewhat question-begging phrase: it resembles the famous definition of orthodoxy given by Vincentius of Lerins – '*quod semper quod ubique, quod ab omnibus*': whereas the very fact that there *are* dissentients proves that the orthodox opinion is held neither always, nor everywhere, nor by all.[1]

Such being the general theory, it was nevertheless inevitable that opinion should be, to a very large extent, moulded, modified, or even metamorphosed, by the energy and prestige of great men. Provided that the great man did not run too plainly against the prevailing spirit of the age, he might, by the charm of his style, by the sanctity of his life, by the strength of his personality, exert an almost unlimited influence on men's minds. He must, of course, be the child of the immediate past, and he must also be in the line of future advance: otherwise his very greatness will be his destruction: he will be like a statesman too far in advance of his time to be able to move the multitudes. But let the hour be propitious, and let the man be born – then, like Napoleon, he will go on from victory to victory.

Such a man we have seen already in Athanasius, who, by his forceful and indomitable character was able to establish the homoousian as the permanent opinion of the Church. It is true that he thought himself a solitary, and spoke of 'Athanasius *contra mundum*'; but, in reality, what gave him

1. The other famous phrase, '*Securus judicat orbis terrarum*', which made such an impression on the mind of Newman, expresses the same idea – that an article of the creed is established by a more or less universal consensus and by a certain permanence. To the sceptic, however, the principle is vitiated by the fact that you have often to rule out half the world from the '*orbis terrarum*', in order to obtain the desired unanimity.

his commanding place in the history of the Church was the fact that the world was with him. Time was on his side – the trend of thought was in his direction – and, as he happened to hit on what was to be the victorious opinion, his greatness had its free course and was glorified. It is no derogation from that greatness to say that he owed as much to his age as his age owed to him. So too the mighty monastic movement not only owed an immense debt to its great men – great in such varied and eccentric ways – Simeon, Anthony, Paphnutius, but lent them no small measure of their power. They were captains who at the same time rode the whirlwind and obeyed it.

Of all these great men, at least in the Western world, the most typical and the most dominating is Augustine, whose spirit still moves on the waters not only of Catholicism but of Protestantism, and who was the master both of Aquinas and of Calvin. We know him better than any other Father of the Church; for he has drawn his own portrait. Most people know the *Confessions*, that strange mixture of vanity and humility, of rant and eloquence, of superstition and commonsense. No one who has read the book can forget the terrible picture of the frightened mother, haunted by the fear that she has committed the unpardonable sin of bringing a child into the world who may be doomed to eternal damnation; weeping, praying, trying every means to drive, to cajole, to attract her beloved boy into the one Ark of safety; worrying Bishops with her anxieties, until they must have dreaded the sight of her. And everybody remembers how one of them, with a touch half of pity and half of impatience, told her 'it could not be that the child of so many tears could be eternally lost'. There must have been many mothers like Monica; and in reading Augustine's pages one wonders, again and again, whether Christianity has not caused more misery than it has alleviated. But perhaps not: the Monicas of today worry equally, though rarely about their children's chances of heaven or hell.

Probably all this fretting defeated its own end; for, though very tender with his mother's memory, Augustine gives plain hints that he jibbed at it, and, like a son of strict Victorian parents, had his fling. With a sort of Rousseauish gusto he describes his youthful excesses. It was not these, however, that terrified his mother so much as his propensity to heretical beliefs. For to mere moral wickedness God was infinitely merciful; but there was no forgiveness for intellectual error. Publicans and harlots might enter the kingdom of heaven; a Manichee never; and the youth showed a strange affection for Manichee doctrines and Manichee associates. For nine years, he tells us, he was 'seduced by this error, and seducing others': and he was plainly, after his conversion, far more ashamed of his heresy than of his debaucheries.

At about the age of thirty he began to be sceptical, and failed to find satisfaction in Manichean theories. He was in search of certainty, and nothing seemed able to provide it. His mind roved to and fro, but found no rest. Even the astounding fact that one of his friends, baptized while unconscious, was converted by the miraculous ceremony, failed to convert *him*. At length, at Milan, he fell under the spell of Ambrose; renounced his profession of teacher of rhetoric, and gave up to others the 'selling of words'. A severe toothache was cured by prayer. He had discovered, in the infallible Church, the sole haven of certainty and safety, and was baptized into it. 'O how I wept at thy hymns and canticles, deeply affected by the voices of thy Church, sweetly sounding! These voices flowed into my ears, and the truth distilled into my soul: and the stream of my devotion broke forth in weeping, that I found relief thereby.' If his faith needed confirmation, it was confirmed by the miraculous discovery of the bodies of the martyrs Protasius and Gervasius, found uncorrupted after many years, exactly at the moment when Ambrose needed a miracle for the confounding of the Arians who were troubling the Church.[1]

1. Those who wish to see two opposite views of this miracle may compare Newman's chapter on it in the *Essay on Miracles* with Rendel Harris's article in the *Dioscuri in the Christian Legends*. Harris points out the remarkable similarity between the performances of these saints and the feats of Castor and Pollux.

His mother had attained her heart's desire. 'Son,' said she, 'nothing in this life gives me delight any more. What do I here any longer, now that my hopes are satisfied? One thing only made me wish to live, that I might see thee in the Catholic Church before I died. My God hath granted me this, and more than this, even that I should see thee despising all earthly happiness, and wholly given to his service: why do I linger?' Within a few days she died.

Amid the multitudinous works of Augustine, not the least important are those that deal with the DONATIST controversy. The Donatists held that evil character and conduct on the part of an official of the Church vitiated not only all the services he performed, but the community to which he belonged: it was thus the first duty of a Church to cast out immoral members. On this question a quarrel arose which split the African Church for hundreds of years. Augustine, remembering his own early heresies, and knowing them to have been sincerely held, was, for a Christian of that time, tolerant in opinion and mild in controversy. But even he could not resist the temptation to bring in the imperial power, and to endeavour to suppress by force and bloodshed what could not be suppressed by argument. No persecution of Christian by heathen was ever more ferocious than this persecution of Christian by Christian, urged on and defended by doctors of the Church, who have since been canonized.

It is clear that, if the ruling theory of the time was in any sense correct, the Donatists were wrong. If, for instance, you cannot be saved without receiving the sacraments, and the sacraments are invalid when administered by an immoral man, then, since God alone knows for certain who is immoral and who is not, no one can feel the slightest security that he is in a safe position. The Donatists were therefore driven to confine their exclusions to cases of flagrant immorality. But this hardly improves their position. The worst of sins is hypocrisy, and this is precisely the one hardest to detect. Are we then to say that a baptism performed by a bold and honest sinner is worthless, while one performed by a man who adds concealment to his other vices is sound? Argumentatively, then, Augustine had an easy victory; indeed the Donatists, remembering his training in rhetorical and dialectic schools, refused to meet him in argument. The Church has decisively established the doctrine of Augustine, that the efficacy of the sacraments does not depend on the holiness of the ministrant; and there can be no doubt that she has acted wisely in so doing. But whether she has been equally wise in maintaining the principle '*nulla salus extra ecclesiam*' is more doubtful. It is strange that Augustine, when contending that the moral tares must be left to grow with the wheat until the harvest, should not have seen that the same sagacious negligence was desirable with the mental tares. He perceived clearly that to *force* the Donatists to seeming agreement with the rest, was merely to fill the Church with hypocrites; why could he not perceive that force employed against heretics would have the same effect as against schismatics? And why could he not see that a heresy, sincerely held, is far less blameworthy, if blameworthy at all, than moral obliquity? He was misled, it would seem, by his inability to distinguish between the visible and the invisible Church of Christ: the one necessarily contaminated with human weakness, the other, wherever it be, and by whatever name it calls itself, consisting of all who follow the Lord in sincerity. With all his mystical and rapturous piety, he yet could not rid himself of a mechanical and ritualistic conception of religion: and this conception is to be seen in his great work, the *City of God*, in which he tried to do for the Christian commonwealth what Plato had done for his philosophic republic. It was this that gradually led him, despite his past and his natural gentleness, to justify persecution and the use of force. On the one hand, the Christian State, like the secular, must tolerate certain vices which it either cannot discover or cannot check without introducing worse evils. On the other, it must punish crimes – treason, murder, *and sacrilege*. Were not, he asked, the Emperors right in inflicting death on those who sacrificed to idols, or in banishing those who would not submit to law? How then could it be wrong for the Church to destroy those who were guilty of the treason of heresy, or to call in the Emperors to help her, by fire and sword, to crush her enemies? 'Compel them to come in,' were the words of Christ; and this involved, surely, in the last resort, the use of compulsion not merely moral but physical. Thus early had the Church, having ceased to be persecuted, learned to persecute others; and thus quickly had Augustine, but lately a heretic himself, learnt to maltreat heretics. That he, like the Inquisition later, persuaded himself that he persecuted them because he loved them – he dwells on his love for them with endless repetition – only makes matters worse.

This mechanical view of the Church, also, is responsible for a doctrine which, perhaps more than any other, has revolted the conscience of the natural man. Since the time of Cyprian, and even before, it had been argued that, as baptism had been instituted by Christ, it was absolutely necessary to salvation. What then of the good heathen, like Socrates or Plato? What, still more insistently, of infants who died without receiving the rite? There were some who went the full length of sentencing these unhappy innocents to eternal damnation; and, unluckily, many of those who, like the Pelagians, could not stomach such an abomination, were heretical on other points. Some postulated a 'Limbo' or intermediate state between weal and woe, for those who, through no fault of their own, had not been immersed or sprinkled – a theory which will be well known to all students of Dante's *Inferno* – but condemned by Augustine on the ground that such a borderland between hell and heaven was unheard-of and inconceivable. '*Hoc novum, prius inauditum, esse vitam aeternam praeter regnum caelorum, esse salutem eternam praeter regnum Dei.*'

About the same time we see the gradual growth of a theory about the other sacrament, which was in time to develop into the *complete* doctrine of Transubstantiation. There can be little doubt that at first, and for long, the elements were considered merely as symbols of the body and blood of Christ. Even a Bishop of Rome had declared that, after consecration, the elements retained their material properties. But now, under the influence of the controversies concerning the dual nature of Christ, the question underwent a more comprehensive examination, and a considerable number of the Fathers recorded their views. The expressions of Augustine are ambiguous. On the one hand, he asserted that Christ's words 'This *is* my body' were Oriental and figurative; that *is* meant simply *signifies* (as Paul's words 'That rock *was* Christ' meant 'that rock was a symbol of Christ')[1]; but on the other, he seems to conceive of a *spiritual* transformation of the elements, in such a manner, and explained in such phraseology, as might admit of translation into the more materialistic doctrine which afterwards became recognized. I do not think, however, that a single one of the Early Fathers ever proclaims a theory which can easily be reconciled with the one elaborated by the Schoolmen of the Middle Ages, and buttressed by a Realist system of philosophy. It will be very hard to find a sentence, in any of these Fathers, stating unambiguously that, at every sacramental service, a miracle is performed when the words '*Hoc est corpus*' are uttered. The doctrine is a 'development' from earlier and simpler beliefs.

I pass over Augustine's views on Free-will and Predestination, where once more he is, I think, ambiguous: it was possible for Calvinism to find authority in his works, and yet the Catholic theory of '*liberum arbitrium*' (Free-will) may be deduced from some of his sentences. The greatness of Augustine does not lie in consistency but in suggestiveness; he resembles Burke, to whom Liberal and Tory may equally repair for the best expression of their views. In learning, and in charity, he was certainly inferior to Clement and Origen: but, through his *Confessions* and other writings, he makes a far stronger appeal to men. We feel him to be a human

1. On this Hebrew use of the substantive verb many controversies turn. No one doubts that 'I am the true vine' is metaphorical; or that 'Hagar is Mount Sinai' may also be thus taken; but there are many cases in which the Occidental mind finds it hard to recognize the Eastern idiom.

being like ourselves, and we listen to him more willingly than to the scholar or the commentator.

We have to travel more than six hundred years down the ages before we find a name to be compared, in doctrinal influence, with his. Anselm is best known to us in England as the man who resisted the tyranny of William Rufus, and wrested from Henry I the great compromise in the dispute as to investitures. But he is even more important as a theologian. If ever any one man changed a popular opinion, Anselm changed the whole view of the Church in one most vital point. Men's minds were busied with the question of the Atonement: Anselm set them at rest. The hour had once again come, and the man. Had he propounded his ideas a little earlier, or had his sanctity been less compelling, he might have been branded as a heretic; as it was, the times being ripe and his position unassailable, he is a saint, and his opinions are orthodox. Just as his support carried the Papacy for Urban against Clement in defiance of the whole force of the Empire and all the avarice of Rufus, so his advocacy of a theory of the Atonement first gained it a hearing and then secured its triumph. But the remarkable point about him is this, that in working this great revolution he was hardly aware of what he was doing. Like other great men, he went far because he did not know whither he was tending. No one was ever a more devoted adherent of the Church as it was, or more fully convinced that it was perfect and needed no improvement. He accepted to the full the idea that the whole Catholic system must be received, as it stood, without argument, by an act of faith which was also a deliberate act of the self-renouncing will. Thus, in all his speculations, he thought himself to be but an interpreter, to be simply drawing out into explicitness and clearness the true and recognized Church opinion; and yet he was all the while revolutionizing it, and revolutionizing it by that which – whatever we may think of it today – was meant to be, and was taken to be, a rigid chain of cogent ratiocination.

About this time the prevailing conception of the 'Scheme

of Salvation' – the doctrine of the Atonement – was roughly this, that by the fall of Adam the whole human race had passed under the dominion of Satan. God, however, had come to the rescue, and had arranged with Satan a composition, by which the Son was offered to death in exchange for the human race: 'God so loved the world that he gave his Only-Begotten, that whosoever believeth in him should not perish.' Satan accepted the treaty, thinking that God's own Son was a full equivalent for what he renounced. But – and here the theory was often put with a full measure of medieval crudity – Satan was deceived – nay, were less august personalities concerned, we might almost say he was cheated. The bargain having been ratified, the Son appeared on earth as man, and duly died in human fashion. Within three days, however, the Devil found that though Christ could submit to death, it was impossible for him to be holden of it: and thus not only was mankind given a second chance of salvation, but the ransom which Satan had accepted in place of man had slipped through his hands.[1]

Against this theory, the grotesqueness of which is not easily to be exaggerated, the whole nature of Anselm revolted; and, in one of the palmary books of the world he gave his own reading of the doctrine of the Atonement; a reading which amid all the various presentations of the doctrine, still holds perhaps the foremost place.

The *Cur Deus Homo*, 'Why God became Man', is to the modern mind, a curious work. It takes the form of a dialogue between a doctor and his pupil, often becoming a rapid alternation of question and answer. We are again and again reminded of Socrates and his interlocutors. But there is little in the logic to convince those not accustomed to scholastic disputations, Boso is constantly assenting to his master's reasonings when, to us, their cogency is very dubious. There are scores of must-be-so's when the utmost

---

1. A mythical expression of this theory is to be found in the 'Harrowing of Hell' – a story found in the apocryphal Gospel of Nicodemus, and one of the favourite subjects of medieval poetry. It is, as all will remember, utilized by Dante in the fourth canto of the *Inferno*.

we should admit is a hesitating 'may be'. But, as with many books, the results are worth more than the process. There is nothing here of a bargain between God and Satan; the scheme of redemption is the product of the divine benevolence towards man. Sin is the failure to give God his due, and therefore leaves man in a state of indebtedness; he must repay the debt with an added satisfaction. Punishment is not revenge but the natural effect of sin, the remedy arranged by God for the confusion which sin has wrought. Nor would man, even if he committed no sin, have done more than his simple duty: he *owes* the living of a perfect life. All, however, have sinned, and the rendering of satisfaction is thus impossible for man as such. No return can be adequate, short of infinity: and thus the return must be made, in a fashion, by God to himself. And yet, from another point of view, it must obviously be made by man. God, then, must become man, and accept the death-penalty which the first man brought upon the race. The Second Adam pays the due of the First.

But how, if Christ thus suffered death voluntarily, can we save him from the charge of suicide? Here Anselm becomes almost metaphysical. Christ endured death because death was involved in that perfect obedience to God which he ceaselessly showed: it was not sought for itself, but *accepted* as a consequence of his submission to the divine plan. Nor, though he endured all kinds of pain and torture, can we call him miserable, for the pain was deliberately chosen as means to an end, namely the conquest of evil. For all this, a recompense was due to him; but what recompense can the All-sufficient desire or receive? At this point we return again to mankind. Christ has no need for a return, but he can transfer the account to men; and, as his perfect work is more than sufficient for all demands, however many there may be who enter into communion with him, and thus share in the benefits he has conferred, there is never any lack. The fund of merit, if we may so put it, is inexhaustible; punishment becomes unnecessary, and harmony is established without the infliction of the pains of the law. It is thus seen that the Atonement involves a vicarious and active satisfaction; and it is clear, from the infinite resources required, that no other being than Christ could have done the work. An angel, after all, is finite; and further, it is due to the dignity of man that he should lie under this tremendous obligation to nothing created, but directly to God alone.

All this may seem to the reader sufficiently abstract; and the theory did not commend itself to all. Somewhat later than Anselm, the famous Abelard[1] took up the question. He too utterly rejected the idea of a bargain between God and Satan; but he could not see how the death of an innocent person could diminish the amount of injustice in the world. He therefore inclined to the view that we are reconciled to God, not so much by Christ's death in itself as by the love of which that death is a manifestation. Of this love, and of the self-sacrifice it involves, we are to be imitators, and in this way attain salvation. But Abelard's theories were pronounced – for the time being at least – heretical, through the overmastering influence of St Bernard. To Abelard a faith that could not be reconciled with reason was worthless: to Bernard the first essential was an unreasoning trust. Since then, there has been a reaction to the principles of Abelard: it is the opinion of Catholic doctors that the creed of the Church can be demonstrated by a chain of argument as cogent as that of Euclid, and that the truly honest reasoner, if capable of understanding it, cannot reject it.

These few examples will be enough to show how narrow and perilous was the path which had to be followed if heresy, on the one side or the other, was to be avoided, and how many must have fallen into the abyss though anxious to keep the right road. Where, for instance, so metaphysical a question – on which Scripture is altogether silent – as that relating to the exact balance between the two natures of Christ, had to be answered, where the utmost nicety of thought and language was necessary; and where the chances

1. Abelard does not appear to have read the work of Anselm; the theory, however, may well have come to him at second-hand.

both of error in oneself and of being misunderstood by others were so numerous – how was it possible for anyone to escape, especially if he had sharp-sighted enemies ready to pounce on the first unguarded phrase? We have seen many such cases, and there are scores of others. Nestorius starts his career in Constantinople with the fixed resolve to root out heresy from the see: ere long he is himself suspected, accused, and condemned as a heretic. Tertullian, perhaps the stoutest defender the early Church ever had, tottered over the verge into Montanism: Origen, one of the greatest of all scholars, and a man to whom we still owe an incalculable debt, made the mistake of thinking for himself, and lost that prefix of 'Saint' which many far less deserving, and some who never existed, have triumphantly borne. Monophysitism, Gnosticism, Sabellianism, were all, as far as we know, honest attempts to discover the truth: all were condemned. Marcion, Novatian, Eutyches, Apollinaris, Jovinian, Pelagius – against all these the dread anathema has been uttered. Some, even of the Popes, have been tainted with heresy, and several others have been threatened with the accusation. How has the Church contrived to escape?

The unbeliever has his answer ready. The Church has avoided heresy simply because heresy is the view she has not happened to adopt. As, in the secular world, treason that prospers is not treason, so, in the spiritual, the heresy the Church accepts becomes *ipso facto* orthodox. For a time, Arianism prevailed in a large part of the Church, and was, within that time and in that space, the right creed. It might conceivably have prevailed altogether, and then it would have been our orthodoxy today. There is nothing particularly wonderful in being always right if you are your own umpire.

The explanation given by Rome herself is very different. A special grace of God has always watched over her to guard her from error: a pillar of cloud by day and a pillar of fire by night have always guided her in her pilgrimage: or, to use another metaphor, the ship of the true Church has had always a divine Pilot to steer it through the innumerable rocks and shoals on which other barks have made shipwreck. It has, it is true, not been the will of God to reveal even to her the whole true doctrine from the first: but in due season he has always done so. Thus a dogma may have had to wait many generations for precise and full definition; several dogmas, indeed, were not thus defined till, in the sixteenth century, the Holy Ghost, by means of the Council of Trent, pronounced the momentous words. The Immaculate Conception of the Virgin, long denied by the Dominicans and others, was found to be true doctrine, but not till 1854; and the infallibility of the Pope, openly contested by good Catholics for centuries, was not established till 1870.[1] Implicitly, it is maintained, the Church has always held these doctrines: they do not become explicit till the Holy Ghost in his own good time, chooses to announce them.

The advantage of this principle is manifest. The simple, ignorant Catholic is safe if he accepts the Church as a whole, and is willing to believe whatever she bids him believe: it is not his business to study her complicated theology. '*Credo ut intelligam*,' he says like Anselm: but even if he never understands, the *Credo* is enough. There are many dogmas, as will be clear from what we have said already, which few Catholics are capable of either accepting or rejecting: they are beyond the powers of all but the highest intellects. But the pious believer accepts them *en masse* on the authority of the Church, and such acceptance is sufficient. The same principle is applied in other ways. Catholics who died before 1854 are not condemned for not believing in the Immaculate Conception; but since that date we are bound to believe it, either knowing it directly as a particular dogma, or if not thus knowing it believing it as part of the general creed of the Church, whose word we take. It is thus that, to the astonishment of Protestants, Catholics are able to digest

1. The Irish Bishops, consulted on the point shortly before the Emancipation Act of 1829, denied that it was the Church's belief; and Hefele declared that though he had studied Church history for fifty years, he had found not a single important authority in favour of it.

propositions which they have opposed. It is certain, for instance, that scores of the ablest and most learned Catholic
Bishops in the world did not believe in the Infallibility of the
Pope; many of them said so openly, and some prayed aloud
that the divine grace might avert the proclamation of so
fatal a doctrine. Yet, when it passed the Council, they read
it to their flocks. *Roma locuta erat*. If, in the Church of England, the authority (whatever it is) asserts a doctrine in
which a certain clergyman does not believe, he still does
not believe it, and either stays calmly in the church preaching his own doctrines, or, if his conscience does not permit
this, goes quietly out.[1]

It is now necessary to trace, as briefly as possible, the
steps by which the Church, not as the depositary of truth,
but as an organized institution, made its way to the commanding position in the world which it held in the Middle
Ages, and which it has not even yet altogether lost. We
have seen how the absence of the Emperor, and the destruction of the Western Empire (usually dated 476),[2] gave the
Bishop of Rome an opportunity of gaining independence

1. After the proclamation of Papal Infallibility in July 1870, most of
the Bishops who had shown opposition submitted: but a number of
Professors of the University of Munich issued a protest, declaring the
decision of the Council invalid. Though there was no desire to separate
from the Church, circumstances were too strong for them, and the result
was the formation of the 'Old Catholic' Church, which, though it undoubtedly possesses the Apostolic Succession, and recognizes all the
decrees of the Council of Trent, has been decisively repudiated by the
Papacy.

A movement was recently started for a kind of federal union between
the Old Catholics and the Anglican Church; and the two Churches are
now in 'communion' with each other.

2. In theory of course, this meant simply that the Roman world was
again ruled, not by two or more partners, but, as before, by a single
Emperor. The Empire was not destroyed, but reunited: the conquerors
called themselves officers of the very Emperor whose dominions they
were attacking. And, under Justinian, an attempt was made, which
temporarily succeeded, to translate the theory into practice, but even
Justinian with Belisarius to help him could not restore the past. An
imperial Exarch ruled, it is true, but in Ravenna; and Rome was ruled,
in effect, by the Pope.

such as never came to the Patriarch of Constantinople. It happened also that in the middle of the fifth century the Pope was one of the greatest of the long line of the successors of St Peter. In the Eutychian controversy, which followed immediately after the Nestorian, and threatened to split the Church into fragments, his influence was decisive, and his legates actually took the lead in the Council of Chalcedon. Almost at the same time his prestige rose still higher. Attila was in Italy, and Rome seemed to lie at his mercy. Leo, if we may believe the story, went out to meet the terrible conqueror, and by the majesty of his demeanour so awed him that he departed and never returned. Though there were other accounts, this one was too picturesque not to capture the popular fancy in preference to prosaic fact: and Leo has the glory of repelling two enemies of the Church – the 'scourge of God' with his myriads of horsemen, and the 'blasphemer' who disseminated false notions as to the nature of the God-man.

Even Leo, however, made no claim to temporal sovereignty: and his attitude to Theodosius is, in comparison with that of later Popes to later Emperors, humble enough. Nor were his successors less submissive. A hundred and fifty years later, Gregory the Great arose, a man recognized by historians as the real founder of the Church of the West. This illustrious man, though still refusing the title of Universal Bishop, ruled all other Bishops, on this side of the Adriatic, with a rod of iron. He compelled the metropolitans of Gaul to submit to his sway, and Spain, which had just been recovered from Arianism, followed the lead of Gaul. In a charter to the monastery of Augustodunum (Autun), he went so far as to use, for the first time, a papal curse as a weapon against royal oppression. As all know, he made a beginning of the recovery of our own island to the Roman obedience, while in Italy he was king in all but name. And yet even he, in his intercourse with the Emperors, shows himself absolutely slavish in his language. His successors for a long while were never consecrated until their election had been confirmed by the Emperor or his representative the

Exarch of Ravenna. Martin I, having offended the Byzantine court, was dragged from Rome to Constantinople, and banished thence to Kherson.[1] There was as yet no thought of equality, and the idea of Papal superiority to the Emperors was too ridiculous for the wildest theorist to entertain.

The opportunity came when the Emperors set themselves against a popular opinion which the Popes could champion with the certainty of receiving strong support. In the eighth century, Leo the Isaurian began his campaign against image-worship. Mohammedanism had extended its conquests far and wide; and the Mohammedan jibe against the Christians – the jibe that stung – was that they were idolaters. Leo felt the taunt, and determined to remove the excuse for it. All the ignorant, in East and West, rose to preserve their precious relics: and there could be no doubt that here at last was a struggle between Church and State. Gregory III, confident in his position, ventured on the portentous step of excommunicating the Emperor (728). This was the decisive advance towards a consummation which had long been threatening – the severance of East and West. Circumstances lent it even greater significance. The Lombards, pretending to be supporting their Lord the Emperor and at the same time, inconsistently enough, to be defending the orthodox faith, moved on Rome. Gregory, at his wit's end, saw nothing for it but to call in the aid of the Franks, then at the height of their prestige through Charles Martel's great victory over the Mohammedans at Poitiers. Charles's son, Pippin the Short, was only too glad to accept the invitation. Charles and Pippin had been nominally but 'Mayors of the Palace' to the Merovingian *fainéants*. In return for the gift of the actual kingship, Pippin

1. A hundred years before this Sylverius had been deposed by Belisarius and Vigilius appointed in his place. The tergiversations of Vigilius in the Monophysite controversy – he wavered from side to side, and finally came out for the heretical opinion – are one of the chief difficulties in the way of the Catholic doctrine of Papal Infallibility. But our point here is that the Pope's vacillations were the result of excessive deference to the imperial authority, which he could not openly dispute.

promised his aid. The Pope released him from his oath of allegiance; Chilperic, the heir of the Merovingians, was deposed; and finally a Pope in person anointed Pippin king at St Denis. The Franks returned the favour with interest. The Lombards were defeated, and the Exarchate of Ravenna, which they had occupied, was taken from them and handed over to the Pope. Thus began that 'temporal sovereignty' about which there have been so many disputes, and so many myths.

Some years later, Pippin's son, Charles the Great, succeeded to the throne. The Lombards again became troublesome; they were crushed, and their kingdom was annexed. For many years Charles ruled Rome, nominally as Patrician under the Emperor of the East, really with absolute power, finding, as he says in a letter, the Pope's humility and loyalty worthy of all praise. In the fateful year 800 the farce was ended. A riot, in which the Pope (Leo III) was all but killed, gave Charles his chance. Leo fled to him for protection. A trial was held under the King's presidency; the charges against the Pope were heard by a lay judge, and pronounced unjustified; Leo was restored to his see. In return, he had much to give. On Christmas Day, Charles was crowned Emperor of the West by the Bishop of the one remaining apostolic see.

While Charles lived, the full consequences of this act were not seen. He was as absolute in Church and State as any Russian Czar in later times; the Bishops and abbots were his liegemen, the Pope his abject slave. He did not hesitate to oppose the Papal notions, even in doctrinal affairs; and he repeatedly censured the ambition and rapacity of the Roman Bishop. But, by the wealth he had given the Church, and by the subjection to Rome which he enforced on the metropolitans in his dominions, he was really laying the foundations of that universal dominion, clerical and secular, which Rome was afterwards to claim and very nearly to win.

The process was aided by a catastrophe which proved to be a blessing in disguise. There had been occasions already on which Eastern and Western Christianity, like the Eastern and Western empires, had seemed on the verge of schism. But now, fifty years after the coronation of Charles, the likelihood became a reality. A quarrel arose between Nicholas I, Bishop of Rome, and Photius, Patriarch of Constantinople. Into the intricate details of this quarrel we need not enter; it had as many changes of fortune as the Wars of the Roses. Photius rose and fell as successive Emperors supported or deserted him, and in fact he ended his days in retirement. Yet before this his cause seemed won; a new Pope had recognized his position. It might seem that the schism was healed. But it was not so; the real question was a deeper one: was Caesar, or was St Peter, the real ruler of the Church? The Emperor had no doubts. Even if he deposed Photius, he did so of his own free will, and not in obedience to Rome; if he restored him it was the business of the Roman see to acquiesce in the restoration. The Pope, on his side, was equally certain: it was he and no one else that set up or pulled down other Bishops. On a point like this there could be no lasting compromise; for the Eastern Emperor was, and meant to remain, the master of the Eastern episcopate.

Both sides, of course, availed themselves of spiritual weapons. Nicholas anathematized Photius; Photius anathematized Nicholas. A long list of charges was brought by Photius against his enemy; the Pope was accused of compelling his clergy to shave their beards, and of observing Saturday as a fast. These accusations were terrible enough, but there were others still worse. He was a heretic, for he added the *filioque* to the clause in the Nicene Creed which declares the 'procession' of the Holy Ghost to be from the Father only; and he was ruining the morals of the Church by insisting on the celibacy of the clergy. But all this was merely the pretext for the war; the real cause was the fixed determination of the East to rule itself and indeed the world. 'These men,' wrote Nicholas indignantly, 'maintain that when the Empire was transferred from Rome to Constantinople, the primacy which the Roman Church had held was transferred with it: with the imperial dignities the Church privileges had also crossed the sea.'

Attempts were made, more than once, to heal the breach; but all in vain. In 1204 the Venetians conquered Constantinople, and thus paved the way for the Turkish conquest two centuries later. Innocent III seized his chance; Latin Bishops were intruded into Eastern sees – an unpardonable offence in Greek eyes, and one that defeated its own end. When it was clear that the Ottomans were advancing upon Constantinople, and that nothing but a crusade of all Europe could save her, the Emperor John Palaeologus made a last despairing effort. At the Council of Ferrara, in 1438, seven hundred Eastern Bishops met their Latin brethren, to discuss terms of reunion. The debates were long and painful; but at last when the council had been transferred to Florence, the Greek delegates accepted the hard conditions. They agreed to the *filioque*, consented to admit the primacy of the Pope, and adopted the Roman theory as to Purgatory. Pope Eugenius broke out into a paean of praise; the schism was ended, the garment of Christ was again seamless. Two obsequious Eastern Bishops were made Cardinals, Bessarion of Nicaea and Isidore of Russia.

The whole thing was empty and meaningless. The Emperor went back, to find no one on his side. The Bishops were assailed with accusations of bribery and corruption. No priest could be found to recite the *filioque* in the Creed. Monks and women joined in the outcry against the traitors, who indeed declaimed against themselves. 'I was forced,' said the Archbishop of Heraclea, 'to vote against my conscience; would my right hand had been cut off before I signed.' Bessarion fled to Italy; Isidore stayed at home, to meet universal contempt. Nor did the West perform its part of the bargain. No crusade set forth; a few volunteers were all that Europe could send to the help of the Lord against the mighty, and John saw that he had given up everything for nothing. The Greeks preferred the Turks to Rome. Within fourteen years Constantinople was taken by Mohammed II, and the Creed, with or without the hated phrase, was heard no more in St Sophia.

Since then, there has been no thought of union. Some

High Anglicans have conceived the idea of joining the Church of England with the Orthodox Church; but no Greek thinks of submitting to the Roman Bishop. The supremacy and infallibility of the Pope were solemnly affirmed at the Vatican Council; were the Greek Church to agree to that it would stultify its whole history.

CHAPTER 7

CHRISTIANITY AS A
SYNCRETISTIC RELIGION

IT was a just charge of the Latin Church against the Greek that it neglected the evangelization of the heathen. The conversion of the Goths was, it is true, accomplished by Eastern missionaries, but they were Arians, and the converts had to be rescued from heresy later; and after the schism it is hard to find a single great missionary effort carried out under Greek direction. The conversion of Russia, vast as was its importance in the history of the world, was due to the accident that one of the Czars was a Christian, and imposed his religion, in good Czarist fashion, on his subjects.

Very different is the case of the West, the glory of which is that it has scarcely ever ceased to evangelize. All have heard how Gregory the Great sent Augustine to England, and know the marvellous success which attended the labours of Augustine and his companions. We must not, however, forget that the way had been prepared by other agencies. Bede, it is true, tells us that the Welsh made no attempt to convert their English conquerors; but it is hard to believe that the British women who became the slaves of the English did not do the sort of work that Naaman's little maid did in Damascus. There is every sign that the English were not entirely ignorant of Christianity when the Roman priests arrived. But, be this so or not, it is certain that the monks from Ireland had done much during the preceding century, and continued to do much for many years afterwards. Neither Welsh nor Irish owed any allegiance to the Roman see, and some of their usages – particularly their observance of Easter at a date said to have been authorized by the Apostle John – differed from those adopted in the Western Church. Augustine and his followers made many efforts to bring these 'sectaries' over to the Roman obedience, but in vain. The Archbishop was not of a conciliatory disposition, and, at a council held near Gloucester, irritated his opponents by his haughty demeanour; nor could even a miracle and a prophecy of disaster as the punishment of contumacy win them over. The dispute lasted yet for many years. Meanwhile the Irish missionaries, of whom Aidan is the best known, continued their devoted labours, especially in the kingdom of Northumbria; the kings and chief men were converted, and a great impression was made on the common people by the humility and sanctity of these evangelists' lives. As Romanism advanced, it became necessary to decide the question between the two Churches. Nor, though it turned mainly on the trifling question of Easter, was it trifling as a whole; for on the decision hung another question – was England to be drawn into the circle of Western civilization, or was she to remain without?

It was settled, at least formally, at the famous Synod of Whitby in 664 – a synod described by Bede with his accustomed force, simplicity, and beauty. King Oswy – and it was with the kings, in Germanic countries, that the real weight rested – chose in favour of Rome; and the English Church was thus brought into relations with the Papacy – relations loose it is true, and neither everywhere nor always recognized – but close enough to mean much in the long run. The decision of the synod was won by the efforts of a man of dauntless energy, often unscrupulously exercised, but on the whole beneficial – the tireless, indomitable, fanatical Wilfrid of York. The organization of the dioceses on a Roman model[1] was carried through with great ability by Theodore of Tarsus,

1. The English dioceses, unlike those of Gaul and the Roman world generally, were large and territorial, by no means limited to cities and their neighbourhoods. Roughly, they covered the area of the old kingdoms, and elsewhere they would have been archbishoprics. But, *as such*, they were organized and controlled from Canterbury by Theodore, who was a sort of English Pope.

who in 669 became Archbishop of Canterbury, and brought the Church still more under Roman dominion by refusing to recognize orders conferred by the Irish missionaries.

In similar ways Rome contrived to appropriate to herself the results of Irish missionary labour in Gaul and Germany. The great Columban, a monk of Bangor in Ulster, went forth to Gaul, where he founded the monastery of Luxeuil, a centre of piety, extreme austerity, and propagandist enthusiasm. Having, however, like John the Baptist, openly rebuked Brunehaut for her crimes, he was expelled from the country. Passing the Rhine, he settled at Bregenz on Lake Constance, in the midst of heathen tribes. Here he assailed the religion of Odin with that mingling of courage and excessive fury which marks so many of these early missionaries, and which so constantly qualifies our admiration. He was, not unnaturally, driven thence by the priests. who resented the breaking of their idols and the hurling of them into the lake. But the work went on. He was followed by his friend St Gall, founder of what is perhaps the most famous monastery in Central Europe, before whose prayers and fastings the heathen spirits fled shrieking to their confines. Scores of monks from Luxeuil carried the Cross everywhere from Brittany to the Black Forest and beyond. But here again Rome stepped in, especially through the agency of the English. Willibrord of Northumbria, working in harmony with Pippin of Heristal and Charles Martel, in the first half of the eighth century, by indomitable labour, converted to Christianity the country round Utrecht; and Willibrord was of the school of Wilfrid, holding the Roman allegiance. At the same time, Winfrith of Crediton in Devonshire, after spending many years in the monastery of Netley in Hampshire, was seized with the missionary impulse. Obtaining a commission from Gregory II, he went out into the vast district between the Rhine and the Elbe, destroying heathen altars, cutting down sacred oaks, disputing with the Irish evangelists who had preceded him, and turning the hearts of hundreds of thousands of heathen to serve the living God.[1] Under the name of St Boniface he is still remembered as the Apostle of Germany. Whether or not he is the author of a ditty of his time:

> *The man slow in deed loseth by delay*
> *In glorious doings, and dieth lonely,*

he acted upon it. Hardly had he finished his work in Saxony when he was, in 738, sent by Gregory III to bring Bavaria, already converted by the Irish, into communion with the Roman Church – a task which he accomplished in a few years. Next, in the double character of Archbishop of Mainz and Papal Vicar, he undertook the hardest work of his life. It is much easier to turn heathens into Christians than to compel Christians to imitate Christ, and at this time the Church of Gaul was corrupt through and through, in heart, head, and limb. Bishoprics and livings were openly put up to auction; the priests were usually runaway slaves who had never been ordained; there were great prelates who could not read, who held many sees together, or who were laymen; no synod had been held for generations; every possible vice was practised by the clergy, to the disgust of the laity, who then, as always, might be vicious themselves, but not unnaturally expected a higher standard from the preachers of virtue. Boniface took up the work with energy and perseverance: in council after council he dealt with these evils, and succeeded at least in securing something like outward consistency between profession and practice. Everywhere he insisted on obedience to the See of Rome. Finally, perhaps desiring a little ease in his declining years, he set forth for Friesland to convert the heathen there. Here, in 755, he gained what he had so often sought – the crown of martyrdom.

It is impossible to read of these devoted labours without the keenest admiration; the courage and endurance of men like Willibrord and Boniface passes the intrepidity of Nelson

1. He would find little difficulty in the language, for his own West Saxon was hardly more than a dialect of the 'Old Saxon' he would meet in Germany.

or the 'bravest of the brave'. With like feelings we read of Anskar the apostle of Sweden, who secured toleration for Christianity in a heathen land by a daring but successful appeal to the decision of the lot, and died, after superhuman toils (855), humbly praying that God would be merciful to a sinner; of Cyril and Methodius,[1] the evangelists and teachers of the Slavs and Magyars; of Wenceslas the royal martyr of Bohemia. But there are many deductions to be made. Such wholesale conversions as were effected by these missionaries – it is said that Paulinus baptized ten thousand in one day and Boniface a hundred thousand in a year – were obviously, in multitudes of cases, merely nominal; indeed the converts of Paulinus reverted in great numbers before long. All remember how the great Mercian king Penda, seeing many of his people falling away to Christianity, remarked sarcastically on the difference between their professions and their lives. Nor were the arguments, used or permitted, always of the best kind. Coifi, the Northumbrian priest, complained that he had served the gods for years, and received little in return: it is pretty plain that, with the first failure of prayer, this argument would lose its force. Too often, a converted king used most un-Christian weapons to compel his subjects to come in. The stories told of Olaf Tryggvason's methods of converting Norway are so unedifying that we may hope some scholars are right in thinking them untrue; but the fact that they are told with eulogy shows that such things were common and were approved.

Again, these triumphs could not be gained without compromise. Every conquest introduced a touch of heathenism into Christianity; the vanquished, in some measure, took the victors captive. The old gods and heroes might be called devils, but they often became saints, and their deeds were told, with slight change, in Christian 'legends'. Old charms were still used, with Matthew, Mark, and Luke in place of Thor or Heimdall. Wells where pagan miracles were wrought were simply handed over to St Winifred or St

1. These were Greeks, but, with certain exceptions, they followed the Roman use.

Ronan, and the miracles went on. Twin gods, like Castor and Pollux, became twin martyrs, like Castoulos and Polyeuctes.

That this kind of transference began very early, and prevailed almost, if not quite, universally, is indicated by the history of Gregory Thaumaturgus or the Wonder-worker, whose life is told by his namesake of Nyssa. Gregory was born of heathen parents, and may well have retained some sympathy with his old beliefs even after he was converted by Origen. Being consecrated Bishop of Neo-Caesarea in Cappadocia, he set to work with immense energy to Christianize the country. It is said that when he began there were only seventeen Christians in the neighbourhood, and that when he died there were only seventeen heathens. His miracles outdid those of the pagan priests, and he had a keen eye to detect conjuring and trickery.[1] But probably he gained still more by the skill with which he made the transition from one religion to the other an easy one. During the Decian persecution he advised his flock to get out of the way, and set them an example of flight. On his return, he held a solemn service in honour of those who had suffered. To this service the bones of the martyrs were brought, and Gregory did not hesitate to substitute these bones for the idols. As his biographer says, 'the people rejoiced in the celebration of festivals in honour of the martyrs.' But, 'seeing that the raw and ignorant multitude adhered to idols on account of bodily pleasures, he slightly relaxed the strain on those who had accepted the yoke of the faith. To secure the most vital ends, that is, to turn their minds to God instead of vain worship, he permitted them to enjoy themselves at these commemorations, deeming that as the Christian faith took stronger hold of them their lives would become more serious and sober'. In a word, he changed the names of the objects of adoration, and little besides. Others followed in

1. A good idea of the miracle-mongers of Asia Minor can be gained by anyone who will read Lucian's story of Alexander of Abonoteichos, who lived about thirty years before Gregory. A Bishop who could expose or outdo an Alexander would be certain of an eager audience.

his steps. Theodoret,[1] two hundred years later, tells us that when the temples were destroyed, the precincts were used for the sepulchres of the martyrs. 'The owner substituted the corpses of his own family for your gods, showing that the latter were gone, and giving to the former the glory once given to the others. In place of the Pandia, the Diasia, the Dionysia, the feasts of Peter, Paul, Thomas, Sergius, Marcellus, Leontius, are celebrated; and orderly assemblies are seen instead of the former ribaldry and obscenity.' The new divinities were supplicated for exactly the same favours as the old – for rain, safety on journeys, productiveness, and the like. New presbyter, in fact, was but old priest writ with different letters. It is to be feared that Gregory was wrong in expecting this to die out with time. Heathenism, to a great extent, absorbed the Christianity which fondly fancied it had been the absorber.

Nor is this heathen leaven expelled even today. The traveller in Southern Italy comes across many things which irresistibly remind him of what he has read in the *Dictionary of Classical Mythology*: things which the educated Catholic does not believe, but which the sagacious hierarchy winks at. Here in England, in France, in Germany, similar survivals are to be found. 'Johannis-Feuer' – the festival of John the Baptist – is simply the ancient sun-worship with a Christian veneer. Christmas is but a mixture of the Northern Yule with the Roman Saturnalia, under a new name. No date is more unlikely for the birth of Christ than the twenty-fifth of December; but it was the birthday of Mithra, and the 'grith-day' of our Northern ancestors; it was a sacrifice well worth the making to adopt that date if by that means some of Mithra's followers could be enticed into the Church; and as it involved also the placing of John's birthday at Midsummer, other sun-worshippers might find their conversion a little easier.[2]

1. I take this quotation from Harnack, *Expansion*, II, 352.
2. The festival of Christmas is first mentioned (by Clement of Alexandria) as being observed by Gnostic heretics (the followers of Basileides). In the East it was long regarded as of much less importance than the

How much besides was adopted from heathenism and more or less transformed by Christianity is a matter of great dispute. There are some who see in the gloom of Good Friday and the rejoicings of Easter too exact a reflection of the ceremonies of the death and resurrection of Attis and Adonis to be accidental: the resemblance is indeed astonishing. There are some again who ascribe the worship of the Virgin to a conscious or unconscious borrowing from the cult of Isis; and there are not a few, both Christians and unbelievers, who have thought the image-worship so common in some branches of the Church an accommodation to the idolatry of the Roman world, some form of idolatry being very natural to man, and very hard to eliminate. As we have seen, the charge of idolatry was one of the chief accusations brought against Christianity by Islam, and one of the most difficult to rebut. At the second Council of Nicaea in 787, image-worship was declared orthodox; but a distinction, still in force, was drawn between Douleia, a pious reverential service to angels, saints and their images, on the one hand, and Latreia, the full adoration due to God alone, on the other. To the vulgar, however, this is a distinction without much difference; the *douleia* includes bowing the knee, kissing the image, and burning of incense; and in many places the saints are thus invoked oftener and with more obvious piety than the Father or the Son. This was certainly not always so: in the early days of the Church the

---

Epiphany. Somewhat later, we find the West celebrating it on 25 December, and the East on 6 January (the date now appropriated to the Epiphany). It would seem then that the Westerners adopted the date of the Roman Saturnalia. By A.D. 386 the December date is spoken of by Chrysostom as adopted in the East also.

In what sense the Gnostics observed it, is difficult to guess, for the birth of the *human* Jesus must have been of little significance to them. It is probable, though by no means certain, that the celebration started with the Jewish Christians; and it may be connected with the Jewish feast *Chanuka*. Be this so or not, it was some time before it was added to Easter and Pentecost as one of the three feasts of rejoicing. No one can doubt that it has many pagan characters; and indeed this is why it was totally rejected by some Dissenting Churches.

Fathers are very severe on the 'cult of the dead'. There is a strong contrast between the words of Augustine on the subject and those of the Council of Trent, which declares that it is profitable and right to invoke the saints for their intercession in heaven and their help on earth. The custom certainly grew very rapidly after the conversion of the Empire and the accession of large hosts of nominal Christians. At the same time, it is but fair to say that among truly pious and educated Catholics direct worship of God is fully as common as among Protestants, and the *douleia* of saints and images is given its due symbolical and subordinate character.

Since so much was to be annexed from heathendom, it is impossible not to be astonished that the missionaries saw so little good in the ancient faiths, and impossible not to regret that their zeal was so intolerant. They must have seen, in barbarous cults, much that was like their own; why did not they show a little sympathy? Boniface roughly cutting down sacred oaks – how would *he* have felt if the barbarians had insulted the Cross? Columban hurling idols into the lake – how was it so good a man did not see that he was behaving as Attila behaved to Christian symbols? Such perceptions, such power of imagining oneself in another's place, are what we never find in these early and most admirable soldiers of Christ. It is true that they are rare at any time, and least of all to be expected *then*; but we miss them none the less. We recognize the courage with which these great saints took their lives in their hands, and the unyielding determination with which they went on, year after year, with their labour; but they did not labour quite as Jesus would have laboured, and they did not show the insight he would have shown. They had, in fact, the defects of their qualities; it is by such men, single-minded and devoted, that great victories are won; but that very single-mindedness and devotion involved an inability to see the good in anything outside their own range. What of good they did see they put down to the sorceries of Satan; and it was therefore worse than evil. All this boded ill for the times to come, when

Christianity would be dominant and heathenism feeble – it was a foretaste of the persecutions that were to prevail in a few centuries, and that were to be all the fiercer because Christianity observed in heathenism something like herself, which in part she had borrowed and which she hated all the more for that very reason.[1]

Apart from the one really important religion of the Roman Empire, with which there could be no compromise – the *douleia* of the Emperor, which the Christians persisted in confusing with a *latreia* – there were many other religions with which Christianity came into contact, and by which it was more or less influenced. As we have seen, there are some who hold that its services were largely tinged with borrowings from the Mysteries of heathen cults, such as the Eleusinian or Orphic: but this is a matter involved in much doubt and obscurity. Paul himself, as is well known, constantly uses the word 'mystery' to denote the esoteric doctrine of the Church – 'God manifest in the flesh'; 'we speak the wisdom of God in a mystery'; 'he hath made known to us the mystery of his will': and he calls the 'marriage' of Christ and the Church by the same name.[2] Jesus also, when explaining his parabolic method of teaching, called them the 'Mysteries of the Kingdom'. But how far these are metaphorical expressions is hard to decide. On the whole, perhaps, the tendency of those who have studied most

1. If anyone desires to form an idea of the extreme crudity of early Christian fancy – contrasting often very strangely with the transcendentalism of the philosophers and scholars who adorned the Church at the very same time – he can hardly do better than look at the pictures in sacred buildings, or at the illustrations in monkish books. The illustrations, for example, in 'Caedmon's' Genesis are astonishing in their *naïveté*, and prove, if proof were needed, that the conception of God was as anthropomorphic as that of the early Hebrews, and the conception of heaven as materialistic as that of an uneducated Moslem. And yet the sermons of Aelfric, based on those of Gregory the Great, are full of allegory, and treat the stories, thus childishly illustrated, in a highly refined and symbolic manner. This contrast is typical of the comprehensive character of the Church generally.

2. Rendered in the Vulgate *sacramentum* – the proof-text of the Roman doctrine that marriage is a sacrament.

deeply these difficult subjects is to believe that if there was large borrowing – which is uncertain – it was rather from Eastern mystery-rites than from Greek.

We have already mentioned MITHRAISM, the sun-religion of the nearer East, a mystery-religion beyond doubt, and one which was for two centuries at least a chief rival to Christianity. Thanks to Cumont's admirable book, we now know much about this religion, monuments of which are to be found in almost every part of the Roman Empire, from the Tyne to the Euphrates. The remains at Housesteads, with the inscription, '*Deo Soli Mithrae, Invicto, Saeculari*' – are familiar to all English antiquaries, and hundreds of similar ones, with the symbol of the Sun-god in the midst, and his attendants Cautes and Cautopates on either side, have been noted and reproduced in photograph or engraving. The wide range of this cult is easily explained: it was *the* religion, or at any rate the favourite religion, of the Roman soldier. The likeness between its mysteries and those of Christianity is amazing; so amazing indeed that the only account the Fathers of the Church could give was that Satan had been mimicking Christ.[1] For me, at any rate, with all deference to the scholars who think otherwise, it is impossible to believe that this likeness is accidental; one must have borrowed from the other, or else the obligations must be mutual. Mithraism had its sacramental service, hardly to be distinguished from ours; it had its 'Christmas' rejoicings, its Easter, its legends of a miraculous birth, and a glorious resurrection. Both Mithraism and Christianity, as Harnack says, were Oriental in origin; they entered the Empire about the same time, and ran a parallel course; they appealed equally to the lower classes; and 'they agreed in several im-

---

1. I take from Harnack, *Expansion of Christianity*, II, 450, the following passage from Tertullian: 'The devil baptizes certain people, his believers and faithful ones, promising remission of sins after immersion. And Mithra there sets a mark on the forehead of his soldiers, celebrates the oblation of bread, introduces a symbol of the resurrection, and wins a crown under the sword. And what are we to say of Satan restricting his high priest to one marriage? The devil, too, has his virgins and his chaste celibates.'

portant features'. But, as Harnack also points out, the map which Cumont gives to show the diffusion of the religion indicates clearly how and why Mithraism failed in the end. Whether because it could not go where the army was not required, or because there was something barbaric about it, the entire domain of Hellenism was closed to it. Christianity, on the contrary, was welcomed by Hellenism, and ultimately became fused with it: thus the one religion had the future which attends a vitalizing civilization, the other had in it the seeds of the death which waits on barbarism. The philosophic Christianity of the East had little, in reality, to fear from this Oriental creed. In the West, on the other hand, Mithraism, after about the middle of the second century, gained notable triumphs. The monuments show that it was strong on the borders of Dacia, Noricum, and Germany – wherever, in fact, the army was particularly necessary – and that it was to be found wherever the veteran, having finished his service, settled down for his well-earned repose. He did not forget the god who had helped him against the Marcomanni, the Chatti, or the Picts. About 180 it made a further advance. As Cumont has shown, the authorities saw that Mithraism and the worship of the Emperor might form an alliance, and lend each other support. All that was needed was to identify the Emperor with the 'invictus et saecularis Deus': a half-sham cult put on new life when the Emperor could be regarded as 'consubstantive' with a holy, invincible, and blessed Eternal King. Rome was not slow to seize this happy chance; and in the third century we find the higher officers of the army, the court, 'Caesar's household', and the chief people of the Italian cities, adopting this religion as the fashionable one, and, we cannot doubt, as the best antidote to the Christian poison. It showed none of the exclusiveness of Christianity; the decaying religions of the Empire could find in it a new hope. Galerius, at last, thought it safe to endeavour to enforce Mithraism as, so to speak, the Established Church.

But it was not destined to endure. In Greece, and the Greek world, it met, as we have seen, with no success. The

Emperors failed to crush Christianity; and the barbarians beyond the borders soon swarmed over and made an end of Mithraism in its transitory settlements along the Danube and the Rhine. It moved backward with the camps of the soldiers, and, not having in it either the spiritual vitality of its rival, or the power of assimilating culture and philosophy, it died gradually away, until its very existence was utterly forgotten.

We need not regret its disappearance. Had it won, it would have won by Imperial help, and would have acquired all the vices, and perhaps more, which Christianity acquired by alliance with the Emperors: under Galerius it showed that it was quite capable of becoming a persecuting religion. Priestcraft, after all, is not a Christian monopoly and appears in almost all religions; when it gains secular power, it is in all cases tyrannical and cruel: there is no reason to think that if Mithraism had gained the day the treatment of heretics would have been less savage, though the sufferers would have been different. Again, Mithraism, as we have seen, had less philosophic basis than Christianity, and less capacity for assimilating the wisdom of the ages past, as well as, probably, less capacity for welcoming the philosophies of the ages to come. It was, when all allowance is made, and with full recognition of its deep spirituality, a crude worship of a celestial body: it would have been impossible for it, like Christianity, to develop a metaphysic which enables men to identify the Christian God with the Absolute, and thus to combine the deepest speculations with a profound faith. No Thomas Aquinas could have arisen in Mithraism. Nor is it easy to see how an advanced astronomy would have been reconcilable with such a worship: Mithraist inquisitors would have been even more severe with a Galileo than were the Roman. Still more important, in spite of the hold which it had on the common soldier and the lower classes, I do not think that it would have had the power, in the long run, of so presenting its doctrines in a simple and intelligible form as to retain that hold. Christianity is at once one of the most metaphysical of religions and one that can be *felt* and *lived* by the poor and the ignorant: this is its real strength, and while it retains this it is not likely to die.

In another sphere, and in another part of the world, Christianity was always borrowing, and had been borrowing from the very first. The same impulse which made Paul talk to the philosophers of Athens in a philosophic style induced men later to adopt from Greek thought as much as they could without destroying their Christian belief. As the Christians were mocked at for building their churches on the model of the temples, so the orator Aristides, in the time of Marcus Aurelius (about 160), accuses them of poaching on the Hellenic preserves and calling themselves philosophers. It is true that he thinks very little of their philosophy. It is Thersites posing as Narcissus or Hyacinthus. But it was a theft nevertheless.

It is unnecessary to say that this philosophizing, and this annexation of heathen thought, started with the higher Christian minds, But gradually, while suffering change in the process, it permeated the lower; and – as we have already seen – the Greek populace had an astonishing turn for finding interest in the most abstruse problems. Like the Scottish people, it loved to discuss dogmas which would weary an Englishman in five minutes. It is a remarkable fact that the religions which proved most dangerous to Christianity were precisely those which were most metaphysical, and which started from a set of transcendental premises. The Christian apologists found little *intellectual* to fear in the ordinary heathenism; but in arguing with religions based on profound philosophical conceptions they always show anxiety, much as the heresies that troubled them most were usually deep Gnostic speculations. And, as is so often the case, they could not help borrowing from the philosophers they thought themselves to be refuting; they were Israelites spoiling the Egyptians whom they regarded as enemies, and many of the brightest ornaments of Christian thought are of foreign origin. It may be desirable to study one or two cases in which this phenomenon is most fully manifested.

One of the earliest, and in some respects the most dangerous, of these philosophic religions, was not of Greek origin,
though, unlike Mithraism, it showed a strange power of
penetrating into the Greek world, and, indeed, of contending on equal terms with Hellenic philosophy; while its high
morality and its asceticism made a strong appeal to the
same elements of society as were attracted by Christian ethic
and Christian monasticism. This was MANICHAEISM,
which, as we have seen, long held captive the mind of so
great a man as Augustine, and which, in some of its aspects,
has even today a certain attraction for persons perplexed
with the problems of the existence of evil in the world. But
it was, I think, less this aspect than the cosmological theory
on which it was based that gave it its chief strength in its
contest with Hellenic Christianity.[1]

This religion, an outgrowth of Zoroastrianism, and to a
lesser degree of Buddhism, was founded in the third century
by Mani, who was born near Ctesiphon in A.D. 215. At a
very early age he began to practise that asceticism which he
afterwards urged on the most aspiring of his followers;
and at twenty-four he had perfected his system. Shortly
afterwards, he announced himself, in the presence of King
Sapor, as the founder of a new religion, which was to be to
Babylonia what Buddhism was to India and Christianity to
the West. Although he is said to have represented himself as
the promised Paraclete, and although, like Christ, he had
twelve special disciples, he appears neither to have imitated
nor to have desired to destroy Christianity: his religion was
for the East; the Roman Empire he scarcely visited. In
Persia he was for a time remarkably successful; but the
Zoroastrian priests, as might be expected, were the deadly
enemies of one who aimed at reforming – which to them was
overthrowing – their religion. On the accession of Bahram,
they persuaded the new king to put him out of the way. In
276 Mani was captured and crucified.

Manichaeism is a kind of Gnosticism: its aim was rather

1. The reader will remember how John Stuart Mill, in his later years,
inclined towards Manichaean dualism.

to give knowledge than to save the soul – though Mani certainly, like Buddha, held that knowledge is ultimately salvation. He proposed, first, to teach the origin of things, and secondly to purify the minds of his followers. We cannot enter here into the complicated details of his speculative system; it is enough to say that he conceived two great principles, the principle of goodness or light, which is God, and the principle of darkness or evil, which is not a God, though it is a person; it is rather the personified Tiāmat or chaos of Babylonian mythology, which develops into the Satan or dragon of active and malignant evil. The conflict between these two principles is the history of the world at large and of the human soul.

Somewhat similar is the practical side of Mani's teaching. He allowed two classes of the faithful: the Perfect, who were to practise the most rigid asceticism, and the Hearers, whose burden was much less heavy. All alike, however, were enjoined to fast at frequent intervals, and to pray almost without ceasing.[1] They had no real priesthood, and no great festival save the 'Bema', celebrated on the anniversary of Mani's crucifixion. After death, apparently, the Perfect entered Paradise immediately; the Hearers had to pass through a kind of purgatory, and unbelievers were claimed by Satan.

Though, as we have said, Mani himself had left the West alone, his followers after his death speedily invaded it, and penetrated Egypt, Africa, and Italy. Like Christianity, Manichaeism had more success abroad than in the country of its birth; it is said that many of the Bishops, especially in the Alexandrian region, were Manichees at one time; and around Carthage, as we know from Augustine, there were flourishing Manichee congregations. Under Constantine it was of course tolerated, and we find many traces of its spread, during the fourth century, in Spain and Gaul. As

1. It is a mistake to suppose that the Manichees worshipped the sun and the moon. They prayed towards them as symbols of the eternal Light; but they recognized clearly the distinction between the symbol and the thing symbolized.

the Church grew stronger, however, and its alliance with
the State closer, Manichaeism was treated as a heresy, and
violently suppressed; the secular arm was called in to help
the spiritual.

It is impossible to doubt that this great religion, with its
philosophical basis, and its strange penetrative power,
strongly influenced the Christianity which opposed it.
Many heresies, unquestionably, were touched by it; and as
late as the thirteenth century the Albigenses held many of
the Manichaean opinions. The sect indeed was not finally
crushed till the great crusade, of which the chief leader was
Simon de Montfort, stamped it out in blood.[1] Nor is it impossible to find some tinge of Manichaeism even in orthodox
Catholicism. For the conquering Roman religion, like the
Roman Republicans of centuries before, knew how to learn
from those it had vanquished.

This 'syncretism', this power of assimilating elements
from anywhere and everywhere, was one of the main secrets
of the success of Christianity. If she was to be a world-
religion, she must be able to adapt herself to the habits of
thought belonging to this nation, that, and the other; she
must avoid the fatal defect of Judaism, a narrow and exclusive patriotic feeling. But universality necessitates some
sacrifice, and Christianity lost something of her original
purity with every extension of her physical dominion. While
we admire her comprehensiveness, we must not omit to note
its cost. A religion that can include a Clement of Alexandria
and an Anthony, an Origen and an ignoramus, has many
virtues. But it took in Clement by adopting much Greek
philosophy of which its founders knew nothing; and it
retained the ignoramus by turning a blind eye upon his
superstitious beliefs and semi-heathen practices.

It was as a world-religion, in this sense, that Christianity
found Manichaeism so dangerous a rival; for Manichaeism
also was 'syncretistic', and transcended the limits of
nationalities. Both religions, as Harnack says, were the final
result of the history of a thousand years, the history of the

1. See note at end of Chapter.

religious development of civilization from Persia to Italy. In both, the old national character of religion was laid aside. For the national cult they substituted a system which aspired to be at once a theology, a theory of the universe, and a science of history, while at the same time it embraced a definite ethic and a ritual of worship. Formally, therefore, they were alike; and they were alike also in having appropriated elements from various older religions. Further, both brought to the front the ideas of revelation, redemption, asceticism, and immortality. Catholicism was a monotheism based primarily on the Old Testament and the Gospel, but built up with the aid of Greek philosophy and ethics. Manichaeism was a dualism (in the sense above explained), based primarily on Chaldaism; but with much of Parsism and some Buddhism added. Christianity was thus full of Hellenism, which was the one element that Manichaeism, at first if not later, almost entirely lacked. It had to be decided, by the course of history, whether Manichaeism could gain a hold, too strong to be broken, on the Graeco-Roman world; and history *has* decided the question.[1]

Only one other religion can be considered a serious rival of Christianity in the Western world; and that was a religion which by its very nature appealed rather to the few than to the many; it was for the learned and thoughtful rather than for the ignorant. This was NEO-PLATONISM, a scheme (or schemes) of philosophic religion which was bound in this final result to fail in its attempt to conquer the world, but which, to an even greater degree than Manichaeism, penetrated into the thought of Christianity, and has left the marks of its influence in the most unexpected quarters. It is not too much to say that men of true piety have found it possible to be at once Christians and Neo-platonists, or that such men exist among us today. 'Plotinus,' says Eucken, 'though a pagan, has influenced Christian theology more than any other thinker': and Dean Inge adds that this

1. On the theme of this paragraph see Harnack, *History of Dogma*, III, 316.

judgement will not seem absurd to those who have traced the ideas of Plotinus in the Cappadocian Fathers, in Augustine, in Erigena.[1] Followers of the Neo-platonists are to be found in every section of Christianity that does not reject learning and philosophy altogether. Henry More, Whichcote, John Smith of Cambridge, Cudworth – these could not have written or thought as they did had there been no Plotinus or Porphyry: Eckhart and Angelus Silesius knew them either directly or at second-hand; Christian mysticism, consciously or subconsciously, owes much to these Hellenic thinkers; and it is certain that their ideas will always have a strong attraction for minds of a transcendental and religious turn.[2]

It is impossible here to give a full account of this system: its teachers are so many, and their variations, within limits, so wide, that a comprehensive analysis would take many volumes; it is the work of specialists. I will confine myself to a very brief account of the work of Plotinus – certainly the greatest of them – and his pupil Porphyry.

Plotinus was almost the contemporary of Origen: he was born in 205 and died in 270. Like Origen, he was a pupil of Ammonius Saccas, but he certainly studied not only Greek philosophy but the wisdom of the East. At the age of forty he settled in Italy, where he gathered round him a small band of disciples, among whom the Emperor Gallienus may be reckoned. Gallienus did him one great service. When Plotinus wished to found in Campania a city called Platonopolis, in which the Platonic idea of a perfect republic of philosophers might be realized, Gallienus refused. Such attempts have often been made, and have rarely succeeded. Plotinus was forced, for our advantage, to confine his plans to the ideal world. He remained in Italy, inde-

---

1. Lecture on Plotinus, 1929, p. 6. I may take this opportunity of saying that I have not studied Plotinus at first hand, but owe my knowledge of him mainly to Dean Inge's two masterly volumes.

2. Plotinus's refusal to go to the temples – 'It is for the gods to come to me' – needs only to be turned into German rhyme to seem an original *sententia* of Angelus Silesius.

fatigably teaching and writing, or, at times, enjoying the Beatific Vision, and entering into the immediate presence of the Godhead.

His three main ideas may be thus summarized. The Real is spiritual, and not, as the Epicureans held, material; the Real is knowable – here he opposes the scepticism of the Academy: and the Real is one and good – here he traverses the dualistic views of the Gnostics.[1] In his system there are two fundamental Trinities: the Divine Trinity of the Absolute (the One or the First), Spirit or Intelligence (*nous*), and the Universal Soul: on the other hand the Human Trinity of Body, Soul, and Spirit.[2] These last are perceived respectively by the senses, the understanding, and intuition or direct spiritual vision.[3] Only by the exercise of this intuition, 'which all possess but few use', can we ourselves become real, or obtain contact with Reality. Nothing actually exists but that which is, in a manner, the unity of the spiritual faculty with the spiritual world. Matter, so-called, is for Plotinus merely that somewhat which we cannot help conceiving as remaining over when we abstract from an object of thought all its qualities – for these the mind bestows on that object: it is arguable that Plotinus would have accepted John Stuart Mill's definition of Matter as 'the permanent possibility of sensation'.

Since the full Real is fully knowable and absolutely good, it follows that there must be a continuous series of degrees of truth, and (as these are more and more fully known) a parallel series of *worths* or values. But for Plotinus this series could not start with a minus quantity of good, or, what is the

1. This has been disputed; but it seems to me clear that Plotinus is a monist; his dualistic expressions are the result of defects of language rather than of inexact thought.

2. This idea of the tripartite nature of man is a view adopted by many Christian thinkers, and may, I believe, be regarded as the orthodox conception.

3. Spinoza's division of ideas into opinion, reasoning or discourse, and intuitive knowledge, will here occur to the reader: but it is not quite the same as that of Plotinus, though these two great philosophers had much in common.

same thing, a positive quantity of evil. This is the chief difficulty of all monistic systems; for the moral sense of mankind revolts against the theory that evil is non-existent; and Plotinus, who will have nothing to do with a Manichaean or any other dualism, is here hard put to it, as is every philosopher who endeavours to reconcile the Manifold with the One. Evil, he says, belongs only to the unreal, to that which has no permanent vitality. It has to do only with the world of sense, which is perceived, if at all, merely by opinion, and not realized by adequate and immediate knowledge. If ever the human soul can rise into a higher region and become spirit, it will see things as they are, evil will be recognized as what it is or is not, and these difficulties will vanish.

Though Plotinus never mentions Christianity, and though there are indications that it did not attract him, yet the language he uses to describe certain experiences is often remarkably similar to that used by Christian saints. His heaven is not theirs: it is attained by perfection of knowledge, the Christian's by perfect imitation of Christ. Yet there are many Christians who could borrow his words: indeed one might fancy that Dante in his *Paradiso* has done so: 'They see all things, not the things that are born and die, but those which have real being; and they see themselves in others. For them all things are transparent and there is nothing dark or impenetrable, but everyone is manifest to everyone internally, for light is manifest to light. Everyone has all things in himself, and sees all things in another; so that all things are everywhere and all is all, and the glory is infinite. Each of them is great, since Yonder the small also is great.[1] In heaven the sun is all the stars, and again each and all are the sun. There pure movement reigns, for the prime mover is no stranger to the movement, and

---

1. Is this Plotinus speaking, or is it Piccarda? (*Paradiso*, III). Compare also *Paradiso* I:

> La gloria di Colui, che tutto muove
> Per l'universo penetra e risplende
> In una parte più, e meno altrove.

does not agitate it: and rest also is perfect, for no agitation mingles with it.'

Again, when he speaks of the direct Vision of Reality which has more than once been vouchsafed to him, his language becomes indistinguishable from that which Christian saints[1] have used in their attempts to describe the Beatific Vision: 'The soul must remove from itself good and evil and everything else, that it may receive the One alone. When the soul turns away from visible things and makes itself beautiful and becomes like the One, and sees the One suddenly appearing in itself with nothing between, then there is that union of which the union of earthly lovers, who blend their being with each other, is a copy.[2] The soul fears no evil while it is with the One; though all things perish around it, it is content, so happy is it. He who has seen it knows what I say. But the vision is hard to describe; for who can describe, as other than himself, that which when he saw it seemed one with him?'

St Paul is said, when he looked on the tomb of Virgil, and thought of his nobility and purity, to have burst out into an exclamation:

> '*Quem te, inquit, reddidissem*
> *Si te vivum invenissem,*
> *Poetarum maxime.*'

He would perhaps have said the same if he could have lived to see Plotinus; for Paul too had had his indescribable vision. 'I will come to visions and revelations of the Lord. I knew a man in Christ (whether in the body or apart from the body I know not, God knoweth); such a man was caught up into the third heaven. And I knew such a man, how that he was caught up into Paradise, and heard unspeakable words,

---

1. And, I may add, such non-Christians or half-Christians as Spinoza, Swedenborg, Shelley, and Wordsworth.

2.
> *Nothing in the world is single;*
> *All things, by a law divine,*
> *In each other's being mingle;*
> *Why not I with thine?*

is Shelley's putting of the converse doctrine.

which it is not lawful for a man to utter.' All the mystics, as Dean Inge says, speak the same language: but here we have a Greek, a loyal disciple of Plato, whose wisdom begins with the cosmic speculations of the Ionians, and ends in a profoundly religious philosophy, resting on personal experience of the Good, and entirely disentangled from any historical events, past or future. That such a man should have had a strong attraction for the higher Christian minds, and that this attraction should have conquered even the almost invincible prejudice against things heathen, is no matter for surprise.

Porphyry, the pupil of Plotinus, is best known perhaps as the author of one of the most powerful attacks on Christianity ever written. Unfortunately this work is lost, for the Church, as soon as she became powerful, started the bad custom of securing the help of the Emperors for the suppression of books attacking her beliefs – a despotic device which she had resented when used against her. We have to detect Porphyry's opinions, like those of Celsus, from references in the works of his adversaries: and how misleading these may be we can guess from Jerome's description of this noble-minded heathen: 'a fool, impious, a blasphemer, mad, shameless, a slanderer of the Church, a mad dog attacking Christ'.[1] We need not attend to these ferocious epithets, which simply prove how powerful was Porphyry's assault upon Christianity. What interests us here is the astonishing amount of agreement between him and those he attacked. The Church had become so largely Hellenic that much of Celsus's 'True Word' was now irrelevant: a hundred years had made a vast difference, and what appears to have saddened Porphyry was that a system which had borrowed so liberally from Plato should not have borrowed still more. It was so nearly a sound philosophy that he wished it had been completely so.

His mistake lay mainly in this, that like Socrates and

1. Augustine speaks differently. To him, Porphyry, although a keen enemy of the Church, was a great and noble philosopher, the most learned of Gentile thinkers.

Plato he believed conduct to depend upon knowledge, and thought that religion was a matter to be argued out. It seemed to his logical mind that if he could demolish the myths of Christianity he could demolish the religion based on them. A close study of the Old and New Testaments showed him that the history was full of myths: the contradictions in the Gospels proved also that the biography of Jesus was largely legendary. The prophecies heaped up by the Evangelists, and said to be fulfilled in Christ, were a tissue of absurdities. For Jesus himself he cherished a high admiration: the gods had declared Jesus to be most pious and had made him immortal; but his followers were a polluted and infected multitude, entangled in error. It is Paul – and here he strikingly anticipated Renan, Nietzsche, and other modern writers – whom he 'cannot away with'. Paul's method of reasoning, so Rabbinic and un-Greek, is unintelligible and utterly repugnant to him. 'Not Paul but Jesus' might have been his motto, as it was that of a critic fifteen centuries later.

What still more strongly roused the antagonism of Porphyry was the separation which Christianity made between God and the world. Accepting the Mosaic system of cosmogony, in all its literalness, Christianity regarded the universe as the effect of a special act of creation *ab extra*, an act performed in time, and involving, or at least combined with, the idea of a destruction also in time. The Christian doctors anticipated a speedy dissolution of the world, in which the elements should melt with fervent heat, and the stars fall from heaven. This appeared to Porphyry not only false but irreligious; for ultimately the All must be One. A similar, or rather perhaps a converse, argument is that which he directed against the doctrine of the Incarnation – for this made a false *union* between God and the world, as the Mosaic account of creation falsely sundered them. As for the Resurrection, this was simply incredible to a disciple of Plotinus,[1]

1. Plotinus *may* have believed in the transmigration of souls; but the orthodox Christian, like Malvolio, 'thinks nobly of the soul', and in no way approves this doctrine.

to whom death, for the Perfect, was an absorption into the One, and to whom a *bodily* resurrection would have meant a relapse into a lower stage of existence.

But it is necessary to note that Porphyry's objections, though profound and far-reaching, stop here, and that his points of agreement are more numerous than his points of divergence. At the time at which he wrote, Christianity was feeling its need of systematizing its philosophy, and was seeking in Neo-platonism some guidance in the task.[1] It was perhaps the very fact that Neo-platonism came so near to Christianity (as Hellenized), and yet did not cross over the bourne, which made Christianity so angry with it. The little more proved so much: and the Church felt towards this creed as if it had been, not an entirely alien scheme like idolatry or Mithraism, but a heresy or a schism which has always aroused more passion in Christians than the lowest paganism. It was certainly felt that the wounds dealt by Porphyry were the more deadly because they were the wounds of one who might, as it seemed, have very easily been a friend. In his mysticism, in his religious feeling, possibly even in his strange belief in the miraculous, the Christians saw the image of themselves, and they could not understand why the likeness went no further.

But, whatever may be thought on this point, enough has been said to show that Christianity, perhaps to a greater degree than any other religion save Hinduism, is 'syncretistic'; it has borrowed from the right and from the left. That is has absorbed and made its own what it has borrowed – that it is no plagiarist, but a royal thief like Virgil or Milton – is true; but we must not on that account refuse to see that its growth, like the growth of any living organism, was accomplished by taking in from outside. Starting as a Jewish sect, with the simplest of organizations and a plain if lofty system of morality, and much of Jewish superstition, it

1. Harnack's dictum may be too strongly put, 'Porphyry in every other respect (than those noted above) was entirely at one with the Christian philosophy of religion, and was quite conscious of this unity': but it is certainly an approximation to the truth.

gradually built up for itself a metaphysic by selecting from Gnosticism elements that it could assimilate, and rejecting others. It then added other elements from Hellenic thought, and modified its cosmological ideas in harmony with both Hellenic and Oriental modes of thought, which, after long struggles, it wrought into something like a coherent whole. Nor did it disdain to adopt many of the more vulgar ideas of the races it converted – the cult of heroes, the worship of beings intermediate between man and God, and image-worship, which, except for higher minds, is idolatry in all but name. Nor has the process yet ceased – new conditions call for ever-new modifications. Much has, in recent times, been borrowed from natural science, and more will assuredly be borrowed in the future. Even those branches of the Church which most pride themselves on the fixity of their creeds, are always changing their real beliefs under the influence of external forces, though they may keep the phraseology of their 'Articles' and symbols unaltered. As, for example, the old crude conceptions of matter give way to more refined ideas, the old ideas of a material hell and of a heaven in space are rapidly vanishing; and as natural law is being more fully understood, the old idea of the miraculous is fading away; even the supernatural is being reduced to law.

Different views will be held as to this process. To some, it will seem that Christianity proves its human character by this human susceptibility to change: others regard it as a proof that it is of divine origin; such adaptation is part of the great cosmic advance over which God presides. One thing is certain, that Christianity cannot live unless it retains this accommodating power, and that, like a sound organism, it must carry on its operations by a process of continual borrowing.

NOTE

The Manichaean heresy was adopted in the East by the 'Paulicians', and spread rapidly over Asia Minor, despite, or because of, the savage persecutions of successive Emperors. At length a considerable number of them were settled, by Constantine Copronymus, in Thrace. From hence their doctrines spread into the West with great rapidity, until, in the eleventh century, they appeared in the south of France, in the dominions of the Count of Toulouse, and made an almost complete conquest of the country, largely, as Catholic historians confess, in consequence of the hopeless corruption and tyranny of the orthodox clergy. Here the sect became known as Albigenses, from the fortress of Albi. They were, like the early Manichees, distinguished by their asceticism, and were often called (by a revival of an ancient name) Cathari or Puritans. They were Docetists, and held, like Mani, to the principle of 'dualism' – the idea of two great contending Powers of good and evil. But their real crime was that they totally rejected priestcraft and the authority of the Pope

Many attempts were made to convert them: St Bernard himself under-took the task; but all failed. Finally, under Innocent III, after preaching, threats, and excommunications had been tried once more in vain, a Crusade was proclaimed; all the princes of France were summoned to extirpate the heretics. The Count himself, who had submitted to every humiliation in order to save his people, was compelled to join the avenging host. Scores of the princes gathered their forces in hope of gaining a share of the spoil; but far fiercer were the Bishops. As a result, the fairest land in Europe was made a desert; whole cities were burned, and the inhabitants, whether orthodox or heretic, ruthlessly slaughtered. Scarcely any of the heretics, when captured, recanted; they bore the flames of martyrdom with astonishing constancy. The leader of the armies, Simon de Montfort, received a large part of the country as his reward. It is said that Innocent himself bitterly repented the horrors he had caused: but the crime remains on record, as perhaps the very worst ever perpetrated in the history of the world.

The Albigenses, who certainly held 'heretical' beliefs, must not be confounded with the Waldensians, though the latter appeared in southern France about the same time, and suffered under the same persecution. The Waldensians, or 'Poor Men of Lyon', the followers of Peter Waldo of that city, had no desire to separate themselves from the Church, and some Popes protected them. Reading the Bible in their own tongue, they returned to Apostolic simplicity, and their only crime was that they insisted on preaching without ecclesiastical sanction. In doctrine they were remarkably similar to the later Mennonites and Quakers. By the Lateran Council of 1215 they were excluded from the Church, and thenceforward their existence was that of sheep pursued by wolves: yet a more or less close connexion was kept up with the Church till the Reformation, when they naturally took the side of the Protestants. Their chief seat was on the slopes of the Alps, half in Piedmont, half in France. According to the political needs of the Dukes of Savoy they were tolerated or persecuted: in 1655 it suited the Duke to persecute them – and the consequent horrors called forth the interference of Oliver Cromwell and Milton's immortal sonnet. Despite banishments, emigrations, slaughterings, the kidnapping of their children to be educated in the Catholic faith, and every device which fanaticism could suggest, they survived, and still exist. In 1848, at last, Charles Albert of Piedmont (which had then become the Kingdom of Sardinia) granted them full equality of rights with his Catholic subjects.

CHAPTER 8

THE CHURCH OF THE WEST

THE schism, though it put an end to even the shadow of visible unity in the Church, yet had its advantages. It was the public confession of what had long been a reality. Inevitably, through the force of circumstances beyond the control of ecclesiastics, the two civilizations had been moving apart. The conquest of province after province of the Eastern Empire by Mohammedanism had accelerated separatist tendencies which had already shown themselves, not only in the political but in the religious world. The culture of the East rested on the past; that of the West was constantly being modified by contact with young and vigorous nations and with developing social systems. Even Italy was more than half Teutonic, and the sympathies of Rome, despite many quarrels, were naturally more with the Goths, the Franks, and the Angles than with the Byzantines.

For the Popes, in particular, the loss was a gain. The union with the Eastern world involved the subjection of the Pope to the Emperor: on that point accommodation was unthinkable. In the West, the theory was equality; or rather Pope and Emperor were two aspects of the same idea. In the crude language of the Middle Ages, each was half of the indivisible God. The Romans swore fealty to both; the image and superscription of both were on the coins; without the one the other was nothing. But it was always within the bounds of possibility that the spiritual staff might assert its supremacy over the corporeal sword.

Almost exactly at the time when Nicholas was contending with Photius, he received a great accession of strength. The famous False Decretals appeared. These were a series of letters, ascribed to Isidore of Seville, a great divine of the seventh century: they were forged for the purpose of releasing the lesser Bishops of Gaul from thraldom to the Metropolitans and to the State. For this purpose, the authors, preferring a distant tyrant to one at their doors, exalted the power of the Pope to the utmost. No Bishop could be cited before a secular court (though a layman could be cited before a Bishop) and the only court that could try him was a provincial synod 'legitimately' constituted; that is, appointed by the Pope. No sooner did Nicholas hear of this work than he seized upon it with avidity, and used all the powers it gave him. But the effect, as so often, was utterly different from what the forgers expected. The Pope did indeed gain power over the metropolitans, and endeavour to gain a similar power over the State; but it was a case of the horse calling in the man to help him against the stag. The little finger of the Pope was thicker than the Archbishop's loins; the lesser Bishops had so far been chastised with whips, but they were now chastised with scorpions. In the fifteenth century Nicholas of Cusa proved that the Decretals were forged; but the Popes did not lay down their power.

When Charles the Great handed over the Exarchate to Leo, the theory was that this was not a gift but a payment of debt. A myth had grown up that Constantine, when leaving Rome for the east, had given Italy to Pope Sylvester. For this story there was not the shadow of a foundation, but it was piously believed for centuries, until Laurentius Valla demolished it at the time of the Council of Florence. Even then, though no article of historic confidence, it remained an article of religious faith. In the fourteenth century, Dante, though thinking the Donation the source of many evils, did not doubt that it had been made.

> *Ah, Constantine, of how much ill was cause,*
> *Not thy conversion, but those rich domains*
> *That the first wealthy Pope received of thee!*

The possession of these 'States of the Church' was a matter of immense importance in history. It was defended as saving the Popes from the necessity of subservience to secular monarchs. It certainly involved them in many secular quarrels, and Dante's opinion has been endorsed by numbers of good Catholics. But it also strengthened the Papacy in its claim to world-wide secular sovereignty. Though, even after the cession of the Exarchate to the Pope, the rule was nominally shared between Pope and Emperor, yet the Emperor was beyond the Alps and the Pope was near: nay, the secular monarch more often saw his subjects as a foreign conqueror than as the native ruler, and the Pope could thus pose at once as a patriotic Italian and as the joint ruler of the world.

It is hard for us in these days, when nationality is even too strong a principle and needs the check rather than the spur, to realize the prestige of Italy in the Middle Ages. Rome was still the object of awe everywhere but in Rome herself, and the name of the Roman Empire still exerted power when the thing was dead. Thus a Roman king – which was what the Pope was – had a power totally out of proportion to his physical strength. And when we remember that, in the vague view of the time, he also had the power of the Empire in him – even though he might be quarrelling with the actual wearer of the Crown, for they were still two sides of one idea – we can guess to some degree what an energetic Pope, determined to press the thing to the utmost, might be able to accomplish.

The first century after Nicholas, however, afforded slight proof that Papal secular rule was either religiously or morally beneficial; and, indeed, it might seem that the Empire gained by the change. This century was the worst in the whole chequered history of the Church: it was a time of murders, riots, robberies, and the 'rule of harlots': a time which made men long for the millennial year which was to see the end of all things.[1] '*Hora novissima; imminet arbiter ille supremus.*' The Pope might be a boy of twelve, a layman, an assassin, a debauchee – even, in the well-known myth, a woman. This is the age in which the corpse of Formosus was dragged from the grave by Stephen, dressed in its robes,

[1]. That the year 1000 was to see the end was an almost universal belief of the time, and led to strange happenings.

tried before the Cardinals, and then thrown into the Tiber:[1] in which Stephen himself was murdered and Formosus rehabilitated, to be anathematized again by one of Stephen's successors; in which another Pope, sick not merely of his place but of the trammels of clericalism, and desirous of marrying his cousin, sold the Papacy for a sum on which he could live in comfort. It was the age in which Peter Damiani called the Bishops heretical brigands, adding that it was easier to convert a Jew (the proverbial impossibility) than one of these Christian prelates.

Twice at least did the Imperial Hercules come in to cleanse this Augean stable. In 962 Otto the Great appeared in Rome, and compelled the Pope to swear allegiance to him. No Pope was to be elected without his consent. Like Charles the Great, he held all the Bishoprics in his hands. It was his policy, while keeping the Bishops as his feudal dependants, to strengthen them as much as he could, that they might be bulwarks of the Emperors against the great lay lords. As clerics could not have heirs, it was possible for Otto, at every vacancy of a see, to provide himself with a new supporter: and of these deferential Bishops the Pope was only the chief. It was the policy pursued later, in England, by William the Conqueror. But, as in England, it depended for success on the strength of the king. Let a weak monarch arise, and the clerics might use against the giver the privileges he had given them. But for many years it might seem that the Papacy was entirely under the heel of the Empire.

A hundred years later, the same evils called for a similar remedy. Rome was distant from the centre of the Empire, and city and Papacy were almost worse than ever. Henry III was called in; and in his train brought a young man named Hildebrand. He knew that Hildebrand would be of inestimable service to him in the work of reform; but he did not know that Hildebrand's ideas of reform were different

1. An incident finely used by Browning in the *Ring and the Book*. Readers of that poem will remember how Innocent XII pondered over it, while meditating on the errors Popes might commit.

from his own. For some time the two worked together. Nothing could exceed the vigour and courage of Hildebrand. On one visit to Gaul he deposed forty-five Bishops who had bribed to get their sees. Many Popes in succession were appointed, practically by his sole will; he preferred to be the power behind the throne. Meanwhile Henry had died, and Hildebrand had the opportunity provided by the long minority of the new Emperor. He was not always scrupulous in the means he employed: he stirred up the great feudatories to put difficulties in the way of the regent; and looked on unmoved while the character of the young Henry was deliberately corrupted by the clerics who had charge of his education. Meanwhile he took the election of the Popes out of the hands of the people, and confined it to the College of Cardinals, over whom his influence was paramount. The Popes thus chosen were puppets in the grasp of a mere archdeacon. In a few years the mighty power of Henry III had been undermined. At length, in 1073, Hildebrand became Pope himself, and the time was ripe for carrying out openly the policy he had matured in his mind, which was simply to assert the absolute supremacy of the Church over all secular authority. He had, as we have seen, allies among the laity, who for personal ends would sacrifice public advantages; and though many of the simoniac Bishops would gladly have seen him defeated, they hardly dared to speak out their desires openly, while the better ones not unnaturally regarded the increase of their worldly importance as synonymous with the advance of religion.

His chief advantage, however, lay in the character of his enemy. Henry was licentious, cruel, and tactless, and had the art of alienating his best friends. When therefore his folly had roused a civil war in Germany, Hildebrand summoned the famous Lateran Council, by which it was declared a deadly sin, to be punished by exclusion from heaven, for any layman – emperor, duke, or the lowest landowner – to give the investiture of any Church dignity. This was, at one stroke, to deprive the laity of about a third of their lands, and to denude feudal lords of half their power. Keeping this blow in reserve, for it might have alienated some of his friends, he summoned Henry to answer for his crimes in Rome. Henry answered by summoning a synod at Worms, in which Hildebrand[1] was declared deposed. It still seemed that the Pope's cause was hopeless; for the clergy whom he had compelled to dismiss their wives, the simoniac Bishops, the great lords, the Lombards, were all against him. But Hildebrand was stronger than men thought. He had with him Matilda of Tuscany, the selfishness of the German princes, the support of the Norman conquerors of southern Italy, whose rights he had allowed, and, as he believed, the favour of God. More than all, he had the weapon of excommunication, the terrible spiritual thunderbolt which made men tremble who trembled at nothing else. He cast Henry out of the Church, and excluded from salvation all who should aid him. One by one, Henry's followers deserted him, until, in 1076, he was forced, attended only by his wife and child, to make his way over the mountains to beg forgiveness. For three wintry days he knocked in vain at the doors of the castle of Canossa, until at last the stern old man, accepting his vows of homage, restored him to the communion of the Church.[2]

But Hildebrand had gone too far, or not far enough. His violence had hardened the hearts of his enemies, and misfortune had strengthened Henry's mind. The Lombards were implacable, and, as Arians, cared little even for anathemas. Henry bided his time, and when, by a series of errors, the Pope had alienated many of his friends, he marched south upon Rome. The Normans, under Robert Guiscard, were away, endeavouring to capture Constantinople. An anti-Pope was chosen, and Hildebrand was besieged in St Angelo, while Matilda was shut up in Canossa.

1. I call him thus, though of course his official name is Gregory VII.
2. Portentous as this incident undoubtedly was, and proverbial as it has become, it is possible that it made less impression at the time than we, with our modern ideas, are apt to imagine. It has been observed that Anselm, though an Italian by birth, and though engaged through many years in a quarrel very similar to Hildebrand's never alludes to Canossa.

At this moment the friendship of the Normans proved fatal. Robert returned from Greece, and rushed to the help of his overlord. Henry's forces, weakened by fever, retired from the city, and the Normans, among whom were many Saracens, entered it. The Romans turned on them, and a frightful street-battle ensued, ending in the destruction of the city under the eyes of its aged master. The Normans drew no distinction between friend and foe; the churches were burnt, the altars robbed, and the converts violated. Thousands of Romans were sold into slavery.

The Pope had made no attempt to stop these horrors. But, afterwards, perhaps in remorse, he retreated from Rome, and took refuge in Salerno, in the dominions of Robert. There, with the words, 'I have loved righteousness and hated iniquity, therefore I die in exile,' on his lips, the indomitable man passed away.

It might seem that his work was undone. But he was a Samson who slew more in his death than in his life. The quarrel went on. In England it was guided by Anselm of Canterbury, who finally gained from Henry I the so-called compromise of Bec, by which the investitures remained with the Church, homage to the King being done only for the temporalities of the sees. The Concordat of Worms in 1122 did the same work for Empire and Papacy. Thus the Bishops and Abbots, instead of being appointed by the King, and obedient feudatories, were in effect the servants, in one kingdom, of the ruler of another. All know how, under Thomas à Becket, the claim was made still more far-reaching, and how it was demanded that every cleric, from Archbishop down to acolyte or lower, should be made independent of State Law. Under John, the King became definitively the Pope's vassal, and Innocent III exercised the right of appointing and deposing kings. The monarch, he said, reigned by divine will; this was universally acknowledged. But the will of God was made known by the Pope; and thus the chief bulwark of kingship was turned into its weakness. The greatest height of all was reached in the first half of the thirteenth century, when the Popes embarked on a contest with the great imperial house of Hohen-staufen. Frederick the Second, the head of that house, was one of the most astonishing men in history – '*stupor mundi*', the wonder of the world, as he is repeatedly called by an his-torian of the time; and his life was as remarkable as his in-tellect. Made Emperor by a Pope, he was engaged, against his will, in constant struggles with the Papacy; no Pope would let him alone; he was excommunicated for not going on one crusade, and excommunicated for going on another; he did what the Church desired, and what Richard Cœur de Lion had failed to do – recover Jerusalem – and the Church hated him for doing it. After thirty years of struggle, he died at a moment when the battle might perhaps be considered drawn; it was certainly undecided.

The strength, and the weakness, of Frederick lay in his Sicilian kingdom, still largely Saracen, and therefore in-different to the thunders of the Church. All the efforts of the Popes, therefore, were directed to depriving his family of this kingdom. Even the help of England was sought, and the Pope actually offered Sicily to an English prince if the King of England would conquer it – a fact which caused a memorable conflict between Henry III and his subjects un-der Simon de Montfort. Finally, Charles of Anjou, brother of the King of France, was called in. The mingling of force and treachery, all under Papal sanction, by which the aim was attained, and the house of Hohenstaufen finally crushed, need not be described here. Suffice it to say that the aim *was* attained, and the Papacy was set on an apparently unassailable pinnacle.

But it could not last. As the spirit of nationality slowly grew, and as kingdoms like England and France slowly con-solidated themselves, a force appeared which in the long run proved itself more than a match for a Papacy that strove to be an Empire also, and to transform kings into mere pre-fects of the new Augustus. Even in John's reign, Stephen Langton, invested by the Pope's fiat against the will of Eng-land, became too English for the Pope. A century later, in a desperate effort to maintain the principles of Hildebrand

and Innocent, Boniface the Eighth came up against the ruthless resolve of Philip the Fair of France, and, after some of the most uncompromising claims ever put forth by ecclesiastics, fell into utter ruin. The Papacy was transferred to the 'Babylonish captivity' of Avignon, and became the subservient minion of France. When Rome again set up a Pope, his French rival did not resign, and the world was scandalized by the spectacle of two successors of St Peter cursing each other. At length, at the Council of Constance, under the guidance of the Emperor Sigismund, both were deposed, Councils were declared superior to Popes, and a new Pope was chosen. Thus were laid the foundations of that Gallicanism which made such pretensions in the time of Louis XIV and Bossuet.

Nor was there, during all this time, any lack of theoretical, as well as of physical, opposition to Papal arrogance. Dante's *De Monarchia* is only the most famous of innumerable works maintaining, on theological and logical grounds, the necessity of a real Emperor in the Christian system. But even more powerful were the writings of William of Ockham and Marsilio of Padua, who, by arguments carried on with medieval logic, and based on Christian premisses, attacked the very citadel of the Hildebrandine policy. Marsilio, in especial, went very far. The clergy had no jurisdiction over heretics or Jews: the decision over these must be left to Christ and the next world. Still less had the Pope authority over the temporalities of laymen, or even of clerics: nay, the clergy ought to renounce their wealth and return to apostolic poverty. The Pope's primacy consisted merely in this, that after consulting with the clergy he might humbly request the sovereign to summon a council, without whose consent he had no power to fix a belief or enact a law. The Pope's coronation of the Emperor was of no more significance than the coronation of a king of France by the Archbishop of Rheims. The famous Bull of Boniface, 'Unam Sanctam', was nothing but a tissue of unimaginable falsehoods.[1]

1. Marsilio even took the extreme Protestant position that the Pope is no successor of Peter. No Apostle was ever a Bishop; if Peter could have

The *Defensor Pacis* is difficult, and Ockham's *Compendium Errorum Papae* still more so; but their doctrines were simplified and scattered abroad by men who knew how to catch the ear of the common people; precisely as, a few years later, wandering friars knew how to popularize the ideas of Wiclif and Hus.

After the Council of Constance, the Popes, Eugenius, Martin, and Nicholas, to a great extent recovered their power; the Council Fathers, by removing the rival Pope of Avignon, had strengthened the single Pope they retained, though they had themselves appointed him; and the decrees of Constance were subsequently annulled. But its work could not be utterly undone: even its greatest error, with which the Popes thoroughly agreed – the condemnation of Hus – by leading to the breaking away of Bohemia from the Church, tended to keep up the spirit of opposition.

Another hundred years, and Henry VIII[1] revived the doctrine and practice of William the Conqueror: remaining orthodox in opinion, he forbade the payment of annates to Rome, destroyed the monasteries which were the chief support of the Papacy in England, and finally, by declaring himself Head of the Church, and assuming the sole power of appointing the Bishops in his realm, severed himself entirely from Roman obedience. From that it was but a step to the declaration of the total independence of England in theological dogma also. In Germany the Reformation, especially as developed by Calvin, carried things much further. Not all the efforts of the Jesuits, nor all the successes of the Counter-Reformation, could restore the past. The secular power of the Papacy is probably broken for ever; so far as it is exerted at all it will, in democratic countries, be exerted in the polling-booths and in constitutional fashion: and even so

---

been a Bishop, he would have been Bishop of Antioch; and if any Apostle could have been Bishop of Rome, it must have been Paul, and not Peter, who cannot be proved to have ever been in Rome at all.

1. A similar step was seriously contemplated by Henry's contemporary, Francis I of France; and a policy not unlike it was carried through by Louis XIV.

it may fail. Even Irishmen have been known to say that they take their religion from the Pope, but not their politics. The decisive act in the long drama, and one which is in all probability conclusive,[1] was played in Italy itself, when Victor Emmanuel annexed first the States of the Church and then Rome itself, leaving Pius IX but a few square yards of territory.

   We have now reached the end of one volume in this strange eventful history. A Jewish religion, hardly in the first instance differing from the dominant Pharisaism of the time, has spread into the Gentile world, and has found itself far more in harmony with that world than with the narrow nationalism out of which it sprang. After some attempts at compromise, it has separated itself from its original, and finally cast it out as a 'heresy'. By successive adaptations to its environment, by half-unconscious accommodations to the heathenism it has displaced, by the influence of the courage and endurance it displays during persecution, by the example which many of its votaries set of brotherliness and charity, by all sorts of forces good or bad, it finally induces the civil magistrate (or rather the military despot) to tolerate it and even to make it the established creed. Meanwhile, it has had to define its beliefs: the accession of a number of men, trained in Greek literature and philosophy, makes this inevitable.

   It is at this point that we mark the first clear and distinct signs of degeneracy on a great scale. Definition was necessary, but it was carried out with an almost total lack of Christian charity. There is no more painful story in the world than that of the way in which ministers professing – nay, loudly shouting – the religion of love behaved to each other in their disputes about points of doctrine, sparing no slander, and hurling anathemas to and fro with reckless bitterness. The second chapter opens with the question whether the State would exert itself strenuously and persistently to suppress these quarrels, or whether it would show itself a partisan.

   1. Mussolini's treaty with the Vatican slightly, but very slightly, enlarged the Papal domain.

The answer was not long doubtful. At the Council of Nicaea, which followed shortly after the conversion of Constantine, orthodoxy was decided by the Emperor, and heresy was confounded with *lèse-majesté*. The whole force of the State was brought in to compel men to profess with their lips what they disbelieved in their hearts, and the Church which had but a little while before been herself persecuted became a persecutor in her turn. Here begins the shameful narrative of factions trying all means, open or secret, of influencing the Imperial court in favour of their peculiar -isms; of creeds changed as Emperors died or varied their ideas; of favourites cajoled into support of this side or that; of Bishops banished and restored by the caprice of Governments; of honest men pursued with rancour in this life and condemned to everlasting punishment in the next, for going wrong or right, as the case might be, on some obscure metaphysical distinction. Worse, if possible, was to come. The heathen were to be dragged into the Church by the same compulsion which they had used to drive men out of it. The arguments which the Christians had employed when they were the victims were forgotten; and the crimes of Decius and Diocletian were avenged on men who had never heard of them. A few voices were raised saying that the weapons of the Church ought to be peaceful; that persuasion, and not force, was alone consistent with Christianity; but few listened, and the Church ran violently down a steep place into a sea of cruelty and self-deceit. The Inquisition and the Statute 'De Haeretico Comburendo' might already have been seen on the horizon.

But the time came when unity, even the nominal unity gained by these means, could no longer be maintained. The removal of the seat of empire from Rome to Byzantium meant that sooner or later the West would sunder itself from the East; and when the West set up an Emperor of its own this consummation drew nearer and became inevitable in the eyes of all thinking men. An accidental dispute proved the occasion of an event whose real cause lay deep in the past: the great schism took place which is not likely ever to be healed.

From that time the history is one of an eternal quarrel between the joint heads of Church and State in the West; a warfare in which there was no furlough, and in which success came to one side or the other as circumstances determined. We find very little Christian feeling on either side. The 'spiritual' party used secular weapons when it found them convenient, and still more unscrupulously used spiritual weapons in its mundane quarrels. The Imperial party, when chance favoured it, was equally indifferent to religion and fairness. But, on the whole, it is safe to say that if the Hildebrandine theory had gained a complete victory, the world would not have been a planet worth living in. By the time of Nicholas V, a few years after the Council of Constance, it seemed as if this undesirable result had been attained: the Pope was, for the time being, supreme. A silent force, however, was even then working for the emancipation of the race. Learning was gradually spreading among the laity; books were no longer the monopoly of the clerks. It became possible to put to the test some of the daring assertions on which Papal and clerical authority rested, and to test them was often to destroy them. Science, also, was timidly pursuing its investigations, and its results were not always in harmony with Church dogmas. The New Testament was being studied, and it is not possible to find there a Christianity closely resembling the Christianity of Hildebrand or Nicholas. Added to all this, the Church was over-confident; she grew corrupt, and the moral sense of mankind was revolted by her immoralities. It might perhaps have been possible for her to reform herself; but the opportunity, if there was one, was missed, and a new schism became inevitable. The schism was aided by the determination of the nationalities to release themselves from Papal interference in their secular affairs: and the Reforming movement, which had it risen some time before, might have been crushed out in blood, had sufficient lay protection to grow too strong for suppression. Europe was thenceforth divided, and will probably remain so.

CHAPTER 9

THE DIVIDED CHURCH

THE Founder of Christianity had not where to lay his head, and his first associates were for the most part poor people. We know that they had a common purse, and that he availed himself of the hospitality that wealthy men offered him; but there is no sign that he ever demanded a single penny from any of his followers. So soon, however, as his Church began to organize itself, money became necessary and was willingly contributed. Nothing more deadly than gentle persuasion was ever used, and we do not hear any complaints of extortion. Paul, for instance, whenever there was any danger of trouble on this account, was particularly careful to provide for his needs by the labour of his own hands. Such disputes as did arise were about the distribution, rather than the collection, of the funds.

As the organization, during centuries, became more and more elaborate, and the Church partook of the nature of a State, more and more money was required, and all sorts of devices were used in order to get it. It was common, for instance, in a newly converted country, to ask a converted landowner to give some land for the foundation of a church and the endowment of a priest: he often gave in haste and repented at leisure, and furious contests ensued between him and the ecclesiastics as to their respective claims. The history of England, France, Germany, and even distant Iceland is full of stories of such contests, in which the lord sometimes resorted to rude physical weapons, the churchman, it was thought, to unfair spiritual ones. Such gifts of land were so frequent – they were regarded as liens on a heavenly mansion – that in some countries the Church owned no less than a quarter or a third of the whole area: and at this point quarrels were inevitable because of the medieval conception of 'ownership'. The theory was that the whole country was the king's, the demesnes, manors, holdings being rented, as we may say, from him as the ultimate landowner. The Church lands were therefore subject to dues like those of any other tenant; but there was one due that they escaped, namely the 'fine' paid when the tenant died and his heir succeeded. The Church never died, and had no heirs: a state of things which led to many sham transfers of land to the Church to escape the death-dues. Hence legislation like the Statutes of Mortmain, to prevent legacies or donations to the 'dead hand': it was felt that the Church had enough, and that the Crown was losing too much. As feudal tenant, the Bishop owed homage for his land: as a supernatural being he owed homage solely to God or to God's Vicar, the Pope. Disputes between Church and king turned constantly on the point at which these two functions diverged, the one party striving always to fix it in his own interest, the other in what he called the interest of religion. Such a quarrel, lasting long, was maintained between Anselm and Rufus, between Anselm and Henry I, between Thomas of Canterbury and Henry II. Under Edward I it was fast and furious, for the King was in desperate need of money, and the Church, in accordance with the Bull of Boniface VIII, *Clericis Laicos*, refused (for a time) to give it. Papal greed also explains other grievances, such as the demand for annates and the frequent filling of benefices with absentee Italians, who received the income but delegated the work. There were other causes of quarrel, in every one of which the scales were weighted against the secular side, and the most powerful lords and kings were constantly defeated, until the capture and ruin of Boniface by Philip the Fair of France taught the Papacy the lesson that the worm would turn: '*spoliatis arma supersunt.*' But the fall of Boniface incidentally introduced a new scandal: the Pope was now a nominee of France, and transferred his see to Avignon, where for seventy years he played the part of a French vassal, and even the show of impartiality was dispensed with.

If, in the disputes about Investitures and other not less

vital questions the Church was usually victorious over such powerful kings as Henry II or Frederick Barbarossa, it may well be imagined that the case was much worse in disputes between wealthy abbots like those of St Edmunds or St Albans and their dependants, and worse still between a poor parishioner and his priest, where all the trump-cards were in the hands of the ecclesiastic. Defended by the unknown terrors of the next world, of which he was supposed to have the keys; with the weapon of excommunication always ready; with the whole ecclesiastical organization behind him, the priest was checked solely by custom, by his own conscience, or by the absolute exhaustion of his victim: and it was not every priest who, like Chaucer's noble poor parson, was 'loth to cursen for his tithes'. In addition to the priest, there was the summoner, whose fearful accusations of heresy could be avoided only by a bribe; and the pardoner, with his sermon on the love of money as the root of all evil, was waiting to persuade more cash still out of the unhappy layman's pocket. Redress was not to be had, for a lawsuit between a layman and a cleric was tried in the clerical courts, which, as was well known, would 'bring in Abel, if lay, guilty of the murder of a clerical Cain'.

We are not surprised, then, that in many cases the first attacks upon the Church had to do with the wealth of the clergy. Acts of Parliament were passed against the extortions of the Pope and his legates; revolts every now and then occurred against the little tyrants of the parish. The better clergy themselves joined in the cry. They looked into the New Testament, and found that the early Apostles were poor men. A demand arose that the Church should return to Apostolic poverty, and – for a short time – the brotherhoods of Dominic and Francis actually set the example of giving up all they had and moving about the country in indigent imitation of Christ and his disciples.

But such a movement could not stop there. From attacks on the wealth of the clergy, in which support might be gained from powerful and not always scrupulous nobles, the assailants inevitably passed to doctrines. Wiclif, for instance, towards the end of his career, expressed more than doubts as to Transubstantiation. He found nothing like that doctrine in the New Testament; the Fathers held all sorts of opinions on the theory of the sacraments; the Schoolmen had varied in their subtle metaphysical interpretations of it; and the dogma was not finally established till it was affirmed by the Lateran Council of 1215. It is obvious that such a dogma enormously increases the power of the clergy. If you believe that you cannot enter heaven without eating the Body of Christ, and if the only man who can perform the miracle of giving you that Body, in the shape of bread, is the priest, you are at the mercy of the priest. He has only to threaten to refuse you the transformed viand, and you must do his will. To attack that doctrine, then, is to attack the very citadel of clerical domination; and the clergy were quick to see the danger. Wiclif and his 'Lollard' followers were branded as heretics. The new Lancastrian dynasty was in need of clerical support; the Statute 'De Haeretico Comburendo' was passed in 1401: some of the heretics were burned, others recanted, and Lollardry was suppressed – though it is said that one or two obscure congregations survived till the Reformation, and though it is likely that a good many people continued to hold Lollard opinions in their hearts while refraining from expressing them with their tongues.

Wiclif's most famous pupil was not an Englishman, but the Bohemian John Hussinetz, generally known as Hus, Rector of the University of Prague. Early in life Hus became acquainted with the works of the English Reformer, and before he was thirty was lecturing on them to throngs of students, and, in accordance with the principles of his master, studying the Scriptures with intense zeal. He was thus led, with a hope more sanguine than practical, to aim at a reform of the Church with the help of his ecclesiastical superiors. For some time his relations with Sbynko the Archbishop were friendly; it is true that in 1403 forty-five of Wiclif's theses were condemned, but Hus was still allowed to lecture, on the understanding that he was not to make

Wiclif's works the text for heretical exegesis. Later, Hus was chosen to investigate some supposed miracles performed by the Blood of Christ, and did not lose favour when he pronounced them fraudulent, and issued a work urging men to cease seeking for signs and wonders, and to search the Scriptures instead. But it was not possible for the friendship to endure. Hus demanded freedom of thought, and freedom of thought was leading to the spread of Wiclifite doctrines: it was his method, rather than his opinions, that terrified the Bishops. In 1410 a Papal Bull was promulgated, forbidding the use of Wiclif's writings, and condemning preaching in unauthorized places. The Archbishop burnt the books, but Hus continued to preach. Finally, he was excommunicated, and the city was laid under an interdict. It then appeared that the force of these tremendous weapons depended solely on the minds of those against whom they were directed. No one took any notice of them, and an ignored excommunication was seen to be a mere *brutum fulmen*.

In 1412 the Pope proclaimed a Crusade against King Ladislaus of Naples. This roused the indignation of Hus and his friends, who openly maintained that neither Pope nor any other Bishop had the right to draw the sword: their kingdom was not of this world. As for the indulgences which were to pay for the war, they were useless; not money, but repentance, could purchase forgiveness. The people listened, assembled in crowds, and burnt the Papal Bull in the market-place. King Wenceslas, however, to prevent civil disturbances, though he refused to deal with Hus as heretic, drove the preacher out of the city, where he occupied himself in reproducing the opinions of Wiclif on the Church.

This was the time of the Great Schism. Two Popes, one at Avignon and the other at Rome, were fulminating against each other. The Council, convened to put an end to these scandals, met at Constance, and, before it separated, deposed both the rivals. But while thus acting, it desired also to show that it had no sympathy with heresy. Hus was summoned to defend his cause. He came, with a safe-conduct granted to him by the Emperor Sigismund, King of Hungary, who desired the eternal glory of restoring the unity of the Church and of purifying the faith. Hus was brought to trial; 'heretical' passages from his writings were picked out and read, and his defence was drowned in shouts of fury. When at last he obtained a hearing, he avowed his respect for Wiclif as a man, but denied that he agreed with him as to transubstantiation. His sentence was already decided on: he was degraded from the priesthood, and condemned to the death of a heretic. As the Church does not, in theory, put to death, but relies for punishments on the secular arm, it was possible for Sigismund to save him. 'I came here,' said Hus, 'trusting in the safe-conduct of an Emperor.' Sigismund blushed; but he had been infected by the priests with the detestable doctrine that no faith should be kept with heretics:[1] and on 6 July 1415 Hus was burned alive at Constance. Within a year, his friend, Jerome of Prague, suffered the same penalty.

It is by no means certain that Hus was a heretic at all: theologians who have studied his works hesitate as to their character. It *is* certain, however, that he did not die for heresy: it was his defiance of ecclesiastical power, and not his errors of belief, that roused his enemies. It is certain, also, that his death was a violation of the law; and in this sense it is far worse than any of the martyrdoms which have made the name of Mary Tudor a byword: all these were at least legal, and followed on an Act of Parliament.[2]

The effect was tremendous and lasting. The indignation of Bohemia broke out immediately, and, though restrained by the universal respect for Wenceslas, could not be checked

1. In a letter to the Bohemians, Sigismund reveals the temper of the assembly. 'If I had not yielded, the Council would have been utterly broken up.' A patriotic Englishman will be glad to know that Robert Hallam, Bishop of Salisbury, strongly condemned the infliction of death for heresy.

2. Milman draws attention to the fact that the Council, though condemning Hus and Jerome, did not dare, through dread of the Duke of Burgundy, to censure the work of Jean Petit, in which the Duke's murder of the Duke of Orleans was defended.

when, in 1419, Wenceslas died and the arch-criminal, Sigismund, succeeded to the throne. The country flew to arms, and one of the most terrible wars in history began, which has made immortal the names of Ziska and Procopius. As so often, the conflict compelled the assertion of principles which had hitherto been latent in the minds of the combatants, and which before they might have denied that they harboured. The Bohemians, or the most determined of them, put forth the Four Articles of Prague, demanding freedom of preaching, communion in both kinds, the return of the clergy to apostolic poverty, and the due punishment of open sins, whether lay or clerical. They had thus passed beyond Hus, who never claimed the cup for the laity.

There is no question either that Christ gave both the bread and the wine to his disciples (who may, it is true, be regarded as in some sense priests) or that for a thousand years the officiating minister always gave both to the participants in the Supper. Pope Gelasius (A.D. 492–6) does, it is true, speak of some who 'held back' from the cup of the sacred Blood; but he censures them as the victims of superstition, and as guilty of sacrilege. Aquinas tells us that the withholding of the cup was usual in certain churches only, and defends it by the argument of Portia, that flesh and blood are 'concomitant', i.e., that flesh is not seen without blood. Some priests, from fear that the sacred blood might be spilt, are said to have kept the cup in their own hand. By the time of the Council of Constance, this custom had become regular, though even the Fathers of that Council could not deny that things had been otherwise in the past. The Hussites now demanded that the old custom should be restored, and were known as 'Utraquists' (Latin *utraque*, 'each') in consequence. This demand, along with the others, may be regarded as the beginning of the Reformation: for though, after ten years of war, a compromise was patched up, and many of the Bohemians gradually returned to the Catholic faith, yet Utraquism never faded out. The design of King George Podiebrad (1460) to found a national Church ended in failure; but Utraquists enough were left to add considerable strength to the cause of Luther, who studied their writings and approved their opinions. 'Not even the ideas of Wiclif and Hus are mistaken,' said Luther very early in his career in his Leipzig disputation with Eck; and the confession was taken both by Eck and by the Utraquists as a proof that he was in sympathy with the Bohemian heresies. When the Reformation had made some progress, the Utraquists recognized the logic of facts, and quietly allowed themselves to be drawn into the main current of Protestantism.[1] It was indeed the obstinate adherence of Bohemia to the Protestant religion that led to the most terrible and fatal struggle of modern times, the Thirty Years' War of 1618–48, which tore Germany to pieces, reduced its population by perhaps half, and laid it open to the aggressions of its neighbours, with consequences of which the end is not yet.

It is an obvious and necessary part of the Roman system that the character of the minister cannot invalidate the efficacy of the rites which he performs, any more than the private character of a secular judge can invalidate his legal decisions. If the priest receives at ordination a miraculous power, that power remains, and the absolution of an Alexander VI is as effective as that of a St Gregory. None the less, the natural sentiment of mankind demands that men professing to hold a sacred office should show a certain amount of sanctity in their behaviour; and the evidence is irrefutable that both regulars and seculars had to a great extent forgotten this wholesome principle during the fifteenth century. Archbishop Morton, Wolsey, Machiavelli, Pope Hadrian, Erasmus, agree in this with the Protestants. The middle classes in almost all nations were either righteously shocked or cynically amused by the open profligacy,

1. The very name is not often heard in later history, though Wallenstein, in the seventeenth century, called himself rather a Utraquist than a Lutheran. The Council of Basle compromised on the question of the cup, and it was not till Trent that a more or less precise definition was formulated. Thus it was long possible to combine Utraquism with Catholicism.

rapacity, and worldliness of the clergy: and the daily sight of men whose conduct was in flagrant contradiction with their professions prepared men to investigate the clerical claims to a divine mission with a critical eye. In Germany, where the general feeling first found overt and widespread expression, it came to a head with the nailing of Luther's ninety-five theses to the door of the church at Wittenberg in 1517. These famous articles were not, though scholastically framed, primarily theological; they were moral, and, so soon as they were translated into German, struck an answering chord in the hearts of thousands of ordinary decent people, who were unable to follow the complicated subtleties of the arguments as to what Indulgences were, but felt instinctively that sin could not be washed away by a monetary payment.[1] The practical mind of Luther broke

1. A full explanation of the theory of Indulgences – or rather of the many theories held on the subject – would take a volume. A very rough and loose outline may here be given. The Christian Church is *one*, and the merits or demerits of its members are contributions to a common stock, or subtractions from it. The merits of the saints are in fact a Treasury of Grace, of such immense wealth that it is open to the Church to draw upon it to a vast and almost unlimited extent. *Sin* may be washed away by Confession and Contrition, but its temporal penalty (including in the 'temporal' the pains of Purgatory) still remains to be paid as a 'Satisfaction', which the priest imposes in his Penance. But the priest cannot know how far his penitent is really 'contrite': he may not have got beyond the stage of what is technically called 'attrition' (which we may broadly interpret as 'regret'). Indulgences come in to compensate the deficiencies of the priest: a man who feels dubious as to his safety may assure himself by purchasing an Indulgence. It was thus that Pope Urban in 1095 recruited his army for the Crusade: fighting against the infidel was a satisfaction, and relieved the mind of the recruit from grave anxieties as to his future fate.

It does not appear that the best theologians such as Alexander of Hales or Thomas Aquinas, vague as their expressions often are, held the view that Indulgences washed away the *culpa* or guilt: this, they maintained, was the work of God alone, proclaimed by the priest in the Absolution: and the Council of Trent, in dealing with the question, abstains from asserting that they do wash it away. (Incidentally, the Council freely recognizes that abuses had intruded, and strongly recommends moderation in the employment of Indulgences. 'And being desirous that the abuses which have crept in, and on account of which this honourable

through the theological technicalities, and went straight to the real core of the question. God alone could forgive sins – a truth not only distinctly asserted in Scripture but written deep in the moral conscience of mankind. As a dialectician, he perhaps showed himself inferior to Eck and the other Romish disputants; but common feeling recognized that the root of the matter was in him.

That his mind was still set on practical evils was yet more clearly shown in the work which he wrote in 1520, three years after the theses, and which had at the time an even greater influence. This is the *Appeal to the Christian Nobility of the German Nation*.

'Reform was impossible,'[1] says the *Appeal*, 'because the straw walls of Rome, formidable only in appearance, were left standing. If the temporal power demanded reforms, it was told that the spiritual power was superior; if Scripture was adduced, it was said that the Pope alone could interpret it; if a Council was demanded, the Pope alone could summon it. Now this Spiritual Power was a phantom: the clergy were marked off from the laity not by a supernatural gift imparted at ordination, but by their

---

name of indulgences is blasphemed by heretics, be amended and corrected, the sacred and holy Council ordains that all evil gains for the obtaining thereof be wholly abolished; and it commands all Bishops diligently to collect all abuses, that, after having been reviewed by other Bishops also, they may be referred to the Sovereign Roman Pontiff.' – *Session* 25.)

It was not, however, to be expected that the common people should draw minute distinctions: a man relieved of a penalty naturally tends to think himself declared innocent; and one who feels 'attrition' exaggerates it into true repentance. There is no doubt, also, that many men of high intelligence did regard an Indulgence as cleansing the soul. Thus in the famous passage of the *Inferno* (27, 99 ff.), Pope Boniface is represented as granting an indulgence to Guido of Montefeltro for a sin not yet committed, and Montefeltro answers, 'Thou washest me from the *sin* I am about to do' – '*tu mi lavi di quel peccato ove io mo cader deggio.*'

The Reformation did much to reform even those who did not believe in it; and one of the benefits it secured was that Indulgences have never since been bought or sold: and Popes have asserted that the enormities of the traffic as practised in Germany were unintended by Rome.

1. I here summarize the analysis given by Lindsay.

special functions, and if they performed those functions badly, they could be called to account, like other men, by the civil magistrate. The Scriptures were open to all, and could be interpreted by private judgement enlightened by the Spirit of God; and all men have a right to agitate for the summoning of a Council.'

Luther had seen Rome, and had been thunderstruck by its corruption. 'There is in Rome a so-called Vicar of Christ who bears no resemblance to our Lord; he wears a triple crown, and requires, to keep up his state, a larger revenue than an emperor: he is surrounded with princes called Cardinals, who must appropriate to themselves convents and benefices to maintain their position. For these and other worldly ends Rome robs Germany yearly of three hundred thousand gold florins; to say nothing of annates, absolution money, and indulgences. No Archbishop can receive his pallium, no Bishop his see, without paying a fine to the Pope; and anyone can purchase impunity for crime by bribing the Papacy. Let Germany, at least, if no other country will do so, form a national Church, abolish clerical dominance, limit the number of pilgrimages, which are an excuse for avoiding honest work, and cut down the overgrown mendicant orders. Let the celibacy of the clergy, which leads to concubinage and immorality, be declared unnecessary.'[1]

Not unnaturally, the issue of this work was followed by excommunication; but this, like the walls of Rome, proved to be but of straw. Luther, amid applauding multitudes, burnt the Bull; and the Church, having exhausted its spiritual thunders, had to turn for help to the State.

Maximilian, the old Emperor, understanding the German

---

1. There were already some who wished to make marriage compulsory for the secular clergy, and voluntary for the regulars.

It is hard to find a single distinguished churchman who had not either a concubine or something worse. Wolsey's provision for his son, to whom he gave several lucrative benefices, is a typical case. At the trial of Cranmer, one of the charges was that he had been married. He answered that he thought it better to have his own wife than, like other priests, the wives of others.

feeling, had warned the Pope not to proceed precipitately against Luther; but he had died in 1519, and his grandson, Charles V, was of another temper. He was an orthodox Catholic, but his zeal was tempered by two stronger sentiments even than his orthodoxy. He was determined to assert the supremacy of the State over the Church, and he was still more firmly set on the aggrandizement of the Hapsburg family. Thus, when he had secured the attendance of Luther at the Diet of Worms in 1521, though he condemned the Reformer's heresies, he refused to imitate Sigismund and violate his safe-conduct. He saw that the divisions among the princes, which the 'firebrand' Luther might kindle, would weaken them in their attempts to assert themselves against the imperial power; and he was not unwilling to see the ecclesiastics busying themselves with internal quarrels. Luther therefore was allowed to go free, and on his way home was 'arrested' by his protector, the ruler of Saxony, and hidden from sight in the castle of Wartburg. In this 'Patmos' he passed through a time of great mental stress, which ended in the confirmation of his convictions, and the strengthening of his resolve. It was in the Wartburg that he began his epoch-making translation of the New Testament, a work the influence of which in Germany is second, if second, only to that of the Authorized Version in England. It is noteworthy that, unlike earlier versions such as Wiclif's or our 'Anglo-Saxon' Gospels, it was made from the Greek, and not from the Vulgate Latin. Already, in 1516, Erasmus of Rotterdam had issued his edition of the Greek Testament, which, with all its avoidable and unavoidable faults,[1] partly due to haste, is the beginning of that critical study of the text which has advanced so far in later years. Almost at the same time the 'Complutensian' edition appeared under the

1. The correct text of the 'Three Witnesses' verse (1 John v, 7) was given by Erasmus in his first two editions. He made a rash engagement with his critics that he would insert the spurious passage if any authority could be found for it; and in his third edition, having found a very late copy with the words, he performed his promise. This incident is characteristic of the man.

patronage of Cardinal Ximenes. Thus Greek scholars had the opportunity of seeing that the Vulgate was not always a faithful rendering of the original; but Luther's translation was the first to give a similar opportunity to the unlearned. It was, indeed, the most powerful agent in spreading the Reformation: and, though Luther himself was far from being a Bibliolater, many of his followers came to attach an even excessive authority to the testimony of Scripture. In their anxiety to find a counterpoise to the Infallible Church, they substituted an Infallible Book. This has involved many of the Protestant denominations in considerable difficulty, and has been perhaps the chief cause of those differences among them which have been utilized by Catholic controversialists like Bossuet. Not until it was recognized that the Bible is not a book but a literature, and that revelation is not static but progressive, did Protestantism begin to understand its own principles. In this respect, though hesitatingly and dimly, Luther saw more deeply into facts than his successors. He declared, for example, that the letter of James was, in comparison with those of Paul, 'an epistle of straw'; he denied the Pauline authorship of Hebrews, and he would have nothing to do with the Apocalypse.[1]

The work of reform did not cease while Luther was in the Wartburg: indeed, in some directions it went on all the more quickly because of the removal of the leader. On the scholastic side it was reinforced by the advent of the learned Melanchthon, whose lectures on the Pauline Epistles had a great influence on those capable of following them. Melanchthon, however, was no revolutionary: the practical side was in the hands of Carlstadt, whose aim was to destroy the Papal system utterly. Carlstadt attacked clerical celibacy, the sacrifice of the Mass, communion in one kind,

1. It will be found, I think, that though in these views Luther had the authority of many of the Fathers on his side (Origen, e.g., denied Hebrews to Paul, and the Apocalypse was rejected by whole Churches for centuries), he relied chiefly on his own feeling. As the books appealed, or failed to appeal, to his higher religious sense, so he accepted or rejected them. But he could not see that others might justly claim the same licence: and many, disregarding his authority, did make the claim.

monasticism, and nearly all the institutions and beliefs in which Papal strength lay; and his friend Zwilling assailed extreme unction as a device of the priests for extorting money out of people's distress and fear. It is at this point that we see emerging what always emerges in revolutionary times – extreme opinions and men who do not hesitate to put extreme opinions into practice. Partly through the influence of Hussites from Bohemia, partly by the natural process of events in Saxony, there arose a party, or confused mass of parties, which carried the doctrine of free judgement to the furthest lengths, began to destroy pictures and images, endeavoured to crush their adversaries by physical violence, and proclaimed that the inner light was as true an inspiration as that of the Apostles themselves. This of course was merely anarchy; and it compelled Luther to assert himself. He saw clearly that unless these factions could be kept in order, reform would lead to chaos, and chaos – at best – to the return of the old despotism. Luther was at heart a conservative; and order was his watchword. He came out of the Wartburg, and, with perhaps the highest exhibition of courage in his whole courageous life, reappeared in Wittenberg – 'most retrograde to the desire' of the Elector. His power was never more conspicuously shown: the extremists either repented or went elsewhere, and above all the appeal to force was refused. The celebration of the Sacrament was referred to the individual conscience, and in one and the same town men could attend the full Mass, take it as Cárlstadt had explained it, or receive both the bread and the wine. Luther himself still retained his cowl, and still lived in his Augustinian monastery.

Two decisive results, however, followed from these disturbances. The men of the Renaissance, headed by Erasmus, were frightened away. Erasmus had hitherto been regarded by many as a reformer, and indeed, when Luther was supposed to be dead, many reformers had called on him to lead them; while the Romanists taunted him with having laid the egg which Luther hatched. He now came out, moderately and timidly, on the Roman side. With his usual skill he chose a theological point on which to debate. Luther was a convinced predestinarian and determinist: Erasmus, in a very able treatise, defended the doctrine of the freedom of the will. Moderate as the tone of this book was, it did not conciliate Luther, whose answer was violent and uncompromising; nor did it satisfy the Romanist party, which expected something much more forceful. The fact was that Erasmus, and almost the whole body of his learned co-adjutors, knew well that the abuses of the Church called loudly for reform, but wished – vainly – that the Church should reform itself.

The second result was perhaps even more important. In his fear of anarchy, Luther began gradually to lean upon the support of the secular princes. He had been defended by the Elector Frederick; in 1524 Frederick came out openly as a Lutheran. Frederick died in 1525, and his successor John, already a Lutheran, was equally willing to defend the Reformer. In the same year, Philip of Hesse, under the influence of Melanchthon, became a convert, and not only permitted but enjoined the preaching of Lutheran doctrines in his dominions. Many others of the princes speedily followed suit: and very soon almost half the Empire, as represented by its rulers, might be said to be Lutheran. This dependence of Lutheranism upon the princes was the first sign of that marked State-Church character which is still so clearly visible in Prussia and other Lutheran countries. Under the influence of the fear raised by the Peasants' Revolt, which started in 1524, Luther's aristocratic leanings became still more manifest; and the horrors of the Anabaptist rising at Münster, ten years later, confirmed him in his conservative principles. His attitude towards the peasants, indeed, whose grievances were many, real, and terrible, was fatal to his attempt to make his movement really national. The revolt was suppressed with savage cruelty: and the cruelty was approved by Luther. It was put down by military force; and the Reformer who had repudiated force now recommended it. 'The ass *will* have blows,' said he: and he regretted that refractory servants could not be treated like 'other cattle'. Thenceforward, Lutheranism utterly failed to make any impression on the peasants, and Melanchthon owned that the populace detested Luther and all his works. To move the multitudes other leaders and other methods were now needed. Luther and Melanchthon were thus constrained to concessions they would once have abhorred, and of which Melanchthon at least was utterly ashamed. To retain the support of Philip of Hesse they sanctioned bigamy: and they came ultimately to regard the decrees of princes as almost ordinances of God. The deification of the State, which has been the central doctrine of so many Germans, and was turned into a philosophy by Hegel and Treitschke, is a lineal descendant of the theories of Luther. Herein we see one secret of the success of the Counter-Reformation.

During the short pontificate of the saintly and scholarly Hadrian VI, it was possible still to hope for a reunion, for the Pope was too noble-minded a man not to recognize the existence of evils demanding remedy. It was ludicrous to deny grievances which the Head of the Church confessed. At the Diet of Speier in 1526, after the death of Hadrian, the grievances were openly emphasized; the princes declared in favour of many of the Reformed opinions; and a demand was put forward for the summoning of a General Council. At the moment, Charles was not unwilling to agree; for his quarrel with the new Pope, who had been forming an Italian league against him, inclined him to hold the weapon of a Council in reserve. At the same moment, 30 August 1526, the 'Destruction of Mohacs', in which the power of Hungary was shattered by Sultan Solyman, and King Louis was killed, opened to Ferdinand of Austria, Charles's brother and later his successor as Emperor, the opportunity of adding the relics of Hungary to his dominions. He accordingly patched up a truce with his Bohemian subjects, and devoted his attention to securing Hungary against his rival Zapolya. Towards the end of the year he had largely attained his ends, and received the crown of St Stephen. In the interval, however, he had been forced to leave heresy alone.

The face of things soon changed once more. The victory of Charles was speedy and decisive: in 1527 the Pope was utterly defeated, and Rome was not merely taken but sacked by the Imperial troops under the Constable of Bourbon. It was open to Charles to destroy the temporal power of the Pope, or even to abolish the Papacy altogether: and he actually considered the question. But he soon saw that abolition, or even the reduction of the Pope to the position of an Italian Patriarch, was likely to be followed by the institution of independent patriarchates in England, in France and in every principality of Germany – the secular rulers in each case being the real Patriarchs, and the Bishops the nominal. What he feared actually came about in England, and nearly came about in France.[1] A few words are therefore necessary to explain what was happening in England.

As early as 1514, it is now known, Henry VIII had felt doubts about the legitimacy of his marriage with Charles's aunt, Catherine of Aragon, who was his elder brother's widow. These were strengthened by the deaths of one after another of the children of the marriage, a sickly girl, Mary, born in 1516, alone surviving. No woman had ever reigned in England; the dangers of a renewal of the Wars of the Roses were present to all men's minds, and the King even contemplated the legitimization of his natural son the Duke of Richmond. There can be little doubt that the execution of the Duke of Buckingham in 1521 was due to these fears; for the Duke, as the direct descendant of Edward III in the male line, might have put forward claims to the crown.

The King's scruples, probably sincere, were certainly strengthened when he saw and fell in love with Anne Boleyn: and by the advice of Wolsey he applied to Pope Clement for a decree of nullification of the marriage with Catherine. Such decrees had been often granted in the past; and Henry saw no reason why one should not be granted

1. It may almost be said to have actually come about in France a century and a half later under Louis XIV, when the Gallican Church established a practical independence of Rome.

now. But the demand arrived when Clement was at the mercy of the Emperor. Charles cared nothing for Catherine, but much for his family interests; and the decree would have meant the exclusion of his cousin Mary, as illegitimate, from the throne. This he was determined to prevent; and Clement understood the situation. The shifts to which the unhappy Pope was thus reduced, the temporizings, the daring when Charles seemed weak and the timidity when he became strong, the promises, the actual granting of the decree and the order to the messenger to keep it secret, the tergiversations and twists of all kinds, must be studied in the minuter histories. They resulted, as all know, in the declaration of independence: Henry, as Supreme Head of the Church under God, took the place of the Pope in England. The nominal Patriarch, Cranmer, did what the lay Pope told him to do. The marriage with Catherine was declared null and void, and Henry married Anne Boleyn. In doctrine the King remained orthodox; but the Bishop of Rome was told that he had no authority or jurisdiction in the realm of England. It is noteworthy that many of the men who afterwards came out most strongly on the Roman side, either strongly or passively supported these measures. One step, however, led to others to which there was less agreement. It had long been widely felt that some at least of the monasteries had outlived their usefulness; many were hopelessly corrupt. They were also rich, and the chief support of the Papacy in England. Already the force of public opinion had compelled the Pope to consent to the suppression of several, and to the application of their revenues to educational purposes. Thus, at the end of the fifteenth century, John Alcock, Bishop of Ely, had turned the nunnery of St Rhadegund into Jesus College in Cambridge; so sound a Catholic as Bishop Fisher had advised Lady Margaret, the mother of Henry VII, as to the similar foundations of John's and Christ's, and as to the endowment of divinity professorships both at Oxford and at Cambridge; Wolsey had, with more than his usual magnificence, endowed in the same way his colleges at Oxford and at Ipswich:

> *one of which fell with him,*
> *Unwilling to outlive the good that did it;*
> *The other, though unfinished, yet so famous*
> *That Christendom shall ever speak his virtue.*[1]

It was now resolved to carry out the work by royal authority. In 1536 the smaller monasteries were suppressed; in 1539 the larger, not without much cruelty and much subsequent suffering. Nor were the spoils rightly used. One or two new Bishoprics, badly needed, were founded,[2] but the lion's share went to the King himself and the rapacious nobles who supported him. The shrewd minister, Thomas Cromwell, who carried the change through, saw clearly what he was doing. These nobles, when the reaction came under Mary, were quite willing to own the supremacy of the Pope; but nothing would induce them to surrender the estates.

It is probably a mistake to imagine that these steps were taken merely through royal caprice. The changes were carried through by Parliament, and – though there were uprisings in different parts of the country – seem to have been not unpopular. Most of them, indeed, were but revivals of measures taken long before. Thus in 1530, when the procuring of licences from Rome for pluralities was forbidden, when annates were withdrawn, when Henry demanded a General Council, when appeals to Rome (one of the chief sources of Papal revenue) were forbidden, and even when some of the monasteries were suppressed, Henry seems to have had the people with him; and, in compelling the clergy to submit to him, the weapon he used was not new, but the Statute of Praemunire passed in 1393. In England, as in Germany, the extortions, the simony, and the flagrant corruption of the Church had excited general odium; and things had long been ripe for drastic reform.

Meanwhile, on the Continent, things had been taking their inevitable course. Charles, after his great victory, had

---

1. *Henry VIII*, iv, 2.
2. And one of these, Westminister, did not last long.

come to perceive that a weakling like Clement might be a useful tool, and that the Papacy was indispensable for his purposes. By the Treaty of Barcelona, 1529, a compact was made with the Pope, and sealed, after the fashion of a merely secular treaty, by marriages and agreements about estates. The Pope's family was to be restored to power in Florence, Ferdinand to be helped in Hungary, and Turks and heretics alike were to be crushed. A peace with France at the same time left Charles's hands free to deal with Lutheranism. At the Diet of Speier the result was soon seen. The Emperor, claiming all the time to be moderate, demanded toleration for Catholics in Lutheran States, but refused it to Lutherans in Catholic States. For Reformers other than Lutherans there was to be no toleration at all. This was, of course, a declaration of war. Against it five princes and fourteen free towns signed the memorable Protest which has given to the Churches which dissent from Rome the name of Protestant. This was followed in the next year by a desperate attempt at conciliation. The Confession of Augsburg, drawn up by Melanchthon, was so framed as to minimize as far as possible the differences between the two parties. Its object was to show that, if the Church only reformed itself, and got rid of the abuses which everybody admitted to exist, the Lutherans would consent to remain in it, and that the Catholics had no right to drive them from it. For a moment it looked as if the compromise might succeed; there were moderate men on both sides who hoped for success and worked for it. But things had gone too far. Melanchthon could not carry his friends with him, and the Catholic extremists refused concession. The Emperor threatened physical force, which merely stiffened the backs of the Reformers: and it soon appeared that his threats were words and nothing more. He had no money; and he knew that his enemy Francis I was waiting only for a civil war in Germany to make an attack on him in Italy. At Schmalkalden, in 1531, a league of the Protestant States was formed to resist aggression, and so many princes and cities joined it that war would plainly have been dangerous and its result uncertain.

For the present, therefore, the two forces watched each other in a sort of armed truce.

No religion has ever been able to escape splitting into sects, and the sects are usually more numerous and more vigorous when the religion is making its first steps. It is even a tenable view that the vitality of a creed may be judged by the number of offshoots from the parent-stem. Such recent and progressive religions as Spiritualism and Methodism might provide examples; they grow rapidly; the number of their members increases – and so does the number of those who break away. Be this theory true or not, the advent of Protestantism was speedily followed by a multiplication of its divisions. Of these the most rabid was the Anabaptist, the most important the Zwinglian: it would be impossible to enumerate all, for there were places in which almost every man was his own church. It was these divisions that constituted Luther's chief weakness, and ultimately checked the advance of Protestantism.

The ANABAPTISTS, whose centre was the city of Münster, went back to early Christianity, proclaimed a community of goods, anticipated the speedy end of the world, and endeavoured to prepare the way for Christ's coming by abolishing civil institutions and social classes. From this point many of them went further: community of goods was held to involve community of wives, polygamy, or the total abolition of marriage. Prophets like Matthys stimulated the fanaticism of the people, and the belief in the coming end enabled them to endure the most frightful hardships in this world without complaining. After the death of Matthys the rule was seized by John of Leyden, who announced that, by the predestination of God, he was to be the king of the whole world, and to inaugurate the Fifth Monarchy of the Book of Daniel. After a terrible siege, the city was at length captured and the inhabitants slaughtered. With the savagery that always goes with fear, John and his lieutenant Knipperdollinck were tortured to death. The Anabaptists, however, were not destroyed. Scattered all over the world, they exerted a powerful influence in England and America, especially during the following century; but their fanaticism and frenzy vanished, and they became the excellent, mild, and harmless Church which we know today.

The Swiss ZWINGLI has been called the most modern in mind of all the Reformers: and it was this modernity that made his quarrel with Luther irreconcilable. He was a classical scholar, and could not deny the chance of salvation to Socrates or Plato. He was a statesman, and had learnt the necessity of compromises and accommodations. Whereas to Luther there was always a clear-cut distinction – one was either for God or for Satan – Zwingli saw that there are many aspects of truth, and that there are many shades of good and evil, making it impossible for a firm line to be drawn between them. There are also many channels of divine grace, and men may reach heaven in various ways. To Zwingli it was impossible to damn the vast mass of men to eternal perdition, and 'original sin', which plays so important a part in the Lutheran theology, he made of little account. As for the demonic agencies to which Luther ascribed such vast power, and with which he waged an almost visible warfare, Zwingli was as sceptical as a man of his age well could be. But it was in the doctrine of the Eucharist that the main differences between the two Reformers were found. Luther, though he did not hold the full Roman view, maintained, in his theory of 'Consubstantiation', something very like it, and clave to the literal meaning of the saying 'This is my body.' Zwingli, on the other hand, pointed out that a similar method would compel Luther to believe that Christ was also a literal vine and a literal door, and the Eucharist became to him no perpetually renewed miracle but simply a commemoration.

Politically, again, Zwingli severed himself from Luther. Far from relying on the princes, or pretending any allegiance to the Emperor, he aimed at uniting the cantons of Switzerland with the cities of south Germany, getting rid of both Pope and Emperor, and establishing a democratic Republic. It was largely with this end in view that in 1530 he met the Lutherans at Marburg, under the protection of

Philip of Hesse, and endeavoured to bridge over the differences between the two wings of Protestantism: for this end he signed all the articles set before him by Luther with the exception of that relating to the Eucharist: and for this end he urged his followers to speak of their Lutheran opponents with moderation. He might have spared his labour. Luther refused to admit that Zwinglians were true members of the Church of Christ, and retorted to the moderation of the Zwinglians by calling them liars, hypocrites, and the very incarnate spirit of lying. When, in the next year, Zwingli was killed at Kappel, he did not disguise his satisfaction.[1] But the split, for which Luther was to blame, was to prove almost the ruin of the Reformation.

It was the desire of Charles, and of all the moderate men on both sides, that a council should be summoned which should deal with practical abuses, to define dogmas, that as many differing opinions as possible might be permitted within the Church, and, at least by implication, allow some rights to the laity. That these ends might be attained, the Protestants refused to have anything to do with a council summoned by the Pope himself, and demanded that it should meet in Germany. The one desire of the Pope, Paul III, was to prevent discussion of abuses, and, by involving the Emperor in quarrels with the Protestants, to hinder any effective practical reforms. For years it was found impossible to assemble a council at all: and when, finally, one was summoned, it was soon seen that no good was to be expected from it. In the first place, it met at Trent, nominally a German city, in the domains of Ferdinand of Austria, but difficult of access to all but Italians, and therefore admitting of being swamped with Italian prelates, who were hardly more than creatures of the Pope. The sounding titles of sacred, holy, and oecumenical were given to it, but it was marked by all the ravings and frenzy which have distinguished ecclesiastical synods from the first, and its universal character was signalized by the fact that Protestants, though

1. Zwingli, he said, must be damned unless God treated him as an exception to his rule.

ironically allowed to come and put their case, were forbidden to vote. The bishops present at first were eminent only for their ignorance; and when the twenty Spanish delegates arrived, though they brought a great accession of piety and learning, they were hopelessly outnumbered, and skilfully outmanoeuvred by the Papal Legate, Del Monte, who took care that the sessions should waste their time in argumentation about minute theological points, and have neither time nor energy left for the scandals that really interested the world. The decrees therefore express the feelings of a number of Italian churchmen, slaves of the Papacy, knowing themselves to be on their defence, and trying every possible shift to prevent the accusations from being pressed home. Such few concessions as the Council made were made only on trifling points, and with reference to abuses which could not be denied: while the really crying scandals remained untouched. Against 'heresy', however, the Fathers were vigorous enough: several Lutheran doctrines were condemned with a force which left little to be desired. Thus, so far from opening the gates of the Church more widely, the Council shut them more closely, and defined many dogmas more rigidly than they had ever been defined before, excluding from the Church thousands whom a certain degree of accommodation might have conciliated. To take but one example, the Vulgate was declared to be canonical, though all scholars knew that its author, St Jerome, had denied that he was inspired, though its text was notoriously uncertain,[1] and though it contained books which Luther

1. The Fathers were aware of the variations of text, and a congregation under Cardinal Caraffa (afterwards Pope Paul IV) was appointed to prepare a correct edition. In 1590 Sixtus V published an edition of his own (still known as the Sixtine) in which all errors, even misprints, were authoritatively asserted to be absent, and an anathema was pronounced on those who should alter it. Unfortunately no fewer than two thousand errors were discovered, and a new edition was issued by so sound a Romanist as Cardinal Bellarmine.

Even if a correct text were possible, and St Jerome's version could be exactly recovered, the question of his accuracy would still remain: for it is certain that he mistranslated some passages, and in others worked on a wrong Hebrew or Greek original.

had declared to be apocryphal, and some of which have very little tendency to edification. A terse and comprehensive anathema, forming the finis to many of the canons, pronounced the eternal damnation of those who could not agree to a series of difficult and obscure theses, while Rome retained for herself all the powers of levying annates, tithes, or fines, and of conferring pluralities on her Cardinals, which were the ground of the charges against her, and the destruction of which had been the end for which the council was summoned.

Even Trent, however, proved after a time too insalubrious a climate for the Papal desires. On the pretence that it was exposed to the plague, the Pope withdrew the Italian Fathers to Bologna: the Spaniards remained, and did not seem to be in danger. No English, and only two French representatives ever appeared at the Council at all; but its oecumenical character was still preserved, though Charles and his friends stoutly denied that thirty or forty Italians could legislate for the world. After a long period of intrigue, the Emperor secured the return to Trent, and there the wearisome process began again. A last desperate attempt at restoring unity was now made – not by the Papacy, but by the Emperor. Luther was now dead, the charity of the time rejoicing that the heresiarch had gone to his own place. Charles therefore invited Melanchthon and his friends to go to Trent and put forward their proposals. Not unnaturally, remembering Constance, they refused until they had received a safe-conduct from the Council itself. The first safe-conduct they received was studiously ambiguous: for the doctrine was still held that a heretic was a wild beast to be entrapped without scruple: and the delay thus caused was utilized to add still more canons and anathemas to the list. Melanchthon did not go, but sent an ambassador, who told the assembled Bishops that the council was called to redress grievances, that the Head of the Church must be called to account as well as the members, that all representatives, Protestant as well as Catholic, should have a right to speak, and that a few Bishops from one or two countries could not settle the faith of the world. This being so, no Lutheran would take any notice of definitions of doctrine formulated by such men and in such a manner. The Council of Constance had asserted its superiority to the Pope: this council should act on that precedent, disregard episcopal allegiance to Rome, and proceed to reform abuses by cleansing the fountain in which they took their rise. Till these things were honestly taken in hand, no Protestant would attend the Council.

We need not follow the history of Trent further. Soon after this, it adjourned, and did not meet again for many years. It has indeed been disputed whether the last two years, 1561 to 1563, should be counted as part of the old council or in fact a new one. In either case, the canons and decrees show clearly that the design of the Fathers was less to reform the Church than so to define its creed as to make reunion impossible and rigidly to exclude heresy from its borders.[1]

But reform was necessary, and to a certain extent reform came. What could not be granted to the demands of heretics was compelled by force of circumstances, and the grosser scandals were gradually removed. Though, for instance, even Pope Hadrian had been a pluralist, pluralism began to decline in his time. Though Paul III had a number of so-called nephews for whom he provided principalities, he was no Borgia. There is a marked difference between Alexander VI and Pius V, and between even so relatively respectable a man as Cardinal Wolsey and Cardinal Borromeo. As the sixteenth century advances, we light on a number of saints, like St Teresa and St Philip Neri, whom Rome adores, and all Protestants can reverence. Associations were formed, the object of which was to promote true piety by precept and example. Such were the order of the Capuchins, founded in 1525, and that of the Theatines, founded a little earlier, and recognized by Clement VII in 1524. For women there were the Capuchines and the Ursulines: nor were

1. By the so-called *Interim* of 1548, Charles V conceded to Melanchthon the use of the cup in the Eucharist and the marriage of the clergy. Both these were condemned by Trent, but Pius IV, in 1564, permitted the cup in Austria and Bohemia.

these by any means the only societies of the kind whose influence spread beyond their own limits and availed to reform the corrupt orders which already existed. The Church, in fact, was an army which, having suffered a defeat through want of discipline, sets to work to reorganize itself.

There was little tolerance in those days, and most of the tolerance that could be found at all was shown, not by the Church, but by the lay princes. It may almost be said that the greater the piety of a man, the less was his willingness to endure what he regarded as heresy. On the Roman side, the lines between heresy and orthodoxy had now been rigidly laid down by the Council: the boundaries of the spiritual kingdom had been once for all delimited. But, as Rome claimed universal dominion, those who refused to obey her were not foreigners but rebels; not members of another State with which a treaty might be made but traitors whose one hope lay in unconditional surrender. Already, the Lateran Council in 1516 had asserted that it was 'necessary for salvation that every human being should own the sovereignty of the Pope': those who refused to own it might be extirpated as pests by any means, fair or foul. Thus the sanctity of Pius V did not prevent him from conniving at the plots to murder Elizabeth, and, by his Bull of Deposition, to release Catholics from their allegiance, thus inciting many otherwise honest men to regicide. There was much to admire in Gregory XIII, but not only did he celebrate a Mass for St Bartholomew; he sent envoys to urge Charles IX not to repent of so magnificent a deed. It is about this time that we note a vast increase in the activity and prestige of the Inquisition, whose work may be compared with that of the Revolutionary Tribunal of 1793. There was a state of war, and there were open or concealed friends of the enemy within the gates: they must be rooted out, and if the process involved the slaughter of a few innocent among the guilty, *vile damnum*. That the Inquisition succeeded, in one sense, is certain: it destroyed heresy in Spain and in most of Italy, and helped to retain half the Low Countries for the Papacy.

Hardly less savage cruelties were common on the other side, and, by the irony of fate, most of them were inflicted by those who ought to have been allies of their victims. The moderation of Zwingli had not, as we have seen, reconciled Luther, who, in the last years of his life, increased in the violence with which he denounced those who did not hold his views of the Eucharist. As a result, the various sects tended more and more to throw themselves on the protection of princes who either held their views or would tolerate them; and the principle, *cujus regio, ejus religio*, which we shall meet again, began to be applied and recognized. It was to this principle that Elizabeth appealed when, in 1563, the Emperor Ferdinand, himself a moderate man, requested her to set aside churches where Roman Catholics might perform their rites. 'Such a concession would foster the designs of the factious, and miserably confound Church and State with party strife.' Who can say that in the circumstances she was wrong? In the very same year, at Amboise, the rights Ferdinand asked for the Catholics had been granted to the Huguenots, and the result was a civil war which did not really cease till Richelieu crushed the Huguenots at Rochelle sixty years later.

Yet another division was introduced into the Protestant ranks by the rise of one of the greatest, most determined, and most ruthlessly consistent men that ever founded a Church. John CALVIN, born in 1509, brought up a Catholic, and intended for the law, became a Protestant and was expelled from France. At the age of twenty-seven he addressed to the King the famous book, *Christianae Religionis Institutio*, in which he laid it down that the Church must have control of its own destinies and authority over its own members. It must obey the King, so far as his commands agree with those of God. After some years of wanderings, he settled down in Geneva, a city whose position, history, and character made it peculiarly suitable for a great experiment. Ruled jointly by its Bishop and by the Duke of Savoy, it was already both a State and a Church. In 1536, however, the citizens accepted the Reformation, and got rid of both Duke and Bishop. It was Calvin's aim to unite Duke and Bishop in one, to make Geneva not a State and Church, but a Church-State; and in this aim, after some failures, he succeeded amazingly.

Theologically, he was inspired by Augustine, and held uncompromisingly to the doctrine of predestination; but Augustine's view had been modified by his conception of the Church, through which alone man had access to God. With Calvin, the Church, in Augustine's sense, was naught: God speaks to men directly, without any priestly inter-mediary. If man is to be saved, God saves him without means; man himself has no share in the salvation; his merits, sacrifices, rituals, count for nothing; the divine Grace is all in all. As to the State, it was the body, and the Church the soul: and without both no ideal life was possible. There might be Emperor, King, or Council; all alike were or-dained by God, and must be obeyed: over the Church were ministers, who also were ordained by God, and must be obeyed. It might seem that Calvin was but repeating on a small scale the Empire-Papacy of the Middle Ages; but the essential difference was that for the Papacy he substi-tuted God himself, whose will could be ascertained and expressed by ministers whom certain signs, rigidly tested, proved to be called by him. When the examiners were satisfied of a candidate's vocation, he was instituted not merely by the Church but by the State. To prevent the tyranny which the minister might well be tempted to exer-cise, he was made to feel that he was one of the people, elected by the people, and liable, if he abused his trust, to be deposed by the people and reduced to the position of one of them. His living, again, was in their hands: he held no glebe, and no certain benefice. Nor, in one sense, was his office any more sacred than that of a secular magistrate. There was no secular magistrate; a town-councillor was as divinely appointed as the most revered of ministers.

Thus Calvin's system was a republican theocracy, on one side like the Platonic polity, on another like the Jewish régime in the days of Samuel – as Calvin understood that régime. It is easy to see that in other hands, and when transferred to other countries, it might degenerate into one of the worst of despotisms: the power which the ministers claimed of inquiring into the private morals of the citizens, of punishing derelictions of duty in the highest and the lowest, of excommunicating malignants, might in time become the phantom, at once terrible and ridiculous, which provoked the furious sarcasms of Burns. His doctrine of election, again, might mean the hopeless despair of those who could not convince themselves that they were of the chosen. But, as he conceived the system and worked it, the discipline he enforced was of incomparable value, not only to Geneva, but to the world; and, as we shall see in the case of Mohammedanism, the doctrine of predestination, received by the right minds and in the right way, lends to men an indomitable courage and an unshakable determination which hardly any other creed can give. Those who wish for examples, need go no further than our own history: the Ironsides and the Covenanters are a sufficient proof of the power of Calvinism: and, with all the modifications which time has brought, Calvinism is still a vital faith, and one not likely ever utterly to die.

To a certain extent Calvin was a reconciler; he tried, with some slight success, to bridge the gulf between Lutheranism and the 'Reformed' Churches. His doctrine of the Eucharist stood midway between Luther's and Zwingli's; and on predestination he did not widely differ from Luther. But not all Calvin's followers were like him; nor was it easy to bring about a union between the Republican Geneva and those Churches which openly relied on the protection of secular princes. Calvin's religion, therefore, like so many mediating religions, merely added one more to the number of disputing sects.

Such being the divisions of Protestantism, a keen eye might see a chance for a concerted counter-attack. Papal Rome, like the ancient Empire, might again rule by playing off one faction against another, and, having removed many of the evils which had alienated her natural allies, might

hope to reconquer the lost dominion. Perhaps the chief
agency in this movement, and certainly one cause of its success, was the famous order called the SOCIETY OF JESUS.
Ignatius Loyola, the founder, was a Spaniard, brought up
in all the crusading ideas of a country which had expelled
the Moors only by crusading enthusiasm, united feeling,
and military discipline. It was not unnatural therefore that
he should conceive the idea of a military order, with the
military virtue of obedience as its first principle. It was with
some difficulty that he obtained the Papal approval; Paul
III may have felt the same fears of a dictatorship as are
always felt when a general demands a free hand. At first, in
1540, he would not recognize it unless its numbers were
limited to sixty: in later years he gave it all the rights of
older orders, and even made the General practically independent of all authority except his own. There have been
times, since then, when the Pope himself has found the military power oppressive and dangerous – the Curia has been
the Long Parliament and the Jesuit not unlike a Cromwell.

As the Society was designed for war, its organization is
that of a professional soldiery. The novitiate lasts two years;
the work of every single hour is regulated; and the whole
system is devised to shatter the lad's initiative and turn him
from a man into a machine. Espionage and delation are encouraged: and the trust which is the mark of our Public
Schools is a thing unknown. At the end of the two years the
novice takes the three vows, of poverty, chastity, and obedience '*perinde ac cadaver*'. Then follow five or six years of study,
all so limited as to make his mind, if possible, still more impervious to dangerous ideas. A second novitiate, devoted to
spiritual exercises, follows. He is then ordained priest, and
takes a fourth vow, either to devote himself to the education
of the young, or to carry out any task whatever which
the Pope may impose upon him.

A man who loves freedom both of intellect and of soul
would sooner die than become a Jesuit: no janissary was
ever such a slave of the Sultan as a member of this order is of
his superiors; and no Soviet despotism was ever half so

severe as the Jesuit rule. But it is easy to see what a powerful weapon this Society was in the hands of one who knew how to use it. The private soldiers have no conscience of their own: right and wrong are decided by their officers, in accordance with a military code: and they no more reflect on the morality of the commands they receive than a Spartan reflected on the orders of his captain. And the whole army moves to one end, the restoration of medievalism, and the supremacy of the Church over the State. From the very first Ignatius made his aims and methods clear: he would not allow even the provincial chiefs to think for themselves; he taught even Lainez, the ablest man in the Society, and Rodriguez the Portuguese General, that they were 'but pieces of the game he played', and might be put back in the cupboard at any moment.

This was the army which, sent forth by Paul III, soon had its soldiers, openly or in any suitable disguise, in almost every country of Europe: nay, in Japan, China, and India. It is impossible to read without admiration the story of the devoted labours of Francis Xavier in the Far East, of the later missionaries in China, or of the band of men who formed a settlement in Paraguay, and rescued from ignorance and savagery the native tribes whom, alas, they could not save from the rapacity of Christians athirst for gold. No danger daunted these heroes, whether it were the traitor's death, the pestilential swamp, the wild beast, or the poisoned arrow of the Indian. Whither they were bidden to go they went, through fire and through water, and when bidden to return they returned, though it were to the lowest position from the heights of glory. But there is another side to the picture. The same zeal which made a Dobrizhoffer[1] made a Ballard. A Jesuit must do what served the Church,

---

1. See Southey's account of Dobrizhoffer in *A Tale of Paraguay*. His words are naïve:

> Blame as thou mayst the Papist's erring creed,
> But not their salutary rite of even:
> The prayers that from a pious soul proceed,
> Though misdirected, reach the ear of Heaven.

be it what others call good or bad. It was Jesuits who engineered the murderous plots against Elizabeth; and Jesuit catechisms were found in the possession of the assassins of William of Orange. Where gentler methods were desirable, they knew how to use them, and their training had made them masters of all the arts of logic, sophistry, casuistry, and persuasion. Perhaps their chief strength lay in their skill as educators. 'Give us,' said they, 'the first seven years of a man's life, and we will guarantee the rest.' As diplomatists or cabinet-councillors they were almost unrivalled. Their one weakness, perhaps, lay in their overweening consciousness of their strength. More than once, when made confessors to kings, they presumed on their position, went too fast, and overreached themselves. They were frequently an embarrassment to the Popes, and were actually, in 1773, suppressed by Clement XIV, though they proved too useful, and were shortly afterwards restored. Few, even of Catholic kingdoms, found them lastingly endurable: they were expelled from Portugal by Pombal, and from France by Choiseul. In Protestant countries their artillery often recoiled upon themselves or on their friends. Their doctrines of equivocation and mental reservation – that it was open to them to swear an oath in one meaning and keep it in another – which were exposed to reprobation and ridicule by Pascal in his famous *Lettres Provinciales*, and which have been attacked since then by other eminent Catholics – perhaps did more harm to their cause than all their missionary zeal did good. Thus, in 1606, Garnet, the English Provincial, when tried for complicity in the hideous Gunpowder Plot, so sophistically paltered and equivocated that 'equivocation' became a proverb.[1] His dodgings were never forgotten, and it was universally believed in England that not Jesuits only but all Catholics, would lie for the sake of their Church.

1. All will remember the allusion in *Macbeth*, which was probably played, in the presence of James I himself, shortly after Garnet's trial: 'Faith, here's an equivocator, that could swear in both the scales against either scale; who committed treason enough for God's sake, yet could not equivocate to heaven: O come in, equivocator.'

Thus, in the so-called Popish Plot, the passionate denials of the unhappy victims were taken as Jesuit perjury, and merely strengthened the conviction of the populace that they were guilty. No small part of the persecution of the Catholics in England was therefore due to the Jesuit doctrines, many of which were utterly repudiated by their co-religionists.

Yet there can be no doubt that the energy and devotion of the Jesuits, added to the physical force of Spain and other Powers, did much to carry through that strong reaction which is known as the Counter-Reformation; a reaction which at one time promised to sweep away the whole work of Luther. To use the 'heightened and telling' words of Macaulay, 'fifty years after the Lutheran separation, Catholicism could scarcely maintain itself on the shores of the Mediterranean. A hundred years after the separation, Protestantism could scarcely maintain itself on the shores of the Baltic.'[1]

The main cause of this change was, as we have said, the divisions of the Protestants, and the unsettlement of belief that comes to many minds when they see everything disputed. On the other hand, those who see a creed they love attacked, tend to hold it more firmly than ever, and to defend it with fanaticism. For a long time the zeal and energy were mainly on the side of Rome: in fact until it too began to show division and dissension. When Church and Empire seemed likely to be entirely victorious, they quarrelled as allies nearly always do.

The first check to the Counter-Reformation came in the Low Countries, where, though Philip won back 'Belgium', seven United Provinces, led by William of Orange, successfully resisted him, and finally asserted their independence. The second was the defeat of the Armada. The third and decisive one was the Thirty Years' War, in which, though it began as a war of creeds, the weight of the Catholic Power of France, guided by a Roman Cardinal, prevented the victory of the House of Austria and its fanatical Emperor,

1. See note at end of chapter.

and compelled the exhausted combatants, by the Peace of Westphalia, to admit the principle of *cujus regio, ejus religio*. There is no doubt, also, that the war had produced a feeling of wearied indifference to religion of any kind, and had led men to cry a plague on both houses. The decline of Spain, and the breach of the close alliance between the two branches of the Hapsburg family, made it quite impossible to renew the struggle in the old form. The Pope (Innocent X) might protest as he liked against composition with heretics; his complaints were disregarded by both sides. Thenceforward religious wars became as dead as the Crusades. In the struggles between Austria and France which followed, the chief ally of the Apostolic Emperor was the Calvinist William III, and the Lutheran Elector of Brandenburg lent his troops to assist his Romish suzerain. Nay, there were times when the Pope himself all but openly sympathized with a Protestant belligerent against a too overbearing son of the Church.

The idea that a State cannot afford to tolerate within its borders members of any but the established religion died slowly. It was the principle on which Elizabeth acted in England, and it is well known that Catherine de' Medici advised her to deal with all the Catholics in England in the same manner as the Protestants had been dealt with in Paris on St Bartholomew's Day. It was on this principle that Louis XIV revoked the Edict of Nantes, thus driving out of his country many thousands of his best subjects. It is to be feared that toleration, when it did come, came rather from feelings of indifference and expediency than from charity. Under Cromwell, it was due to the necessity of keeping together an army largely recruited from sectaries, whose valour and discipline the general could not afford to lose. The Toleration Act of 1689 was a slight recognition of the services done by the Dissenters to the Revolutionary cause. During the eighteenth century all churches had more or less given way to the prevailing apathy: even in Calvinist Scotland a Moderate party had arisen, which could associate comfortably with Hume, and studied Gibbon without repulsion. In France, though there were sporadic outbursts of persecution, the general tone was, to use a modern term, so 'agnostic' that they rarely lasted long, and the Revolutionary decrees of toleration roused little opposition. In Prussia, Frederick the Great, an open scoffer at religion, though a Protestant by hereditary necessity, admitted men of any and every belief or no-belief into his dominions. The attack and defence of the creeds were both conducted on rationalistic grounds; there was, comparatively, little passion in it, and nothing of the frenzy which is seen when men hold their creeds by a faith supposed to be communicated directly from the deity. Toland, Tindal, and Collins lived their ordinary lives after publishing their 'infidelity': Whiston, whose views were those of Servetus, lost his fellowship, but ran no risk of being burned alive. The most furious outbreak in our country during the eighteenth century – the Gordon Riots of 1780 – was the outbreak of an ignorant and lawless mob: the educated classes had few prejudices. The penal laws were not repealed, for fear of exciting popular risings, but they were administered with mildness, and dexterously interpreted by the judges into meaningless verbiage. There was, to speak generally, and without forgetting many exceptions, a religious peace in the world: enthusiasm, on any side or for any cause, became unfashionable, and to show zeal in the defence of one unintelligible creed against another was of all enthusiasms the most absurd and futile.

NOTE

A brief account is necessary to explain the position of the Jansenists, long the most powerful enemies of the Jesuits.

Cornelius Jansen was a Dutch-born professor of theology at Louvain, who, through zealous study of St Augustine, had been led to adopt opinions totally opposed to those of the Jesuits. His great work, *Augustinus*, was published after his death in 1638. He had already incurred the hostility of the members of the Society by preventing them from securing a foothold in the Louvain University: in this book he stirred their still keener hatred, though death had made him personally secure, by showing that their doctrines were practically equivalent to those of Pelagius whom Augustine had refuted and who had therefore been declared heretical by the Church. Five of Jansen's Propositions, extremely technical in their language, were specially obnoxious to the Jesuits, and were selected by them as sufficiently heterodox to be submitted to the Pope (Innocent X) for condemnation. Roughly, they turned on subtle points relating to the vexed question of the freedom of the will. In 1653 the Pope, urged on by the Jesuits, pronounced the Five Propositions heretical.

Now it happened that St Cyran, the head of the famous monastery of Port Royal in Paris, had been a close friend and coadjutor of Jansen at Louvain. Through him, the Port Royalists, the well-known Antoine Arnauld among them, had learned of the doctrines, and certainly sympathized with them. They were, however, devoted Catholics, and were quite willing to submit to the Pope in matters of doctrine. When, therefore, the condemnation was published, they declared their full belief that the Propositions, in the sense ascribed to them by the Pope, were heretical; but denied that Jansen, if rightly understood, could be accused of holding them. Whether they were actually to be found in *Augustinus* or not was a matter not of faith but of fact, and to matters of fact the Pope's infallibility did not extend. It was a neat point. When the Pope replied that the heresies *were* in the book, and that Arnauld and his friends must sign a statement to that effect, they refused, and were expelled from their posts. The new Pope, Alexander VII, confirmed the expulsion: and Port Royal would have been suppressed, but for the intervention of a miracle. A thorn from Christ's crown was placed on the high altar of the nunnery. The niece of Blaise Pascal, the illustrious mathematician, was suffering from a disease of the eye. A nun took the thorn, touched the eye, and by evening it was found to be healed. It was desirable to take heed before attacking people so highly favoured.

Then ensued one of the most famous disputes in the history of the world. Pascal, though not a full member of Port Royal, was in close communication with it; he had given up science and Montaigne, and was now the devoutest of men: but he retained his genius. With the assistance of many theologians among his friends, he now entered the lists with his immortal *Provincial Letters*, which, beginning with a defence of Jansen's theological position, soon passed into an attack upon the casuistical system of Escobar and the Jesuits in general. This is the work which Gibbon used to read through every year in order to keep his ironic powers in good trim. For his materials, Pascal relied on the Jesuit books themselves, and on information gathered by conversing with some of the Society in person – often at considerable risk. The *Letters* were, of necessity, published anonymously, but they had not long to wait for recognition. They constitute the first masterpiece of modern French prose. Their admirable style, their liveliness and vigour, the relevance and abundance of their deadly quotations from Jesuit writings, and their consummate skill in ridicule, made them immensely popular. There had been nothing like them since the *Dialogues* of Plato: the sarcasms of Erasmus had been less effective.

But even Pascal could not avail against the master of thirty legions. The royal power was called in, and the Jesuits had the ear of the King. A formula was drawn up, declaring the Five Propositions to be heretical, and asserting that they *were* in Jansen: and all clergy were required to sign it. A cruel persecution followed; the Jansenists had to hide themselves, and the nuns of Port Royal were imprisoned. Four Bishops, who desired to maintain a 'respectful silence' as to the point of fact, were arraigned for contumacy; but before they could be brought to the bar, the Pope died, and his successor, Clement IX, not wishing either to condemn the Bishops or to compromise the Holy See, arranged a peace, allowing it to be maintained that Jansen had not meant the Propositions in a heretical sense. This was really a Jansenist victory; and the Jesuits did not intend to sit down under it. The fight went on long after most of the original disputants were dead. Could those who maintained a 'respectful silence', asked the Jesuits, be really honest in signing the formula? At last, in 1705, they found a Pope to their mind, and an opportunity for moving him. Quesnel's *Moral Reflections on the New Testament* was a well-known Jansenist text-book: it had been suppressed, and a demand was now made for a new edition. If it could be condemned, the Jansenists would be overthrown. In 1713 Pope Clement XI issued his famous Bull *Unigenitus*, in which no fewer than a hundred and one propositions in Quesnel's book were anathematized. This split the French Church into two irreconcilable parties: but Louis XIV, now drawing near the end of his long reign, decided to support the Bull with the whole force of the State, and the Jansenists were rigorously repressed. For years the controversy raged; but in 1720 the Bull was formally made part of the law, both religious and secular, of the French kingdom. Even so, Jansenism was not utterly destroyed. Miracle, which had already aided it, came again to its assistance. A Jansenist deacon, François de Paris, died in 1727, and was buried in the cemetery of St Medard: here, it was said, wonders and signs were performed, and pilgrims resorted thither in crowds. But miracle proved, as so often, a broken reed: the pilgrimages degenerated into carouses, and – not for the first time – the State authorities had to proclaim that 'miracles were not to be performed in that place'. From that time Jansenism ceased to trouble France; its few adherents migrated to Holland, where a small Church, Catholic in everything but acceptance of the Bull *Unigenitus*, may still be found.

CHAPTER 10

MOHAMMEDANISM

MOHAMMEDANISM may be considered from various points of view. It has often been regarded as but one more of the many Christian heresies, more dangerous and powerful than Arianism or Gnosticism, but of the same general kind: and indeed Mohammed's ideas as to Christ are occasionally such as might be adopted by some who, though unorthodox, yet profess and call themselves Christians. To Jews, in similar fashion, Mohammedanism may well appear as an heretical development of Judaism; and there is much to be said for this conception. As we shall see in more detail later, Mohammed accepted the inspiration of the Old Testament, and claimed to be the successor of Moses. From another standpoint we may view Mohammedanism less as a religion than as a political institution. The Prophet was also a warrior and a statesman: his kingdom was emphatically of this world, and he seems to have desired before all things to weld the quarrelling tribes of Arabia into a single whole. It is true that he demanded the allegiance of the rulers of all nations, and that his successors went a long way towards securing that allegiance; but they were forming an *empire* with Arabia as its centre. They were missionaries, but missionaries of the stamp of Cortes or Pizarro rather than Pauls or Xaviers. Mohammedanism, like other great movements, had many sources, took many characters, and availed itself of many means of propagating its doctrines and enlarging its dominion.

Almost more than other great movements, it was the work of one man. There is no more astonishing career in history than that of the founder of this religion, and scarcely any man has more profoundly influenced the destinies of the world. He was, of course, favoured by circumstances, but he knew how to turn them to his purposes, and he faced adversity with the determination to wring success out of failure. While he could not have succeeded in another place or at another time, it is tolerably certain that no one else could have succeeded at all.

He was born at Mecca, in A.D. 570. Mecca was a kind of lesser Rome; all roads went to it and from it. It lay on one end of the great caravan-routes from Yemen to Syria, and was the meeting-place of men from a score of nations. It was a centre of pilgrimage: from time beyond the memory of man it had been associated with the names of Abraham and Ishmael, and the mysterious glamour hung around it which overshadows sacred places: it was holy ground, and within its walls, for four months in every year, feuds had to be forgotten and swords to be sheathed. Then, as now, sanctity was acquired by visiting it. It had one god, Allah, who had acquired a sort of supremacy over the innumerable idols and fetishes of the peninsula; and it had a rough municipal government, which marked it out amid the clans around, who were ruled paternally by their sheikhs. Like Delphi it had proved itself by supernaturally overthrowing an invading army: the god had protected his own when others had been overwhelmed, and his prestige was great. But there were Christians, Jews, and Mandaeans either in the city itself or in the neighbourhood; and the religion of Allah may have borrowed elements from them all. Learned men may have known the Christian and Jewish scriptures; for the Arabic system of writing had been recently introduced. As with Venice later, the trade and prosperity of the city depended on many peoples; merchants from Syria, Egypt, and Abyssinia constantly visited it, and merchants from Mecca in turn visited far lands, to bring back not only goods but knowledge. Mohammed himself was a tradesman, and himself conducted a caravan: how much, with his receptive mind, he picked up on his journeys we can only guess.

Mohammed was left an orphan at six years old, and his uncle, Abu Talib, became his guardian. Though the family, that of the Hashimim, was noble, Abu Talib was poor, and was glad to procure for the youth a trading commission from a wealthy widow named Khadijah. So well did the youth perform his task that Khadijah, though many years older than he, fell in love with him and married him. They had two sons and four daughters, of whom only the daughter survived.

So far, the life of Mohammed had been ordinary; he seems to have been remarkable for nothing except success in business and an uprightness in dealing which gained him the name of the Faithful or the Trustworthy. But beyond doubt he had been learning and meditating; and in his thirty-fifth year an incident occurred which it is natural to believe made him regard himself as called to a mission. The great shrine, the 'Kaaba', had been injured by an inundation; when it had been rebuilt, the sacred Black Stone[1] had to be set back in its place. The decision as to who should perform this act was left to the lot, and the lot, disposed by Allah, fell upon Mohammed. Whether inspired by this divine omen, or from other causes, he soon began to show signs of a high religious feeling; retiring into the desert for solitude, which he 'preferred beyond choicest society', and for meditation, which often rapt him into ecstasies and drew heaven into his view. A cave in Mount Hira, not far from the city, is still shown as the scene of these solitary communings with God. From them he came back to earth with the settled conviction that he was formed to be a prophet of righteousness and to call back his degenerate countrymen to the ancient ways. In one of his visions an angel gave him the direct command to go forth and proclaim the message. After this, as we might well expect, he fell into a deep depression: for a long period the Lord answered him neither by omen nor by vision, and Mohammed was even tempted to cast himself headlong from a cliff. At length the darkness was

1. Such stones are everywhere regarded as homes of the deity, or even as deities themselves. We think of the image of Artemis at Ephesus, or of Bethel in Israel, as well as of the 'Baetyls' which abound in Greece. The god of Delos, before the arrival of Apollo, was a stone. Compare the stone at Delphi marking the *omphalos* or navel of the earth. It is a noteworthy fact that Mohammed, with all his hatred of idolatry, never hesitated to kiss the Kaaba stone.

dispelled; again the angel appeared to him: 'Arise and preach, magnify the Lord, cleanse thy garments, and wait patiently for him.' Thenceforward the visions came to him almost regularly.

Meanwhile, he had adopted one of Abu Talib's sons, named Ali, who became a devoted friend, and who afterwards married Fatima, one of the Prophet's daughters; and two other friendships appear to have had a strong influence upon him. Zeid, a slave of Khadijah's, captured from a Christian tribe, he manumitted and adopted; and Zeid is known as the son of Mohammed. Waraka, a cousin of Khadijah, was an 'Inquirer', that is, a searcher after truth, who is said to have known the Christian Gospel, and may have communicated to Mohammed something of the Christian tradition. It seems certain that at this time, as at the time of Christ's birth six hundred years earlier, there was a widespread expectation of great things shortly to be; and there were men who already saw in Mohammed the Prophet of the new dispensation. Unlike others of his class, he had honour in his own house: Khadijah[1] was a fervent believer, and Zeid and Ali were among the very first to acclaim his mission. Ere long a tiny band, or rather family, of adherents gathered round him, including these relatives, some freed slaves, and a few friends.

The first step was sufficiently daring. Mecca was wholly given to idolatry, and Mohammed's spirit was stirred within him. He announced openly his great message, 'There is but one God.' This roused the furious hostility of the townsmen, and not least of the Koreish, the powerful tribe in whose

1. Mohammed's feeling for Khadijah is illustrated by a well-known anecdote. Years after her death, his young wife Ayesha asked him about her. 'Was she not old, and has not God given you a better in her place?' 'No, in God's name,' replied he, 'there never can be a better: she believed in me when men contemned me; she supported me when I was poor and persecuted.' When she died, he set her among the Four Perfect Women, along with Miriam the sister of Moses, the Virgin Mary, and his daughter Fatima, Ali's wife – a list that might symbolize the eclecticism of his religious system. It is said that Khadijah was slow to yield belief; but she clung uncompromisingly to it when once given.

hands were the ceremonies of the Kaaba. Anywhere else, the flame would have been speedily quenched in blood; but no blood could be shed in Mecca. It was, however, possible to starve the heretics to death,[1] or it was open to the head of the tribe to expel the Prophet from the city, that he might be killed outside its borders. But Abu Talib was head of the tribe, and, though no believer in Mohammed's claims, threw his aegis over him. The Prophet himself was thus safe, but his followers had to flee to Axum, the capital of the Christian part of Abyssinia, where the King received them kindly – a rare thing in those days of fanaticism – and where they lived for fourteen years, till the triumph of Mohammed recalled them from their exile.

Shortly after this, Mohammed was for a moment reconciled to the Koreish. As they sat under the Kaaba, he recited to them a revelation[2] he had just been vouchsafed, in which he admitted three goddesses, the 'exalted ones', to share divinity with Allah. With this compromise the Koreish were satisfied, and agreed to worship Mohammed's God. But conscience speedily troubled him: he felt that the revelation came not from Allah but from Satan, and Gabriel confirmed him in this belief. For the hateful concession he substituted a terrific denunciation of the no-gods whom the heathen had invented; and persecution arose again. He and his followers were compelled to withdraw to the Hashimite quarter of the city, where under the protection of Abu Talib, they lived in seclusion, emerging to preach the doctrine only at the times of pilgrimage. It was at these times that he won over a number of pilgrims who had come from Medina. But he had little else to comfort him, save the memories of Jewish and Christian heroes, and repeated visions. Khadijah died, and was soon afterwards followed by Abu Talib. A

1. A very common way of making 'killing no murder'. Thus the Romans got rid of Jugurtha without shedding his blood.

2. This was contained in the fifty-third *Sura* or chapter of the Koran, but afterwards suppressed. The original meaning of *Sura* is uncertain. If it meant a line or row, as of bricks in a wall, perhaps the word 'set' is the best rendering.

mission to a city called Taif, sixty miles east of Mecca, totally failed: like Paul at Iconium he was driven from the place, and narrowly escaped being stoned to death. His fortunes seemed to be at their lowest ebb.

But hope returned. Omar, the Saul who had been one of the worst persecutors, came over to him, and soon proved one of his most active supporters. A band of Jinns appeared to him in vision, and showed themselves eager to listen to his preaching. At Medina the faith spread rapidly. There were many Jews in that city, who recognized in the new teachings much of what they had been taught by Abraham and Moses; and one of the two factions which had split the people was eager for help, which Mohammed was willing to give. If Mecca was obstinate, Medina might be ready to welcome him. Seventy of his Medinese disciples, at the time of pilgrimage, swore that they would receive him and defend him with their lives. The faithful slipped out one by one from the Quarter of Abu Talib, and made their way safely to the refuge. Mohammed and his family were left almost alone, and the Koreish held a council, plotting to take him: 'The unbelievers conspired against thee,' says a *Sura*, 'to hold thee, or slay thee, or expel thee: but God conspired also, and the best of conspirators is God.' He escaped from the city, hid for three days in a cave of Mount Thaur, and finally reached Medina. This is the Hégïra or Departure, A.D. 622, and it marks the beginning of the Mohammedan era.[1]

At Medina, despite strong opposition from the faction which his advent had deprived of the chance of power, he gradually asserted his strength, and ultimately became the virtual ruler of the city. A mosque was built, his little band of refugees was welcomed, and the opposition, though not growing any less bitter, was forced to conceal its feelings. Mohammed's keen eye, however, detected their furtive machinations: in the *Suras* of this time he denounces the 'hypocrites' of Medina as fiercely as he had denounced the

1. As the Mohammedan year is 354 days, a small calculation is necessary to accommodate Arab dates to ours.

idolaters of Mecca. He attempted to increase his strength by
the conversion of the Jews; but here he failed. It was his
doctrine that Abraham was a Moslem, that he himself was
the prophet foretold by Moses, and that anyone studying
the Old Testament with unprejudiced eyes could not fail to
recognize his claims. But the Jews were obstinate; their
hearts were seared; seeing they refused to perceive, and
hearing they refused to hearken. After long-continued
efforts, Mohammed gave them up as reprobate, and turned
from entreaty and persuasion to force and denunciation.
The ritual, which had hitherto been Jewish in character –
thus, for instance, the prayers had been towards Jerusalem –
was altered: Friday took the place of Saturday as the Sabbath: the fast of Ramadan displaced the feast of the Atonement; and the rites of sacrifice were assimilated rather to
those of Mecca than to those of Judaea. The Prophet assumed more and more decisively the character of a theocratic king, whose orders it was at once impious and
treasonable to disobey. A messenger from Mecca was astonished at his authority. 'I have seen,' said he, 'Chosroes of
Persia and Caesar of Rome; but never did I see a king
among his subjects like Mohammed among his companions.'

It is probably this sense of kingship, combined with irrita-
tion at opposition, that accounts for the change of tone in
the *Suras* of the Medina period. Hitherto, violence had been
forbidden; conversion was to be accomplished by persuasion. But now we find revelations which not only permit
but urge the use of force to compel submission. The unbelievers have been offered their chance; through stubborn
wickedness, inspired by Satan, they have rejected the offer,
and it is right to slay the perverse and crooked generation.
The first battle was against the Koreish at Bedr, where
three hundred of the Faithful totally defeated an army out-
numbering them by three to one. Such a victory could be
explained only as a miraculous interposition of the Deity: the
decision had been gained by the help of legions of angels;
and Mohammed's hold upon Medina was immensely

strengthened. Next year, 625, the Prophet showed that he could turn defeat to the same end as victory. At Ohod, largely through the treachery of Abdallah ibn Obey, the chief of the opposing Medina faction, he lost the day, and was himself severely wounded. But, said he, God was with him; his life was saved, and the disaster had been a mercy in disguise, intended as it was to sift the false brethren from the true. His followers listened to his words, and were nerved to yet greater exertions. Two tribes of Jews were besieged, forced to surrender, and sent into exile, their goods were confiscated and divided among the conquerors according to a law which Mohammed, like David long before him, had promulgated. A third tribe met a worse fate. The Beni Koraidha were suspected of having stirred up the Koreish against the True Believers. They were attacked, and after a siege of twenty-five days surrendered at discretion. To the number of seven hundred they were all massacred under the eyes of the Prophet; their property was divided, and their arms were a welcome addition to the spoils. All this was in accordance with a new revelation. 'The sword is the key of heaven; a drop of blood shed in the cause of God, a night spent in arms, avails more than two months of prayer or fasting: he that falls in battle, his sins are all forgiven: at the day of judgement his wounds shall shine as vermilion and smell as musk; angels and cherubim shall give their wings to restore the limbs he has lost.' Every war was thus a 'crusade'; the warriors went to battle as the followers of Peter the Hermit afterwards went against *them*, with the certainty that death was the gateway to Paradise. But the Moslems had one great advantage over the soldiers of the Cross. Never was the doctrine of predestination preached more uncompromisingly than it was by Mohammed. All was determined from all eternity in the counsels of God. No sword could slay, no arrow could smite, those who were not fated to receive the blow: and if the blow *were* doomed, no cowardice could avoid it. This is the creed which paralyses weak natures, but doubles the strength of the strong. It explains the conquests of the Norsemen and the unyielding resolve of the Scottish Covenanters: and it lies at the root of the victories of Islam.

Having ceased to worship towards Jerusalem, the prophet now turned his eyes towards Mecca – a symbol of his desire to recover the Holy City. More than once he made the attempt in vain; at last, having secured the alliance of the Arab tribes, he assembled an irresistible army, and marched suddenly and unexpectedly – his detractors might say treacherously – upon the city. Resistance was vain; the keys were delivered up to him; the chief of the Koreish owned that Mohammed was the prophet of God; the three hundred and sixty idols of the Kaaba were destroyed: and the law was laid down that no unbeliever should ever set foot in the Holy City. Having accepted Islam, the vanquished were spared, and we find later the Koreish marching in his armies. Shortly afterwards, the whole peninsula came under his dominion. The year 631 is known as the Year of Deputations, which came in from all sides, acknowledging his suzerainty, and asking for instruction in his doctrines. His last expedition was to Tebuk, to check certain Syrian tribes which had been incited by the Romans to give him trouble. Despite the recalcitrance of some malingerers, who dreaded the discomforts of the marches, the campaign was successful, and some Christians and Jews submitted to him.

Arabia being thus united, Mohammed took the opportunity of the Pilgrim Month for holding a solemn ceremony. The multitude being assembled at Medina, Ali was commissioned to recite the 'Release' – that is, to free Mohammed, after a short interval, of all other duties, and to command him to go forth and make war on all unbelievers, who were to be offered the choice between receiving Islam with Paradise, and death by the sword in this world with hell in the next. But it was not predestined that Mohammed should be the Joshua of the new dispensation. In the tenth year of the Hegira (632), he made his farewell pilgrimage, attended by his wives and an enormous throng. No vestige of idolatry stained the rites. Then, ascending his Pisgah, Mount Arafat, he pronounced his Deuteronomy, ending with the words, 'This day I have perfected my religion unto you.' Next, in Medina, he added advice as to the social duties of the people; all believers were equal, life and property were sacred. Like Paul at Miletus, he warned them to beware of the wiles of Satan. 'I have fulfilled my mission: I leave behind a plain command, the Book of God, and manifest ordinances, which if ye keep, ye shall not err.'[1]

Shortly afterwards, he was seized with a fatal illness, which, according to some, was due to poison administered by a revengeful Jewess.[2] So soon as he knew his danger, he mounted the pulpit, and asked any man whom he had wronged, despoiled, or slandered, to make his grievance known. 'You owe me three drachms of silver,' said a voice. Mohammed paid the money, and thanked the man for enabling him to settle the debt here rather than in the next world. Before he died, he enfranchised his slaves, and almost till the very last continued the service of public prayer. He awaited the end with perfect calmness. He had been assured that the Angel of Death would not come without asking his permission: as his weakness increased, he gave it, and died in the arms of Ayesha, the best-beloved of all his wives. His last words, distinctly heard, were, 'O God, pardon my sins; I come – among my fellow-citizens in heaven.'

His character will probably always be viewed variously according to the varying opinions of students. The old crude theory of sheer imposture, however, is unlikely to be held again save by fanatics. We understand more now about the phenomena of ecstasy than was understood two or three hundred years ago: and if a Paul could have ecstatic visions, the still more Oriental mind of Mohammed was likely to be subject to them. No visions, however, transcend the nature of the man who experiences them: they tell him what he

1. In this and some previous paragraphs, ignorant as I am of Arabic, I have availed myself largely of the works of Sir William Muir. I have of course consulted many others.

2. The well-known tale runs that she gave it to him in order to test whether the prophet's knowledge could detect the future when it concerned himself: the result decided that he was an impostor.

knows already, and are but sublimations of his waking thoughts. It cannot be denied that many of Mohammed's revelations were extraordinarily convenient. Thus, when he had fallen in love with Zeinab, wife of his adopted son Zeid, the revelation came at the right moment, telling him to fear not the face of man, and assuring him that believers might lawfully marry the wives of sons who were sons only by adoption. Again, when scandal had touched Ayesha, and he had become estranged from her, a vision assured him of her innocence and she was taken back. In both these cases it is easy to see that the subconscious mind asserted itself in dream: he desired to have Zeinab, and his love for Ayesha was still there. The wish was father to the vision. Similarly, we can trace in the increasing severity of the *Suras* which deal with Jews, Christians, and other infidels, the effect on his mind of the obstinacy with which they resisted his claims. He was, when waking, exasperated with them, and his exasperation produced the revelation. That it came to him as a supernatural voice was inevitable in one to whom God, angels, and devils were as real as the rocks of Arafat. There is no reason to think that the visions were ever other than genuine to his mind. If they represented him as a privileged being, they were but God's confirmation of a deeply felt conviction. Such trances can be paralleled in the lives of almost all great religious saints and teachers: Paul, Peter, Böhme, Swedenborg, the Yogis of India – time would fail to mention a fraction of the number of those who have enjoyed them, and who have received them as direct manifestations of the divine purpose.

Not all visions give righteous commands. But there was much in Mohammed's surroundings that might well stir him to moral indignation, and make him feel that in attacking it he was doing the will of God. The task he undertook in this regard was manifold. First, he swept away idolatry, which, as we have seen, was deeply rooted in Arabia, and more especially in Mecca. How far there was, at the time, an undercurrent of revolt against it we cannot tell; but it is certainly a proof of extraordinary courage that he should have put its abolition in the forefront of his schemes: he set his life on the cast, and but narrowly escaped with it. Along with the idolatry, and almost indistinguishable from it, was a rich congeries of taboos, superstitious rites, and more or less detestable practices. These Mohammed could not alto- gether sweep away, any more than Christianity could sweep away similar practices in the Western world; but his pro- clamation 'There is but one God' would in time, if fully understood, have gradually abolished them. Believing, as almost all the ancients did believe, that mankind had de- generated from an earlier purity of religion, and finding in the traditions that Abraham and Ishmael, the fathers of the Arab race, had known but one God, he wished to recall his people to that primitive simplicity; and nothing in the his- tory of the world is more remarkable than the determination with which he pursued his aim and the success which he achieved.

To Mohammed the statesman there was another evil which was as repugnant as polytheism to Mohammed the theologian. Arabia was hardly even a geographical expres- sion. It was a set of warring tribes, at that stage of civiliza- tion in which the tribe is held responsible for the crime of an individual member of it. Hence constant blood-feuds, battles, murders, ceasing only with the utter exhaustion of the two sides. Nothing but an ordered central government could put an end to this fatal state of things: and it would seem that Mohammed, in making himself virtual king of the whole country, had in mind the extinction of vendettas and private wars, a purpose which his doctrine of the equality of all Moslems might have aided him to realize. In a sense, also, his proclamation of a 'crusade' or Jihad against all unbelievers may be taken as a scheme for busying the minds of the people with foreign quarrels, and thus turning their attention from private dissensions.

Some of the old customs – in particular circumcision[1] –

1. This rite, the origin of which has so greatly exercised students, seems to be a healthy one in hot climates, and may have been started for medical reasons. It is a curious fact that Mohammedanism has scarcely

Mohammed retained. Against infanticide – the almost universal practice of the ancient world[1] – he set his face like a
flint. Here he stood far in advance of the heathen opinion of
the time, and apparently on a level with the Christian.
'Morality' was grossly disregarded, and Mohammed,
though he allowed himself so many wives, endeavoured by
every means to discourage sexual vice, with, as far as can be
judged, a considerable measure of success.

The means employed for the achievement of these reforms was a book, or rather a series of disconnected revelations which were gathered together into a book after his
death. Every one of these revelations was taken to be the
direct voice of God: as it fell from the lips of Mohammed –
either during the ecstasy or later – it was taken down by one
or other of his followers who was able to write: in later
years, apparently, by a professional amanuensis. As Baruch
the scribe thus copied the prophecies of Jeremiah, so the
writer of Mohammed's words would make a record. But
even when the words were written, the scribe's memory
would be required to read them, for the writing resembled
a set of shorthand notes rather than a full transcription: and
the materials on which they were entered were often of the
most perishable character – palm-leaves, ostraca, or bones.
It must have been a matter of almost as much difficulty to
put these scraps together as to arrange the oracles of the
ancient Sibyl; and in any case few reciters would know the

---

ever gained a firm hold on populations outside the zones in which circumcision appears to be desirable – roughly, thirty degrees north, and
thirty degrees south, of the equator. Judaism, however, flourishes almost
everywhere.

1. Dean Inge's paragraph on this subject (*Outspoken Essays*, Series I,
p. 63) will be recalled by many. The famous Oxyrhynchus letter, 'When
– good luck to you – your child is born, if it is a boy, rear it, if a girl,
expose it', is typical. Of all Greek towns, Ephesus alone put some restric-
tion – and that slight – on the practice. Our own ancestors were hardly
better. 'I deem,' said Thorsteinn to his wife (*Gunnlaugs Saga*, cap. 2),
'that thou art about to bear a child: carry it out, if it is a girl, and foster
it, if a boy': and the sagaman adds that poor parents often did so in
heathen days.

whole series; some might be able to repeat one set of Suras, and others another. We must not, however, imagine that for this reason the Koran as we possess it does not represent the original teaching of the Prophet. In countries where books scarcely exist the memories of story-tellers and rhapsodes are very retentive and exact, and with the help given by the copies the longest discourses could be remembered and recited verbatim, as the author of *Parsifal*, who could neither read nor write, recited his enormously long epic. The real danger lay elsewhere – that the records might be destroyed in a hostile raid, by fire, or by some other accident. There seems to have been no one place where the revelations could be stored. Mohammed himself had no scriptorium; it has been supposed that they were kept in the harem. But it is known that at times Mohammed would call for a particular Sura in order to add to it, and that it could be found. Some portions were probably arranged in tolerable order before the Prophet's death, and read or recited at the public services: and we may believe that, though very few would know or possess a complete collection, such parts as individuals did possess would be far more accurate than, in these days of libraries, we are inclined to think. When the Arab tribes, in the Year of Deputations, asked to be instructed in the new doctrines, there were plenty of men fully competent to go forth, with or without written notes, and give them not merely the substance, but the precise words of the revelations.

But this could not last. As among the Christians the demand arose for authoritative written records of the sayings and doings of Jesus, so among the Moslems: and the demand became vocal after a battle in which many of the reciters of the Koran were killed. The caliph, Abu Bekr, perceived that if such a slaughter happened again, there was great risk that a large proportion of the revelation might be lost. He therefore commissioned Zeid, the chief of the Prophet's secretaries, to collect all the fragments. Zeid set to work with indefatigable energy: he sought out the Suras 'from palm-leaves, tablets, and *the breasts of men*', and succeeded in compiling what was practically a complete Koran. There is no reason to suspect that anything of importance was lost. Nor were the caliphs content even with this. As it was found that copies of Zeid's work were beginning to differ in such matters as dialect and phraseology, the third caliph, Othman, appointed a committee to form a standard text. This was done by searching out all the various readings, and reducing them to the standard Meccan dialect in which Mohammed had spoken. All other versions were burnt; copies of the final recension were made with rigid care, and sent out to the chief cities of the empire. From that time the Koran has been preserved exactly[1] as Zeid and his co-adjutors left it. No other book, written before the invention of printing, can in this respect compare with it. Such additions to Mohammed's own words as may have been made (there is, for instance, a prophecy of the Persian War which occurred after his death) were probably made, more or less deliberately, *before* Zeid began his work. Moslems believe that they have in their hands the very words of God as received by the Prophet, unchanged and unabridged. It is their boast, as against the Christians, that while the manuscripts of the New Testament contain many thousands of variations, their Scripture contains none. They are further relieved from the difficulty which confronts all thoughtful readers of our Bibles – the question how far the revelation has been modified by the personal peculiarities of the human transmitter. The styles and characters of the various authors of our sacred books are so different that we may suspect some human error in the version they give of the divine message. But the author of the Koran is not even one man, Mohammed: he is the One God, Mohammed being

1. Modern improvements in script, diacritical marks, the filling in of abbreviations, and the like, have of course been admitted. It must be remembered that the official copies were written rapidly without the vowel-signs, and that in many cases the reporter himself had difficulty in reading them. A copy of today may be compared to a printed edition based on an author's shorthand. It has been suggested that Zeid was employed on both recensions because he alone would be able to remember the *precise* interpretation of the symbols.

merely the pen which the deity held in his hand, or the gramophone record of his speech.

But, while Mohammedans have this great advantage, every word being known to be plenarily inspired, they have to face a difficulty from which the critical student of our Scriptures is free. A contradiction between John and Luke *need* not trouble a student who realizes that John and Luke were both men, and subject to the limitations of men – greatly as it *has* troubled rigid literalists in the past. The Koran, however, is full of worse contradictions than those between two Evangelists – and God cannot be accused of inconsistency. This perplexity is resolved, and was in fact sometimes resolved by Mohammed himself, on the theory that a later revelation may abrogate an earlier.[1] Thus, as we have seen, he revoked his permission of idolatry, and expunged certain compromising phrases from the Sura in which the permission was given. But here we light on what is perhaps the greatest embarrassment of all. There is no real order in the Koran: and that first principle of all interpretation, that a passage should be read in the light of the context, and with due consideration of the circumstances in which it was written, can hardly be applied at all by readers of this so-called book. It is true that we have something of the kind in our own Scriptures, which are not always by the authors to whom they are ascribed and not always chronologically arranged. But our troubles are as nothing compared with those of the Moslems. We can read an Epistle or a Gospel straight through from end to end, and, though we may find great difficulty in understanding it, we can always compare a passage with its surroundings – which *are* its surroundings. Roughly, we always know what it is talking about, and can interpret it in relation to the circumstances that gave it birth. We may, for example, be unable to explain every verse of the Epistle to the Romans: but we can

1. As Ezekiel changed the law that 'the fathers eat sour grapes and the children's teeth are set on edge' into the new one, 'The soul that sinneth, *it* shall die.' But Ezekiel and Moses were *two* prophets: Mohammed had to correct his own ordinances.

see its drift, we perceive that, though it is the work of a busy and impulsive mind, it is an ordered and profound argument, addressed to a definite set of readers, and adapted to a particular situation. The whole Testament, again, though the work of many writers, has plainly been put together with a certain purpose. But the Koran, though the work of one man, is entirely without system, and he who reads it as it stands has no chance of understanding it at all. The latest chapters are clearly in many cases the earliest in date, and the chronological confusion throughout is astonishing. Some even of the individual Suras do not appear to be complete, while others seem to be pieced together from different fragments. A holy awe prevented the editors from interfering with the Providence which had given them the *disjecti membra gigantis*: and the result is an almost hopeless confusion. The tireless labours of scholars have contrived to reduce the chaos to a semblance of order; but, when all is done, much uncertainty remains.[1]

A further characteristic troubles the Western mind more than the Oriental. The style is lyrical, resembling to some degree that familiar to us in the Hebrew prophets, but still more exclamatory. Even the narrative portions are not in the mode we associate with history: it is rarely we come across a passage of any length with its full equipment of subject, verb, adverbial adjuncts, and object. The Arab literary art is usually in one of two forms, rhymed prose – which, to the native ear, is exceedingly beautiful, but of which of course the special beauty does not survive translation – and verse of a highly technical and elaborate kind. The Koran is written in a style of its own, intermediate between the two. It may be that the differentiation between them had not yet been completed when Mohammed spoke: in any case the Suras bear, as a rule, every mark of improvisation, and reveal a highly impetuous and poetical mind, with all the merits and all the defects of such a

1. 'Even,' says Muir, 'in a chapter which is rightly classed as a Medina Sura, we not unfrequently meet with passages evidently given forth long before at Mecca, and *vice versa*.'

character. There is little care for consistency, and, with many flashes of deep insight, little philosophic precision of thought. The Arab is captivated by the beauty of language – the dialect, as we have seen, is the pure Meccan of Mohammed's time; the ordinary European has to read it in the dull medium of translation: and, as Margoliouth has put it, 'the Koran *has been* translated, but never *can* be'. We have to study the content without the glamour; and the loss is as great as if we should read a song of Shelley in a prose paraphrase.[1]

The content is curiously mixed. Some of it is in a sense autobiographical: it describes the occasions in the life of the Prophet which led to the revelations. These references, as for example those to the battle of Bedr or the capture of Mecca, are the chief guides to scholars in their attempts to assign dates to the Suras. From time to time we have actual mentions of names, as of Zeid, Mohammed's adopted son, or of one or another of his wives. But such clear allusions are rare: as a rule they are obscure, and it is exceedingly perilous to build conclusions upon them. As, moreover, they are almost exclusively found in the later portions of the book, they throw very little light on what we chiefly wish to know – the growth of Mohammed's ideas from simplicity to a certain measure of complication. We can, however, see that very early in his career he had proclaimed the main doctrines of Islam – the unity of God and the wickedness of idolatry, the Future Life and the coming rewards and punishments. A large fraction of the book, which also may be early, is taken up with narratives of the kind which the Hebrews called Midrashim, that is, stories in which the literal truth is subordinate to the moral or religious lesson they are made to convey. Many of these refer to Old Testament heroes, and are confessed to be drawn from 'the former pages, the pages of Abraham and Moses'; for, as we have seen, Mohammed regarded himself as a successor of those patriarchal prophets, and 'a preacher like one of the

1. Compare the effect of Racine upon an Englishman who can just read him, with the effect upon a cultivated and tasteful Frenchman.

preachers preceding him'. We find thus, alongside of traditions of Arabian saints, accounts of the Fall and of the
Flood, histories of Abraham and Isaac, sometimes in the
very words of Genesis, the story of Sodom and Gomorrah,
lives of Joseph and of Moses. The Jews are constantly
spoken of as the People to whom We (i.e. God) have given
the Book; the People possessing the Revelation. Where the
stories add to, or differ from, those familiar to us, they become specially interesting to the student of legendary lore.[1]
What is still more remarkable, the Christians also are
spoken of as Possessors of the Revelation; Jesus is alluded to
with reverence as a prophet of Mohammed's own kind. 'If,'
says the Fifth Sura, 'the People of the Book believe and fear
God, We shall expiate their sins, and introduce them into
gardens of delight: and if they observe the Gospel and that
which hath been revealed unto them from their Lord, they
shall eat both from above and from under their feet.
Among them is a righteous people, but evil is that which
many of them do.'[2] One Sura gives the history of the early
years of Christ – perhaps obtained from Waraka – much as
it is given in the Gospel of Luke, with additions which remind us of the tales told in the Apocryphal Gospels. We find
here the account of Zacharias, of the birth of John the Baptist, of the Annunciation, the Conception, and the birth of
Jesus: a passage which, it has been conjectured, was designed to explain to the Abyssinian king the attitude of
Mohammed towards the Christian tradition. It was his aim
to prove to Jews and Christians alike that while their Scriptures were inspired, and were sufficient for the place and
time in which they were composed, they were essentially
temporary: his religion was the divinely appointed fulfilment of the earlier incomplete dispensations, a development
of the old rather than something entirely new. 'Verily,' says
one Sura, 'the Koran which We have revealed unto thee is
held as certain among them [the Jews and Christians]: it is

1. They are constantly made use of by Stanley in his *Jewish Church* to
increase the picturesqueness of his narrative.
2. The translation is that of Muir, *The Corân*, p. 207.

revealed in their writings, in the same manner as that which We have revealed unto thee. Summon the witness of the earlier Books; ask those who read the Book revealed before thy time.' In another Sura we have a list of the ancient saints, David, Solomon, Job, Moses, Aaron, John the Baptist: 'these are they to whom We have given the Book, and Wisdom, and Prophecy: and if these men (the Koreish) reject it, verily we make it over to a people who will not disbelieve.' Like Paul or Apollos, 'opening and alleging' from the Scriptures that Jesus was the Christ, Mohammed appealed to the same authority to prove that his mission had been foretold long before by those whom his hearers acknowledged to be inspired.

In later passages we find rather legislation and direction for the guidance of believers than appeals to the unconverted. The legal code, though confused in its arrangement, is often exceedingly minute, reminding us of Exodus or Leviticus. There are regulations as to fasts, feasts, and prayers, and even as to the posture to be adopted in the devotional exercises. Unlike Jesus, who trusted rather to the power of a few main principles than to particular precepts, Mohammed – though the single formula, 'There is one God and Mohammed is his Prophet', was taken as a sufficient proof of conversion – plainly considered that religion was aided by the performance of precisely ordered ceremonies, and that uniformity of worship was a strong influence in keeping his disciples together.

Nothing in all history is more astonishing than the onrush of the arms of Islam in the first century after the Prophet's death. It is true that circumstances were favourable. The two great Empires, Rome and Persia, had exhausted themselves by long and indecisive wars: the King of Persia, Chosroes, had just died, and his successor was a weakling: his great enemy, Heraclius, the Roman Emperor, had survived himself, and was but *magni nominis umbra*. The various provinces of Rome owed the throne but a shadow of allegiance, and were in many cases torn by religious dissensions: Christianity had to a great extent lost its reality, and its adherents were often willing to accept the alternative of tribute and toleration rather than that of war to the bitter end. The Moslems were fighting not with Caesar nor even with Belisarius: their enemies, when once the army was broken, were unable to offer strenuous resistance, and a single battle repeatedly meant the submission of a whole province. None the less, the conquest of the whole vast region between the Himalayas and the Pyrenees, within the space of a single century, remains to show what can be done by discipline, religious enthusiasm, and indomitable perseverance. Nothing but the invention of 'Greek fire' prevented these furious warriors from capturing Constantinople itself only fifty years after the Hegira. Our own country has had instructive experiences in recent times. Nothing but machine guns and dum-dum bullets saved Egypt from being overrun by the Mahdists at the end of the nineteenth century.

After Mohammed's death, disputes at once began. He had no son. The candidates for the succession were three: Ali, the husband of the Prophet's daughter Fatima, son of Abu Talib and head of the Hashim clan; Abu Bekr, father of the beloved Ayesha; and the fiery Omar. Omar retired in favour of Abu Bekr, who was accordingly chosen: but Abu was old and infirm, and 'was taken to the Mercy of the Merciful' within two years. On his deathbed he nominated Omar, adding a prayer that God would ratify the choice, and that peace and harmony might reign in the Moslem world. Ali was thus again disappointed; but he took his rejection with calmness: the troubles that arose were due rather to his followers than to his ambition. After a dozen years, Omar was mortally wounded by an assassin: he lived long enough to leave the election of the caliph to six councillors, who again passed over Ali and chose Othman, one of Mohammed's amanuenses. At last, when Othman in turn was assassinated, Ali succeeded to the throne which many thought he might have claimed from the first as his undoubted right. The schism thus begun has lasted ever since: the Shiites of Persia still maintain that Ali was the true vicar of the Apostle, and that his three predecessors were usurpers. The orthodox or Sunnite creed claims that the order of succession was determined by the degrees of sanctity of the three competitors. Very early in the career of Islam the schism led to a desperate civil war, which was not terminated by the murder of Ali. His son Hoseyn, also, was murdered by his enemies in a cruel and treacherous manner. He is the St Stephen of Islam: on the anniversary of his martyrdom the Persian Shiites 'abandon their souls', to use the phrase of Gibbon, 'to the religious frenzy of sorrow and indignation'; and the name of the murderer Shamer is still pronounced with curses.

Despite these internal discords, the work of conquest began and continued with almost unvarying success. Irak was subdued in a single battle; Persia almost as speedily; and the Zoroastrian religion was suppressed with it. Ere long the Mohammedan empire reached the borders of China. Meanwhile, the vast province of Syria was wrested from the weakened hands of Heraclius by Kaled, the sword of God. 'I send you,' said Abu Bekr, 'into the land of Syria, to take it out of the hand of the infidels. So to fight is an act of obedience to God, in whose presence you are, and in the hope of whose Paradise you strive. Spare the monks, the women, and the children: cut not down the palm-trees, nor other trees of fruit; destroy not the fields of corn.[1] But when you find the men with shaven crowns, who are of the synagogue of Satan [thus he describes the Christian priests], you shall cleave their skulls, nor give quarter till they either accept Islam, or pay tribute.' The army was to be holy; prayers were not to be forgotten in the camp, wine was forbidden on pain of fourscore strokes of the bastinado; and all profane language was as rigorously checked as in the army of Cromwell. Kaled, nominally second in command to Abu Obeidah, but really the general in chief, went forth to war with the determination to conquer or enter Paradise. The first victory was

1. Compare the commandment of Moses, Deuteronomy xx, 19: 'When thou shalt besiege a city, thou shalt not destroy the trees thereof: for is the tree of the field man, that it should be besieged of thee?'

the capture of Bozrah, through the treachery of the commander Romanus, who admitted the enemy and embraced Islam. From Bozrah Kaled marched to Damascus, which after a siege of seventy days, was taken. The inhabitants, with a few exceptions, were spared, but tribute was exacted. The disaster roused Heraclius, who gathered an army of eighty thousand men, and placed it under the command of an Arab, who, he hoped, might understand, and be able to meet, the tactics of the Arabian archers and horsemen. At the terrible battle of Yarmuk this mighty host was overthrown. The victors had thus leisure to carry through the siege of Jerusalem, which, after four months, followed the example of Damascus. Aleppo was taken by an extraordinary feat of daring; Heraclius left the country to its fate; Antioch, the famous capital, purchased safety at the price of servitude and three hundred thousand pieces of gold. Caesarea, which the Emperor had left under the care of his son Constantine, ought to have been impregnable: but the prince deserted it in the night, and the city surrendered. Within six years of the death of the Prophet, the whole of Syria owned the sway of his successor. Nor did the conquerors stop here: they speedily added Cilicia to their dominion, and their raids brought them into sight of Constantinople itself. Nay, not content with victories by land, they took to the sea, and chased the fleets of the Emperor into the Sea of Marmora.

A yet speedier conquest was that of Egypt. A captain named Amrou, who had gained great glory in the Syrian wars, obtained permission from Omar to attempt an attack upon Egypt, the fame of which was commemorated in the Koran. Starting from Gaza, Amrou advanced along the ancient route to Pelusium, the key-fortress of the country, and took it in a month. Much more difficulty was found in the siege of Memphis, which was not taken for more than half a year; but after that the invaders found allies among the people of the country. Many of them were 'heretics', who had been persecuted by the Emperors, and preferred the mercy of the Moslems to the cruelty of their fellow-

Christians.[1] They willingly consented to pay tribute in return for toleration; and – by no means for the last time –
the hatred of Christian sects towards each other proved a
help to the foes of the faith. Thus relieved from perils in the
rear, Amrou turned to assault Alexandria itself, which was
captured after a beleaguerment of more than a year. Thus
the greatest commercial city in the world was added to the
dominions of the caliph. The news is said to have been fatal
to Heraclius, who died within a few weeks of the catastrophe (641). Great as was Amrou's achievement in itself,
it has been embellished by legend. The story goes that he
sent to Omar to consult him as to what should be done with
the great library of the Ptolemies. 'If,' replied the caliph,
'the books agree with the Koran, they are useless; if they
differ, they should be destroyed.' If Omar really said so, he
was running counter to the principles of his creed; but the
tale is first told six hundred years later.[2]

The conquest of North Africa, which followed, was not
achieved without many disappointments and vicissitudes of
fortune. Some energy was shown by the Roman generals,
and the native tribes were often as stubborn and elusive as
their ancestors had been in the days of Jugurtha. At least
once the invaders were compelled to renounce all their ac-

1. The majority of the Egyptian Christians were 'Monophysites' –
that is, they refused to give Christ two natures. As such, they were declared heretical by the Council of Chalcedon in 451; but their descendants, the Coptic Church, still hold Monophysite opinions, and refuse
to accept the Council as oecumenical. The persecutions to which the
Church was subjected by the orthodox, and the consequent hatred, are
almost enough by themselves to explain the success of Amrou. Unfortunately, the Mohammedans in later days were as intolerant as the
Catholic Christians themselves.

(Reasons of space compel me to say nothing of the interesting religion
of ancient Egypt. Little influence, so far as I know, was exerted by this
religion on Christianity; but it is possible that the Coptic practice of circumcision, which is still maintained, was carried over from the ancient
religion.)

2. 'If,' says Gibbon with his customary sarcasm, 'the ponderous mass
of Arian and Monophysite controversy were indeed consumed, a philosopher may allow with a smile that it was ultimately devoted to the
benefit of mankind.' Gibbon, of course, does not accept the story.

quisitions, and to retreat to the very borders of Egypt. But finally the work was done, and Islam stood on the edge of the Atlantic, in sight of the mountains of Spain. The Moors had already begun to intermarry with their conquerors, and to learn the Arabic language; they were fully as fanatical devotees of their new religion as the first followers of the Prophet; and they rejoiced to swell the armies of propagandism. Musa, the Arab chief, therefore, though so far from home, was not destitute of troops, and could rely on recruits.

The story of the conquest of Spain is one of the most famous and romantic in the history of the world: it has been the theme of poets, of tale-tellers, and of preachers. Shakespeare may have been thinking of it when he said that 'boundless intemperance in nature' had been the emptying of thrones and the fall of many kings. The illicit passion of the Gothic King Roderic for the daughter of Count Julian led the Count, so it is said, to ask Musa for assistance, and to betray the country to the Moors. In any case, it would seem certain that, as so often, the Mohammedan invaders could rely on some native help. Musa sent his lieutenant Tarik across the straits; Tarik landed, in 711, at the rock which still bears his name. The Goths were no longer what they had been under Alaric or Theodoric: but they might easily have defeated the invaders, who were vastly inferior in numbers, had there not been treason in their ranks. At Xeres, the Archbishop of Toledo and the two princes whose hopes of the kingship had been disappointed by the election of Roderic, chose the decisive moment of the battle to desert: the confidence of the army was broken, and Tarik won a crushing victory. Roderic himself perished in the flight; urged and guided by Julian, Tarik pressed on to the chief city of Toledo. Cordova was taken after a brave resistance; Toledo offered none, and capitulated so soon as Tarik consented to grant toleration to the Christian religion in return for tribute. To the Jews, who had suffered horribly from persecution, and who had given him willing aid, he was much more favourable: he entered into an alliance with

them, and established that friendship which lasted un-
broken till the expulsion of the Moors delivered the unhappy
nation once again to the cruel mercies of the followers of
Jesus. Never was a conquest more rapid. The divided realm,
accepting the single battle of Xeres as decisive, submitted
tamely to the victor; the few stubborn recusants retreated
to the mountains of Asturias, and the cities which Tarik had
left unassailed were captured one by one when Musa,
jealous of Tarik's successes, arrived in person to prevent him
from monopolizing the glory.

Spain was, in effect, the final acquisition of Islam in the
West. A desperate attempt was indeed made to conquer
Gaul. Under Abdurrahman, twenty years later, an enormous host penetrated far to the north. On the Garonne they
met and totally defeated Count Eudes: advancing further,
they captured Tours. But here, after what the monkish
chroniclers say was a seven-day battle, they were utterly
overthrown by Charles Martel, in 732, exactly a hundred
years after the death of Mohammed. It is impossible to
exaggerate the importance of this defeat; its significance was
felt at the time by both victors and vanquished, and has
been more clearly perceived since. Not only did it establish
the fame of Charles Martel, and thus make possible the portentous achievements of his son Pippin and his grandson
Charles the Great, but it put a limit to the progress of Islam,
and perhaps actually saved the Church of the West from
total destruction. It was as if Providence had a second time
said to the almost irresistible flood, 'Hitherto shalt thou
come, but no further, and here shall thy proud waves be
stayed.' Islam retired behind the barrier of the Pyrenees,
and was not finally driven from the Peninsula till more than
seven hundred years had passed.

It may be asked both why the new religion made such
marvellous progress, and why it did not carry its conquests
still further. Apart from the obvious weakness of its dis-
tracted enemies, the ability of its generals, and the frenzied
enthusiasm of its soldiers, one very important cause lay in
the policy of the caliphs. Omar laid down the principle that

while in Arabia itself there must be but one religion, in the rest of the world submission, as shown by the material token of tribute, was to be sufficient. The Roman Empire, accustomed to peace within its borders, and relying on standing armies, largely recruited from barbarians, to keep out the foreigner, was helpless when once that barrier was broken. For more than three hundred years it had been inured to invasion from Goth, Frank, and Hun, and had learnt to acquiesce in the constant change of masters. The distant parts of the Empire were very loosely attached to the centre: many of them were already in the hands of Germanic tribes, whose chiefs called themselves Roman officers, but were in fact independent. Christianity, again, in many places, had degenerated; it was torn by furious factions which hated each other more than they hated the heathen, and some of which were willing to welcome the help of any external force in order to obtain vengeance on their adversaries, or to secure, at a price, the toleration which their fellow-Christians would never allow them. Some, perhaps, wearied with perpetual disputes about metaphysical points, might be glad to find refuge in a religion which, whatever it was, was not over-metaphysical. Mohammed's argument against the Divine Sonship of Christ, that God has no wife and therefore cannot have a Son, is crude and childish enough, but it has its appeal to men who are sick of hair-splitting and wire-drawn subtleties. To another class of minds Mohammedanism might prove attractive by its plain and direct prohibition of image-worship, into which the Church was more and more rapidly falling. We have seen already that the charge of idolatry brought by Islam against the Church stung Leo the Isaurian into iconoclastic fury: there must have been many before Leo's time who cherished similar feelings.

It is, indeed, not mere reasoning from the event to detect in the success of Mohammedanism a proof that the religion was remarkably well adapted to the minds of those to whom it came. It answered the questions which men were subconsciously asking in the seventh century, as Christianity had answered the questions men were putting in the first. In some respects Christianity had risen too high for many of its adherents, in others it had sunk too low. Islam hit the happy mean. It is impossible to explain the multitude of conversions by fear of the sword or care for the pocket. Doubtless, then as ever, there were plenty of people willing to accept any religion rather than face poverty or trouble: but poverty and trouble had not prevented the Christians from holding out in the times of Decius and Diocletian. Had there been the same spirit in the seventh century as in the third, they would have held out against Kaled and Amrou. It is clear that thousands were either dissatisfied with Christianity and quite content to try another religion, or else so indifferent that one religion seemed to them as good as another. The Moslem missionaries came upon them when they were in this mood, presented them with a creed that appealed to them, and found them receptive. As compared with the symbols of Nicaea and Chalcedon, Mohammedanism was incomparably more intelligible to the plain man. It must be remembered, for example, that Spain, when Tarik invaded it, had not long renounced Arianism: to such Arians as still remained, Mohammedanism would not appear so repugnant as to a Trinitarian.

But there were weaknesses in Islam which, when the first enthusiasm had waned, were bound to show themselves. In the first place, on its political side, it was a despotism; and despotism, however successful for a time, always fails in the long run. There was no law outside of the Koran, and, as has been well remarked, Mohammedanism has never produced a constitutional lawyer. A legal system like that which, when Rome itself was in ruins, still survived, and lives now as the greatest legacy of Rome to the world, never arose in Islam. Mohammed, like Augustus, contemplated a single king for the whole world. Both failed – the Roman Empire was partitioned, and there were times when Islam had two, three, or four caliphs – but Augustus gave his world an organization which outlasted its external unity; Mohammed had nothing to give his realm but the caprice of an absolute monarch. Thus we find his empire strong when the caliphs were strong, and lapsing into anarchy when the caliphs were weak. This fact is specially illustrated in the history of Turkey. An amazing succession of able sultans made the Turks the terror of Europe: but so soon as the happy accidents ceased to occur, Turkey ceased to advance and began rapidly to recede, till finally nothing but the mutual jealousies of the European Powers allowed her to retain a precarious hold even of the Propontis. It is noteworthy also that the doctrine of predestination, once, as we have seen, so mighty a force in driving the hosts of Islam to victory, works the other way when once failure seems to declare that the will of God is not victory but defeat. The Moors accepted the disaster of Tours not as an incentive to renewed effort, but as the sign that Allah did not design them to conquer Gaul. In later times we have seen a similar feeling active – or rather passive – in the Turks. No people fights more bravely when conscious of divine help; no people accepts the decision of God, however revealed, with more fatalistic resignation; and as, according to their Prophet, Allah is God of hosts, it often seems to them that his decision is shown them by the result of a single battle.

Again, the very extent of the dominion had its weaknesses; the outlying portions, in accordance with a universal law, speedily became lax in their obedience, and finally asserted a virtual or actual independence. National characteristics inevitably reappeared: as the conquerors intermarried with the conquered, the Spaniard emerged as the Spaniard, the Moor as the Moor. It is a strong testimony to the superiority of persuasion over force that while the attachment of the provinces to the Caliphate, in its political aspect, grew looser and looser, the *religion* retained its strong hold. No religion, in fact, has altered less from its original form, has suffered less corruption, or would be more easily recognized by its founder as being what he meant it to be, than the religion of Mohammed; and in none have the precepts of the founder been more faithfully obeyed.

But no religion can escape external influences, or the

clash of mind on mind within itself; and Mohammedanism is not an exception to the rule. There have been heresies in Islam as in other religions, and sects by the score. We have already seen the great schism between the Shiites and the Sunnites: this division is only one among many. Mohammed, in one of his most truly inspired moments, had declared that the thoughts of the heart are known to God only; the mere profession of faith with the tongue is sufficient. But, as in Christianity, there arose men who desired to probe into the most secret recesses of the mind, to assert their own opinions alone as orthodox, and to crush out those who did not agree with them. As in Christianity again, and perhaps in part through contact with it, there arose discussions, which often led to bitter disputes, on metaphysical and transcendental points – points on which the Prophet had refused to touch; he is indeed said to have forbidden metaphysical argument altogether. But you may expel philosophy with a pitchfork; it will recur. A sect of Mutasils or Separators – itself subdivided into smaller sects – asserted even the freedom of the will, and contrived somehow to reconcile their doctrine with the Koran. Some of them wearied themselves with discussions of the relations to God of his Attributes; others 'reasoned high' as to whether the Koran was created or uncreated; and, as with Arianism and Athanasianism, what was orthodox in one age became heterodox in the next. The eternal question as to the destructibility or permanence of matter was talked 'about and about' by Moslems as by Greeks, and was left, after many thousand pages, as dubious as ever. Some minute philosophers endeavoured to decide whether the wicked would be driven into the flames of hell, or whether they would be attracted to the fire by their own impulse towards it. Another great sect, the Murjites, dealt with the problem which has split our own religion in twain, the comparative worth of faith and works.

The Prophet himself 'came eating and drinking', and, apart from his ecstatic visions, was most certainly a practical man of the world. He had, of course, made provision for other-worldly saintship, and he admitted that the man who lives to gain the favour of God is higher than he who labours for the rewards of Paradise. But he was too much of a statesman not to encourage to the utmost the soldier, the man of action, and the common toiler. By contact with Christian asceticism on the one hand, and with Indian mysticism on the other, Mohammedanism speedily made room for ideals which would have astonished its founder: we find in Islam St Anthonys or Benedicts, and mystics like Tauler; and there are lives of saints like those of the Bollandists, describing miracles as wonderful as those of Cuthbert or Gregory. Though Mohammed himself laid no claim to miraculous powers – apart from the one miracle of the Koran – these saints made up for his deficiencies; and, by a natural tendency, that which the Prophet's followers claimed to possess was in time ascribed to their leader.

On the whole, however, while Islam has its full apparatus of saints, prophets, preachers, wonder-workers, monks, and visionaries, its main characteristic seems to be a common-sense adaptation to the needs and powers of ordinary men, as they live and move in the tropical countries where it has found its proper home. There is something of pragmatism about it. You may be a saint if you can and wish so to be: but you are a sound enough Moslem for all practical purposes if you follow some plain and perfectly intelligible rules, say prayers at the proper times, abstain from pork and strong drink, and hold firm to the belief that there is one God and Mohammed is his prophet: and this, which is within the reach of everybody, is for the most part done. There does not seem much likelihood that, in its own regions, the faith will die out for a long time yet. There are about two hundred and fifty millions of Mohammedans in the world; their conversion will take many years, if indeed it is ever accomplished. It may be that it will yield to a universal scepticism: it is not likely to give way to Christian missions as long as, by the side of the missionary, the Mohammedan sees the 'Christian' adventurer and the 'Christian' drink-seller. Prophecy, however, is gratuitous. The religion grew up almost as rapidly as Jonah's gourd: revolutions are often very sudden; and it may, like Jonah's gourd, perish in a night. Whatever happens, it will always remain one of the wonders of the world.

No history of religion, or of religions, would be complete without some account of BĀBISM, that remarkable movement which, starting less than a hundred years ago, numbers already perhaps a million adherents, which has already passed through innumerable vicissitudes, which has endured and triumphed over the most cruel persecutions, but which, like other movements that begin with the noblest aspirations and the highest hopes, has not been able to resist the more dangerous influences of internal dissension and slow corruption. No religion shows more strange parallels to Christianity, not the least noteworthy being the martyrdom of its youthful founder. And, as that martyrdom took place so late as 1850, we are able, in the case of Bābism, to mark, with more clearness than usual, the process by which a religion rises, attracts notice, then arouses hatred, remains united while its founder lives, and is torn to pieces when he is removed from sight. History never exactly repeats itself; but the history of such a movement as Bābism may well throw light upon the dark places of the history of movements not unlike it.

In the 1840s there appeared in Shiraz a young man claiming to be the latest incarnation of the Highest Reason, and preaching a religion which was to supersede all other religions. His name was Mirza Ali Mohammed, but he was universally known as the 'Bāb' or Gate – a title which had before been given to religious leaders: but also as the Point, his Holiness the Proof, and whatever else the picturesque and poetical genius of Persia could suggest.

There had been forebodings of this 'Insuperable Matter'. Some years before the manifestation, Sheykh Ahmad, a doctor of Kerbela, had prophesied in his lectures and books that great things were about to happen: and after Ahmad's death, Seyyid Kazim of Resht announced the approaching

Theophany, which, he said, would be just after he had died: and he used to say, 'Do you not desire me to depart, in order that the Truth may be made manifest?' These two men are known as the Two Preparatory Gates of God.

And when Seyyid Kazim had departed this life, Mohammed Hoseyn began to teach in Shiraz, and said, 'Such a one must surely appear, and these shall be his tokens'; whereupon his Holiness the Point, who sometimes came to hear him, stood forth and said, 'See whether these tokens be not in me.' And that one word was enough for Mohammed Hoseyn, who was the first to believe, and was the 'Most Mighty Letter of the Book'.[1] One by one, disciples were added, until the 'Letters' were completed, thus making what is called the First Unity. The last to enter the band was 'His Holiness the Sacred'. Next to them was a second company, less highly honoured but equally devout and faithful, among whom appears a woman called by the chronicler 'the much-wronged Tahira'. Almost all these were subsequently martyred, enduring their afflictions with a constancy not surpassed by the followers of any religion.

After 'the promulgation of the Matter' and the 'affirmation of the Letters' the Lord, as a devout Mussulman, set out for Mecca, sending his disciples forth in all directions to preach the new gospel. Immediately the persecutions began; for all the Mohammedan fanaticism not only of Persia but of the surrounding countries was stirred against the missionaries. One of the 'Unity', starting for Turkey, was seized and cast into prison at Baghdad, and shortly afterwards was poisoned. Another, bearing a book of the Bāb's called 'The Best of Stories', set forth for Teheran. The Bāb himself, returning to Shiraz from his pilgrimage, was

1. An allusion to a mystical Book which the Bāb had already written, containing the substance of his doctrines. These doctrines are extraordinarily obscure – according to Professor Browne they are more intangible than those of the Kabbala or of Spinoza. Yet this is no obstacle to the success of an Eastern religion; as Brahmanism, Buddhism, and Manichaeism are sufficient to prove.

arrested by Hoseyn the governor of the city, and grievously
maltreated. Such was the virulence of his enemies that they
even violated the sacred peace of Ramadan, and, on the
very night on which Mohammed received his first revelation,[1] on which the Prophet forbade all tumults, they fell
upon the house of the Bāb and despoiled it. Fortunately
Hoseyn was held for a time in check by the governor of
Ispahan, who saved the Lord from his foes, requested the
gift of his books that he might study them, and even offered
him riches, which the Lord refused to take.

Thenceforward, for many months, the story is one of
journeyings, imprisonments, scourgings, and preachings;
of the conversions of enemies, and of tormentors turned into
believers by the sight of the constancy of the sufferers. Thus,
to take but one example, a man named Mohammed Beg,
sent to escort the Lord to prison at Maku, 'on the way
thither became sincerely attached to him, and spoke often
afterwards thereof'. In Shihrik, which is called the Grievous
Mountain, the Bāb was thrown into a house without win-
dows, and not allowed a lamp. Shortly afterwards the Crown
Prince[2] arrived at Shihrik, summoned the Lord into his
presence, 'entreated him shamefully', and then ordered
him to receive chastisement. What this meant is too plainly
hinted by the name given to the chapter in which the Bāb
described it – 'The Place of the Blow'.[3]

From scourgings the transition was soon made to slay-
ings. A murder having been committed, suspicion fell on the
sect, many members of which were arrested and put to the
torture. At length the murderer came and confessed, saying,
'I slew the man, what have you to do with these others?'
None the less, some of the saints were still detained, and,
with the connivance of the chief official, three of them were
cruelly murdered. The name of the first martyr, Salih the

1. This is called the 'Night of Worth' in Mohammedan countries, and
is as sacred as Good Friday in ours.

2. Afterwards the Shah Noureddin, famous for his visit to England in
1873.

3. Such seems to be the meaning of this obscure title.

Arab, is remembered in the sect like that of St Stephen among Christians.

It was not always that the believers submitted with patience. When armed bodies of men were sent against them, they sometimes drew the sword, and indeed won a number of victories. After one of these battles a truce was made; the King's troops swore on the Koran to observe it, and the saints laid down their arms, whereupon they were at once massacred. No faith was to be kept with heretics; indeed, as the Shah himself said, these men, though Mohammedans, and though many of them had been more than once to Mecca, were treated worse than utter infidels.

The final scene is described with almost tiresome prolixity by the author of the Tarikh-i-jadid, or New History, which was written more than thirty years after the event. The 'Holy Point' was seized and carried to Tabriz. There, after cruel interrogations and torments, he was thrown into prison for the last time. The merchant Aka Mohammed Ali desired to share his martyrdom. The Bāb replied, 'Let all have regard to their own safety, for it is better that the bond of friends should continue than that all should perish': nevertheless he cried in a loud voice, 'Verily, Mohammed Ali shall be with us in Paradise.'

When the time came, the Lord and his followers were led out to die. Aka Mohammed Ali's kinsmen said to him, 'Recant, and say you are not of them'; but he replied, 'If you love me, bind me opposite to the Lord.' Then they were bound, and hung up. Ali was killed at the first volley; but, by what was supposed to be a miracle, the Lord was not hurt; the bullets did not strike him, but severed the rope by which he hung. Seeing this, the Mussulman soldiers refused to fire; a Christian regiment was brought up, three bullets struck him, 'and that holy spirit, escaping from its gentle frame, ascended to the Supreme Horizon'.[1] This was on

1. It is typical of the way in which legends grow that the 'New History' asserts that the Christian volley also failed at first to touch the Blessed Figure; and the author indulges in a lengthy digression saying that the

8 July 1850, six years and a few weeks after the first Manifestation of the Bāb.

The list of martyrdoms is by no means complete: it would indeed take a Bābi Foxe to enumerate them all. It is said that the King desired to save 'the much wronged Tahira'; but the Queen-mother and the Prime Minister dragged her from prison and 'compassed her martyrdom, in different manners according to different accounts': the truth is known only to the executioners and to those who urged them to the work. The tale of the next few months is one of killings, lootings, exiles, chains, and imprisonments: so many captives were brought to Shiraz that the city could scarcely hold them. 'It is strange,' says the successor of the Bāb, 'that a man's chief foes were those of his own household.' All this robbery and wickedness, he adds, was done for the wealth of a few transitory days; 'but the life of the world is naught in comparison with the Hereafter, and the decision resteth with God the Lord of the Worlds'. The persecution culminated in a frightful massacre in the year 1852, in which nearly all the still surviving apostles of the new faith perished.

Mirza Ali Mohammed had already nominated as his successor a lad of twenty, whom he named Subh-i-Ezel, the Morning of Eternity. Subh-i-Ezel escaped from the massacre of 1852, and fled to Baghdad, beyond the reach of the Persian Government. Here, along with his half-brother Behaullah, he lived in comparative peace; but ten years later, apparently in consequence of representations from the Shah, they were transferred by the Turks to Adrianople: and now the schisms set in which seem to be the inevitable fate of all religions after a few years. Behaullah, who had for some time been working to supplant his brother, now broke out into open opposition. Subh-i-Ezel was a recluse and a visionary; Behaullah a man of action. The split became violent; and

---

kings of England, if the bolts fail to fall, always respite a condemned murderer. He might almost have foreseen the famous case of Lee, the Babbacombe murderer. The earlier history, by Mirza Jani, says the *second* volley was fatal.

the Turks, fearing trouble, packed off the Beha party to Acre, the Subh party to Cyprus.

The result was that the whole community, throughout the nearer East, was sundered. Beha proclaimed himself the true Manifestation of God, and called upon all the faithful, including Subh, to obey him; and when Subh refused, branded him as the First Letter of Denial. What was still more astonishing, Beha began gradually to undermine the authority of the Bāb himself, announcing that he was not the true Manifestation, but merely the harbinger of the perfect theophany of which Beha was the embodiment. He stuck at nothing to attain his ends. One by one the followers of Subh-i-Ezel, some of whom had been personal attendants of the Bāb, disappeared – in certain cases by assassination, and the 'Letters of the Living', as they were called, were soon reduced to Subh himself and one other. Nay, Beha tampered with the Sacred Word itself: the doctrines of the Bāb were speedily no longer recognizable in the form which Beha gave to them. Whatever we may think of his conduct, he was a practical man. He cut out the mysticism, expunged the metaphysics; made overtures to the Shah, and let it be known that the Bābis were to conform their life not to an impossible transcendental system, but to the ordinary standards of mankind. History was quietly falsified; the accounts of the earlier movement were altered so as to conform with what Beha desired his followers to believe.

Now, as Professor Browne says, if we once admit Beha's right to assume this position of supremacy at all, there can be no doubt that he acted wisely. The doctrine of the Bāb might suit certain Persians, but totally unfitted it for mankind in general, and must be altered if Bābism was to be a world-religion. The books in which they were written were not even in Persian, but in bad Arabic, full of grammatical errors, repetitions, and unknown words. The sense, when disinterred from this farrago, was found to be unintelligible; there was a worse than Pythagorean theory of numbers, in which 19 was chosen as the basis of all calculations; there was strange play made with the divine names and attributes;

there were doxologies and poetical rhapsodies so wild that none could follow them. There was much dogma and little precept; and what precept there was was childish – as the command that after two hundred and two years the books should be copied afresh and the old destroyed, or elaborate rules, which could not be kept, as to the burial of the dead. Moreover, the Báb had discouraged travel and the learning of foreign languages, had ordered the destruction of books of science and philosophy, and had, by the narrowness of his ideas, made it all but impossible for Bábis to live peacefully with the adherents of other religions. His kingdom, in fact, was emphatically not of this world: it was noble, subtle, and lofty in aspiration, but it is certain that few, when the first enthusiasm had worn away, would be able to live in it. Beha gradually accommodated it to mundane minds. He employed scribes to write his new revelations, and their books were intelligible and comparatively concise; the writings of the Báb sank into oblivion; in fact but for the fortunate survival of the work of Mirza Jani, which was written in 1851, immediately after the Báb's death, the true history of the 'Point' would be unknown; and that work, when Professor Browne wrote, existed in but a single manuscript.[1] *The New History* (Tarikh-i-Jadid) dated *c.* 1874, represents one long step in the transformation of Bábism into Behaism; the *Traveller's Narrative*, written by Beha's son in 1886, represents yet a further step. In this the Báb is reduced from the 'Point' or the 'Mahdi' to a somewhat inferior John the Baptist; the real founder of the religion, whose words are quoted with reverence, is Behaullah.[2]

1. This manuscript was found in Teheran by the famous Count de Gobineau about 1856, and deposited in the Bibliothèque Nationale. Strictly, there are *two* MSS, but one contains only a third of the book.
2. As an example of the obscurity of the early Bábi writings, I give here a few lines from a letter of the 'much-wronged Tahira' as translated by Browne in *The New History*, p. 438:

'The heart of the Za was gladdened, and the Letter Fa rejoiced, and the bosom of the Ta was elated, for that she saw the signs from the red leaf arising.

'God the True hath willed to see the Tree cast down on the dusty

After the death of Beha in 1892 there was another schism, his two eldest sons, Abbas Effendi and Mirza Mohammed Ali, disputing the succession. The elder maintained that the Manifestation was continuous, and had passed directly from his father to him; and he appears to have at least this to say for himself that Beha had announced him as his heir. The younger, however, refused to acknowledge any *authority* in the heirship, and, apparently, so far as doctrine was concerned, he was right: for, though the Bāb had preached that the Imam-Mahdi, or he who is manifested, must appear at intervals, yet he himself did not arise till exactly a thousand years after his predecessor, and certainly had not contemplated a series of rapidly repeated manifestations. Moreover, he had urged his followers, if ever anyone should claim to be the Imam, to subject him to immediate tests: and these tests Mohammed Ali maintained that his brother signally failed to pass. The strife, as usually is the case when brothers fall out, was exceedingly bitter; but it ended in the victory of Abbas. Despite all these quarrels, the religion continued to gain ground, and, it is said, has some adherents even in America and France.

---

earth in most great abasement, and from all, in all, by all cut off; His then is the command, and his the decision, universally, partially, particularly, all-consuming.'

The Za (Zahra, the Bright), Fa (Fatima the daughter of Mohammed, who, in Bābi belief, was reincarnated in Tahira), Ta (Tahira): all these mean Tahira the much-wronged herself: the 'signs of the red leaf' are the letter she is answering. Thus she simply means she had been glad to receive her correspondent's communications.

The 'Tree', again, is Tahira, the Pure: and 'cast down on the dusty earth' refers to her imprisonment and sufferings before her martyrdom.

If we imagine a style like this employed to express the mystical dogmas of the Bāb, we shall have some idea of the difficulties which students of his work have to encounter.

CHAPTER II

ZOROASTRIANISM

THE religion of Zoroaster (Zarathushtra) was at one time among the most important in the world. It was the religion of the great Persian Empire, which for two hundred years included twenty provinces from Egypt to India, and which, when revived by Ardshir or Artaxerxes about two hundred years after Christ, disputed the nearer East on equal terms with Rome till Roman Emperor and Persian Sultan alike gave way to the irresistible advance of the Mohammedan Arabs. In the interval between the destruction of the first Empire and the rise of the second or 'Sassanian', the religion had been depressed but not abolished; and no sooner had Ardshir overthrown the Parthian power than he called the priests to consultation in order to restore the pristine purity of the creed, which had been corrupted by mixture with foreign beliefs and made dubious by the disputes of innumerable sects. It is said that no fewer than eighty thousand came to the assembly; and the arguments of these vast throngs seemed likely to have no result, when, the historians tell us, one of the priests received the truth in a miraculous vision, and his authority, backed up by the force and prestige of Ardshir, established the doctrines on a firm basis. Thus the great Empire once more revered its great prophet; and despite wars without and schisms within, the religion maintained itself until it was ruthlessly stamped out by the Moslems. In the seventh century the last of the Sassanians was defeated, driven from his kingdom, and finally killed. The conquerors did not spare the 'infidels'. The worshippers of Fire, as they were called, were extirpated wherever found. A large band of them fled to India, where, as 'Parsees', they have made themselves, in spite of the smallness of their number, indispensable as bankers, financiers, and men of business. In Persia itself a few thousands

managed to survive, and are still to be found in scattered
societies.

Though once so great, and now numerically so insignificant, neither the importance of this religion, nor its un-
importance, is to be measured in arithmetical terms. Its
influence, outside its own borders, had been profound;
Zoroastrian doctrines penetrated into Judaism, mainly of
course when Persia ruled in Judaea itself and in the other
lands where the Hebrew exiles had been planted; nor less
noteworthy have been the results of its contact with Christianity. Many of the Gnostic systems show plain traces of
their Zoroastrian origin; and, though anathematized by the
Church, left their mark upon it: the powerful heresy of
Montanus was not untouched by Avestan influence;
Mithraism, that dangerous rival of Christianity, is an im-
pure Zoroastrianism[1] adapted to the needs of the Western
world and to the culture of the Roman soldiery; Manichaeism, though branded as a heresy by Zoroastrian priests,
was a heresy and not an entirely new religion; and the
Christian Church, while rejecting Manichaeism with even
excessive vigour, could not prevent itself from being to a
considerable extent affected by it. Even when the last overt
relics of Manichaeism, detected or suspected among the
Albigenses, were sought out and savagely destroyed, the
creed lived on in secret, and insensibly made its way into the
minds of its persecutors. If for no other reason, therefore, yet
in order to understand our own beliefs, we as Christians
ought to endeavour to obtain some notion of the ideas promulgated, two millenniums and a half ago, by the great
Persian sage and prophet.

When and where the prophet lived cannot be determined;
and the contradictions of the legends have led some authors
of high repute to hold that he never lived at all. Others have
maintained that there were at least two of him. In the face
of the disagreement of the doctors it does not become laymen to decide; but it is perhaps not rash to place his date

1. Probably, rather, a descendant of the original Iranian religion as it
was before Zarathushtra had reformed it.

somewhere about the seventh century before Christ, and, roughly, a hundred years before Cyrus began his career of conquest. Zarathushtra speaks of himself as living in the reign of Vishtashpa or Hystaspes, who may have been an ancestor of the great Darius: and on the whole the linguistic criteria derived from the study of the Avesta (or Revelation) are not inconsistent with such a date. As to his home, we are able to guess with more probability; he was born in the region of Adairbaijan; and his mother's family was connected with the Median town of Rhagae (so familiar to us from the Book of Tobit), which lay not far from Teheran. We know the name of his father, Pourushashpa, and the name of his clan, Spitama, also occurs very frequently in the sacred writings. Some poems tell us of his wife Hvovi, a member of a noble family at the court of Vishtashpa: if this is correct, it may imply that the prophet also was of noble birth: but Hvovi is spoken of in a peculiar way, as if she were rather a mystical abstraction than a woman.[1]

Neither the exact place nor the exact date of Zarathushtra, however, is of much importance to the student of his system. It is certain that his doctrines were not wholly new, but were based upon ideas commonly held in Persia, and running back, in an elementary and often childish form, to immemorial antiquity. These ideas are, in fact, not even peculiarly Iranian; their likeness to many of those held by the Brahmans indicates that they are 'Aryan', and must belong to a time when the Aryans had not yet penetrated into India, but were still one people with the Iranians. We have to go back at least to a period before the Vedas were composed – that is, fifteen or sixteen hundred years B.C.: and the fundamental conceptions may have been dimly adumbrated still earlier. The likeness of certain divine names in the two systems, Indra and Andra, Mitra and Mithra and others, would be by itself sufficient to prove a

1. I owe my knowledge of Mazdeism primarily to the works (*Early Religious Poetry of Persia*, etc.) and to the conversations of my lamented friend J. H. Moulton, who introduced me to translations of the poems, and gave me my first acquaintance with the system.

community of origin. But after the separation, as was inevitable, the two peoples developed their primary ideas along different lines; and Iranianism cannot be considered a mere form of Hinduism, any more than the Iranian languages can be considered dialects of the Sanskrit. They are kindred systems, springing from the same root, and modified according to the character and environment of the peoples among which they grew. Zarathushtra himself was the reformer who gave the Iranian ideas definiteness and a certain consistency, purified them from vulgar accretions, and – it is almost certain – systematized though he did not originate that metaphysical theory which is so characteristic of Eastern religions, and which makes them so difficult for Western minds, even when specially trained, fully to appreciate. But it remains a matter of great delicacy to disentangle Zarathushtra's own ideas from those which thus seem to have existed in more or less crude and undefined or corrupted state, before his time. It is, I believe, easier to distinguish his ideas from those which were added *afterwards* by the Magians. In the writings (the Gathas), which are held on independent grounds to represent Zarathushtra's thoughts, or even to give us his actual words, there is singularly little ritual: the sage was a prophet, not a priest. In the later portions (the Vendidad) there is ritual and little besides. Analogy, if nothing else, would indicate that the Gathas give us the pure religion, and the Vendidad the accretions; this is the almost invariable order in religious history. From inscriptions and other evidence we gain confirmation of this conjecture. We know that, in the early days of the Persian Empire, the Magi made an attempt to seize the rule, and actually succeeded in putting one of their number, for the moment, on the throne. It is clear that they were in alliance with the subject-nations, but we can also see that they were aiming at the restoration of the old unreformed religion as it was before the rise of Zarathushtra. They were foiled by the energy of Darius, a convinced Zarathushtrian, who in the Behistun inscription relates the story, and speaks of their attempt as the 'Lie' (a phrase characteristic of the prophet's style): and during his reign of nearly forty years they were held in check. But priestcraft may be expelled with a pitchfork; it ever returns; and it returned in Persia. Retaining the name of the prophet, and even exaggerating his claims to reverence, the Magi gradually re-introduced into the religion what he had rejected, adding much (from Babylon and elsewhere) that had never been in the old Iranianism at all. Thus Zoroastrianism, like every religion that has lasted long and spread widely, is 'syncretistic'.

On the other hand, as I said just above, the exact nature of the religion which Zarathushtra found prevalent among his countrymen, and which he felt himself impelled to purify, cannot be determined with precision. For one thing, both in Iran and in India, the Aryans were a dominant and conquering tribe – almost certainly a minority; and the beliefs of the subject-races – what they were is totally unknown – must have profoundly affected their conquerors. Like all other invaders, the Aryans would for the most part spare the women, who became slaves and nurses; and it is the habit of such women to propagate their ideas, often in the crudest form, among the children they are set to tend. Some Babylonian traits have been detected in the later Zoroastrian writings, and a few of these ideas *may* have penetrated Persia at very early times. But, using all the means at our disposal, comparing for example the Zoroastrian records with the Vedas, we can see with some clearness that the Iranians, like the early Romans and other peoples, were nature-worshippers, but had scarcely yet discriminated fully between the natural object and the deity residing in it. They certainly worshipped Father Heaven and Mother Earth, and we learn that they had a god actually named Mithra, who may have been the sky, or rain, or air, and who was later to become the sun-god; but whether he was their own or borrowed is uncertain. A river-genius, Anahita, would appear to be non-Aryan, and to have come to the Iranians from a neighbouring or subject people. But as a rule the deities are nameless – that is, their names are not 'proper', but 'common'.

It is likely that the distinction between gods (Ahuras) and demons (devas), which Zarathushtra made the basis of his system, already existed, at least in germ, before his time; and it is certain that ancestor-worship, whether originally Aryan or not, prevailed among the Iranians, to be transformed in the later Zoroastrianism into the conception of the Fravashi or guardian-spirit,[1] which, as we have seen, was taken over by the Jews and made a permanent element in the Jewish religion. These, as has been pointed out, were the real guardians of morality, and the source of social custom; for while the sky and the elements generally were far

1. Next, perhaps, to the doctrine of Angels, of which, indeed, it may be said to be a part, the idea of the Fravashi is the most important of the Persian conceptions which penetrated first into Judaism and thence into Christianity. The derivation of the word is unknown, but it may be connected with a word meaning to impregnate. This, if true, would account for the influence of the Fravashis, as originally ancestors, in presiding over births. They are also very prominent in war; and we have not to go far for examples of the worship of ancestors as a means of securing victory. As spirits of the dead, they are naturally identified with the stars. At the annual feast of All Souls, held at the end of the year, the Fravashis were invited to share the meal with their living descendants. They are, in fact, the Manes or Good People.

But from this conception we pass to another. A verse, probably early, tells us that the Fravashis of the Living are more powerful than those of the dead. They are now regarded as part of a good man's self, living in heaven and reuniting with the soul at death. They are the External Souls of men, exactly like the body, but of a more tenuous substance, and liable to be mistaken for the real man, as the household of Mary thought that Peter's Fravashi was mistaken by Rhoda for Peter himself. The universality and tenacity of this belief is illustrated by Frazer in his *Golden Bough*; and, as will be seen later, the idea lies at the basis of the modern Spiritualistic religion, has its place in Swedenborgianism, is a fixed tenet in Theosophy, and is indeed rooted in the minds of our own people. Whether it is original in Iranianism has been doubted: some suppose that it was tacked on to the Aryan ancestor-worship by the magians of an earlier race with whom the Aryans came in contact. The Fravashis are never mentioned by Zarathushtra himself.

The prevalence of demonic beliefs in Judaism needs no explanation; but it may be worth mentioning that the Asmodaeus of Tobit (a book full of Persian ideas and proverbs) is the demon Aesma, Wrath, with deva added: he is one of the helpers of Angra-mainyu: though the Tobit-tale is rather Median than Persian.

off, and took comparatively little interest in the affairs of men, the Fravashi's were close at hand. As in Rome Jupiter was in heaven, but the Penates in the household, Mars distant, but the Manes near, so with the Iranians. True, the Sun beheld all things – but then it was just the 'all things' that he did behold; the ancestors watched over *each thing*. Nearer than the Sun was the Earth-spirit, for which the people had gone so far as to invent a proper name, Aramati; but even she – though all early races feel very strongly their sympathy with Earth – was less close than the father who a short time before had watched over pasture and homestead, and who could not be conceived as having lost his affection for it, or as being unable to show his resentment if his children neglected it. He had presided at the feasts and sacrifices, and he was still interested in keeping up the orders and customs on which prosperity depended.

There is clear evidence of a cult of Fire, but a cult of a peculiar kind. The Fire-god in most religions consumes the sacrifice, which – as it is the nature of fire to ascend – he carries up to heaven. But in early Aryan days the sacrifice was not burnt at all; the Fire (Atar) was the messenger who invited the gods down to partake of the feast. Ancient myths seem to show that the stars received worship: the star Tishtrya has a terrible combat with the drought-demon Apaesha, lasting three days and three nights; and we may guess that in times of famine the help of Tishtrya was invoked. Relics are found of the worship of the ox – the animal on which, in all nomad peoples, the prosperity, and indeed the very life, of man depended. There is a legend that Mithra, at the final regeneration, is to make man immortal by giving him of the flesh of the primeval cow from whose slain body mankind was made; and it has been suggested that this is connected with another myth, which tells how man fell by eating forbidden food – that is, possibly, by eating the flesh of the cow, in order to obtain immortality, before the time decreed by Ahura-mazda.[1]

1. The reader will be reminded of the Genesis-myth of the Forbidden Fruit and the Fall. This, however, though probably in origin the same as

We must not, however, hastily assume that, simple as the religion was, the people were incapable of higher thought. Some of the lowest savagery is often found to go with extreme subtlety, and the Iranians were not savages. It is likely that the great conception of a spirit of Good, over against a spirit of Evil, had been dimly visualized by the more reflective among the people, and lay there ready to be taken over by the prophet when he arose, and to be sublimated by his genius. It is not conceivable that he should have met with the success which he gained had there not been something already *there* to which he could appeal: and his own words seem to imply that he regarded himself not as bringing something new, but as restoring what was old, and as reforming what had degenerated. To say this is not to impugn, but to enhance, his greatness; not to deny his originality, but in the truest sense to assert it.

Thus, on the whole, the old Iranian creed was, as we might expect, animistic; there were in it strong elements of anthropomorphism; and, to a certain extent, when Zarathushtra appeared, there had grown up a kind of Pantheon. All the gods thus developed the prophet relegated to the world of demons, and even the nameless ones suffered the same fate. He never mentions Mithra and Anahita; had he mentioned them, we can guess what he would have done with them. His reformation was, in large measure, a repudiation of idolatry; and it met with the fortune which such a reformation almost invariably encounters. Not long after the prophet's death Mithra and his crew returned, and priests who nominally revered Zarathushtra might have

---

the Persian, was worked out differently. As Frazer has suggested, it may have once run thus: There were two trees in the garden, one of life and one of death: and God sent a message by the serpent telling man which to choose; but the cunning animal perverted the message, ate the fruit of life himself and told man to eat of the other. Thus man became subject to death, but the serpent is immortal (as, in many countries, he is still supposed to be: his habit of changing his skin has deceived observers).

The alteration of the tale into the form in which we know it may, just possibly, be due to Persian influences received at second or third hand by the Hebrew sages.

been seen worshipping the very deities whom he had, overtly or implicitly, denounced. None the less, his religion, as he left it, is the purest in the history of the world, early Christianity and early Mohammedanism alone, perhaps, excepted.

This purity, and the freedom from idolatry which thus mark Zoroastrianism in its earlier phases, struck foreign observers. Herodotus notes with admiration that the Persians have no temples or altars, and look with contempt on those who build them; 'as it seems to me,' says he, 'because they do not, like the Greeks, think the gods to have a human nature. But they do not hesitate to ascend to the highest points of mountains and sacrifice to "Zeus", meaning by that name the whole circle of the heaven; and they sacrifice also to sun and moon, earth, fire, water, and winds.'[1] Similarly, both Plato and Aristotle knew, and apparently approved within limits, the dualistic system, and show acquaintance with the names and natures of Ormuzd, Ahriman, and some of the subordinate spirits. Plutarch's account (written four or five hundred years later) is well known.

The doctrines of Zarathushtra are contained in the Avesta, which is written in a very ancient Iranian dialect known conveniently as Zend. Much of this is poetical in form, though the character of the metre has not yet been accurately determined. Of the mass which at one time existed, at least two-thirds have been lost, whether through the destruction of Persepolis by Alexander,[2] or, as is more likely, through the fanaticism of the Moslem conquerors of the seventh century, who offered the choice between the Koran and death. The main portions are the Yasna ('worship'), including the Five Gathas;[3] and also the Yashts or

1. According to Herodotus, the Persians had already borrowed from the Assyrians (or Syrians) the worship of Aphrodite (by whom he means Ashtoreth or Astarte).

2. A story used by Dryden as the basis of his famous ode; but almost certainly false.

3. Properly, hymns; but also applied to prose explanatory notes or rubics, or to short sermons.

hymns of praise addressed to angels. The rest consists chiefly of the Vendidad or code of ceremonial law. All this was probably originally taught orally, and preserved in the memory for many centuries – a fact which will surprise nobody who is familiar with what the human mind can retain when there are no books. It is said that it was not written down till the first century of our era; Ardshir and his successors (the Sassanian dynasty) certainly saw to it that copies were multiplied; and the canon was finally settled in the fourth century.

These poems are excessively obscure, partly because of the difficulty of the language, partly because of corruption in the text, but also because of the extremely metaphysical cast of the prophet's mind. They must have been obscure even to the original disciples, and would require, like so many 'mysteries of the kingdom', explanations given in private. I choose an example from Moulton – by no means the hardest:

'He that in the beginning thus thought, Let the blessed realms be filled with lights, he it is that by his wisdom created Right. Those realms which the Best Thought shall possess, thou dost glorify through the spirit, O Lord, who art evermore the same. I conceived of thee, O Wise One, in my thought, that thou the First, art also the Last, that thou art Father of Good Thought, for so I apprehended Thee with mine eyes; that thou didst truly create Right, and art the Lord to judge the deeds of life.'

Here the scholars are not agreed as to whether the blessed realms are those of the visible heavens, or the ultimate Paradise into which the good shall be drawn when Ahriman is finally overthrown. Again, does Right mean simply moral excellence or the ordered cosmos, the 'duty that preserves the stars from wrong'?

Once more, there is a hymn containing a dialogue in heaven, in which Ahura-mazda, the highest spirit, is one speaker, Zarathushtra another, and the 'Creator of the Ox' a third. The ox-soul complains that he (i.e. the cattle) receives no care from men. Even Ahura fails to give help; but

Zarathushtra undertakes to protect the beasts, and the Ox-soul accepts the service. Whatever this means, it reveals how Zoroastrianism has sublimated the crude worship of the ox, of which we spoke a short while since. The Creator of the Ox was, in the old mythology, probably Mithra; he now appears as a spirit or abstraction in the midst of other equally transcendental principles.

But all this strange language has a genuine ethical tendency. No religion, in fact, is more closely bound up with morality than Zoroastrianism, and none insists with more determination that morality is not mere convention but something eternal. It has its roots in the immemorial past, and points to the infinitely distant future. 'Now,' says the prophet in the thirtieth Yasna, 'the two primeval Spirits, who revealed themselves in vision as Twins,[1] are the Better and the Bad in thought and word and deed. And between these two, men of understanding chose aright, the void of understanding not so. And when these two Spirits met in the beginning they ordained Life and Not-life, and declared that at the end the worst existence should be to the followers of the Lie, and Best Thought (apparently a symbol of Paradise) to the followers of Right. Of these two Spirits he that held to the Lie chose the doing of the worst things; the holy Spirit chose Right, he that clothed himself with the massy heavens as with a garment. So likewise do the men who desire to please the Wise Lord by deeds of truth. And Aramati, the Spirit of Earth, gives to men continued bodily life, so that at the end they may be victorious over their enemies. Thus, when the punishment of these evil ones cometh, then, O Wise One, at thy command shall Good Thought establish the Dominion in its fullness for those who deliver the Lie into the hands of Right. If, O mortals, ye mark the commandments, that the Wise One hath ordained, then hereafter shall ye have bliss.'

At times we light on a practical precept, untouched by metaphysics or theology, like the one which moved the ad-

1. The rendering is disputed. Others translate, 'Who as the Directors guide the Better and the Bad': and for 'in vision' read 'automatically'.

miration of Gibbon: 'He who sows the ground with care and diligence acquires a greater store of religious merit than he who repeats ten thousand prayers'; and, whether these are Zarathushtra's own words or not, there is no doubt that he would have agreed with them. The Persian threefold rule, spoken of by Herodotus, to ride the horse, to draw the bow, and to speak the truth, would have appealed to him: but he would have added, 'and to treat the horse and all other animals kindly'. The good deeds on which he insists are not the performance of futile ceremonies, but the doing of acts which promote social well-being. We might compare him with Spinoza, whose ethics, starting with the most profound metaphysical ideas, lead to the inculcation of plain and simple virtues, such as are possible to the most ordinary men, and such as, if steadily pursued, would hold the frame of society together in unbreakable unity.

No sooner, however, had the Prophet been taken away than, as usual, degeneration began. 'The step,' says Moulton, 'from Gathas into Yashts is a step into a new world.' We still meet the old familiar names: Ahura-mazda is still supreme, with his Amesha-Spentas or holy spirits around him, and lip-service is still paid to Zarathushtra. But the sage has been degraded into something very like a divinity. He is 'no longer a man of like passions with ourselves, a fervid Reformer, eagerly pressing his lofty doctrine of God and duty against opposition, and exhibiting very human emotions of elation and discouragement as the fortunes of the campaign sway to and fro.' He has undergone the fate which so often befalls great religious leaders; his personality is exalted and his precepts and doctrines are neglected. Ahura-mazda himself is changed: he is a more or less anthropomorphic deity, surrounded by other deities only nominally inferior. Sacrifice, which in the Gathas is hardly mentioned, assumes a vast importance; prayer is a matter of magic, and the gods are *constrained* by the use of the correct names and spells, rather than entreated. Apart from the eschatology, which has suffered little change, Zarathushtra, had he returned to earth, would have felt that his work had to be done all over again. A process of continuous degeneration set in; the religion was split into a multitude of sects all equally superstitious; and, though the reformation under Ardshir recovered much of the lost ground, yet the tendency of human nature once more reasserted itself, the eternal circular process was repeated, and even the Mohammedan persecution, fiery as it was, did not altogether purify the beliefs.

The Yashts are hymns of praise, comparable in some small measure to the so-called Hymns of Homer, being addressed not to Ahura-mazda nor to the eternal principle behind him, but to individual deities, to the Sun and Moon, to Tishtrya or Sirius, to Druaspa the horse-goddess. To pass from the Gathas to these is as if, after reading the Hymn of Cleanthes to his almost Pantheistic Zeus, we suddenly lighted on the myth of the birth and baby-doings of Hermes. But there is one Yasht which is more curious; it is the Praise of Mithra. We know how, in parts of Iran which escaped or resisted the reforms of the Prophet, the cult of the old Light-god still lingered on, and how in times to come it was to take on itself new features from Semitic religions and dispute supremacy with Christianity. In this tenth Yasht we find him penetrating into Zoroastrianism, and he does so in a very remarkable way. He is paired with Ahura as one of the two imperishable Holy Ones, but not as the Sun-god. He is the Lord of Truth, the great Zoroastrian virtue; he is the one who sanctions contracts, the enemy of the Lie. Instances are given to show how he punishes the 'Mithra-druj' or breaker of agreements, and saves him who keeps his promises: and it is often hard to be sure whether the promise itself (*mithrem*) or the god is meant:

'Spitama [Zarathushtra], break not the *mithrem* made with sinner, made with faithful, for Mithra stands for sinner, stands for faithful: Mithra, Lord of spacious pastures, true of speech, wise in council, with a thousand ears, and myriad eyes, from his world-wide watch-tower gazing, strong, unsleeping. If a lord of a house, a town, a province, lies unto him, then fierce and angered he crushes house, town, and province: the steeds of these liars fling their riders from the saddle; though they run, they stir no step, though they ride, they move no pace.' As for the liar, his strokes, though well and truly aimed, avail nothing; his spear is turned backward and hurts the thrower. On the mountain Alburz, Ahura builds for Mithra a glorious palace, where it is always light, where no clouds ascend, nor ever wind blows loudly, not sickness nor death enters, nor the pollution born of devils. There are evil men who say in their hearts that Mithra sees not the ill deeds nor hears the lying words: but they err grievously. How far all this prepared for the fuller entrance of Mithra into the Zoroastrian world, and for the worship of him as the material sun, is hard to tell. But the poem shows how a deity not even mentioned in the earlier Avasta contrived to slip back into the hierarchy from which he had been expelled.

We are now, perhaps, ready to give a brief sketch of the form which, after the Magians had had some centuries of predominance, the Zarathushtrian doctrine assumed, and of the ritual which they added to it. Much, as will be seen, is retained from the Gathas, much borrowed from other religions. Something of Brahmanism – when taken over is hard to say – can be detected in it. There is even, in the later writings, an attack upon 'Gautama', who may be either Buddha himself, or one of the Buddhist missionaries: in any case, we may suspect that Buddhist influences were at work and were feared, perhaps with good reason.

As in Brahmanism there is a neuter principle (Brahmă as distinct from the masculine Brahmā), so in the Zoroastrian creed there is an abstract entity, unlimited and apparently incapable of definition, lying as the substratum of the universe. This conception may well go back almost to primitive Aryanism. But, as being utterly inactive, and as possessing no ethical content, this principle can excite neither affection nor aversion; it neither attracts nor repels: nor, on the intellectual side, can we predicate anything of it. If we must speak in terms of time, it was before all things. Yet, so soon as we pass from eternal vacuity, and reach the

beginning of time as we understand it, we recognize two
vast areas of light and darkness, sundered from each other
by empty space. As, in one sense, light itself, and in another
inhabiting light, we find an essence which the poverty of
human nature compels us to picture as almost a Person
(Ahura-mazda, the Wise Lord),[1] the spirit of light and
truth; and similarly at the opposite pole Angra-mainyu
(hostile spirit), the principle, also half-personified, of darkness, falsehood, and evil. (The names are often corrupted to
Ormuzd and Ahriman.) For untold years the two spirits
lived apart; but, when Angra-mainyu learned of the existence of Ahura-mazda, he was filled with fury and rushed
upon him to make an end of him. At first the two spirits
were equal in strength; but in the *potentiality* of growth
Ahura-mazda was the greater. Foreknowing what was to
come, he knew that the contest would endure for thousands
of years, for, as he himself was the perfection of good, so
Ahriman was the perfection of evil; and, indeed, whatever
was positive in the one was balanced by a negation in the
other. Thus, as it is expressed Ormuzd thought first and
acted after; Ahriman acted first and thought after: and
whatever Ormuzd did, Ahriman counteracted. For three
thousand years the terrible war endured, Ormuzd knowing
that the victory could come to him only by length of time.
To aid him in the battle, he created spirits – Bahman, the
protector of living beings; Amerdad, the spirit of the waters
and the others – but Ahriman always met him with a
counter-creation: everyone of these expressing the Zoroastrian philosophy that good is the everlasting Yea and evil
the No which, if the struggle goes rightly, will not be everlasting. At length came a symbolical truce of nine thousand
years, the meaning of which is not easy to discover. Ahriman
seems to have forgotten his cunning in yielding to the proposal, for no sooner did he see what he had done than he
was seized with despair, and flung himself into the abyss
where he remained for three thousand years in darkness
silence, and inactivity, while Ormuzd, helped by the spirits

1. Hence the religion is often called Mazdeism.

created the heaven, the waters, the earth with its planets, trees, and animal life, and finally mankind. The heaven he filled with four hundred and eighty-six thousand stars, a mighty army for the defence of the realm of light. Earth, in a manner which will remind the reader of the cosmogony of the Middle Ages made familiar by Milton, was suspended from the lower surface of heaven, in the space between the dominions of Ormuzd and Ahriman: and on it were set two human beings, the Adam and Eve of the Iranian Genesis.

At this moment Ahriman awakes from his trance, and realizes with horror and indignation what has been happening. 'The egg of Ahura-mazda' has been hatched while he has been sleeping. Should he linger, he will be destroyed; but all is not yet lost; he will not slip the occasion. Against the stars of Ormuzd he sets hostile stars; he pierces the egg, and appears on the surface of the earth, where he finds Urstier and Gayomard, innocent but weak, and unable to contend with him; they are utterly destroyed. Ormuzd creates a second pair, Mashia and Mashiana, but they too are swept away, and disease, death, famine, with all the other ills of life, enter through their fall.[1] Thenceforward the centre of the great strife – the Belgium of the ever-contending powers – is our unhappy earth; and the lesser nature of man feels to the full what it is to come between the pass and fell, incensed points of mighty opposites.

As in almost all cosmogonies, there are dates, and the periods are equally divided, the numbers, one would fancy, being half conventional and half magical or symbolic. The world is to last twelve thousand years. Of these the first quarter covers the creation; the second, as we have seen, the sleep of Ahriman. The third is the time of the worst and most savage conflict; on the one side the great heroes of light – Kaikobad, Jenjib – on the other dragons, monsters, and evil men of renown – Zohak, Afrasiab. But

---

1. Is it possible that in the Hebrew traditions, also, there was once a double creation of mankind? In the Talmudic legends Adam's first wife was not Eve but Lilith; and in the genealogies we seem to see two lines of descent, one from Adam and one from Enos.

Ahura-mazda is biding his time. Not till the end of this third quarter, three thousand years before the final judgement, can Zarathushtra be born. Ahriman knows his danger; he tries every means to prevent the birth, but he is too late, and the Prophet appears. As a token of the joy he is destined to bring, he is the only babe that ever smiled on first seeing the world.[1] Many times did Ahriman strive to destroy him, but always in vain.

When he was thirty years old, Ormuzd summoned him into his presence, and gave him the revelation which was to renew the world. Thus filled with the divine spirit, he appeared before Vishtashpa, and the signs and wonders which attended him convinced the King that the true prophet had arisen. From that time the doom of Ahriman, though it may be delayed, is sealed. The Devas, or spirits which aid him, are smitten by the words of Zarathushtra as with swords: they lose their power of appearing in bodily form, and act invisibly. Nor, though this first prophet may pass from the earth, will he be without successors. Every thousand years another will arise with equal or greater power;[2] slowly the forces of evil will be overcome, and when the final catastrophe overtakes the world, when the elements shall melt with fervent heat, and the ocean roar with flame, Ahriman and his hosts will sink for ever into the abyss,[3] good will

1. Some have thought that Virgil had heard of this myth when, in his prophecy of the golden age which was to follow the birth of the mysterious child, he cried, 'Incipe, parve puer, risu cognoscere matrem.' (Eclogue IV: a line applied by Gray to the birth of Shakespeare.)

2. Compare the reincarnation of the Buddha.

3. According to some theologians, the victory will be still more complete: Ahriman will be reconciled to his enemy, his evil heart will be changed; the fire will purify him from every taint, and he will be called to the abode of light, to join the choir invisible of those who never cease to chant hymns of praise to the Timeless One in whom all things live and move and have their being. Apparently this was the real conception of Zarathushtra: and thus he can only loosely be called a dualist.

Such a system, of course, lends itself to many variations. Modern Parsism is said – perhaps under the influence of Mohammedanism or even of Christianity – to have transformed Ahura-mazda into the Original First Cause, and to have degraded Ahriman into a mere Eblis or Satan – a rebel against God.

triumph, and mankind will be drawn up into the region of eternal light, to reign with Ormuzd for ever and ever.

The Vendidad, which is in prose (in itself a fair indication of date), is largely later than Zarathushtra's time, and consists almost entirely of a code of laws and of regulations as to ritual. Righteousness, which is backed by supernatural sanctions, is inculcated with extreme minuteness. Already the Prophet had declared that there was, in the other world, a 'Bridge of the Separator' (like the Moslem Arch of Al-Sirat), which would part the righteous from the wicked, and beyond which lay the 'House of Song'. We now find this bridge more exactly described; it was a broad path for the good, and a razor-edge for the bad, with hell yawning beneath. The Separator is now named; he is Rashnu, weighing with scales our good deeds against our evil.[1]

For guidance in order to escape a fatal verdict from the scales, the believer found plain rules. He must have faith in Ahura, but the faith must show itself in works. He must avoid arrogance, pride, and jealousy; and, of course, the Lie', which involves unchastity, magical arts, slander, and falsehood of every kind. Next, he must revere the Amesha Spentas, the spirits which Ahura used in the work of creation, and which dwell in the things they have created; and here also actions must follow. His reverence for these spirits must lead him to maintain the fire, to keep metals pure, to spare all clean animals, to care for plants, trees, and rivers. He must *help* the spirits by destroying weeds, by curing diseases in men and cattle, by extirpating poisons and harmful beasts: and he must keep *himself* pure from all contamination, especially from corpses, in which Ahriman's evil spirits reside in strength. Every failure introduces into his soul a Druj, or agent of Ahriman; and the Druj can be expelled only by confession to a priest and by performance of the purifications and penances he enjoins. For the priest

1. Some would see in the Zoroastrian eschatology the origin of Jewish, and so of Christian, Apocalyptic literature, which dominated the world for centuries, and has not yet lost its power. (See on this the chapter on Judaism.)

now appears as the appointed mediator between God and man, and his power is as great as that of his antitype in Buddhism or in Roman Catholicism. He certainly earns his place, for he has to learn the law by heart, and the ceremonies over which he presides are very laborious. As now performed by Parsee ministers in India, divine service begins at midnight – for, as everywhere, 'only more so' in Mazdeism, the demons have their hour in darkness – and lasts till dawn. Hymns, the recitation of the law, sacrifices, and prayers, pass the gloomy and perilous time. Every family is expected to keep a confessor, and to pay a tithe for his maintenance. His power is great, for he is both tutor and spiritual guide. He it is who watches over the young Parsee till his fifteenth year, when, by a kind of Confirmation, he admits him into full communion with the Church in a solemn ceremonial, and finally fastens on him the sacred symbolic girdle, which is never to be laid aside.

Though, as we thus see, much has been retained by the Zoroastrian, both of doctrine and of practice, since the expulsion of the religion from its native Persian home, there are of course some parts of the Sassanian code of laws which are inapplicable in a distant country and under a foreign domination. The Persian legal system was part of the Persian religion, and was based on the Vendidad : it could no more be transferred in its entirety to India than the Mosaic code could be carried unaltered to Russia or Germany. Nevertheless, in its essentials it remains. Founded on the great rule of honesty and truth-telling, it not only permits, but urges, the Parsee to make a living, or even a fortune, by straightforward dealing, to accommodate himself, as far as possible, to the social organization in which he lives, and to preserve the sanctity of the family. Thus the Parsee has contrived, without the sacrifice of principle, to maintain himself in the midst of an alien population, and, though never *of* the world surrounding him, dwells *in* it, and gives none offence.

CHAPTER 12

THE RELIGIONS OF THE
FAR EAST

OF the hundreds of religious cults practised in the Eastern hemisphere, it is impossible here to speak. It will be sufficient if we deal with the three which, if the numbers of their adherents were the criterion of importance, would be reckoned the three most important religions in the world. All three of them date from times long before the birth of Christ, and show as yet no sign of giving way to Christianity. Unless one of those sudden upheavals occurs which have repeatedly upset the most confident prophecies, it is likely that for many centuries yet these three creeds (if such they may all be called) [1] will still be disputing with Christianity for the allegiance of some of the most populous countries in the world.

Of these what is commonly called Hinduism [2] is the most ancient. Its origin is lost in utter obscurity, though there are indications that it sprang, in the first instance, from the same sources as certain other religions – that is, Ignorance and Fear. Men felt their subjection to the mysterious powers of Nature, and the need of propitiating them. In the Hindu Bible, however, those Vedic hymns which date from fifteen hundred to a thousand years before Christ, these 'primitive' ideas have been largely discarded. Many of these hymns reveal that years had brought the philosophic mind, and clearly rest on very lofty conceptions. It has even been maintained, with some plausibility, that they proclaim a monotheism as firm and unflinching as that of the Hebrew prophets. In any case they are the product of a fairly

1. Confucianism may perhaps be better described as a code of social behaviour than as a religion in the ordinary sense.
2. The Hindus do not call it Hinduism, Brahmanism, or Vedism, but Arya-Dharma, the Religion of the Aryans.

advanced civilization and of deep and long-continued thought.

Whatever was the original seat of the Aryans – whether on the Baltic, by the Caspian, or somewhere to the north of the Hindu-Koosh – they, or rather one of their many branches, migrated from it, and pushed, at some unknown date, into the Punjaub, where they found and subjected tribes of entirely different races from their own. They brought with them the Sanskrit language, a member of the great Indo-Germanic family, which, to some extent, they succeeded in imposing on the subject-peoples. Their religion, also, they made the dominant one; but, as in all such cases, not without sacrificing something in the process, or – which is the same thing – not without admitting many alien elements. The religion thus inevitably suffered contamination, and a process of degradation may, with more or less certainty, be traced through the centuries. There is, for example, no idolatry in the Vedas; but there is no more idolatrous religion in the world than the ordinary Hinduism of the peninsula; and, if the Vedic poets were in truth monotheists, they would be astonished at the many thousands of gods that are worshipped in India today.

It is this contamination which has led scholars to divide the Indian religion under three heads[1] – Vedism, Brahmanism, and Hinduism as generally understood: though of course these divisions are not altogether exclusive, and though in each of them stages of development may be detected.

The Veda, or Divine Knowledge, is supposed to have been revealed to the Rishis, or inspired men, and by them passed on to the people at large, by means of Mantras or hymns. Three great collections of these Mantras were made at different times. The first is the Rig-Veda, a kind of Book of Psalms, including chiefly prayer and praise. The second is a sort of liturgy, in which some of the psalms of the Rig-Veda are collected to be used in sacrificial services. In the third, the Sama, the hymns were arranged for chanting at

1. Some find six or even more.

the services in which the juice of the sacred Soma-plant (the draught of knowledge, brought by Indra, and since then believed to have been removed from earth to heaven) was offered for special purposes. A fourth collection, made much later, is partly old, but to a great extent new, and consists of texts and formulas used as charms and spells: this, as it was compiled by priests called Atharvans, is known as the Atharva-Veda.

When we dissect the Vedas to find the theological ideas on which they are based, we light, as might be expected, on much confusion. In some passages the gods are treated as one family, children of Dyaus (Zeus or heaven) and Earth (Privithi). In others Varuna (Uranus) is occasionally addressed as supreme deity. But the prevailing conception is that of a trinity – Agni (Ignis, Fire), Indra (Rain), and Surya (the Sun), one each for earth, air, and sky. All the other gods are either modes of these, or associates of them. Thus the twin Açvins (Equi, horses) are children of the Sun, driving his car and heralding the Dawn.

The special friend of man was Agni, manifested (naturally enough) by the friction of two pieces of a fig-tree, present (like Vesta) in every household, the father of sacrifice, and (for the sparks fly upward) the bearer of messages from the homestead to heaven.

Apart from these stand Yama and his twin-sister Yami.[1] Yama was the first of men to die; he therefore (like Michael and Hermes) guides souls to the spirit-world. He has two terrible Cerberuses, which guard the way to his dwelling. In later myths he becomes the Minos and judges the dead.

As for the Vedic sacrifices, they consisted of simple gifts to the gods, as a sign of gratitude for favour; but later they became propitiatory offerings to secure assistance or to ward off harm. To the feasts, the gods were invited, and a share was always left for them. Particularly they were supposed

1. We have already seen the tendency to call twins by the same or similar names. For this see Rendel Harris, *The Dioscuri in Christian Legends*. Thus, e.g. Crispin and Crispinian, the saints of Agincourt, were twins.

to 'smell sweet savours', and to enjoy the scent of the Soma-juice. Not till later, apparently, were animal sacrifices introduced,[1] which gradually developed into enormous rites in which whole hecatombs were slaughtered, and gods, priests, and people banqueted together to the chanting of hymns. By diligent performance of this ceremonial, which was called Yajna, a man might gain admittance to the heaven of Indra.

As the female principle was seen to be necessary not merely to natural reproduction but to creation, we find, though not in the early hymns, all the great deities furnished with wives, whose names, however, being derivative (Indraui, Agnayi), show clearly that they are not yet of primary importance, and who are not the objects of worship.

The cosmogony of the Vedas, their stories of the origin of things, and their accounts of the birth of the gods, bear a striking resemblance to those told in the Babylonian myths, in the Scandinavian Edda, and indeed in many other creeds; they show how men, reflecting on the world around them, tend to think in the same way and to come to similar conclusions. I quote here but one example, from Monier-Williams's translation in his *Indian Wisdom*:

> *In the beginning there was neither naught nor aught:*
> *Then there was neither sky nor atmosphere above:*
> *What then enshrouded all this teeming universe?*
> *In the receptacle of what it contained?*
> *Was it enveloped in the gulf profound of water?*
> *Then was there neither death nor immortality:*
> *Then was there neither day, nor night, nor light, nor darkness,*
> *Only the Existent One breathed calmly, self-contained.*
> *Then first came darkness hid in darkness, gloom in gloom:*
> *Next, all was water, all a chaos indiscrete,*
> *In which the One lay void, shrouded in nothingness.*

Let the reader compare with this either the Babylonian Creation-Myth, from which the first chapter of Genesis is

1. Compare the story of Cain and Abel.

derived, or the words in the Icelandic 'Volu-spa' or Song of the Sibyl: 'In the beginning there was neither sand nor sea, nor earth nor heaven above: there was a yawning chasm, but no grass; till the sons of Bor, who made the glorious earth, raised the ground. The Sun knew not his habitation, nor the Moon her dominion, nor the Stars where they had their place.' It is clear that the authors of the Veda had a more metaphysical conception than our concrete-minded ancestors; and it would seem that their morality also was of a by no means low kind.

As men of high mentality began to reflect on this Vedic religion, they gradually conceived the idea of a spirit – something deeply interfused, which breathed in the mind of man, inspired the hymns of the Rishis, and yet rolled through all things. It was no Person, though it gives life to persons; it was not limited by individuality, yet it moved and gave being to individuals. This they called Brahmă (something expansive), because it diffuses itself through the universe, and all gods, men, and things are but modes of it. This conception gave rise to Brahmanism, which has so deeply affected the ritual, the philosophy, the mythology, and the law of India. The idea of the necessity of sacrifice gradually strengthened itself, until it was believed that by duly-performed sacrificial rites one could extort favours from the most unwilling gods, obtain superhuman powers, or even enter heaven. Hence a system of unequalled elaboration: the sacrifices were to be performed by the proper classes of priests, every one of whom received his appointed guerdon; and the songs were to be chanted with the correct intonations; the prayers, which might last for weeks or even years, must be according to rule; and the whole was 'like an intricate piece of mechanism, or a chain of which every link required to be perfect in all its parts'.[1] But the power of such a machine was infinite. Passively, it maintained the universe in its full energy; actively, it could secure any benefit, even admission into the heaven of Indra, or a welcome, on equal

1. Monier-Williams, *Brahmanism and Hinduism*, p. 23.

terms, into the company of the gods: nay, the gods themselves had gained their deity by such sacrifices. The Creation
itself was brought about by cutting up and sacrificing the
primeval Male.[1] There is reason to think that human sacrifices were not unknown; and it seems as if men might gain
some sort of immortality by sacrificing themselves: such
immolations, at any rate, occur from time to time.

A reaction from this was of course certain; and the next
phase of Brahmanism emphasized knowledge rather than
act. In the Upanishads, the Scriptures of this phase, or, as
they have been called, the New Testament as contrasted
with the Old Testament Mantras, the essential doctrine is
that the universal desire to be reunited with the One Spirit
(the Atman or Brahmă) can be satisfied by pursuing the
path of knowledge (jnina). Man's spirit is already part of
the Atman, limited by the illusion (Maya) of personality:
it is eternal like the Atman: it is not mind, which is a function of the body, but an essence accidentally tangled with
the body. As it acts, it does good or evil; these actions receive rewards or punishments; and the spirit in consequence
migrates into lower or higher bodies until it is finally absorbed into the One universal Spirit. This is the doctrine
which Pythagoras introduced into the Greek world. But it
must be remembered that there is nothing positive in this
great Spirit: it is a Trinity of negations. It is Existence as the
negation of nonentity, Thought as the negation of non-
Thought, Happiness as the absence of misery. It has no self-
consciousness, no will: it exists in individuals through
Illusion only, and takes no share in their thoughts and feelings. Thus it has but numerical likeness to the Christian
Trinity, the essence of which is personality and will in triune
harmony.

Similarly, the ordinary European conception of the Ego
and the Non-ego is totally opposed to Brahmanism, which
regards the two as only illusorily separate: a theory which,
as may well be imagined, it finds it hard to maintain con-

1. Compare the similar cutting up of the giant Ymir in the Scandinavian mythology: his bones were the rocks, his blood the sea.

sistently; the external world, like cheerfulness, is continually breaking in, and the illusion is treated as practically a reality. At times, indeed, the duality is openly recognized and there are schools of Brahmanism which directly teach it. But all alike, apparently, inculcate abstinence from action of every kind, good or bad, and from feeling, whether 'wrong' or 'right': thus only can we draw near to the final consummation in which both will disappear. For action and feeling are alike products of the ignorance which deems the illusory real. And that final consummation is indeed hard to attain; for the path to bliss (i.e. to non-sentience) is through eight million successive births: a creed which, more than anything else, crushes the heart out of the Hindu believer.

The myths of Brahmanism are contained in great part in the two great epic poems, the Mahabharata and the Ramayana, two immense mountains of words which the ordinary European finds its exceedingly difficult to master.[1] In this mythology abstraction disappears, and the ethereal essences put on personality. We find a series of demigods, superhuman beings, lower gods, higher gods, reaching to Brahmā, who now appears as a male personal divinity: and associated with him are Vishnu the Preserver and Siva the Destroyer; the three perhaps developed from the earlier Vedic Earth, Water, and Fire; or from Earth, Air, and Sky. All these three are, in strict Brahmanic theory, but one: each first, each last, each supreme, and each at times doing the work of the others. Even when, as happens in ordinary thought, they become three gods, their superiority over all others is never denied. But they, and especially Vishnu, may become incarnate, as Vishnu, at one descent or Avatar, became Krishna (one of the heroes of the Mahabharata): or as half of Vishnu's essence descended into Rama (the hero of Ramayana). Every great man possesses, at least in part, an infusion of the divine essence; Brahmans, in particular, are in a sense human representations of Brahma, and

1. The present writer has toiled through them in mercifully abridged translations.

receive reverence on that account, and that though every man, and every thing, is also, in another sense, a portion of the divine. All three deities have wives, which represent them in their female aspect; and Brahma and Siva have even sons.[1]

We shall see later, what we should expect, that while these great gods are owned as supreme, the smaller ones are those of whom the Hindu thinks most, and to whom he prays most frequently. This is, of course, the common feature of all religions: the Lar was more nearly present than Jupiter, the troll than Odin.

Finally, we reach the legal or preceptive phase of Brahmanism, the chief source of which is the so-called Code of Manu, though there are others of only slightly less authority. It is on these codes that the caste-system, the decisive element in Hindu social life, is based. So long as the caste-system prevails, so long will Hinduism maintain itself. According to Manu, God created distinct orders of men, as he created distinct species of animals and plants, and these orders – Brahmans, soldiers, agriculturalists, and servants, must remain apart, as lions are distinct from dogs, or wheat from barley. But, as a Brahman may marry a wife from any of these three lower castes, there arises, from the offspring of such marriages, an endless number of castes within castes, each limited to its own occupation. It matters not how wealthy a man of one caste may be, or how learned; he can never rise into a higher.

The connexion between Indian morality and religion is peculiar. No Hindu believes that God will help him to live a moral life: his prayers are not directed to this end. But his belief in metempsychosis naturally leads him to try to live such a life by his own unaided efforts. If theft, for example, means that he will become a rat after death, he will try, with more or less success, to avoid being a thief: and if murder means he will become a cobra, he will try to spare the lives of others. No other motive is set before him: he is not told

1. Vishnu does not appear to have sons in the strict sense. His Avatars (Krishna, Rama, etc.) have many.

either that to do right will please God, or that 'because right is right, to follow right were wisdom in the scorn of consequence'. None the less, the code of Manu, with a noble inconsistency, contains some of the highest moral maxims that are to be found in any religion; some of them, indeed, might be read in the New Testament without stirring a sense of incongruity. I give here two or three. 'Wound not another, though by him provoked': 'Be not angry with the angry, give blessings for curses': 'Give to the poor, but talk not of thy gifts; the merit of alms melts away by ostentation': 'No study of the Veda, no sacrifice, no alms, can lead to heaven him who is inwardly depraved': 'Long not for death, nor hanker after life; calmly expect thy own appointed time, even as a servant reckons on his hire.' 'Thou mayest think thyself alone, but within thee resides a Being who knows thy goodness and thy wickedness.'[1]

And out of this philosophical, ethical, and transcendental Brahmanism grew the modern HINDUISM, in which the transcendentalism has largely disappeared, and into which all sorts of elements, from here, there, and everywhere, have been introduced. Hinduism, as has been tersely said, is 'Brahmanism run to seed'. It is the philosophy as adapted to all the races, Dravidian, Kolarian, with which it has come into contact, and as assimilating all their superstitions and practices. Nor is Brahmanism to be blamed. Merely spiritual ideas, impersonal abstractions, are totally unintelligible to half-barbarous populations; concrete, visible things must be offered to them, or they will turn away.

Thus the first distinction between Hinduism and its parent is that the worship of the too spiritual Brahmā has all but disappeared; Vishnu and Siva, in their various manifestations, have usurped his place; and such is the comprehensive and receptive character of the religion that there is practically no idea which it cannot assimilate. It is like the Ganges itself, which welcomes waters from a thousand tributaries. It does not reject the fetishism of the aborigines, or the demon-cults of the savages; it permits animal-

1. For more of these see Monier-Williams, op. cit., chap. xxi.

worship,[1] and does not spurn the most horrible or degrading rites, wherever found; while on the other hand it is ready to borrow the loftiest ideas from Mohammedanism or Christianity. It is so amorphous that it can scarcely, by any conceivable means, be destroyed – it is like a vast country without a capital, a ruler, or an organization. Thus, when Buddhism appeared, and for a long time seemed likely to be a dangerous rival, Hinduism quietly and imperceptibly expelled or absorbed it. Not unnaturally it regards itself as the universal religion, destined to absorb, in similar fashion, all others that come within its reach. There have been many great teachers, like Sankara and Sayana, who have proclaimed high and profound doctrines; Hinduism accepts the doctrines, and reconciles contradictions in a unity of multiplicity. A missionary of some unknown creed may arrive in India; the pundits will tell him with truth that the essentials of his creed are already there, and have been known for thousands of years: the only difference is that his creed, to him, is exclusive; to them it is only another ingredient in the witches' cauldron.

It is but a further characteristic of this comprehensiveness that Hinduism should be not without its sectarianism. With such a multitude of ideas to choose from, it is clear that some men will choose a certain set, and others another. Some will prefer to worship Vishnu, others Siva; and as these gods have many manifestations or associates, there will be worshippers of the same god who prefer to adore him under different names and forms. It has taken scholars long and patient study to reduce these cults to a manageable number, and to detect something like system in the chaos. With difficulty they have succeeded so far as to disentangle two main strands. The worshippers of Vishnu may be set apart from those of Siva: this is the great and main division. Secondary are the worshippers of the female personifications of energy or reproductiveness, regarded as the wives of the deities; this is called Saktism. Here again there is every form of be-

1. Thus the fish and the boar are worshipped, being very simply accepted as incarnations of Vishnu.

lief from the highest to the lowest: there are those who regard Sakti, or force, as the power of Nature, which is but
one manifestation of the energies of the single supreme
Spirit; but this degenerates in others into the worship of individual female deities. 'The whole world,' says a text, 'is
embodied in woman. One should be a woman oneself.
Women are gods; women are vitality.' Hence the worship
of Siva's wife Kali rather than of Siva, or of Krishna's wife
Radha rather than of Krishna. Hence the countless rami-
fications, spreading down from the worship of Kali to the
worship of female deities of the lowest kind, all of whom are
conceived as partaking of the primal Sakti. If you get a
thoughtful devotee of one of these to tell you his views, he
will say that he worships her as a form, or incarnation, or
other exposition of the Maha-Devi or great goddess, who is
herself, as the wife of Siva, only a manifestation of Siva himself. For all gods are both male and female. And, if you
question him further, he will tell you that Siva is, in turn,
but a mode of the One Spirit Brahmă. He will give you a
long list of Matris or mothers of the Universe: Vaishnavi,
Brahmi, Indrani, Yami, Devi or Kali, Lakhshmi, and
dozens more; he will add a crowd of 'mistresses', who preside over illegitimate love, and sorceresses, and female
fiends; but all are one. None the less, the ordinary man
thinks of them as many, and the result is that Saktism has
produced as licentious and horrible a multitude of rites as
any of those which gathered round Ashtoreth or Derkěto.
The most famous, and the most striking, as no visitor to Calcutta can avoid seeing them, are the rites of Kali, with her
terrible gaping mouth and unkempt hair.[1] 'She has four

---

1. The form of Kali-worship called THUGGEE (Thagi from a root
meaning to conceal) is familiar to all. The Thugs, who lasted for centuries, and at times even included some Mohammedans in their society,
were a band of initiates who sacrificed victims to Kali by strangling them
with a scarf or handkerchief. The murder was a religious service, and
was undertaken after a special ceremonial. There was no image of Kali
at the ceremony; though it is said that the pickaxe used to bury the
victims was a symbol of the goddess.
The cult was suppressed by W. H. Sleeman, with almost incredible

hands and a garland formed of the heads of the demons she has slain; she holds a sword, and is without fear; her throat is besmeared with blood; she is Kali, or Black, for she is dark as the clouds, and has the sky for her garment; her necklace is skulls and her ear-rings dead bodies; she smiles with her lips but her teeth are terrible; she dwells among the tombs, and she tramples on her husband.' The rites are drinking[1] and eating, followed, as in those of the Syrian goddess, by Maithuna or sexual union. This last, which so horrifies Europeans, and which, as practised by the Canaanites, was an 'abomination' in the eyes of the Hebrews, is (theoretically) a symbolic action, representing the union of the Self with Energy, from which the world originally came: but it is to be feared that this symbolism is not always kept before the minds of the worshippers. In a similar way the two symbols, Linga and Yoni, which are to be met with everywhere in the Hindu world, represent the divine principle of reproduction, but do not always retain their divine character.

Another very important cult is the worship of Fortune.[2]

skill and daring, in the Governor-generalship of Lord William Bentinck (1828–35); the task took seven years. Sleeman's own account shows clearly the religious enthusiasm of the Thugs: none of them showed the slightest remorse, and, when punished, all of them, with hardly an exception, exhibited the courage and devotion of martyrs.

Bentinck, following up the work of Lord Wellesley, also abolished Suttee.

1. Drinking brings knowledge; all Brahmans, therefore, according to some 'Tantras' or sacred verses, must drink arrack as the gods drink nectar. But this does not prevent the inculcation of extreme temperance or total abstinence; drunkenness is indeed not an Indian vice. Similarly, in old days cows and other animals were eaten at the sacrifices, and that in accordance with a code: what is the custom today is too well-known to need mention.

2. It takes much reflection, and a good deal of science, before chance or fortune is understood, before we can say ' Nos facimus, fortuna, deam, caelogue locamus': nor is the lesson by any means learned yet. The Hebrews, as we saw above, 'prepared a table for Fortune, and filled up mingled wine unto Destiny' – two gods, Gad and Meni – while nominally worshipping Yahweh (Isaiah lxv, 11), and Christians carry mascots and amulets, and trust in the luck of particular cricket-grounds. Next to Mammon, Fortune is perhaps the favourite deity of the West. It is to the credit of Brahmanism that Mammon has little power in India; a Fakir who owns nothing is more highly honoured than a millionaire.

For, as has often been observed, while the higher minds among the Hindus desire, like the higher minds in all religions, to be freed from sin and the inclination to sin, the lower pray to be delivered not from sin but from the evils that assail them, and especially from those to which they are exposed from the universal presence of demons. There is not an atom in the universe but is the abode of such demons, actively malignant or merely mischievous, fiendish or Puckish. These are the agents that cause plagues, famines, sickness, inconvenience, annoyance of any kind: and, as might be expected, it is the village that is most terribly infested by them. Hence the worship of Siva's sons Ganesha and Skanda or Subramanya. No two gods are greater favourites than these. Just as in all nations the lesser spirits and fays are more omnipresent than the Jupiters and the Thors, so in India. There is nothing that Ganesha does not control. If a poet cannot manage his verses, this is not because of his own inability; a demon has been at work; he therefore calls on Ganesha. If a tool breaks, a demon has done it, and Subramanya is invoked. Both, of course, are deputies of Siva, who is the real master of the armies of the demons: but this is usually forgotten. Subramanya, the Sacred One, is the captain of the good demons, and attacks the evil ones openly in battle; Ganesha – the well-known elephant-headed and four-armed god – is, as his form shows, the shrewd and strategic deity of craft, who *circumvents* the demonic hosts. He often rides on a rat, the wise animal, or appears in company with Nag, the serpent, that most subtle of all the beasts of the field. He is in fact the deity of Success in Life, and he is invoked first in all ceremonies except those of death, the final failure. It is said that there is not a single sect which, whatever other god it primarily worships, does not take care to offer constant prayers to Ganesha.

Part and parcel of all this is the worship we have already incidentally mentioned – that of the Matris or Mothers, which is universal. Every mother is in a sense a deity to her children; much more are the divine Mothers deities. The father is venerated, but the mother, as more clearly the source of life, is adored; and Earth, or Space, more than all.[1] Everywhere in India are to be found shrines, however humble, containing stone symbols of the union from whence life comes, which, to the educated Hindu, typify the primeval union of Spirit and Matter: and everywhere the female principle is regarded as the more potent. Hence the care taken in every village to keep her in good temper, as when angry she can and will do unlimited mischief. One

1. Nothing is more frequently misunderstood than the position of Indian women. Child-marriages, the perpetual mourning enforced on widows even of twelve years of age, the (now abolished) Sati (Suttee), the confinement of high-class women in Purdahs, have given a false idea to many foreign observers. As a matter of fact, women in India enjoy a higher position, and exert a greater influence – on the whole – than, till recently, they did in Europe. Wilful ill-treatment of wives is almost unknown: though of course they have to submit to conjugal caresses at too early an age, and are compelled to go through a weary round of domestic service. But the early marriage is religiously necessary: without children there can be no proper performance of the funeral ceremonies which are essential to the peace of the soul. Wives, it is true, never pronounce their husband's names, nor do husbands ever allude to their wives save by a circumlocution. But this is part of a superstition common to Brahmanism and scores of other beliefs. It is true, also, that women are never formally admitted into the faith, and never read or hear the Vedas: they are in a sense 'Sudras' – of the servant-caste – and outside of the Hindu scheme of salvation. But they gain it in another way, simply through marriage, which is itself sacred. The position of a Queen-mother, or still more of a grandmother, is one of the most influential in the world; and mothers and grandmothers in lower spheres often exercise a similar despotism, which is rarely disputed. A passage quoted from the *Mahabharata* by Monier-Williams (op. cit., p. 389) is here in point:

> *A wife is half the man, his truest friend;*
> *A loving wife is a perpetual spring*
> *Of virtue, pleasure, wealth; a faithful wife*
> *Is his best aid in seeking heavenly bliss;*
> *A sweetly speaking wife is his companion,*
> *A mother in all seasons of distress,*
> *A rest in passing through life's wilderness.*

In a word, women are the mainstay of Hinduism; without their support, which at present shows no signs of failing, the whole edifice would crumble.

Mother may *be* small-pox, *cause* small-pox, and *expel* small-pox; another is similarly cholera or whooping-cough. To please such a goddess, or to control her by means of spells, is therefore the first duty of the wise man of the village: and such is the power of faith that sometimes a few spells, duly muttered, actually have driven the disease away. A single such case is sufficient to fix firm as a rock the belief of many generations, and to make them look on the sanitary inspector as either an atheist or a madman.

Naturally, among the more benevolent Matris are those who preside over childbirth,[1] and some are the special patrons of infants. Others, again, with an inconsistency that will surprise no student of religion, are virgins, and yet protectresses of motherhood. As a rule, their images are simple stones, like the Ephesian image of the virgin Artemis – who also watches over '*Laborantes utero puellas*'.

It is impossible to separate all this from the worship of demons: for gods and goddesses may at any moment become hostile fiends. Ninety per cent, it is said, of the people of India live under the dominion of spiritual fear, and their worship is a worship of terror. If they do believe in beneficent beings, they feel they hardly need to worship them: they are kind enough already; but the demons are here, there, and everywhere, and are crouching in every corner to pounce on the unwary. For the most part they are princes of the powers of the air, especially in that one of the seven upper worlds which is nearest to our own, or in any of the twenty-one hells which lie beneath. They may have relations of any kind with men; there are many stories, like that in the sixth chapter of Genesis, of their taking to themselves the daughters of the human race. Some were created by God at the beginning; others are the spirits of dead men; some, by a sort of transmigration, inhabit serpents or apes, others seem to be personifications of human passions, as Ravana is

1. Their help is certainly needed; for in some parts of India, as in many other countries, the mother is expected to set to work immediately after the birth, while the father takes to his bed, groans with pain, and demands the best of food.

Ambition, and his brother Vibishana Content. As in Icelandic and other mythology, the soul of a man killed by an evil beast becomes a demon and haunts the neighbourhood: a man-eating tiger is a cannibal devouring his own people. Nay, a criminal may die and depart, but his crime remains as a person, malignant and fearful. Thus the murderousness of a murderer walks the earth unseen but powerful, the perjury of a dead perjurer survives him, the blasphemy lives when the blasphemer's body has been burned, and his ashes scattered to the winds: all these tempting living men to commit the crimes they have themselves committed. Thus the armies of the evil demons are ever increasing: luckily, they are to some extent counteracted by the armies of good demons, recruited from the ranks of saints.

These, of course, are in multitudes of cases survivals of cults which existed long before Vedism or Brahmanism appeared. They have been adopted into the higher creed by the device of representing all demons as in some form or other manifestations of Siva, or – what is much the same thing – of his sons Ganesha and Subramanya. There is in fact no limit to the assimilative power of Hinduism. The old cults, especially in the South[1] – the last region to be penetrated by Aryanism – remain; but Aryanism has taken them up into a higher form.

There is also, as might be expected, no lack of the worship of the hero, or deified man. Of this an example may be found in the veneration paid to Rama, the hero of Ramayana, who was probably once an actual man, or at any rate as much a man as Achilles or Agamemnon, but who like them was worshipped. (Few names appear oftener than his as an element in Hindu proper names: as English boys were called Thomas to secure the favour of St Thomas of Canterbury, so Hindus are Ramas to gain the help of this hero.) Another case is that of Hanuman, who appears in the poem as the

1. In many villages the doors never open towards the south, lest the demons from that region should find an easy entrance: and, if any distinction can be drawn, the south is more fully penetrated with fear of demons than any other part of India.

levoted friend of Rama, and who, having been deified in
he familiar fashion, is worshipped as the giver of bodily
trength, and as the type of the '*Treue Diener Seines Herrn*'.
He has many temples throughout India, and may almost be
egarded as one of the greater gods. His form is peculiar. It
s possible that he was originally a chief of a savage tribe
vhich the Aryans regarded as hardly distinguished from
apes; he is in the poem represented as actually an ape, and
as leading armies of monkeys to the help of Rama. His worship, then, may be connected, as cause, effect, or both, with
the universal veneration in which monkeys, like other animals, are held. At any rate, whatever mischief they do, they
are never injured: whether it is thought that Hanuman will
resent an insult to his fellows does not, so far as I know,
appear. This unwillingness – I use a mild term – to interfere
with the animal creation is one of the chief obstacles in the
way of the advance of material civilization in India, and one
of the most frequent causes of hostility between Mohammedans and Hindu.

To sum up this necessarily meagre sketch of one of the
most intricate and contradictory religious systems in the
world: Hinduism is a species of pantheism, 'Spinozism', it
has been said, 'before Spinoza'. God is One, but he manifests himself in all things; he expands himself, so to speak,
first into the three great deities, and through them into innumerable energies or principles, which may be, and are,
constantly personified. But personality and consciousness
are imperfections, to be got rid of though it take millions of
transmigrations to effect the riddance. Every man's destiny
has been decided for him, by what we may call *himself*, in a
previous incarnation, and cannot be changed till another incarnation begins, at, or some time after, death. A Brahman
is a Brahman, a potter a potter, an untouchable an untouchable, and can no more become something else than,
in this life, a bird can become a beast. But the God who has
thus – to use a poor metaphor – portioned himself out, does
not love the portions: he imposes on them intolerable
burdens, and requires to be placated by impossible oblations.

The most pious Hindu, though knowing himself to be a manifestation of a god, will appease that god by endless ceremonies: and he regards that god not as kindly but usually as angry. Siva will not cease to destroy, or Kali to devour, unless somehow his or her wrath be turned away, it may be but for a moment, by the sacrifice of thousands of goats and hecatombs of bulls. Equally terrific are the demands made by the inferior supernatural beings, and even by the animals, trees, and stones in which the godhead resides.

How then can the highly educated and intellectual Hindu – and there are few more keenly intellectual men in the world than many of these – reconcile himself to a system so childish, superstitious, and barbarous as this? If East can never meet West, it would seem impossible that the loftiest culture and the lowest savagery could find a common ground. Yet when we remember how in certain Christian lands the mystic and the half-idolater live side by side, and the metaphysician can join us in worship along with the crudest of materialists, the case may perhaps not seem so inexplicable. To the intellectual Hindu there is but one God, by whatever name he may be called: impersonal, without consciousness, revealing himself in endless shapes and personalities, secretly working in every individual thing throughout the universe. The separateness of these individuals, even though they may speak of their 'selves' as independent, is Maya, illusion. When the ignorant man sets up an idol, he is trying, in his childish fashion, to form some idea of one or other of the manifestations of God. Not being educated, men perforce make God like themselves, or like something they see around them: this is their weakness, for which we must make allowance. According to the disposition of the intellectual Hindu will be his attitude to these more feeble brethren. It may be pitying, it may be an intellectual interest, it may be – as it has been called – contemptuous accommodation; or it may even be pride in the liberality of a religion which can find room for so many varieties by virtue of its all-embracing charity.

A few words are necessary on the SIKH sect, which may be regarded either as a reformed Brahmanism or as a separate religion. It is, in any case, one of the most remarkable of all Indian creeds. It was started by Kabir, a Mohammedan by origin, about 1500. He is, like so many other religious leaders, said to have been born of a virgin. Feeling dissatisfied with Moslem bigotry, he became a Hindu of the Vishnu persuasion, but carried over the monotheism and the hatred of idolatry of Islam into his new faith. Thus he formed an eclectic religion, combining, in a way the reader will now fully understand, pantheism with the oneness of God, and mingling a God who has will and personality with the God who is, so to speak, Nothing and Everything at once. He claimed no more for himself than the Socratic wisdom of a searcher: and he constantly urged his 'Sikhs' or disciples to test the truth of his words. Some indeed hardly need testing – they appeal to all: 'When the blind lead the blind, both will fall into the well. All can see a drop fall into the ocean; few know that the drop and the ocean are one. There are many words: take the pith of them.'

He was followed by one of his Sikhs, called Nanak, who was almost the exact contemporary of Erasmus and Luther. Around Nanak also myth has gathered: at his birth all the gods assembled in the sky and proclaimed that a great teacher was born that day. A great teacher (Guru) he certainly was, and, like other great teachers, he was a learner. A Hindu, he studied Mohammedanism, and proclaimed the singleness of God, who may be called God, Allah, or Vishnu, but is always the same: Nanak preferred to call him by one of Vishnu's many names, Hari. He aimed at reconciling Hindu with Moslem by getting rid of caste, superstition, and idolatry, while retaining the Pantheistic ideas of the higher Vishnuism. There is no creation – the universe is an expression of God; all things are one with him, and it is only Maya or Illusion that makes us think otherwise. Yet Nanak retains some childish superstitions – the repetition of the name of Hari will secure salvation, and is the only means of escaping the miseries of metempsychosis. So long as the

Sikhs merely proclaimed spiritual ideas, the Emperors left them alone, and there was something in their religion which was likely to appeal in particular to such a ruler as Akbar, who was, as is well known, desirous of forming a religion which should reconcile Hindu and Mohammedan. Thus a succession of Gurus or Teachers was able to continue the work without molestation for some years after Nanak's death in 1538. They were able to establish the great Sikh centre at Amritsar, which became a rallying-ground for the community, and they were further bound together by the compilation of the Granth, or Sikh Bible, and by the organization which the Guru Arjun gave to the hitherto isolated bands. It was not till the reign of the fanatical Mussulman, Aurungzbe, that the hatred between Sikh and Moslem became marked, and that the movement put on that military character which has marked it ever since. The Guru Govind was driven to make himself a warrior. To strengthen his armies he abolished caste; and to signalize their bravery they were to add Singh or Lion to their names. Like the Achaeans, they were to wear their hair long, and like the Templars they were admitted to the Order by a special rite: for they were to engage in a perpetual crusade against Islam. No Sikh must turn his back in battle; a new Granth was issued with the pacific sentences of Nanak left out, which was even personified and called Sahib. Large deductions were made from the Hinduism retained by Kabir and Nanak, and Sikhism became totally severed from its parent-stem.[1] The Punjaub was practically turned into a camp of religious warriors, and war became the real Sikh religion. To the desperate force which this religion gave to the nation our own army can bear eloquent testimony. And yet such is the absorbing power of Hinduism that it has all but reconquered the lost ground. Thousands of Sikhs now wear the Brahmanical badge, keep Hindu festivals, and worship Hindu idols: indeed it is difficult for any but the most enlightened to go to an assembly at Amritsar and not fancy he

1. Retaining, however, the idea of the sanctity of the cow – indeed to kill a cow was worse than murder.

is in a lovelier Benares. Hinduism is, as the air, invulnerable, and the sword-strokes of Sikh fighters are but malicious mockery.

As to the Jains, though one of the most interesting and widespread of Hindu religions, an even shorter notice must suffice. These too, like the Sikhs, are regarded as heretics by the Brahmans, but they are perhaps best regarded as independent, though their religion certainly has its roots in Brahmanism. Founded by Vardhamana about five centuries before Christ, it rejects the authority of the Vedas, modifies the doctrine of transmigration by asserting that saintliness of life secures immortality immediately after death, abolishes whole hosts of Brahman deities, and even despises caste-distinctions. Their sacred books – the Agamas – proclaim these doctrines freely; and their twenty-four immortal saints largely take the place of the deities: it is indeed maintained by some that Jainism is practically monotheistic; but, as so often in Eastern religions, the language of the books on this point is ambiguous.

In many respects Vardhamana approximated to his contemporary Buddha: like him he parted company with Brahmanism, and like him maintained the sacredness of all life: even insects must not be killed, and the plants must be regarded as the brothers of mankind. But there are also marked differences, particularly in his conception of Nirvana, the ultimate repose of the saints.[1]

1. I cannot forbear quoting here, as an expression of higher Hindu thought, a few words from Mulk Raj Anand's *Hindu View of Art*:
'The lofty idealism of its original impulse may have become coated with a thick crust of mendacity and superstition, but I believe that the truth conceived by the sages of ancient Hindu thought and practised by their followers during the ages is in the blood of India. . . . If it does not come out in its purity and strength today, if it has been polluted by the accretions of wrong thinking . . . it will emerge intact one day when Indians search within their hearts for the truth, or lifting the veil of sensualism and materialism . . . look for it in the soil of India. For Hindu idealism is not only in the blood of India, it is also in the soil of India. . . . Was it not India's vast expanses . . . and the deep immensity of its forests, that evoked from the ancient sages the gospel of the Veda and the Vedanta, of Buddhism and Jainism, and of the Ramavana and the

We now turn to BUDDHISM itself, which demands a fuller survey.

The difficulties a Western mind has to overcome if it is to understand Buddhism are very great. First, the basic ideas of the system are not ours: the intellectual landscape is as different from that to which we are accustomed as the Himalayas from the Sussex downs. Again – what is another aspect of the same thing – the phrases in which Buddhism clothes its thought scarcely ever admit of exact translation into other languages. Thus, for example, the two words which are perhaps central in the doctrine, *dharma* and *karma*, each demand at least three or four English words to cover their full connotation: *dharma* includes right, good, law, system, and *karma* is work, function, doing, making. Thirdly, though the Buddhist writers certainly aim at precision, and to a large extent attain it, yet they, like other philosophers, cannot help accommodating themselves, at times, to conventional modes of thought. To them, for instance, there is no such thing as a permanent self;[1] all is

---

Mahabharata? ... A few at least of India's men and women still know the Truth and worship it. These are the real and genuine Indians who live in the poor little villages and humble towns ... greeting the bright sun at dawn with sweet Rig-Vedic hymns, or ... crowding the corridors of their temples when, their day's work finished, they go to offer formal prayers to the Deity whose name has been on their lips all day.'

Mr Anand's book, which seeks to explain Indian art as the expression of Indian religious feeling, gives an admirable, though too brief, account of Hindu religion as an ideal.

1. Here, at once, we meet with doubt; for there are some scholars, and those perhaps the best, who hold that Buddhism does not deny permanence to the *true* Soul or Ego: it is the phenomenal or illusory Ego that has no real permanence or identity. Some of the apparent contradictions in Buddhist philosophy may be due to the failure, in reader or writer or both, to keep clear in the mind this distinction between the illusory and the real: what is true of the one may be false of the other.

Thus it is hard to see that an entity which is *already* non-existent can *attain* Nirvana: and there are many other doctrines which can be understood only when we keep this distinction – between the phenomenal and the real – carefully before us. In my opinion, which I give for what it is worth, not only European, but some Asiatic interpreters, have sometimes failed in this regard.

eternally changing; yet they cannot help speaking of 'I' and 'me' in the ordinary fashion. They believe in some sort of transmigration of souls, and yet there is no Buddhist word for the soul or self in our sense of a personal and individual entity: the word we have to translate by soul may perhaps be rendered better by 'disposition' or 'tone of life'. Nor is the 'soul' in one incarnation the same thing as the soul in another. 'Nirvana', the final absorption of the saint, is usually rendered 'annihilation' or 'nonentity'; but there is no doubt that, at least in some Buddhist theories, it carried with it an idea of actual experienced happiness. To all these difficulties is added that which Buddhism has in common with all religions: it has vastly modified the doctrine of its Founder, it has annexed much from other systems, and it is at the present moment shedding some ideas, adopting others, and silently changing all. Like Christianity, it has practically ceased to exist in its native home, and its transference to a country so different from India as China has inevitably meant that it has put on a new character in accordance with its new nationality.

We must, then, be content here to give a rough and general outline of this extraordinary creed (if philosophy be not its more appropriate title), amazingly interesting as it is, and immensely important, not only because it has more adherents than any other, but because of the influence which it has exerted on other religions, and not least on Christianity itself.

The life of Buddha is told in comparatively simple fashion in early Pali writings; but it is perhaps best known to most people from translations or paraphrases of the long poem of Asvagosha, written about the middle of the first century of our era – that is, five or six hundred years after the Master's death.[1] Much legend or myth has entered into the story, of which the poet avails himself to the full; but there is no reason to doubt that it rests on a substratum of fact. Gautama, afterwards to be one of the Buddhas, was a prince

1. We do not know Buddha's exact date: his birth may be placed between 550 and 450 B.C. Many put his death about 480.

of Northern India. His mother, Maya, 'pure as the water-lily', saw in a dream a spirit descend into her from heaven; and the Brahmans, consulted by the King her father, told him that the child to be thus miraculously born would either be ruler of the world or else, if he so chose, its Buddha or saviour. Accordingly, in the garden called Lumbini, the child was born under a fig-tree; and Maya hastened back to her father, but died almost immediately. The child was named Siddhartha, the Completion of Purposes, and was brought up as a prince, and trained in all royal duties. He was duly married to his cousin, a princess of a neighbouring kingdom, 'majestic as the Queen of Heaven, cheerful as night and day': and a son, Rahula, was born to them. But amid all this happiness, the misery of the world, and the approaching end, death, troubled him. All things hastened to decay. He longed for that which never perishes, and began to fix his thoughts not on earthly things but on Nirvana. At length, at the age of twenty-eight, he abandoned all, and went forth to seek wisdom for himself. Six years he lived on the banks of the river Nairanjana, eating each day but one grain, till life nearly departed from him. Seeing that this was not the way to gain wisdom, he changed it, and took fuller nourishment; wandering forth alone, he found the Bodhi tree, or tree of knowledge, and sat under it in meditation. Here he was sorely tempted by Mara, the spirit of sense, and all his hosts: but these tried all their arts in vain, and at length fled from him. As they flee, he falls into a trance, in which true and perfect knowledge is revealed to him, and he is thenceforth known as the Buddha, the Enlightened One, and realizes that he, like all the Buddhas who have preceded him, is sent to convert the world. From this time forward he moves from place to place, teaching the doctrine which has been revealed to him: *devas* or spirits, as well as men, listen to his words. He proclaims the 'eightfold path' to bliss: he shows that asceticism on the one hand can only give confused thought, and excess on the other is the fool's bar to enlightenment. The true way is the *via media* of temperance. Four 'sublime truths' are what is necessary and sufficient:

(1) Pain is due to the self and its desires; banish self, and pain will depart; (2) pain is a *growing* thing: unless checked by the annihilation of self, it will increase and multiply; (3) but it *can* be checked and utterly destroyed: there is no iron law of necessity that constrains men; (4) and the means by which it is destroyed is the Eightfold Way (Right Belief, Feeling, Speech, Action, Living, Effort, Memory, Meditation). The poet tells us that when Tathāgata (the 'Duly Come', for such was now his name) preached these doctrines in his first sermon, the men who heard him, and eighty thousand of the *devas*, gained enlightenment, put away all that defiled them, and 'received sight': while the earth-spirits raised a shout, 'Tathāgata hath set revolving that which never yet revolved, and hath opened the gate Amatam.'[1] Nor did the *devas* and men alone receive the gospel; all living things, which had groaned and travailed in pain till then, were stirred by the teaching and welcomed it.

After more than forty years thus spent, he was sitting in a grove of trees beside a pool of water, when Mara again visited him, and said, 'Long since, by the Nairanjana, when thou hadst attained enlightenment, thou saidst, "When I have done all that I have to do, then will I pass to Nirvana." Now thou hast done all thou hadst to do, therefore shouldst thou depart.' Then answered Buddha, 'The time of my departure is nigh; within three months I shall go hence': and Mara, rejoicing, left him. And Buddha said, 'I live now only by the power of ecstatic vision; my body is as a shattered ear.' So saying, he passed on slowly, attended by the beloved disciple Ananda, and the rest, till he reached Kusingagara. There he bade Ananda prepare his couch, which Ananda did weeping. Then Tathāgata lay down, his hand beneath his head, and his feet crossed as it were a lion-king. All is over: from this sleep he shall not rise again. Amid the utter silence of the world, while the flowers and leaves dropped mournfully, he passed away: and then the

1. Here again we have difficulty, for neither 'immortality' nor 'eternity' appears to give the meaning of 'Amatam'. It seems to imply that which neither is born nor can decay and die.

earth quaked, the sun and moon ceased to shine, the forests quivered, and the rain fell sadly to the ground.

They burned the body as men burn the bodies of kings, and the ashes were sent to eight kingdoms, each of which built a monument over its portion of the holy relics.[1]

Buddha himself left no writings. It is said that after his death a number of his disciples met together, and contributed what each could remember of the Master's teachings. These, according to Eastern fashion, were retained in the memory, and finally collected in the three 'Pitakas' or 'Baskets of Tradition', and in other sacred books, which appear to have been written about a hundred years before Christ. These were in Pali; the later documents are in Sanskrit or in the Chinese versions. There are ancient Pali commentaries or expansions, the work of Buddhaghosa and Dhammapala, dating from the fifth century A.D.; these treat the Pitakas as canonical and authoritative. But the literature now known, printed, and translated into European languages, is enormous: it must amount to hundreds of volumes. More will doubtless be published as the libraries of Burma and Siam are more thoroughly searched, and as the monasteries of Tibet are opened to the outer world.

Memory, where there are no books, is much more retentive and reliable than among peoples accustomed to taking notes. None the less, it is common, even in the East, for men to imagine they remember what they wish to remember, and this is particularly the case when a theory has to be buttressed with the authority of a beloved teacher. It can thus be seen how easily a doctrine might be inserted into the canon, with a 'Buddha said' prefixed to it. We can, however, make out with some degree of probability what were the main elements of the Master's teaching. Buddhism cer-

1. In the older records, it is said, the story is different. Buddha is not born of a royal family; no Mara tempts him before his enlightenment; he works no miracles; and he is not presented as the saviour of the world. If the growth of the legend could be traced in full, it might throw light on the way in which such stories accumulate around famous names.

tainly arose as a protest against Brahmanism. Perhaps the first and most important of its assertions is that there is no such thing as a soul: there is nothing *permanent* behind our mental states; the mind is merely a bundle of impressions. 'The world,' said Buddha, 'is empty of self; therefore it is a foolish doctrine that the so-called *I* shall live eternally.' Even the gods are without selves; they are everlastingly changing, and if they think they are immortal, there is no real *they* to think it. We cannot help talking of *ourselves*, but the true philosopher knows that this is but a way of speaking without real significance.

This is not exactly atheism: it is the very fact that the gods 'exist' which proves that they are subject to the law of eternal change. There is no such thing as 'same' and no instant at which we can catch the fleeting essence, and say, 'That is that': the god, and the man, of this instant is already different from the god or man of the last. Thus Buddha made no attack on the Brahman idea of Brahmă as an *impersonal* principle of world-order: it is when it is personified, and said to be pleased or displeased with man, that Buddha parted company with the Brahman creed. Even when it was called the world-soul Buddha would have nothing to do with it. As a result of this doctrine, paradoxically enough, Buddhism contains a most elaborate system of psychology: the sense-impressions are fully analysed. No true disciple of Buddha could dispense with this analysis; for it was solely by understanding these sense-impressions that the impermanence of the 'soul' could be fully realized: the 'soul' *is* these impressions. And, on the ethical side, man cannot control his sensuous impulses unless he knows them and discriminates them one from another. When once he has gained the perception that all is transitory, he becomes willing to resign earthly ambition and to accept with tranquillity whatever comes to him. We may sum up this theory by saying that to the Buddhist 'man is a heap of happenings': mind is an ever-flowing river, not one drop of which keeps its place for an instant; it is a vulgar error to imagine that the Ganges *is* the Ganges. It was this doctrine which

Buddha preached as a way of escape from the over-sensuous life which he saw in the people around him.

From this conception of eternal change, Buddhism naturally passes to consider what *makes* the change. It has been laid down that we must not ask *who* it is that feels; there is no *who*. But there *is* a cause, or, as it is metaphorically called, an incline, a door, a way in, an association. As water follows the slope of the ground, and does not issue a command to the next drop to follow it, so with the mind. An idea follows the slope of the mind; as we habitually walk along a street to a gate, so ideas run along a beaten path. Nothing happens unless something has happened before without which it would not have happened. Thus ignorance is the cause of action, action of consciousness, consciousness of mind and body, these of sense, and thence of desire, rebirth, decay, death, in endless succession. This is the famous Buddhist Wheel or Chain; Life, which has never begun in time, going on, dying, being reborn, and so on for ever; but all in obedience to the law of causation. It is an infinite process of coming to pass and passing away; cause producing effect, and the effect in turn becoming cause. Acquiescence in this law is the first necessity of the man who would be truly free. A saying ascribed to Buddha illustrates this conception in picturesque manner. 'If a man should desire to cross a brimming river, and should say, O further bank, come over to this side, would the bank, by reason of the man's praying and praising, come over to him?' Even so do the Brahmans who invoke Indra or Brahma err; for things are as they are, and will be what they will be: it is our duty neither to rebel nor to pray, but to *consent*.

Every act, then, brings its natural consequence. There is, in a sense, no reward, no punishment: it is no reward for the acorn to become an oak, no punishment for the leaf to decay and fall. 'According to the seed that is sown, so is the fruit; the doer of good will reap good, the doer of evil evil: the seed is sown, and thou shalt taste its fruit.' This is the law of karma: the great rule of the universe: the '*bija-niyama*', or order of seeds. The law applies as much to con-

scious actions as to the process by which a rice-seed produces rice. Thus – to use a rough Western paraphrase –
Buddhist morals are utilitarian. 'Dost thou wish, Rahula,'
says Buddha to his son, 'to do a deed? Bethink thee, will
that deed tend to thy harm, or mine, or that of others? If so,
do it not. Will it bring good to thee, to me, or to others? If
so, do it.' Karma, or action, affects not merely other actions,
but the doer – in a *natural* way. Beings are owners of their
deeds, they are heirs of their works; their works are their
mothers' wombs, their children, their fathers, their inheri-
tors: nay, the works we did in a former incarnation are bearing their fruits now; what we were makes us what we are –
or rather, what the imaginary 'we' is at this instant becoming. Yet it is necessary to avoid the conception that what
another did *we* are feeling: the succession and change is the
evolution of *one* individual who is yet never the same; he is
marked off from others as the Ganges is marked off from the
Indus. But what the Ganges is at Calcutta is decided by
what he is at his source. 'Neither the same, nor another':
'I teach,' said Buddha, 'the mean between two extremes.'[1]
The illustration used by some of the later Buddhists, who
deny transmigration in the strict sense, and yet allow rebirth, is that of a lamp lit from another lamp: the new light
is *born* from the old, but the old has not migrated into it. Or,
still more subtly, when an idea is conveyed from master to
pupil, the idea is *born anew* in the pupil, but has not trans-
migrated. None the less, it has 'passed across', and any admixture of truth or error there was in the teacher's idea will
pass into the mind of the disciple, and bear its good or evil
fruit.

Thus, despite appearances, the convinced Buddhist feels
an almost stronger motive impelling him to good deeds than
the adherent of any other religion. Recognizing that his

1. That the Buddhists *must* use terms like *I* and *self* while denying their
validity has been compared to the astronomer's habit of saying 'the sun
sets' and the like: but the fact is that the astronomer *can* speak scientifically, while no manipulation of language will enable the Buddhist to
avoid question-begging terms.

present state is the result of an infinite series of acts and dispositions in the past, and that what he does in this life will have repercussions through an infinite series in the future, he strives so to regulate his conduct that the sum of future evil may be diminished and the sum of future good may be increased. A being[1] who, in a sense, is 'himself', is to be born, whose career will be modified for good or ill by his behaviour: he can by no means release himself from the invisible chains which tie him to that being, or from the obligation to save him anxiety and pain. To employ a Western parallel, he is like a father who desires to give his son a good start in life.

It was thus that, without inconsistency, Buddha could proclaim his five practical precepts: kill not, nor slay the lowest of creatures; it may be struggling upward to a higher existence: Give cheerfully, and receive gladly, but take nothing from anybody by force or fraud: Bear not false witness, the lie defiles the inward man:[2] Shun all intoxicating drinks, for these dull and bewilder the mind: Avoid all sins of the flesh, touch not the wife of thy neighbour. They who keep these laws have their feet upon the first rung of the ladder; and they who break them cannot even begin the ascent, nay, they will compel their successors to begin the climb from a lower level. It has been, and will be disputed whether Buddhism is a *religion* in the sense of a reverential fear of the divine; but it cannot be denied that, with all its

1. I need not say that the Buddhist philosophy avoids, as far as possible, the word Being (atthita) and substitutes Becoming (bhava): it shuns *est* and says *fit*.

2. This phrase, 'the inward man', which I take from certain translations, seems to me to be, probably, scarcely satisfactory, seeing that Buddhism would not recognize an inner self. Possibly better would be something like this, 'the lie defiles the ever-flowing stream of mind, as a fragment of mud defiles the Ganges, which yet is never the same.' Similarly with the word 'mind' just below.

We do not notice that Hume, to whom as to Buddha, the mind was nothing but an endless succession of 'impressions', found himself incapable of developing a moral philosophy: nor, though dubious as to Self, was F. H. Bradley unable to lay down principles adapted to social life.

metaphysical subtlety, it is a system of social ethics, taught not merely by direct commands but by the example of its Founder: it is indeed that example, as shown in innumerable anecdotes, which gives it its imperishable charm.

Having thus got rid of a personal soul, Buddhism inevitably also dispensed with gods, at least with the sort of gods recognized by the crude Brahmanism which Buddha saw around him. The wheel of nature turns without a maker, without a watcher. There is not even that sort of ' Pre-established Harmony' which Leibniz postulated to explain the apparent reign of law in the world; for there is no ' establisher', and no time before in which the harmony could be determined. The universe has no beginning and no end; cause, effect, cause, effect, work out their will-less way from eternity to eternity. This has led to the assertion that Buddhism is atheistic; that, as has been said, it substitutes cosmism for theism. But here again, as I have hinted above, it seems to me that uncompromising dogmatism is impossible, and that European phrases fail to express the full meaning of the Asiatic. At any rate, whatever be Buddha's esoteric doctrine, he allows for the weakness of the uninitiated, and here and there uses words which seem to involve accommodation to the ordinary view. Thus in one place – and probably here we light on his own words – he compares life to a stormy river, which the traveller essays to cross by means of a raft. The river once crossed, he abandons the raft. This apparently implies that the belief in God, and even the laws of ethics, are useful means to transitory ends, but should be discarded as soon as those ends are attained. Evil (*drukka*), in all its forms, may be entirely overcome, and finally *ignored*, by the saint, and when once overcome will leave him with neither the idea of morality nor that of immorality, neither with theism nor with atheism: these distractions will fret him no longer; he is in one sense in a state between them, in another sense far above them. As in the Brahman cosmogony, before the worlds there was neither light nor darkness, so in this transcendental world. This state may be confused with utter apathy, and has been variously appraised by scholars according to their different points of view. To some it appears a dull and despairing acquiescence in evil, an utter pessimism, and a sad contrast to the cheerfulness inculcated by Christianity and often attained by Christians. To others it appears more as serenity, the calmness of the man who has gained the victory over his desires. There is no doubt that Buddha emphasized the existence of evil in the world, and made it the starting-point of his whole philosophy: he would have nothing to do with the doctrine that evil is a *mere* negation: and so strongly did he emphasize it that many have seen nothing else in his religion. But he also emphasizes the possibility of suppressing evil. Evil arises from natural cosmic causes: suppress the causes, and the evil vanishes. All evil was due to the 'karma' of our past lives; in our present life we must follow the right path, and we shall at least make progress towards ridding the world of the evil that besets it. No one would say that Christianity was a pessimistic religion because a great Pope could write a *De miseria conditionis humanae*, in which the horrors of this world are pictured with unsurpassed force, in order to induce us to fix our thoughts and hopes on the next. The same purpose inspired Buddha and his early followers. In one aspect he was more optimistic than many European teachers. So far from asserting that to travel is better than to arrive, he declared that attainment is possible, and that when we have attained we are satisfied, and abide in a state of content without monotony. This state is variously termed Arahatta (the man who has reached it is an Arahant), Anna or knowledge, and Nirvana. By four stages we approach, and finally gain, this consummation. Some reach the Stream, down which they no longer drift, but of which they are the masters. Others are in the last incarnation but one; they will return to life once more only. Others are the Never-returners; this is their last sojourn in the vale of tears. Finally there are the Arahants. This ultimate, Nirvana, is the putting out of the fire of life. From one side it is mere extinction. From another it is the putting out of the fires of desire, of hatred, of illusion. But such extinction

might, by an opposite metaphor, be equally well figured as
the lighting of a candle which shall never be put out. It is
emancipation, which may be thought of as the negation of
imprisonment or as the fullness of a free existence. In one
place it is called health – and health is something more
than the simple absence of disease: elsewhere it is called
enlightenment, which is not the mere negation of ignorance.

Thus the saintly Buddhist, though he has often to express
his feelings by the use of negative terms, reveals clearly that
he has realized something active, positive, direct, and blissful. His language is – allowance being made for Eastern
modes of thought – exactly like that of Western mysticism.
But we must remember that to the Eastern mind the rigid
distinctions familiar to us carry no weight. It can conceive
a state between being and not-being, neither life nor death:
and it can conceive a state of bliss which, if we should try
to describe it, would appear as hardly to be discriminated
from annihilation. Thus in one poem Buddha speaks of Nirvana as the *destruction* of death: in another he calls it
oblivion. Perhaps we may best represent it as a condition
neither mental nor bodily, out of time and out of space, but
none the less real because it falls into no category expressible
in words. It is the final contradiction, the union of opposites,
at which all metaphysic ultimately arrives.

To reach this consummation the Buddhist system of discipline proposes a threefold training: the *sila* or higher
ethics, in which the novice practises the morality enjoined
in the Five Rules; meditation, which leads to tranquillity of
mind; and thirdly, knowledge of the causes of evil and of the
way by which it can be made to cease. In other words, social
life, solitary thought, philosophical study.

Buddhism made great progress in India during some centuries, but it was finally in part absorbed, in part expelled.
But about 200 B.C. there began to be frequent, if tedious and
difficult, intercourse between India and China, and –
largely indirectly through the barbarous tribes of the North-
West – Buddhism penetrated into the Celestial Empire. We

hear of the king of one of these tribes, Kanishka, as becoming a Buddhist; and in the first century of our era it is clear that reports of the religion had spread about the Empire. At any rate the Emperor Ming-ti, about A.D. 60, is said to have had a dream which was interpreted by one of his ministers as meaning that there was a divine person of India called Buddha; and Ming-ti accordingly sent a mission to inquire about this person. The mission collected sacred books, and, in company with two Buddhist priests, returned in safety to China. There, according to the tale, a number of miracles convinced the Emperor of the truth of their message. The two priests, after learning the language, translated the books, including a Life of Buddha, into Chinese. Then began a great missionary movement, which lasted for hundreds of years; men, stirred with the desire to convert the world, poured into China, preaching, writing, translating. By A.D. 335 it is said that more than forty monasteries had been built in the capital city of Lo-yang: the search for real or imaginary relics of Buddha was incessant and the progress of the religion was rapid. Inevitably all this provoked hostility from the dominant Confucianism. There were many persecutions, hardly less violent than those which the Christians suffered under the Roman Empire. In the eighth century thousands of priests were compelled to return to ordinary life; in the ninth, nearly fifty thousand monasteries were suppressed and their property confiscated. But the persecutions failed, and as soon as the zeal of the persecutors waned, the advance began once more. There are some who believe that in the reign of Kublai Khan (about 1280) an actual majority of the Chinese people were Buddhists. About 1660 the Emperor issued an edict against them, and the religion was forbidden; but the edict, though periodically read in the cities for two centuries, remained in effect a dead letter. From China the religion was carried to Japan; and though, as we have seen, it was driven out of India proper, it has never ceased to flourish in Ceylon, Burma, and Siam.

As may be expected, transplantation to another soil has

had a vast influence upon the creed; and the Chinese form of Buddhism shows many points of difference not merely from the original teachings of Buddha himself, but from the later Indian developments. It is impossible to mention even a fraction of these sects and divisions; but some account is necessary of the most important and remarkable of all – the LAMAISM of Tibet, which is, to many, the very type of Buddhist orthodoxy.

Even before A.D. 600, when Buddhism began to penetrate into Tibet, the central doctrines of the creed had been perverted. The conception of a saving Buddha who reappears at intervals of five thousand years as a *man*, and who by successive reincarnations had gained perfection, was being vulgarized into that of a phantom, hovering in the interspace between earth and heaven, attended by a host of demonic beings. The discipline imposed by Buddha on his followers, the necessity of conversion by means of meditation, study, and philosophy, had largely given place to a formal monasticism and sacerdotalism, which substituted ritual action for sancity of life and thought. This degeneration has, since the religion established itself in Tibet, greatly advanced, doubtless in some measure through contact with the original Tibetan demon-worship, which indeed for a time succeeded in banishing Buddhism from the country or driving it underground. Such Buddhists as remained appear to have conformed to the dominant cult. When the religion returned, although persecution had revived many of its virtues, it could not escape contamination. In the fifteenth and sixteenth centuries the metamorphosis into Lamaism was complete.

In this, the religion has become a polity. The Dalai Lama, who is the reincarnated Buddha of India, is at once King and High Priest; Pope and Emperor in one. He rules despotically in both civil and religious affairs. Under him is an ordered series of spiritual officers, ending with the monks. The country is a vast 'State of the Church': it is said that one man in every six or seven is a monk; and the whole force of the State is directed towards obtaining the revenues which maintain the monasteries and the church-offices. How far Lamaism has departed from the original Buddhism is shown by the fact that when the Dalai Lama dies, and his successor is elected, he in turn becomes a Buddha. At the same time, though the oppression of such a government was severely felt, the prestige of the Lama, and of the holy city of Lhasa, was so great that, despite the rigid seclusion of the land – which, till recently, only a few daring travellers from other countries ever penetrated – Lama-ist influence, more or less attenuated, was felt in remote parts of China, and even in Southern India.

There is no doubt that both monachism and coenobitism are in harmony with the spirit of Buddha, who not only knew the value of solitude as an aid to meditation, but permitted certain of his pupils, who found the stress of life too great for them, to withdraw from the world; but there is no way of living which more easily degenerates and forgets its ideal: and it is to be feared that Buddhist monasticism is no exception. No one can foresee the future; but it is likely that if Buddhism is to survive, either some Benedict must arise to reform the monastic rule, or some new incarnation of Buddha must appear to enlighten the world and to send forth a band of disciples as devoted as those who followed Siddhartha two millenniums and a half ago.

Buddhism is, and will probably yet be for some time, best known to Englishmen through Edwin Arnold's poem *The Light of Asia*. Arnold, of course, as becomes a poet, does not endeavour to sift legend from true history in his narrative of the Life; but in his sketch of the doctrine, vast as is the amount of knowledge accumulated since his day, he has probably caught the essential points. Thus, for example, in the Eighth Book we read:

> *Ye who will tread the Middle Road, whose course*
> *Bright Reason traces and soft Quiet soothes,*
> *Ye who will take the high Nirvana way,*
> *List the Four Noble Truths.*

The First Truth is of Sorrow. *Be not mocked!*
Life which ye prize is long-drawn agony:
Only its pains abide; its pleasures are
        As birds which light and fly.
The Second Truth is Sorrow's Cause. *What grief*
Springs of itself and springs not of Desire?
Senses and things perceived mingle and light
        Passion's quick spark of fire.
The Third is Sorrow's Ceasing. *This is peace,*
To conquer love of self and lust of life,
To tear deep-rooted passion from the breast,
        To still the inward strife.
The Fourth Truth is The Way. *It openeth wide,*
Plain for all feet to tread, easy and near,
The Noble Eightfold Path; *it goeth straight*
        To peace and refuge. Hear!

There is no sharper contrast in history than that between
Gautama and his contemporary CONFUCIUS (Kung-fu-tse,
the Master-King). The system of Buddha was based on
transcendental metaphysics; Confucius was the least metaphysical of men. Buddha was original; there is hardly a saying of Confucius that is not confessedly borrowed. Buddha
worked by influencing individuals, whose personal conversion was his first aim; the method of Confucius was to reform the governments, in whose power to promote the
happiness of their subjects he put a trust which was quite
pathetic, and which resisted the most crushing disappointments. A student of history, looking back into the far past,
he fancied he had found a golden age, in which he traced all
the prosperity of the people to the virtues of the Emperors
Yao and Shun. This golden age he hoped to restore by inducing the rulers of his own day to imitate those Emperors.
It is as if, in the time of the Wars of the Roses, a philosopher
had urged Richard III to follow the example of Edward
the Confessor. Yet the writings of Confucius, having by
imperial authority been made into a combination of
Scripture and the classics, and having become the sole

subject[1] of study for those who desire political advancement, have profoundly influenced the thought and conduct of hundreds of millions of people during more than two thousand years.

The life of Confucius is thus, by the nature of the case, a more exact exemplification of his theories than that of any other philosophical teacher. It is as if Plato, instead of lecturing to pupils, had gone from court to court endeavouring to persuade princes to act up to the precepts of the *Republic*. One such experiment was enough for Plato: but Confucius never tired of passing from dukedom to dukedom, or of accepting State offices in which he might put his theories into practice. 'That is good government,' said he, 'when the prince is prince, and the minister is minister.' Never was man more sanguine. 'Let a prince employ me,' he declared, 'and in a twelvemonth much would be done; in three years the government would be perfected.'

He was born in 551 B.C., the son of a distinguished soldier and politician, who had been childless till the age of seventy, and who therefore (for childlessness is the worst of evils to a Chinaman)[2] celebrated the birth of the boy with great rejoicings. Miracles, of course, were in later years remembered to have accompanied the appearance of the sage on earth. We may leave these on one side. As he grew up, he showed great devotion to learning, and particularly to the study of history. At nineteen he married, but his marriage was not a happy one, and shortly after the birth of a son[3] he divorced his wife. Hence in part, perhaps, the low opinion of women which he always expresses.

While still very young, he was appointed keeper of the stores of grain, and later, controller of the public fields. It

1. With them are included the works of Mencius (Mang-tse), who, two hundred years later, developed the Master's doctrine, and enjoys an authority second only to his.

2. The performance of due funeral rites, and that by a son, is a necessity to the Chinese.

3. The son, Le by name, does not seem to have received much affection from his father.

Descendants of Confucius are said to be still living in Shan-tung.

was doubtless through these public offices that he became so rapidly known. We find him, at twenty-two, attracting to him a considerable number of pupils, and welcomed at the court of the prince of Chow (the 'Middle Kingdom'). It was here that he met Lao-tse, who was at that time treasurer of the realm.

A word is here necessary on this remarkable man. He is said to have been fifty years older than Confucius; and he had already formulated his religious scheme, which is that known as TAOISM, and which is still, in a degenerate state, one of the great Eastern creeds. As this creed is highly meta-physical – *Tao* is 'Ultimate and Unconditioned Being' – and is in fact as transcendental as Buddhism itself, it is not sur-prising that Confucius found Lao-tse the most uncom-promising of his critics. 'You talk,' said the old sage, 'of your admiration of the ancients. These men have mouldered into dust; all your historical knowledge is vain and empty. Resign your study; cultivate virtue and seek Tao: learn that talk breeds only confusion of mind; enter on that way which can never be forgotten.' Shortly after this, Lao-tse resigned his office, for he foresaw that the state of Chow was beyond redemption, and went into retirement to meditate still more deeply on the nature of Tao.[1]

---

1. The subsequent history of Taoism is instructive; for it is that of all religions, and not least of those which start from metaphysical premisses. Having learnt from Brahmanism, Lao-tse taught that Tao was impalp-able, invisible, inexpressible in words. But it can be attained by virtue – through compassion, thrift, and humility. Violence is the sure way to fail of attainment: out of weakness comes true strength. There is no personal God: such gods as men imagine are mere emanations of Tao, which gives life to all things. Demons and spirits, if they exist at all, are subject to him who follows Tao. Works are valueless; one act of internal resignation out-weighs a hundred thousand deeds that follow from our own will. Non-existence is better than existence, the inner man infinitely better than the outer. As for our relations with others, they are summed up in the one word benevolence: 'Recompense to none evil for evil: repay evil with good': 'Forgo much, take little': 'Sorrow over the sorrows of others, and rejoice with them when they fare well': 'Do good, expecting no return': 'Give cheerfully': 'Pity the orphan, and compassionate the widow': these are but a few of the maxims in which Taoism need fear no com-

Though Confucius was not convinced by Lao-tse, he yet owned that in his presence he felt the dominance of a master-mind. 'I know how birds fly,' said he, 'how fishes swim, and how beasts run. But I cannot tell how the dragon mounts on the winds and rises into the heavens. One can snare the beast, and hook the fish, and shoot the bird with an arrow. But Lao-tse is the dragon; him I cannot overcome.' It may have been the memory of this conversation that strengthened the peculiar humility characteristic of him. For though his whole system rested on the doing of good works, and though he was conscious of his own merits, yet he appraised them with a certain disinterestedness, listened modestly when his own pupils questioned his behaviour, and always ranked himself below the ancient sages.

Returning from Chow to his native Lu, he soon found himself at the head of a large band of disciples – it is said three thousand in number. But the times were singularly unfavourable to a philosopher. China was then the prey of anarchy. Not only was it split up into a multitude of princi-palities, but almost all the principalities were torn by the quarrels of clans and warlords. In Lu there were three of these clans, which, after long and desultory fighting, sud-denly patched up a reconciliation, united their forces, at-tacked Chaou the reigning prince, defeated him, and drove him to take refuge in the neighbouring State of T'se, where the ruler received him hospitably. Confucius followed his lord into exile, and endeavoured to impress his theories on the ruler of T'se. Meanwhile the victorious factions of Lu

---

parison even with Christianity itself. Lao-tse allowed no shrines, no images: there was in his system no room for idolatry, and little enough even for worship. Yet no religion fell more rapidly into the depths of superstition. He himself was the first deity to be adored – and as a Trinity, each of the three persons having an idol. Next came Shang-te, the Supreme God; then star-worship, thunder-worship, the cult of seas and tides, the adoration of gods of learning, of domestic services, of a thousand deities of every kind, whose number is ever increasing. Soldiers worship the god of war; nay, some Taoists adore Confucius himself. Lao-tse certainly would not recognize his own religion if he could return and see it.

fought for the spoils among themselves, while the unhappy commons, like the Greeks of old, were ground in misery through the madness of the chiefs. It was not for some time that Ting, the head of one of the contending clans, was able to restore some semblance of order. When Chaou died in exile, the position of Ting was greatly strengthened, and Confucius returned to Lu, where Ting offered him the post of Minister of Crime. The Platonic scheme was now put into practice: the philosopher was, if not actually a king, yet a ruler; and, if we are to believe the story, the success of the experiment was complete. There was no crime, from the day of Confucius's appointment, in the whole country of Lu. Yet this can hardly be literally the case; for we hear that Confucius had to try a lawsuit brought by a father against his son; and that he settled it by throwing both into prison, the son for his unfilial conduct and the father for having failed to bring the lad up properly. 'Had you trained him in the way he should go,' said he, 'he would never have behaved in this wicked manner.' At another time he put a man named Shaou to death for disturbing the public peace.

A curious idea of his was that people are led by example. If therefore the ruler sets a good example, his subjects will follow it: a naïve belief which was not always justified by the event. But it accounts perhaps for the punctiliousness with which, all through his life, he insisted on ceremonial observance, which was regulated by the most rigid etiquette. To the prince he behaved with subservience, speaking to him in low tones, and trembling as if the sight of majesty was too much for him. To his equals he spoke freely but always politely; to his inferiors he bore himself with lofty courtesy: and he imposed similar observances on others. So only, he thought, could authority be maintained, and the due subordination of ranks be kept up. But he found it impossible to induce the prince himself to assume the dignity befitting the highest post. Ting, surrounded by dancing-girls, gave himself up to frivolous pleasures; the example of the court was not one which the people could follow with credit; and Confucius at last left Ting to his own devices.

This failure, however, did not daunt him, nor did he for a moment waver in his conviction that if he could but gain full authority for a year or two social evils would cease from the land. He went imperturbably on, trying prince after prince, never succeeding in getting the employment he desired, but always hopeful. From Lu he went to Wei, where the ruler received him kindly, and gladly heard his discourses, but consistently refused to treat him as a practical statesman. From Wei he journeyed to the town of Kwang, where he nearly lost his life; from Kwang back to Wei; thence to Ch'ing, where he was received 'like a stray dog', thence to Ch'in, and so, after months of travelling, to Wei once more. Men would listen to him, and consult him, but his advice they would never take. Weary at last, he settled down in retirement in his native country of Lu, and blessed himself with the composition of the *Spring and Autumn Annals*. According to legend, he had been warned by the reappearance of a unicorn or 'K'e-lin', which had appeared before at his birth, that his time was short. He therefore desired to leave behind him some written memorials; and he presented the *Annals* to his followers saying, 'By these I shall be known, and by these I shall be judged.' They are a history of the principality of Lu: he had returned in his old age to the passion of his youth.

One day, in the year 478, he was overheard by his faithful disciple Tse-Kung murmuring, 'The great mountain must crumble, the strong beam must break, and the wise man withers like a plant.' Tse-Kung hurried into the house after him, and Confucius told him of a dream he had had, presaging his death. Characteristically enough, he added that the dream had had to do with the funeral rites of former ages – the love of ceremonial was strong in him. That day he took to his bed, and within a week he died. He was buried to the north of the capital city of Lu, on the banks of the river Sze, where his tomb is still shown. His followers mourned for him for three years – the beloved disciple Tse-

Kung for six, drinking, as he said, of his master's wisdom as a man drinks of a river, not knowing its depth.

Confucius, as we have said, was not an original teacher. All his works, except the *Annals*, were compilations from the sayings of his predecessors. The *Analects*, the *Great Learning*, and the *Doctrine of the Mean*, which his grandson is said to have put together, are all the 'passings-on' of the known teachings of earlier sages. Nor indeed did he claim to be himself a sage; he even modestly declined the title of 'Higher man', though he aimed at acting as 'Higher men' ought to act.

The sage is he who is born to perfect purity, and to whom knowledge comes directly: he is at once the Abyss and the equal of heaven. Thirteen only were recognized as sages; Confucius was added to the list, but not by himself, nor till after his death. A sage, through the charm of his nature, draws men after him, and adds his power to that of earth and heaven so as to shape their destiny. He is a river of pure and living water, refreshing whatever it touches.

Next to the sages are those who, not having intuition or inspired knowledge, yet learn, and so attain to knowledge. Some are apt students, and learn easily and quickly; others, though dull, struggle and contrive to learn. Lowest of all are those who never learn.

It is Destiny that decides to which class a man shall belong: and Destiny is but another name for Nature, which sends forth Life in all its forms. Thus prayer is unnecessary; for man, having once received his destiny, can demand from Nature, and receive from it, that which he chooses: his own will, his own efforts, determine all things.

Between heaven and man is the army of spirits and demons: and these, from time immemorial, had been worshipped. Among them were the spirits of the dead; and the worship of these Confucius took over from the common beliefs and customs of his countrymen. Particularly did he permit the cult of the spirits of their ancestors, who still took interest in the affairs of their children: and, right down to the end of the Empire, the Emperors regularly consulted the spirits of their fathers when any important decision was to be taken. But Confucius was not inclined to emphasize the necessity of this worship: his mind was set on earthly things. 'Reverence the spirits,' said he, 'but keep them far off. As to serving them, how, if you know not to serve men, can you serve their ghosts?' Similarly, he would have no worship of Shang-te, the ancient supreme God, whom he hardly ever mentions, and whom he waters down into a mere impersonal heaven. To him the example of the sages was sufficient for guidance in the path of virtue: no divine help was needed.[1]

The most frequent, and the most characteristic utterances of Confucius are those which deal with the 'Higher Man' – the class below the sage. It does not appear that he found this conception – at least fully developed – in earlier teachings: in any case he was the first to draw it out clearly. Unlike the Sage, this Man does not know intuitively nor do right without effort; but he *learns*, and he makes himself righteous. As we have seen, Confucius did not regard himself as having fully attained to this stature. 'These marks of the Higher Man,' said he, 'I do not claim to possess: I have not fully learned to serve my father as I would have my son serve me; to serve my elder brother as I would have my younger brother serve me; to behave to my friend as I would have him behave to me.' The Higher Man is ever aiming at making himself better; when he fails, he is like the archer[2] who, having missed the target, studies to find where and how he went wrong. But the chief point about him is that he cultivates himself in order to give peace to the people: both by example and by service he strives to raise the commonalty, to enlarge their minds, to elevate their souls, and to relieve the hardships of their lot. Few indeed

1. But the worship of Shang-te could not be rooted out: he still remains, if not the object of the commonest worship – *that* is always the cult of ancestors – yet the object of the highest devotion. He has the noblest temples, and his service is the most splendid.

2. We are told that, in earlier years, Confucius spent much time in the practice of archery.

can be sages, but to become a Higher Man is within the power of all who will make the effort and carry through the needful training.

The training consists in study. If a man does not learn to play in tune, said Confucius, drawing an image from his favourite science of music, he can never make beautiful harmony: if he does not study colour, he can never dress with propriety. But learning without thought is wasted labour, as thought without learning is dangerous. Mere meditation is utterly vain: the thoughts must be nourished on the works of the ancient sages – thus only can substance be given on which the mind can duly exercise itself.

The first object of study is truth, and truth involves the accurate knowledge of one's own faults. Here again the sages must be studied; for by comparing oneself with them one learns the imperfections of one's own nature, and is prepared to begin the task of amendment. Thus of all studies that of history is the most important; Confucius himself attained his virtue by contemplating the lives of early kings, their laws, and their conduct: it was thus that he knew the 'destinies of heaven'. When you know a thing, said he to his pupils, hold that you know it; when you do not know it, confess your ignorance. Thus at last a man becomes 'four-square to all the winds that blow', or, in the homelier language of the sages, he stands firm like a chair with four strong and equal legs.

With knowledge must go (here Confucius is anticipating St Paul) the will to virtue, which is variously called *E*, intention, *Tsing*, desire, and *Che*, purpose. This will must be fixed and determined; he that wavereth is like a ship without a compass or a horse without a bridle. Well for him whose will is strong – a king may be driven from his throne, but the man of will is immovable in himself, though he be the poorest of the poor. But the heart of man is restless and changeable, prone to error, and ready to pursue the pleasures of the moment, as the rulers of Yin, in the pride of their hearts, displayed to men the beauty of their robes and walked boastfully and arrogantly, thus falling into utter evil.

On the other hand, King Wau, by keeping a steady purpose to do right, made his reign glorious, and filled the land with good.

This good will expresses itself in outward action: it will be *visible* to the world by the way in which the man behaves, by his deportment and carriage, by his way of speaking and walking, by his performance of ceremonial acts. A good man will be dignified in manner, respectful to his superiors, courteous to all. Especially is this lofty and yet humble deportment the mark of a good ruler, who, by acting in due fashion, constrains the loyalty of his people, and by the force of his example leads them to behave with dignity also. Words and behaviour must be simple. No crime is worse than hypocrisy, or than an appearance put on to deceive. 'When I was young,' said Confucius, 'I judged men by their words; now I judge their words by their conduct.' None the less, words must not be despised; the Higher Man uses words with precision, and it is the duty of all men to make their words clear and accordant with their thoughts.

If a ruler, like Kaou-Yaou, possesses the virtue thus described, it will flow over his whole land like a river; he will be like the Pole-star round which all stars revolve, fixed itself, and 'unchanged of motion': his example will be followed, and prosperity will come to his subjects; the neighbouring States will love him, and wars will cease. For, like the early Hebrew prophets, Confucius maintained that virtue inevitably brought its reward in this world: happiness emanates from it as light from a lamp. Virtue, like wisdom, is better than life, and riches and honour are not to be compared to it. Its hands are filled with length of days – for man is the cause of his own death, and he who lives in truth virtuously lives long.

No man can rule a State or teach others who cannot rule his own family. The ruler whose family is united sets an example to the whole State; if his family is rebellious the State is rebellious. The son must show filial piety; the younger brother must treat the elder with reverence and honour; the wife must obey with willingness. It was thus that Yaou and

Shun, by the example of their families, guided their people towards right: and it was by the violence and discord of the households of Ke and Show that their kingdoms fell into ruin. Of all virtues, perhaps, Confucius insists most strongly upon filial piety; and, in characteristic fashion, he lays down minute rules as to how it should be shown in externals. The sons must treat their parents during their lives with reverence expressed in *demeanour*: they must perform the funeral rites in regular and decorous fashion; and they must sacrifice to them 'according to propriety'. Thus, for instance, the son must rise at dawn, and having washed and dressed, should make it his first duty to see his parents and ask what they desire for food and drink. He should enter no room without his father's leave, and respectfully request permission before he departs. Almost every detail of conduct, in fact, is laid down and ordered: Confucius often speaks as if 'etiquette' and religion were but aspects of the same thing.

Similar rules are laid down as to the marriage-relation; but here the subordination is all on the side of the wife. Her first duty is to provide children, that the sacrifices at the parents' tombs may be correctly performed: and among the seven reasons for divorce barrenness is one. Jealousy and talkativeness are others; and thus the power of the husband is increased. Polygamy is sanctioned; and as among the Hebrew patriarchs a Bilhah may be taken to raise up seed if a Rachel proves a failure: and this permission is specially given to kings, who need heirs more than others if the State is to be preserved. This regulation, as in most Eastern countries, has largely defeated its own object; for the multitude of sons makes the heirship a matter of contention, and the size of the harem is an almost inevitable cause of quarrels.

Similar minuteness marks the rules as to friendship, to which Confucius attaches immense importance. All men, from the Emperor down, need friends, and should not omit, for a single day, to have intercourse with them: for friends halve our sorrows and double our joys. Those are the truest friends who are united by a common love of literature: 'make friends,' says Confucius, 'of scholars, and choose among scholars him who is most virtuous; watch a man who is dutiful to his parents, and take him for your friend.' Having gained a friend, trust him; if he needs admonition, admonish him gently, and if he admonishes you, receive his rebukes with meekness. 'Behave towards a friend as you would have your friend behave towards you.' Unlike Christ, however, Confucius did not enlarge this rule to include strangers and enemies.

Having learned to rule his family, and to regulate his friendships, the Higher Man is ready to rule a State. But Chinese scholars have pointed out that the advice given by Confucius to governors is excessively vague, and indeed far vaguer than that of the earlier sages on whom he drew. He had, of course, no notion of government other than paternal and, as we have seen, he had an unbounded confidence in the power of a wise ruler to make his people happy. The aim of the ruler is to cherish the people; and this is to be done first by enriching them and then by teaching them. There must be enough food for them to live, a soldiery sufficient to protect them, and a government which the governed can trust. It is plain that this does not carry us very far; and Confucius seems quite unaware of the limits of the prince's powers. He would never, like the modern poet, have exclaimed:

> How small, of all that human hearts endure,
> The part, that laws or kings can cause or cure.

He would seem to have fancied that all ills are due to bad government, and that a good government can cure them all. It is true that there has probably never been a nation more docile than the Chinese or one more content to go on with its daily tasks so long as it has a modicum of security from oppression: and the fact that Confucius's somewhat crude doctrines were accepted by millions for so many centuries is a proof that they were adapted to his people:[1] but they are not likely to suit societies more highly advanced, or

1. It is curious to reflect how much Confucianism a thoughtful Chinaman might detect in certain twentieth-century European modes of government. The idea of Mussolini and of other recent dictators is that the ruler knows better than the people what is good for them.

those in which the people have been accustomed to think for themselves. It must be remembered, however, that the country for which Confucius was legislating was less a great empire than a small principality, in which the ruler might be known to almost all; and hence, perhaps, his confidence in the efficacy of the prince's example. As the ruler behaves, so will the people behave: for they see him daily.

There are, he says, plain rules which the good prince must obey. He must be beneficent without excessive expenditure; the people must see that the money he takes from them is employed better than they could employ it themselves. He must similarly impose tasks on them which they perceive to be useful. He must at all times avoid covetousness – his taxes must not be put to *his own* purposes. He must always maintain a dignified demeanour, whether in the presence of many or of few. He must never punish without explaining why, or exact work without giving previous warning. And, above all, he must choose good men as advisers and administrators. Unfortunately, as Confucius saw, the princes of his time too often employed the wrong officers – 'jackanapes, not worthy of respect, little men, incapable of ruling themselves, and bad rulers of others'.

Nothing is more remarkable in the system of Confucius than the importance he attached to the due performance of ceremonies. He seems indeed to have thought a ceremony as important as righteousness or justice. His ceremonial code is full and precise: rules are laid down for the due behaviour of sons to parents, of inferiors to superiors, of classes to classes. The right complimentary phrases are taught, the precise depth of a bow, the correct bend of a knee. He held that if a man had been accustomed from his youth to address others in a regulated fashion, jealousy would diminish, suspicion would cease, and quarrels be all but impossible. You cannot easily fall out with a man whom you are at the moment, from mere habit, addressing in terms bordering on flattery. That there is something in this view may be admitted; but Westerners, who see how barristers can quarrel with their 'learned friends', or Members of Parliament contrive to abuse 'right honourable gentlemen', may be inclined to think less of it than Confucius, who does not seem to have appreciated the fact that forms easily lose their vitality, and that politeness may be but a cloak for extreme hatred. It is said that there is but one passage in all his writings in which a dim perception of this truth is to be detected.

Of all 'ceremonies', or 'proper things', as Confucius would have called them, the final and most perfect is music, of which he was passionately fond, and in whose soothing and healing virtues he profoundly believed. He delighted in the musical gifts of his disciple Tse-yew; and it is related that, at a place called Wu-shing, where the people were wild and turbulent, he reduced them to order by setting a band of his followers to play and sing. If music, said he, be performed virtuously and with sincerity of heart, it will work wonders beyond the scope of anything else in the world.

Should the ruler fail in his duty, and should it become clear that he is beyond redemption, the people may rebel and depose him. Kings are kings by divine right: but this very divine right means that they hold their position only so long as they act rightly. 'The right divine of kings to govern wrong' is not for a moment recognized. In all the revolutions which took place in China before the Communist revolution, the appeal of the rebels was to the principles of Confucius, enforced as they were by Mencius. The *office* of king is sacred; his *person* is sacred only so long as he is worthy of the office. In a sense, Confucius would have maintained that *vox populi* is *vox dei*: so long as the Emperor retains the good will of his people, so long does he rule by the will of heaven. There are, of course, times when this doctrine is of immense and beneficial weight: the Ming dynasty, and such Emperors as Kien Long, could not have reigned so gloriously without it; but it has often led adventurers to disturb settled rule, in the hope that the sword, and the chances of war, may seat them on a throne which they may claim as a heavenly gift. Such a doctrine generally arises and flourishes in times of discord and upheaval: it was proclaimed by the Jesuits in Protestant countries and repudiated by them in Catholic kingdoms. There can be little doubt that Confucius was led to hold it by seeing the multitude of princes around him who were unworthy to rule, and whose constant wars and oppressions made life almost intolerable to the common people.

If, as we have so often emphasized, there is little that is original in the system of Confucius, and if his predecessors were so often more clear and precise in their maxims, it may be asked how it is that he has gained an authority almost unquestioned for more than two thousand years, and only recently seeming likely to be shaken. The causes appear to be both historical and psychological. Confucius is the typical Chinaman, neither too high nor too low for his people. He is of the earth, earthy – born of the Chinese soil. Unlike Christ or Buddha, he does not demand that which is attainable only by the chosen few. He bids you love your friends, but he also bids you revenge injuries; and he bids the son or brother of a murdered man never rest till he has punished the slayer. In a word, he can be understood, and his precepts can be obeyed. But also, in the anarchy which prevailed over a large part of China for centuries, the works of older sages were lost, except so far as they had been preserved in the compilations of Confucius. His fame therefore eclipsed theirs, as the fame of borrowers has so often eclipsed that of the real discoverers. America still bears the name of Amerigo Vespucci; and China still reveres the name of Kung-fu-tse. But, when all deductions are made, he remains one of those 'whose is the praise if mankind hath not as yet in its march fainted and fallen and died'.

In some respects the most interesting religion that has come to the front in recent times is THEOSOPHY. I use the phrase 'come to the front' deliberately; for it is maintained by its adherents that it has existed, at least in the background, from the very earliest ages. Both in Asia and in Europe its doctrines have been known and its precepts have been practised, sometimes by societies like the Rosicrucian, sometimes, more or less imperfectly, by members of other religions.

But, till recently, it attracted comparatively little attention.

The interest it has excited during this century is due to many causes. Partly, perhaps, the repute of some of its teachers may have had to do with it. Partly also, we may trace it to the growing dissatisfaction with the *spiritual* results of ordinary science. Splendid as the material achievements of this science have been, it has failed to meet the demands of the soul, and this failure becomes constantly more obvious, especially as men see how chemistry and physics are applied to purposes of destruction and mischief. To meet the demands of the soul Theosophy comes forward, and makes the most daring and magnificent claims. It those can be substantiated, it will satisfy certain rooted instincts in human nature, and will meet, in a comprehensive and inclusive manner, not a few difficulties in other religions. Thus, to take obvious examples, it solves the question, to which so many desire a clear and precise answer, as to what death is and as to what happens after it: while, on the other hand, it explains many of the miracles found in other religious schemes, by subsuming them under the laws of the 'higher physics'. So wide is its range, that it is possible to regard Swedenborgianism, Spiritualism, much Mysticism, and even, in a sense, Christianity itself, as covered by it. That it is capable of producing saints few impartial persons who have met Theosophists will deny.

We may roughly date its emergence, or rather re-emergence, about 1875, when Mr A. P. Sinnett, who had spent some years in India, began to publish a series of works which speedily attained notoriety. The times were not unfavourable; interest was being taken in Eastern religions, and the old ignorant contempt was giving way to an almost exaggerated reverence for Indian wisdom. In 1879 appeared Arnold's *Light of Asia*, which met with amazing success; Marion Crawford's *Mr Isaacs* gave novel-readers some notion of occultism; and more serious students were being influenced by the works of Max Müller, Monier-Williams, and others. When Annie Besant, previously well-known as a powerful assistant of Bradlaugh in his 'Secularist' campaign, announced her conversion to Theosophy, the public was still more keenly interested, and the movement began to gain adherents in England and America. Its success elsewhere has not been great; but among 'Anglo-Saxons', to use the convenient phrase, it has a considerable number of intellectual believers. The interest redoubled when, a few year afterwards, Mrs Besant proclaimed that she had discovered a young Indian who was to be the Christ of the new dispensation.

It is unfortunate that, as with Spiritualism and Christian Science, the public has been compelled to listen to somewhat embittered controversy as to the trustworthiness of some of the chief propagators of the creed. Grave doubts have been openly expressed as to the character of Madame Blavatsky, who may perhaps be called the founder of modern Theosophy: she has been accused of fraud and worse; nor perhaps have her defenders succeeded in clearing her of suspicion. It may be that, as has been asserted in the case of others of her kind, she really possessed occult powers, which, however, worked intermittently; and that, when she felt them failing, she had recourse to more ordinary methods for maintaining her credit. Be that as it may, I pass it on one side. I shall try to give an account of the religion as it is, an account necessarily brief and imperfect, but, I trust, tolerably accurate as far as it goes.

As Theosophy is not a Church, but a science, it is possible for a man to be a Theosophist without seeking association with others. Naturally, however, people holding similar views tend to sympathize with one another and to form a kind of brotherhood. For admission to this brotherhood nothing is necessary but belief in God, the determination to live an upright life, and the endeavour to seek truth and to love and benefit others. The foundation-doctrines, also, are simple. They may be summarized under three heads. God is good, and can be perceived by any man who wills to perceive him. Man is immortal – and the true man is a soul. The world is ruled by absolute justice – good is *naturally* rewarded, and evil has *inevitable* evil consequences. Thus, to put it at its lowest, it is *desirable* for man to live well and control his appetites.

The Infinite God is beyond us, but he has chosen to manifest himself to us as that which philosophers have called the Logos – and the Logos *can* be known. When we speak of God as love, or as light, or as personal, we are not limiting *him*; we are speaking of the Logos: and the trained Theosophist not only thinks he knows the Logos, but has actually seen him, and has recognized him as a certain scientific fact. He has discovered, scientifically, that God is a Trinity in unity; that he is within us and around us; that in him we live and move and have our being.

Theoretically, and in some degree practically, a member of any religious organization may be a Theosophist. No peculiarities of custom, dress, or language are compulsory. Many Theosophists are vegetarians (the common belief is that all are such), but the end of the religion being attained by health of body and of mind, a person is not excluded who finds that vegetarian diet injures him, and who therefore eats like others. Even smoking is not forbidden, though here again the majority would practise abstinence. A Theosophist, though bound to live a sanctified life, will not hesitate to do in Rome as Rome does.

The doctrine is largely Buddhist in origin, as the title of one of the earliest books, Mr Sinnett's *Esoteric Buddhism*, clearly indicates: but it avails itself of light from Brahmanism, Christianity, or any other system which seems to have a contribution to make to knowledge. The distinctive doctrine is that of Reincarnation, which is closely allied, as in Buddhism, with that of Karma or (to use an inexact paraphrase) Life-labour. Spiritual progress is a matter of many ages: and three score years and ten can carry us but an infinitesimal step forward to perfection. None the less, he who does his duty in this life will be able in the next to start again where he left off. A baby, it is true, having not yet reached full consciousness, must wait awhile; but at seven years or thereabouts, it begins to realize its position, at fourteen it is well on the way, and at twenty-one it takes up the task where it was broken off. When, after death, we wake up to our surroundings, we find a region exactly suited to our capacities, and one in which we can resume the work with hope and joy. This region is known as the 'Astral Plane' – an unfortunate expression, for it has little, in some stages, to do with the stars. It is a vast sphere surrounding our globe, very various in its character, but containing nothing to terrify the immigrant, who, if he has developed his 'ego' in due fashion, will pass immediately into an environment in which the ego has full scope. This plane, though beyond the ken of the ordinary man, has been actually beheld by theosophic clairvoyants, who, while alive, have 'sent their soul into the invisible' and brought back news of it, as the spies brought to the desert-wanderers their report of the Holy Land. The living may hope, or rather may be sure, that they will meet in that plane their beloved dead; and thence they will return in due time to work once more for the divine far-off event.[1]

As in Swedenborgianism, Spiritualism, and other schemes, the geography of this supernormal world is worked out in great detail: and it is possible to draw a map of it. Around our globe are seven concentric spheres, known as 'sub-planes' – a phraseology which irritates the mathematician, but need not annoy the ordinary man. The two nearest the earth – in fact, partially involved in it – are regions of suffering reserved for those who, having deliberately offended against divine law, receive the just penalties of their sins. Even for these, however, there is hope; they pass upwards as soon as the punishment has had its due effect of leading them

1. The Astral Plane, unless I am mistaken, is defined variously by different authorities. Some would define it as a region of dream-like repose, between reincarnations, in which there is neither Karma nor any actual progress, except so far as progress is involved in the realization of the aims and capacities of the last earthly life. As, however, this realization may involve many degrees of completeness, it is clear that the progress may, in the view of some, be very considerable. Nor is repose – as we may conjecture from the analogy of sleep – without its element of advance. Both physically and mentally we constantly awake from sleep at a stage far ahead of that at which we retired the night before.

to hate the sin. There is nothing either arbitrary or merely retributive about it; it is curative and purifying, and free from any taint of vengefulness. The third sphere, a kind of purgatory, is also painful, and is designed for the end of ridding the soul of the love of lower things, in which during the earthly life it may have been too deeply absorbed. But this also need not terrify us: if we have lived lives on the whole honourable, or if by some eminently good deed we have redressed the balance, we shall pass through it easily and quickly. A man, for example, who had given his life in an attempt to save others, or who has perished in a noble and unselfish war, will pass rapidly through this region. In the fourth sphere, a world of infinite variety, are those who have done great work on earth – the artists, the poets, the musicians – who find there the impulse and the opportunity for still higher achievement. At the present moment the Miltons and the Beethovens are thus working, *ohne Hast, ohne Rast,* on greater poems and on yet more perfect symphonies. For Theosophy recognizes in art and craft a religious quality: the doubts which sometimes assail men of genius as to whether they are serving God are charmed away. No Pascal will renounce his mathematics in order to devote himself to more specifically holy things – there is nothing holier than the selfless pursuit of knowledge; and in the fourth sphere full scope will be found for pursuing it, with pure and unalloyed pleasure and with entire freedom from distraction. The learned man will lose nothing of what he has learned; his memory will be clear, and his intellectual powers keener even than they were. And so on to the still higher regions.

If, then, a soul has reached one of the highest sub-planes, and has gained a stock of virtue and knowledge corresponding to the stage thus reached, it is hard to set any limit to its possibilities of attainment, and the more so when we remember that it has had thousands of years in the past, with many reincarnations, in which to increase in knowledge. It will now, therefore, be a Mahatma or Master of Wisdom; and, as its self-abnegation is complete, it will be a source of wisdom for all who can gain access to it. The Master, in fact, is waiting and willing to communicate of his fullness: and, if we can but reach him, the toil and time ordinarily spent in the attainment of knowledge may be avoided. His range of experience will vastly surpass anything that we, in this earthly stage, can conceive: is it *possible* for him to share it with us? The answer is twofold. The Mahatma may be able to put himself into a human body, and thus come into contact with us; or we may, in certain circumstances, as we have just seen, send our soul out of our bodies into the astral world, and thus have what may be called interviews with the Masters. The amount of knowledge thus placed at our disposal is vast; for the Adept, by the very fact that he has attained such a rank among the hierarchy of beings between the Lowest and the Highest, has solved all 'the myriad enigmas of good and evil, of sin and sorrow and hope; and neither life nor death holds any riddles from his understanding'. At this stage he can quit his body at will and assume, if he chooses, a new incarnation: and, if it suits his benevolent purpose, he may take the form of a carpenter, live a humble life, and die a painful death, although he might, by the slightest act of will, remove himself from danger and vanish, by occult means, into thin air. And these services the Masters render 'all for love and nothing for reward'. While inhabiting the humble body, they will not be recognized as Masters: but it is none the less our duty to remind ourselves that, unknown and invisible, these beings are working on our behalf in the war with the Powers of Evil. They do not *ask* gratitude, but – if only for the sake of heightening our own spiritual experience – we should be grateful to them. Mr Sinnett illustrates all this by quoting from Tennyson's early poem 'The Mystic':

> *Angels have talked with him and shown him thrones:*
> *Ye knew him not, he was not one of ye:*
> *Ye could not read the marvel in his eye,*
> *The still serene abstraction he hath felt.*
> *How could ye know him? Ye were yet within*
> *The narrower circle.*

It must be allowed that the knowledge communicated by these Mahatmas is very astonishing, and the manner of its communication no less so. By a kind of supersensual wireless telegraphy it may be passed over thousands of miles, though the Master may be hidden in Tibet and the pupil be living in London. It is thus that the material for a large work, with maps and diagrams, dealing with the history of Atlantis thousands of years ago, was obtained by the author. Atlantis has long been submerged and not a trace of it remains; a 'myth' given by Plato in his dialogues, the *Timaeus* and the *Critias*, almost alone preserves its memory: but its story has been recovered and published. 'The few qualified to carry on super-physical research are enabled to get into touch with still more abnormally developed Beings who, though lost to sight as regards ordinary mankind, have not lost their sympathy with humanity'; and thus we trace the origin and progress of Atlantean civilization. We learn that the Atlanteans had in some respects advanced much further than ourselves; but they used their science, not for spiritual ends, but to gratify sensual desires; the Mahatmas abandoned their country, and they fell. They understood aviation and chemical transformations; but we – *mirabile dictu* – understand moral progress better than they.[1]

Again, clairvoyance enables the skilled Theosophist to *see* the atom and count its electrons; it gives knowledge about the planets, how far they are inhabited and by whom; and it reached many scientific discoveries before the men of science made them; radium before Madame Curie, the meaning of atomic weights before the physicists.

The chief of these discoveries is that the world is a vital organism, that evolution is a moral unfolding of the natural powers, and that physics therefore is a branch of theology – or rather, to avoid confusion, of what must be called Theosophy. The five senses, by which ordinary natural science works, are by no means all the senses we possess. All of us, or nearly all of us, have others in an undeveloped state; the

1. From another side, the reader might consult Mr Spence's *Problem of Atlantis*.

Theosophist cultivates them into activity, and may reach a high skill in their use – even in the present life. Thought and effort will put these super-senses at his disposal if he wills: but their full use can be gained, if ever, only in the higher planes. At this, as at many other points, the Theosophist comes into contact with the Spiritualist; yet, for some reason, the two, though so near, do not harmonize, and there seems little likelihood that they will ever coalesce. Both avail themselves of the clairvoyant and the medium; both claim to be able to hold intercourse with the spirit-world; and yet there seems to be the same antagonism between them which we so often observe in religious history between a creed and a heresy not easily distinguishable from it.

Among the powers claimed by both alike is that of overcoming the force of gravity. The phenomenon of 'levitation' is constantly observed in séances, and its principles are thoroughly understood by the Mahatmas. It is thus that they are able to transport themselves, if they so desire, even in bodily form, from place to place: and it is maintained by many Theosophists that it was through their instructions that the ancients were able to lift the huge masses of Stonehenge into their places, and even to convey them for scores of miles from their original quarries. It is, of course, one of the enigmas of history how this and other similar feats of mechanics were in fact performed. Readers of Fuller will remember his remark on the old legend that Merlin by his magic conjured the vast rocks of Stonehenge out of Ireland – 'and brought them through the skies (what, in Charles's Wain?)' – but to the Theosophist the legend is but an ignorant distortion of the truth. 'Merlin' represents a Mahatma, and his magic is but a poetic travesty of occult powers constantly wielded by astral souls, and at our own disposal if we but know how to avail ourselves of the services of Mahatmas.

Similarly, as we hinted above, certain of Christ's miracles accommodate themselves to higher Theosophic science. His walking on the sea is merely an instance of prolonged levitation; the success, and the failure, of St Peter show equally how the Mahatmas help the trusting and how they refuse help when the trust gives way and the line of communication is broken. As for the Ascension, it is a phenomenon by no means rarely observed, when the Mahatma reveals himself in bodily form, rises into the air, and then vanishes from sight.

It is clear that, when this system is taken up by ignorant or half-educated people, it may run into extravagances which can only increase scepticism and provoke ridicule. The theory, for example, is that there is a Master, not unlike the national Angel of the Book of Daniel, who watches specially over the interests of a particular country; there is an English Master, a Scottish Master, and more than one American Master: though it does not appear that there is one for the whole Union, presiding over the fifty who guard the separate States. Such a Master takes incarnation in a body belonging to the people concerned; he is a Frenchman in France, an Italian in Italy. A theory like this needs only to be taken up by inferior minds to be involved in all sorts of absurdities. On the other hand, some of the Masters find it convenient to abide, so far as their bodies are concerned, in Himalayan retreats, and to employ subtler means to spread their influences abroad over the world at large. If we ask who they are, and how we are to recognize them, the answer is that it is impossible for them to be identified by ordinary people: an 'adept' can be detected only by other adepts, or by those who have discovered the right means of approaching him and learning from him. Sometimes the revelation does not come till the adept has disappeared from the world, perhaps by what common medical science would suppose to be death. Thus it is the belief of many that Jacob Böhme, the inspired cobbler, was an adept: but the fact was not known, despite the extraordinary nature of his life and writings, till Theosophy revealed it. 'Count St Germain' was busy in Russia, trying to restrain the violence of the revolution – not always, it is to be feared, with success. The same Master, we are assured, or another, took the form of Francis Bacon. If we object that

Bacon's life, though on the whole of immense benefit to the world, shows some very obvious flaws, we are told that only a third of the Master's personality entered into him. The 'Great White Lodge', a sphere of the highest order, has purposes, and uses means, which our intellect is unable to understand: it may find it consonant with the evolution of morality to limit its operations, and to moderate its energies. It may even be, in some obscure way, hampered by opposition; thus, in pouring the light of Theosophy upon the world, it has had, as we saw, to contend with the scepticism of Spiritualists, who, while accepting the doctrine of the Spheres and the after-life, refuse to acknowledge even the existence of the Masters. No knowledge can be given except to willing pupils; unlike most ordinary teaching, that of the adepts always comes as a response to eager inquiry; they will never, as a schoolmaster is often driven to do, force it upon the recalcitrant. Thus the infidel never receives it; and the Spiritualists, though so near, remain afar off. We must consciously *look up* to the Masters in our search for knowledge: and thus it was not for some years after the first promulgation of the doctrine, in *Esoteric Buddhism*, that men were in a condition to apply for help, or the Masters able to give it. Since then, the transmission has gone on at an accelerated speed; restrictions to intercourse are more and more rapidly removed, and students like Anna Kingsford, A. P. Sinnett, and Annie Besant have been able to make successive revelations which enlarge and correct previous hints into clearer and more accurate knowledge. Not that it is necessary for all members of the Society to keep abreast with this ever-advancing erudition. The Masters themselves, so it appears, do not desire it. Enough if a general acquaintance with Occult Science is attained: as it is not necessary for a workaday Catholic to know his Thomas Aquinas, so a Theosophist, whose leisure is limited, may content himself with a broad outline of the creed, trust in his leaders, and earn his daily bread like other people.

The knowledge, therefore, does not admit of verification, except by the Theosophists themselves. The system, unlike

that of physical science, does not, and scarcely can, offer itself to be tested, by the external and unbelieving world. A
Newton or a Faraday puts forth his theory, and *invites* criticism; if he is proved wrong, he accepts the correction and
experiments again. The Theosophist proclaims that his
teachers will not impart their teaching except to the initiated; you must take the plunge before you can expect to
swim. The wise and prudent find the mysteries shut to
them: and when they inquire, 'How do you know?' the
answer is, 'Come to our school.' It is clear that there is an
irreconcilable antagonism between those who say, 'Give us
some facts that we can test *before* we believe,' and those who
say, 'Believe first and the facts will be supplied afterwards:
they *cannot* be supplied except to believers.'

This is well illustrated by the astronomical lore of Theosophy, which is such that the ordinary astronomer cannot
easily subject it to his tests. Let us consider, for example, the
doctrine of the 'Planetary Chain'. The planets are the
abodes of life, partly of life below our level, partly beyond
it. The unhappy world condemned to harbour the laggards,
not fit even for our earth, is Mars. The inhabitants, of course
many millions in number, have 'failed to make the exertions
required for the acquisition of superior vehicles': they are
on the whole lower than our lowest savages both in intellect
and in morals. In bodily frame they are ugly and repulsive;
and even the animals share their degradation; they are rep-
tiles swarming in those 'canals' over which our astronomers
dispute, but which the Theosophist knows to be great inland
lakes. There are, however, some Martians whose 'egos' are
higher than those of the rest; the souls of these are allowed
to transfer themselves to our earth where they take up their
abode in the Aboriginals of Australia or in the negroes of
Central Africa.

After a due probation in our world, the souls pass, not, as
perhaps might have been expected, into Venus, but into
Mercury, which is thus peopled by the very best of the
human family. Information gained from the Masters who
roam the lucid interspaces of world and world enables us to

say that the Mercurians are intellectually and morally far in advance of us; and it will please feminists to know that the female half of mankind (so far as the word 'female' is at all applicable to such a lofty life) is distinctly though not inconveniently, ahead of the male population.

The planetary order is not that either of Dante's system or that of the Copernican. From Mercury the souls advance to Venus, the first of the higher Astral spheres. Here they live in the contemplation and practice of Beauty. And so on to yet higher levels, called 'Manasic'. But it must be noted that souls *may* reach these levels prematurely; there may be 'Venus-failures' who revert to Mercury, and assist in elevating the life of that sphere, and Mercury-failures who revert to earth, to do similar service here.

In all this the number seven plays its ancient part: the spheres are seven – three 'physical', two 'Astral' in a special sense, two 'Manasic'. In the higher, there are no troublesome entanglements; life is developed to the full without hindrance; and the souls can pass upward or downward at will.

It is unlucky that the assistance given by the great souls inhabiting these sublime peaks is often useless and even apparently childish. It may, of course, like Herodotus in Beloe's version, have suffered in translation from the higher language to the lower; but, as with the messages from the dead to the living as transmitted by mediums, the communications of the adepts are, to the uninitiated at least, somewhat disappointing. A patient applying to a doctor whose qualifications come from the Astral Plane sometimes fails as utterly to receive a cure as the woman with the issue of blood who tried the prosaic doctors of Palestine. Nor are the messages, as they reach this lower sphere, always couched in good, or even grammatical, language. Several of those which reach the Logos-Observatory in America are very poor in style, however elevated they may be in substance. And this is the more remarkable as, if we may believe certain Theosophic writings, the Astral intelligences have had centuries in which they might have acquired a tolerable knowledge of the English tongue: and even those who live, so far as their bodies are concerned, in Tibet, might have learned at least some grammar.

But this, one is willing to believe, is due to the attempts of inferior minds to assume positions to which they are not entitled. There is little to complain of in the style of Mrs Besant: and it is possible that if the more ignorant can be kept in their place, some of the revelations may reach us in a more attractive form. At any rate, whatever we may think of the intellectual results of occultism, it certainly succeeds, as a rule, on the humdrum plane of earthly moral conduct.

CHAPTER 13

THE REFORMED CHURCH OF ENGLAND

MUCH dispute has arisen as to the exact effect of the Reformation on the Church of England. According to one school of thought, she is the old Church reformed. Certain modifications have been made, abuses and errors corrected, the supremacy of Rome repudiated: but she is not changed in any essential feature. She is thus a branch of the Church Catholic, coequal with the Roman and the Orthodox Churches, and differing *toto caelo* from those Churches, like the Calvinist, that have no Apostolic Succession of Bishops – for Bishops in this view, are of the *esse* and not merely of the *bene esse* of the Church. Doubtless there were many, at the time of the Reform, who held these views in one or other of their numerous possible varieties. The Act of Supremacy of 1535, which by declaring the King the Supreme Head of the Church, broke decisively with the Pope, was followed, of set purpose, by the Act of the Six Articles, which retained all the essential *doctrines* of the Papal Church. The Act of Uniformity, passed in 1559 under Elizabeth, is likewise consistent with the view that no destruction, but only renovation, was intended.

'There is no other difference,' wrote Joseph Hall, Bishop of Norwich, 'between us and Rome, than betwixt a Church miserably corrupted and happily purged. Be it known to all the world, that our Church is only reformed or repaired, not made new.' 'The Roman Church and the Church of England,' said Laud, 'are but two distinct members of that Catholic Church which is spread over the face of the earth.' 'We do not innovate,' said Andrewes, answering a Romanist; 'it may be we renovate what was customary with the ancients, but with you has disappeared in novelties.'

There was, however, and still is, another view, which the Puritan branch of the Church desired to express in action, and which is to some extent countenanced by the opinions of many Church divines of authority, that the Pope was Antichrist, and that the corruptions of the Papacy had gone beyond mere mending. The Church of England had therefore severed itself utterly from the Roman, and had become distinctly Protestant, in sympathy with Geneva if not entirely in agreement with her, and not far removed, in many respects, from Lutheranism. It was the view of many members of the Church that she made an entirely new start at the Reformation, that her Episcopacy was, at most, a convenient and desirable form of Church government, and that her doctrines were in the main those of the Reformed Churches. This view, with the modifications caused by the lapse of time and the growth of tolerance, is still held by eminent authorities, but is probably less widely spread than formerly. Something in favour of it may be found in the writings of Jewel, of Archbishop Ussher, and of Chillingworth.

In any case, from the *legal* point of view, the Church is the creation of Parliament; and this was fully recognized at the time of the great change. Many Romanist Bishops, such as Tunstall and Gardiner, repeatedly declared their willingness to obey laws passed in due fashion, and to give at least verbal consent even to *doctrines* affirmed by law, while stubbornly holding out against mere ecclesiastical decrees. In 1547, just after the death of Henry, it was an Act of Parliament that ordained communion in both kinds; it was an Act of Parliament that permitted the marriage of the clergy; and it was an Act of Parliament that enforced, or tried to enforce, the use of the revised Prayer Book of Cranmer in place of the half-dozen 'Uses' which had been permissible before. On the other hand, the use of the Book of Homilies, and other ordinances which the ruling Council put forth on its own authority, without Parliamentary sanction, met with considerable opposition, on the ground that they were not 'legal'.

Similarly, the Marian reaction was carried out, almost entirely, in a legal manner, and it was an Act of Parliament (1 and 2 Philip and Mary, c. 8) which restored the supremacy of the Pope: indeed, till that Act was passed, Mary, devout Papist as she was, retained the title of Supreme Head of the Church. It was not till the old Statute 'De Haeretico Comburendo', passed in 1401 against the Lollards, had been re-enacted, that Rowland Taylor, Hooper, Ridley, and Latimer, were burnt.

Under Elizabeth the same course was pursued, and no pains were spared to make it evident that the Church was to be controlled by the State as represented by the Queen in Parliament. Despite the efforts of Romanists on the one side and of Puritans on the other to reverse the order of precedence, all attempts at freedom on the part of the Church were sternly repressed. The Crown was armed, *by Parliament*, with almost unlimited powers against the clergy, and the Queen was authorized to give commissions to such persons as she pleased to visit and correct all errors, heresies, and abuses which demanded redress. And this system, in effect, still remains. The ultimate appeal is not to the Archbishops, but to the Crown as Supreme Head, and all ecclesiastical authority is defined by law. The Crown appoints the Bishops by what is ironically called a *congé d'élire*[1] (or 'permission to elect') sent to the Dean and Chapter of the cathedral. The test of belief is the Thirty-Nine Articles, which are as much an Act of Parliament as the Reform Act of 1832: the order of religious services is regulated by the Prayer Book, which also is an Act of Parliament; and, what is still more important, it is the State, and not the Church, which settles the degree of orthodoxy required of a lay or clerical member. If a layman is excluded from the sacraments on what he deems unlawful grounds, his appeal will be to the State: and, if a clergyman is accused of heterodoxy, it will be State lawyers that will decide the case. All

---

1. The *congé d'élire*, said Dr Johnson, 'is such a recommendation as if I should throw you out of a two-pair-of-stairs window, and *recommend* you to fall soft'. Boswell, *sub anno*, 1784.

these facts can be easily illustrated from history. After the Revolution of 1688, a number of Bishops were removed from their sees for refusing the oaths to William and Mary. There is no doubt that, *ecclesiastically*, these Non-jurors remained Bishops, and the clergy whom they consecrated to the episcopal office were as truly Bishops as Dr Lang or Dr Temple; but there is equally no doubt that *in law* those who took their places, and whom they regarded as schismatics, were Bishops, and their ordinations valid. In 1850, Dr Phillpotts of Exeter refused institution to Mr Gorham because Mr Gorham held Calvinistic views on baptismal regeneration: the Judicial Committee of the Privy Council instituted the heretic despite the Bishop.[1] In 1848 the Dean and Chapter of Hereford objected to the appointment of Dr Hampden as Bishop (Dr Hampden had already been in trouble on account of his opinions). Lord John Russell replied to them that he took note of their intention of breaking the law; and Hampden was duly consecrated. There was a similar useless opposition to the appointment of Frederick Temple as Bishop of Exeter (1869).

There can be no doubt that all this was the deliberate intention of those who engineered the Elizabethan settlement. No counsel was taken with Convocation, which, in 1559, held Romish views on Transubstantiation, and declared that the spiritualty alone had the right to settle things relating to the doctrines, ritual, and discipline of the Church. It was therefore ignored, and, after the comedy of a discussion between representative clergy on both sides, the Act of Uniformity restored, with a few alterations, the Second, or more Puritan, of Edward VI's Prayer Books. Those of the Bishops – and, to their credit be it said, they were all but one – who refused to countenance these changes, were deprived of their sees.

The 'continuity' of the Church, in the Anglican view, depends on what next followed – the consecration of Matthew Parker as Archbishop of Canterbury. He was, un-

1. This was the famous occasion on which the Privy Council 'dismissed hell with costs'.

questionably,[1] consecrated in a perfectly regular fashion, by four surviving Bishops of King Edward's reign, according to the order prescribed in the Prayer Book which had just been legalized by the Act of Uniformity. The regularity, in the Anglican view, of the consecration of the other Bishops, rests on that of Parker's; in the Papist view they are all schismatics, as the Roman Bishops had not been duly deprived. Thus, on the one side, the State had broken with Rome: on the other it offended the Puritan party both by retaining episcopacy and by certain decrees against 'disorders'.

Convocation, having been duly purged in this manner, was permitted to meet, and drew up the Thirty-Nine Articles, which, however, were not regarded as binding till they had been ratified by the Queen. The constitution and doctrine of the Church as thus decided were stated and defended by John Jewel, Bishop of Salisbury, in his famous *Apology*, the tone of which is far from High Anglican, and represents in many places the Genevan views which he had acquired abroad during the Marian persecution. For example, it treats episcopacy as a matter of expediency. This work had the honour of being considered and read by the Council of Trent as the standard expression of Church of England ideas. Jewel later, by his patronage of Richard Hooker, made possible the still more famous defence of the Church which is to be found in the *Ecclesiastical Polity*. These two books, one putting the case against the Church of Rome, the other against the Puritans, sum up between them

1. The old story of the 'Nag's Head' consecration, set on foot by some Romanist enthusiasts about 1600, has long since been rejected by all historians, of whatever belief. It was to the effect that the nominees to Bishoprics met at the Nag's Head in Cheapside to be consecrated by Dr Kitchin, of Llandaff, the one Marian prelate who conformed to the new system. Kitchin, however, being threatened with excommunication by Bonner, refused to perform the ceremony, which was accordingly carried through by John Scory (who had been Bishop of Rochester under Edward VI) in a highly irregular manner. There is not a word of truth in the tale, as is sufficiently shown by the fact that the nominees were not consecrated together, but at intervals from December 1559 to April 1562.

the conception of the English Church which were entertained by her adherents till the rise of the Latitudinarians and the modern High Anglicans.

In 1571, again by Act of Parliament, subscription to the Articles was made incumbent on all ministers. It is true that the Queen herself, in many cases, chose to act rather by royal decree than by statute-law[1]; but the general anxiety was always to secure Parliamentary sanction both for ritual and for doctrine. Parker, in particular, was careful to proceed legally; it is said that though he was personally indifferent as to cap, tippet, surplice, and the rest, the use of which by the clergy was so obnoxious to the Puritans, yet he felt it his duty to insist on them, 'as being by the law established'.[2]

These vestments, though to us today they seem matters of quite secondary importance, were to the Genevans the very symbols of Popery; and, though doctrinal differences were of course emphasized, yet questions of clerical dress and etiquette, of postures and places, inevitably came to the fore, and, to a superficial view, might seem to have been the main points at issue. The whole of Elizabeth's reign was one long struggle between these objectors, who are conveniently and comprehensively called 'Puritans', and the Established Church. The majority of the Puritans, despite their opinions, remained within the Church, and it is astonishing how, though the Queen, the law, and the hierarchy (for the most part) were against them, they contrived not merely to exist

1. It was by the Queen's special direction that, in 1575, two foreign Anabaptists were burned for heresy.

2. It must be remembered that Nonconformist Churches, also, are subject to the law as regards their chapels, the trust-deeds of which are legal documents, and in fact as regards their material possessions generally. No State can afford to give up control of such things. Again, the Church of England has gained a considerable measure of self-government of recent years, more especially since the Enabling Bill and the establishment of the Church Assembly; and the State is naturally cautious about interfering with her spiritual functions. But what has been said above is true as to the past, and is in theory, if not in practice, true as to the present.

but to increase in strength. They would perhaps have been suppressed but for the support of some of the most powerful laymen in the country: Burghley, Leicester, and Nicholas Bacon strongly favoured them, and contrived, with great skill, to convince the Queen that the growth of Puritanism, which she regarded as lawlessness and semi-treason, was due to the slackness of the very Bishops whose work they were hindering. Some of the Bishops themselves, notably Pilkington of Durham, were zealous Puritans, and steadily refused to enforce the law. There was a strain of Puritanism, also, in Parker's successor Grindal, who, indeed, was so little to the liking of Elizabeth that she was dissuaded from deposing him only by the urgent representations of the Council, and did actually suspend him for many years. His successor Whitgift, who became Archbishop in 1583, was more to her mind, and, for the twenty years of his rule, waged a bitter war with the Genevan party. He was naturally a man of an imperious temper, to whom force was more congenial than persuasion: and he was met with equal determination by his opponents. He began by drawing up Articles aimed at compelling Puritan ministers either to submit or to go out: the Queen's supremacy must be acknowledged, the Prayer Book must be followed in the services without alteration, omission, or addition, and the Thirty-Nine Articles must be accepted whole-heartedly. For those who refused, there was suspension, or deprivation; and the High Commission court, which he strengthened to the utmost, was there to support him. Where all else failed, he could fall back upon the Queen. No Archbishop has been more violently hated: but he had also the friends whom a strong man generally gathers round him. It was against him that the famous Marprelate tracts were directed, and, virulent as they were, they did not exaggerate the feeling that he had aroused.

Externally, Whitgift had a large measure of success; but, to judge by what was to follow, he had really but driven the disease inward. With the slightest relaxation of severity, the Puritan feeling openly manifested itself. He died in the year

(1604) of the Hampton Court Conference. With the accession of James, who, it was hoped, would favour Presbyterianism, it was at once seen that the snake was not killed but only scotched; for at that Conference a very large number of clergy boldly defended Presbyterian views: and even when it appeared that James took the other side, they were not checked. The work of Whitgift was carried on by Bancroft, in whose time the Bishops appointed were mainly of Arminian views in theological matters,[1] and absolutist in politics. Under Abbot, who was Calvinistic in his ideas, the Puritans again raised their heads; but Abbot soon lost royal favour, and was reduced to a cipher, while the real influence lay with William Laud, Bishop of London. There is much to be admired in Laud; his zeal and energy in introducing some sort of order into the Church services, his true piety, and the patience with which he bore his later misfortunes, even his enemies will admit, and there is no one who does not regard his death as an inexcusable and tyrannical crime. But his friends are compelled to own that he was harsh, tactless, and hasty. His treatment of those who differed from his views was utterly ruthless; many of his words and actions were such as to excuse the common belief, held both by Romanists and by Puritans, that he was a Papist at heart; and he was totally without insight into other men's minds. Supported by the King, however, he went on his way, endeavouring to compel uniformity in creed and ritual not only in England but, with results fatal to himself, in Scotland also. Nothing is more characteristic of the man than his absolute confidence that the people had accepted his ideas, and that all was quiet, at the very moment before the storm rose which was to sweep all his works away.

There is no need to re-tell the oft-told tale. The attempt to introduce the Anglican liturgy (with a few modifications) into Scotland led to an instant upheaval, which ere long

1. The chief, and in every way most admirable, of these men was Launcelot Andrewes, Bishop of Winchester, in whom we may see this form of Churchmanship at its best.

brought about a still more dangerous revolt in England. The Civil War followed, in which State and Church fell together.

During the Commonwealth it was soon seen that the Puritan party understood toleration as little as Laud himself. Everything was to be suppressed except what suited the Presbyterian divines. But this did not last. The army, which had overcome the King, was neither Presbyterian nor Episcopalian, but of every sect or none: and, under Cromwell, the churches fell into the hands of clergy who did as they or their congregations pleased. Many of them were 'Independent' in opinion – that is, they held that every congregation was its own master. The result was an anarchy which greatly shocked the more sober part of the nation. Cromwell himself, who was a statesman, but also an Independent, and who would have tolerated all sects, was in the difficulty that the one sect he could not tolerate was the largest. The Episcopalians, whom, as was shown at the Restoration, the populace still preferred, could never forgive the man whom they regarded as the murderer of their sainted King; and it was all but impossible for them to keep the 'Engagement', under which, if they took an oath of allegiance to the Protector, they would be permitted to preach. A few acts of insubordination convinced Cromwell that they were not to be trusted; and in the last years of his life they were suppressed as sternly as the Puritans had been suppressed by Laud – with similar success. No sooner was the Protector dead, than the crushed party rose in its might. At the Restoration, the Church returned, and it was soon seen that the King himself could not protect the Puritans from her natural, if un-Christian, vengeance. The Clarendon Code followed: in 1662 a new Act of Uniformity was passed and nearly two thousand clergy were driven out of the Church. The Five-Mile Act of 1665 retaliated on the broken cause by reissuing, *mutatis mutandis*, a regulation of Cromwell's: no Nonconformist minister was allowed to teach within five miles of a corporate town. To the King himself, who before his return had promised 'liberty to tender consciences' involving a measure of toleration, and who was a Catholic at heart, all this was deeply repugnant. There was no hope, however, of inducing Parliament to alter it; and his attempt to do so, in 1672, by royal prerogative, but led to the stern and tyrannical Test Act of the next year, which compelled all officials, civil and military, to receive the Communion according to the rites of the Anglican Church. His Majesty was plainly told that such matters belonged not to him alone, but to King, Lords, and Commons in conjunction.

The alliance between Catholics and Dissenters, as being equally oppressed by the Church, is seen again in the reign of James II, whose two Declarations of Indulgence, like that of Charles, were meant to secure toleration for the Catholics by binding up their cause with that of certain Protestants. Here also the law stepped in; these Acts were declared illegal, and were one main cause of the King's ruin. Parliament was determined to retain the right of regulating ecclesiastical affairs, as well as secular, in its own way.

During the Stuart times, a doctrine of Non-Resistance had gradually grown up, and had been proclaimed in season and out of season by the High Church clergy. It was asserted with vigour by two such different writers as Robert Filmer, a devotee of Charles I, whose *Patriarcha*, published at the time of the Exclusion Bill (long after Filmer's death), had a vast influence, and as Thomas Hobbes, whose *Leviathan* was eagerly read, but who was shrewdly suspected of 'atheism'. The idea was known as the 'Doctrine of the Cross', and was to the effect that, whatever the conduct of the King might be, he must be at least passively obeyed. Men pointed out that, when St Paul bade his converts honour the King, the King was Nero. The powers that be were ordained of God, and the King was King by divine right. This doctrine gained greatly by the too visible results of rebellion. Disobedience to Charles I had led ultimately to his murder; his subjects had disputed his commands, and thence sprung the terrible anarchy, both in Church and in State, which had marked the annals of the Commonwealth. It is probable that, in 1680 (the year of the publication of

Patriarcha), this was the one great distinguishing tenet of the High Church party, and that it was held by the majority of Tory laymen.

The policy of James II put it to a severe strain. His treatment of Cambridge and Oxford – the latter was a stronghold of the dogma – shook the faith of many, and the Trial of the Seven Bishops that of many more. At the accession of William, those who still held it were put to a test of a different kind: for they had to decide between the King *de facto* and the King *de jure*. Some, like Dean Sherlock, openly abandoned it, and endeavoured to prove that the Church had never held it. Others, like Archbishop Sancroft, persuaded themselves that James had, by his departure, abdicated the throne, and that they might, in a sense, still obey him by accepting his abdication. William and Mary might be named regents, and might, nominally, act on behalf of the King they had actually turned out. A Non-resister, therefore, might conscientiously submit to their rule, and yet save his darling doctrine. Nearly all the Bishops were in favour of this expedient. It was soon clear, however, that they would not be allowed to apply it. The Convention Parliament began by declaring the throne vacant, though James was still alive; it then went further, and, after much discussion, offered the crown to William and Mary jointly. The 'Doctrine of the Cross', therefore, was now overtly denied; and, when Parliament followed on to insist that all clergymen should take the oaths of allegiance to the new sovereigns, the consciences of many were sorely perplexed. When the time for administering the oaths came, nine Bishops, including Sancroft and the saintly Ken of Bath and Wells, refused to take them.[1] Of these, three died shortly afterwards, but the remaining six, and four hundred other clergymen, were deprived. The result was the 'Non-juring Schism'. On High-Church principles there can be no doubt that the Non-jurors were right: the real schismatics were not the expelled incumbents, but those who, by mere State

1. Five of them were among the famous Seven who had so nobly resisted King James in the matter of the Indulgence.

action, were intruded into their places; and a large number, even of the clergy who had yielded, strongly sympathized with the martyrs. By the same High-Church principles, however, the intruders would become canonically legitimate the moment the rightful holders of the benefices died; and it was the wish of Ken, and Frampton of Gloucester, that no steps should be taken to make this peaceful solution impossible. Sancroft was of another mind, and others agreed with him. Accordingly, in 1694, Dr Hickes and Mr Wagstaffe were secretly consecrated Bishops of Thetford and of Ipswich. These in their turn consecrated others, and the little Church, which consisted almost entirely of clergy without congregations, lasted for about a century. Among its members were Jeremy Collier, the famous author of the *Short View of the Stage*, Charles Leslie, author of the *Short and Easy Method with the Deists*, and William Law, whose *Serious Call to the Unconverted* had, directly or indirectly, an enormous influence on English religious history. A few years after the Revolution, their numbers were somewhat increased by the accession of the 'Nonabjurors', that is those who would not take the oath *abjuring* the right of the Pretender, James III, to the throne. Approaches were made towards union with the Greek Church; but these came to nothing. Small as the body was, it divided into yet smaller bodies; a split occurred between those[1] who desired a change in certain sacramental usages which would have brought the Church nearer to Roman practice, and those who, like Charles Leslie, wished to retain the Anglican service.

This Church included in its ranks some of the most learned and pious men of the day; but it made no impression on the great mass of the people. As Jacobitism died away, its influence, such as it was, waned, and the movement faded out almost unnoticed.

---

1. Led by Collier, then a Bishop. Collier's obstinate, fearless, and masterful nature is well known. Readers of Macaulay will remember how he openly and solemnly absolved, on the scaffold, men who had conspired against the life of William III.

During the eighteenth century the controversies of Churchmen were chiefly with the Deists, the Quakers, the Latitudinarians in their own body, and – towards the latter half of the time – with the Methodists. Few of these controversies still live; but the great work of Bishop Butler of Durham (1736), the *Analogy of Religion with the Constitution and Course of Nature*, directed against Deism, is still read for its masterly reasoning, based on the premisses of the Deists themselves.[1] With the Methodists there was little doctrinal dispute; the chief charge, as laid by Bishop Lavington and others, was that of 'enthusiasm' – the *bête noire* of the age.

It was inevitable that many men of free spirit should revolt against the thraldom in which the Church was held by the State, while the State maintained that as she was established, she must be willing to pay the price. A clergyman who felt that his mission was divine could not but chafe at the bonds which held him in. Such clergy as those described by Jane Austen might go comfortably on, performing their mechanical duties with even less sense of responsibility than the squire his functions as Justice of the Peace. There were, however, others of a different stamp.[2] The feeling might be restrained as long as the State was governed by Tories and Churchmen. But when, in 1832, by the Reform Act, the power fell into the hands of Liberals and Dissenting shopkeepers, it broke out. Lord Grey showed signs of intending to lay sacrilegious hands on the Ark. He bade the Bishops set their house in order, and even brought in a Bill for reducing the numbers of Irish prelates. This, said

---

1. It must be remembered that the Deists – Toland, Tindal, Chubb, Anthony Collins, in England, Voltaire and his disciples in France – believed in a God as revealed by Nature, while they (with various degrees of emphasis) rejected the God of Revelation. Butler took them on their own ground. He does not, except incidentally, argue against atheism.

2. Note the dexterous title of the organization which, later, urged Disestablishment – 'Society for the *Liberation* of Religion from State Patronage and Control': a Nonconformist society, it is true; but the phrase expresses the sentiments of many Anglican clergymen.

Keble, the author of the *Christian Year*,[1] in the famous Assize Sermon of 14 July 1833, was National Apostasy. The Oxford Movement had begun. Within a few days a meeting was held at the house of Hugh Rose, Vicar of Hadleigh in Suffolk, to concert measures for repelling the enemy. The call rang out to the clergy to magnify their office. In the *Tracts for the Times*, which were delivered – if necessary by voluntary carriers – at every parsonage in England, and some of which had a circulation of sixty thousand, the parsons were told that they were not civil servants, but successors of the Apostles, chosen vessels for the transmission of mysterious powers. Pusey, the learned Professor of Hebrew; Keble, the author of the sermon; Isaac Williams – and above all Newman – carried on the work, which was aided in other ways by such men as Palmer, the erudite liturgical scholar, and the vigorous but rash and hasty Hurrell Froude. By degrees it became manifest to many that the Tractarian doctrines meant more than a return to the High Anglicanism of Andrewes and Laud; they tended, if not actually to Rome, yet Romewards; and when, in the ninetieth and last tract, Newman showed how, by a dexterous manipulation of words, the Articles themselves, which the Evangelicals regarded as bulwarks of Protestantism, could be made to square with Roman doctrine, the uproar was great:[2] the tract was formally censured by the Bishops. But the movement had done its work. Even when in 1845 Newman went over to Rome, those who remained were not dismayed, and a succession of distinguished or undistinguished men – the undistinguished perhaps with more effect – gradually transformed half the clerical body into 'Anglo-Catholics', intro-

1. An enormously popular volume of religious poems on the days of the Church Calendar. Its poetic merit is slight, but it suited the times, and some of the poems still suit certain minds.

2. Thus, for instance, Article 22 says 'the Romish doctrine of Purgatory is a fond thing vainly invented'. Newman said that we are permitted to believe in a doctrine of Purgatory so long as it is not 'Romish'. This was in 1841. In 1844 W. G. Ward, a daring and go-ahead pupil of Newman's, threw oil on the flames by publishing *The Ideal of a Christian Church*, in which it appeared that the ideal Church was the Roman.

ucing Romanist ritual into the churches, and proclaiming
octrines Roman in everything but actual submission to the
ope. Some of them, such as Mr Mackonochie and Mr
reen, carried their Ritualism so far as to suffer imprison-
nent in the cause: thus, ultimately, gaining a victory over
ie State by forcing it to assert an authority which public
pinion refused to sanction. Many of the clergy introduced
ie practice of confession, and some of them began to claim
ie right of inflicting punishments on transgressors.[1]

A movement like this, being human, is mingled both of
ood and of evil. The services were certainly more orderly
nd more beautiful; the churches revived the old Gothic
armony and grace; the easy-going, secular-minded, hunt-
ig and drinking 'squarson' disappeared; and the devotion
f the parish priests was often beyond praise. Some, in par-
cular, of the London High Church clergymen gave their
·hole lives, without thought of self, to the service of the
oor, despising wealth and scorning preferment. For those,
gain, to whom the symbolism of the sacraments is a means
f grace, the insistence of these clergy on such ceremonies
as been of incalculable spiritual value. But the exclusive-
ess of the creed, the bitterness with which the Evangelicals
vere spoken of,[2] the 'Jesuitry' of some of the interpretations
iven to the Prayer Book, alienated many honest British

1. It is a mistake to think that the early Tractarians were Ritualists.
he services at St Mary's, where Newman preached, were simple and
ven bald. Pusey disliked ritual, and censured those few of his followers
ho introduced candles and vestments. But his private practices – his con-
·ssions and his austerities – were in the line of Romish developments;
nd, though he never showed the slightest desire to submit to Rome, it is
ard to deny that the later Anglo-Catholics have understood his
rinciples better than he understood them himself.

It must be confessed that Pusey was very badly treated by his oppon-
nts. He was condemned unheard for his sermon on Baptismal Regenera-
on. Nor was this the only occasion in which the authorities acted hastily
nd tyrannically.

2. As, for example, by Hurrell Froude, whose 'Remains' were pub-
shed by Newman and Keble. The mingled mawkishness and un-
haritableness shown in this book did the Movement much harm among
ealthy-minded people.

minds; and the relations with the Dissenters, which under
the Evangelical régime had been growing steadily more
friendly, were almost hopelessly shattered. It was widely felt
that a few more of these clergy might have done better to
follow the example of Newman and Manning: and, indeed,
many of them did so. A more liberal tone began to be heard
in the eighties and nineties: when, in 1889, Charles Gore
and his friends brought out the collection of essays called
Lux Mundi, it was seen that it was possible for High Anglicans to take note of the results of the critical study of the
Bible, and to hold their own views without being unchari-
table towards others. This book shows an approximation to
'Modernism', and marks a great advance since the time when
a Bishop urged Churchmen to treat Colenso as a heathen
and a publican because of his views on the Pentateuch.

The strength of the Movement lay mainly with the
clergy, with large numbers of the 'lower classes' in the great
cities, and with women. The educated laity, and the middle
classes, with many notable exceptions, looked on unmoved.
The pretensions of some of the more inexperienced ministers
raised at best a tolerant smile, at worst contemptuous or indignant laughter. It is hard for average men of the world to
believe that a young man of twenty-three, whom they have
known as the quintessence of mediocrity, has, by the ceremony of ordination, suddenly developed into a supernatural
being, who can perform a miracle every time he celebrates
'Mass'.[1]

1. This is of course a crude and superficial view. I take the following
from Bishop Headlam's *Church of England*, p. 67:

'The Sacraments are performed not by the Bishop or priest, but by the
Church; and the Minister of the Sacrament is Christ. The priest is but
the minister of the Church through whom it acts. Khomiakoff, the
Russian theologian, says, "The Seven Sacraments are not accomplished
by any single individual, but by the whole Church in the person of an
individual". And Thomas Aquinas says, "The priest in consecrating the
Eucharist acts as the representative of the whole Church". In the second
place, the form of the Sacrament is a prayer. The priest does not *make*
the Sacrament, but the whole Church prays, through its ministers, that
Christ will give us the spiritual food of his body and blood'.

Thus, strictly, the priest claims nothing for his office more miraculous

This sentiment was very plainly shown when the Bishops, in 1927, appealed to the State to sanction a new edition of the Prayer Book, which, permitting a certain number of ritualistic practices, would enable – so it was said – the Bishops more easily to put down those not sanctioned. The House of Commons, of which a large proportion was Nonconformist, threw out the Bill; and once again the Church was brought up against the stubborn fact that she is a State department.[1] Many clergymen, therefore, appeared to be willing to accept Disestablishment as the only way out of the impasse. But the difficulties and dangers of such a step gave them pause. What will happen none can foresee.

A totally different view is that of the Evangelical, Protestant, or 'Low' Church, which still preaches, with the inevitable modifications due to time, the doctrines proclaimed by Charles Simeon of Cambridge a hundred years ago, and by Jewel three centuries earlier. The party is, perhaps, weaker than it was, especially among the clergy; but it is still very strong among the laity. The difficulty of both parties is that neither can sign the Articles without some reservation; and, if any reservation at all is allowed, the point at which conformity becomes dishonesty is hard to define with accuracy. The Prayer Book as a whole, again, bears every mark of compromise; it was drawn up to include as many moderate Catholics, and as many moderate Puritans, as possible: and it cannot therefore be said that the Low Church alone represents the views of the Reforming Fathers. Nearer as the Low Churchmen unquestionably are to Cranmer and his coadjutors, the High Church is nearer, perhaps to Hooker, and certainly to Andrewes and Laud.

The Articles thus being accepted in general and not in particular, there is room for a third party, the 'Broad'

---

than the rest of the Church possesses. His power is derivative, and *representative*. If this were always emphasized by the clergy, and understood by the laity, much that is regrettable might be avoided.

1. In the following year an amended form of the Book was submitted, designed to remove some of the protestant objections, but this too was rejected by the Commons. It was nonetheless issued, and continues to be used, though without formal authority.

Church, which of late years has tended more and mor
to adopt 'Modernist' views, to explain away miracle an
prophecy, to accept the results of natural science, and in
deed to be, so far as doctrine is concerned, almost Unitarian
This section of the Church includes some of the most able
learned, and eloquent men in the country; and it perhap
makes the strongest appeal to the educated layman. But
is open, as much as the High Church party though in the
opposite direction, to the charge that it translates the for
mulas of the Church in a very liberal fashion. Such eminen
divines as Bishop Barnes and Dean Inge make no pretenc
that they accept a literal rendering of the Articles; man
'Modern Churchmen' reject the Virgin Birth of Christ, an
welcome the Higher Criticism as freely as a German Luther
an. Despite *Lux Mundi*, there can be no accommodation be
tween them and the extreme Anglo-Catholics; while th
Low Churchmen, many of whom retain the old ideas o
plenary inspiration, are afraid that the Broad way leads onl
to destruction. Nothing but the Establishment holds thes
contending parties together: and to some the Establishmen
appears like a Mezentitus-chain binding, in torturing union
the living with the dead.

On the other hand, there are many to whom this com
prehensiveness is the chief charm of the Church. Th
Church is national, and as the State tolerates Liberal, Tory
Socialist, and Independent, so the Church not only toler
ates, but gladly welcomes, the widest diversity of views. Sh
is, indeed, comprehensive. At the very moment when New
man and his friends were driving on the Oxford Movement
an entirely different set of men, some of whose leaders wer
from Cambridge, were preaching a very different creed and
following very different lines of action. Deriving their in
tellectual inspiration from the somewhat nebulous philoso
phy of Coleridge, Frederick Denison Maurice, his followe
Charles Kingsley, and others, developed a Broad Church
system in which – though it differed widely from late
Latitudinarianism – a view of the Church was involved
utterly opposed to that of Newman and Pusey, and which

was entirely antagonistic to Roman claims. Yet the leaders
remained in the Church. Maurice, indeed, lost his professor-
ship at King's College because of his rejection of Eternal
Punishment; but he was at once given a Cambridge living,
where he remained impregnably entrenched. Kingsley,
whose detestation of Rome was undisguised, and was proclaimed in more than one of his novels, kept his living of
Eversley and was a Cambridge professor till his death.
Meanwhile, Robertson of Brighton, perhaps the greatest
preacher the Church of England has had for centuries, was
influencing thousands by his sermons, which were published
posthumously and circulated very widely: and Robertson
had no sympathy either with Newmanism or with Evangeli-
alism. He founded no school, but his disciples were count-
ess. Arnold of Rugby, again, who hated the Oxford school
and was hated by it, desired to enlarge the Church till it
should be practically synonymous with the State; he would
have included all Nonconformists except Unitarians. As
Rugby admitted all sorts, so should the State-Church com-
prise all Christian believers.

Along with all these, and many others, there is a party
which regards the Establishment as a confession that the
State recognizes religion; which emphasizes the advantage
of having 'a gentleman in every parish'; which troubles itself little about dogma, and adopts ritual, so far as it does
adopt it, not as an essential symbolism, but merely as a decent and attractive ornament of the service, which carries on
the tradition of the eighteenth century, and does its duties
quietly and inoffensively, regarding the clergy as good
sound citizens, elder brothers and advisers of their parish-
oners. This party, holding that every Englishman is, poten-
tially, a member of the Church, excludes none, and welcomes to the services any who like to appear. Its bounds
often cross those of the other parties, for its determining
character depends rather on the temperaments of the individual ministers than on their dogmatic or ecclesiastical
views. It is a tribute to the liberality of the Church of England, as by law established, that it can find room for men

of all these different kinds. How long it will be able to do so is hard to say, and whether this comprehensiveness would remain if Disestablishment came is still more uncertain.

Of the marvellous missionary work which the Church of England has done during the last eighty or ninety years, space prevents us from speaking at length, but must not prevent us from speaking with admiration. The number of Bishops has been multiplied many times over, and scarcely a region in the world but has seen their labours. If this growth continues at the same rate, it will not be long before the centre of gravity of the Church is transferred elsewhere. In this, all schools of the Church have engaged in usually generous rivalry; and perhaps nothing does more to reconcile differences and to reduce non-essential doctrines to their proper proportions.

CHAPTER 14

THE CHURCH OF SCOTLAND

THE reformation in Scotland, as elsewhere, began as a moral reform. The corruption of the older Church was rank and smelled to heaven. Its wealth, in comparison with that of the country, was monstrous, and was monopolized by the higher clergy, the Abbots and Bishops keeping up the state of earls, while the vicars almost starved, and kept themselves alive by oppressing their parishioners. The celibacy of the clergy was a farce, and a farce dangerous to the honour of the common families. Cardinal Beaton's illegitimate children were at least five in number; and a clergyman who lived decently with one woman was a blessed exception. Benefices were purchased for money, and were conferred on laymen or on children: they were, indeed, the common means of providing for noblemen's younger sons. Indulgences, the sale of sham relics, the worship of images, had been seen through and denounced long before the Reformation; but they still went on.

When, therefore, Luther's writings came into Scotland, they were welcomed, and were circulated, along with Tyndale's English Bible, in defiance of all that Church and State could do. Some of the heretics were burned, some fled, but others took their place. Violence was answered by violence. The burning of the reformer Wishart in 1546 was followed within three months by the murder of Cardinal Beaton, who had been Wishart's judge: and from that time forward there was confusion, in which the only thing clear was that Reformation doctrines were making rapid headway. James V had supported the Church against the nobles, who were eager to seize the Church lands; but his early death left the State in the hands of men inclined to Lutheran opinions. When, in 1554, Mary of Guise assumed the regency, the troubles were further complicated, for her aim was to make Scotland an appanage of France, and many of the Catholic nobles refused to follow her: thus the Church party was divided and weakened at the time when its enemies were daily gaining strength. The clergy saw their danger; a number of enactments tending to put an end to the scandals (and incidentally proving how terrible they were) were passed in 1549, and others in 1552: but it was too late. The majority of the people were now determined not merely on a reform of manners, but on a root and branch change of doctrine, discipline, and worship. Unlike Henry VIII of England, they would not stop with the substitution of Crown for Pope. Most of the preachers had learnt, not from Luther, but from Calvin: and in particular their leader, John Knox, who had worked in Geneva with Calvin himself, was resolved to introduce the full Calvinistic system into Scotland. Along with this great man, to a considerable extent, went the 'Lords of the Congregation', who in 1557 signed the Covenant to maintain the 'blessed Word of God and his congregation' against their enemies, and demanded the right of holding services in the manner they desired.

At this moment the tangle was still farther ravelled by the accession of Elizabeth in England. To the Catholic party she was illegitimate; the rightful Queen was Mary of Scotland, now married to the Dauphin of France. If then Scotland could be won back to Catholicism, and Mary made Queen of England, it might be possible to gain a decisive victory at once for France and for the Papacy. Accordingly, the Scottish Protestants made an appeal for help to Elizabeth, which, after her usual delays and tergiversations, she at length granted. English troops were sent to aid the Lords of the Congregation, and as a result the French troops departed. Mary of Guise died almost at the same time, and the Estates met, in August 1560, to settle their affairs, free from foreign pressure. This is the real date of the Scottish Reformation. No sooner had the Estates met than the Confession of Faith, drawn up by Knox and five other ministers, was presented to them, and was almost unanimously adopted: the authority of the Pope was abolished: and the celebration of Mass was declared a penal offence. When, however, an attempt was made to apply the lands and revenues of the old Church to the support of the ministry, the Estates – many of the Lords and smaller barons being already in possession of the Church lands – refused to give them up. Thus the new Church failed as yet to gain legal recognition; but the meeting of the first General Assembly of the Kirk, in December of the same year, provided a good substitute for Parliamentary sanction: indeed, for many years, the Assembly was a much better representative of Scottish opinion than Parliament itself.

The ideas on which the Reformed Kirk was based are found in the Confession, in Knox's Liturgy, and in the Book of Discipline. The Confession is strongly Anti-Papal: the 'Kirk malignant' is denounced in several places; Apostolic Succession and Transubstantiation are repudiated; Christ is the sole head of the Kirk; the Papist priests are not ministers at all; and the Mass is a blasphemy. The Liturgy, which was practically the same as one used by Knox when serving his Geneva congregation, was of course in English: it was intended to secure order and regularity in the services throughout the country. It remained in general use till the reaction caused by Laud's attempt to force an Anglican liturgy on the Kirk led to its abandonment, and to the substitution of 'free' prayers. The Book of Discipline contains a most elaborate set of rules for the election of ministers, for the provision of their maintenance, for the appointment of schools and masters, for the reorganization of the universities, and in fact for the ordering of everything connected with Church affairs – which, indeed, were not always sufficiently distinguished from secular.

The whole was based on the Word of God: and here the want of a critical study of the Bible is easily to be discerned. Old Testament and New were equally inspired, and the example of Jewish prophets was adduced to justify the most savage persecution of the 'Amalekites' and 'hosts of Midian' whom the Protestants saw reincarnated in Papists and Prelatists. Here, unfortunately, they were retaining precisely those Papist opinions which they would have done best to reject. In another matter, also, lay the seeds of future conflict. The State was recognized as divinely appointed, and as coequal with the Church; but there were not wanting signs that the Church would stretch her claims beyond the point at which the State could admit them.

The admission of the laity to a share in the Church order is a special mark of the Scottish Kirk. The deacons took charge of the funds; but the elders had, like the ministers, the oversight of moral and spiritual affairs; nay, they might, at times, sit in judgement on the ministers. The people elected their own pastor, after testing his learning and character; and that extraordinary feature of Kirk life, the public rebuke of offenders, is due to the fact that at first the congregation had the right of dealing with moral transgressions.

Although there were 'Superintendents' who to a certain degree exercised authority over their brother-ministers, and who have often been regarded as Bishops under another name, yet it was made clear that the Superintendents were, at best, *primi inter pares*: all ministers had the same status. Whether the original reformers, nearly all of whom had been Romish priests, meant to pave the way for a modified Episcopacy is uncertain: what is certain is that, in the confusion of the time, such authorities were absolutely necessary, for the number of men qualified for the ministry was small. In later days, their work has been done by the Church-courts, which are one of the most powerful engines of discipline in Presbyterian Churches.

The history of Scotland has been largely affected by the fact that for two whole centuries her kings died young, minorities succeeded, and the nobles were therefore able to gain a power which was often too much for the Throne itself. The Reformation-time was no exception. The Queen, who had nominally reigned for eighteen years, had been in France for thirteen, and Queen-consort there for a year. Her husband, however, died, and she returned to the country of her birth, to which she was in fact a total stranger. She was a mere girl, and the problems before her were such as might have overtaxed the energies of a Robert Bruce. Had she arrived a year or two earlier, they would yet have been too hard for her; but she came at the very moment when Protestantism had consolidated itself by the vigorous steps we have described. To her, brought up a strong Catholic, the movement was unintelligible, and she vastly underrated its strength, imagining that a dexterous mingling of force and craft might restore the old faith; for it seemed possible, by setting one faction of the nobles against the other, so to weaken the Protestant Lords as to make the royal will prevail. For a moment her hopes ran high, and indeed, to one who could see in the whole dispute only a contention between great and ambitious men, the hopes might appear justified. She refused to summon the Assembly; and some of the Protestants who still retained some respect for the Crown therefore refrained from attending when it met unsummoned. A number of the Protestant lords were driven into banishment, and, had the Reformation really, as she thought, depended on them, it might have been suppressed. But this was far from being the case. The Kirk, though deprived of its secular leaders, was quite capable of defending itself; and very soon a series of events, too well known to need recapitulation, led to the utter ruin of the Queen's cause. Her fatal marriage to Darnley, the murder of Rizzio and that of Darnley shortly afterwards, her marriage to Bothwell, her imprisonment in Lochleven Castle and her escape, the battle of Langside, and her flight to England, all these are known to every schoolboy. They were, to a great extent, affairs of personal hatred, of vulgar intrigue, and of very unchristian passions; but, evil as they were, they inevitably tended to the strengthening of the Kirk, for the nobles who had defeated Mary needed Church support, and bought it by promising to complete the work of establishment and to root out what was left of 'Popish superstition'. They fulfilled that part of their engagement which did not affect their own material advantage. The Parliament of 1567, led by the Regent Murray, re-enacted in a stronger form the Act of 1560; but, ultra-Protestant as it was, found itself unable to stomach the Book of Discipline. During the three years of Murray's rule, he worked on the whole in harmony with Knox, and the Protestant lords, secure of their gains, supported him with a zeal tempered by covetousness.

By now nearly every parish had a Protestant minister; a large number of Romanist priests had come over and formed the nucleus of the new hierarchy; and the Protestantism of England assured the Scottish nation that there would be no attempt from the south to overthrow the new system. Knox, in particular, who had been an Anglican, and who had even been offered an English bishopric, did his utmost to foster friendship with England, and thus to hinder the return of Mary. A succession of Protestant regents, Murray, Lennox, Mar, and Morton, gradually obtained the mastery over Mary's party, and broke the power of Romanism. The Massacre of St Bartholomew, which so terribly weakened the Huguenots in France, strengthened the determination of their friends in Scotland: and when, a few months later (November 1572) Knox died, he might feel that his work was done.

In the same year, however, there came a curious change. Under the Regency of Morton, episcopacy was introduced: and, if the new Bishops had been worthy of the name, the Scottish Kirk might be episcopal today. It soon appeared, however, that though the Bishops were determined Protestants, they were really but tools of the State. Morton and his friends, who were resolved to keep the Church in their hands, appointed the Bishops on the clear understanding that a large portion of the revenues should come to the State. The Bishops were known as 'Tulchans' (straw-stuffed calfskins meant to induce cows to give milk); and the Church in general was seen to be but a milch-cow for the State. This made men more willing to see force in the arguments of Andrew Melville, who went everywhere proclaiming that episcopacy was not only unnecessary but unscriptural. As Morton's power waned, it became possible for the Church to assert itself; and in 1581 the Second Book of Discipline passed the Assembly. This book, unlike the first, came gradually to be accepted by the State. Its effect was to define the Church, to assert its independence of the State, to describe and delimit the powers of its rulers (among whom neither Bishops nor Superintendents appear),[1] and to secure, after a time, the mapping-out of the whole country into Presbyteries, which were grouped into Provincial Synods, and were all controlled by the General Assembly, to which they sent both lay and clerical representatives. This was in the main the work of Andrew Melville.

Episcopacy, however, found a strong supporter in the King, who was now, theoretically, of age to rule. Though only sixteen years old, he saw clearly that the Kirk, as thus organized, must prove a too powerful rival of royalty, and that a Bishop was the natural ally of a King. A confused struggle ensued, lasting for several years, and interrupted, but not ended, by James's consent to the Act of Parliament of 1592, which ratified the liberties of the Kirk, permitting her to legislate for herself, and accepted, in effect, Melville's new Book of Discipline. This Act was regarded as the charter of the Church, and was the basis on which, after a hundred years of struggle and the final expulsion of the Stuarts, she organized herself under William and Mary. But James, as usual, was deceptive. While outwardly maintaining the Act, he was secretly working for the full establishment of Episcopacy: and the publication of extracts from his book *Basilicon Doron* (containing advice to his son Henry) showed the people how little his protestations were to be relied on. When, in 1603, he became King of England, he was in a position to throw off disguise. The episcopate was restored, and three Bishops were summoned to London to be consecrated after the Anglican pattern, in order that they might duly consecrate others. Finally, in 1612, the Act of 1592 was repealed: shortly afterwards, at Perth, 'Five Articles', which to many seemed to open the gates to 'Popery, were passed at a packed General Assembly; and

1. 'Bishop' is declared to be only another name for minister.

for the next twenty years not even a packed Assembly was allowed to meet.

What happened in the next reign is well known. Charles, with more obstinacy and openness than his father, carried on the same work. By his own fiat, in 1637, he transformed the whole Church system into one practically Anglican: and in the same year the Anglican Liturgy (slightly altered by Laud) was made compulsory. The result was the Covenant of 1638, by which, after a recitation of the Acts of Parliament which Charles had violated, all the signatories, that is, nearly all in Scotland who could write, bound themselves to support each other in defending the true religion. The King was compelled to agree to the summoning of a General Assembly, which abolished Episcopacy, deposed all the fourteen Bishops from the ministry, and restored the whole Presbyterian system. This meant civil war; but Charles, unable to control England, was forced to accept the demands of the Assembly: in 1641 he granted everything that was asked, and the new settlement was legally ratified.

After the defeat of Charles, which was largely due to the Scottish help given to the Parliament, it looked for a time as if Presbyterianism might be established in England also, but this hope was destroyed by the English army. Even when Charles was dead, and his son, in his desire for Scottish support, accepted the Covenant, the attempt was crushed by Cromwell at Dunbar and Worcester. Scotland became for a time a province of England; and, though there was little interference with worship, the General Assembly again ceased to meet.

Before Charles II's Restoration, he had promised to retain Presbyterianism; none the less he proceeded to break his promise. The Drunken Parliament of 1661 rescinded all the laws passed since 1633; Episcopacy was restored. Two presbyters, James Sharp and Robert Leighton, were summoned to England, and were consecrated Archbishops of St Andrews and Glasgow respectively: the Covenants were declared treasonable, and all public officers were required to abjure them: even the Act of 1592 was repealed, again

For a quarter of a century the country was torn to pieces; rebellions, executions, dragoonings, followed in interminable sequence. An indulgence granted in 1669 merely led to greater bitterness on the part of the extreme Covenanters; it was in vain that men like Leighton tried to reconcile Presbyterian and Episcopalian; Sharp, the chief object of hatred, was murdered in 1679, and a serious revolt followed, which was put down, not without difficulty, by Monmouth at Bothwell Bridge, and punished with frightful severity. Under Richard Cameron and others a guerrilla war was carried on for years; and the Cameronians, in their rage and despair, finally deposed and excommunicated the apostate King.

Under James VII things were no better, though, in his desire to obtain toleration for Catholics, he endeavoured to conciliate the Presbyterians by offering an Indulgence – illegal, because not passed by Parliament. With this the Cameronians would have nothing to do: but the more moderate Presbyterians availed themselves of it, and preached openly in conventicles, to be dubbed for their pains, by the irreconcilables, Judases and traffickers with the Scarlet Woman.

No sooner was James declared to have forfeited the crown of England, than the Estates of Scotland followed suit. The 'Convention' declared that he had 'forfaulted' the crown of Scotland also, passed a 'Claim of Right' similar to the English 'Declaration of Rights', and proclaimed William and Mary King and Queen. The full Parliament which succeeded abolished Episcopacy, and a year later the Westminster Confession was adopted as the doctrinal symbol of the Kirk, while the Presbyterian system of government was restored according to the basic Act of 1592. All the Presbyterian ministers – there were sixty survivors out of hundreds – who had been expelled since the Restoration, were recalled, and, after a lapse of forty years, the General Assembly met again.

There was, not unnaturally, some harshness. Great unwillingness was felt to permit Episcopalians to remain in the Church, even if they conformed to the new order. William, one of whose chief glories is that he refused to be a persecutor, strongly objected, and dissolved the Assembly. Had it met again without his permission, there would have been a serious breach between Church and State: but William was wise, and there were wise men on the other side. In the Parliament of 1693 an 'Act for settling the Quiet and Peace of the Church' was passed, which provided that all ministers who would take the oath of allegiance, subscribe the Westminister Confession, and accept the Presbyterian system, should be admitted into the Kirk. An Assembly, duly summoned by the King, followed up the Act by admitting such ministers. It is said that about a third of the ministers were Episcopalian in opinion, though they loyally kept their oaths. The Settlement, of course, did not satisfy the extreme Covenanters, and there were some unfortunate secessions, as well as some 'rabblings' or mobbings of unpopular pastors: but on the whole the Parliament, the Assembly, and above all William himself, had acted with exemplary moderation and prudence. From that time no year has passed without a meeting of the General Assembly, which – within limits carefully defined – acts in entire independence of the State. Communication with the State is maintained by the presence, along with the Moderator, of the King's Commissioner, who, after the Moderator has dissolved the Assembly in the name of Christ, and fixed the time and place of the next meeting, formally repeats the phrases in the name of his Majesty.

At the Union of England and Scotland in 1707, the rights of the Kirk were clearly and fully asserted. Before coronation, in fact immediately on his accession, every new sovereign, as his first official act, must take an oath to 'maintain the government, worship, rights, and privileges of the Church of Scotland'. One more Act, of great importance, followed in 1712, forbidding any civil penalty to follow excommunication. This, though it might seem to weaken the Church, really marks still more clearly its independence: it is the recognition of the principle that Church offences are for the Church alone, and civil offences for the magistrate.

In the same year, by a gross violation of faith, the Tory

majority in Parliament passed the Patronage Act, restoring to the ancient patrons the right of presenting to livings. Against this Act, fruitful of much evil, the Church did not cease to protest, claiming that the 'call' of the congregations was the real essential in the election of ministers. Considerable trouble also arose from the uncompromising attitude of the extreme Covenanters; and a secession, in the Covenanting sense, took place about 1740 under Ebenezer Erskine, who protested against the non-renewal of the Covenant in 1692, against the retention of Episcopalian ministers in the Church, and against other 'Erastian' tendencies and un-Scriptural practices which were detected in the Kirk as re-established. Other secessions followed, most of which were the natural consequences of the Act of 1712 and of the abuse of patronage.

Though the Church for the most part retained its Presbyterian orthodoxy, yet it could not resist the influences which were so powerful everywhere in the eighteenth century. This is shown by the rise of the Moderate Party, which, by the end of the century, had become powerful in the Church, and showed, within certain limits, the same features as those which marked the Church of England about the same time; a Latitudinarianism of view, an inclination to tone down the rigid Calvinism of earlier days, a willingness, perhaps tainted with Erastianism, to work with the State, and an absence of intolerance even where freethinkers were concerned. It was this Moderate spirit that to a great extent explains the continuance of patronage, and the toleration of the Episcopal Church in Scotland, which was finally confirmed in 1792. Some Moderate ministers, like 'Jupiter' Carlyle and Alexander Jardine, were friendly with even so daring a thinker as David Hume: and the views of the historian Robertson, one of the most influential ministers of the time, were unquestionably very broad.[1]

1. At the Greyfriars Church in Edinburgh, Robertson, the Moderate Leader, and John Erskine the Evangelical, were joint ministers, preaching differing views from the same pulpit. They remained close and trusting friends; but it was not likely that such harmony in difference would be possible everywhere.

The strength of the Moderates lay chiefly in Edinburgh and the Universities; the old stubborn orthodoxy remained in the country parishes; and it might have been suspected by clear-sighted observers that great tact would be necessary if secessions, on a larger scale than any yet known, were to be avoided. It was practically certain that, as in England, a revival of Evangelical religion was coming, that dissatisfaction with a Church of which the mark was a dislike of enthusiasm, and a certain easy-going worldliness, was increasing, and that an upheaval was more than possible. The French Revolution perhaps delayed the crisis, but the nineteenth century saw its arrival. We shall briefly speak of that crisis elsewhere.

CHAPTER 15

THE SECTS

THE early Reformers, like most revolutionaries, did not understand their own work. Beginning with a revolt against a practical evil, they passed on, as was inevitable, to attack some of the doctrine of the Church. But they did not see that they were starting a movement in favour of freedom of thought and freedom of the expression of thought, which must lead to the expression of ideas far more advanced than their own. Luther, for instance, could never see that men would demand, and use, the right of dissenting from him as he had dissented from the Pope, and his arguments on this head become strangely wriggling and illogical. He usually, in fact, avoids argument and contents himself with denunciation. It is hard to see why, if he might modify the Papal doctrine of Transubstantiation, however slightly, Zwingli might not modify the Lutheran; yet Luther could never be brought to admit that Zwingli, being obviously wrong in his opinion, was nevertheless entitled to hold it, if he believed it. There are many places in Calvin's writings where he asserts for himself the power of interpreting God's will through a sort of inward illumination: consistently, he ought to have permitted to others the same gift; but he never, except in comparatively unimportant points, could be brought to such a concession. Not the Church of Rome herself was more intolerant than the Church of Geneva. Of this intolerance the worst and most celebrated example is the case of Servetus. Michael Servetus was a Spaniard who had started life in the service of the confessor of Charles V. Beginning to study the Bible, he convinced himself that the doctrine of the Trinity was not in it; and at the age of twenty published a book on the Trinitarian errors, which made a great sensation. The book was burnt, and he was forced to change his name and adopt the profession of a physician.

For twelve years he lived at Vienne, surrounded by Roman Catholics, unsuspected and honoured. But he still held to his views, and, hoping to lead the Reformation along the Anti-Trinitarian path, opened a correspondence with Calvin, whom he utterly failed to move: Calvin, indeed, became more and more exasperated as the arguments developed. When, in 1546, Servetus, thinking a personal conference might have some effect, asked for a safe-conduct to Geneva, Calvin uttered the ominous words, 'If he comes, and my influence has any weight, he will not leave the city alive.' Six years later, the heretic published anonymously his second work, reiterating with more force his former arguments. Through Calvin's instrumentality the authorship was revealed; he was imprisoned at Vienne, and held for trial. Escaping thence, with the object of practising as a physician at Naples, he ventured into Geneva, and was recognized just as he was about to leave it. There he was tried for heresy, Calvin pressing the charge with furious eagerness; and on 27 October 1553 he was burnt at the stake. It is painful to think that the vast majority of the leading Reformers, Melanchthon included, approved of the murder; but the instinct of the common people was on the other side, and Calvin was driven to defend himself. The Marian persecutions in England followed soon after: if there is a preference possible as to such horrors, the Marian are preferable to the Calvinian.[1] Twenty years later, another judicial murder of the same kind occurred in the Calvinist Palatinate.

Whereas, however, men whose whole position was due to having thought for themselves, thus refused to allow others to imitate them, there were, fortunately for the world, men who, despite all dangers and insults, persisted in exercising the right, and others who, though not sharing the 'heretical' views, maintained that the heretics ought to be left free to express them.[2] It is to the courage and persistency of men

1. A monument has been erected to Servetus, 'by followers of Calvin', close to the spot where he died.

2. Trechsel, an authority on the case of Servetus, mentions a severe criticism of Calvin's action by 'Vaticanus', and a 'very remarkable

like these that we owe the greatest blessing of modern times, the right to utter openly what we think sincerely: a right, it is true, fully conceded only in theory, and not by any means always recognized in practice, but, imperfect as it is, exceedingly precious.[1]

It is impossible to mention a tithe of the sects which, exercising the right of private judgement, and sometimes refusing it to others, appeared in Britain and on the Continent during the century and a half after Luther. In some respects, the most important is the PRESBYTERIAN, which is nothing but Calvinism transplanted to another soil; which, under the leadership of John Knox and his successors, became dominant in Scotland; and which, for a long time, disputed with Anglicanism the supremacy within the English Church itself. The story is well known how the exigencies of war compelled Pym, in order to secure the aid of the Scots against the King, to consent to the Solemn League and Covenant, by which for a moment Presbyterianism was established in England, and showed itself as intolerant as Laud had been before it. To Milton the new 'Forcers of Conscience' were fully as obnoxious as the old; 'presbyter'

---

book', published in 1554, entitled *De Haereticis an sint persequendi, sententiae*, a collection of opinions on the right to persecute.

1. In times of excitement, the proud claim made by Tennyson, that England is a land 'where, girt by friends or foes, a man may speak the thing he will', is too often falsified. During the Boer War, for instance, a man who openly opposed the Government's policy did so at peril of limb or even life: and in the war of 1914 there was an intolerance scarcely less virulent. In religious matters, too, there has been less freedom than is commonly supposed. Richard Carlile was repeatedly imprisoned for what was called blasphemy, though his views differed from Palmerston's chiefly in being honestly proclaimed: and three instances of persecution, all from the single year 1857, are collected by Mill in the second chapter of his *Liberty*. The suppression of the free discussion of *political* questions, which is now so common in half Europe, is too familiar to need mention.

The Church of Rome has not only never renounced the right of persecuting, if 'necessary' even to death, for heresy, but repeatedly asserted it during the nineteenth century. The eulogy of Ferdinand of Arragon, as a zealous persecutor of heretics, still remains in the revised (1911) Breviary.

turned out to be merely a lengthened spelling of 'priest'; and the tyranny was checked only by the rising power of the army. After the return of Charles II, many of the Presbyterians were absorbed into the Church, and became the ancestors of the present 'Protestant' party. Others, by the Act of Uniformity of 1662, were driven out – nearly two thousand clergy among them – and had a hard life till the Toleration Act of 1689 gave them a measure of relief. Their subsequent fate we shall describe in a moment.

The doctrines and institutions of combined English and Scottish Presbyterianism were defined in the famous Westminster Assembly of Divines, which began in 1643 and faded away almost unnoticed in 1652. This, it is important to remember, was an advisory committee; the final voice remained with Parliament, which, in full Erastian style, claimed control over Church affairs. The doctrinal standards are contained in the Westminster Confession, which was approved by the Church of Scotland in 1647 and by the Long Parliament in 1648. With certain modifications, it is still the foundation of the belief of Scottish, American, and English Presbyterianism, and is the most thorough and logical statement in existence of the Calvinistic creed. It bears some marks of compromise; episcopacy is not absolutely condemned, and even a presbytery is not declared to be *jure divino*, but stated to be 'agreeable to the word of God'. The dogma of election, however, with its concomitant predestination, is rigidly affirmed; and the final perseverance of saints, once assured of their election, is clearly and positively laid down. The Confession was summed up in two catechisms, the longer for the use of ministers, and the shorter to be taught to children.[1] This little work is perhaps the most widely known catechism in the Protestant world; and the influence it has exerted, both by attraction and by repulsion, can hardly be exaggerated.

Against the Calvinism of the Presbyterians the 'sover-

1. All readers of Sir Walter Scott know the 'shorter Carritch', and most are familiar with its opening words, 'what is the chief end of man?'

eign drug'[1] of ARMINIANISM was found a potent remedy.
Arminius, a professor in the University of Leyden, is one
of the very rare cases of men converted to an opinion which
they have set about to refute. He had been appointed to expose the errors of a heretic named Koornheert on the question of free-will, and his investigations made him doubtful
as to predestination. He did not, however, live long enough
to develop his doctrines; and the importance of his work
was not seen till after his death. A disputation having arisen,
his followers presented a 'Remonstrance' of five articles to
the Estates of Holland and Friesland. These articles stated,
in opposition to Calvinism, that God has determined to
save, not a definite number of persons, but those who
through grace believe in Christ; that Christ died not for
some men but for all; and that the doctrine of the perseverance of the saints must be more particularly proved from
Holy Scripture before it can be preached with confidence.
The question was thrashed out in the famous Synod of Dort
in 1618; and, partly for political reasons, the Remonstrants
were condemned. The quarrel between Maurice of Nassau
and Oldenbarneveldt was then at its height, and Oldenbarneveldt sympathized with the Remonstrants. Maurice
was not scrupulous: the Synod was both advocate and judge,
and two hundred Remonstrants were deposed. After
Maurice's death, however, they were tolerated, and, as is
so often the case, when no longer oppressed, they ceased to
increase in numbers. But the influence of Arminianism is
not to be measured by the size of the nominal Arminian
Church. The doctrine penetrated Anglicanism, and strongly
swayed the minds of Laud and his followers, who recognized
its use as a weapon against the aggressive Calvinism of the
Puritan party. Among the Methodists a hundred years later,
the disputes of Dort were renewed. Whitefield, Toplady,
and others were strong Calvinists: Wesley, Fletcher, and
the majority, were Arminians. In the controversy that
ensued, the violence was nearly all on the side of the Calvinists. Fletcher's *Checks to Antinomianism*, a model of calm

1. The phrase used by Archbishop Laud to describe Arminianism.

argumentation without a touch of bitterness – a book worthy in every way of one of the most saintly men in history – remains perhaps the best statement and defence of the Arminian position ever written. He did not, however, convince his opponents: the Calvinist ministers and their followers separated themselves from Wesley and formed a Church of their own, which still flourishes, especially in Wales.

It is not easy to define UNITARIANISM, for the best theologians of that denomination are unwilling to be bound, or to bind others, by any creed, and leave room for the development of ideas not merely in the society itself but in the individual member. We thus find among Unitarians opinions ranging from an Arianism closely approaching orthodoxy to beliefs in which Christ is reduced to the status of a great and holy man, purer and higher than Socrates or Zoroaster, but of essentially the same kind. Every Unitarian, then, has the right, and exercises the right, of tracing his beliefs to any master or to none. Some may incline to the view of the third-century presbyter SABELLIUS, to whom the three Persons of the Trinity were but aspects of the one Monad, and whose favourite image for the mystery was the sun as the Father, the light as the Son, and the heat as the Holy Ghost.[1] Others may recognize their views as much the same with those ascribed as Arian or semi-Arian heretics of the fourth and fifth centuries. Yet others, like the well-known Andrews Norton, may derive their opinions from a study of the Scriptures, and may own no other teacher.[2] Thought, among Unitarians, is perhaps freer than in any Church that has ever existed, and the thinkers more inde-

---

1. Sabellius was excommunicated in A.D. 261; but his opinions have never died out. They resemble those of Schleiermacher and Herder; and I have myself heard a Church of England clergyman preach them (using the very illustration mentioned above) from the pulpit of a consecrated church.

2. Norton's *Reasons for not believing the Doctrine of Trinitarians* is almost entirely based on the Bible: he was a thorough believer in inspiration and in the supernatural, but could find no evidence for the Trinity in the sacred Books.

pendent. Everyone is *nullius addictus jurare in verba magistri*, and thus it is quite impossible to mention any name as that of the father of the church: nor is 'church' perhaps the best word to describe a society, which is deliberately compacted very loosely. But, though Unitarians do not swear to the tenets of any man, they are willing to learn from them, and it may be legitimate to mention names they hold in honour, if none can be mentioned which they idolize. Strangely enough, Servetus is rarely referred to by modern Unitarians. The Reformer whom it is less dangerous to call their master than any other is Faustus Socinus – a name at one time the very type of heresy. Socinus is an example of the freedom of speculation which, as I said above, the Reformers detested but of which they were themselves the originators. Born in 1539 at Siena, he was compelled by family circumstances to migrate to Zürich. Here, while working through the papers of his uncle Laelius, a man no less hardy in his heresies than Faustus, he found statements and arguments which set him thinking, and suggested to him theories which he afterwards drew out in full. At a very early age – in revolutionary times men are often extraordinarily precocious – he published some of these views, but anonymously. As the authorship and the heresy became known, he thought it advisable to leave Western Europe and betake himself to the more congenial atmosphere of Poland, where there was already a society of Anabaptist Unitarians, and where a strange chaos of beliefs was to be found. He was unable to join the Anabaptists, who insisted on his re-baptism; and – despite serious persecution – busied himself with the propagation of his peculiar views. Such was his success that they were accepted in 1603 by the synod of Rakow, and he was engaged after the fashion of the time, in formulating them in a catechism when, in the next year, he died. The catechism was finished and published soon afterwards by some of his friends.

Socinus based his system, boldly and uncompromisingly, upon reason, which, to him, is man's supreme gift. By reason, we decide that the Scriptures are inspired, and that miracles are credible. We therefore accept what the Scriptures tell us, but not on the authority of Pope, or Church, or the witness of any other Christian; where the Scriptures tell us things *above* reason, we admit them, but on rational grounds, for they can never contradict reason. But the doctrine of the Trinity, and that of the union of the divine nature with the human in Christ, *are* contrary to reason, and are therefore false. We are not, however, in this respect put to the task of reconciling reason with revelation, for the doctrine of the Trinity is not to be found in the Bible, which distinctly asserts that God is one. Those proof-texts so often adduced by Trinitarians are all misinterpreted: the three 'Holies' in the sixth chapter of Isaiah are merely emphatic; of the three men who visited Abraham before the destruction of Sodom only one is called Lord; and the Three Witnesses text in the Epistle of John is spurious. Christ is more than man, but he is not divine; when he said 'I and my Father are one', he simply meant that they were one in will and intent, as we say two people are of one mind. In a work on St John's Gospel, the stronghold of the Trinitarians, Socinus subjects every supposed proof of Christ's divinity to searching analysis, and reaches the conclusion that there is not one word which, properly understood, or rationally interpreted, asserts the doctrine. Everywhere, in fact, Socinus shows himself the father of modern Rationalism, maintaining the right and duty of testing everything by the touchstone of reason: and readers of the eighteenth-century Deists will notice many points, apart from his strict acceptance of Scripture, in which he anticipates their ideas.

Unitarianism has never been popular, and many men who have held Unitarian views have never called themselves by the name. When the Toleration Act was passed, a declaration of belief in the Trinity was exacted. But, by a gradual and insensible process, the Presbyterian Dissenters who received the benefit of that Act became infected with Socinian ideas, and the descendants of men who would have burnt Socinians at the stake preached Socinian doctrines. Priestley and Price, for instance, who occupied Presbyterian pulpits, were Unitarians, and Priestley was attacked as such by Bishop Horsley. Later, such was the unpopularity of the sect that a determined effort was made to deprive them of their chapels and endowments on the ground that the preachers did not hold the views of the original founders. This attempt was foiled by the Dissenters' Chapels Bill of 1844, passed by Sir Robert Peel with the weighty support of Macaulay and other enlightened Whigs.

Since then, they have been unmolested, but the strange unpopularity continues, nor, though one of the most intellectual of Churches, do they largely increase their numbers. Many of their ministers maintain themselves by lecturing and writing, their congregations being too small to provide adequate salaries. The power of the creed or no-creed which they profess, however, is not to be reckoned by the number of open adherents. There have been, and are, thousands of Unitarians who are nominally members of other Churches, and thousands besides who belong to no Church at all. There have been men like Milton, Arian in opinion, but not attending public worship; laymen of the Church of England like Isaac Newton, who privately incline to Unitarian views; clergymen like Samuel Clarke, who are 'unsound' on the Trinity, or like Conyers Middleton, who believe in 'Free Inquiry' while still holding preferments: and there still are such men. Neither Jowett nor Dean Stanley would have been out of place in a Unitarian pulpit. Liddon's Bampton Lectures on the Divinity of Christ were answered by a Church of England clergyman who went further in denial than Socinus, and was less of a Trinitarian than Martineau. Dr Edwin Abbot, the author of the *Kernel and the Husk*, in which the husk was the miraculous, was a Church of England minister, and stated that he knew personally four hundred of his brethren who substantially agreed with him. It is hard to distinguish the views of many Modernist churchmen from those of certain Unitarians. In the orthodox Nonconformist churches there are Unitarian laymen, who, being 'sensible men', keep their ideas to themselves.

In America there has been little of this concealment, and little need for it. In Boston, the centre of American enlightenment, almost all the distinguished laymen, and the most influential clergymen, fifty or eighty years ago, were Unitarians and avowed it – I was about to say 'boldly avowed it', but there was no necessity for boldness. Emerson – in his own highly individual fashion – Longfellow, Charles Eliot Norton (the son of Andrews), Oliver Wendell Holmes, James Russell Lowell, and all the élite of that intellectual society, were Unitarians not only in belief but in name. But by far the most eminent and representative member of the Church was William Ellery Channing, whose moral and religious influence in America was unequalled during the first forty years of the nineteenth century, and whose works were for a long time as well known in England as in his native country. Along with James Martineau, he stands as the chief exponent of modern Unitarian doctrine, and as the best exemplification of its character.

American Calvinism had been passing through similar phrases to those we have already seen in the English Church; by slow gradations it was moving from orthodoxy to some form of Anti-Trinitarianism, and the Calvinistic doctrines were being shed entirely or greatly modified. Channing felt the influence of the times. Born in 1780, he was brought up in a Calvinist atmosphere, and might have been regarded as a disciple of Jonathan Edwards, the most able and logical of American Calvinist theologians.[1] Edwards's works are what Coleridge said those of Berkeley and Spinoza are: if the premisses are granted, the argumentation is a 'chain of adamant' as consecutive and logical as a demonstration of Euclid. But Channing's nature was not of the kind to be bound in logical fetters: he revolted against the Calvinistic scheme because it appeared to him to lower the character

---

1. Jonathan Edwards's great work on the Freedom of the Will appeared in 1754, and remains one of the standard presentations of the Calvinistic doctrine. He died in 1758. His Life was written by his friend and disciple Samuel Hopkins, with whom Channing, in his youth, was closely intimate.

of God; and very early in his career he came out decisively
on the Liberal side, for reasons which he afterwards developed in an essay, 'Moral Argument against Calvinism'.
Against the common doctrine of the Atonement he was
equally emphatic, and nothing would make him believe in
the total depravity of the natural man. He was a sincere and
convinced Anti-Trinitarian, and regarded Christ not as
God but as the ideal of humanity, offered by God to us as
an example, sinless, performing miracles by virtue of his
sinlessness, and literally raised from the dead in token of
the immortality of mankind and of the future blessedness of
believers. Thus, as he often said, he was scarcely a Unitarian, but rather a member of the Universal Church: the
somewhat harsh doctrines of Priestley and Belsham he refused to accept.

As will have been perceived, Channing was less of a theologian than a philanthropist: and the amazing influence he
wielded was due not to his doctrines so much as to his eloquence, his moral fervour, and the transparent beauty of his
character. There was not a good practical cause of the time
into which he did not put all the energy he could command,
and no abuse which he did not fearlessly expose. The annexation of Texas brought forth from him a public rebuke,
though Chauvinism and greed were here too strong for
him; he was one of the keenest, if sanest of the enemies of
slavery – his words, as Longfellow wrote, were like those of
Luther, 'half-battles for the free'; he was active in the cause
of prison-reform, and a worker for temperance. For theological subtleties he had little aptitude. Yet the effect of such
a man's life could not fail to win sympathy for the theological views he held:[1] and, mainly through reverence for
Channing, Boston became and long remained the centre of
a Unitarianism which dominated the religious mind of the
whole of New England. It was not, in fact, till the Episcopal

1. I have known some English Nonconformists who have confessed
that reading the life and works of Channing has made them Unitarians;
and I have heard some stubborn Trinitarians say that he was a saint in
all but his creed.

Bishop, Phillips Brooks, appeared above the horizon, that there was any strong opposition to the ruling creed.

Hardly less influential than Channing, and equally distinguished for his support of all good causes, was Theodore Parker, who, however, went further in free thought than Channing, and had finally to separate himself entirely from the Church, and to form a congregation of his own. Parker's theological views may be roughly summed up as a belief in God, and a profound faith in the ability of the soul to commune with him, combined with a disbelief in supernaturalism as commonly understood. His nearest English analogue is perhaps Francis Newman, the brother of the Cardinal. The Hebrews had a natural religious genius, and were thus able to grow out of idolatry and anthropomorphism into the lofty monotheism and morality of the later prophets, and to become the leaders of mankind in religious thought: but there is nothing miraculous in their history. The Gospels, similarly, need to be purged of their wonders if we are to gain a true idea of Christ. Christ, thus divested of actual divinity, becomes a man of the highest spiritual insight and of moral perfectness; his words on this side are therefore infallible. But in matters of science, and intellectual things generally, he was subject to ordinary human limitations; his prophecies were guesses, often falsified, and his ideas as to the authority of Scripture were frequently mistaken. Thus, for instance, he was utterly wrong – through ignorance of pathology – as to demoniacal possession.

Many of Parker's views are now freely proclaimed not only by members of the Church which rejected him, but by clergymen of more orthodox societies.

We must now go back several generations, and take up our tale again in the age of Elizabeth. As we have seen, the aim of the Calvinists was not to form a society outside of the Church of England as established by the Act of Uniformity in 1559, but to reform it, in their own sense, from within: and the aim of the Bishops, especially of Archbishop Whitgift of Canterbury, was to make the Church coincident with the nation, to suppress all teaching not in harmony with her formulas, and, if necessary, actually destroy or drive out all obstinate dissidents. We thus find many Puritan teachers *within* the Church, who are from time to time silenced by the Bishops, but return to the assault as the pendulum swings back. Often they were able to rely on the support of powerful Puritan laymen, such as Leicester, Burghley, or Walsingham: and the issue of the conflict remained uncertain till the death of the Queen and the accession of James I. For the most part the quarrel, which at times was exceedingly bitter, is of little interest to all but professed students of the times; very few are those who can read through the literature of the Martin Marprelate controversy. Nor is it easy for us today to follow with much enthusiasm the dispute, which lasted for more than twenty years, between the Puritan Cartwright and the Anglican Whitgift, in which the one desired the Church government to be based entirely on Scripture, and the other insisted on the power of the State to settle the Church constitution – and incidentally employed that power to silence his adversary.[1] The quarrel, however, assumed another character when the defence of the Elizabethan settlement fell into the hands of Richard Hooker. Hooker had been brought up a Calvinist, and indeed speaks of Calvin as 'incomparably the wisest man that ever the French Church did enjoy'.[2] He had been particu-

---

1. Cartwright's *Six Propositions* sum up the Puritan position. They are, briefly, as follows: (1) Archbishops and archdeacons should be abolished; (2) Bishops and deacons, as in the first ages, should respectively preach and take care of the poor; (3) Every individual church should be governed by its own ministers; (4) Each minister should confine his work to his own congregation; (5) No man should be a candidate for the ministry – he should be *chosen*; (6) and, consequentially, Bishops should not have the sole voice in the creation of ministers.

It is clear that a plan like this would destroy the authority of the Crown as far as the Church was concerned.

2. The whole passage, *Ecclesiastical Polity*, Preface, § 2, is well worth reading. 'Calvin's bringing up was in the study of the civil law. Divine knowledge he gathered by teaching others. For though thousands were debtors to him, yet he to none but only to God, the author of that most blessed fountain, the Book of Life, and of the admirable dexterity of wit, together with the helps of other learning which were his guides.'

larly struck with the unity and discipline which Calvin introduced into the anarchical city of Geneva; and, though he came to differ from the Reformer's theological creed, he never ceased to admire him as a statesman. England, he conceived, if the wars of the sects were to be permitted, would also fall into anarchy, and it was the 'polity' of Elizabeth's settlement that alone could save her. He must have formed these views before his appointment as Master of the Temple in 1585 compelled him to give them public expression. He gained this post through the influence of the two Archbishops, Whitgift of Canterbury and Sandys of York: but a strong effort had been made to appoint Travers, a vigorous and able Puritan, who was already afternoon lecturer, and was supported by Burghley. Thus, in the morning, as Fuller puts it, the pulpit spoke pure Canterbury, and Geneva in the afternoon. This led Hooker to consider more deeply the question of the relation between Church and State; and the result was the immortal *Ecclesiastical Polity*, a book which churchmen can read for its doctrines, and students of literature for its language and style. It was the first, and still the greatest, attempt to justify the Elizabethan settlement as not merely a political expedient, but a scheme with a philosophical, historical, and religious basis. It endeavours to show that Puritanism, consistently carried out, would mean the dissolution of society: and the appeal is everywhere to the practical reason.

Though a controversial work, and directed against a particular band of adversaries, it takes a philosophical line, and appeals to general principles. Admitting the authority of Scripture, it will not declare everything unlawful which Scripture does not mention or expressly forbid, and allows weight to considerations of political expediency. Hooker stands midway between the Puritanism of Jewel and Grindal on the one hand, and the High-Churchism of Whitgift on the other. There are passages which show that he might consent to alter the Church constitution if circumstances demanded it, and others which insist on the necessity of obedience *at the time*. Thus, as Burke, whose mind was in some respects like his, has been claimed both by Whigs and by Tories, so Hooker has been appealed to both by High Churchmen and Low. But he is entirely, or nearly, free from the passion which Burke constantly shows: he was tolerant by nature, and if the Church had imitated his spirit, we might have been spared many instances of tyranny and oppression.

The book did not check the advance of Puritanism. Cartwright, the real leader of the party, and Travers, still continued their work:[1] and the spirit of the time was with them.

Both parties in this controversy regarded uniformity of religion as not only desirable but necessary: their difference was as to the particular form of religion which should be enforced. We now, however, begin to meet with sectaries *outside* the Church, some of whom can hardly have hoped to make the State adopt their doctrines; and they were dealt with not by mere silencing but by savage persecution. The most important of these were the BROWNISTS and the ANABAPTISTS.

Robert Browne was a relative of Burghley, to whom at times he owed protection. Educated at Corpus Christi, Cambridge, he took orders in the Church, and became chaplain to the Duke of Norfolk. But very early he formed the view that Bishops were not only unnecessary but pernicious excrescences on the Church, and refused to accept from their hands the license to preach, though he did not hesitate to preach without it, especially in the diocese of Norwich. Finding Norwich a dangerous place of residence, he fled with his followers to Middleburg, where, at the moment, Cartwright, for similar reasons, had gathered a

1. A reconciliation was patched up between Whitgift and Cartwright, who in his later days lived quietly in Warwick, preaching, according to a promise given to the Archbishop, temperately and moderately. His stormy life ended just before the Hampton Court Conference of 1604. (Fuller tells a story that in his last days he was compelled by infirmity to study on his knees; which his opponents considered as a judgement. He had constantly censured as idolatrous the adoption of that posture in public worship; God had now made him adopt it himself.)

Church. Here he produced the works in which he laid down his peculiar doctrines: dissensions not unnaturally arose, and he removed with a few families to Scotland, where he came into conflict with the Kirk, and suffered imprisonment. Returning to England, he was again imprisoned, and, despite the favour of Burghley, was excommunicated for contumacy. Summoned by the Bishop of Peterborough to answer for his offences, he refused to appear, and paid the penalty. Suddenly, however, he made a complete *volte-face*, submitted to the Church, and received preferments in it. From that time forward, during forty years, the fiery preacher and determined Dissenter lived the life of an Anglican clergyman: when given a living in Northamptonshire he not only said nothing against the authorities, but said nothing at all: he never preached. This remarkable ending has led the Congregationalists to refuse to call him their founder: but it seems now to be established that before he took the fatal step his mind had to some extent given way. It is at any rate certain that a final imprisonment, during which he died, was due to an act that can be accounted for only as the result of lunacy.

Be this as it may, the principles of Browne are in the main those of the CONGREGATIONALIST body. His mantle fell on two very remarkable men, Henry Barrow and John Greenwood, who carried on his work with some success, despite imprisonments, till the stringent Act of 1592, 'for the punishment of persons obstinately refusing to come to church', was passed mainly for the purpose of suppressing this sect. Under this Act they were, at the instigation of Whitgift, arrested, tried, and hanged at Tyburn – as truly martyrs for their faith as any who suffered under Decius or Diocletian. At the same time, their principles certainly ran contrary to those of the Church of England as by law established, and, in days when it was considered necessary that the State could be united only if its Church was one and indivisible, they could scarcely be tolerated, harmless though their tenets may seem when that theory has long since been abandoned. They asserted, for instance, that the

only head of the Church is Jesus Christ – thus implicitly
denying the supremacy of the Crown. The only statute-
book, they said, was the Word of God, whereas the Articles
of Religion, and the Common Prayer, are Acts of Parliament. They maintained that the Church must be wholly
separate from the world, whereas the Elizabethan doctrine
was that Church and State were one. Each congregation of
godly believers, said they, was independent of every other,
and had the power of choosing its own ministers, whereas
the established system first put the whole Church under the
Crown, and then organized it into provinces, dioceses,
arch-deaconries, and parishes, all under the same discipline,
and set up officers whom it was totally out of the power of
the laity either to elect or to dismiss.

Thus oppressed, a large number of the Brownists removed
to Holland, the one country in which some degree of religious freedom was permitted. Here, in Amsterdam, a
Church was formed, under Francis Johnson as pastor. Later,
this body was joined by the illustrious John Robinson, who,
though holding fast to his own views, showed a liberality
rare in those days, and found it possible to work with men
of a different persuasion. For several years he laboured in
peace at Leyden, and his Church increased in numbers and
in 'grace'. But the members felt themselves exiles, with no
continuing city; they longed for a country where they could
not only worship God in their own fashion, but convert
the heathen: and in July 1620, the 'Pilgrim Fathers', a
hundred and one in number, set sail in the *Mayflower*, to
and in December on Plymouth Rock. Robinson intended
to follow them, but died before the second band of pilgrims
had left the country. Of the incredible hardships they
endured, and their final success, this is not the place to
speak.

Not all the Congregationalists left Holland: and when,
under Charles I, a new company of exiles came over to escape from Laud and Wren, they found men to welcome
them. These were not Congregationalists: the zeal of Laud
was directed against the Puritans; but the majority of them

speedily adopted Congregationalist views. Having left England because of 'the urging of Popish ceremonies and the silencing of divers godly ministers, in the hope of enjoying liberty of conscience', they joined themselves to the Church in Rotterdam, where, to use their own phrase, they 'saw a new light' – that is, came to believe that independent congregations were according to the will of God. Among these the most famous was Thomas Goodwin, afterwards President of Magdalen College, Oxford, and the minister who attended Cromwell on his deathbed.

When the news of the assembling of the Long Parliament arrived, they returned to England, 'not without hopes of finding liberty there'; and many of them were welcomed with honour. Some indeed became members of the Westminster Assembly, Goodwin being actually a 'commissioner for inventory'. In the debates they were hopelessly outnumbered; but they have the immortal glory of being among the first to plead for liberty of conscience against the Presbyterians, who wished to enforce their system, in good Laudian fashion, upon the whole country. As Cromwell and the army gained in power, the 'Independents' increased in influence: and finally they were able to allow liberty of prophesying to all except – a considerable exception, it must be confessed – Episcopalians, Roman Catholics, and 'wild sectaries' such as the Quakers.

With the return of royalty in 1660, they suffered along with other Nonconformists, the fear of them being especially keen as so many of Oliver's soldiers were of the Independent persuasion. The persecution was very severe, but it had one good result, that the common misery drew together Presbyterians, Baptists, and Independents, and largely mitigated the animosities which had been previously felt. All alike were Nonconformists, and could not help having to some extent a common feeling.

The conception of the isolated independent Church has its attractions for many, and appeals specially to the English love of liberty: but it also involves disadvantages, which for obvious reasons, are most strongly felt in the poorer congregations. Inevitably, therefore, steps have been taken by which the benefits of union may be secured to any extent short of the sacrifice of freedom. County unions have been formed, to which, in cases of difficulty, the separate Churches *may*, if they desire, refer: but any semblance of compulsion has been rigidly suppressed. In 1833, after many searchings of heart, the Congregational Union of England and Wales was formed, which has been of vast use in making ministers and laymen acquainted with each other, and encouraging the exchange of ideas. Under its auspices many important works have been published, including the collected writings of Robinson and the well-known *Congregational Union Lectures*.[1] But the Union has no legislative power, useful and informative as its deliberations may be. It has issued a Declaration of Faith, but no minister is bound by it – he is responsible to his own Church, and to no one else.

Congregationalism has always been strong and vigorous in the United States, where, of course, the memory of the Pilgrim Fathers is held in special honour. Like all religions, it has had its periods of stagnation and degeneracy, but it has always been able to recover itself. As with the Presbyterians, so with Congregationalists, there was at one time a tendency towards Unitarianism; but, both in England and in America the controversies that arose in consequence have strengthened the intellectuality of the Church. Few denominations have produced keener, more learned, or more influential theologians. The system, in fact, while perhaps less favourable to average or inferior talents in ministers than unitary Churches, lends added power to men by nature powerful. No Bishop could desire to wield more influence, for example, than was wielded by R. W. Dale in Birmingham during the years between 1860 and 1890.

Like other Nonconformist Churches, the Congregationalists have been accused of devoting too much attention to

1. Some of these have been very influential: I may mention in particular those of Pye Smith on Geology and Scripture.

politics, and the sermons have been said to be Liberal propaganda rather than Gospel discourses. It is at any rate
hard to exaggerate the influence of Congregationalists,
along with other bodies, between 1832 and the end of the
century. As one example, Edward Miall, who had been minister at Leicester, and became editor of the *Nonconformist*, led
the opposition to the Education Bill of 1870, and drew from
Gladstone the famous exclamation, 'if he cannot give us
his support, in God's name let him take it elsewhere'. The
challenge was accepted, and the Nonconformist defection,
led by Miall, Dale, and Joseph Chamberlain, brought about
the Liberal defeat of 1874.

We have already seen that after the capture of Münster
the ANABAPTISTS scattered in all directions over the Continent. As, to live, they had to hide in dens and caves of the
earth, it is difficult to trace their history; but one branch of
them we may briefly describe. Menno Simons, a Fries-
lander, who began life as a Catholic priest, about 1536,
through the study of the Scriptures, adopted the principles
of the Reformers, with three notable differences. Infant
baptism was wrong; the congregations of the Church ought
to be separate and independent; and – here he anticipated
George Fox and the Quakers – the use of force was contrary to the spirit of Christ. It is one of the ironies of history
that a people repudiating war should have suffered from
their connexion with a set of men who had fought at Münster one of the most savage wars ever waged. In all places,
where discovered, they were brutally tormented: chased out
of Geneva, sold for slaves in Bern, crushed at Basel, oppressed at Zürich, persecuted at Danzig. But through all
they maintained their doctrines, and when after many years
the storm blew over, they emerged with garments hardly
singed by the burning, a Church (or many Churches) without a confession, without a priesthood, and without an
organization. They found their safest abode in Holland,
where the Liberal policy of William the Silent left them unmolested, and here they lived quietly, refusing to take oaths,
never taking up arms, bearing no part in civic offices, and

known only by their plainness of dress and their simplicity of character. It is a remarkable fact that even Napoleon exempted the Mennonites of the Vosges from his all-embracing conscription.[1]

Nothing is more noteworthy than the way in which, at these times of stress, men exiled from one country contrived to find out sympathizers in others, from whom they learned much, and whose ideas, more or less modified, they brought back with them to their own country when the calamity was overpast. It was thus that Genevan notions were acquired during the Marian régime and brought to England under Elizabeth. By some such communication, it would seem, Baptist ideas came into our country, whether through wandering refugees from Münster, or through returning Englishmen from the Continent. By the time of the Civil War, the BAPTISTS had grown strong, and their similarity to the Congregationalists made them stronger. Their creed, which was embodied in the Confession of 1644, was found to be so nearly identical with that of the General Assembly that it was adopted, with few changes, and has been retained (as revised in 1689) ever since.

Under the Commonwealth they flourished, and after the Restoration suffered with the rest of the Nonconforming bodies, the Act of Uniformity (1662) and the Conventicle Act (1664) perhaps bearing more hardly upon them than upon any sect except the Quakers. The persecutions endured by Bunyan, the most illustrious of their name, are familiar to all; but Bunyan's troubles, though severe, were scarcely typical; he seems to have been less harshly treated than many others. There is no sadder story in the world than that of the afflictions and torments of these men, 'of whom the world was not worthy': and it would be unendurable but for the instances of benevolence, disregarding the law, which constantly brighten the tale and restore one's belief

1. That Spinoza, after his expulsion from Judaism, was much attracted by the Mennonites and the allied sect of the Kollegianten is practically certain. Some of his letters are addressed to Jarrig Jellis, a leading Mennonite.

in human nature.[1] As so often, the sight of the patience of the martyrs repeatedly made converts of their persecutors: nor was it possible for all the magistrates to bring themselves to enforce the law with more than the minimum of rigour.

At the Revolution, the Baptists shared the benefits of the Toleration Act, and they are the one of the three denominations which are allowed the privilege of petitioning the King in person. They still remain one of the most important of Nonconforming bodies, and the services done to Christian thought and practice by some of their chief divines, such as Robert Robinson, John Foster, Robert Hall, and Charles Spurgeon, are beyond price.

Their distinctive doctrines in one very important respect resemble those of the Congregationalists – a fact which has permitted a measure of federal union in certain places. Holding that the Scriptures are the sole standard of faith and practice, they maintain that the Holy Spirit is the only source of regeneration,[2] that justification is by faith alone, and that the church-order as described in the New Testament is that to which we should conform. Thus their congregations are independent, appoint their own ministers and deacons, and receive advice, but not commands, from the general assembly. Though the Church has been far from unaffected by 'modernist' influences, and though it has produced many scholars of high rank, the main tendency

1. Thus Tillotson, as one might expect, befriended and protected the Baptist Francis Holcroft, who had been his fellow-student at Clare Hall, Cambridge.

2. A distinction must be drawn between the 'General Baptists' and the 'Particular'. The latter hold Calvinistic views, the former Arminian: but the Confession of 1689, and the independence of the Churches, allows considerable latitude, and it is not uncommon, even now, to find ministers of the General Baptist Church holding more or less modified Calvinistic views. The Seventh-Day Baptists, who retain the Saturday sabbath of the Jews (as do the Nestorians and the Arminians), still exist in England and America. During the Reformation days they were subjected to severe persecution: among the expelled ministers of the English Church in 1662 were several men, then called 'Sabbatarian Baptists', of this persuasion. It is said that there are churches in Holland, and a mission-house in China.

has been to cleave to the old paths, and to interpret Scripture more literally than do some other Churches.[1]

But the really distinguishing mark of their creed lies in their doctrines as to baptism. They refuse entirely to baptize infants, holding that not a single example of the practice can be found in the Apostolic writings. Baptism, they say, presupposes conversion, and a profession of faith which of course cannot be expected from infants. This involves a denial of the Augustinian dogma that unbaptized children cannot be saved, and of any magical virtue in the ceremony itself, which is valueless without the living faith that ought to accompany it. No 'sponsors' can take upon themselves to guarantee the faith which only the candidate himself can feel.[2] Here the Baptists part not only from the Roman belief but from the Lutherans, who, according to the Augsburg Confession, declare that 'children ought to be baptized, being by baptism offered to God, and received into his favour'. All other Churches (the Quakers and a few others excepted) lay it down that at least the children of believing parents (or the godchildren of believers) are accepted as themselves believing.[3]

On the question of ritual, again, the Baptists differ from

1. Spurgeon, the great preacher of the 1870s and 1880s, was a strong champion of this orthodoxy.

2. I quote the following dialogue between Dr Gunning, Bishop of Ely, and Henry Denne the Baptist (whose answer to Featley's *Dippers Dipt, or Anabaptists Ducked and Plunged over Head and Ears* is still known to students) from Mr Nutter's *Story of the Cambridge Baptists*, p. 37:

'*Gunning:* Infants unbaptized (where there is no desire of their baptism in their parents or friends) shall be shut out of heaven.

'*Denne:* If unbaptized infants be shut out of heaven, then God punisheth some creatures for that which they cannot help. But God punisheth no creatures for that which they cannot help. Therefore unbaptized infants are not shut out of heaven.

'*Gunning:* I deny the consequence.

'*Denne:* Then shutting out of heaven is no punishment.'

3. The question was settled for the Catholic Church by Augustine, in his *De Baptismo*, a work written against the Donatists. Here he laid it down not only that the baptism of children was necessary, but that baptism, even if performed by heretics, was binding and could not be repeated.

other Churches, though here, apparently, they are not heretical. Looking back to Apostolic times, they find the practice to have been invariably immersion – the methods of 'affusion' (single or triple pouring on the head, as observed by Romanists and Lutherans) they reject, along with 'aspersion' or sprinkling, which is widely practised in many Churches, and permitted by Rome in the case of the sick or weakly. That immersion was the custom in the Western Church till about 1300 (the Council of Ravenna in 1311 allowed a *choice* between immersion and sprinkling), and that Thomas Aquinas *preferred* it, while the Eastern Churches still adhere to it, is certain: and here the Baptists appear to be primitive.

Accepting, of course, the Sacrament of the Lord's Supper, the Baptists, in common with almost all Reformed Churches, reject the other five sacraments of the Roman Church.

Amid the multitude of sects bred of the ferment of the Revolutionary period in England, perhaps the most interesting is that of the Friends, or, as they are commonly called, the QUAKERS. Here we have the inestimable advantage of being able to read the journals of the founder himself, and to hear him out of his own mouth. We have also full information as to the life of the most famous of the founder's followers, and an *Apology* from the pen of Robert Barclay, an able and highly educated man, who published his work – still the standard exposition of the Quaker faith – while the movement was in its infancy. The Friends, further, are distinguished by the thoroughness and care with which they have registered the names of practically all the members of their society, and recorded all the essential facts about them.

George Fox, who was born in 1624, and died in 1691, began to feel doubts as to the primitive character of the Church when about twenty years of age. His conversations with the clergy rather strengthened than solved these doubts; and in 1647 he began to preach the true and simple Gospel, going on foot, and at his own expense, into every corner of England. His teaching inculcated a return to the Christianity of the earliest days, and proclaimed that every believer had the power of direct communication with God, who by his Spirit would enlighten the souls of his servants, and guide them into all truth. This is the essence of Quakerism, but what drew special attention to Fox and his followers was a number of external peculiarities. Their dress, when they wore any, was such as inevitably to attract notice: Fox himself was known as the man in leather breeches; and the broad-brimmed hat which the Quakers wore, and refused to take off even in the presence of royalty,[1] informed everybody that somebody was about who would speak of the 'inner light' and denounce the 'steeple-houses'. The polite 'ye' and 'you' were never uttered; 'thee' and 'thou' – usually the former, however ungrammatical – were held alone appropriate to single human beings; 'yea and nay' were the farthest they would go in the direction of an oath, and they refused utterly to engage in war, or to resist evil in any manner. It is probable that this passive endurance irritated their opponents more than any other of their peculiarities – an Englishman understands a man who hits back, but not one who turns the other cheek. When they detected idolatry in the names of the days of the week, and spoke of 'First

1. The hat was to the Quakers a symbol, to their enemies a provocation. 'They haled him out of the Door into the Field (where was a Man they called a Justice), and with a Pitchfork struck off his Hat' (Braithwaite on Nayler, p. 112).

'*Justice Pearson:* Put off your Hats.

'*Nayler:* I do it not in Contempt of Authority, it being forbidden in Scripture.

'*Justice:* That is meant of Respecting Persons in Authority.

'*Nayler:* If I say to one in fine Apparel, Sit thou in higher Place than the Poor, I am partial, and judged of Evil Thoughts.

'*Colonel Brigs:* If thou wert in the Parliament House, wouldst thou keep it on?

'*Nayler:* If God should keep me in the same Mind I am now, I would.

'*Colonel Brigs:* I knew thou wouldst contemn Authority.

'*Nayler:* I do not contemn Authority; but I am subject to the Power as it is of God, for Conscience sake.

'*Justice:* Now Authority commands thee to put off thy Hat, what sayst thou to it?

'*Nayler:* Where God commands one thing, and Man another, I am to obey God rather than Man' (Fogelklou, p. 93).

Day', 'Seventh Day', a touch of contempt mingled with the exasperation. Fox himself, with his trances and visions, and his claims to a kind of inspiration, was easily taken for an impostor. He certainly suffered from that kind of hysteria which makes one impervious, for the time being, to pain: he tells us how he was struck violently and not hurt: this he ascribes to divine protection. It is a pity that he and his followers were not thus hysterical at all times, for their sufferings were terrible. Like the Baptists, they had to endure persecution from other sects, and even in the Commonwealth days were horribly ill-treated. They were accused by those who had themselves only recently been persecuted, of blasphemy and witchcraft, fined, imprisoned, put in the stocks: and, whatever their treatment, they accepted it with meekness. It was a repetition, in very truth, of primitive Christianity: not the martyrs of Nero's day were more patient or more forgiving than the Friends of the seventeenth century. The large-minded Protector, it is true, saw through the outside into reality. In the famous interview which Fox describes in his journal, Oliver listened to the uncouth prophet as he discoursed of the 'Light that is from above and the Darkness that is from beneath', and as he incidentally pleaded for his suffering brethren. Several times Oliver exclaimed, 'That is very good, that is true' and finally, as they parted, he said, 'Come again: if thou and I were but an hour of the day together, we should be nearer one to the other. I wish no more harm to thee than to my own soul.' But the persecutions continued,[1] nor were they likely to diminish when the Royalists and Episcopalians regained power. We are told, in the accurate account of the Society, that between 1650 and 1688 fourteen thousand Friends were imprisoned in the noisome dungeons of the time, and that, of these, three hundred and sixty-nine died in jail, including more than half of the ministers. This

1. As Fox's journal is undated, we cannot tell whether Cromwell was then near his end or not. It seems to me probable that he died soon after, otherwise Fox would have visited him again, and the persecutions would have been checked.

was in England: in America, where one would have hoped
there might have been some mercy, their treatment was, if
possible, worse still.[1] But the progress of the sect, partly perhaps as a result of the martyrdoms, was astonishingly rapid.
Among Fox's converts (and at first he was the only preacher)
were not only multitudes of the poor, but persons of the
highest consequence, clergymen and ministers, men of
wealth and education. In eight years there were sixty
preachers, and Quaker missionaries were to be seen in Asia,
Africa, and America; nay, in Hungary, Malta, and Rome
itself. Despite, or because of the persecutions, there were in
England alone, within thirty years, not less than sixty
thousand Friends. The story of the intimacy between Charles
II and William Penn, which led to the foundation of
Pennsylvania, is too well known to need repetition. The proverb that extremes meet is well exemplified by the semi-
alliance which existed between James II and the Quakers.
Both alike being persecuted, Catholics and Friends could
unite in endeavouring to drag toleration out of the dominant
Church of England.[2] One of the keenest supporters of James
was the Quaker William Bromfield, who, strangely enough,
gave the King sound military advice and much help in the
Boyne campaign, and figured prominently in Barclay's
plot to assassinate William.[3] Bromfield, somehow, contrived to remain a Quaker, and wrote an excellent defence of the Quaker creed and practice: but there were
members of the Society who were not altogether satisfied
with him.

1. The terrible punishment of James Nayler, after his triumphal entry
into Bristol in imitation of Christ's entry into Jerusalem, is fully described
Miss Fogelklou's *James Nayler*, pp. 215 ff. We learn that it roused pity
many of the bystanders. That Nayler's mind was not quite sound I
think certain: but his Christianity was unaffected. This was in 1656.
2. Macaulay's account of William Penn's conduct under William, in
1691, in which Penn cuts a somewhat poor figure, seems to be affected by
confusion between William and another Penn with the Christian name
George.
3. See an account of this extraordinary man in Hine's *Hitchin Worthies*,
97 ff.

After 1688 the persecutions ceased, and the Society settled down quietly, both in England and in America, to its proper work. Rapidly as it had progressed at first, however, it made comparatively few converts in these later years. It became, indeed, one of the least propagandist of Churches, and one, in comparison with its influence and repute, of the smallest. No body of Christians has retained more of its ancient purity, or deserved and gained greater respect.[1]

The Friends have no formulated creed, though their doctrines are fairly clearly stated in the works of Fox and Barclay. Their main positive belief is in the direct personal communion they enjoy with the Holy Spirit, which inspires them and guides them both in speech and action – a doctrine often known by the name of the 'Inner Light'. This, of course, might easily lead to the wildest travesties of truth, but it is clearly laid down that any act or utterance contrary to the Holy Scriptures is a diabolical delusion. Negatively, this spirituality causes the Friends to disuse the two Sacraments, no outward and visible sign of the inward and spiritual grace being, in their view, either necessary or commanded by Christ.

Their organization is of the simplest. Ministry, in the ordinary sense, they have none, though any man or woman plainly called by God to any special service, may speak, preach, or be set aside for a mission of any kind. The congregations are independent, but unite with one another in monthly, quarterly, and yearly meetings. The 'Quaker meetings' on Sundays are also unorganized – there is no regular order of service. Silence is preserved until the Spirit moves someone to utter his or her message. Theoretically

1. I cannot refrain from calling attention here to the Life of John Woolman, a saint of the Universal Church, worthy to be compared with Francis of Assisi. (The book was a favourite of Charles Lamb's.) Though not free from the superstitions of his sect and time (1770), he is a model of Christian virtue. By mere persuasion, and we may add by the transparent beauty of his character, he induced every Quaker in the American colonies to emancipate his slaves. Had there been a hundred Woolmans in other Churches, there would have been no Civil War in the 1860s.

the Spirit may move the ignorant thus to speak; but, as everywhere, the influence of scholarship and position makes itself felt; and a person of known learning speaks with authority. In late years, there has been a considerable advance in the freedom with which Scripture is interpreted; and many of the external peculiarities of the society have been quietly dropped. Of the contributions to knowledge made by men like Hodgkin, Seebohm, Rendel Harris, and Eddington there is no need to speak.[1]

Merely to enumerate the sects that sprang up in the Commonwealth era would be difficult; to describe them would be an impossibility. Most of them, like Jonah's gourd, arose in a night and perished in a night, nor have they usually found a prophet to bemoan their fate. Some of them would strain the indifferent tolerance of our own day. A few words on one of them, the MUGGLETONIAN, will suffice. Lodowick Muggleton and John Reeve were journeymen tailors, who, like so many others, found in the Book of Revelation a mine of dross which they mistook for gold. Deciding that they were the Two Witnesses of the eleventh chapter, they agreed that Reeve represented Moses and Muggleton, the orator, represented Aaron. Without knowing it, they repeated the Patripassian heresy, that the Father died on the Cross; but they added to it the remarkable statement that he left Elijah as his vicegerent while he sojourned on earth. As will be seen, they rejected the doctrine of the Trinity, and maintained that God has a human body. Yet such was the spirit of the time that they had a large number of followers.

Whether the LEVELLERS, the DIGGERS, the FIFTH-MONARCHY MEN, the MILLENNARIANS, or others of the kind should be viewed as religious sects or as political parties, is a difficult question. Politics in those days were inextricably entangled with religion, and a man who wished

1. Hodgkin, author of *Italy and her Invaders*; Seebohm, author of the *Oxford Reformers*; Harris, editor of the *Codex Bezae* and author of innumerable theological works; Eddington, the mathematician and astronomer.

to depose Oliver and substitute Christ[1] might be regarded, according to different points of view, as a martyr or as a mutineer when he came to suffer. Thus Trooper Lockyer, shot in April 1649, was a martyr in the eyes of the thousands who followed his corpse to the grave, a mutineer in Cromwell's: and the Fifth-Monarchist Venner, who, after revolting against Oliver in 1657, revolted against Charles in 1661, was treated by both less as a theologian than as a rebel. Whichever he was, this doubt gives the historian of religions an excuse for 'jumping o'er times' and passing rapidly from the seventeenth century to the eighteenth.

The policy of the Toleration Act was not accepted with enthusiasm by the High Church party, and when, in 1711, the Tories came into power, measures were passed (the 'Occasional Conformity Act'[2] and the 'Schism Act'[3]) seriously limiting the liberties of Dissenters. In the eyes of the Whigs, to whom the Dissenters, with their mercantile wealth and sound Protestant principles, were a source of strength, these steps were anathema; and, when the accession of the House of Hanover restored them to their old position, it was their aim to maintain the friendship. For this reason, among others, they pursued through many years the system of appointing Latitudinarian Bishops, and of relieving Nonconformists from their disabilities (without

1. The 'Digger', Everard, had a vision 'which bade him arise and plough the earth and receive the fruits thereof'. Thus the Diggers started, in April 1649, to dig on St George's Hill and elsewhere, claiming the right to take any common or untilled land. They proclaimed community of goods, and announced a doctrine familiar enough in our own time that the English are of Jewish descent. Their chief spokesman, Gerard Winstanley, dedicated his book, *The Law of Freedom*, to Oliver Cromwell. When brought before Oliver, the Diggers refused to remove their hats. For this and other reasons, Winstanley has been held by some to have been the real founder of the Quakers. (See Carlyle, *Oliver Cromwell*, 20 April 1649.)

2. Dissenters, to obtain civic office, often chose to attend a Church service and to take the Sacrament at the hands of Church clergymen, for the nonce: after which they returned to their chapels. The Act forbade this.

3. Forbidding Dissenters to teach.

ising a storm by actually repealing the Test Acts) in more
less surreptitious ways. We thus meet the phenomenon
a hierarchy far more tolerant than their subordinates,
d dioceses ruled by men who were but sullenly obeyed by
eir clergy. Nevertheless, the first half of the century was a
me of comparative peace, which has often been censured
sluggishness and indifference. The Church, like the State,
der Walpole's administration was content to 'let sleeping
gs lie'. When Convocation began to stir up trouble about
e 'Bangorian Controversy',[1] it was suppressed, and did
t meet again for a hundred and thirty years. As for
ueen Caroline, whose interest in theology was keen but
ademic, and untainted by any strong religious belief,
e appointed Bishops for their learning and liberality,
ithout regard to the depth or shallowness of their Church-
anship. She made Butler Bishop of Durham, and is even
id to have tried to make Samuel Clarke, who was more
an suspected of Arianism, Archbishop of Canterbury.
he Church, thus ruled, was not likely to suffer from over-
uch enthusiasm, though there was perhaps rarely a time
hen it did more service to knowledge.

It was upon a Church in this somewhat torpid condition,
d upon a country ruled by Walpole, that METHODISM
irst with startling effect. The history of this portentous
ovement would require volumes: only the slightest sketch
n be attempted here.

No system, intellectual or religious, is without ancestry.
ethodism owes its origin to Moravianism, and Moravian-
m was a revival of the Church of the 'Bohemian Brethren'.
ng before Luther, the Brethren had formed their Church,
hich may be called, without undue inaccuracy, a kind
Quakerism: it rejected all force, would not take the oath,
d had no hierarchy. When the Reformation came, it made

1. Hoadly, Bishop of Bangor, preached in 1717 a sermon in which he
oclaimed, in the most uncompromising terms, the doctrine of tolera-
n for all creeds: 'My kingdom is not of this world.' Fifty or sixty
swers, more or less ferocious, were published. Walpole, in accordance
th his usual policy, promoted Hoadly first to Hereford and finally to
nchester.

approaches to Luther, but appears to have felt more sym pathy with Calvinism. Like all other forms of Protestantism it was ruthlessly persecuted by the fanatical Ferdinand I and only fragments of it were able to survive in dens and holes of the rocks. In the eighteenth century the Church was re-established by Count Zinzendorf, who offered it a refuge in Saxony, where a town was built called Herrnhut or the 'Protection of the Lord'; and this was the centre from which the 'Moravians', whose missionary zeal has never been surpassed, spread rapidly all over the world. The chief distinguishing doctrines may be gathered into one that faith is a direct and supernatural illumination from God assuring us, beyond all possibility of doubt, that we are saved, and that no morality, no piety, no orthodoxy is of any avail without this 'sufficient, sovereign, saving grace'.

John Wesley, hitherto a High Churchman who had been chiefly influenced by the very different views of the Non juror William Law, fell in with Moravians on his ill-fated mission to Georgia – for the Moravians, who left hardly any part of the world unvisited, did not omit America. He was much struck with their ideas, but was not actually converted to them till his return to England, where his brother Charles who had already become an adherent, introduced him to Peter Böhler, a Moravian minister in this country. After a short but very intense struggle, in which he passed through the extremes of despair and hope, he found the light at a small meeting in Aldersgate, 'where one was reading Luther's preface to the Epistle to the Romans'. This was in May 1738, a date of the first importance in English and American history. From that time Wesley devoted his immense energies and great abilities to the one object of saving souls. There is no comparable example of tireless and long-continued exertion on record. Similar labour wore out Napoleon in a dozen years; Wesley kept them up for fifty, and said at the end that he remembered but one wasted quarter of an hour in the whole time – that spent reading a worthless book. Till past eighty he rose at four and toiled incessantly the whole day.

At the same time, Whitefield was preaching in every part
of the country, with an unsurpassed passion and eloquence,
and Charles Wesley was enriching the Society and the
world with his hymns. But to no small measure of their
talents John added powers totally absent in them – those of
organization, prompt and firm decision, rule, and states-
manship. The system on which he organized the 'People
called Methodists' was to arrange them in a number of
societies, these societies being united into 'circuits' under a
superintendent minister, the circuits into 'districts', and all
into a single body under a conference of ministers, which has
met annually without a break since 1741. To maintain the
services in the outlying parts of a circuit, local lay preachers
were utilized. The ministers were itinerant, and, to prevent
their freshness from being lost, were removed from circuit to
circuit every year.[1] The chapel-services were not intended
to oppose those of the Church of England, in which Wesley
hoped to remain: they were supplementary, providing 'that
which was lacking' in the clerical discourses. In many
places, almost within living memory, the Methodists
attended church in the morning and chapel in the afternoon
or evening: nor, for a long time, did they count themselves
nonconformists.

The unit of the organization was the class-meeting, at
which, under a chosen 'leader', members met and told their
'experiences', being often subjected to an examination as
stern as that in any Roman Confessional. At the end of every
quarter they received a ticket of membership, which enabled them to present themselves at monthly Sacramental
services. Wesley was extremely rigid in insisting on regular
attendance at these meetings; and class-books remain in
which names are ruthlessly excised, in Wesley's handwriting,
after three or four absences. No one was counted as a member whose name was not on these lists: for Wesley cared
nothing for numbers, nor did he regard the 'penny a week
and shilling a quarter' which was the price of a ticket as

1. Mitigated later to three years, and today subject to considerable
relaxation.

being worth receiving from anyone not enthusiastically d
voted to the cause.

Two other steps, of considerable importance, were take
by Wesley, which have left their mark on his own Chur
and on others. He threw himself heartily into Robe
Raikes's Sunday-school schemes;[1] and practically eve
Methodist chapel had its Sunday-school, the importance
which, especially in the days before the Education Acts, ca
scarcely be exaggerated. He also revived the 'Agapae'
'love-feasts' of the early Church, which were fellowshi
meetings for relating 'experience' and deepening the sen
of brotherhood in the members of the Society.

Two other innovations, which seemed to many Churc
men dangerous and almost schismatic, were forced on hi
by circumstances. Whitefield, excluded from the church
had taken to open-air preaching, in which his magnifice
voice (he could be distinctly heard by thirty thousar
people) and his marvellous eloquence produced the mc
amazing results. After some hesitation, Wesley follow
Whitefield's example, and, though his speaking was d
liberately calm and restrained, his sermons had simil
effects to Whitefield's – tears, groans, fainting-fits, and eve
form of emotional excitement. Not unlike were the scen
beheld when his lay-preachers stood on a mound and pr
claimed the Gospel-tidings. These men, again after hesit
tion, Wesley induced a Cretan Bishop to ordain; and l
even, when sending Dr Thomas Coke out as missionary
America, ventured himself to consecrate him Bishop.[2] Tl
justification must be found in the fruits. Few lives, an
where, are so astonishing as those, usually written by ther
selves at Wesley's request, of these early Methodist preacher
who, 'through peril, toil, and pain', travelled from end
end of England, or (when kidnapped and forced to l

---

1. He started these schools even before Raikes.
2. This was too much even for his brother. 'Wesley his hands
Coke hath laid but who laid hands on *him*?' cried Charles. The ti
used was 'overseer' or 'superintendent', but Charles saw its mea
ing.

oldiers or sailors) carried their message[1] wherever the army et foot or the navy touched.

All this did not exhaust Wesley's energies. He is the pioneer of the cheap book and of the propagandist magazine, as well as of the education of the common people. His Book-Room put at the disposal of his people all sorts of works, provided their tendency was safe. When he saw a book he thought likely to be useful, he edited it and published it. Thus he gave to Methodists, Young's *Night Thoughts*, Thomas à Kempis, Brooke's *Fool of Quality*, and even a Unitarian work which seemed to him, despite its authorship, good and true: while manuals of history, medicine, biography, science, often written by himself, poured from the press. The *Arminian Magazine* (1778), which still exists in another form, was perhaps the first monthly of its kind ever issued.

As may be imagined, the influence of the movement was not confined to the 'People called Methodists'. Many Church of England clergymen, such as John Newton of Olney, Grimshaw of Haworth, Romaine of London, Augustus Toplady, the author of 'Rock of Ages', the saintly Fletcher of Madeley, Thomas Scott, the commentator, were, to all intents and purposes, Methodists, and the great Evangelical movement associated with the names of Wilberforce, Zachary Macaulay, Charles Simeon, and so many others, owed its strength to Methodism.

Like other great religious movements, it had its schisms. We have already mentioned the first – the alienation which took place between the Arminian and Calvinistic sections, which ended in 1811 in complete severance. After Wesley's death in 1791 the main disputes turned on the position of the laity, or on the relation of the Connection with the Church of England. In 1797, under Alexander Kilham, the METHODIST NEW CONNECTION was formed, differing in

1. I might mention specially John Nelson and Thomas Walsh. The latter, whose work lay chiefly in his native Ireland, made himself, in spite of eternal journeys, preachings, and prayers, the finest Hebrew scholar Wesley ever met, and died, worn out, at twenty-eight.

no respect from the old, except that it gave the laity equal representation with the ministers. This body remained always small. In 1810 the more important secession of the PRIMITIVE METHODISTS took place, which admitted the laity to still greater power, and, under the leadership of Bourne and Clowes, reintroduced the camp-meeting, which had been falling into desuetude. Under O'Bryan, in 1815, the Bryanites or BIBLE CHRISTIANS were formed, who became strong in the south-west. Even these were far from the last disputes and secessions. A quarrel on a comparatively trifling point (but really, in all probability, inspired by the same resentment on the part of the laity) led, in 1834, to the expulsion of Dr Samuel Warren. The real ruler of Methodism at that time was Dr Jabez Bunting, a man of great ability but somewhat masterful nature, whose methods inspired jealousy and animosity in certain quarters. When it was proposed to establish a theological college, Warren protested, and finally led large numbers with him out of the main body. This case caused great interest, and even came before the courts of law.[1] As the ministers were still in the main Tory, and the laity were gradually growing more and more Radical, the breach inevitably widened. At the same time as Warren, Joseph Rayner Stephens[2] was driven out for joining the Chartists, and one or two eminent ministers were censured for appearing on Liberal platforms. It was evident that a still more dangerous storm was brewing: and this came to a head when James Everett issued his anonymous *Fly-sheets*, attacking Bunting and his supporters with great virulence. After some years of agitation, Everett was expelled in 1849, along with Dunn and Griffith, two Radical ministers. This led to the secession of a full quarter of the members of the Church, including some of the most distinguished laymen. The seceders, for the most part

1. Warren ultimately joined the Church of England, and became rector of Ancoats. He was the father of the once-famous author of *Ten Thousand a Year*.

2. Stephens had been chaplain to our embassy in Stockholm: he was brother of George Stephens, the author of *Runic Monuments*.

joined with the Warrenites to form the United Methodist Free Church.

There were, of course, many who felt this as a terrible disaster which might have been avoided; and, as the denomination grew more and more Liberal, approaches were made towards reunion. In 1878 the Wesleyans admitted the laity to the Conference, and thus removed one great cause of ill-feeling. In 1881 the great Methodist Oecumenical Conference was held in London, at which representatives of thirty or forty million Methodists from all over the world met together. It is noteworthy that Griffith himself attended, and received the Sacraments from the hands of Dr Osborn, who had been the chief agent in his expulsion thirty-two years before: nor was this the sole proof that the old bitterness was dying down.

The tendency to diminish the number of sects, and if possible to reunite all Churches whose doctrinal differences were slight, was at this time evident all over the country, and indeed in many parts of the world. Several Scottish sects had already joined, and formed the United Presbyterians. Towards the end of the nineteenth century the Scottish Free Church[1] and the United Presbyterians resolved to combine. The resulting lawsuit, in which the House of Lords decided that a few Highland congregations, which dissented from the scheme, and which were known, appropriately enough, as the Wee Frees, were entitled to all the colleges, churches, and revenues of one of the most learned and important denominations in the Empire, will be fresh in the memory of the reader. Legislation was urgently called for; under Balfour's ministry most of the injustice was removed, and the United Free Church was legally established. Nor was this all. As there was no doctrinal difference

1. Founded, under the influence of Chalmers, Candlish, and others, after the great secession of 1843, which turned on the question of patronage. The decisive case was that of Marnoch, where a minister whom only a single member of the Church desired to 'call' was forced upon the congregation. As a result, four hundred and seventy ministers, led by Chalmers, the most eminent minister of the time, resigned their livings.

between the United Church and the Established Kirk, it was strongly felt that the time had come for the schism of 1843 to be healed: and, after protracted negotiations, the reunion was accomplished in 1929 amid universal rejoicings.

Methodism, more especially as its organization is Presbyterian, and as there is great sympathy between its members and those of the Kirk, could not help feeling the influence of these great movements. But the lesson of the Scottish lawsuit was not forgotten: it was desirable to proceed with caution. The movement began with the union of the smaller Churches: the New Connection and the Bible Christians set the example: and others followed. Since the legal position of the 'Wesleyan', or parent body, depended on trust-deeds guaranteed by Act of Parliament, and the ultimate government, fixed by John Wesley and similarly guaranteed, rested in a hundred ministers called the 'Legal Conference', it was necessary to obtain Parliamentary permission to remove these barriers to union: and this, with no greater delay than usually attends Parliamentary procedure, was granted. Finally, after the most careful preparation, and ascertainment of the desires of every single District Synod, the scheme was carried through, and in 1932 the first Conference of the reunited Church was held amid demonstrations of extreme friendliness and harmony. Qualifying adjectives are henceforth dropped – the Church is no longer 'Wesleyan' or 'Primitive', but Methodist *sans phrase*.

The subject of Methodism in America is so vast that we must be brief precisely because of its vastness. Founded in 1784 by Thomas Coke, ordained Bishop or superintendent by Wesley, and by Francis Asbury, it met at the 'Christmas Conference', and organized the great Methodist Episcopal Church, on the doctrinal basis of Wesley's Twenty-Four Articles selected from the Thirty-Nine. Its spread was astonishingly rapid, and it is now one of the largest Protestant Churches in the world. It retains the itinerant system instituted by Wesley, even the Bishops being required to move from place to place. At first it covered the whole dominion of the United States, but in 1844, on the burning question of the right to keep slaves, the Methodist Episcopal Church South was formed, the first Conference meeting in 1846. Long before the Civil War, there were many 'Coloured Methodist Churches' both in America and in Canada; and the German Methodists are numerous and powerful. The Canadian Methodists, now united, are very strong. Taken all together, the Methodists are by far the largest Protestant Church in the world.

Although the Methodists have always emphasized a distinction between themselves and Dissent, yet the tendency of the last century has been to cultivate friendly relations with the Dissenting bodies, and the rise of the Anglo-Catholics in the Church of England, amid all the good it has done, has inevitably widened the breach between an Evangelical body like the Methodists and the Church. Endeavours at reunion, which have recently been again and again made, always break down on the question of the Apostolical Succession and the recognition of Presbyterian orders, on which neither the Scottish Kirk nor Nonconformists Churches can yield without stultifying their whole position.[1] The movement has not, however, been without its effect. Intercourse between divines who, to use Carlyle's phrase, 'agree in everything but opinion', cannot fail to bring about natural respect, and there is an increasing tendency on the part of Churchmen to recognize the great services to theological learning which Nonconformists have rendered and are rendering. The removal of University tests in 1871 inevitably improved the understanding between the two great sections of Protestantism, mitigated prejudice, and promoted friendliness. As early as 1870, Nonconformists were invited to join the company of Biblical Revisers – a contrast to the spirit which, in 1604, refused the services of Hugh Broughton, the greatest Hebraist of the

---

1. Similar considerations impede the union of the Anglo-Catholics with Rome, which demands absolute submission to the Pope, and refuses to admit the validity of Anglican ordination. This refusal was made definite in 1896.

age.[1] It has been more and more clearly recognized since that, if corporate union is impossible, co-operation is not only possible but desirable; and occasional interchange of pulpits had been recommended and practised; and it was a great symbolical act of friendship when Dr Lidgett, President of the reunited Methodist Church, was asked to preach in Westminster Abbey. How far, and how rapidly, this movement may spread, none can tell: at present the signs are favourable.[2] Few Methodist Conferences, or Dissenting Assemblies, now meet in a town but the Bishop, either personally or by deputy, conveys friendly greetings, and the Church Congresses are similarly welcomed by Nonconformist ministers. It is not likely that all differences of creed will be settled, but, if these happy omens prove true, the old antagonisms will disappear.

Of all the outgrowths of Methodism, none is better known, or more worthy to be known, than the SALVATION ARMY, which was, indeed, at first nothing but the application of primitive Methodist principles to new conditions. Every doctrine of the Salvation Army, including those of instantaneous conversion and Christian perfection, is Wesleyan; and the movement, though so portentous, sprang quite naturally from its Methodist surroundings. There was much of John Wesley's spirit in William Booth. Without the wide and deep scholarship, without the extreme dialectical subtlety, and without the theological profundity, of his great predecessor, Booth had the same consuming zeal for saving souls, the same organizing capacity, much of the personal magnetism which was so conspicuous in Wesley, and the same dominating temperament. Wesley's Society, while he lived, was an absolute monarchy; Booth attained

1. Though Dean Stanley incurred much obloquy by admitting one of the Unitarian Revisers to the sacramental service in Westminster Abbey, yet the act, which would have been impossible even to a Dean Stanley a few years before, remains a sign of the times.

2. For many years past, it has been the custom for *Nonconformist* ministers to interchange pulpits, especially on Hospital Sunday. Methodists have thus learned to respect Congregationalist ministers, and Baptists to see the virtues of Presbyterians.

the same end by forming his followers into an army, with ranks and degrees so duly subordinated that they would have satisfied Ulysses himself. He enjoyed, however, one advantage which Wesley never had. Wesley's wife, during twenty years, was his thorn in the flesh. Mrs Booth was her husband's right hand; a devoted Christian, an ideal mother, and probably the greatest woman-orator of the nineteenth century.

As a lad of nineteen, Booth was a member of the church in Nottingham which was presided over by Samuel Dunn, the very minister who was shortly to be expelled, along with Everett and Griffith. Dunn, who objected to the despotism of Dr Bunting, was a despot himself, and ruled his people with a rod of iron. When he heard that the youth had been preaching in the streets, he said, 'And who gave you leave?' but he saw the young man's talents, and urged him to train for the ministry. The General, who knew an autocrat when he saw him, ever afterwards spoke of Dunn with mingled affection and respect. When the great schism came in 1849, however, he took no part in it, nor did he follow his pastor into the wilderness. Many offers were made to him by the 'Reformers', and he worked in loose alliance with them for some time; but he finally found refuge in the 'Methodist New Connection', the body which, as we have seen, had been established by Alexander Kilham fifty years before and which now welcomed some of the new exiles from the parent Church.

It certainly welcomed Booth. After a very short period of study (he never became a theologian) he was admitted into the ministry, and was released from the ordinary 'circuit' work in order to travel from place to place as an evangelist, and to conduct revivals and special services all over the country. In these labours his talents and energy had full scope; his popularity was immense and his success prodigious. The chapels were always crowded, and the conversions numerous. Not unnaturally, however, the regular ministers were not always pleased: these services upset the routine of work; and it was not easy for elderly gentlemen to see themselves eclipsed by a young man of twenty-eight, who appeared like a comet, turned the little world upside down, and then vanished, leaving the pastor to straighten things out as best he might. Some of them closed their chapels to him. It says much for their forbearance that they endured it for several years, and that he was ordained in 1858 without a dissentient voice.[1] Many compromises were proposed; but Booth, knowing what his real call was, refused them. At the Conference of 1861, such a compromise was moved. Mrs Booth, who was in the chapel, met it with a loud and decisive 'No'; and, amid cries of 'Order', Booth moved down the aisle, took his wife by the arm, and left the assembly. At the next Conference his formal resignation was accepted.

It was a daring step for a man of thirty-three, without a penny and with a wife and several children. At first, indeed, Booth was in despair; even a successful revival in Cornwall did not raise his spirits. But some wealthy laymen came to his aid;[2] and for many months he went about preaching in the chapels of any denomination that would admit him, in circuses if chapels failed, and out of doors if he could not find a circus. His wife, defying all the conventions of the time, preached also; and their names speedily became famous all over the country, in Cardiff, Walsall, Leeds, Sheffield,[3] to say nothing of Nottingham. A chance call of Mrs Booth to Rotherhithe, however, led to a more permanent settlement. Her mission there was a wonderful success, but it revealed what an enormous field of labour was open to Evangelism in East London. In 1865 the family

1. The New Connection, like other Methodist bodies, required a probation of four years before a minister could be given full status. Thus Booth, who had been admitted in 1854, was not ordained till 1858. An exception had, however, been made in his case. Though a probationer, he was allowed to marry.

2. Despite his poverty, he refused thousands of pounds that were offered him on conditions. He would preach as he thought right, and would be in bondage to no man.

3. It was the sight of the unconventional 'Hallelujah Band' in Sheffield which seems to have suggested the formation of the Army.

moved to Hackney, and thenceforward the life of both was wholly devoted to the salvation of the submerged classes, whose terrible degradation was ever present to their minds. The difficulties and dangers were great: both of them ran daily risks of losing their lives, and money was hard to find. Booth was to learn, too, like every evangelist, that it is easier to make converts than to keep them. It was two years before it was possible, by engaging a theatre, to give the 'Christian Mission' a regular home; and Mrs Booth found it impossible to make ends meet without taking in lodgers.

Booth's aim at first was not to form a separate organization, but to send his converts to the Churches they preferred. Discovering, however, that these 'low-class' people were not welcomed, he decided at length on a policy which led ultimately to absolute independence: and in 1878 the Salvation Army was founded. Attempts had been made, by wealthy men who supported the Mission, to obtain control of it; these Booth would not tolerate, and made it plain that he, as 'General Superintendent', must be free to act as he chose. From this it was but a step to the establishment of military discipline. He had already, in jesting allusion to his imperious character, been nicknamed the 'General' by his intimates: in 1878 he accepted the title in earnest. The Mission was entirely reconstituted; and the movement was announced as a war. The magazine of the society proclaimed that a Salvation Army had been organized 'to carry the Blood of Christ and the Fire of the Holy Ghost into every part of the world'. The Army was indeed organized. Booth himself, no longer Mr or the Reverend, was Commander-in-Chief: under him, in regular gradation, were staff-officers, commissioners, majors, captains, adjutants, all sworn to obey their superiors without question. Uniforms, bands, marches, were all on the military pattern; and thus began that series of battles which made the Army and its warfare one of the most familiar sights in this country and ultimately in the world. The persecutions endured in the first few years were terrible; the 'Blood and Fire' of the Salvation banner might seem a symbol of the trials through which the

Army passed. Mobs, encouraged, it is to be feared, by the police, assaulted the Salvationists; and the magistrates, next day, too frequently punished the victims. In one year fifty-six buildings belonging to the Army were wrecked, and over two hundred and fifty women (not to mention men) were knocked down and seriously hurt.

It is true that there was much vulgarity, much rant, much unnecessary noise, and much besides to shock the respectably minded, in the Salvation services and in their writings. The *War Cry*, the Salvation paper, was full of crudities, signed perhaps by 'an individual calling himself Devil-walloper'. Occasionally, too, the Army showed itself too careless of the religious feelings of others: once at least its behaviour was such as to rouse just offence on the part of adherents of the Greek Church; and more than once it wounded the susceptibilities of Catholics and Anglicans. But, on the whole, if we consider the class from which it drew its recruits, and the treatment it received, we shall be astonished at its good behaviour. The conduct of the ministers of the law, on the other hand, was as a rule without excuse.

Persecution did not thin its numbers. As usual, the blood of martyrs was the seed of the Church; converts came in regularly after every instance of mob-savagery or the injustice of tribunals: and gradually the violent hostility ceased. Men of the highest distinction, like John Bright, Archbishop Tait, Bishop Lightfoot, used their influence to check disorder and to call attention to the good work that was being done. 'I hope,' wrote Bright to Mrs Booth, 'that the language of the Home Secretary will have some effect on the foolish and unjust magistrates. I suspect that your good work will not suffer materially from the ill-treatment you are meeting with. The men who mob you would doubtless have mobbed the Apostles.'

About this time it became still more clear that, whatever the General's personal desires might be, the Army was developing into a separate Church. He had, as we have seen, aimed so far at supplementing the work of the Churches,

and was not unwilling that his converts should attach themselves to such denominations as suited them. For a time he
seems to have hankered after some sort of federal alliance
with the Church of England. But a few conversations with
eminent men in that Church showed him the difficulties in
the way of such a connexion, however loose. Had the
Church taken over the Army, the control would have passed
from the General to the Bishops,[1] who must have claimed
the authority of a War Office; and to such an abdication
Booth would never consent. Again, neither he nor his converts cared much for things that lay close to the Anglican
heart. Many of them, of course, had never been baptized;
and Booth did not insist on their baptism. The Eucharistic
service was a 'breaking of bread', very informal, never administered by ordained ministers: nor was it considered of
importance that it should be regularly taken even by officers
of the Army. It is certain, further, that vast numbers of
Booth's followers would have revolted sooner than enter the
Church, while, on the other hand, the Church would have
been much embarrassed by the vagaries and irregularities
which were constantly seen in the Army, and equally by the
obloquy attending the offences which were falsely laid to its
charge. Any idea of fusion, therefore, was speedily abandoned. Cardinal Manning, also, who was sympathetic with
the movement and may at one time have dreamed of drawing it within the ambit of Rome, saw early that it was bound
to become a separate sect. Some very successful missions in
America strengthened the General in his conviction that
independence was necessary.

We now reach a critical period in the history of the Army.
Hitherto, Booth had confined himself to Evangelistic work:
he had been convinced that all that was necessary to raise
the degraded was to convert them: and it is true that conversion is an immense step forward in social regeneration; if
it does no more than put an end to intemperance it has done
much. 'Bring a man to Christ, and then set him to work for

1. A 'Church Army', under the Rev. F. S. Webster, was subsequently
formed, on the Salvation model, but subject to episcopal control.

Christ,' was Booth's motto. He stood aside when his son Bramwell, now Chief of the Staff, threw himself whole-heartedly, along with W. T. Stead, into the great campaign against organized vice and for the raising of the 'age of consent' – a campaign which led to Stead's imprisonment and nearly involved Bramwell in the same penalty. Mrs Booth, also, though keenly sensitive to the horrible conditions in which the poor lived, confined herself to the proclamation of the Gospel.[1] But suddenly, as if by a Damascus-vision, the General was enlightened. He had seen the misery for years; he now felt it as a compelling obsession, and he perceived that external conditions must be reformed if conversion was to have its perfect work. The result may almost be called a complete metamorphosis in the character of the Army.

There was already, everywhere, a sense that the horrors of the slums were a disgrace to civilization. Even the Universities had been stirred, and those 'Missions' had been started, like Toynbee Hall and that associated with the name of Canon Barnett. That terrible book, *The Bitter Cry of Outcast London*, had stirred the conscience of the people, and Stead's *Maiden Tribute of Modern Babylon* had revealed some of the worst effects of poverty. Charles Booth was working at his monumental survey, which, with astonishing thoroughness and accuracy, marshalled every relevant fact. But General Booth was the first to propose a vast and comprehensive scheme on a scale at all commensurate with the evil. In 1889, with the willing assistance of Stead, he published his epoch-making work, *In Darkest England and the Way Out*.[2] In this he proposed to found three sets of 'Colonies'; City Colonies 'to stand as harbours of refuge in the very centre of the ocean of misery'; Farm Colonies, or agricultural estates

1. This great and noble woman died in 1890, after a long and painful illness. Whether she would have lent her influence to the new movement is uncertain; her death took place before it was fully thought out.

2. The title took advantage of the popularity of a recently issued book called *In Darkest Africa*. Stead, a born journalist, knew how to catch the public eye.

in country districts, to which men prepared by the City Colonies should be drafted; and Oversea Colonies, in South Africa, Canada, Western Australia, or elsewhere, which the Salvation Army would make ready for settlement, and which should be ruled on equitable principles. For the carrying out of this scheme he boldly appealed for a million pounds.

The scheme met, as was to be expected, with furious opposition and with enthusiastic support. There were many, like Professor Huxley, who saw in it merely an insidious device for hiding sectarian propaganda under the cloak of a plan for social regeneration: 'Corybantic Christianity' was to masquerade as philanthropy. The chief objection lay in the fact that the money would be entirely at the General's disposal; but Booth was convinced that in such cases autocracy was essential. Despite all difficulties, he received the preliminary hundred thousand within a few months; and the Army entered on the new phase which is now, perhaps, its chief claim to honour. Whereas at first it was viewed with suspicion by the police and the magistrates, its help is now constantly sought by them, and the Army shelters, the Army colonies, and the Army farms, are freely made use of. Again and again in the courts, when a distressing case arises, an Army officer is there to take charge of it, and his help is willingly accepted by the authorities. During the First World War, the occupants of the shelters, if of military age, voluntarily enlisted, and the shelters were handed over to the Government to be put to any national purpose that might be desired. There are, in fact, many people who regard the Salvation Army rather as a philanthropic society than as a religious organization.

This was certainly not the General's opinion: indeed, he was at times troubled with doubts whether the social work of the Army was not inconsistent with its proper functions. He kept the two sides rigorously apart, and, after some years of labour over his great scheme, left the control of the shelters and colonies largely to others, and turned back with relief to Evangelization.

In his later years he had lived down antagonism, and had become a venerable and familiar figure, who was saluted with respect in the streets, and was welcomed in the houses of rich and poor alike. He died, full of years and honour, in 1912. His son Bramwell succeeded him as General. Bramwell, though equally devoted, was of a totally distinct character from his father, less dominating and more susceptible to external influences. Under him, though there was certainly no neglect of the Evangelistic side, it is perhaps true to say that the social work became the chief interest of the community: but there were some unhappy disputes, largely due to the feeling that the power had been long enough in the hands of the Booth family. These disputes, most unfortunately, came to a head when the General fell seriously ill, and the reins of government were in consequence slackly held. At last, in 1929, he was deposed, and Edward John Higgins, who had been in the Army for forty-seven years, was elected General by a variously composed High Council. In 1931 the Salvation Army Act was passed which laid down, *inter alia*, that the General should be elected by a two-thirds majority of the High Council, membership of which was restricted to the higher-ranking officers.

CHAPTER 16

SOME OTHER SECTS

IT would be impossible even to mention the vast number of religions, more or less based on Christianity, which have sprung up, especially in Britain and in America, during the last two hundred years, and which have often gained a large number of adherents. The Glassites or SANDEMANIANS will always be remembered as counting among their members the illustrious Michael Faraday, who never failed, after spending the week doing his epoch-making scientific work, to attend the service at an obscure chapel of this sect. Of the Swedenborgians (the New Jerusalem Church) we shall speak later. The SOUTHCOTTIANS are notable for the extraordinary audacity of their foundress, and for the expectations, forgotten during the First World War, of great revelations to be made in the centenary year of her death (1914). She proclaimed that, though she was fifty and more years old, she was to give birth to a divine man named Shiloh; Shiloh has never appeared, but there are still people who expect him. Christadelphians and others may still be met – enthusiastic devotees of their peculiar views. The IRVING-ITES (the Catholic Apostolic Church) date from 1830, when the strange phenomena (exact repetitions of the scenes at Corinth described by St Paul) began on the Clyde, to be repeated shortly afterwards in London. The leader was that remarkable man Edward Irving, under whose eloquence the hearers were excited to prophesy and to 'speak with tongues'. Sceptics who visited the church observed that these tongues were scraps of Latin or French, mingled with unintelligible gibberish; to believers they were inspired utterances. By 1832 the Church had begun to be organized, on the principle that the Apostolic office should be restored. Irving himself died in 1834, but the organization was completed in the next year, with its full complement of twelve

Apostles, prophets, or evangelists, 'angels' or Bishops, and deacons. The ritual is highly elaborate,[1] and the liturgy, based on the Anglican and the Greek uses, is solemn and majestic. The creed is in fact a strange mingling of the highest Anglicanism with views borrowed from all sources. The Church holds that the Second Coming of Christ is near at hand: its Sacraments are sacrifices, hardly to be distinguished from masses; the symbols of Nicaea and Chalcedon are rigidly maintained; and baptismal regeneration is preached. Though Irving was a Presbyterian, the majority of the original members were Episcopalians; and though the pretensions of the Church are unbounded, the piety and humility of the individual adherents are beyond question. As the imitation of the early Church is complete, the number of the Apostles was never increased, and as each in succession died off, his place was not filled.

The PLYMOUTH BRETHREN, whose origin is mainly associated with the name of John Nelson Darby, began about 1827. Darby was a clergyman of the Protestant Church of Ireland.[2] Dissatisfied with the want of spirituality both in Church and in Dissent, Darby joined with Edward Cronin, an ex-Romanist, in small meetings in Dublin every Sunday for the 'breaking of bread': and very soon his influence, due to his piety, learning, and force of character, made itself felt. By his writings, the movement was made known to the outside world, and adherents began to come in. Visiting Paris, Oxford, and Cambridge, he attracted more, and finally settled in Plymouth, which became the centre of the society, and has given the popular name to the 'Brethren'.

No Church has split up more rapidly into smaller bodies, and hence it is difficult to give a succinct account of its beliefs. It began with an 'endeavour to keep the unity of the

1. I have attended some of these services, which with their singing, their incense, and their symbolic vestments, are among the most impressive in the world.

2. He is the 'Irish clergyman' repeatedly alluded to by Francis Newman in *Phases of Faith*.

Spirit': and indeed it welcomed the accession of any who were inspired by Christian spiritual feeling: but very soon it exercised the right of excluding any who held heterodox views. A large fraction of them, itself sundered into three or four groups, is in fact generally known as 'Exclusives': others, the Kellyites, the Newtonites, and 'Bethesda', differ according to their views of Church government or of prophetical powers. Nevertheless, we may perhaps give, as fairly authoritative, a sketch of the creed laid down in Darby's various works. As Judaism apostatized, so had Christianity fallen from New Testament purity. All Christendom is under God's displeasure. Catholicism, Lutheranism, the Church of England, Nonconformity, are alike corrupt: they have, for instance, established ministerial offices which hinder the direct approach of every believer to God. Ministers are not officials; they have their special gifts, granted them from above, 'Charismata' which they are bound to exercise, assigned them by the Holy Ghost according to his will: these Charismata have no connexion, *as such*, with episcopal or other posts, though, as in the case of Stephen, they may happen to coincide with such an office. No man, or body of men, since the time of the Apostles, has the right to appoint to such offices: in the Churches where such exist, corruption has taken place, and the true believer must withdraw.[1] The whole doctrine, in fact, depends on the freedom of *direct* spiritual access to the Divine: intermediate agency, as of priests or presbyters, is not only a hindrance but a sin. There is no fundamental objection raised if members of other Churches join the Brethren, and yet retain their former allegiance: but it is clear that Darby's views make it difficult for such cases to be common: and indeed the usual charge against the Brethren is not any lack of piety or virtue – they are indeed one of the purest Churches in the world – but their uncompromising assertion of their own views as the sole certainties,

1. Not necessarily *openly* withdraw, but withdraw into himself and into communion with God. The corruption of a Church does not necessarily demand cessation of brotherhood with its members.

and the sternness with which they maintain the corruption of others. No Church has taken more complete possession of the 'Ladder of Acesius'.

None the less, their services to the world have been great. The work of S. P. Tregelles in New Testament criticism has never been surpassed: no philanthropist has ever been more devoted than Müller of Bristol; and the scientific achievements of Philip Gosse, though he naturally refused to accept Darwinism, have been of permanent value. The missionary Groves, one of the earliest adherents, well deserves the epithet of 'noble-hearted' which Francis Newman gave him.

But if England has been prolific in its sects (as the religious censuses, incomplete though they are, bear witness) America has been much more so. Churches of every kind spring up like towns in the Territories – one year a barren waste, the next a flourishing colony. It will be possible here to deal, and that briefly, with but two or three of the most important of these recent growths. We may take first the MORMONS or Latter-Day Saints, of the State of Utah.

Joseph Smith, a youth of eighteen, living in the State of New York, having been much influenced by a religious revival which took place in his native county, was, he tells us, praying for guidance in September 1823, when two heavenly messengers appeared to him, and forbade him to join any existing Church, but to prepare to be the prophet of a new one. Later, a series of heavenly visions informed him of a revelation written on golden plates, which he was to find. In a hill near by, he says, he found the plates, and, by the help of 'Urim and Thummim', translated their message into English. This, the 'Book of Mormon', was published in 1830. In the same year the little Church, numbering six believers, was started in Fayette, a small town of New York State; and the first of Joseph Smith's miracles – the casting out of a devil – was performed.

As a matter of fact, Smith was almost certainly an impostor, whose relations with the police in his native district were the reverse of friendly; and the Book of Mormon, far from being the work of angels, or even of Joseph himself, was probably written by a Presbyterian minister who had conceived the idea that the Red Indians were the lost Ten Tribes. Hence the strange 'history' which fills a portion of the book. But Smith, like other men of his class, had the power of winning over people of greater intellectual force than his own; and among his first associates was Samuel Rigdon, a man of considerable knowledge and literary skill. It would seem that Smith, with Rigdon's assistance, added to the book the chapters speaking of Christ's appearance in America after his ascension, and of his organization of the Church. Another book, *Doctrine and Covenants*, collects together the revelations Smith claimed to have received.

The society grew, and as it grew encountered constant opposition and persecution, chiefly because its members boasted of being the Chosen People, while all others were Gentiles, but largely also because they took a violent part in politics, voting solidly as their inspired prophet dictated.[1] They were expelled from one city after another, until they were forced to build themselves a dwelling-place at Nauvoo on the Mississippi, in the then thinly inhabited Illinois.

They would probably have soon died out but for the atrocious murder of Smith in 1844, which, as so often happens, gave him the halo of martyrdom. What was even more important, it gave the Mormons a leader of an entirely different stamp. Brigham Young, who succeeded him, was a man of practical sense, indomitable energy, and iron will: he was, in fact, a statesman. Under him, the warring factions which had torn the sect to pieces were reconciled – hopeless recalcitrants were driven out, and the submissive were ruled for their own good. Finding that the persecutions did not cease, he determined on the stupendous 'trek' to Salt Lake, then outside the United States; an opportune 'revelation' came to him, ordering the faithful to migrate; he himself led the way, and, after a frightful desert march of more than a thousand miles, reached Salt Lake on 24 July 1847. Four thousand of the society followed him; Salt Lake City was

1. In 1843 they actually nominated Smith for the Presidency.

built; the Church was rigidly organized, and Brigham Young, a king in all but name, ruled Church and State for thirty years, dying in 1877.

Almost the only fact known to the majority of people about the Mormons is their former sanction of polygamy.[1] Curiously enough, polygamy was at first forbidden by Joseph Smith, and was not formally permitted till Smith had been dead several years, by Brigham Young in Salt Lake City. Their other doctrines, however, are not less remarkable. They practise baptism by immersion, but no child under eight is baptized: they celebrate the Lord's Supper with water instead of wine. They preach plainly that God is of human form, that Christ, though the Son of God, is of different substance from the Father; that the Holy Spirit is not a person but an influence; that souls have existed before birth, and wait (like the souls in Virgil) anxiously for human bodies into which to enter, for only through such means can they attain final bliss. Hence the justification of polygamy; he who, by having a number of children, provides bodies for these souls is conferring a benefit on the spiritual world. They are Millennarians: at a time not far distant Christ will appear and reign a thousand years. As the dead are still alive, they may, by repentance, obtain admission into the true Church; hence the Mormons 'baptize for the dead'. They practise certain mysterious rites, known as 'endowments', which are in fact a kind of sacred drama, not unlike the old Orphic Mysteries: God and Satan, Adam and Eve, are persons in the drama, and there are endless ablutions, anointings, hand-claspings, and the like. No marriage is complete, or will be blessed, unless both the parties have been through these endowments, which, if duly performed, will qualify the faithful to face the Father after death without fear.

Miracles, it is needless to say, are still performed; for the Latter-Day Saints have recovered all the powers possessed by the early Church.

The Bible, the Book of Mormon, and the 'Doctrine' are

1. This practice was renounced in 1890.

equally inspired; but the Old Testament was meant for the Jewish Dispensation, the New for the Christian, the other two for the consummated Church. But, as has been truly said, the real inspiration and guidance came from the leaders – from the Melchizedeks, the higher order of the priests, and the Aarons, the lower. The Melchizedeks include the apostle, the patriarch, the high priest, and the elder: these, for the most part, undertake the spiritual duties; the Aaronic order, though also spiritual, yet for the most part, like the deacons of the early Church, 'serves tables', and attends to the temporal affairs of the Church.

Whether the SHAKERS should be counted among American Churches is doubtful; for they are of English origin – if indeed they should not rather be traced to the south of France. A body of Revivalists from Dauphiné migrated to England about 1700, and formed a small community there. Ann Lee, the daughter of a Manchester man, moved by strong conviction of sin, attached herself to this society in 1758, when she was a young woman of twenty-two. From that time forward she was the subject of many remarkable revelations, which increased in intensity and vividness when she was imprisoned and brought near to starvation during a severe persecution. In consequence the little sect received her as their leader; and, under the inspiration of prophetic visions, she set forth with no more than nine followers for 'Immanuel's Land' in America. A holding was purchased not far from Albany in New York, and there the Church made its home. The community was known in ridicule as 'Shakers', from the peculiar motions which, at times of religious excitement, they were observed to make; but, like so many other nicknames – Christianity itself among them – it has been adopted in all seriousness. 'Yet once a little while,' says the prophet, 'and I will shake all nations, and the Desire of all nations shall come': the sect believes the prophecy to be fulfilled in themselves.

Ann Lee died in 1784, but the Church remained, and is

still well known in New York and New England. There is nothing ridiculous about either its polity or its theology. The Shakers bear considerable resemblance to the Society of Friends; they will take no part in war, but every peaceful demand of Government they willingly meet. Men and women are on perfectly equal terms; in their meetings, which often include sacred dances, women preach as often as men: but, as in certain Dissenting Churches, the two sexes keep apart, and even in the dances remain separate. The doctrine is in a sense Unitarian; God is both heavenly Father and heavenly Mother; Christ is not God, but the Son of God, one of the many intelligences by which God reveals himself to man; he did not become the Christ-spirit till his baptism. As man, he is our Elder Brother; but as the Christ-Spirit he is both man and woman; and we have Daughters of God as well as Sons, equally baptized with that spirit. There is no bodily resurrection, and no Second Coming of Christ except as the Christ-spirit: nor is there vicarious atonement: man is rewarded or punished according to his works, for man has free-will, and is responsible for his deeds. Heaven and hell are spiritual states, in which the rewards and punishments are dealt out to all; but there is an intermediate condition after death, in which man can still further prepare himself for his destiny. 'Election', though all things are chosen of God, is determined by the fitness of the receiver: he that wills, may take of the water of life freely.

As may be expected, the Shakers are Spiritualists, basing their belief on the teachings of both the Old and the New Testaments. It has even been thought by some that their beliefs are touched with Essenism, and their way of living in families lends some colour to the theory; on the other hand they are strongly anti-monastic.

Nor can we count the DOUKHOBORS, any more than the Shakers, as strictly an American sect, though their present seat is in Canada. They are of Russian origin, and were founded, paradoxically enough, by a Prussian non-commissioned officer who happened to be stationed in the Governorship of Kharkof, about the middle of the eighteenth century.

As their name – 'Spirit-wrestlers' – indicates, they show how almost indestructible is that desire for direct communication with the divine which has given us the Quakers, the Mennonites, the Moravians, and a score of other Churches. They deny the need of secular rulers, absolutely refuse to sanction war, and act by the dictates of the 'inner light' as confidently as George Fox himself: nay, they will admit to their body, be his beliefs what they may be, anyone who has seen and obeyed that illumination. They will have no marriage-ceremonies; 'Love is enough'; and the union may be broken off as soon as love ceases. Like the early Quakers, too, they sometimes cause embarrassment to their neighbours by the perfect simplicity with which they 'put off these troublesome disguises which we wear'; a custom which was of no account when they lived far from the rest of mankind, but which has caused some trouble as the advance of civilization brings people near them. Not believing in government, they refuse to pay taxes; they do not engage in commerce, and confine themselves to agriculture. One of their sects – for, few as they are, they have had their share of schisms – remains communist: their lands belong to the whole community: others are making timid approaches to the private possession of property.

For a considerable time their harmless lives secured them from Government interference, and they gradually spread southward towards the Black Sea. But in 1797 the Czar Paul, hearing of their views as to monarchy, refused them toleration; after Paul's death in 1801, Alexander I removed them to the neighbourhood of the Sea of Azov and left them to their own devices. Some years later, however, whether they had really degenerated, or whether their increasing numbers (they were now at least twenty thousand) aroused the fanaticism of their neighbours, sinister rumours reached the Russian Government. It was said, probably with truth, that they held strange doctrines. Their leader, Kapoustin, was supposed to have called himself Messiah; the society was believed to assert that God has no existence apart from man; and – what was probably false – it was whispered that Kapoustin's successors got rid of their opponents by murder. At any rate, in 1841 the authorities made a rigid investigation into these charges and ended by banishing them to Georgia. Here the half-savage tribes were greatly amazed at their quiet disposition, and at the way they never resisted evil.

Yet another crisis came in 1887, when Russia introduced conscription. To this the 'wrestlers' utterly refused to submit, and no severity made the slightest impression upon them. For more than ten years they endured the full weight of Czarist tyranny. At length, in 1898, Tolstoy, whose own principle, as is well known, was 'Resist not evil', took up their cause. He knew nothing about the theocratic claims of their leader, and looked on them simply as followers of the Sermon on the Mount: and he used his immense influence to have them quietly removed from Russia. The Canadian Government was induced to make them a grant of land in Assiniboia, to which seven or eight thousand betook themselves. There, for a long time, they lived 'quiet and secure', remote from the centres of population. Recently, however, their peculiar views and customs have caused a little stir. It remains to be seen whether they will be absorbed into the general life of the Dominion, or whether they will be able to resist influences which have always proved more subtle and more powerful than persecution.

The other Russian sects are very numerous. The one which has raised most interest is perhaps that of the STUN-DISTS. This interest was keenest about forty years ago, when the Czarist system was coming up for criticism before the tribunal of public opinion, and when not only the political but the religious tyranny of the old régime was being subjected to strong censure by all the Liberal forces of Europe and America.

As the name shows, the sect was of German origin: its adherents were 'holders of hours of devotion' – *Stundenhälter*. About 1824, a German Lutheran named Bohnekämper started meetings, in the district of Kherson, which soon developed into a Church of considerable dimensions. Its principles were similar to those of the Baptists, and, when it formed an alliance with the already existing Russian Baptists, it spread fast, and drew upon itself the attention of the Holy Synod. When the notorious Pobedonostseff, about 1870, became Procurator of the Synod, persecution became rigorous, and stirred great indignation. It must be confessed, however, that the actions of some of the Stundists were provocative, and would in any civilized country have been dealt with by the law. They strongly objected to the worship of images, and, like the Puritans of the Reformation times, entered churches and broke the offending 'idols' to pieces. Pobedonostseff was alarmed, and when his agents, during a dozen years, reported that the Stundists were rapidly increasing, he took vigorous steps, not merely against the law-breakers but against the sect generally. His punishments were very severe; and not even the horrors suffered by political offenders roused more feeling than the treatment of these sectaries.

Since the Revolution of 1905, and still more since that of 1917, little has been heard of them, and accurate knowledge of what is happening under the Soviet domination is almost impossible of attainment.

Among the many religions that have sprung up during the last hundred years, far from the least important is the SPIRITUALIST. Its growth has been rapid, not only in America but in England: and its strength is not to be measured by the number of declared adherents. In the 1930s six hundred churches were claimed on the west side of the Atlantic, and more than four hundred and fifty on ours; but there are multitudes of more or less convinced believers who are attached to none of them, while many Spiritualists prefer to regard their belief as rather a science than a religion. Members of the Psychical Research Society, founded by Frederic Myers and Edmund Gurney in 1882, may or may not be believers; the society was founded for the purpose of making impartial and objective investigations into spiritualistic and allied phenomena; but there can be no doubt that the work of the Society has aided the growth of the Religion.

As a Religion, properly so-called, Spiritualism may be said to owe its origin to Andrew Jackson Davis, who, when a very young man, published *Nature's Divine Revelations* – a book which, since it appeared in 1847, has gone through more than forty editions. Davis was undoubtedly influenced by Swedenborg, but his mode of expression was coloured by the mesmeric and magnetic theories in vogue at the time, though now largely superseded. Accepting the common theory of the tripartite nature of man, he defined the 'spirit' as essentially one with the Divine, and a process of it. The 'soul', the intermediate substance linking spirit and body, is animal in origin, and may be regarded as a sublimation of the body. Through work we are constantly losing part of our vital energy; hence the need of food, which, after being assimilated by the body, is refined into the more ethereal substance of the soul. But the soul is the exact counterpart of the body, with all its limbs, organs, and senses: the body itself is nothing but the material covering by which the soul communicates with the rest of the material world; and the messages the soul thus receives it is able, by its greater tenuity, to pass on to the spirit.

It will be easy, after this, to see what, in Davis's conception, is the nature of old age and death: the one is the slow wearing away of the material machine, the other its complete severance from the soul. As we grow older, spirit and soul gradually withdraw themselves from the fleshly wrapping, and, when the process is finished, they quietly and peacefully abandon it. If, however, death takes place prematurely, either by violence or by disease, the shock is proportionately great, and the released principles find it difficult, at first, to accommodate themselves to the new sphere of life. Davis tells us how, in one of the clairvoyant states to which he was subject, he beheld clearly the normal process of death – which, indeed, has been illustrated by means of 'spirit-photography'. The soul-body visibly removed itself from the corporeal frame, and stood above it; the exact mage, in a kind of gaseous form, of its counterpart. There still remained, however, a stream of vital electricity uniting the two shapes, which did not vanish for some time; and Davis, boldly comparing this with the umbilical cord, deduced that death is not merely figuratively but literally a birth from a lower to a higher plane.

In passing to describe that higher plane, Davis to a certain extent parts company with Swedenborg, to whom that world was entirely spiritual, whereas to Davis and his followers it still retains something, at least in the primary spheres, of its relation to the material, and can therefore enter into communication with it. This communication is effected through mediums, whose successes and failures depend on the degree to which the relation between the earthly sphere and the spiritual has been affected by lapse of time or other causes. Davis himself was able repeatedly to enter into *rapport* with departed spirits; the Fox sisters, whose experiences gave the religion a vogue which all Davis's philosophizings could never have gained, passed on innumerable messages from the next world to this; and multitudes since have given séances which have been the subject of wide curiosity. There is hardly a spiritualist religious service at which a séance is not one of the chief features; it is this, unquestionably, which has drawn the attention of the public. That many of the mediums are Sludges is certain; but many others have as certainly given some very remarkable messages. Among those as yet unexplained, the messages sent by the old monks of Glastonbury, as described in the book called *The Gate of Remembrance*, may be specially mentioned. They were accurate to the last detail.

The dead pass slowly from sphere to sphere, but, as spirits, they are not troubled by distance, and of course are not excluded by corporeal bar. There is, in Davis's idea, a correspondence between the advance of the spirits in moral perfection and its advance from sphere to more distant sphere, until ultimately it is absorbed, without losing its identity, into the divine. Some later Spiritualists represent this advance pictorially by reference to the Rings of Saturn. But, though these rings, zones, or spheres are spiritual, they – or at any rate their stellar types – can be measured in material scales, and their distances from the centre of the earth have been calculated in miles and metres. In the books of Davis and his successors there is a most elaborate mapping-out of this cosmic system.

The organization of the Church is simple: there are ministers and lay-officers, with of course the mediums, who do not always attach themselves to particular churches, but move from place to place. The services are unliturgical, with extempore prayers, sermons, and hymns usually of no high literary merit. At present, though so many men of intellect are *interested* in Spiritualism, the intellectual level of the Church is mediocre, even the ministers, for the most part, being poorly read. Not many of them have studied Davis, or could understand him if they did study him. What the seekers desire is the satisfaction of their hopes as to a future life, a proof that their dead are not sundered from them for ever; and this they believe they find in the revelations of the mediums. At the services and séances they receive what professes to be proof; and the 'will to believe' is strong in them. They admit the ease with which fraud may be practised, but they are too hopeful to be scrupulously on their guard. It is not always that the evidence which satisfies even such men as Lord Dowding convinces the outsider; and men of less scientific mind than he are much more credulous. Yet the Church is growing, and will probably long continue to grow.

The religion which has probably made as rapid advance as any other during the last fifty years is the Church of Christ, Scientist, commonly called CHRISTIAN SCIENCE. Like all religions which have attracted wide attention, Christian Science has been a subject of acute controversy, which has at times not hesitated to attack the sincerity and personal character of the Foundress. Fortunately, with all this we are not here concerned. We shall briefly relate her life as she herself tells it in her book *Retrospections and Introspections*, and as it is authoritatively told elsewhere: and afterwards we shall, as succinctly as possible, summarize the doctrines of the Church.

Mary Baker was born in New Hampshire in 1821, of a family many of which had been famous in American history for two hundred years. Her parents were well-to-do and highly respected members of the Congregational Church at Tilton, in New Hampshire. From her earliest years, though of delicate health, she showed remarkable intelligence, and her teachers predicted for her a distinguished future. At the age of twelve she discarded the Calvinistic doctrine of pre-destination in which she had been brought up, but she con-tinued her membership of the Congregationalist Church for many years afterwards.

In 1843 she married Major Glover, a contractor and builder of South Carolina; but Glover died within a year. During the following years she devoted herself to journalism and teaching, and gained a considerable reputation: not, however, neglecting theological and religious studies. In 1853 the great misfortune of her life occurred: she married a Dr Daniel Patterson, who proved a faithless and neglectful husband. She endured his vagaries for twenty years, but finally secured a divorce on the ground of desertion and in-fidelity.

It was during these evil times that she made the great discovery which so many of her followers have made since. In 1866 she had a terrible accident, and was carried to a house close by, where the doctor found that her injuries were internal and very serious. 'For years,' she tells us, 'I had been trying to trace all physical effects to a mental cause: and my immediate recovery from the effects of this injury was the falling apple which led me to the discovery how to be well myself and how to make others so.' On the third day, when the physician was in despair, she called for the Bible, and read Matthew ix, 2, the story of the cure of the man sick of the palsy; the healing Truth dawned on her sense, she rose, dressed herself, and ever after was better than she had been in her life. From that moment she began a renewed study of the Scriptures, and saw in them clear proof that spiritual healing had been practised by the early Christians. 'I beheld with ineffable awe our great Master's purpose in not questioning those he healed as to their disease or its symptoms, and his marvellous skill in demanding neither obedience to hygienic laws, nor prescribing drugs to support the divine power which heals. The miracles recorded in the Bible, which had before seemed to me supernatural, grew divinely natural and comprehensible: Jesus of Nazareth was a natural and divine Scientist.' This discovery, after some years of seclusion, she gave to the world in a book entitled *Science and Health with a Key to the Scriptures*, published at her own expense at Boston in 1875. No publisher would undertake the risk; but by 1891 it had reached its sixty-second edition.

For some months after this she healed, preached, and taught unofficially, receiving no pay and living on a small annuity. One incident caused a great sensation. A woman was said to be dying in childbirth: Mrs Patterson went to the bedside, stood there for a quarter of an hour, and 'treated' the case. The woman rose up, dressed herself, and was well.

In 1877 she married for the third time. Dr Asa Gilbert Eddy was the first of her students publicly to announce himself a Christian Scientist; he gave up his ordinary medical practice, and devoted himself to spiritual teaching, to metaphysical healing, and to Sunday-school work. He died in 1882, leaving a memory which his widow faithfully treasured for the rest of her life. From the time of this marriage she is known as Mary Baker Eddy.

Though she had been preaching and lecturing for several years, and had founded a college as well as a 'Christian Scientist Association' in 1876, the actual Church was not started till 1879, with a membership of twenty-six. Of this Church she was elected pastor, and her sermons soon attracted large congregations. This is the First Church of Christ, Scientist, Boston, the mother of a very large family: it is said that there are now some thousands of churches scattered over many countries of the world.

Like so many other religious leaders, Mrs Eddy had a

first no wish to found a separate Church; she hoped that existing Christian denominations would welcome her interpretation of Scripture, and would see that it was not inconsistent with any theological dogmas they might hold. Some ministers did, in fact, admit Christian Scientists to their pulpits; but there was so much opposition, and even persecution, in many quarters, that separation was seen to be inevitable. Nevertheless, when the Church had been completely organized, it was found that the jealousies and quarrels which seem inseparable from a hierarchy of ranks and offices, were creeping in. It was accordingly dissolved into its elements, and what Mrs Eddy calls a 'spiritual organization' was substituted. 'When the material form of cohesion has accomplished its end, continued organization retards spiritual growth, and should be laid off.'

During the following years, Mrs Eddy's life was one of incessant labour. The *Christian Science Journal* was started in 1883; there was constant teaching of classes; and the Church expanded so rapidly that, though she was able to train up others to relieve her of much of the detail, her days were overcrowded with toil. In addition to her journalistic labours, she brought out between 1886 and 1902 a large number of more permanent works, of which *Christian Healing* is perhaps the most important. She died at Newton, Massachusetts, in 1910.

The doctrines of Christian Science are not, as will be already obvious, put forth as new; they profess to be a *recovery* of certain main conceptions of original Christianity which had been lost sight of. Since Christ's time his ideas have become distorted by materialism: we must draw out the full implications of his saying, 'God is a Spirit'. By this is meant that God is Mind or Principle, all-inclusive. The word Person may be used to denote him, but not as implying anything anthropomorphic. He is all-pervasive, and the mind of man is in a sense the mind of God, but not in such a fashion that man loses all individuality. We are, and have been created to be, *ourselves*. Similarly the universe has been created by God to be itself. God pervades it; but neither is the universe God nor God the universe.

All this can be drawn from the teaching of Jesus, who is the Guide, or 'Way-shower', to his brethren: and this is why his religion was called the Way by his early followers. If we study his teaching, and follow his example, we cannot fail to discover and keep the right path. This Way is constantly spoken of in the New Testament as 'Living': and hence Mrs Eddy, though not forgetting the death of Jesus, lays more emphasis on his life. The Church rejects utterly the idea that the righteousness of Jesus was 'imputed' to man, who had lost at the Fall the righteousness he had once possessed; nor will it have anything to do with the conception that Christ, by his death, bore in himself the whole punishment due for the sins of man. The words of Jesus are, 'Because I live, ye shall live also': and his whole career on earth, *including* his death and his conquest over it, was the bringing of life and immortality to light.

From another point of view, in expressing which Mrs Eddy seems to prefer to speak of 'Christ' rather than of 'Jesus', we may regard God as manifesting *himself* to the world, and as putting on flesh for the destruction of error. This is the 'mystery of godliness' of which Paul speaks; and Christian Science claims to have unfolded this mystery and made it clear to the world after it had been forgotten or but confusedly understood. Christ is at once the Teacher of the Way and the Way itself, at once the Guide to Truth and the Truth. The Atonement thus becomes a reconciliation between man and God; man is saved through realizing his unity with Him. Salvation comes 'through Truth, Life, and Love as demonstrated by the Galilean Prophet in healing the sick and overcoming sin and death'.

Once again, Christian Science claims to have discovered, or rather rediscovered, the real meaning of the Scriptural saying that man is made in the image of God. This does not mean that God is like a human being: it means that man, ideally conceived, is like God; that is, that man is Spirit. Everything material about man is mirage or illusion, and cannot originate with God; and, conversely, whatever does not originate with God cannot have a real existence. This is the primary doctrine of Christian Science. True religion is true knowledge: 'this is life eternal, that they might *know* thee, the only true God'. When man learns his true relation to God, he is saved, he has Religion: as the false and material man disappears, the real, that is the ideal, man reappears in proportion. Could we rid ourselves of erroneous conceptions, we should cease to sin; or, to put it more accurately, the very idea of sin is an error. From the subjective point of view, sin is mistake; from the objective, it is illusion.

Sin then being due to ignorance, Christian Science seeks to *educate* men in spiritual knowledge. It points out that the pleasures of sin are illusory, that the temptation to sin always comes as a deception, that its punishment is certain. But let us cease from sinning and the penalty immediately ceases. Get rid of what St Paul calls the 'carnal mind', and life, health, and peace result. Positively, also, the cultivation of a healthy mind, the practice of good deeds, will leave no room for sin, exactly as the acquisition of truth drives out falsehood.

We thus arrive at that feature of Christian Science which has attracted most strongly the attention of the outside world – Spiritual Healing. Here again the religion professes to teach nothing new; it simply reaffirms a main conception of primitive Christianity. The Gospels and the Acts are full of narratives of spiritual healings, which are spoken of as perfectly natural occurrences *in the circumstances*. Causation is spiritual: death, and ill health, are 'carnal', that is material and illusory. Make your escape from the illusory carnal plane, and ill health is seen at once to be imaginary. Disease is a proof of false belief: it is to think that real which is essentially non-existent: see things as they are, and ill health is seen not to *be* at all. As truth destroys and must destroy error, as science has driven out erroneous views of nature, so Christian Science drives out the false idea that man is material, and raises him into the sphere of the spiritual, which can know no pain. This does not imply that the religion refuses natural aids; a clean body is an assistance to the attainment of a clean mind: but hygiene and sanitation are the cleansing of the outside of the cup and platter: 'these things are not to be left undone', but the first thing to do is to cleanse the inside – that is, to gain a sound and healthy mentality, and a clear notion of our relations with the divine. In the Gospels and Epistles the close connexion between disease and sin is constantly emphasized; Christian Science also emphasizes the connexion; but by defining sin as ignorance it makes the healing of disease the certain result of perfect knowledge.

This Spiritual Healing must be marked off from other kinds of healing with which it has sometimes been confused. The Church of Rome, for example, claims to retain the Apostolic power. No canonization takes place until the saint has been shown to have performed miracles, which are, perhaps in the majority of cases, miracles of healing; and the multitudes who have thronged to Lourdes or La Salette testify to numerous cures, as the Canterbury Pilgrims bore witness that the holy blissful martyr had 'holpen them when they were sick'. But these, in the view of Rome, *are* miracles, special manifestations of divine power allowed to specially sanctified members of the Church, or else (as at Lourdes) direct exertions of influence by heavenly beings. They are not performed, naturally and constantly, by ordinary believers. Christian Science, on the other hand, regards such cures as effects of 'natural law in the spiritual world': the name 'Science' is deliberately adopted in order to indicate that they are as normal as the processes by which chemical or electrical experiments produce their expected results. Catholicism recognizes the uniformity of nature, but says that God, as he wills, may break the uniformity; Christian Science declares that these cures no more break the uniformity than the succession of day and night breaks it.

The cures, again, must not be confused with those wrought by hypnosis. They depend upon faith, that is knowledge: whereas hypnosis is an affair of power. An invalid restored to health by Christian Science retains full control of himself; his will is still his own. The Christian Scientist, also, asserts that his cures are permanent – in this sense, that the patient who keeps his faith and retains right knowledge will *not* be ill; disease is not only cured but – to use ordinary language – prevented, by the steady exertion of belief. One who knows, and knows so thoroughly as to be practically intuitively conscious that sin and its attendant diseases are illusion, cannot be cheated into thinking himself ill.

This does not imply, as is sometimes thought, that Christian Science totally rejects ordinary medical aid. It is true that no member of the Church is permitted to learn hypnotism – such an offence is punished by excommunication. But the help of a physician may be called in for certain specified purposes. 'If a member of this Church,' says one of Mrs Eddy's By-laws, 'has a patient whom he does not heal, and whose case he cannot fully diagnose, he may consult with a Doctor of Medicine on the anatomy involved. And it shall be the privilege of a Christian Scientist to confer with a Doctor of Medicine on Ontology or the Science of Being.' This explains what has often been regarded as an inconsistency, that in such cases as broken limbs Christian Scientists have been observed to call in physicians. These are advisers, not healers.

In the words of a distinguished exponent of the doctrine, 'When Jesus cured the man whose right hand was withered, declaring that it was lawful to do so, he proved two propositions: First, that there is a principle and a rule by which such a healing is possible; second, that he had acquired the understanding thereof. The principle and rule of Christian healing must be eternal and universal, and must be available to all who possess the necessary understanding. The only personal factor is the understanding; and in the last analysis it is personal only in the sense of being individual. The belief that Jesus exercised a power peculiar to himself is one which he refuted explicitly and repeatedly.'

This healing power is, as might be expected, a source of great happiness and confidence to the believer; for it is the outward and visible sign of dominion over evil. When Jesus said, 'That ye may know the Son of Man hath power to forgive sins,' and healed the sick of the palsy, he was stating this truth for all time. Every disease healed is the expulsion of a sin, and justifies the hope that, as cure after cure is performed, evil will in time be entirely banished from the world.

The dissemination of this religion, which, as said, above, has been amazingly rapid, is accomplished not by ordinary advertising methods, but by quiet talk between man and man, and especially by the 'testimonies' borne in the weekly meetings – usually held on Wednesdays. The constitution is peculiar. It is emphasized that the First Church is unique – 'it occupies a position that no other church can fill': the other churches cannot, except within defined limits, adopt the Mother Church's form of government. We said above that the Mother Church broke up its original organization: but in 1892 it once more organized itself in a fashion which, it was hoped, would obviate the old evils, and it was insisted that there should be 'no ecclesiastical monopoly'. There is no settled ministry, and the branch churches may be said to be as independent of the First Church as Congregationalist societies are of the Union; but they are subject to the control of the 'Christian Science Board of Directors', and the creed and discipline are pretty rigidly fixed by Mary Eddy's 'Church Manual', which primarily concerns the Mother Church, but indirectly, of course, regulates the subordinate congregations. There is a recognized order of officers – Teachers, members of the Board of Lectureship, Readers, directors of Publication, and the like, the qualifications for which are defined.

The services are simple and uniform; music of a religious character, hymns, prayer, and the reading of portions of Scripture with Mrs Eddy's comments. No sermon is preached, and nothing may be said except in authorized words: the members must reserve their own speaking for the week-day testimonies.

Not least influential in making the religion known has been the *Christian Science Monitor*, an international daily (the *Journal* is a monthly) founded by Mrs Eddy in 1908, 'to injure no one, but to bless all mankind'. This paper is of the highest character;[1] its news and comments are sound, and its literary columns, in particular, are of outstanding merit. The whole publishing system, indeed, shows high efficiency. The various shops and reading-rooms (it is a law that every church must have a reading-room attached to it) also deserve mention: here information is freely and courteously given to all who desire it. No literature, however, but that of Christian Science is to be found in these rooms.

Whatever may be thought, in fact, of the doctrines of this religion, all must admit that it is 'run' in a most competent and attractive manner; and its rapid growth is not in the least surprising.

The SWEDENBORGIANS (or New Jerusalem Church) regard their religion as bearing the same relation to Christianity as Christianity bears to Judaism: their Church is not a sect, but a new dispensation, in which the old receives its fulfilment. So far from recognizing the finality of the Christian revelation, they view it as the necessary, but imperfect, groundwork of their own. Thus they use the Christian Scriptures as Paul used the Old Testament – as inspired, but as needing a new interpretation.

The founder of the Church, though it was not formed till eleven years after his death, was Emanuel Swedenborg, unquestionably one of the most remarkable men that ever lived. A mathematician of very high rank, he anticipated many modern discoveries. But his intellectual curiosity was boundless. He attached himself to watch-makers to learn their craft; to cabinet-makers, to makers of mathematical instruments. He travelled abroad to study the manners and disposition of other nations, and to converse with learned

1. It refuses to tell of crimes or horrors – the popular element in so many papers – and it will have nothing to do with sensationalism of any kind.

men in every part of Europe: and he bettered their instructions.

He was born in 1688, the son of the Bishop of Skara, in Sweden, and a member of a noble family. The Bishop was a man of admirable character, and his influence on his son was profound.

In 1716 Swedenborg was appointed by Charles XII assessor in the College of Mines. Here he was brought into close contact with the King, who, being himself interested in mathematics, was greatly attracted by him, and to whom he did service by his skill in practical inventions. The office stimulated Swedenborg still further to carry on his indefatigable researches; he made investigations into the nature of heat and into the best methods of mining, the results of which he revealed to the world in a large number of publications. It is probable that no one has contributed more to the advance of applied science than this extraordinary man, whose mind seemed capable of absorbing knowledge from every source, and of analysing and developing it to the utmost.

But all this time his chief interest was in religion, and he had already written books on the subject. All his scientific achievements he considered of little value in comparison with the discovery of the soul, and, like Pascal, whom in some respects he resembles, he finally, after thirty years of service, resigned his post in order to devote himself exclusively to this search. He had already had the experience which changed his whole life, and dictated the course of the studies which he pursued unremittingly till the end of his days. The spiritual world was opened to him by God in vision; he was enabled to converse with spirits and angels; and from that time forward the other world remained free to him.

But there is a marked difference between Swedenborg and some other religious visionaries. He believed himself subject to divine illumination, but he did not imagine that this relieved him from the necessity of intellectual work. He learned Hebrew, and studied the Scriptures in the original languages with all possible diligence. Believing thoroughly

the existence of God, and in the divine character of the
ew Testament; believing also that he was appointed to
veal God to men and to give the true explanation of his
ord, he poured out volume after volume describing his
sions, unlocking the hidden secrets of the Bible, and asking
o more than that his claims should be tested by each
ader in the only just way – by their harmony with the
vine order and by the appeal they make to the individual
nscience. He died in 1772. His personal character is emi-
ntly attractive; he was gentle, modest, unassuming, and –
good criterion – always beloved by children.

The doctrines of the Church[1] must be briefly summed up.
od is one, and personal. His essence, which also is single,
love; this, when it issues in action, may be. *described* as
isdom, but the wisdom and the love are but aspects of the
me principle. Yet God is a Trinity; and here Sweden-
rg's doctrine is very remarkable. The Father, or Jehovah,
God in himself, absolute and unconditioned: the Son is
e humanity which Jehovah assumed when he determined
save mankind; the Spirit is the Power of God as expressed
that humanity. But God put on humanity with all its
fects: it began in ignorance, and grew in knowledge; it
as subject to real, and not merely imaginary, temptation;
consciousness was its own; and, like the rest of humanity,
could make approaches towards perfection. When per-
ction was reached, Christ ascended to his Father, thus
uniting his human nature with the divine, and making it
ossible for mankind in general to be reconciled to God.

Man is not precisely *created*. He is a form so made as to be
pable of receiving the constant inflow of life from the one
urce of life – or, more accurately, from the Love-Wisdom
hich *is* Life. According as he is willing to receive this in-
ow, such is the degree of fulness of his life. Before the Fall,
ere was this receptiveness; man and God were in har-
ony; the concord was broken when man, forgetting his

1. They may be found in Swedenborg's books, or, more shortly, in the
peal on behalf of the New Church by Samuel Noble, one of the earliest
ondon Swedenborgian ministers.

dependence upon God, exercised his will independentl
For life was so granted to him that it seems to be his ov
possession; his will is free. To use the symbolism of Genes
he gave way to the serpent of sense, to human affections
that is, to woman, to his own intellectual arrogance:
deemed himself a God. The penalty was spiritual death
the discontinuance of the inflow of life. But God did n
leave him alone. Recognizing his weakness, he gave him tl
Mosaic Law – a dispensation adapted to his powers, ar
gradually drew him upwards, until, in the fulness of tim
he appeared to man as himself man; in order that tl
inflow might again be fully possible. Not that Gc
actually *became* man; he invested the divine in a huma
covering.

Man's spirit is the real man; it is (here Swedenborg reli
on his visions) an exact replica of the body, with its shap
organs, and functions: the body is the husk, which, if sin ha
never entered the world, would have been naturally di
carded when the corn appeared. Death was but one ste
into a higher plane; now, through sin, it has become a dif
cult step, but, as we more and more come to regain ov
sense of dependence upon God, it becomes more and mo
an easy and gentle rebirth.

The spiritual world, which includes the spiritual forms
every material thing and much besides, is free from the lav
of time and space; but symbolically it may be divided in
heaven, hell, and the intermediate plane. In this plane v
live lives at first similar to those we have lived on earth, b
we are gradually drawn, according to our sympathies, eith
upward or downward. Once drawn upward, we are eter
ally impelled nearer to perfection; in the lower sphere v
fall ever lower. The knowledge of these states came
Swedenborg in actual vision; his eyes being enlightened,
saw the spiritual world, and his descriptions are often ama
ingly clear and precise.[1] The knowledge thus revealed is tl

1. No better idea of them can be easily attained than by studying t
pictures of Blake, who was for a time a member of the Swedenborgi
Church, and in whom the Swedenborgian influence was never lost.

econd Coming of Christ, which was mistakenly supposed
o be a physical manifestation, but is in truth spiritual, and
will be realized by believers as they attain spiritual know-
edge, which will finally pass into spiritual vision, such as
was vouchsafed to Swedenborg himself.

A very few words must suffice to describe the system called
OSITIVISM or the Religion of Humanity: though had we
been writing seventy or eighty years ago it would have demanded to be treated in some detail. It was founded by
Auguste Comte, a distinguished French professor of mathematics. Starting as a disciple of the Socialist Count St
Simon, Comte gradually drew away from him, and in his
Cours de philosophie positive, the first volume of which appeared in 1830, he elaborated the thesis that there are three
great stages of human thought, the Theological, the Metaphysical, and the Positive or Scientific. In the first stage men
seek for 'divine' causes to explain nature, inventing gods
and demons; in the second they seek abstractions and metaphysical entities; in the third, which is probably final, they
proceed by experiment and gradually reach 'positive' truth.
Comte's analysis of the sciences, and the generalizing acumen with which he coordinated them, gained him a considerable following. But later, in strange fashion for one who
had got rid of the supernatural, he substituted the transcen-
ental idea of Humanity for that of a personal deity as an
bject of worship, and claimed to have discovered a new
eligion, issuing a Positivist Catechism and a treatise on
ociology in which he declared himself the High Priest of
he cult. The worship of a pale abstraction proving practic-
lly impossible, he drew up a list of historical characters
whom he regarded as worthy of the same sort of reverence as
Catholics render to saints; and a very curious list it is.
Whereas Comte's scientific work was highly appreciated
by many eminent men – not least by John Stuart Mill – and
was popularized in England by George Henry Lewes with
onsiderable effect, his religion attracted comparatively
ew adherents. A small school, mainly consisting of Oxford

scholars, J. H. Bridges, Dr Congreve, Professor Beesly, and
Frederic Harrison, adopted his scheme with varying degrees
of fidelity, as did Littré in France: and Harrison continued
to preach Comtist doctrines to audiences in London
throughout his long life. But large numbers who had looked
on Comte with respect as a man of science, regretted the
vagaries of his later days. The Church has never been large
– it repels at once those who believe in supernaturalism and
those who uncompromisingly reject it.

CHAPTER 17

CONCLUSION

THE religions we have been surveying may seem many, but they are few in comparison with the actual number that now exist and have existed in the world. At one time, it is hardly too much to say, every independent community had its independent religion; and when external pressure, like that of Rome, had forced the religions, along with the communities, into some sort of unity, there was always a tendency for the unity to be dissolved into sectarianism. Within one religion, again, even though apparent unity might be maintained, there was immense diversity of view. Nor is there any reason to believe that the process will stop. At the present moment there is a clear desire to merge smaller bodies into larger organizations; but the old differences will probably remain: and, while there are many signs of very keen interest in *religion*, there are as many of dissatisfaction with *religions*, and we may well see shortly another arise, more in harmony with the prevailing feeling of the age than any of those now existing – and others after that. There are some able observers, it is true, who anticipate a very different result – the division of the religious world into two hemispheres, the one Catholic, the other sceptical, scientific, rationalist, or atheistic. I do not think this is probable. First of all, there is little sign that the great masses of population in the East have the smallest desire to embrace Christianity. Secondly, within the Christian world itself, there are multitudes without number who will never, I think, be able to reconcile themselves to the act of submission which the Papacy – rightly if its claims are just – continues to demand. To them the first duty is to retain control of their own reason, and they will not part, at any price, with the right to follow their reason wherever it may lead them. To them, as to Milton, 'if a man believe things because his pastor says so, or the assembly so determine, though his belief be true, yet the very truth he holds becomes his heresy.' This spirit the Church of Rome regards as sinful pride: and there will probably for a long time be many who will agree with her and yield up their judgement to her disposition. But there will equally be many who will regard such a surrender as the worst of treacheries.[1] They may excuse such treacheries in others; never in themselves.

But if our study has led us to doubt whether there will ever be unity of religion in the world, and even whether such unity is desirable, we have none the less been struck, again and again, with the strange likeness which exists amid so much dissimilarity. Religion seems to follow much the same path, though it may start up in very different surroundings. Thus it begins, as we have seen, in the sense of fear, and though, like Tragedy, it often seeks to drive out one terror by substituting another, it makes some sort of effort to rid men of it. But it soon goes on to an attempt at satisfying *curiosity*. Men are afraid of the unknown; and religion, to diminish their fear, tries to let them know. Thus the religions, almost without exception, tend to develop an intellectual element: they become philosophical and in a sense historical. They tell their adherents how the world came to be, what is the nature of the divine, what happens after death, and how a friendly relation to the gods, or a tolerable condition after death, may be secured. They provide a cosmogony, a theology, and an eschatology: and it is astonishing what similar theories on all these points the most diverse nations have produced.[2]

1. I know no better examples of these two classes of minds than Spinoza and his former pupil Albert de Burgh, who entered the Roman Church and endeavoured to convert his teacher to it. Every word written by Spinoza indicates that he was determined, at all risks, to retain his own freedom of judgement, which had withdrawn him from the Jewish communion and prevented him from joining any other. Yet Spinoza was one of the best and most religious men of whom history holds record.

2. Still greater is the likeness between the *saints* of diverse nations, who seek not merely to know *of* God, but to know God himself. The Buddhist

Next, the majority of peoples, though not all, have gradually learned to add morality to theology. At first, as we have seen, the two had nothing to do with each other. There was nothing moral about the thunderbolt or the tornado, which gave man the sense of irresistible power, but assuredly not of power used for moral ends. When a primitive Odysseus was hurled to and fro by a primitive Poseidon, he did not think of Poseidon as working for a noble ethical end. Now, however, the fusion of ethics with religion has often gone so far that many regard the two as identical. This view, though it has commanded the assent of distinguished names,[1] is probably erroneous. Without disputing as to words and definitions, we may hazard the statement that what is generally understood by Religion implies at least some reference to a power or powers higher than man, whether that power be personal or not.

That reference, in early stages, may involve a feeling even of abject terror, and lead to the most despicable of ceremonies and sacrifices: in later and more refined times, or in stronger minds, the terror gives way to awe, reverence, or a sense of mystery. These feelings, of course, will move different people in different ways, and will act on them in varied

---

saint is, in all essentials, indistinguishable from the Christian. Men who met Fletcher of Madeley felt the same awe and attraction as men who met Francis of Assisi. And, as we have seen, the mystics of all religions have the same experience and speak the same language. The same Beatific Vision is beheld by Plotinus, by St Paul, by St Catherine of Genoa, by the Brahman, by the Buddhist, by the nature-worshipper Wordsworth, by the 'atheist' Shelley. When we read the descriptions these holy dreamers give of their raptures, we are inclined to think that the differences of creed are nothing, and that sectarian disputes are quarrels about straws.

1. There was formerly an 'Ethical Church' in London, presided over by Dr Stanton Coit; and the church in South Place, where Moncure Conway preached from 1864 to 1897, was the home of a 'religion' in which prayer was abandoned and Theism rejected. To such a Church, I think, had it existed in Königsberg in the eighteenth century, Kant would have belonged. The movement still exists, but has split up into two groups: the Ethical Society, and the West London Ethical Society.

proportions. To some they will be quite compatible with the filial emotion of love. God is their Father, and fatherhood is the constant image under which the divine presents itself to them: while they acknowledge that his infinitude is far beyond their ken, yet they approach him with the confidence of children. 'Dark with excess of bright his skirts appear'; and yet they can gaze undazzled on one aspect of his being. It is this aspect that Jesus dwelt on with engaging emphasis; and he compelled his followers, by setting it in the forefront of the prayer they use continually, never to forget it. Even here, however, there are differences due to difference of environment and temperament: to some, fatherhood will connote a measure of sternness; God is the Father who judges, and assigns penalties for offences. In some forms of Christianity, therefore, in which legalism plays its part, he is perpetually present as watching jealously over us, ready at any moment to detect and punish; in others he recedes into the background, and his place is taken by more gentle and placable personalities, such as the Son or the Virgin Mary.

Curiously enough, feelings of this kind can be excited not merely by a deity conceived as paternal. Some men have, apparently, the capacity of feeling awe, reverence, or even affection, for a deity which they have denuded of every vestige of personality: they can worship an abstraction with perfect ease, and rise strengthened and ennobled from the prayer. This is unquestionably the case with certain Brahmans and Buddhists, whose meditations and supplications, though concerned with a mere *Quale*, lack nothing of the rapture which Dante describes St Bernard as finding in the contemplation of so personal an object of worship as the Virgin herself. There are many who, regarding God as identical with the All, worship with equal devotion not a deity *immanent* in the universe, but the universe itself, matter and spirit, extension and thought; contriving to speak to it as though it heard, and to approach it as though it were 'closer than breathing, and nearer than hands and feet'. In converse manner, many Christian mystics, starting with the conception of God as a person, go on in their exalted moments to *lose* this conception of his personality, and to be absorbed in a trance in which they are rapt away in a union with a transcendental Absolute. But wherever there exists anything which deserves to be called Religion at all, there never fails to be found in it what has been denominated 'Numinousness', the feeling of awe inspired by the recognition of something which, while it can be more or less dimly envisaged by the human mind, is yet felt far to surpass it.

All religion recognizes the helplessness of man, and seeks aid from something above him and outside him. The savage asks protection from the terrible forces of nature, and finds it, or at any rate strives to find it, in creating gods like himself but stronger. The malignity of some of these forces may be soothed by flattery, of others evaded by craft, of others overcome by summoning even greater force. As the savage evolves into civilized man, he asked for other things, but always for what he wants. He has overcome some of the natural forces: he asks no help against these: it is the unconquered forces that still compel him to pray for supernatural assistance; and he has found some which his savage ancestor never suspected to exist. For example, he has discovered that he cannot conquer *himself*: 'he feels the weight of chance desires', and realizes that his own strength is insufficient to remove them. It is against these, more than against any others, that the saintly man prays, if so he may become more saintly: the Christian that by the help of Christ he may tread this inner Satan under his feet, the Buddhist that he may pass into a region beyond desire, the Brahman to realize that desire is but Maya, or illusion. The religious man of science, unlike the savage or the ignorant man around him, asks for yet other things. He does not pray for rain or for fine weather: these, he knows, depend on immutable natural law. He does not think of malaria and cholera as gods to be placated by offerings or cajoled by spells; he studies germs and attends to the drains. But the 'religious' man, though his science be of the most exact or profound, yet feels himself in the presence of 'Another', to which, or to whom, he responds, and which, he is somehow conscious, responds to him. It is this responsiveness, in the man, that we call Religion: in the 'Other', it is the self-communication of the divine.

We cannot, with our utmost endeavours, avoid anthropomorphism. 'We cannot step out of our own shadow'; and the man who strives, with all the metaphysical thought at his disposal, to fashion a god unlike himself, yet retains the likeness. That God created man in his own image is only another way of saying that man creates God in *his*. Deny as we please that God is human, we must yet think of him with human thoughts, and define him in human phrases. And man is ever changing, sometimes moving upward and sometimes tending downward. As he thus changes, his God inevitably changes with him. The gods of the savage are savages: the God of Sir James Jeans has been called, with an approximation to truth, a mathematician. To the ancient Chaldeans, we are told by Habakkuk, their own might was their divinity: and of whole nations, a few years ago, a Habakkuk would have said the same. To the Hebrews, when they were a fighting tribe, God was Yahweh Sabaoth, Jehovah of the Armies: the Jewish God today is very different. After an experience of the horrors of war, horrors which stagger the consciences of men, God is to myriads, whether Jews or Gentiles, a deity of peace, to whom, because war is detestable to *them*, war is also detestable. A *Te Deum* after a victory appears no longer as a religious service, but as the worst of blasphemies. It was not so to Handel in the days of Dettingen.

Similarly, it has not been through an advance in logical power, but through a change in moral feeling, that Christians – even those who accept Calvin's premisses – have gradually modified Calvinism. Nothing is more certain than that if you accept Calvin's premisses you must accept his conclusions: his reasoning is as cogent as Euclid's. Nothing again, is more certain than that Calvinism is to be found in the authoritative documents of Christianity. But the moral sense of today rejects the conclusions; and men, acting on the subconscious assumption that God is like themselves refuse to believe that he will act as a good man would not act. In the same way the doctrine of eternal punishment has either been entirely thrown over, or so whittled down as no longer to affront our *human* sense of justice. If *we* would not sentence even a Nero to eternal torture, we assume that neither would God do so. Dante, following Thomas Aquinas, could honestly assert that the 'primal Love' created hell: we, believing that God loves as we do, disagree with Dante.

The process works curiously, in what we may call a circular fashion. We first create a God in our own likeness, and then make that God the model and the sanction for our own actions: we strive to imitate that which is really a mimicry of ourselves. Because men love, they figure God as loving, and then, because God loves, they urge themselves to love. In old days, Samuel was stern and unforgiving. He therefore felt himself bound to be stern and unforgiving because Yahweh bade him be so, and hewed Agag in pieces *before the Lord* – an act which *our* Lord forbids us to commit. In the Southern States of America, eighty years ago, many of the sincerest Christians approved of slavery; they fashioned therefore a God who approved of it; and then, arguing from the nature of that God, strengthened their conviction that they were right to hold slaves. God had cursed Canaan, and made him a servant of servants: it was therefore their Christian duty to make slaves of the descendants of Canaan. In the Northern States, many equally sincere Christians were revolted by slavery; their God therefore was also revolted by it; and they found, in the very same Scriptures on which the Southerners relied, the command to destroy the accursed thing. A thousand other examples could be given. It is this that explains the horrors of the Inquisition, the frenzy of the Mohammedans against the infidel, the counter-frenzy of the Crusaders against Islam, the cruelties of the saintly Bernard, the atrocities of Drogheda, the Marian persecutions. *You* hate something, therefore God hates it, therefore it is your religious duty, as followers of God, to hate it yet more. Thus finally the worst of all crimes are committed in fancied obedience to divine commands.

God, then, is that which men conceive, more or less clearly, as the highest expression of their own most exalted feelings. He is morality at the loftiest point to which they can project themselves. And, as their own personality is that to which they cling with the most stubborn tenacity – the last thing they would give up – they inevitably conceive of God as a person. They give him what is the sublimest attribute in themselves – a self: and, if philosophically-minded, they say that he must at least *include* personality, though what more he possesses they confess it is beyond human power to tell. They will own that this is anthropomorphism, but they claim that in giving the highest human attributes to God they are justified precisely as they are justified in the assumptions on which all human knowledge is based. You cannot *prove* the axioms of Euclid: nor can you prove the personality of God. All knowledge begins with mystery and in mystery it ends: that religion is no exception merely indicates that it is a human function and is limited by the imperfections of humanity.

The evolution of mankind is thus, to use modern jargon, accompanied by a revision of 'values': what our ancestors regarded as of worth we often regard as of little consequence; and even when it retains its absolute value its relative value declines. We therefore tend to correct our idea of God in accordance with these changes: for God must, we are inclined to believe, possess those qualities which are of the highest value. In old days, for instance, God was a national god. When you stepped beyond the borders of your country you escaped from his dominion. The only way in which Naaman could worship Yahweh in the land of Rimmon was by carrying thither two mules' burden of earth from Yahweh's territory. Standing on that, he could expect an answer to his prayer; leaving it, he must have recourse to Rimmon. But gradually, as nationality, though still strong, was felt to be of less relative importance than other principles, God transcended national boundaries, and was discovered to be the God of the whole earth, then of earth and heaven, and finally even of the dead. The most fanatically

national of modern peoples will hardly now deny, at least in
words, that God belongs to other peoples as well; though
there are still Germans who harbour the idea that he has a
special affection for Germany, and still Englishmen who
hold, with Milton, that when God has something specially
great to be done, he hands it over to 'his Englishmen'.
Four hundred years ago, when sectarianism was stronger
than today, the feeling was often different: the Catholic
Frenchman would unite with the Catholic Spaniard, and
expect the help of the Catholic God against the heretic:
while the Protestants of all nations would unite against the
Catholics, trusting in the 'Lord of Hosts, from whom all
glories are'. The pendulum has swung in another direction;
but it may return.

As philosophy has tended to monism, so has theology to
monotheism: and this, at one stage or another, is the characteristic of all religions. Even those which in words say
there is no god, find a unity in atheism: there Nothing is a
single Nothing. The advance is first from a multitude of
gods to 'henotheism' or 'monolatry' – one god for the race;
and thence to one god for the universe. The Greeks gradually gave Zeus a supremacy over his rivals or colleagues,
and then reduced the colleagues to practical non-existence.
There can be no doubt that monotheism has a strong religious appeal, as the discovery of the One within the Manifold appeals to philosophers. The strength of Mohammedanism lay in its proclamation that there was one God,
and that Mohammed was his prophet. But here again the
pendulum swings, and lesser deities constantly creep in, to
the embarrassment of the theologians who teach the unity
of the divine. The reality of evil presents an ever-recurring
problem to those who maintain that the One God is good:
and we find Matter, Satan, or Ahriman elevated into stubborn unconquerable principles, gods in all but name:
while the common people worship all sorts of lesser deities –
saints, demons, ghosts, or mere luck. As we have seen, the
Jews in their monotheistic days yet contrived to worship
Fortune or Destiny; the Buddhists adore innumerable demi-

gods; the Brahmans, though they insist that there is but one
divine Being, bow down to its 'manifestations'; Christians
carry mascots, and devout cricketers keep amulets in their
pockets.

All this may be put from the other side. We may conceive
of God as gradually revealing himself both to men and in
man; as slowly enlightening the eyes of their conscience,
and in mysterious ways bringing moral order into the chaos
of their hearts. The higher ethic which makes them envisage
a higher God is the effect of his working upon their minds.
As they yield more and more to his influence, they learn
more and more about his nature, and the knowledge of his
nature, in its turn, further elevates their souls. From whichever side we regard it, whether as God's revelation to men
or as man's discovery of God, it is certain that the better a
man is, the nobler is his conception of the divine. And, by
the leavening power of a few good men, the idea of God
which the community holds is gradually and imperceptibly
raised, until a whole nation refuses to admit that God can
approve actions or devices which once it unhesitatingly
ascribed to him. Those who killed the martyrs thought they
were doing God service: a man of very commonplace morals
today will never try to serve God in that manner. No nation
in the Middle Ages and later, admitted that Jews had any
rights. Today, the persecution of Jews has aroused an almost
universal condemnation of the persecutors; and the condemnation is voiced by many as ratified by God. God de-
tests today what we never till recently imagined he detested

But we have to remember that the conscience of the better
men in a community often succeeds in establishing a higher
conception of God than the ordinary man could ever have
formed; and to a certain extent these better men succeed in
imposing that conception upon their less saintly fellows. We
thus find men, vaguely and feebly it is true, holding a view
of God far in advance of their own personality, and feeling
the stings of conscience when their actions fall short of the
standard which a God created for them by others is supposed to demand. Men's conscience thus always runs far

ahead of their actions. But the conception of God must not run *too* far ahead. A religion must fit the society in which it is to take root, or in the long run it will either be driven out or suffer mutations hardly to be distinguished from corruptions. If it demands too much, it will accomplish less than if its demands are moderate. This is a discovery made by every religion after the first enthusiasm has begun to wane. It would seem that there is *no* asceticism, no sacrifice, too severe for a religion to impose upon its early converts: pleasure will be renounced, marriage declined, pain welcomed, at the bidding of the founder; nay, hard intellectual study and profound meditation will be eagerly faced. Most religions gain their early triumphs by insisting on renunciation: they flourish, not by saying 'You may', but by the stern veto, 'You must not'. Wait, however, a few years, and the scene is changed: the forbidden pleasures creep in, the banned practices are winked at, the compulsory ceremonials become merely voluntary. This is the almost universal law. Thus the rule of St Benedict is relaxed, the strictness of St Francis is quietly mitigated. It was thus that Mohammedanism accommodated itself first to the warlike spirit of Arabia and then to the disposition of the North African tribes; Buddhism to the Chinese character; and Christianity assumes a different aspect in the different lands where it prevails. If any of these religions should conquer the world, it would do so at the expense of still more drastic accommodation.

The strength of Christianity lies perhaps in the fact that it can thus accommodate itself, better than any other, without altogether losing its essential character. By its very nature it is a comprehensive, a vital, and an elastic religion. Or rather, because it is a Life, it retains its identity in passing from childhood to youth, and from youth to age. It may change its sky, but it does not change its soul. Being, of course, a human thing, it suffers from different diseases in different countries, and finds its health in different ways as it passes from land to land. To the Greek it was largely a matter of philosophy; to the Roman largely a matter of law;

but it was Christianity still. In later times it has shown the same unity in diversity, the same power of eternal development. If we may liken it to that which, though great, is nevertheless comparatively small, it resembles the plays of Shakespeare, in which every new generation discovers something fresh which the previous generation had failed to detect. High poetic genius, we are told, has a way of saying things of a deeper content than the poet meant: he reaches forth to regions beyond his ken. So in Christianity we can find truths of the profoundest import which even Paul or John did not realize: the truth is greater than its greatest teachers. Thus a modern theologian finds it possible, without undue straining, to adapt Christianity to the most recent philosophy and ethics – or, to put the case in another way, he discovers, hidden in the heart of Christianity, what was already there, but what could not be found there till the advance of knowledge and morals had made the explorers capable of unearthing it. The treasure was in the earth, but the excavators have only lately found the tools wherewith to dig it out.

Particularly does this seem to be true of the character of Christ. Whether we look on him as God, as man, or as mysteriously both, it seems as if men will never exhaust him. Thus many who are dissatisfied with every existing form of Christianity appear able to find in the study and imitation of Christ a religion which appeals to them. On the other hand, there seems to be an increasing number of people who, though born and bred in Europe and under Christian influences, have been led by natural and acquired sympathy to adopt in some form one of the Eastern religions. They find there the answer to questions, and the satisfaction of longings, which they cannot find here. Buddha seems to respond to their needs more fully than Christ.

What is certain, and is being more and more clearly recognized, is that Buddha and Christ were touched in similar manner with a feeling of the infirmities and miseries of men, that they did what in them lay to help the weak and to comfort the miserable; and that their works and words have been sources of almost infinite consolation to millions during two thousand years. There have been many lesser teachers who have similarly striven, and who, with all their defects of mind or heart, have yet lightened the load of humanity, and strengthened those hopes without which it would have fainted and fallen. If our study has led us to honour these teachers as they deserve, and to rid ourselves of the narrow parochialism which thinks itself in sole possession of all truth, it will not have been in vain.

INDEX